The Big Show

The Big
SHOW

HIGH TIMES

and

Dirty Dealings

BACKSTAGE

at the

ACADEMY AWARDS®

STEVE POND

*Photographs by Art Streiber,
Lara Jo Regan, David Strick,
and Antonin Kratochvil*

Faber and Faber, Inc.

A division of Farrar, Straus and Giroux / New York

This book is not affiliated with the Academy of Motion Picture Arts and Sciences.

Faber and Faber, Inc.

An affiliate of Farrar, Straus and Giroux

19 Union Square West, New York 10003

Copyright © 2005 by Steve Pond

All rights reserved

Distributed in Canada by Douglas & McIntyre Ltd.

Printed in the United States of America

First edition, 2005

Library of Congress Cataloging-in-Publication Data

Pond, Steve.

The big show : high times and dirty dealings backstage at the Academy Awards / Steve

Pond.— 1st ed.

2211908

p.   cm.

Includes index.

ISBN-13: 978-0-571-21193-7

ISBN-10: 0-571-21193-3 (alk. paper)

1. Academy Awards (Motion pictures)   I. Title.

PN1993.92.P66 2005

791.43'079—dc22

2004013294

Designed by Abby Kagan

www.fsgbooks.com

1   3   5   7   9   10   8   6   4   2

Contents

Contents

The Big Show

Prologue

A True Tragedy

THEY COULD ALWAYS HEAR HIM COMING. A big man with a bum hip, Allan Carr walked slowly through the rooms of Hillhaven Lodge, his sprawling brick mansion down a private road in Benedict Canyon, a mile north of the Beverly Hills Hotel. His feet dragged a little, and his cane squeaked, then thwacked into the hardwood floors. The house was dimly lit, quiet, and warm, with a gleam from the fireplace reflecting off the polished floor. In the winter of 1989, staff members for the 61st Academy Awards often sat in the study waiting for Carr, and they heard him a couple of rooms away: the shuffle of his feet, but mostly the sound of the cane skidding on the floor, then slamming down. Creak . . . *whap*. Creak . . . *whap*. Creak . . . *whap*. He arrived in his robe and in pain, but the man knew how to make an entrance.

Everybody said the same thing about Allan Carr: he was a *showman*. Carr was short and rotund, swathed in custom caftans when he wasn't wrapped in a robe or a smoking jacket; his baby face was topped with a tousled blond mop and framed by oversized designer glasses. At fifty-one, he had been a manager, a publicist, a producer, and a master promoter, self-

and otherwise. He'd had a hit movie, *Grease*, and a Broadway smash, *La Cage aux Folles*. He knew how to make a fuss, how to attract the press, and especially how to throw a party. In fact, he'd installed a fully functioning disco in the basement of Hillhaven Lodge, which had been a more sedate estate in the hands of its former owner, actress Ingrid Bergman.

But the history was beside the point, because Carr, in the early months of 1989, was producing the Academy Awards. Friends said he looked at it as the pinnacle of his career, as his crowning achievement. In interview after interview, he promised that it would be the biggest, the most glamorous, the most beautiful, the most star-studded, the most *fabulous* Oscars ever.

Carr had been dying to tackle the Oscar assignment ever since he'd put on a particularly festive Governors Ball after the fiftieth-anniversary show in 1978. Expecting a call back then, he was disappointed when it didn't come; a decade later, though, he eagerly took the unpaid job when it was offered to him by Richard Kahn, the president of the Academy of Motion Picture Arts and Sciences. Kahn had originally offered the job to director Gilbert Cates, but when he and Cates couldn't agree on a direction for the show, he turned to the more flamboyant Carr. "Allan was a showman of the first degree, and I wanted to invest our show with the kind of excitement he brought to everything he did," says Kahn. "And we got a lot of excitement, much of which we did not expect."

The new producer was not always in the best of moods: between the hip replacement surgery he'd had in October and the torn knee cartilage he suffered in mid-February, he hurt and he was often cranky. He was overly protective of the stars he considered his friends, and sometimes seemed not to trust anybody but himself to deal with them. He seldom appeared at the dingy, windowless, drab green production office on La Cienega Boulevard, preferring to hold court at Hillhaven, where he'd installed a six-foot Oscar statue by the front door. On the occasions when he left the house on Oscar business, associate producer Michael Seligman drove him around. Carr was a heavy, rough passenger: when the show was over, Seligman had to replace the front seat in his Mercedes SLC.

Carr thought fast, talked fast, made decisions instantly. Some of his staffers were inspired and invigorated by his energy and creativity, but he also kept people off-balance, ill at ease, and wary of slipping and setting off his volcanic temper. Douglass M. Stewart, who put together film clips for the show, was reminded of the character played by William Castle in *The Day of the Locust*, the 1975 film based on Nathanael West's novel about the excesses of Hollywood. "Allan was a flamboyant producer the likes of which are often depicted on-screen," Stewart says. "He was the colorful, charismatic figure screaming from the top of a crane before the whole thing came crashing down around him."

What Carr wanted in an Oscar show was old-fashioned, fabulous glamour. "I remember going with him for our first survey of the Shrine," says Jeff Margolis, the director of that show, which was held at the aging Shrine Auditorium in downtown Los Angeles. "He walked in, and I remember him saying, 'I'm not doing the show here unless they redo all the bathrooms. I want the bathrooms redone, and I want all the hallways and the lobby painted. I want it to smell like it's brand-new.' " Carr got his renovations, whereupon he had a million tulips flown in from the Netherlands and fifty thousand glass beads affixed to the Shrine's curtain. There were names for production designer Ray Klausen's elaborate sets, names that captured the elegance Carr envisioned: "Stars and Diamonds," "Tiffany Jewels with Crystal Beads and Chiffon Swags," "Beaded Victorian Flowers," and "The Grand Drape" among them.

Off the stage, occupying a corner of the adjoining Shrine Exhibition Hall, was perhaps the grandest space of all. The green room at previous Oscar shows had usually been a utilitarian area where stars could relax during the show; Carr dubbed his version Club Oscar and turned it into the most elaborate green room anybody had ever seen. "You never would have known that you were backstage in a theater," says Margolis. "It was like you were in some highfalutin club in West Hollywood or New York City."

Some crew members wondered about the producer's fanatical attention to Club Oscar. "Everybody felt he was more concerned about the green room than the show itself," says stage manager Dency Nelson. "We thought, The guy knows how to throw parties, but does he really know how to produce an awards show?"

But Carr was determined to take care of his stars. He was proud of the people he'd attracted, and proud of the way he was putting them together as part of an overall theme: couples, costars, companions, and compadres.

Sure, not all of his plans worked out: Warren Beatty and Jack Nicholson declined his offer to be presenters, Paul Newman and Joanne Woodward didn't want to fly, Brigitte Bardot would do it only if she could talk about animal rights, Loretta Young only if she could give out best picture by herself. But Demi Moore and Bruce Willis said yes, as did Michael Caine and Sean Connery and Roger Moore, Kim Novak and Jimmy Stewart, Melanie Griffith and Don Johnson, Bob Hope and Lucille Ball.

To kick off this fabulous assemblage, Carr knew he needed a particularly fabulous opening—something to get 'em talking the next day, to announce that these were *his* Academy Awards. Lavish production numbers had long been an Oscar staple, but in recent years they'd been heavy on technical flash and high-tech trickery. "He wanted to simplify it a little bit," says Margolis. "He wanted the production numbers to be big and grand like the old Hollywood movie musicals, without laser beams or flash pots or smoke and mirrors."

The answer, Carr decided, lay 350 miles to the north in San Francisco, where the satirical, campy musical revue *Beach Blanket Babylon* had been a hit for fifteen years. Simultaneously spoofing and celebrating pop culture, creator Steve Silver threw dozens of pop icons together in a deliriously silly extravaganza. Carr persuaded Silver to adapt the show for the Oscars—whereupon, says Seligman, "that hellacious opening number just grew and grew."

Silver did much of his work in San Francisco, while Carr remained in L.A. The number became a trip through old Hollywood as taken by a wide-eyed Snow White, a central character in the San Francisco show. She started by speaking with *Variety* columnist and Oscar greeter Army Archerd, visited the legendary Cocoanut Grove nightclub, went on a "blind date" with the young star Rob Lowe, and wound up surrounded by dancing usherettes at Grauman's Chinese Theatre. "Steve kept expanding it, and Allan did not take charge and tell him when to stop," says Seligman. "He brought in Merv Griffin, he brought in Rob Lowe . . . I told him he had to shorten the number, but Allan let it go."

For the Cocoanut Grove section, Carr lined up several tables full of classic stars, including Doris Day, Dorothy Lamour, Cyd Charisse, Vincent Price, and Roy Rogers and Dale Evans. But his biggest coup was to cast the ultimate Oscar-night host, Irving "Swifty" Lazar, as himself. The reticent Lazar agreed to leave Spago, where he traditionally hosted the hottest Oscar party in town, to table-hop in the number.

At the Shrine, though, even Carr eventually had to face the fact that Silver's production was too big. "It ended up way, *way* too long," says Margolis. "It became a special in itself. We had to cut it, because we knew you could only push the envelope so far in terms of length and style." Some of those who'd watched rehearsals thought the cuts hurt the number and made it more confusing. Late in the game, Swifty Lazar changed his mind and opted not to leave his own Spago soiree.

By the day of the show, the theater was gleaming and Carr was ready. Elaborately costumed and coiffed dancers from Steve Silver's number filled the aisles the broadcast began. "I sat down at the Shrine, and the curtain was a dazzling, shimmering, huge piece of sequins and velvet," says Douglass Stewart. "Then these *characters* filled up the aisles. The whole house was just so intrigued, so curious, so excited about what was going to happen."

Bruce Davis, who would soon assume the post of executive director of the Academy, sat nearby not knowing what to expect. "He wanted it to all be a surprise, not only to the audience but to us," says Davis. "And when I saw Snow White walk down the aisle and kind of brush by me, I thought, Oh, my God, I wonder if anybody's cleared that. I knew there were some things you have to do some checking around on."

The squeaky-voiced princess, played by a twenty-two-year-old actress named Eileen Bowman, greeted stars in the orchestra section, then sauntered onstage to sing what quickly became an infamous duet with Rob Lowe, who looked shell-shocked as he butchered a rewritten version of the Creedence Clearwater Revival rocker "Proud Mary." "Used to work a lot for Walt Disney / Starring in cartoons every night and day," Bowman warbled, and then Lowe picked up the story: "But you said good-bye to Doc and Sleepy / Left the dwarf behind, came to town to stay . . ." The impossibly cheesy number, which went on for an agonizing twelve minutes, also included dancing tables, a high-kicking chorus line of ushers, and Merv Griffin singing "I've Got a Lovely Bunch of Coconuts" in front of a batch of legendary stars sprinkled across the stage like so much window dressing. "His mistake was having that first number go on for so long," says Gilbert

Cates, who would in subsequent years produce the Oscar show himself. "When you see something that doesn't work, by four minutes it's terrible, by five minutes it's outrageous, by eight minutes it's the kiss of death, and by twelve minutes it's the worst thing you've ever seen in your life."

Not long after the opening number, Carr visited the press tent behind the Shrine. "How's the food?" he asked the reporters, some of whom were simultaneously trying to watch the show on monitors, interview winners and presenters, and grab sandwiches from a modest buffet. When asked his opinion of the show so far, Carr beamed. "We couldn't be happier."

Midway through the evening, another fifteen-minute production number showcased twenty "stars of tomorrow" singing a regrettable anthem entitled "I Wanna Be an Oscar Winner." (A "super-trouper, super-duper Oscar winner," no less.) The youngsters included Corey Feldman doing a Michael Jackson impersonation, Christian Slater sword fighting with Tyrone Power, Jr., Patrick Dempsey undertaking a soft shoe, Chad Lowe emoting ("I'm a thespian in the classic sense!"), fifteen-year-old Savion Glover tap-dancing (one bit of actual talent on display), and other offerings from Blair Underwood, Holly Robinson, Joely Fisher, Keith Coogan, Patrick O'Neal, Carrie Hamilton, Ricki Lake, Tricia Leigh Fisher, Corey Parker, Tracy Nelson, D. A. Pawley, Tracy Edwards, Melora Hardin, and Matt Lattanzi, most of whom looked vaguely embarrassed. For the record, none of the twenty have come close to winning an Academy Award in the ensuing years, though Christian Slater won an MTV Movie Award for "most desirable male" and Chad Lowe watched his wife, Hilary Swank, pick up an Oscar for *Boys Don't Cry*.

Elsewhere on Carr's show, the chitchat between his carefully matched presenters was cutesy and interminable. The best-picture award was entrusted not to Loretta Young but to the less legendary but (to Carr's mind) more fabulous Cher, who dressed for the occasion in a fringed, strapless mini. Reading from the TelePrompTer and addressing his wife, Geena Davis, Jeff Goldblum could have been speaking for most of the participants when he asked, "Have we lost our sense of dignity . . . here?"

Still, many of those present were swept up in the sheer exuberance of the producer's outlandish vision. When the show ended and the credits began to roll, it was quiet in Club Oscar until Carr's name appeared on the screen. Then Bruce Willis began to applaud, quickly joined by most of the stars in the room. At the Governors Ball, remembers Margolis, "Everybody was flying high. There was a buzz in the room, people were talking about how different it was. And then the shit hit the fan the next morning."

It began early, as Academy president Richard Kahn was sitting at his desk. "I was basking in the terrific ratings and the reaction we'd gotten," remembers Kahn. "And at about 9:15 I took another phone call, which I thought would be somebody else telling me what a great show it was." The caller was Frank Wells, the president of the Walt Disney Company and one of the most respected executives in Hollywood. "I think we have a real problem," Wells said.

Carr had not cleared the use of Snow White, and Wells wanted a formal apology. By midday, Disney lawyers were threatening to sue for copyright infringement; by the end of the day, they'd carried out the threat. Kahn drafted an apology that was delivered at a press conference eleven days later. Carr attended the press conference, and then the devastated producer called Jeff Margolis in tears.

Critics savaged his show: "one of the most grotesque television broadcasts in recent memory," said film critic David Ehrenstein in the *Los Angeles Herald-Examiner*. Gregory Peck wrote Kahn a letter saying "it looked like the Photoplay Awards," a reference to a tacky show put on by the now-defunct movie magazine, and threatening to give back his two Academy Awards if subsequent shows were going to look like Carr's. Seventeen Academy members, including Peck, Paul Newman, Billy Wilder, and Julie Andrews, wrote an open letter calling the show "an embarrassment to both the Academy and the motion picture industry"—although Kahn says, "I collared the people one by one, and most of them expressed no recollection of putting their names on that letter."

Carr never knew what hit him. He briefly tried to come to his own defense, claiming that former president Ronald Reagan called it "the best television show I've ever seen," and showing *Los Angeles Times* reporter Charles Champlin a stack of laudatory letters and telegrams. One came from agent Michael Ovitz, for whom the night had been a particular triumph: the movie Ovitz had shepherded through years of adversity, *Rain Man*, had been the big winner. "You brought show business back to the movie business," Ovitz wrote.

But the complaints overwhelmed the kudos, and Carr sank into a depression that gripped him for years. "He was blindsided completely, and it devastated him," said Seligman. "His biggest mistake was to tell everybody beforehand that he was going to do a show better than any other producer, because that set every previous producer against him. And when he failed, he completely lost respect in the community. He never got over that."

Gil Cates sympathizes with his predecessor as well. "I think Allan got a bad rap, and I think it hurt him beyond measure," says Cates. "Had that first number been three minutes long, Allan Carr might still be alive and still be producing the show."

Years later, Carr briefly surfaced for the twentieth-anniversary rerelease of *Grease*. Otherwise, he stayed out of sight. He died ten years after his Oscar show, without having done much in the interim. The cause of death was liver cancer, but some thought that other factors contributed.

"It's a true tragedy," says Seligman. "It killed him. Frankly, I think, more than anything else, the reaction to that show really killed him."

IF IT WAS A DISASTER ON MANY LEVELS, Allan Carr's show shaped the modern Academy Awards in more ways than the producer could have realized. Much of what has happened to the Oscars since then has been a reaction against the Carr show: the Academy convened a panel to figure out what went wrong and how to keep it from happening again, and then hired the man who headed that panel, Cates, to produce eleven of the next fifteen shows. Carr's show caused a backlash that restored dignity to the Oscar show . . . if you can call David Letterman's Top Ten List or Whoopi Goldberg's double entendres dignified. It doomed large-scale production numbers . . . but only until Debbie Allen and Paula Abdul began choreographing battalions of dancing fish, genies, and lions. It did away with cute chat between presenters . . . briefly, if at all. Carr's, in fact, was a night whose excesses weren't all that far removed from some of the excesses seen on shows produced by the guy who was hired to be the anti-Carr, or the others who followed him.

"He brought the show into the new era," insists Richard Kahn, "and did things that had never been done before but are now tradition." Carr was the one who replaced the phrase "and the winner is . . ." with the less exclusionary "and the Oscar goes to . . ." He was the first to hire a fashion coordinator and stage an Oscar Fashion Show, the first to hand out Oscar nominee sweatshirts, the first to take the crucial step of finding corporate partners for promotional tie-ins. He was the first to turn the green room into a glamorous showpiece, a true sanctuary for stars. He was the first producer to hire writer Bruce Vilanch, who has been the chief comic voice of the show ever since.

"That was widely felt to be a disastrous show, both inside and outside the Academy, but it's amazing how many of the innovations that Mr. Carr introduced are still with us today," says Bruce Davis. "He was selected because he was a showman, and by God, he did some things that were fun, and that we still do. It's hard to change the Oscars, but he was an energizing force."

Jeff Margolis defends the show even more avidly. "There was a sameness to the shows before that, and Allan really turned it on its ass," he says. "People were walking out of there going, 'What the hell just happened?' which was great. Allan was just what the show needed."

"To me, there is no question that Allan Carr's show paved the way for what has happened since then," says Chuck Workman, an Oscar winner who has made short films for most of the shows since 1988. "Often, I think that it takes a terrible disaster to let people see what is possible. You see that in politics: at Kent State, four students got killed, but that was the point where the hippies won. And you see that in popular culture all the time. Something is totally disastrous, somebody went too far, but the next person senses what is possible. We have to give Allan Carr his due for that."

THE PAST FIFTEEN YEARS have been a period in popular culture in which Allan Carr, under different circumstances, would have felt at home. The flamboyant, outsized producer, enamored of glamour and excess and celebrity, had embraced the hedonistic indulgences of the disco era and the shiny consumption of the eighties; had he been a participant rather than a broken man during the nineties, he could have enjoyed the pace of an era in which the media and the public eagerly built up, knocked down, embraced, and discarded celebrities and wannabees with astonishing speed.

The show that helped destroy Carr has been a significant part of the process. From the rise of the independent film to the decline of the major television networks, from the success of brain-dead blockbusters to the burgeoning of movie marketing as a contact sport—over the past fifteen years, the Academy Awards have been a battleground in which the themes running through the entire entertainment industry have played out.

At stake is the most widely recognized symbol of excellence in the entertainment industry—and also, clearly, one of the most potent marketing tools ever created. The monetary value of an Academy Award varies widely from film to film—generally speaking, the more successful a movie is before winning an Oscar, the less it benefits—but in most cases it reaches into the tens of millions of dollars. For the city of Los Angeles, the state of California, the movie industry in general, the value of the show is even harder to quantify, though the *Los Angeles Times* once estimated the figure at nearly $650 million, factoring in everything from the cost of trade advertisements to the money spent on pre- and postshow parties.

Advertising during the Oscar show alone brings ABC more than $75 million, of which as much as half goes to the Academy for broadcast rights. The Academy of Motion Picture Arts and Sciences pays for the production of the show, which costs more than $10 million; events surrounding the show add many more millions to the cost. What's left from ABC's fee is enough to cover virtually all of the Academy's annual operating budget.

The Academy has other sources of income: its membership dues bring in more than $1 million each year, while the organization built up an endowment worth tens of millions through fund-raising efforts that began in the early 1990s. But just as the Oscar show brings in the lion's share of the Academy's income, so has it become to most people the public face of the organization, and of Hollywood. The Academy operates a world-class film archive, awards screenwriting fellowships, and runs year-round screenings, exhibitions, and lectures—but to the public, it has a singular identity as the group that hands out Academy Awards.

The irony here—that an organization devoted to motion pictures supports itself by selling the rights to a TV show—is not lost on Academy officials. But they've embraced it, making sure that the Oscar show is always designed with TV viewers rather than the theater audience in mind.

Most years, the Oscars attract more of those viewers than any other nonsports program on television. The best-picture winner is usually seen by far more people on the Oscar show than in theaters; in recent years, only *Forrest Gump*, *Titanic*, and *The Lord of the Rings: The Return of the King* have boasted the kind of attendance figures that might rival their Oscar-night audiences. The party line that the Oscars are watched by a billion people is a lie, as the Academy will admit when pressed—but viewers still number well into the hundreds of millions, making the show a rival of the Super Bowl as the most watched telecast around the world.

"The Super Bowl kills us in the United States, and we don't have accurate figures for the rest of the world," concedes Bruce Davis. "But if you think about it, what's more popular around the world—American movies, or American football? I think we catch up to them in other countries."

Particularly over the past ten years, scrutiny of the event has increased on nearly every level. Dozens of magazines and nearly as many television shows are devoted to the lifestyles, foibles, and missteps of the rich and famous, and to them the Oscars are the main event. No other night is quite so resplendent with the top echelon of stardom, quite so grand a showcase for celebrity in all its finery and its absurdity. But in a culture highly attuned to competition, as witnessed in everything from the Super Bowl to *American Idol*, the Oscars are also irresistible in the way they ruthlessly turn the stars into haves and have-nots, supplying far more of the latter than the former. When those five boxes appear on the screen showing the faces of the nominees as the envelope is opened, who doesn't want to catch the losers in that moment of disappointment that proves impossible to hide? The show also fits neatly into the desire to track celebrities through every predictable moment of the *Behind the Music* or *True Hollywood Story* arc: Winona's down, Nicole's back, Whitney's heading for a fall . . . The Oscars can serve equally well as the moment of redemption, or as the pride that goeth before the fall.

The Academy Awards also reflect, more and more fully, the vicious side of Hollywood. In the 1980s, as the post–*Star Wars* blockbuster mentality firmly took control of Hollywood's major studios, the Oscars were one time of year when the studios could tell themselves it wasn't all about money. Even if studios were desperate for the next *Top Gun* or *Rambo*, Hollywood could point to Academy Awards for smaller films like *Kiss of the Spider Woman* or *Tender Mercies* as proof that the business was still about art *and* commerce.

But a business accustomed to the cutthroat pursuit of money could easily adapt to the cutthroat pursuit of gold statuettes. Over the past fifteen years, Oscar campaigns have displayed a nearly unprecedented ferocity. Ironically, more than a few of the campaign tricks came straight from Allan Carr's strategy for landing *The Deer Hunter* a best-picture win in 1979. Carr persuaded EMI and Universal to open the movie late in the year, building the buzz through special screenings and making it the movie of the moment precisely at the time when Oscar ballots would be in the mail. A decade later, this would be a strategy frequently used to great effect by Miramax as the company revolutionized Oscar campaigning.

But the strategy of opening late was only a start. Ad campaigns relying solely on genteel "for your consideration" ads in the Hollywood trade papers became a rarity, replaced by multifront campaigns encompassing parties, talk shows, celebrity endorsements, and the use of occasional underhanded tactics that ranged from artfully obscuring the true nature of your film to quietly bad-mouthing an opponent's entry.

The Academy finds the very thought of Oscar campaigns to be distasteful, along with the idea that those campaigns have any influence on voters. The organization is well aware that the importance and significance of the Academy Awards is tied to the perception that they genuinely are awarded for merit. When Halle Berry broke down sobbing after winning the best-actress Oscar in 2002, she was not doing so because her win meant another $20 million in box-office grosses and video sales for *Monster's Ball*, or because her asking price had just gone up; the numbers that affected her were the 6,000 voters who'd chosen her as the best, rather than the 600 million viewers who watched it happen. To safeguard that prestige, the Academy had spent much of the last decade fine-tuning its regulations that relate to campaigning, reacting as studios have violated the letter and the spirit of the law, and punishing the most serious transgressions.

At this point, though, even the Academy would not pretend that its annual awards are, or ever were, an artistic oasis unsullied by the mercenary zeal of the movie business. Oscar statuettes are the most valuable prizes to be accumulated by companies determined to accumulate both money and prizes by any means necessary.

At the center of these questions about intention and competition is the Academy Awards show itself. Whether you celebrate the Oscars as a sincere effort to honor artistry, or condemn them as a symptom of all that is wrong with Hollywood, the show is often irresistible television. It's a glitzy, glamorous, frequently god-awful display of fashion; it's a variety show, an increasingly rare commodity on TV, in which big stars sing songs you probably don't recognize; it's a chance to watch rich and famous people attempt to act pleased when somebody else wins an award. For three and a half or four hours, Hollywood's (and, often as not, a handful of the world's) brightest, most beautiful, and occasionally best get all dressed up, parade in front of cameras, and then pretend to be pleased as 80 percent of them go home losers.

In the last decade and a half, the Academy Awards broadcast has reached record lengths on three separate occasions, while battling a trend of declining ratings for network television. It has showcased four different hosts, and served as a sometimes eager, sometimes reluctant vehicle for the coronation of such outsized egos as James Cameron and Harvey Weinstein. At times, it has seemed irrelevant to the battles waged elsewhere in Hollywood; other times it has been a perfect case study in those battles. It is still the grandest, wildest celebration, dogfight, fashion show, and circus ever staged by the movie business. And just as in Allan Carr's day, dance numbers are still roundly panned, viewers still go to the refrigerator during the endless procession of technical awards, and presenters still look lost when they try to talk to each other.

IN EARLY 1994, the Academy agreed to give *Premiere* magazine unprecedented access to production meetings and rehearsals for that year's Oscar show, as well as backstage access during the show itself. While the rest of the massive Oscar press corps was invited to staged events and sequestered in the press room during the show, I was allowed to cover the event from the inside. Although the arrangement was initially envisioned as one time only, the Academy and the producers of the Oscar shows continued to allow me access in ensuing years. The degree of that access has varied slightly, but for the most part I have been allowed near-total entrée into an event that receives saturation coverage, but only from the outside; that draws intense scrutiny for about two months, then fades.

"It has the most glorious short life of any enterprise that I've ever been involved with," said Gil Cates, the most frequent producer of Oscar shows over the past fifteen years. "When you finish shooting a movie, you have to edit it, and afterward there's a life on television, on cable, on tape, in foreign markets. If you do a play, even if it closes there's the potential of an afterlife somewhere. The Academy Awards show lives gloriously in over a hundred countries for three and a half hours, and then it's gone. And I guess the reason I keep coming back to the well is that the process just astonishes me."

The goal of this book is to look inside that process, at the unseen, unguarded side of the Oscars. In studying the negotiations and machinations, the politics, the compromises, and the excesses of a strange, extraordinary event, I also hope to sketch a portrait of fifteen years of shifting currents, adjustments, and upheaval in the motion picture industry.

A NOTE ON DATES: The Academy refers to Oscar shows by the year during which the eligible movies were released. The show that takes place in February 2005, for instance, is officially the 2004 Oscars. I have tried to avoid that labeling as often as possible, because I'm dealing more with the Oscar shows themselves than with the movies under consideration. Thus, if I mention the seventy-fifth Oscar show, which took place in March 2003, I've tried to call it "the Oscars in 2003" rather than "the 2002 Oscars." I know that's not how the Academy likes to identify its shows, but I find it less confusing.

Introduction

History Is Made at Night

IT DIDN'T LOOK LIKE MUCH ON PAPER. Tucked away in the middle of a statement of aims drafted by the newly formed Academy of Motion Picture Arts and Sciences was a modest suggestion, almost an afterthought. The organization, it suggested, should encourage its young industry in a variety of ways, including handing out "awards of merit for distinctive achievement."

Awards weren't the point of the new Academy, which was formed in 1927 in large part to consolidate power in the hands of Hollywood studios and producers, and by doing so to stem the tide of unionization by workers in the fledgling industry. The document drafted by the group's thirty-six founders, which emphasized the noble more than the practical, put the emphasis on ideals like promoting harmony among movie professionals, protecting "the honor and good repute" of the industry, and "meeting outside attacks" from both church and state. In fact, the idea of awards wasn't even pursued until a year after the organization's founding, during which time the Academy had already intervened in a looming labor dispute, raised

$35,000 for victims of floods along the Mississippi River, and begun a library of material related to motion pictures.

Initially, Academy Awards were given out in a dozen categories: actor, actress, director, comedy direction, cinematography, interior decoration, the catchall engineering effects, three writing awards (adaptation, original story, and title writing), and the confusing tandem of best production and artistic quality of production. The winners were chosen by a committee of five, one from each of the Academy's branches. The committee was overseen by MGM chief Louis B. Mayer, hardly a disinterested observer.

Mayer, the driving force behind the formation of the Academy, was an autocratic boss who ran the most influential of Hollywood's studios, and by extension much of the town as well. Born in Russia but raised in Canada, the conservative and moralistic Mayer controlled the contracts of an enormous collection of stars, painting himself as a father figure while keeping a tight hand on the purse strings. The idea of the Academy had been floated during a small dinner at Mayer's home, and while he stayed out of the limelight (the actor Douglas Fairbanks, the organization's first president, having been deemed a better public face for the Academy), Mayer was known to cajole, argue, and otherwise pull strings behind the scenes.

The first Academy Awards took place on May 16, 1929, in the Blossom Room of the Hollywood Roosevelt Hotel. The midsized banquet room, which sits across the street and less than a block west of the current site of the Oscars, the Kodak Theatre, hosted less than three hundred Academy members and guests, who partook of dinner and dancing before Fairbanks handed out statuettes to the winners and scrolls to the runners-up. The only recipient to make a speech was Darryl F. Zanuck, who accepted a special award for *The Jazz Singer*—which, as a talking picture, had been ruled ineligible for the regular awards. Another special award—and, in a way, another consolation prize—went to Charlie Chaplin, who'd failed to be nominated after writing, directing, producing, and acting in *The Circus*.

At that first ceremony, there had been no attempt to create suspense: the winners had all been announced three months before the banquet, and two of those winners—best actor Emil Jannings and Paramount head Adolph Zucker, accepting the best-production award for *Wings*—had already been given their statuettes.

Slowly, though, the awards and the presentation underwent a metamorphosis. The second year, the Academy tried to clear up the problems caused by two de facto best-picture awards, consolidating best-production and artistic quality of production categories into a single best-picture award. The engineering award was eliminated, the three writing awards reduced to one, and the two directing awards to one. Four of the seven awards went to founding members of the Academy, including one to art director Cedric Gibbons, the man who also designed the statuette. Mary Pickford was named best actress for *Coquette*, a movie that had not been well received, intensifying criticism of the committee system. After the ceremony, the Academy decided that all its members would henceforth be allowed to vote.

But raising the number of voters from five to four hundred did not end complaints about the results, or about the pervasive influence of studio bosses. The following year, Greta Garbo's acclaimed performance in *Anna Christie* was overlooked for best actress in favor of Norma Shearer, the wife of MGM executive Irving Thalberg. Rumors flew that the studio, which released both Garbo's and Shearer's films, had urged all its employees in the Academy to vote for the latter. "What do you expect?" snapped Joan Crawford of Shearer's win. "She sleeps with the boss."

Throughout much of the 1930s, the Academy Awards remained a collegial event, designed more for the industry pals who filled banquet rooms than for the general public. Although a local radio station broadcast segments of the show beginning in its second year, postdinner entertainment usually consisted of nothing livelier than protracted speechmaking. In 1931, in fact, so many notables got up to talk—beginning with the vice president of the United States, Charles Curtis—that the awards weren't handed out until after midnight. By the time Marie Dressler was named best actress for *Min and Bill*, ten-year-old nominee Jackie Coogan had fallen asleep on her shoulder. Dressler had to gently dislodge him before accepting her award.

Over the next few years, the Academy saw its award grow in stature and importance, and also acquire the nickname of Oscar—though it's still uncertain whether the moniker came from Academy librarian Margaret Herrick, actress Bette Davis, or gossip columnist Sidney Skolsky, all of whom claimed responsibility. Those years also produced the show's first dead heat (Fredric March won the 1932 best-actor race by a single vote over Wallace

Beery, but Academy rules considered anything closer than three votes a tie) and the only write-in winner in its history, cinematographer Hal Mohr for *A Midsummer Night's Dream*.

Mohr had not been nominated, he believed, because of the ill will caused by his activism in the labor disputes that threatened Hollywood in the mid-1930s. The Screenwriters Guild and the Screen Actors Guild, both formed in 1933, were initially populated by writers and actors who'd quit the Academy, angry at its tacit support of Depression-era regulations that would have imposed salary ceilings and restricted the ability of actors to switch studios after fulfilling their contracts. The Screen Directors Guild was formed three years later, and like the other guilds encouraged its members to skip the Oscar ceremony. When the major studios followed by withdrawing their financial support of the floundering Academy, it fell to new president Frank Capra to right the sinking ship.

Capra, the thirty-eight-year-old, Sicilian-born director of *It Happened One Night* and *Mr. Deeds Goes to Town*, had gotten off to a rough start with the Academy. He'd first been nominated for best director for his 1933 movie *Lady for a Day*, and had attended the ceremony badly wanting to win. That night's emcee, Will Rogers, had a folksy, conversational way of announcing the winners, and when he got to Capra's category he rambled for a bit before announcing, "Come on up and get it, Frank!" In his autobiography, Capra said he got to his feet and was halfway to the stage before realizing, to his enduring embarrassment, that Rogers had been addressing *Cavalcade* director Frank Lloyd. But Capra made the walk for real the following year, when *It Happened One Night* won Oscars for best picture, actor, actress, adapted screenplay, and director.

After rewarding his movie with that unprecedented sweep of the top categories, the Academy made Capra its president during the stormiest time in the organization's brief history. In an attempt to save the show in 1936, Capra turned the evening into a tribute to film pioneer D. W. Griffith, attracting stars who might otherwise have boycotted. He also moved to ensure the integrity of the voting process by hiring Price Waterhouse & Co. to collect and tabulate the votes.

In order to meet the deadlines for late newspaper editions, though, the Academy continued to give the results to the press at the beginning of the festivities. In 1937, this allowed an impatient best-actress nominee, Gladys George, to stroll through the press room and learn she'd lost to Luise Rainer; a disconsolate George headed for the ladies' room, where she shared the bad news with fellow nominee Carole Lombard. Three years later, after the *Los Angeles Times* published the results in its 8:45 p.m. edition, which was carried into the show by late-arriving guests, the Academy decreed that envelopes would henceforth remain sealed until they were opened onstage.

Since the ninth Oscar show in 1937, those envelopes had included the new categories of supporting actor and actress. Character actor Walter Brennan won three of the first five supporting-actor Oscars, a record attributed in part to the fact that in 1938 the Academy had opened voting to members of all Hollywood guilds—including the populous Screen Extras Guild, whose members liked to honor those who, like Brennan, had come up through their ranks. The extras were also instrumental in the best-picture win for *Casablanca* in 1944. *The Song of Bernadette* had more nominations and was the odds-on favorite coming into the awards—but in an unusual if not unprecedented attempt to make it a prestige picture, 20th Century-Fox limited *Bernadette* to a few theaters in Los Angeles and New York, with tickets priced significantly higher than the nationwide average of 29 cents. After the Oscars, a survey of the Screen Extras Guild members, not the most well-heeled group of voters, showed that only one in four had even seen *Bernadette*, while almost all had seen *Casablanca*.

The show at which *Casablanca* won was also the first to be held in a theater rather than a banquet room, an expensive dinner dance having been deemed unseemly in wartime. Oscar winners during World War II received plaster statuettes, which were replaced with the gold-plated metal ones after the war ended. (Since 1941, the statuettes had carried a stipulation that still stands: winners were forbidden from reselling them without first offering them back to the Academy for ten dollars.)

As the war ended, another battleground heated up. Returning to prominence with the title role in *Mildred Pierce* after nearly a decade of lackluster, largely unsuccessful movies, actress Joan Crawford hired press agent Henry Rogers, who masterminded what might have been the first true Oscar campaign. While open solicitation of votes had proved fruitless when MGM became the first company to take out trade ads on behalf of the Eugene

O'Neill drama *Ah, Wilderness* in 1935, Rogers's style was subtler. Planting items in gossip columns, calling friends at the studios, and making sure Crawford was available and cooperative with anyone who wanted to talk about her maturation, by Oscar night he'd turned his client into the odds-on favorite—at which point a terrified Crawford refused to attend the show because, she said, she knew she was going to lose.

Undaunted, Rogers notified the press that his client was in bed with a 104-degree fever, while dispatching a hairdresser and makeup man to her house, just in case. Crawford won and director Michael Curtiz accepted on her behalf; back home in Brentwood, the actress managed to get out of bed, don an appropriately photogenic negligee, and sit with her groomers. When Rogers delivered her Oscar after the ceremony, Crawford was ready for her close-up. Said the admiring publicist later, "The photo of her in bed clutching the Oscar pushed all the other winners off the front page."

The following year, members of the actors, writers, directors, and extras guilds were removed from the voting rolls. The guilds were still invited to participate in the nominations, but only Academy members made the final choices. Even with an influx of new members that more than doubled the size of the Academy, to sixteen hundred plus, the electorate was far smaller than the previous year's total of more than nine thousand. With fewer voters to influence, campaigning by the studios picked up. That year, Rosalind Russell was the prohibitive best-actress favorite for *Mourning Becomes Electra*, but when Fredric March opened the envelope and read the name of Loretta Young, the audience was shocked—none more so than Russell, who'd already begun to rise from her seat in anticipation of a triumphant walk to the stage. Thinking quickly, Russell simply stayed on her feet and started clapping, appearing to graciously lead the standing ovation for her opponent.

Within two months of that ceremony, the five major Hollywood studios were dealt a blow by the Supreme Court, which ruled that it was a violation of antitrust laws to own both movie studios and theater chains. The studios became desperate to cut costs after the loss of what had been as much as 50 percent of their income, so they decided they could no longer underwrite the Oscar ceremony. Faced with canceling the show in 1949 for lack of funds, the Academy instead downsized, moving from the 6,000-seat Shrine

Auditorium to the 985-seat screening room in its Melrose Avenue headquarters. That night, in a move that some saw as payback for Hollywood's stinginess, six awards went to British films, including best picture to *Hamlet* and best actor to Laurence Olivier. The following year, the studios restored their financial support and the show moved to the ornate, twenty-eight-hundred-seat Pantages Theater in Hollywood.

The post–World War II years were rough ones for the movie business, battered not only by the court's ruling but also by a substantial slump in movie attendance largely attributed to the new medium of television. Unwilling to aid the enemy, the Academy had always resisted the idea of televising its show—but by 1953 it had little choice. In the face of uncertain support from the studios, a $100,000 offer from the National Broadcasting Company was irresistible. Men were warned that white shirts didn't photograph well under TV lights, women were told that pale colors worked best, and many stars took the easy way out and stayed home. Still, the likes of Mary Pickford, Jimmy Stewart, Ginger Rogers, and Olivia de Havilland appeared, and the bond between the Academy and the young medium was cemented when the ratings came in. The show had drawn the biggest audience in the five-year history of commercial television.

The move to television also marked the return to the Oscars of Bob Hope, who'd hosted all or part of five shows before his own television show had briefly rendered him unacceptable to the Academy. With the organization now committed to TV, Hope would return to host thirteen more times over the next twenty-five years. Over that time, Hope would perfect a standard shtick made up of wild political and movie-industry gags and countless jokes about how he'd never won an Academy Award (never mentioning that he'd been given five honorary awards).

Another milestone came with the best-picture winner *Marty* in 1956: the low-key drama, which began life as a television play, became the first film whose production cost ($340,000) was less than the price of its Oscar campaign ($400,000). With extensive prerelease screenings to foster word of mouth; ads bearing endorsements from actors such as Charlton Heston, Dean Martin, and Jane Russell; nonstop personal appearances by the film's likable star, Ernest Borgnine; and an unprecedented offer to send a 16-millimeter print of the movie to the home of any Academy member, the film's promotional blitz netted it four Oscars, including best picture and best actor.

By the end of the decade, the alliance between the Oscar show and television was becoming a comfortable one. The Hollywood studios even agreed to buy all the advertising for three years running, from 1958 through 1960. Still, adapting to the new medium was not entirely smooth: Bette Davis, for instance, fumed in 1958 when the network cut away before she handed out five honorary awards. The following year, emcee Jerry Lewis ran into the opposite problem: the show was twenty minutes ahead of schedule when it went into its final number, a rendition of "There's No Business Like Show Business" sung by actress Mitzi Gaynor. Lewis shouted "Another twenty times!" and desperately mugged for the cameras until NBC mercifully ended the broadcast early.

Beginning in 1961, the Oscars headed for the beach for seven years, to the Santa Monica Civic Auditorium. One of the few larger venues that could give the Academy enough setup time, the three-thousand-seat Civic was the first Oscar venue well outside the Hollywood–downtown Los Angeles axis. The inaugural show there was notable for the first public appearance of Elizabeth Taylor following an illness that had caused her to undergo a tracheotomy in London. Taylor had been nominated for her role in *Butterfield 8*, a seamy potboiler in which she hadn't wanted to appear—and though she continued to insist that she hated the movie, the sympathy vote helped win her the best-actress trophy over Shirley MacLaine in *The Apartment*. That film's director, Billy Wilder, sent MacLaine a telegram that read, YOU MAY NOT HAVE A HOLE IN YOUR WINDPIPE BUT WE LOVE YOU ANYWAY.

The controversy over Taylor's win was minor compared to the flap that surrounded John Wayne's three-and-a-half-hour epic *The Alamo*. To support his expensive, flag-waving film, Wayne mounted one of the most excessive Oscar campaigns in history, with ads essentially suggesting that it would be unpatriotic not to vote for his film. His campaign resulted in six nominations—including one for supporting actor Chill Wills, who proceeded to outstrip his costar with a campaign of unparalleled tastelessness. One Wills ad purported to name every Oscar winner for which the actor had ever voted; another listed every single Academy member and said, "Win, lose or draw, you're all my cousins and I love you all." Groucho

Marx couldn't resist the setup: the comedian took out his own ad, which read, "Dear Mr. Wills, I am delighted to be your cousin, but I'm still voting for Sal Mineo." The last straw, though, was an ad that pictured the cast of *The Alamo* and suggested that they were praying for a Wills victory "harder than the real Texans prayed for their lives at the Alamo." Wayne blasted Wills, press agent W. S. "Bow-Wow" Wojciechowicz took the rap, and in the end *The Alamo* won only a single Oscar, for sound.

The following year, the Academy's board of governors was forced to issue its first major statement on Oscar campaigning. Condemning what it called "outright, excessive and vulgar solicitation of votes," the board urged that nominees eschew ad practices "which are irrelevant to the honest evaluation of artistic and technical accomplishments." It declined, however, to set specific guidelines, leaving that to "the good conscience of the nominees."

George C. Scott, a supporting-actor nominee for *The Hustler* the following year, also claimed to be repulsed by the nature of the Oscar races. "I take the position that actors shouldn't be forced to out-advertise and out-stab each other," he said, asking the Academy to withdraw his nomination. The organization refused, and others pointed out that Scott's distaste for the Oscars came only after he'd been nominated for *Anatomy of a Murder* in 1960 but lost—unjustly, many felt—to Hugh Griffith from *Ben-Hur*, which set a new record that night by winning eleven awards. Scott lost again in 1962, this time to George Chakiris from *West Side Story*, on a night when Stan Berman, the self-described "world's greatest gate-crasher," managed to sneak onstage and hand presenter Shelley Winters a homemade award for Bob Hope.

To some, another unwelcome visitor to the Santa Monica Civic stage was Joan Crawford, who in 1962 costarred with longtime rival Bette Davis in the melodrama *Whatever Happened to Baby Jane?* Davis had been nominated for best actress, while Crawford was overlooked. While all involved denied any friction, Crawford immediately wrote congratulatory notes to the other four nominees, gallantly offering to accept the Oscar in the event they couldn't attend. The night of the show in 1963, Davis stood in the wings, confident she'd go home with the third statuette of her career; instead, the absent Anne Bancroft won for *The Miracle Worker*, and Crawford accepted on her behalf. It was, Davis said later, "despicable."

For all the backstage strife, the Academy Awards managed to ignore the battles being waged in the streets and in popular culture for much of the 1960s. Rock 'n' roll was never seen on the show; civil rights consisted of Sammy Davis, Jr., joking about calling the NAACP when he was mistakenly given the wrong envelope. In 1967, though, the show was almost canceled by a strike of the American Federation of Television and Radio Artists, which was settled only three hours before showtime. The following year, the fortieth Oscar show was postponed for two days after the assassination of Dr. Martin Luther King, Jr. That night, the big winner was a drama about race relations, *In the Heat of the Night*.

It wasn't until the end of the decade, 1969, that a serious attempt was made to overhaul and update the Oscar show. Gregory Peck, the president of the Academy, brought in Broadway director and choreographer Gower Champion, who'd made his name with shows like *Hello, Dolly!* and *Bye Bye Birdie*. The show was moved to the newer, more elegant Dorothy Chandler Pavilion in downtown Los Angeles; Champion tried, but failed, to eliminate the bleachers full of fans. He also gave Bob Hope the boot as host in favor of ten "friends of Oscar," including Jane Fonda, Sidney Poitier, Diahann Carroll, Frank Sinatra, and Natalie Wood. He couldn't do anything about the voting, though: the best-picture winner was the distinctly old-fashioned musical *Oliver!* while the riskier likes of *2001: A Space Odyssey*, *Rosemary's Baby*, and *Belle du Jour* weren't even nominated. Bob Hope, meanwhile, got a standing ovation when he showed up to present the Jean Hersholt Humanitarian Award to Martha Raye.

The following year, the voters managed to walk an artful middle ground: they gave John Wayne his first Oscar for *True Grit*, a genuine career-achievement gift to one of the old guard, but then handed the best-picture trophy to the edgy, X-rated *Midnight Cowboy*. The 1971 ceremony got another jolt courtesy of George C. Scott, who again tried to decline a nomination for *Patton*, and this time had to decline the Oscar statuette as well. Marlon Brando refused his Oscar for *The Godfather* two years later, but Brando sent along an actress named Maria Cruz to decline on his behalf. Claiming to be a Native American named Sacheen Littlefeather, Cruz lectured the audience about the shameful "treatment of American Indians today by the film industry . . . and on television in movie reruns."

By this point, politics had infused much of the Oscar show. When Charlie Chaplin was coaxed into receiving an honorary Academy Award in 1972, his acceptance became one of the most emotional moments in Oscar history partly because the eighty-two-year-old actor hadn't been in the United States for twenty years, dogged by criticism over his neutrality in World War II and his nonpayment of U.S. taxes. Three years later, open warfare spilled onto the stage after producer Bert Schneider, who won for his Vietnam documentary *Hearts and Minds*, read a telegram offering the thanks of the Viet Cong delegation to the ongoing Paris Peace Talks. Backstage, Bob Hope was incensed that Schneider had proffered greetings from the group U.S. forces had been fighting. Hope persuaded cohost Frank Sinatra to read a statement apologizing for "any political references made on the program." But Sinatra's apology infuriated a third cohost, Shirley MacLaine, who proceeded to berate Sinatra in the wings. "I'm a member of the Academy," she raged, "and you didn't ask me!"

In the early 1970s, a pair of executives began long stints at the helm of the Oscar show: Howard W. Koch produced the first of his eight shows in 1972, while director Marty Pasetta began a seventeen-year run the same year. Koch had a real sense of glamour, while Pasetta was determined to always use the latest, most advanced technology on every show. But neither Koch nor the show's other producers seemed to know what to do about Oscar hosts: the first eight shows of the decade all had multiple hosts, from a low of four to a high of thirty-two. Those who took a turn onstage ranged from Helen Hayes to Goldie Hawn, Fred Astaire to Burt Reynolds, Myrna Loy to Richard Pryor.

Of the seventy-four stars who tried the gig during those years, the best moment probably belonged to British actor David Niven, who in 1974 had the wit—or, some insisted, the script—to respond to the sight of a streaker with the line, "Isn't it fascinating to think that probably the only laugh that man will ever get in his life is by stripping off his clothes and showing his shortcomings?"*

---

*The streaker, thirty-three-year-old Robert Opal, made some TV appearances, was hired by Allan Carr to streak a party for Rudolph Nureyev, tried to make it as a stand-up comedian, and five years later was murdered in a San Francisco sex shop.

Between 1977 and 1979, a trio of Oscar telecasts revealed deep divisions between approaches to the show. The first of those years, film director William Friedkin was persuaded to produce the show. Friedkin was notoriously difficult to work with in those days, and his films—among them *The French Connection*, *The Exorcist*, and *Cruising*—were notably lacking in sentimentality. As might have been expected, he proved to be a hard-nosed, jaundiced overseer: he brought in Richard Pryor, Warren Beatty, Jane Fonda, and Ellen Burstyn to host, and vetoed a plan for Loretta Young to salute the recently deceased Rosalind Russell. He also asked *Network* writer Paddy Chayevsky to accept the Oscar should the late actor Peter Finch win for best actor; the last thing he wanted, he told the writer, was to have a weeping widow on his stage. But Chayevsky double-crossed Friedkin when Finch won, immediately summoning Elthea Finch to the stage.

Friedkin's show drew the lowest TV ratings of any Oscar telecast, and the director wasn't invited back. The following year, the job went once more to Koch, who produced a fiftieth-anniversary show long on tradition and sentiment. Bob Hope was back as emcee, while legends like Fred Astaire, Bette Davis, Greer Garson, and William Holden also participated— as did past Oscar winners Ernest Borgnine, Dorothy Malone, and Burl Ives, among others unfortunately lumped into an awkward opening sequence. And while actress Vanessa Redgrave caused another furor with a speech that included a condemnation of "Zionist hoodlums" in Israel, the Academy was able to shrug off the controversy when the ratings came in: the show had drawn the largest television audience of any Oscar show.

The following year, the Academy began its sixth decade with a new approach—or, to be more specific, a new host. Unlike most emcees, Johnny Carson was not a movie star, but the host of *The Tonight Show*. He had an easygoing manner that had been pleasing the television audience for more than fifteen years. The Academy found a style and sensibility in the fifty-two-year-old Carson that was comfortable to the public; he had enough of an edge to separate his material from the predictable patter of a Bob Hope, but he didn't make the Academy nervous the way the likes of Richard Pryor did. (The first line of Pryor's monologue the year he hosted the show had been, "I'm here to explain why black people will never be nominated for anything.")

Still, Carson had a tendency that did not endear him to all the branches of the Academy: he'd tell the home audience "this might be a good time to make some dip" before the reading of the rules, and even worse he wasn't shy about mocking the occasional nominee or winner in the technical categories. For instance, when the recipient of the sound effects editing award for *The Black Stallion* couldn't make it in 1980, Carson seized the moment. "It always happens," he said. "First George C. Scott doesn't show, then Marlon Brando, and now Alan Splet."

The branches always bristled at that kind of belittlement, but Carson kept it up. To make matters worse, his first turn as host included a medley entitled "Oscar's Only Human," which was designed to showcase great movie songs that hadn't been nominated for Academy Awards.

When members of the music branch heard about the medley, they tried to convince producer Jack Haley, Jr., to drop it. It had been a rough few years for the branch: in 1976, after Diana Ross's hit song "Theme from *Mahogany* (Do You Know Where You're Going To)" failed to win a nod from the special committee that picked the best-song nominees, the outrage had been so widespread that the branch changed the rules, threw out the committee's choices, and had all its members quickly vote a new slate of nominees. (The Ross song made the cut.) Two years later, similar howls ensued when not a single song from the Bee Gees' landmark *Saturday Night Fever* soundtrack was nominated; this time, though, the branch had no real recourse but to endure the complaints. But when the members learned of plans to make an Oscar-night medley of their most notable errors in judgment, they immediately cried foul. Haley branded the music branch "thin-skinned," threatened to quit and take Carson with him, and got his medley, one of the best-received moments of that particular show.

Carson brought a steady voice and a stability to the show during the five years he hosted between 1979 and 1984. Those years included a one-day postponement of the show in 1981, after an attempt on the life of President Ronald Reagan, as well as a sillier contretemps two years later when Polish director Zbigniew Rybczynski, a winner in the best animated short category, stepped outside the Chandler for a smoke, then couldn't talk his way past an overzealous security guard to get back in. Rybczynski kicked the guard, who promptly had him arrested and carted off to jail; there, the director called the only American lawyer whose name he knew, celebrity divorce specialist Marvin Mitchelson.

During the Carson years, Academy membership crept toward the five thousand mark, and the length of the Oscar show crept toward, and past, the three-and-a-half-hour mark. When Carson walked away from the gig, producers struggled to find the right tone. Actor Jack Lemmon opted for brevity in 1985, the year of Sally Field's famous "You like me, you really like me" speech, while legendary musical director Stanley Donen booked the mismatched host trio of Robin Williams, Jane Fonda, and Alan Alda the following year, and stumbled with an elaborate production number featuring actress Teri Garr and a crew of wing-walking high-steppers. By 1987, producer Samuel Goldwyn, Jr., was forced to face the fact that the Oscars were no longer considered a prestige booking: he wanted to open the show with a version of the *Guys and Dolls* standard "Fugue for Tinhorns," but got turned down by everyone from Frank Sinatra and Dean Martin to Steve Martin and Rodney Dangerfield. In the end, he settled for the distinctly bargain-basement threesome of TV's Kojak, Telly Savalas, *The Karate Kid*'s Pat Morita, and rotund comic actor Dom DeLuise.

Goldwyn, who loved producing the Oscars, was one of several producers to tackle the show during this era. (Another, film director Norman Jewison, told friends he hated the job.) The one constant, though, was Marty Pasetta. The director and the highest-ranking paid employee on the production staff, Pasetta was responsible for many of the procedures that Oscar staffers—and those who worked on all other awards shows—would come to take for granted. "Seat-fillers, stand-ins, picture cards, camera techniques—a lot of the ways awards shows are now done started with Marty," said Danette Herman, who worked closely with Pasetta for several years.

"He had this great kind of bigger-than-life feeling of what a ringmaster should do," said Michael Seligman, who began working with Pasetta on the fiftieth Oscar show in 1978. But Pasetta also had a temper. "No no no no no," he'd snap if an underling did something he didn't like. "*Wrong*. Nonononono. *Wrong*." When the day of the show rolled around, Pasetta rarely had a voice left.

By 1988, Pasetta had directed seventeen consecutive Oscar broadcasts, and according to many who worked on the shows, he often acted as if he alone were running the show. That year, though, the director overstepped his bounds for the last time. Pasetta loved to stage elaborate musical numbers, and started the show with a routine set to a song from the musical *A Chorus Line*. Producer Samuel Goldwyn, Jr., hired Michael Kidd, a legendary Broadway choreographer who'd also worked on films including *Seven Brides for Seven Brothers* and *Hello Dolly!* But Pasetta and Kidd had some disagreements about how the number should be staged. Kidd pleaded his case to Academy president Robert Wise, for whom he'd choreographed sequences in the 1968 film *Star!* On one of the final days of rehearsal, in an incident still legendary within Academy and production circles, Wise approached Pasetta on Kidd's behalf—and Pasetta dismissed the president of the Academy with a curt, "I think we can take it from here, Bob."

"It's not like Bob didn't have any credentials to sit in on a music discussion," said one Academy official of Wise, the Oscar-winning director of *West Side Story* and *The Sound of Music*. "And he was the president of the goddamn Academy. When the story went around, that was that. The board was just appalled." Howard Koch continued to hold out hopes that the board might someday relent, but Pasetta's run at the helm of the Oscar show was over.

At that point, the Academy Awards were long and glitzy, by turns glamorous and silly, occasionally ponderous and sometimes almost elephantine. At a time when MTV was revolutionizing the look of music and entertainment on television, the Oscars were determinedly old-fashioned. Ratings were still good, but the trend was downward, not upward; stars, especially younger ones, were not as easy to corral for the show as they had once been.

Richard Kahn, who took over as Academy president from Wise, knew the institution needed an infusion of energy. He brought in Allan Carr. A year later Carr was a bad memory, Gilbert Cates was in charge, Billy Crystal was on board, and the modern Oscars had begun.

1

≡

Putting It Together

The 66th Academy Awards

"THE PELLET with the poison's in the flagon with the dragon," Chuck Warn muttered to nobody in particular as he walked down a long central hallway in the Academy Awards production office. "The vessel with the pestle has the brew that is true." Dressed all in black and cutting an imposing figure at well over six feet and three hundred pounds, the bearded, longhaired publicist for the show's producer paused, then picked up the pace. "The pellet with the poison's in the flagon with the dragon, the vessel with the pestle has the brew that is true . . ."

The lines, first uttered by actor/comic Danny Kaye in the 1956 comedy *The Court Jester*, had nothing to do with the 66th Academy Awards, which would take place in six weeks. Most of those weeks would be filled with steady, sometimes frantic activity: yet to come was flash and furor and spectacle beyond anyone's control, the Oscar carnival in all its finery and silliness. For the moment, though, on the third floor of a nondescript high-rise office building on Wilshire Boulevard in West Los Angeles, things were calm enough that staffers who wanted to spend a few minutes declaiming Danny Kaye dialogue could do so.

Inside the largest of the offices that lined the hallway Warn was pacing, Gilbert Cates sat behind his desk and looked out the window, across Westwood Village and toward the UCLA campus. "I've always been a fan of the circus," he announced. "And this is the greatest circus." He returned his gaze to the room, where pages of schedules, notes, and numbers sat on the desk. Behind him, over his right shoulder, a shiny metal gong hung within reach so that he could notify staffers of each new booking with an appropriately dramatic flourish. Across the room, a bulletin board, protected from unauthorized eyes by a set of white miniblinds, broke down the show and sported the names of presenters and performers, some already booked and others merely coveted. "This show presents great opportunities, great highs and great lows," he said. "It requires a tremendous effort, but it's a lot of fun." Cates paused, allowing a small grin to crease the corners of his mouth. "And I use that word *fun* carefully."

The spectacle was a familiar one to Cates, who had produced every Oscar show since Allan Carr's momentous mess of five years earlier. "I think Gil totally saved the Oscar show," said Chuck Workman. "It was moribund. And he was the perfect man at the perfect time. He was able to make it a much more modern show, keep it very much about Hollywood but also catch up with the rest of entertainment."

A member of the Academy's board of governors for eight years, as well as a two-term past president of the Directors Guild of America, the fifty-nine-year-old Cates had started his career in 1955, after graduating from Syracuse University. Originally a premed student at Syracuse, Cates became fascinated with the theater almost by accident: a member of the school's fencing team, he'd been drafted to teach the actors in a campus production of *Richard III* how to wield swords. He switched his major to theater, stage-managed on Broadway after graduation, and then worked on a string of largely forgotten TV game shows (*Haggis Baggis*, *Picture This*, *Camouflage*) during the 1950s and early '60s. Cates broke into the movie business in his midthirties with the circus-themed 1966 film *Rings Around the World*. He continued to move between theater, television, and film; in that last arena, his most notable successes were a pair of Oscar-nominated early '70s dramas, *I Never Sang for My Father* and *Summer Wishes, Winter Dreams.*

Cates's film career cooled off after those movies, and he turned largely to television, where he was allowed to make the kind of socially themed movies in which he was most interested. While directing TV movies about mental illness, domestic abuse, and the like, he remained active in Academy affairs. In 1989, after six years on the board of governors, he was asked to head the Awards Presentation Review Committee formed to scrutinize Allan Carr's show.

Cates's committee recommended using a single host whenever possible, relying more on film clip packages than on production numbers, and booking single presenters to prevent awkward chit-chat. In many ways the most dramatic suggestion, though, was to pay the producer of the Oscar show. "The idea that we didn't need to pay because the producer's job was a great honor was a double-edged sword," said Bruce Davis, who assumed the executive director position the year after the Carr show. "It *is* a great honor, and only the top directors and producers in town had ever been asked to do it— but if you ask a guy to put that kind of time into a project and don't pay him, you almost lose your ability to rein him in. We would frequently get the reaction, 'Look, I'm doing this for free and now you guys are gonna nickel-dime me?' To pay the producer put the show on more of a business footing."

The first year, the job carried an honorarium of $150,000. New Academy president Karl Malden, also a member of the review committee, figured that the man who chaired the panel ought to do the job (and pocket the paycheck) himself. Cates took his share of ribbing as both the man who recommended the producer be paid, and the man to benefit from that recommendation—but four years later, with four Oscar shows under his belt, he was still the only man who'd ever been paid to produce the Academy Awards. "It's embarrassing, being the first producer to be paid," Cates said at his first board of governors meeting after taking the job. "I can only say that had I known it was going to be me, I would have said the pay should be much higher."

As a producer, Cates had certain tendencies: he felt that each show should open with a film clip, but he also loved staging those oft-maligned dance numbers (though he subscribed to the theory that each individual element should last no longer than three minutes). He liked to give themes to his Oscar shows, and he was fond of surprise appearances by both people and animals. But despite his penchant for dogs and horses and Debbie Allen, Cates was also a steadying, calming influence—particularly when compared with the likes of Carr. As befitted a college dean and an occasional teacher, Cates had a professorial manner. But when the mood struck him, the generally soft-spoken producer delighted in sprinkling his speech with expletives.

On the slow Monday morning in early February, Cates conferred briefly with Chuck Warn, then walked back down the hall toward his own office. Outside the door, he stopped to look over the schedule kept by his assistant, Debbie Olchick.

"Oh, this is a very important meeting that demands all my attention," he said as he ducked back into his office. "It's hard work, figuring out if the fucking jackets and hats should be red or black."

THE PAST FOUR YEARS had been a smooth stretch for the Academy Awards. When he took over on the heels of Allan Carr's show, Cates tried to streamline the operation and unify the staff. Where previous producers had often worked in separate offices from much of the production staff, he brought everyone together in one office.

He also had a different sensibility, one formed by a background that included theater, film, and live television. "Gil had produced television and produced motion pictures and directed television and directed motion pictures, and he had some Broadway experience as a producer and director," said Jeff Margolis, who returned to direct his second show. "He also had a whole different philosophy from Allan. He wanted to do it bigger and better, but he knew the limitations of television. He knew we weren't making a movie, we were doing a television show, and that was a whole different way of approaching the show."

His first year on the job, Cates took the crucial step of lining up Billy Crystal to host. Crystal's brief routine had been one of the best-liked moments of the Carr show; the comic had a stand-up background, but movies like *When Harry Met Sally* had also given him a cachet in the movie business.

Initially, Crystal had been enamored by the gig, but reluctant to commit. To make his pitch, Cates took Crystal to lunch at the Friar's Club in Beverly Hills—where the producer received an unexpected assist from the eighty-one-year-old comedian Milton Berle, who dropped by their booth to say hello and, when he learned why the men were meeting, launched into an enthusiastic monologue about why Crystal simply *had* to take the job.

Although Cates had heard from some naysayers who felt that Crystal's humor might be too ethnic for Middle America, the comic immediately found the right tone. At his first show, in 1990, his monologue was filled with Hollywood jokes that were inside enough for the audience at the Chandler, but broad enough for the millions at home. His first line, though, alluded directly to the previous year. "Is that for me," he said as the audience applauded, "or are you just glad I'm not Snow White?"

In fact, Ms. White had already made an appearance on the show, which had opened with a breakneck montage of famous movie clips put together by Chuck Workman. Among the more than three hundred scenes crammed into five minutes was an entirely deliberate shot of the Disney heroine. "I asked, 'Do you think this will offend anybody?'" said Workman, "and Gil said, 'Fuck 'em, it's good.'"

Cates was determined to make his Oscars a classy one—and since the Cold War had essentially ended in 1989 and the Iron Curtain had come down across Europe, an international event as well. He sent crews to London, Moscow, Sydney, Tokyo, and Buenos Aires, enormously complicating the technical side of the production.

"Nothing like that had ever really been attempted before, and we went on the air not knowing if we were ever going to have any sound coming from Russia," said Margolis. "During all the setup and all the rehearsals, we never got the audio and video together at the same time. I thought, poor Jack Lemmon. We've shipped him all the way to Moscow, and now nobody will be able to hear him. But it worked. I loved it."

Cates's initial show was well received, both within the Academy and outside it. "We could do no wrong that year, because we were following Allan Carr," said Roy Christopher, the production designer for the show in 1990. "It was much more what the Academy, and the public, seemed to want." The show was nominated for five Emmy Awards, with Christopher winning; over the next three years, Cates's shows would secure twenty-six nominations and six more wins.

During those years, the producer continued to trot out variations on his Oscar formula. Each year he gave the show a theme ("100 Years at the Movies" in 1991, "The Pure Joy of the Movies" the following year, "Women and the Movies" in 1993), and each year he used Crystal as host, relied heavily on film montages, but also threw in dance numbers, often as not choreographed by Debbie Allen.

Some of those numbers were gruesome (including a 1991 opening that purported to trace the history of film and involved lots of people jumping back and forth through screens), and sometimes the real world intruded on the relatively smooth machine Cates was running. In 1991, the recent Gulf War caused security to be far tighter than usual, as for the first time Oscar guests (with the exception of Bob Hope) were run through metal detectors on their way to the red carpet.

Cates initially figured he'd produce no more than three shows, but by 1994 he was on something of a roll. "It's very hard to conceive of a producer agreeing to do it again while he's in the throes of it, or within a month or two afterwards," said Bruce Davis. "But when they calm down and relax, you can sometimes talk them into doing it again. And considering that Gil had done the show before and done it well, that he'd actually succeeded in cranking up the ratings little bit, and that ABC embraced him, the talk within the Academy was along the lines of, 'Do you think we can talk him into doing it again?' "

ABOUT FOUR MILES EAST of the production office, it looked as if a hurricane had hit the Beverly Hills headquarters of the Academy of Motion Picture Arts and Sciences. In fact, the disarray—missing ceiling panels, soiled carpeting, dented furniture—had come from a 6.7 magnitude earthquake that hit Los Angeles just after 4 a.m. on Martin Luther King Day, January 17, 1994. Throughout the seven-story building, bookcases had been toppled and the emergency sprinkler system had drenched desks. In subsequent days, the closet in Bruce Davis's office filled with Oscar statuettes that were returned to the Academy for repair (or, more often, replacement) after the quake: Oliver Stone's Oscar for *Platoon* was bent at the base, while Jack Nicholson's for *One Flew Over the Cuckoo's Nest* had been dented when it fell on its head.

Amid fallout from the temblor, bookcases and tables were piled high with boxes of publicity photographs, slides, bios, and press kits. In preparation for the next morning's announcement of Oscar nominations, studios had sent over promotional materials for all who had a shot at a nomination, and some who didn't: near a stack of bios of Holly Hunter, considered a lock for a best-actress nomination for *The Piano*, was a box that Touchstone Pictures had supplied in the unlikely event that Kathy Najimy won a supporting-actress nod for *Sister Act 2: Back in the Habit*.

For most of the day, a team from the accounting firm of Price Waterhouse had locked itself in the sixth-floor copy room, where they compiled lists of the nominees, copied those lists, and double-checked spellings and punctuation with Academy staffers. Of course, they couldn't just come out and ask, "How do you spell *Spielberg*?" So they'd pass Academy officials a list of several names to be checked; one name would belong to a true nominee, while the others would be decoys.

Just after 6 p.m., the building was cleared of all but essential personnel, and the switchboard was shut down. At the same time, the Price Waterhouse reps came into Davis's office and officially presented him with the list of nominees. In a ceremony whose formality was at least partly tongue in cheek, the executive director thanked the accountants for doing another meticulous job of counting, whereupon his staff descended upon the lists of nominees and tore through them.

The list contained the names of thirty-seven feature films and thirteen shorts, eighteen different actors and actresses, and close to 150 other nominees. To the surprise of no one, the film with the most nominations was Steven Spielberg's *Schindler's List*, the Holocaust-themed drama that had been considered the Oscar front-runner since its December release.

Spielberg had a troubled history with the Academy, which sometimes seemed mistrustful of the kind of zestful popular entertainment in which the director specialized. In 1975, his film *Jaws* became the top-grossing movie ever made, and the twenty-nine-year-old wunderkind was considered such a strong candidate for a best-director nomination that a TV crew went to Spielberg's home to record his reaction when the nominations were announced. But there is often a discrepancy between the five films nominated for best picture by the Academy's entire membership and the five directors nominated by the smaller directors' branch—and more often than not, that discrepancy manifests itself when a director responsible for a successful popcorn movie is bypassed in favor of an artier auteur. Such was Spielberg's fate: as the film crew watched, he found that *Jaws* was up for best picture, but he had been left out in favor of Italian legend Federico Fellini, whose autobiographical *Amarcord* had won the Oscar for best foreign film the previous year but was eligible in other categories in 1975. "I can't believe it," said Spielberg, head in hands. "They went for Fellini instead of me."

Spielberg had other reasons to complain in subsequent years. He was nominated for *Close Encounters of the Third Kind*, *Raiders of the Lost Ark*, and *E.T.*, but lost to Woody Allen (*Annie Hall*), Warren Beatty (*Reds*), and Richard Attenborough (*Gandhi*); his 1985 film *The Color Purple* won eleven nominations, including best picture, but was passed over in the best-director race. The following year, the board of governors' decision to give Spielberg the Irving Thalberg Award carried the unmistakable air of an apology.

But with *Schindler's List*, the feeling was that Spielberg had finally made a movie the Academy could not help but embrace wholeheartedly, whatever reservations it may have had about the director's youth, commercial success, and populist instincts. Competing with *Schindler* for best picture was director Jane Campion's austere but erotic *The Piano*; *The Remains of the Day*, from the high-toned Merchant Ivory team; *In the Name of the Father*, director Jim Sheridan's fact-based story about a young Belfast man falsely accused of being a terrorist; and the action film *The Fugitive*, adapted from the '60s TV series. Campion became only the second woman to receive a nomination for best director (following the Italian director Lina Wertmuller in 1976), while eleven-year-old supporting-actress nominee Anna Paquin was the youngest performer to be nominated since eight-year-old Justin Henry fourteen years earlier.

Final voting for the Academy Awards was conducted in a simple, straightforward manner. But the nominations were arrived at in a far more complex way, through a method known most commonly as the preferential system.

The system had been recommended to the Academy by Price Waterhouse in the 1940s, after the accounting firm had studied the pitfalls of alternatives. Academy members were asked to vote for five nominees, in order of preference, in each of their branch's categories, plus the best-picture category. Initially, a small group of Price Waterhouse employees, working at a location the firm kept secret, separated the ballots into stacks based on the film listed first. Nominations automatically went to films receiving first-place votes on one-sixth of the ballots, plus one; with five nominations in a category, it would be impossible for five other films to receive more votes.

Films that received no first-place votes were eliminated from contention, while the ballots of voters whose first-place choices received the smallest number of votes were redistributed into the remaining piles based on their second choices. (If a voter's second choice was no longer in the running, the third, fourth, or fifth pick would be used.) The process was repeated, with the films drawing the least support eliminated in each subsequent round, until only five piles remained.

To complicate matters, if a film received far more first-place votes than it needed to secure a nomination, all of the ballots in its pile were redistributed into the other piles, with the second choices listed on those ballots given a fractional value based on the percentage of that member's vote required to ensure the first choice a nomination. (For instance, if *Schindler's List* received twice as many first-place votes as it needed, it earned a nomination and the second choice of all *Schindler* voters counted as half a vote.)

The idea was to allow each member to vote for favorite films without second-guessing or worrying about electability. "The problem with the usual weighted system," said Davis, "is that the two points you give to a guy lower on your ballot might be just enough to push him past the guy you really want at the top of your ballot. It leads to a certain amount of game playing, because if you're afraid of other candidates you might put them way down." Under the preferential system, a member didn't have to worry about a third or fourth choice hurting a film listed higher on the ballot—because the third choice can't be counted unless the voter's first choice is either out of the running or already assured a nomination. "I don't think a very high percentage of members could describe exactly how it works," conceded Davis. "When I hear them talking about it, I can tell that they don't understand."

ON FEBRUARY 17, the week after the nominations were announced and five weeks before the Oscar show, Cates convened a production meeting in a conference room across the hall from his office. Sitting around the long table were the core members of the Oscar team. Director Jeff Margolis was a barrel-chested veteran of five Oscar shows and dozens of variety telecasts. Danette Herman, the show's executive in charge of talent and in Cates's words "the heart and conscience of the show," was a soft-spoken woman who nonetheless was known to quietly exercise steely control over her province, which ranged from booking performers and presenters to making sure that the stars on the show were well treated. Associate producer Michael Seligman, short and sharp, was the money man. Production designer Roy Christopher had designed three of the past five Oscar sets, between his day job as the art director of TV series like *Frasier* and *Murphy Brown*. Composer and conductor Bill Conti, Cates's usual choice to head the Oscar orchestra and an Oscar winner himself, was a slight, sardonic man who invariably played his best-known composition, "Gonna Fly Now (The Theme from *Rocky*)," at least once during every show. Chuck Workman was the master of fast-paced montages of film clips—one of which, *Precious Images*, had won him an Oscar in 1987. Costume designer Ray Aghayan, diminutive and deeply tanned, was one of the oldest (and during production meetings, quietest) members of the Oscar crew.

As aides brought in a modest selection of sandwiches and soft drinks, Cates went over the show's musical numbers. The songs were always a key part of the Oscar show, and one over which the producer had no control: whatever the music branch nominated had to be performed. Since he took over, Cates had gone out of his way to book the original performers on the show; he knew that viewers had cringed in the past when the songs were handed over to less suitable interpreters.

This time, three of the five nominations had gone to major stars in the fields of rock and pop music: Bruce Springsteen and Neil Young for "Streets of Philadelphia" and "Philadelphia," respectively, both from Jonathan Demme's film *Philadelphia*; and Janet Jackson for "Again" from *Poetic Justice*, a film by director John Singleton. The final two nominations went to the light pop tune "A Wink and a Smile" from *Sleepless in Seattle*, which was sung in the film by the popular jazz-pop singer and pianist Harry Connick, Jr., and to the formula love song "The Day I Fell in Love," a duet by country diva Dolly Parton and soul crooner James Ingram from the comedy *Beethoven's Second*. With one exception, the original performers had already agreed to appear—and the one who declined to do the song was the demanding Connick, whose absence had caused no great dismay in the production office. Conspicuously missing from the nominees was anything from an animated Disney movie, although that studio had recently dominated the category, winning seven nominations and three Oscars in four years.

"Janet Jackson is going to do her song," Cates said, looking at the first item on his agenda. "She also wants to do it on the *Jackson Family Honors* television show, which is coming up before us, so we're trying to discourage that." Cates then summed up a conversation he'd had with Rene Elizondo, who directed many of Jackson's videos and was her husband of three years, although the couple had kept the marriage secret. "Rene says he and Janet want to do it with five violins, very simply, and with candles," Cates said. "Armani's going to dress her. He said they have a sense of it being *bluish*."

"Got it," said Christopher. "Five blue candles playing violin."

Margolis had worked with Jackson many times before. "She's sweet as can be," he said, "but fairly inflexible. Rene is sweet as can be, but he's a killer also."

Bill Conti frowned. "We're not gonna have another rehearsal like Madonna pulled, are we?" he asked, remembering a 1991 run-through of legendary difficulty.

"I hope not, Bill," said Cates calmly. "The thing to remember with them is that they're guests on our show. Give them all the courtesy we can."

Conti grimaced. "Okay," he muttered.

"Next up is 'Philadelphia,' " Cates said. "Neil Young's going to do it. He wants to do it with an acoustic piano, by himself."

"As opposed to the way he does it on the record?" asked Conti.

"I guess so."

"I wonder if he wants to use that funky, incredibly bad piano he uses on the record," mused Conti.

"Well, they told me he's bringing down his own piano from Northern California, so that's probably the one," said Cates. "Now, Roy, I think we want to keep this pretty straightforward. Nothing too fancy on the stage behind him."

"I'll come up with a simple, strong look," said Christopher. "Do you want to contact him about clothes? That could be a sensitive issue."

"I don't think he'll listen," said Aghayan.

Herman shook her head. "Let's not tell Neil Young how to dress," she suggested.

After dealing with "The Day I Fell in Love" and "A Wink and a Smile," Cates got to the final song. "Last but not least," he said, "is Bruce. He does what he does. He has four people. I'm expecting that he wants to do it just like he did it at the AIDS Project L.A. show last month, which was great. It's a very powerful song. I'm very excited about it, and his people say he's really thrilled to be doing the show."

"So what do we have to do about it?" asked Conti.

"Nothing, for the moment," said Cates.

"No dancers in any of these?" asked Christopher.

"No," said Cates. "We only have two dance elements on the show this year, the opening number and the ballet."

Conti frowned. "Ballet?" he said. "What's that?"

Cates looked incredulous. "You're not aware of that?"

"No."

"Oh, what a hole in the loop." Cates explained that Allen was choreographing a ballet to accompany selections from the five nominated scores, to be performed by pairs of dancers from several of the world's leading ballet companies.

This was Herman's territory. "The biggest problem," she said, "is logistics. The Africans speak French, the Chinese barely speak English. Twelve dancers come into town on February 28, but six of them leave on March 6 and don't come back until the seventeenth or eighteenth. The Shanghai dancers arrive on the twelfth, the Paris ballet not until the eighteenth. The

Cubans, the Central Ballet of China, and the Africans will be in town the whole time."

"This has to be very organized," said Cates. "It can't be last minute."

"And it's going to be a hard number to design," said Aghayan. "I can't just load it up with sequins and send it out there."

The last musical number on the agenda was the first one in the show: an opening sequence set to Stephen Sondheim's "Putting It Together" and sung by Broadway star Bernadette Peters. "Bernadette will be arriving in L.A. next Monday," Cates told the staff. "And as is her custom, her assistant will be driving her around in a sedan without a phone."

The song would be recorded the following Tuesday night; later in the week, Workman would shoot a movie that would introduce, incorporate, and illustrate the song. "One thing to remember, though, is that it's a little too long now," Cates said. "We might want to cut some of it. But if we see things we think need to be changed, we need to let Bernadette and Sondheim know at the same time. They're best friends, and they talk on the phone constantly, so we don't want one of them feeling left out if the other knows something first."

WHEN IT WAS FIRST HELD IN 1982, the nominees' luncheon was designed to be little more than another photo op. "Somebody thought there was a lull in the publicity between the nominations announcements and the show itself," said Bruce Davis as he waited to greet nominees near the entrance to the ballroom at the Beverly Hilton Hotel. "It was originally proposed, I think, out of fairly cynical motivations. But it was such an immediate hit among the nominees that we realized, Jesus, everybody says it's a great honor to be nominated, but the only time we ever bring the people together is on this terrible night when four out of five of them will walk away feeling like they've lost something."

Enter the luncheon, which had become a supposed respite from the competitive air and frayed nerves of Oscar season. Nominees, their guests, Oscar staffers, Academy officials, and members of the board of governors were spread out across two dozen tables on three levels of the same ballroom that had hosted the Golden Globe Awards six weeks earlier. The seating chart was drawn up so that no nominee sat at a table with anyone else nominated in the same category, or anyone else who worked on the same film.

The crux of the lunch came just after the appetizers were served, when Academy president Arthur Hiller officially welcomed everyone. "It's unfortunate," he added, "that in less than two weeks, 80 percent of you are going to, how shall we say, perceive yourselves as losers when your name isn't called." The nominees were asked to stand on a riser that curved around a huge Oscar statue. When they'd jostled into place, the annual group photo was taken, after which the nominees came to the stage in alphabetical order to receive a certificate of nomination and an official Oscar nominee sweatshirt.

The shirt was another innovation of Allan Carr's, though he'd insisted that each shirt be personalized with the name of the nominee. A couple of years' worth of inevitable omissions and misspellings later, Bruce Davis prevailed upon Cates to hand out generic sweatshirts, in this case gray ones sporting a small gold Academy Award and the inscription OSCAR NOMINEE.

After lunch was served, Cates gave a short speech. "Veterans of this lunch know that this is the time when I get to talk to you nominees about your speeches," he said. "I've had my fantasies: a trapdoor behind the podium, or a treadmill going from one side of the stage to the other, thirty-five seconds and you're out . . ." But those remedies, he said, shouldn't be necessary. "Forty-five seconds is a long time, ladies and gentlemen. You can do a lot of things in forty-five seconds."

In the press room at the luncheon, composer Marc Shaiman, who'd been nominated for writing the song "A Wink and a Smile," needed less time than that to cause a minor furor. Shaiman had been annoyed when Harry Connick, Jr., declined to perform the song on the Oscar show, and frustrated at how long it had taken to secure a replacement. He'd spoken to David Bowie, who'd briefly entertained the idea, and watched while the likes of Bob Hope and George Burns were approached. He was happy when Tony Bennett agreed to perform the song, then irked when Bennett suddenly cited a prior commitment.

At the luncheon, Shaiman had just learned that actor/singer Keith Carradine would be performing the song. The composer knew Carradine's voice was well suited for the light, bouncy tune, but he was also smarting after a couple of weeks that had left him feeling, he said, "like such category-filler." When the publicist he'd hired plopped him in front of the assembled press, Shaiman figured they didn't care what he had to say—especially when he looked toward the door and saw Steven Spielberg and Tom Hanks waiting their turns at the microphone.

"I was like the kid in school who wants to make the bullies laugh," he said. "So when someone with a real edge in his voice said, 'How come Harry Connick isn't singing your song?' I said, 'Well, he's busy recording, and he has social commitments, and he's a schmuck.' "

Having gotten his laugh, Shaiman didn't think anything of it until the following evening, when the phone in his hilltop Los Angeles home began ringing off the hook. "I finally turned up the volume on the answering machine and heard a musician in New York going, 'Good for you, Shaiman! Tell it like it is!' It had already been on *Entertainment Tonight*: 'Songwriter gets into Yiddish name-calling with pop star!' " Suitably embarrassed, Shaiman apologized to Connick in a letter that, he said, "should be studied as an example of self-effacement."

THE AFTERNOON of the nominees' luncheon, a new schedule was distributed to the production staff. A running joke had been added to what was normally a dry, straightforward document. Under the heading SATURDAY MARCH 19, there was a new entry for 8:00 a.m.: TUNE NEIL YOUNG'S PIANO."

A little later, at 12:30 p.m.: TUNE NEIL YOUNG'S PIANO.

Sunday March 20, 8:00 a.m.: TUNE NEIL YOUNG'S PIANO.

Sunday, noon: TUNE NEIL YOUNG'S PIANO.

Monday, March 21, 8:00 a.m.: TUNE NEIL YOUNG'S PIANO.

Monday, 9:00 p.m.: STRIKE NEIL YOUNG'S PIANO.

"THEY'D SAVE a *fortune*," said Douglass M. Stewart, Jr., "if they knew who the winners were ahead of time."

For more than a decade, Stewart and his company, DMS, had been responsible for most of the short film clips that ran throughout Oscar shows—

and for the more numerous clips that were prepared but never shown. DMS assembled the clips of nominated films and performances, the brief montages used to explicate categories like costume design, makeup, and visual effects, and the footage that was shown on-screen while some winners (i.e., the lesser-known ones, whose trips to the stage were not of intrinsic interest to most viewers) walked to the podium. Every time one of those last clips was shown, it meant four others went unused.

Stewart also prepared a reel of historical footage about the Academy Award and the Oscar show, which was kept on hand in case something disastrous happened and the producer needed to cut away from the stage. Though the emergency reel had never been used, it was reworked and updated every year, in order that it could fit as seamlessly as possible into each new show.

With less than three weeks to go before the show, Stewart called the DMS staff into his office at a nondescript two-story complex south of Beverly Hills. To begin the meeting, he showed a montage of dog clips designed for an interlude in the Dolly Parton–James Ingram duet from *Beethoven's Second*. "We spent a month looking at seventy to eighty dog films," he said, "and started with a list of forty dogs we wanted to include. But finally, I think we've got a lock on it." He cued up a montage that included only six celebrated canines: Toto from *The Wizard of Oz*, Asta from the *Thin Man* movies, Sandy from *Annie*, and from the films that bore their names, Lassie, Old Yeller, and Benji. "Gil thinks that Old Yeller ought to be last," said Stewart. "Does anybody think that Old Yeller has more emotion than Benji?"

"No, Benji's much more recognizable," said Stephanie Sperling, a DMS film coordinator. Around the room, the other staffers nodded.

"I like it the way it is, too," said Stewart. "So we'll keep it this way." He paused. "If we can use it."

"Is Disney still a problem?" asked one staffer.

"Yeah," said Stewart. This wasn't a surprise: famously protective of its properties, as the Academy had learned when Allan Carr didn't get permission to use Snow White, Disney had declined to make any of its footage available for a montage celebrating the history of film animation unless the piece showcased nothing *but* Disney animation. Now the company was making similar dog demands. "They say they don't want Old Yeller and Benji to be included in a bit honoring another studio's dog," said Stewart. "We told them it's about famous dogs, and there are no shots of Beethoven in it. It's on approval."

He paused. "We didn't mention that Beethoven's going to be onstage."

Stewart looked at a five-page list that included the status of all the film clips needed on the show, and brought up a litany of problems. ABC wouldn't allow a scene from *In the Line of Fire* in which John Malkovich put his mouth around a gun barrel . . . They needed better footage from the making of *The Piano*, which had such a small budget that there wasn't enough money for the usual behind-the-scenes crew . . . They were still waiting for Steven Spielberg's okay to use footage from *Jurassic Park* for the sound effects editing category . . . And they had no access at all to any footage from *Schindler's List*, but were simply waiting for the director to assemble his own clips from the suggestions they'd given him.

"We're getting close," said Stewart as the meeting wound down. "Until the next train wreck happens."

After the meeting, Stewart called a staffer at Miramax, which had released *The Piano*. The independent studio, notoriously aggressive when it came to campaigning for Academy Awards, had scored ten nominations—two for the Chinese film *Farewell My Concubine* and eight for *The Piano*, including crucial nods in the best-picture, best-director, best-actress, and best supporting actress categories. But as zealously as Miramax campaigned, the company was difficult to work with when it came to supplying film clips. Miramax worked slowly, and worse than that it tended to offer the same scenes that had already been seen in every ad or on every talk show.

"We're running out of time, and I need a ten-second shot for cinematography," Stewart said into the phone. "Pick the most beautiful shot in the movie, and give me ten seconds. It's better with stars in it, if you've got it."

"LOOK!" said Cates, pointing to the call sheet in his hand. "I'm listed as *talent*. All my life I've wanted to be listed as talent."

The producer was standing in a small television studio located on the outskirts of Culver City, south of Beverly Hills and only a few blocks away from the old MGM studio lot, now home to Sony Pictures. He'd arrived at the complex at 6:15 a.m. for the domestic satellite press tour, in which he and actress Laura Dern would do short interviews with shows on eighteen different ABC affiliates around the country. Dern showed up fifteen minutes after Cates, fully made up and camera ready; this impressed staffers who remembered that for a similar press tour a week earlier, Nicole Kidman had arrived at 4:30 a.m. for two painstaking hours of primping.

Cates's priority was to sell the show, something he felt ABC hadn't been doing as effectively as usual. The network had long since sold all its Oscar ads, at a cost of $630,000 for each thirty-second spot, and the show did not carry a ratings guarantee—meaning if the viewership slumped, as it had for many recent awards shows, ABC would not have to make it up to advertisers. But nobody wanted to concede a ratings slump that in truth had been going on since the mid-1980s. The solution, the Academy's Public Relations Coordinating Committee had decided at a meeting two days earlier, was to use every opportunity to emphasize the heavyweight musical talent on the show.

Cates and Dern took their places in a small studio, one of several in the complex. Behind them was an Academy Awards backdrop; in front of them were several cameras and a group of placards listing the nominees in all major categories, lest they forget anybody.

The first interview was with a morning show in Cleveland. "What's the most distressing part of the awards for you?" asked the host. "When the stars go off on their own?"

Cates admitted he found that distressing, but in about thirty seconds he'd worked the conversation around to the musical performers. "Now, this year we've got Bruce Springsteen, Janet Jackson, Neil Young, Dolly Parton, and James Ingram . . ."

The questioner addressed Dern, who was nominated in 1989 for *Rambling Rose*. "What's it like as a nominee, Laura?" he said.

"It's great," she said. "Hopefully you can just concentrate on the event, and not worry about the competition . . ."

Then the next morning show came on the line, and the routine began again. Interviewers and cities changed, but some things remained constant:

Dern described what it was like to be nominated, and Cates turned the conversation to music.

Columbus, Ohio—*"Laura, you've been nominated. What goes through your mind waiting for the envelope?"*

Dern: "It's a great opportunity to enjoy a celebration of the work. Hopefully you can do that and not think about the competitive aspect of it . . ."

"How do you make sure two presenters don't wear the same dress?"

Cates: "If they're interested in finding out, they can call Fred Hayman. Oddly enough, sometimes it happens with singers. This year we have Bruce Springsteen and Janet Jackson and Neil Young . . ."

Houston, Texas—*"Laura, how do you make sure no two outfits are the same?"*

Dern: "Well, Fred Hayman is the fashion coordinator . . ."

"Gil, how's it going with Whoopi?"

Cates: "Okay. By the way, the question you asked Laura is interesting, because sometimes it happens with musicians. For instance, this year we have Bruce Springsteen and Janet Jackson and Neil Young . . ."

Buffalo, New York—*"Laura, what is it like to find out you're nominated?"*

Dern: "It was great, because I really cared about the movie . . ."

"But you didn't win."

Dern: "Guys!"

Cates: "You know, who wins is just caprice. For example, this year we have Bruce Springsteen and Janet Jackson and Neil Young . . ."

In the control booth, this transition—or, to be more accurate, this non sequitur—got big laughs. "He's taking that corner on two wheels," said Chuck Warn. Afterward, Cates and Dern took a short break, and Cates shook his head. "I feel like a used-car salesman," he said. "All I want to do is plug Bruce Springsteen."

A GRAY-HAIRED WOMAN who looked more like a suburban grandmother than a Hollywood insider, Bethlyn Hand spent more than eleven months out of each year working for the Motion Picture Association of America, the lobbying arm of the film industry. The MPAA and its chairman, Jack Valenti, were perhaps best known for creating, implementing, and zealously defending the movie rating system, which had been designed in the 1960s to keep legislators from trying to exercise control over the content of Hollywood movies.

The two most recognizable organizations serving the film industry, the Academy and the MPAA had a cozy relationship. The slick, dapper, pint-sized Valenti was almost always booked as a presenter on the Oscar show, and he was usually given the pleasure of copresenting with an attractive young actress. As for Hand, her MPAA duties included rating movie trailers—but come Oscar time, she was also in charge of Oscar escorts.

These were publicists, most of them recruited from the ranks of the major film studios, who led winners through the press rooms during the show. The job of an Oscar escort usually fell to young studio publicists; for more experienced flacks, the joys of hobnobbing with Oscar-toting celebs were more than outweighed by the grind of spending four hours dragging dazed winners through corridors and up and down elevators and stairs.

Inside the Dorothy Chandler Pavilion for an escort walk-through, Hand loaded two dozen publicists into two elevators for a trip to the fourth floor, where the press rooms were located. "This floor is where all the winners will be taken," Hand told them. "Near the end of the night, you may have a wife or spouse with you, because they're not going to want to wait in the hall after the show is over. If you do, make sure you know who you've got, because they won't have a badge." She laughed. "They almost threw out Larry Fortensky last year, until somebody realized that he was Elizabeth Taylor's husband."

Personal publicists, she added, were generally not allowed upstairs; neither were agents. "According to my memo," said the Academy's John Pavlik, "if Steven Spielberg wins, Mike Ovitz will be coming up here with him."

"I hope he's got a badge," said Hand.

"If he doesn't, I'm throwing him out," laughed Pavlik. "He's not *my* agent."

Hand led the group down a narrow hallway and into a tiny room with a small stage and a rudimentary set of bleachers. This was the room for deadline press, mostly newspaper and wire photographers who needed to file their work during the show. Behind a curtain was a larger room, with far more spacious bleachers facing another stage. "I lovingly call this my animal room," said Hand, "because it's a zillion photographers from all around the world, and they all act like animals."

In the two photo rooms, she explained, the winner and the presenter would be photographed together. "Photographers are not allowed to take pictures of the presenters without the winners. If Robin Williams comes in here with somebody who won for his short film, we can't have the winner being insulted because everybody just wants pictures of Robin." After leaving the photo rooms, she explained, the presenters would head back downstairs, leaving the winners to continue through the two interview rooms. This would spare lesser-known winners the humiliation of facing a battery of reporters interested only in their famous presenters.

The first of the two interview areas was a spacious room holding almost two dozen long tables for print and radio journalists. Beyond that was a final, smaller room for television reporters.

"If a winner isn't very well known," Hand added, "you'll send a runner ahead to the general press room to make sure that people want to interview them. If there's no interest, the runner will come back and tell you that, quietly I hope, so you can bypass the room. Obviously, we don't want the winner to know that nobody wants to interview them. You'll do that again for the television room—and in the television room, you most assuredly will have bypasses."

Before the escorts left to go downstairs, Hand offered a final instruction. "You've got to remember to stay with your winners," she said. "They are absolutely euphoric, or numb, so they'll follow you *anywhere.*"

THE DOROTHY CHANDLER PAVILION sat on a hill in downtown Los Angeles, anchoring one end of a block that also contained the Ahmanson Theatre and the smaller Mark Taper Forum. The block was known as the Music Center—and it was there, home to the Los Angeles Philharmonic, the L.A. Opera, and the Center Theatre Group, that twenty-two Academy Awards shows had taken place in the last quarter century.

Built in the early 1960s, the Chandler was beginning to show its age. But for the Oscar production staff, it worked. It had dressing rooms downstairs, on the same level as the artists' entrance; it had a few offices on the stage level, along with enough extra space to erect a green room and a production office; and outside the building was enough room for a series of production trailers and trucks, most notably the command truck that would serve as Jeff Margolis's home base while he directed the show.

Four days to show time, Margolis sat in the truck and stared at a wall of monitors, which showed him the view from more than a dozen cameras inside the theater. To help him plot camera moves for each entrance, exit, and acceptance speech, a full complement of stand-ins waited for instructions from the show's stage managers. Most of the stand-ins, who covered a wide range of ages and looks, were hired from local theater companies; many returned to the Oscars in this capacity year after year, working for AFTRA scale of about twenty dollars an hour.

To make the rehearsal as real as possible, the stand-ins who subbed for presenters were given dummy Oscar envelopes to open. Inside each envelope was the name of a winner, along with one extra, and crucial, line of text: FOR THIS REHEARSAL ONLY. For the next four days, no one would announce an Oscar recipient without using that phrase. Other stand-ins were positioned in the audience, occupying the seats of that category's nominees. The "winner" would come to the stage, give an acceptance speech, and then exit into the wings.

By this point, large seat cards occupied the chairs of every nominee, presenter, and performer on the show. Block letters listed the names and categories of lesser-known nominees, while movie stars' cards sported black-and-white photos as well.

Virtually all the stars were seated in the first eight rows, the section located in front of the TelePrompTer and the only area of the audience that received significant on-screen exposure. Mixed in with the actors were a few agents and studio heads, plus blocks of seats for Cates, Hiller, Goldberg, and other Academy and show executives. Nominees were placed close to the side or center aisles, for easy exit in case they won. And along the side aisles beginning about eight rows back were the nominees in the less glamorous categories.

By placing all the nominees for the craft categories in one or two rows, Margolis only needed one handheld camera to cover all the possible winners—as opposed to the awards in the acting categories, where the nominees were spread out across the orchestra section and a different cameraman would be assigned to each.

Seating decisions were more difficult in years when the Oscars were held at the Chandler, as opposed to the show's less elegant but far more cavernous alternate home, the Shrine Auditorium. Though its stated capacity was on the high side of three thousand, camera placement and the needs of the production reduced the usable size to about two thousand eight hundred people, less than half the capacity of the Shrine. Around one thousand seats went to nominees, presenters, and guests of the Academy, including small blocks to sponsors of the television broadcast. Each nominee was officially given two seats, though some ended up with more. The rest were distributed by lottery to Academy members, who paid $50, $100, or $200, depending on the location. The lottery system was supposed to ensure that members who didn't get tickets one year were more likely to get them the next, but it invariably left plenty of disgruntled Academy members.

By this point, the seating chart had been eyed by Margolis for camera placement, and by Academy controller Otto Spoerri, who allocated tickets and seated the organization's guests around the nominees and presenters. Then Cates looked things over to avoid a different kind of problem. One year, he remembered, one nominee had in the audience his wife, his current girlfriend, and two former lovers, one of whom had remarried. "Sometimes, you just have to spread certain people out," he said with a laugh. "I think I get at least one of those phone calls warning me about that every year."

SATURDAY AFTERNOON, Whoopi Goldberg made her first appearance at the Chandler. She walked out of the wings accompanied by Cates and Bruce Vilanch, who had been writing for the Oscars since the Allan Carr show. Burly and frizzy-haired, Vilanch hitched up his pants and buckled his belt as he followed Goldberg to the podium, then took a seat in the front row alongside Cates, Seligman, Warn, Herman, and senior executive consultant Robert Z. Shapiro.

The houselights were darkened. Susan Futterman, an ABC director of broadcast standards for comedy and variety shows (or, in her own words,

"Madame Censor Lady"), sat a few rows farther back, a script in her lap and a pen in her hand. And then Goldberg sashayed onstage, a smug grin on her face, and delivered her entire opening monologue in a high-speed, falsetto mumble that rendered her jokes completely unintelligible, except when she slowed down for the last word of her punch lines: "Schindler!" "Nicholson!" "Tonya Harding!"

She went on to practice her intros and transitions, this time taking them at normal speed. "This next presenter," she read from the TelePrompTer, "was Madonna's friend in *A League of Their Own*, Meg Ryan's friend in *Sleepless in Seattle*, and my friend all the time." She stopped. "Rosie O'Donnell? I don't *know* her."

And so it went: Goldberg moved through her lines quickly, mocking most of them, adding her asides, eliminating lines, or rewriting them on the fly. When a few bars of "Help Me Make It Through the Night" inexplicably played over the sound system after she introduced Al Pacino, she stopped dead.

"If this mother comes out singing that song," she said, "I'm goin' home. Al Pacino doing country western? I couldn't handle it." Then she grinned again. "I know: you're just trying to see if you can throw me. Well, we'll see where the power is Monday night."

AFTER DINNER, the first thing the crew did was tune Neil Young's piano. For real.

It was a night for rock stars at the Chandler. First there was Young, who arrived in a 1954 Cadillac limousine and took his time onstage, virtually ignoring the needs of Margolis and his camera crew. Then Bruce Springsteen's band showed up for their own rehearsal—without their boss, who'd spent the day in New Jersey, at the wedding of his nephew. With a stand-in taking the place of Springsteen, the band set up and ran through the song "Streets of Philadelphia" a couple of times. Behind them on the stage were two enormous boxes, lit from the inside and shining brightly against the black backdrop.

Springsteen's manager, Jon Landau, didn't like the look of the set, but initially he decided to wait until the next day and let Springsteen himself decide. But as the band continued to rehearse, Landau watched closely on a monitor at the production table, shaking his head when the light boxes showed up on the screen. "I don't want Bruce's first impression of this show to be a set that he's not going to like," he said.

The manager told Margolis and Seligman that he'd rather Springsteen sang in front of a plain black backdrop. Christopher resisted. "That's one of the key looks of the whole show," he said.

Cates had gone home for the night, leaving no one with the authority to resolve the dispute. The next morning at 8 a.m., though, Landau received a phone call from Cates. "If you don't want a set," the producer said, "then we won't have a set."

THE FIRST DRESS REHEARSAL was always a moment of truth. The rehearsal took place the night before the real show, after a day that had been devoted to star presenters dropping by to rehearse their lines at fifteen-minute intervals. Until the dress, the show had been rehearsed mostly in bits and pieces, seldom for more than five minutes at a stretch. Calculations made in the production office gave an idea of how long the show might run, and past experiences suggested potential trouble spots—but much of the planning remained guesswork until the crew ran through the entire show in as close to real time as it could manage. It was the last time that significant changes could be made: a second full-show run-through would follow the next morning, but if anything major was still wrong at that point, it would likely remain wrong.

Dress rehearsal featured the host and the musical performers, with stand-ins taking the place of presenters and winners. But Goldberg was still determined to keep her jokes fresh, so she once again delivered her monologue in a high-speed mumble. Midway through, she grinned, "You know they're really sweating now."

The host did some sweating of her own a few minutes later, when stagehands took far too long resetting the stage for Janet Jackson. "They're asking me to stretch," Goldberg confessed after ad-libbing a few extra jokes. "They want me to do an act, basically." She looked into the audience, scanning the seat cards. "How cool is it that the Boss is here?" she said. A long pause. "So,

Bruce Vilanch," she said, turning and looking into the wings. "This could be the tampon bit." In the audience, Futterman laughed nervously.

Aside from the botched changeover and some sound problems with Neil Young, the rehearsal ran fairly smoothly. The show seemed long—though without a real audience or any gushing Oscar winners, it was hard to tell if the length would be a problem, or if the emotion of the evening would compensate.

Throughout the run-through, the "for this rehearsal only" winners were assigned almost randomly. But some crew members were making guesses—and plans—accordingly. While a stand-in for *In the Name of the Father* director Jim Sheridan made an acceptance speech after receiving the best-director award, a couple of cameramen huddled in the center aisle, mapping out their moves so they wouldn't block Steven Spielberg's walk to the stage the next night. "I'll drop back quickly and he can go around you this way," said one. "Does that sound okay?"

"THE WORLD SERIES. The Olympics. The Rose Bowl. None of them mean anything." Joseph DiSante stood in front of a room of 126 well-dressed men and women seated at long tables draped in white tablecloths. "Because *tonight* is the night. Let's go to the Oscars, folks."

At 10 a.m. on Oscar morning, DiSante was holding his yearly indoctrination of the Academy Awards' seat-fillers. These were volunteers deployed to make sure that when the cameras turned toward the audience, viewers would see smiling faces rather than empty seats. DiSante was ABC's head of guest relations, but for twenty years he had also selected and trained seat-fillers, choosing them from as many as 550 letters and 1,200 phone calls he'd received from those who aspired to the gig.

DiSante had already eyed each of the chosen as they entered a sound-stage at ABC Prospect, the network's lot on the eastern edge of Hollywood. Most were dressed well (and tastefully) enough to pass muster, though he'd sent home a fortyish blonde in a peach miniskirt, asking her to change into something more appropriate. (She came back sporting a floor-length lime number.) In lieu of actually being paid, the seat-fillers received Oscar hats, posters, and programs when they signed in.

Around the perimeter of the room, buffet tables were laden with chafing dishes of hot food, plus cookies, brownies, and beverages that included milk, water, and coffee, but nothing alcoholic. Red, white, and gold balloons decorated the room. A bus was parked outside, ready for a trip to the Music Center.

But first, DiSante picked up the microphone and delivered what was partly a pep talk, partly a lecture in the art of seat-filling. "It is a very tough, hard process, getting to be a seat-filler," he said. "You are hand-picked because I think you can look like you belong."

Wearing a gray Oscar sweatshirt, DiSante asked the seat-fillers to stand up, introduce themselves to each other, and compliment each other on how good they looked. "It's very important that you know one another," he said. "We're asking you to be part of our security. Through the course of the evening, there will be people who will try to sneak into your lines. We need you to spot them and point them out to us."

Then he outlined the logistics. A team of seat-fillers would be stationed on each side of the house. The team would include "sitters," who would fill the seats; "spotters," who'd point out the seats that were emptied at each commercial break; and "runners," who'd hustle the sitters into position. Their territory, he added, would include everything from the front row to the TelePrompTer, behind which the camera rarely ventured. Seat-fillers would be issued laminated passes, which they were not to remove. "But when you sit down," added DiSante, "you need to hide your badge so that the camera doesn't see it. Men, tuck your badge inside your tuxedo jacket. Women, turn it so it's hanging down your back."

Some of them, DiSante said, would wind up in a seat for the entire show. "If that happens, God bless you and enjoy the show." Some would be challenged by the people they sat next to. "Just tell them you're temporarily filling the seat for camera purposes." Those who filled a winner's seat, DiSante said, could count on about forty-five minutes before the winner finished the press run and returned.

"In the first seventeen or eighteen rows of the Dorothy Chandler Pavilion," he said, "the entire power structure of Hollywood is sitting. This is not your night. This is *their* night."

The two most veteran seat-fillers then demonstrated what DiSante called "the Groucho Marx walk," a quick, hunched gait designed to get people into seats unobtrusively, and "without stepping on people's feet or putting your lovely butt in their faces."

Then he covered the etiquette of sitting next to a movie star. "Let's talk about autographs," he said. "Absolutely not. No autographs. If they talk to you, knock yourself out. But do not initiate the conversation." A few seat-fillers groaned. "Sorry, but it has to be that way. Most of them will talk to you. And if you sit next to a nominee and feel the urge to wish them good luck, go ahead."

DiSante looked around the room. "Is anybody getting nervous?" he asked. A few people raised their hands, so he called one woman, Linda Sanderson, to the front of the room. "What are you nervous about?" he said.

"Being on television," Sanderson said. "Sitting next to Alec Baldwin."

"You're not gonna sit next to Alec Baldwin," he said.

"Why? You're not going to let me?"

"Kim is gonna sit next to Alec Baldwin."

"Maybe she'll go to the bathroom."

After suggesting that the seat-fillers help start standing ovations for the show's two honorary Oscar winners, Paul Newman and Deborah Kerr, DiSante issued a warning.

"If you're down there and any of the press want to talk to you, I consider that an unauthorized interview," he said. "You're gonna hear and see a lot of things that most people never hear or see. Please, don't embarrass yourself, don't embarrass the Academy or the talent. If you're interviewed, remember: what the press really wants to know is what did Clint Eastwood say when you were sitting next to him? He might have said, 'Jesus, it's so hot I can't wait to get outta here.' But that's not what you're gonna say. If you embarrass the Academy or any of the talent, it's going to be all over, and you're not going to be back next year.

"If somebody from the press gets ahold of you," he concluded, "remember: only positive, nice things."

AT THE MUSIC CENTER, the day underwent a slow metamorphosis. Jeans and T-shirts were commonplace when the morning rehearsal began, but as the day wore on more and more staffers would show up in gowns and tuxedos. Security guards and Los Angeles Police Department officers began to survey the hallways and check the doors more frequently. During the lunch break that followed the end of the rehearsal, about 3:00, almost the entire staff vacated the area around the stage, the green room, and the production offices; when they returned, the women sported formal dresses or suits, the men tuxedos.

This was an ironclad rule at the Oscars: everyone working on the show was required to wear formal dress. It didn't matter if you'd be seen on camera, or if you were anywhere near a winner, nominee, or presenter. A wardrobe bank below the stage provided tuxedos for all who wanted them, depleting the supplies of several tux-rental shops around town.

By 3:30, traffic had been diverted on all the streets surrounding the Music Center, while fans in the bleachers outside grew more impatient as they awaited the first arrivals at the red carpet. A bus stop on Grand Avenue, near the artists' entrance, was taken out of service. An airplane flew overhead, towing a sign that contained a phone number and a promise: WORLD'S FUNNIEST SCRIPT. Lower in the sky, half a dozen police helicopters circled the block continuously. In front of the Chandler on Hope Street, an army of parking valets was ready to take cars to an underground garage beneath the Department of Water and Power building across the street.

The valets sprang to action when guests began arriving about 4:00. The bleacher crowd screeched for each new star, while emcee Army Archerd hauled as many of them as possible to his platform midway down the red carpet. Archerd coaxed a few words out of reluctant nominees, plugged *Variety* every chance he got, and asked a hundred variations on the question "How do you feel?" Sometimes, though, his job was easy: he simply stood back and watched when veteran actress and forty-nine-year-old blond bombshell Sally Kirkland, who'd received a best-actress nomination for *Anna* in 1988 after waging one of the most aggressive campaigns in memory, launched into an unprompted monologue about how it was the first year Hollywood was raising people's consciousness, and how her dress was designed by an African American designer, and how she was making a movie called *Wrestling Monty*.

———

6:00 P.M., PACIFIC DAYLIGHT TIME: *"From Los Angeles, it's the 66th annual Academy Awards."*

As the traditional montage of arriving celebrities began, Whoopi Goldberg left her dressing room and waited in the wings of the stage. Backstage, Tom Hanks emerged from the men's room.

In the lobby, the crowd of late arrivals included Kurt Russell and Goldie Hawn, Ralph Fiennes, Pete Postlethwaite, and Daniel Day-Lewis. Standing amid a crowd of unused seat-fillers, Fiennes, Postlethwaite, and Day-Lewis decided they weren't comfortable watching the first twenty minutes of the show from the lobby. They slipped through a nearby door and walked down a small corridor that led backstage. Seeing that things were even more chaotic there, they changed their minds and tried to get back into the lobby, inadvertently causing a huge traffic jam outside an office used by the show's writers.

"So, they gave me a live microphone for three hours," said Goldberg early in her monologue. "There haven't been so many showbiz executives so nervous, sweating over one woman since Heidi Fleiss, honey." Backstage, Al Pacino walked down a hallway muttering "One Mississippi, two Mississippi, three Mississippi . . ."

Twenty minutes into the show, Hanks presented the first Oscars of the night to the art director and set decorator for *Schindler's List*. After Allan Starski gave a fifteen-second speech, his partner Ewa Braun leaned to the microphone to say a few words of her own. Before she could speak, Cates gave the cue to Margolis, who instructed Conti's orchestra to cut her off. (Any time the producer was in the command trailer, he made the call to play off winners; during the infrequent occasions when he was elsewhere, the decision fell to the director.)

Cates kept Conti in check for the first big winner of the evening, Tommy Lee Jones, even though the supporting actor committed the unpardonable (to Cates) sin of reading his fifty-three-second speech off a piece of paper. To make matters worse, Jones kept his head down while doing so, giving the TV audience an unfettered view of his gleaming, nearly bald head, which had been shaved for his role in the film *Cobb*. "The only thing a man can say at a time like this is, 'I am not really bald,' " he explained. "I'm lucky enough to be working."

One floor above the stage, Janet Jackson left her dressing room. A beefy security guard watched her walk by, then sighed. "Me, being that close to Janet Jackson?" he said, grinning. "I'll get over this tomorrow."

During commercials, Goldberg huddled with Vilanch in her dressing room stage left, or in a small room lined with black curtains in the wings of the stage. Nearby were tables covered with Oscar statuettes. Two Price Waterhouse representatives stood in the wings, one on each side of the stage; each carried a full set of envelopes, and each had memorized the results and had orders to immediately interrupt the show if an incorrect winner was announced. One of the two "trophy ladies," models hired to carry statuettes onstage and escort winners off, waited by each table of Oscars. (Officially dubbed "trophy ladies," the women were nonetheless called "trophy girls" by virtually everyone involved with the show.)

A little more than an hour into the show, Gene Hackman gave the supporting actress award to the evening's most stunning, and stunned, winner: eleven-year-old Anna Paquin. The hyperventilating Paquin managed to blurt out a short speech, then ignored the trophy lady trying to steer her into the wings, instead fleeing down the stairs and back to her seat.

Outside the Chandler, the tiny foyer of Jeff Margolis's command truck contained a table laden with junk food: Baby Ruth bars, Pepperidge Farm Goldfish, Oreos, peanuts, rice cakes, M&M's, raisins, Fig Newtons, salsa, peanut butter, chips . . . Above the buffet, someone had pasted a cartoon of two surgeons. One was sweating and wiping his forehead, while the other said, "Relax, man, it's not television."

Watching monitors that showed the view from each of the more than a dozen cameras, Margolis yelled out the camera numbers: "Four! Now . . . Cue her! Cue her! Cue her!" As he made each command, he snapped his fingers, and assistant director Wendy Charles Acey yelled her own orders into her headset at exactly the same time. During Debbie Allen's dance number, Margolis dispensed with spoken commands almost entirely; when he wanted a camera move, he waved his hand at the screen, and Acey translated and ordered the appropriate cut or fade. At the end of the routine, Margolis broke his silence. "Roll playback," he said, "ba-bing!"

"Good job, boys," said Cates from his seat directly behind Margolis. "Good job."

On the other side of the building, Christian Slater stepped outside the Chandler for a smoke. Springsteen got a quick touch-up in the makeup chair, then headed for the green room muttering, "Nervous, nervous." As he walked away, Geena Davis took his place in front of a makeup mirror. She was so tall that she couldn't see her face in the mirror, but it wasn't her face she was interested in. Davis was instead eyeing her cleavage, carefully patting and adjusting the folds of her dress around it.

Two and a half hours into the show, Springsteen performed. Pages immediately rushed him back to his seat, and a few minutes later he won the Oscar for best song. "This is the first song I ever wrote for a movie," he said. "So I guess it's all downhill from here."

As soon as he walked off the stage, Springsteen was hustled into a crowded elevator, along with a group that also included Whitney Houston, who'd presented him with his award. In the elevator, a page asked Springsteen for an autograph. "I guess so," he muttered, looking dazed. "I'm a little excited right now."

Upstairs, Chuck Warn, acting on the orders of Springsteen's management, rushed the press-shy winner through the four media rooms as quickly as possible. As Springsteen left the last room and headed for the elevator, the film critic and TV personality Gene Siskel pursued him down the hallway, yelling, "Bruce! Congratulations! But I just want to ask you one question about the process. What comes first, the words or the music?"

Bruce stopped to consider the oldest and dumbest question in the book, while a security guard stationed in the corridor shouted at Siskel, "No interviews in the hallway!" Springsteen gave a tentative answer—"Well, it really depends on the song"—before he was rushed away. As he waited for an elevator, he heard from a nearby monitor that Tom Hanks had won the best-actor award for *Philadelphia*, the same movie for which Springsteen had written his song.

"Is there someplace we can go to see Tom's speech?" he asked. Knowing that the Chandler's elevators were notoriously slow, Warn quickly came up with an alternate route. "We can take these stairs," he said, pointing to a door. The men dashed down four flights of stairs, only to find that the first-floor doors that would lead them back to the green room were locked.

"Shit!" yelled Warn. "They told me that this door was going to be unlocked!" After pounding on the door to no avail, Warn ran up one flight; that door was locked, as well. Finally, he found an open door that led to a nearly empty corridor on the third floor. A lone man stood in a doorway at the end of the corridor. "Do you have a monitor down there?" yelled Warn.

"Yeah," yelled the man. Springsteen ducked into the room, a makeshift headquarters for staffers from Eastman Kodak, which was shooting each winner with a large-format instant camera in one of the upper balconies.

On the screen, Hanks was giving an emotional acceptance speech, which began with thanks to a high school classmate and a drama teacher, whom he identified as "two of the finest gay Americans" he'd ever met. "[T]he streets of heaven are too crowded with angels," he said. "They number a thousand for each of the red ribbons that we wear here tonight . . ."

In the doorway of the room, a Kodak staffer watched Springsteen rush by and take a seat on the couch. "Um, does that guy have an Academy Award?" he asked.

"Yes," said Warn.

A pause. "Who is he?"

When the Kodak employees finally figured out that they had an Oscar-winning rock star in their midst, they asked for autographs and photos. Springsteen finally made it back to the first floor right about the time that Holly Hunter picked up the best-actress award for *The Piano*, completing a sweep for that film's female stars—as well as its writer-director, Jane Campion, who won the Oscar for her original screenplay.

But Campion didn't walk away with the other prize for which she'd been nominated: to the surprise of nobody, Steven Spielberg continued what had been a very good night (five Oscars so far for *Schindler's List*, plus three for *Jurassic Park*) by winning the best-director award. "Am I allowed to say that I really wanted this?" Spielberg asked.

A few minutes later, *Schindler's List* won for best picture. In the backstage hallway, a large crowd clustered around a monitor to watch the speeches of Spielberg and producer Branko Lustig, himself a Holocaust survivor. "It's a long way from Auschwitz to this stage," said Lustig, as Neil Young walked through the crowd on his way out the back door.

"Well, that's Oscar sixty-six, baby," said Goldberg a minute later. Spielberg came offstage, Oscars in hand, and was herded toward the elevator. The director, famously wary of elevators, stopped. "Can we walk?" he said.

"Yeah," said his escort. "We can walk."

Most of the crowd had begun making its way toward the Governors Ball, but the bulk of the Oscar staff stuck around. On the side of the stage, Cates was approached by ABC's John Hamlin. "I think this Oscar show will go down in history," said Hamlin, who had supervised Oscar shows for more than a decade. "It wasn't a big, showbizzy, Broadway-type show. It was a great, emotional show."

Cates made a detour into the production office to thank his staff, then slipped into the Governors Ball by a back entrance. He quickly did a few interviews, telling the handful of reporters allowed inside the ball how delighted he was with the show. Then he left the tent the same way he came in, rejoined his wife, and made his grand entrance through the front.

Soon, the ball was crammed with people. Hanks and Spielberg spent more than an hour talking to the press; other winners and nominees dispersed to their tables. Bruce Springsteen stood at the bar, waiting without much luck for a bartender to notice him and take his order. "Ya win an Academy Award," he said with a grin, "and ya still can't get service at the bar."

MANY HOURS LATER, Springsteen, Spielberg, Hanks, and Goldberg were among those who ended up at a private party at Dani Janssen's Century City apartment. Janssen, the widow of actor David Janssen, attracted that crowd partly because the Oscar party scene was undergoing a seismic shift: Irving "Swifty" Lazar had died at the end of December, and Spago, the site of his legendary Oscar party, had closed for the night out of respect for the agent.

Janssen had stepped into the void with a small, private party, while other events made a more public play for the A-list. While Elton John had drawn a good crowd the year before with a Maple Drive party that benefited his own AIDS foundation, the most serious newcomer was *Vanity Fair* magazine, which cohosted a bash at Morton's restaurant with producer Steve

Tisch. The Academy, meanwhile, took notice of the absence of Spago on the scene, and took steps to increase attendance at its own soiree: it asked Spago's owner, Wolfgang Puck, to supervise the menu at the following year's Governors Ball.

The morning after the show, Cates read all the reviews, but he didn't pay them much heed. *The New York Times* wrote the show a love letter, the *Los Angeles Times* was lukewarm, others found the evening bland. "The first time I ever produced the show, I spoke to Samuel Goldwyn, and he told me something great," said Cates. "He said, 'It doesn't matter what kind of show you do. Some of the reviews are going to hate it, some of them are going to love it, and there's nothing you can do about it. So do the show *you* want to do, and forget about everybody else.' "

Ratings did not slide the way some had feared. In the months leading up to the Oscars, the Grammy Awards, People's Choice Awards, and American Music Awards had all scored their lowest ratings in years, but the Academy Awards show held its own, dropping off only slightly from the previous year and managing its second-highest rating in a decade. At three hours and eighteen minutes, it was also the shortest Oscar show in five years—a change that could be attributed in large part to Whoopi Goldberg, who spent considerably less time on her entrance and her monologue than Billy Crystal would have done.

One interested viewer of the show was writer Paul Rudnick, who wrote a satirical film review column for *Premiere* magazine under the name of Libby Gelman-Waxner. Under his own name, Rudnick had recently written the script for the comedy *Addams Family Values*, and he was struck by Tom Hanks's disclosure that his high school drama teacher was gay. Though Hanks did not, as some publications charged, "out" the teacher against his will—he'd called the retired, sixty-nine-year-old Rawley Farnsworth and asked permission a few days before the show—Rudnick was inspired to begin work on a script about a deeply closeted drama teacher who's outed by a former student at the Oscars. Three years later, that film, *In & Out*, would win an Oscar nomination for actress Joan Cusack.

2
≡

Restraint and Decorum

The 67th Academy Awards

AT FIRST, IT SEEMED LIKE A GOOD IDEA. Gil Cates had chosen "Comedy and the Movies" as the theme of the 67th Academy Awards show, and nobody doubted that David Letterman knew comedy. True, his comic sensibility was the sort that might have made him a long shot most years, and he might not have been a movie star the way Billy Crystal and Whoopi Goldberg were—but Letterman was funny and his late-night show was on a roll, so Cates won plaudits for making what many thought was a gutsy, inspired choice that might put a fresh spin on the Oscars.

To go with Letterman, Cates had to break his informal rule: usually, he looked for a host who was both a movie star and a live performer capable of working a room. Those qualifications essentially limited the pool to a handful of stand-up comics who'd gone on to have movie careers, though Cates's short list also included Tom Hanks, an actor with no stand-up experience.

Letterman was by no means a movie star: his film debut, such as it was, consisted of a one-line part in his friend Chris Elliott's disastrous 1994 comedy *Cabin Boy*. Still, Letterman's *Late Show* was the undisputed champion of late-night television, regularly trouncing Jay Leno's *Tonight Show* in the ratings and winning over critics with a sardonic and occasionally absurdist wit far sharper and smarter than Leno's market-tested gabfest. Letterman had badly wanted to host *The Tonight Show* himself following the retirement of its longtime host, Johnny Carson, but after much deliberation NBC went with the safer bet, Leno; Letterman, who'd been on NBC following Carson at 12:30 a.m., jumped to CBS and the 11:30 time slot, where in the eyes of many he'd been making NBC regret its decision.

The *Late Show*'s rating encouraged Cates that Letterman might well attract new viewers to the Oscars, and he also knew that there was ample precedent for handing the ceremony's reins to a talk-show host. The most successful host between the Bob Hope years, which ended in 1978, and the Billy Crystal stint that began a dozen years later was Johnny Carson, Letterman's idol and mentor.

Carson stayed away from his usual *Tonight Show* gags but retained the easygoing, self-deprecating charm he had on that show. He also liked to puncture the pomp of the event: his first monologue, in 1979, began with a classic line that called the Oscar show "two hours of sparkling entertainment . . . spread over a four-hour show." Carson hosted five times in six years, before walking away from the gig and resisting subsequent entreaties to return.

Letterman, the Oscar staff hoped, would follow the lead set by his hero fifteen years earlier. Still, some observers and insiders worried about the clash of cultures between Letterman and the Academy. NBC had opted for Leno largely because the network thought Letterman's humor was better suited to the 12:30 time slot. With his self-mocking wit, his perpetually sour expression, and stunts like his "stupid pet tricks," Letterman simultaneously hosted a talk show and mocked the entire enterprise. The Academy Awards, on the other hand, took themselves seriously. Comedy was fine, but propriety mattered.

Immediately, Letterman's presence changed a few things about the institution of the Oscars. Academy press releases were usually predictable documents, sporting the expected harmless plaudits that Cates could dish out with the best of them: "Whoopi Goldberg has all the qualities of a great Oscar host," "Jeff is a great television director," that sort of thing. The press release announcing Letterman, though, actually slipped in a bit of deadpan facetiousness, a commodity usually in short supply in Academy corridors. "David Letterman . . . is punctual, well groomed, and knows how to keep an audience awake," it quoted Cates as saying.

Added Letterman, "We're changing the format this year. The whole show will be forty minutes long, and I'll be giving away cars."

IN A WAY, the tension between the host and the event fit the tone of the Academy Awards race in 1995. The previous year had been a stormy one, one in which Kurt Cobain committed suicide, O. J. Simpson was charged with the brutal murders of his ex-wife and her friend, and Disney Studios chairman Jeffrey Katzenberg left the company on the heels of his biggest triumph, *The Lion King*, when CEO Michael Eisner refused to give him the job of president, which was left empty after longtime executive Frank Wells died in a helicopter crash.

While *The Lion King* was the top-grossing movie of the year, two other films dominated the Oscar race. One was the blockbuster hit *Forrest Gump*, a paean to blissful ignorance starring Tom Hanks and helmed by *Back to the Future* director Bob Zemeckis. The tale of a good-hearted southern-born simpleton who stumbles through many of the key events of the past forty years, *Forrest Gump* took pains to emphasize the personal and political destruction wrought by the sixties counterculture. Jenny, the free spirit played by Robin Wright and loved by Tom Hanks's title character, embraced the protest and hippie movements and paid for it with an early death, while Forrest Gump himself became an uncomprehending hero almost by accident.

The other film was the profane and bloody *Pulp Fiction*, the second feature from Quentin Tarantino, the young director of *Reservoir Dogs*. Tarantino reveled in the freedom to craft an entertaining movie out of staggeringly violent and offensive material. He and cowriter Roger Avary littered their screenplay with obscenities and vulgarities, gunfights and savage beatings, while never quite losing a sense of fun. *Pulp Fiction* became the first $100 million movie ever released by Miramax, and a milestone in the world of independent cinema.

When nominations were announced in February, the best-picture competition quickly boiled down to a race between *Gump* and *Pulp*—"Life is like a box of chocolates" in one corner, "Any of you fuckin' pricks move and I'll execute every motherfuckin' last one of ya" in the other.

Publicly, Zemeckis and Tarantino played nice, incredulously painting *Gump* and *Pulp* as films cut from the same cloth. "I don't see them as being drastically different," said Tarantino to Zemeckis in the *Los Angeles Times*. "I actually think [*Gump* is] a black comedy." (Away from tape recorders, meanwhile, Tarantino was known to be dismissive of much of *Gump*.)

With those two films battling it out, perhaps the Oscars were ready for a tougher, more sardonic host. Still, there were danger signs early on, caused largely by Letterman's independence and inaccessibility. Often, Cates couldn't even get Letterman to return his phone calls. "I remember Gil calling me," said stage manager Dency Nelson, who'd been the cue card man on Letterman's morning talk show in 1980 and had stayed in touch with the host ever since. "Gil said, 'I can't get through to him. He's an odd duck, isn't he?' "

At a production meeting in mid-March, Cates acknowledged that communications with his host had been sporadic at best. "I actually even spoke to Dave last week," Cates said to his staff, who responded with a round of knowing laughter. "So I'm real confident that he will be here."

FOR MIRAMAX PICTURES, the 67th Academy Awards were a milestone. The company, founded in 1979 by two brothers from Queens, Harvey and Bob Weinstein, had become a brazen, inescapable force in the world of independent film, and by far the most successful of the companies that distributed what were largely low-budget movies. The brothers, particularly the corpulent, flamboyant Harvey, were known for abusing staffers, bullying filmmakers, throwing tantrums, driving hard bargains, and a host of other sins both common and uncommon in the movie business—but they also pushed art films like *sex, lies and videotape*, *My Left Foot*, and *The Crying Game* into the mainstream.

By the early 1990s, Miramax was beginning to work its scorched-earth marketing techniques to perfection on the Academy Awards. They were one of the first companies to aggressively send out screener cassettes to Academy members, an area that had become one of the prime campaign battlegrounds of the time. "The advent of video distribution afforded studios the opportunity to do more than just send a video out in a cardboard mailer," said Richard Kahn, the former Academy president and member of the committee that oversaw campaigning. "Suddenly we were seeing studios spend enormous amounts of money packaging their videos and including fifty-, sixty-, seventy-dollar coffee table books." In 1994, Sony had enclosed eight of its videos in a black laminated wooden box that Kahn called "something any bride would be proud to put her dowry in." The Academy discussed instituting stricter rules about packaging, but in 1995 the likes of *The Lion King* were still going out in elaborate packages, with extra goodies thrown in.

Most of the studios sent out videos and included extras; Miramax distinguished itself by going further, by making sure their filmmakers were seen with the right people and at the right parties during Oscar season. They also hired consultants to spread the word about their movies—and, rivals always charged, to spread dirt about the competition. Among actors and filmmakers eager for the kind of exposure, cachet, and cash that comes with an Oscar, Miramax's stock rose every time another one of its films racked up the nominations: five for *My Left Foot* in 1990 (and a win for its leading actor, Daniel Day-Lewis), six for *The Crying Game* in 1993 (including best picture, best director, and two acting nominations), eight for *The Piano* in 1994 (with three wins, all in big categories).

By the time the Oscar nominations were announced in 1995, Miramax had been acquired by the Walt Disney Company, though it still operated with a large degree of autonomy. The nominations were a triumph for the Weinsteins: Miramax garnered twenty-two nominations, which was twelve more than its parent company and five more than Paramount, its closest rival. In two categories, supporting actress and original screenplay, Miramax had four out of the five nominations; in the best-director competition, the company had three out of five.

As Miramax celebrated, the Academy was dealing with a firestorm of criticism. One of the most acclaimed films of the year had been *Hoop*

Dreams, a three-hour documentary that followed two high school basketball players from inner-city Chicago, both of whom hoped to make it into the National Basketball Association. The film, directed by Steve James, received the kind of acclaim and mainstream attention rarely given to documentaries; Fine Line Features even mounted a campaign to win the movie a best-picture nomination, which the company knew was a long shot.

But not only did *Hoop Dreams* not win a best-picture nomination, it also wasn't chosen as one of the five nominees in the feature documentary category, where many observers had expected it to win easily. That was a category in which a special committee chose the nominations—but since the Academy did not have a documentary branch, the documentary screening committee was comprised of volunteers from all thirteen branches of the Academy.

With sixty-three movies in contention for nominations, committee members needed to be available every Tuesday and Thursday night for three months; the requirement skewed its membership toward the aging and retired. Bruce Davis called them "a very eccentric group of individuals" with strong opinions and unconventional manners. One woman, for instance, would routinely start crying during the discussions that followed screenings.

At those screenings, committee members were asked to "vote" with flashlights fifteen minutes after each documentary began. If three-quarters of them turned on their lights, the movie was stopped. If a documentary passed the fifteen-minute mark, a new vote was taken every ten minutes, and the power to stop the movie shifted to a simple majority.

"A lot of very good movies were turned off because people didn't want to spend the time," said Chuck Workman, a member of the committee. "These people were smart and they were dedicated, but their documentary experience was basically older films or films on PBS. There was a whole world of nonfiction film going on from about the late eighties, exciting stuff, that they just kind of missed."

The failure to nominate *Hoop Dreams* caused an uproar that dwarfed the outcry when the committee had previously overlooked commercially successful documentaries like *Woodstock*, *The Thin Blue Line*, and *Roger and Me*. Critics found it particularly disheartening that one of the nominations went to *Maya Lin: A Strong Clear Vision*, a documentary that won mediocre reviews but was directed by Freida Lee Mock, a past chairwoman of the documentary committee. (Mock had disqualified herself from voting because her film was in contention.) "Leaving out *Hoop Dreams* is like leaving out *Schindler's List*," Lianne Halfon, executive producer of the acclaimed but snubbed documentary *Crumb*, told the *Los Angeles Times*.

The day after the nominations were released, Arthur Hiller announced that he would take "a close, hard look at the procedures of the documentary committee." Bruce Davis followed by taking what was for him an unprecedented step. He called Price Waterhouse and asked to see the complete results of the voting. The accounting firm prepared a rundown for Davis that left out the names of the voters, but showed how each voter had scored every movie in contention.

In voting, members of the committee were asked to rate each documentary on a scale of zero to ten—a departure from other Oscar categories scored by committee, which used a scale of six to ten. "What I found," said Davis, "is that a small group of members gave zeros to every single movie except the five they wanted to see nominated. And they gave tens to those five, which completely skewed the voting."

Choosing his words carefully, Davis summed up the results. "There was one film that received more scores of ten than any other, but it wasn't nominated," he said. "It also got zeros from those few voters, and that was enough to push it to sixth place."

AFTER FIVE YEARS at the Dorothy Chandler Pavilion, the Oscars had returned to the Shrine Auditorium. The Shrine was a seventy-year-old theater that sat in a dodgy part of town just south of downtown Los Angeles, nestled next to the University of Southern California and across the street from the venerable Felix Chevrolet auto dealership.

Cates preferred the Chandler because it was more elegant and looked better on camera, but that twenty-eight-hundred-seat theater simply didn't have enough room for all the Academy members who wanted to attend the show. Moving to the six-thousand-seat Shrine allowed the Academy to clear its backlog of members who'd lost out in annual lotteries for seats at the Chandler.

Six days before the show, crew members worked to turn the cavernous building into a usable theater for the Oscars. Bleachers were erected and the red carpet laid in front of the Shrine; production trailers, trucks, and a huge press tent filled the parking lot behind the building. Inside the Shrine, tables were laid across seats in the orchestra section to create command posts for the producer, the network, the design crew, and the stage managers. Stage left and downstairs were dressing rooms. Through the wings stage right was the green room, nestled in a corner of the Shrine Exhibition Hall, which doubled as the site of the Governors Ball.

Seats near the stage sported seat cards that indicated who would be sitting where come Monday night. The front row contained Rene Russo, Samuel L. Jackson, Andie MacDowell, Hugh Grant, Annette Bening, Julia Ormond, John Travolta, Jeremy Irons, Arnold Schwarzenegger, Tom Hanks, Sharon Stone, Denzel Washington, Jodie Foster, Jack Nicholson, Holly Hunter, and Anthony Hopkins. Also Uma Thurman and Oprah Winfrey.

As work proceeded, the host of the Oscar show was nowhere to be seen. Letterman had arrived in Los Angeles, but he was spending his time with the twenty-odd *Late Show* staffers he'd brought with him. Occasionally, word of Letterman's doings filtered down to Oscar staffers, some of whom said they'd heard that the host really was planning to raffle off a car onstage, just as he'd promised in the initial press release. The raffle, of course, was to be rigged. "They wanted Jessica Tandy to win," said an Oscar staffer with ties to the Letterman camp. "They didn't realize that she died six months ago. So now they're looking for somebody else to give the car to."

Letterman was expected to make his first appearance at the Shrine the next day. In the meantime, the TelePrompTer he would use displayed a more philosophical bent: IF THERE ARE WORDS ON THE PROMPTER AND NO ONE READS THEM, it read, ARE THEY REALLY THERE?

THREE DAYS BEFORE THE SHOW, during a dinner break, Bruce Vilanch walked into the production office wearing a T-shirt that read: THANK YOU

FOR NOT BEING PERKY. Vilanch picked up a phone message that had been pinned to the board all day: "D. Letterman," it read, with a return number. "8:35 a.m." Vilanch laughed. "He called me at home at 8:36," he said. "I don't think I need to return this."

The frizzy-haired, three-hundred-pound, openly gay Vilanch had been a common sight (always in baggy pants and humorous T-shirts) at Hollywood awards shows for years. The former journalist began writing for Bette Midler's stage act in the early 1970s, spent some time on variety shows like *The Brady Bunch Hour*, and over the years had written material for the likes of Diana Ross, Lily Tomlin, Richard Pryor, and Joan Rivers. He had been writing for the Oscars since the Allan Carr show in 1989, mostly for the host but also on occasion for presenters.

"With Billy, we wrote material and refined it over weeks," Vilanch said as he tossed Letterman's phone message into the trash can beneath his desk. "With Whoopi, I wrote it and she said it. But Dave doesn't work like that. He wants *tons* of material. And then he goes off by himself, sifts through it all, and digests it on his own."

CATES USUALLY FELT that the Oscar show should begin with a piece of film rather than a production number, but he did make an occasional exception for a routine that mixed film and dancing. In 1991, for instance, he'd hired Debbie Allen for the first time, and she'd choreographed a frenetic number in which live dancers burst through a movie screen and danced onstage. In 1994, Allen and Chuck Workman had collaborated on another tricky routine, which found Bernadette Peters appearing both in film footage and, at the conclusion of the song, on the stage of the Dorothy Chandler Pavilion.

And in 1995, Workman and Allen were collaborating on an even more difficult blend of live action and film. Set to "Make 'Em Laugh," Donald O'Connor's tour de force from *Singin' in the Rain*, the production number featured a barrage of film clips illustrating the art of film comedy. Several singers and dancers, chief among them *Sister Act* actress Kathy Najimy, *Rocky Horror Picture Show* star Tim Curry, and the seven-year-old star of *Mrs. Doubtfire*, Mara Wilson, jumped in and out of a huge screen, which was slit to accommodate their entrances and exits. The three singers would be seen live onstage, but also in new footage, shot by Workman, which depicted them watching classic film comedies. Occasionally, they'd be inserted into those classic clips as well.

The live audience wouldn't be able to see the entire number; they'd be looking at the performers come and go through a large blank green screen. Only at home would viewers be able to fully appreciate the number—and then only if Margolis could find a way to shoot it without simply confusing the audience. "It was one of those openings that was *way* too difficult to do on a live show," said the director, "but it's the Oscars, so you push the envelope and do what you can. I had to keep cutting to the stage in a way that would remind the audience at home where we were."

From the start, the number had been a mess. Workman didn't want to use Najimy, and thought the actress was "only concerned with her own image." As he tried to make the piece work, the filmmaker grew more argumentative and difficult. At one point, he went to Cates and suggested dumping the number entirely. "No, keep working on it," the producer insisted. "It'll be okay."

On the stage of the Shrine, though, take after take got no closer to making the routine smooth, or even comprehensible. "The thing about the Oscars," said Workman later, "is that it's like turning around an aircraft carrier." On his own, the filmmaker was used to sitting in an editing room, trying out tricky cuts and juxtapositions, and quickly revising or jettisoning ideas that didn't work. But working within the context of an Oscar production number, where his film was only one part of a mammoth undertaking that also involved dancers, actors and their agents, a director, a choreographer, and many others who had to be alternately challenged, coddled, and consulted with, Workman found that he could no longer work as efficiently or effectively as usual; change came as slowly as if he were a Navy captain piloting an eleven-hundred-foot vessel. "And you can't blame it on the machinery," he said, "because if you work on that show you have to understand that you are on an aircraft carrier."

As staffers watched the performers struggle to sync their moves with the film clips, and Margolis fight to find the right camera angles and cuts, the intricacies of "Make 'Em Laugh" seemed overwhelming. "Man, if this thing works it'll be a miracle," said one viewer. "It's so friggin' complicated."

RANDY NEWMAN was a six-time Oscar nominee, but so far the prize had eluded him. Partly, that was because the songs he wrote for movies were rarely as distinctive—or, for that matter, as tough and as mean—as the work with which he'd made his name. The songs on Newman's pop albums, including the deceptively gorgeous anthem to slavery, "Sail Away," the nihilistic "God's Song," and the cracker anthem "Rednecks," were often barbed and cruel; his big pop hit had been "Short People," in which the six-foot Newman was presumably joking when he proclaimed, "Short people got no reason to live." By contrast, his movie tunes tended to be jaunty, even pleasant. His latest nominated song, "Make Up Your Mind," from the Ron Howard movie *The Paper*, was typical: bouncy, professional, and forgettable.

Still, Newman remained a formidable talent and intellect. He may not have had a pop hit since 1977, but he'd written some classic film scores and found a lucrative niche following in the footsteps of his uncles Alfred and Lionel, both notable film composers.

Newman arrived at the Shrine on Saturday afternoon to rehearse "Make Up Your Mind." Before sitting down at the piano, he walked over to his background singers and addressed them solemnly. "Remember," he said, "give me at least 64 percent."

"Hi, Randy," said Margolis over the P.A. system as Newman took his seat. "How are you?"

"Really good," said a characteristically deadpan Newman. "I've got my speech all ready in case *The Lion King* vote cancels itself out."

This was, of course, a long shot. After a year in which the song nominations had gone to the likes of Bruce Springsteen, Neil Young, and Janet Jackson, Disney had returned with a vengeance. Its blockbuster animated film *The Lion King* dominated the music categories: not only did composer Hans Zimmer win a nomination for his score, the film captured three of the five nominations for the best song. One of those nominations, Elton John's ballad "Can You Feel the Love Tonight," was the only hit among the nominees, and the odds-on favorite.

Sitting at the piano, Newman turned his gaze to the audience, scanning the seating cards until he spotted the star of *The Natural*, for which Newman wrote an acclaimed (and Oscar-nominated) score. "There's Robert Redford," Newman joked to no one in particular. "He belched his way through the movie I did with him."

Newman performed his nominated song once, then looked into the orchestra pit and located conductor Bill Conti. "That was a little faster than it should go," Newman told Conti, "but it was pretty good. And it was good enough, since I've lowered my standards so much."

After Newman left, Margolis prepared to rehearse another of the nominated songs, Patty Smyth's "Look What Love Has Done" from the Arnold Schwarzenegger comedy *Junior*. The director sat in his truck behind the Shrine, staring at a wall of some sixty-five different TV monitors. The three largest screens sat directly in front of Margolis's seat, where they showed him the camera being used at any given moment, along with the next two he was planning to use. Smaller screens surrounding those three featured the view from each of the sixteen cameras that would be used during the show. Beneath those screens were pieces of masking tape with the camera number and the name of the cameraman: CA-1 BILL . . . CA-2 HECTOR . . . CA-3 LARRY . . .

With a background in music and variety shows, including *The Gong Show*, the American Music Awards, and Dolly Parton's short-lived variety show, Margolis had first been hired after Marty Pasetta had proved too imperious for the Academy's taste. Margolis didn't have Pasetta's temper; he grinned a lot and kept quiet when things went wrong. His crews tended to like him, and not just because he'd hired his son as a stage manager and his father as a stand-in; even those who weren't related found him loose and open to outside ideas. Among the higher echelons of the Oscar staff, though, occasional doubts were raised about the director's agenda. It didn't help when Margolis's own press agent began to solicit the attention of the media, which was eager for any Oscar-related access.

Margolis was in his booth going over the plans for "Look What Love Has Done" when he got a call from stage manager Ken Stein. Patty Smyth, said Stein, didn't want to make her entrance by walking down a small stairway that had been placed on the stage.

"Why not?" asked Margolis.

"I don't know," said Stein. "I think it's a female thing, because we get it from all of them."

The woman who sat to Margolis's right in the truck, associate director Wendy Charles Acey, quickly chimed in. "Because she'll be wearing three-inch heels and she's afraid she'll trip in front of everybody, of course," said Acey.

Smyth was the coquettish former lead singer of the pop band Scandal, who had two small hits a decade earlier with "Goodbye to You" and "The Warrior." She'd already caused one problem by asking that her boyfriend be allowed to play guitar in her band on the show; the trouble was that her boyfriend was the temperamental tennis player John McEnroe. Cates nixed the request on the grounds that McEnroe's presence would be a distraction.

When Smyth said she didn't want to use the stairs, Margolis left the truck to speak to her. While he was gone, Bill Conti radioed the truck. "Does this girl cause as much commotion as Streisand, or what?" he asked.

"Yeah," said Acey. "I guess I should find out who she is."

Conti laughed. "*Exactly*," he said.

A few minutes later, Margolis returned to the truck. "Oh, boy," he sighed, sinking back into his chair.

Margolis had planned to begin the number with a slow pan to Smyth as she walked down the stairs. With that option gone, he watched her run through the song, shaking his head as he tried to figure out how to shoot it. None of the camera angles seemed interesting to him, nobody cared much for the song itself, and the director seemed defeated by how to make it work on-screen.

After the first take, Smyth leaned into the microphone. "It's really muddy up here," she said to the sound mixer.

"Okay, just give us a couple of minutes," Margolis told her over the P.A. system. Then he shut off his mike and leaned back in his chair. "A couple of minutes to find another song," he muttered.

"Another singer, maybe," added Conti, whose headset allowed him to hear conversations in the truck.

For the next fifteen minutes, Margolis studied the script in front of him, jotting down notations for each dissolve, cut, and camera move. Finally, he came up with a plan for the song. "Okay, here we go for rehearsal," he said into his microphone. "Thank you for your patience." Then he addressed his cameramen. "Guys," he said, "try to give me something here you didn't do on the other song."

But the next take was no better than the last, and Margolis stared back at his script. Smyth paced the stage, idly singing the Bobby Gentry hit "Ode to Billy Joe," then questioning the crew about when they'd be ready for her again.

"Kenny, you better go talk to her," said Margolis to Ken Stein. "She's getting really impatient, and I need some time here."

"What should I tell her?" asked Stein.

Margolis sunk his head in his hands. "Just tell her," he said wearily, "I'm redesigning the whole fuckin' thing because she wouldn't come down the stairs." He stopped. "No, just tell her to relax for a minute. Tell her we're lighting or something."

Unaware of the mood in the truck, Smyth stretched out her arms and did a little dance. "We have some choreography we'd like to show you next time through," she announced.

"Just as long as it starts with you walking down the stairs," said Margolis.

"*Falling* down the stairs is what I'll do," said Smyth, a notorious klutz who swore she once broke a rib putting on her bra. "But I'll try it if you want."

"No," said Margolis. "This'll be fine."

Slowly, Margolis puzzled it out. "Camera twelve's got the first shot, four's got the second, three's got the third . . ." They tried Margolis's new plan, but cameramen kept getting in each other's way. "Forget it boys, it's not working," said the director. "Let's try something else. If anybody's got a good shot, show it to me."

Over the next few takes, Margolis slowly found a handful of shots and camera moves he could live with. He clearly wasn't happy with the number, but neither was it a complete disaster. "If I stop after this one," he said to Acey at the beginning of one take, "am I on schedule?"

"No," she said. "But you're closer than you were."

"Okay," sighed Margolis when the take ended. "Thank you very much, Patty. Thank you, guys. Let's move on."

In the trailer, Acey shook her head. "Well," she said, "it's been a slow year for music."

"THE IRVING THALBERG AWARD," read Arnold Schwarzenegger, "is given to people who have devoted their lives to making movies of lasting value." The action star looked at the TelePrompTer, which displayed the lines he'd be using to present a special Oscar to Clint Eastwood. He started to laugh. "Heck," he ad-libbed, "I don't think they're going to be giving *me* that one."

Near the production table, Susan Futterman from ABC approached the show's senior executive consultant, Robert Z. Shapiro. Futterman had an open script in her hands. She pointed to the second page of the script. ITEM # 2, it read. OPENING COMMERCIAL BILLBOARDS. On it were the voiceovers that announcer Randy Thomas would read at the top of the show. Four companies had paid for plugs: Revlon, American Express, Chevrolet, and Coca-Cola. The problem, Futterman told Shapiro, was that while the first three companies had short plugs ("Revlon: Revolutionary products for revolutionary women . . . American Express: For life, for living . . ."), Coke had altogether too much copy.

"Look at it," she said, jabbing her finger toward the lines: "And Coca-Cola, in the genuine Coca-Cola bottle. Nothing looks like it. Nothing tastes like it. Because it's always Coca-Cola."

"It's more than five seconds," Futterman insisted. "It's seven."

"Is that really a problem?" asked Shapiro.

"Yes it is. You have to cut the line, 'in the genuine Coca-Cola bottle.' "

"Are you sure?"

"Yes," she said firmly. "Why should they get seven seconds, when we're selling everyone else five?"

WITH DAVID LETTERMAN and his staff on the premises, communication had improved between the host and the production team—though that's not to say that Dave and the Oscars were always on the same page. For one thing, Letterman wanted to wear a suit, while Cates insisted on the usual tuxedo. Letterman wanted his own drummer in the orchestra pit to punctuate his jokes with the kind of rim shots the Oscars had always done without. He wanted sound effects and slow motion and instant replays, all mainstays of his television show.

"We talked to him about a number of ideas we didn't feel were really appropriate," said Margolis, whose wrath Letterman had incurred by suggesting that Hal Gurnee, the director of *The Late Show*, would have been able to provide a slow-mo replay effect Margolis didn't want to use. A subsequent meeting in Letterman's trailer had ironed out some of the differences, but a gulf still existed between the Oscar staffers and their host. "A lot of the stuff that he does in the Ed Sullivan Theatre is brilliant there," said Margolis. "But it wasn't going to translate to the Shrine, to our audience."

On Friday afternoon, Letterman had breezed through a few introductions and gotten the feel of the stage (while his head writer, Rob Burnett, had taken note of the seat cards, particularly the ones that indicated where Uma Thurman and Oprah Winfrey would be sitting). At 8:30 p.m. on Saturday night, he took the stage once more; as if to show that this rehearsal was more serious, he entered to the strains of Richard Strauss's "Also Sprach Zarathustra," aka the theme from *2001: A Space Odyssey*, aka the portentous music with which Elvis Presley announced his arrival onstage for much of the last half-decade of his life.

Letterman wore jeans, a T-shirt, and a San Francisco Giants cap and jacket. He sported several days' growth of graying beard. Almost immediately, the rehearsal took on the look and feel of a *Late Show* broadcast—though not, it seemed, a particularly inspired *Late Show* broadcast. He showed a lackluster film package of New York City taxi drivers talking about the movies, and a funnier one of stars reinterpreting Letterman's one line from *Cabin Boy*: "Would you like to buy a monkey?" His punch lines were punctuated by the sounds of breaking glass, and by drummer Anton Fig's rim shots. He read a Top Ten List, "Top Ten Surprises in Kato Kaelin's Testimony." (Word quickly spread among the crew that the list was from a recent Letterman show, and that he'd have a new, custom list ready for Oscar night.) He called Bill Conti "the world's most dangerous Oscar orchestra leader," a line borrowed from his traditional introduction of the band on his own show. He even did a Stupid Pet Trick, bringing out Sadie, The Dog That Spins When You Applaud. As the title suggested, the hyperkinetic German Shepherd spun madly in circles when the audience applauded.

And as he promised in the initial press release, Letterman held a raffle. "Some lucky nominee," he said, "could be driving Oscar home in a brand-new car." With Jessica Tandy out of the running, Letterman's writers had decided to give the vehicle to Sally Field instead. Margolis, Letterman, and *Late Show* producer Robert Morton spent a great deal of time trying to figure out how to drive the car onstage so that the winner could immediately get behind the driver's seat (the only solution was to back it on), and how to position the raffle cage from which one of the show's trophy ladies would pull the winning name.

As Letterman's rehearsal wound down, many of the Oscar staffers began repeating a line that would come to sound like a cross between a mantra and a plea: "Well, I'm sure he's saving his best stuff for Monday night."

Still, the rehearsal left more than a few people disappointed and disconcerted. "I'm a little surprised," confided Roy Christopher. "I had hoped that he wouldn't do so much of his usual stuff. Carson didn't do that, you know."

KEANU REEVES ducked into the green room, a script page in one hand and a motorcycle helmet in the other. Unlike most of the other stars due to rehearse on the afternoon before the show, Reeves hadn't come to the Shrine in a town car provided by the Academy. Instead, he rode his motorcycle there.

Army Archerd said hello to Reeves and then nodded at the script. "What are you doing?" he asked.

"One of the best-picture things," said Reeves, who had been given the plum task of introducing the film clip from *Pulp Fiction*.

"Oh, that's good."

"Is it?" asked Reeves. "I'm out there by myself. I wanted to give out an *award*, and be with a *girl*."

Reeves spotted Vilanch, whose T-shirt du jour read, MIGHTY MORPHIN FLOWER ARRANGERS. "You're one of the writers," he said to Vilanch, holding up his script. "In this line, 'This shocking, brutal, hilarious adventure is called *Pulp Fiction*,' can I say 'entitled' instead of 'called'?"

"I don't see why not," said Vilanch.

"Okay, good," said Reeves. "Also, don't they mention the names of the directors in these things?"

"In the clip intros?" asked Vilanch. "I don't think so. Quentin will be mentioned lots of other places."

With his concerns about the script assuaged, Reeves began pumping Vilanch for information about the show. "What's Dave been like?" he said.

Vilanch laughed. "Oh, you should see it," he said.

Reeves caught something in Vilanch's tone, and frowned. "He's not doing stuff like he does on his show, is he?" he asked.

"Well," admitted Vilanch, "there will be a Top Ten List."

"No."

"And he's got some of those film clips he does. There's one with taxi drivers."

"No!"

"And there is a Stupid Pet Trick."

"No! He *can't*!" said Reeves angrily. "Whatever happened to restraint and decorum?"

Before long, the green room was cluttered with stars who'd arrived for the rehearsal ritual that took place the day before every Oscar show. Sarah Jessica Parker was casual in black sweats and sneakers; Annette Bening was elegant in a maroon suit. Anna Paquin wore an oversized T-shirt; Sylvester Stallone jeans, sunglasses, and an open shirt. Radiant in pastels, Andie MacDowell carried her baby daughter, Sarah. Sharon Stone wore a long, filmy dress, causing (and to all appearances basking in) a huge commotion everywhere she went. Sigourney Weaver bemoaned the fact that she didn't bring high heels to wear as she rehearsed her walk across the stage. Tim Allen stopped to chat with the stagehands on his way off the stage, while Paul Newman charmed everyone he encountered. Everywhere Matt Dillon went, he was shadowed by his publicist. In fact, lots of the stars were shadowed by their publicists—which led to some tense scenes, since the past few months had seen an abnormal amount of publicist-switching among actors. At one point, a press rep for a small firm walked out of the green room, made a U-turn, and quickly came back in, shuddering and looking for refuge. "All of PMK's out there," she said, referring to the huge PR firm that, according to its chief, Pat Kingsley, had twenty clients on the show.

The action-film star Steven Seagal, whose last big hit movie had been *Under Siege* three years earlier, walked in the artists' entrance wearing black and looking serious. In his wake, many staffers were heard to mutter, "Why is *he* on the show?" Some suggested that the answer had to do with the fact that Seagal and Letterman shared the same agent, CAA's Michael Ovitz.

All afternoon, Vilanch and his fellow writers, Hal Kanter and Buz Kohan, had been hastily rewriting lines to suit the stars. For the most part, introductions were simplified, stripped of jokes, and shortened. Steve Martin's bit, though, was lengthened to include a routine about the power of movies. "I remember sitting in a darkened movie theater with seventeen-year-old Mary Jo Rasmussen, trying to get to second base," he said. "I even remember the name of the movie: *The Lion King*." The joke got big laughs—just as it had the first time he'd used it, a couple of months earlier on *The Tonight Show*.

"WELL, at least we're going to get a sense of timing," said Michael Seligman, standing in the aisle of the Shrine. "We're very long at this point."

With a few minutes to go until the first dress rehearsal, the length of the show was only one of a series of question marks. The theater was cleared of most guests, and then rehearsal began with a stand-in reading Arthur Hiller's welcoming speech and introducing the "Make 'Em Laugh" dance number. The singers and dancers slipped smoothly through the slit screen that stood center stage, and got through the song without any notable technical goofs. But the blend of live performances and filmed footage went by so quickly, and involved such a complex blend of media, that it remained confusing.

Still unshaven, Letterman made his appearance in a blue blazer, blue T-shirt, and tan slacks. His opening monologue was truncated and uninspired. "If life really is like a box of chocolates," he said, "I think it's safe to say that Dom DeLuise has eaten every one."

This time through, Letterman asked for Paul Newman's help with the Stupid Pet Trick; a stand-in subbing for Newman helped the host unroll the carpet on which Sadie spun. Letterman scrapped the car giveaway and delivered a new Top Ten List, "Top Ten Things Overheard at Last Night's Rehearsal." It included, "We'll just be ready in a couple of weeks," "According to my stopwatch, the running time of the show is exactly eight hours," "Margolis grabbed my ass," "Why don't they let that spinning dog be the host?" and "What does Gil Cates do?" Number one was, "Is it too late to call Billy Crystal?" Immediately, crew members asked if they could get the list printed on T-shirts.

Besides the inside jokes in that Top Ten List, though, Letterman's material did not go over particularly well. The phone in front of Cates rang more and more frequently. At one point Cates and Seligman huddled intently with Robert Morton. "For the first part," Cates told Morton, "it *has* to be a tuxedo."

Clearly, the Letterman camp was as anxious as the production staff. Midway through rehearsal, Vilanch walked to the production table, sat down near Cates, and turned on his laptop. "They're getting nervous," Cates said.

"I know," said Vilanch. "I was paged."

AT MIDNIGHT, Cates and Margolis met in the production truck. "Well, Jeff, you did a good job," sighed Cates, who always tried to keep his complaints to a minimum after the dress rehearsal, because there wasn't enough time to make major changes. "Very, very, very nice run-through, given everything."

Margolis nodded. "It's a good show," he said. "I don't know what Dave's gonna do tomorrow, but I love him."

"They may well come back tomorrow and change things," said Cates. "They may switch the order of the film bits."

"The way we just did it felt like the right way to do it to me," said Margolis.

"I don't feel that way," said Cates with a sigh. "But ultimately, it's their decision."

Bill Conti entered the truck, and Cates patted the conductor on the back. "Wonderful job," he said. "But Billy, if you ever do this again, you've got to change the music when people walk onstage." Cates hummed the familiar fanfare, and then grinned. "*I'm* at my wits' end," he said, shaking his head, "but I'm sure that you'll do this again."

Outside the truck, a few high-level staffers gathered to kibitz about the show, and to grumble about the aloof and difficult Letterman. "The man," said one high-level staffer, "is a major neurotic."

They looked toward the trailer where Letterman and his writers were watching a tape of the rehearsal. "Should I go over there, shake the trailer, and yell '*Earthquake*'?" asked one. The idea garnered significant support.

Meanwhile, a publicist for Tim Allen called the production office to ask how she could guarantee that Allen would be included in the montage of arriving stars that opened every show. "Be aware that traffic will be very heavy," Chuck Warn told her. "And get him here on time."

MONDAY DAWNED HOT AND BRIGHT. Letterman still hadn't shaved.

The second run-through was a little faster, a little funnier, than the first—though to cover a delay in resetting the stage for Elton John, Letterman resorted to an encore appearance by The Dog That Spins When You Applaud.

Rehearsal ended just after three o'clock. A few minutes later, Letterman walked across the stage with Rob Burnett, tossing a football back and forth. In an aisle near the side of the theater, Gil Cates looked around the nearly deserted theater.

"The playwright Robert Anderson had a great quote," he said quietly. "He said he feels best about a play when he's finished writing it, just before he sends it off to anybody. He's done it, but nobody's seen it so nobody can say anything about it, nobody can piss on it. I feel the same way. Right now the show is ready, and nothing has gone wrong yet. All we can do now is wait and see what happens."

An hour or so before show time, Dency Nelson dropped by dressing room number one, which sat just off the wings stage left. Letterman had shaved, but he was still wearing a T-shirt. He had a joke he wanted to try out on Nelson.

"What do you think, Dency?" Letterman asked. Pretending that he was onstage, the host looked toward an imaginary audience. Uma," he said, pointing toward the spot where Uma Thurman would be sitting. Then "Oprah," pointing toward Winfrey's seat. "Uma, Oprah," he repeated. "Oprah, Uma." He looked at Nelson. "Should I do it?"

Nelson thought the gag sounded like a typical David Letterman goof; it was dumb, but he loved how Letterman was unafraid to be dumb. "Yeah, I like it," he said, laughing. "You should do it."

In front of the Shrine, meanwhile, the storm had already begun. In the back, by the artists' entrance, crew members with walkie-talkies communicated with others out front, keeping track of precisely which nominees and presenters had arrived, which ones were on their way—and, most seriously, which were unaccounted for. With several walkie-talkies open, though, what emerged was confusing as often as it was clarifying.

"John Travolta is here."

"Thank you."

"Rene Russo."

"Thank you."

"Two of Patty Smyth's musicians are missing."

"Is Jamie Lee here?"

"Yes."

"Steven Seagal?"

"No."

"Do you read me?"

"David Alan Grier's limo is at Thirtieth and Figueroa in the limo line."

"Did anybody call Sharon Stone's car?"

"Sharon shut off her communication with us. We cannot reach her."

"Can you hear me, Danette?"

"Has Paul Newman arrived in back?"

"No, Danette, we have not seen him."

"Someone should try to reach Steve Martin."

"Danette, do you copy? Steve Martin is two minutes away."

"Hugh Grant, Denzel Washington, are those confirmed?"

"Yes."

"Arnold Schwarzenegger has arrived. Hugh Grant has arrived."

"I can't hear anything. Can you hear me?"

"What's the status on Steve Martin's car?"

"Danette, can you read me? Steve Martin's two minutes away."

"Winona Ryder has arrived."

"Winona? This is a new one."

"I know."

"Steve Martin . . . with Diane Keaton!"

"That's something to tell the seating people."

"Got it. Steve Martin and Diane Keaton."

"Has Helen Mirren arrived? She's the only nominee that we haven't heard from."

"Anybody we're missing, get on the phone and start calling those cars."

"Who are we missing?"

"Ellen Barkin, Tim Allen . . ."

"What?"

"Ellen Barkin's coming in."

"Thank you."

"Can you guys hear *any* of this?"

As this went on, Jack Nicholson strolled by the green room, a bottle of water in his hand and a platinum-blond Rebecca Broussard on his arm. Anthony Hopkins returned from the men's room, tucking his shirt beneath his cummerbund. Former teen actor Corey Feldman showed up at the back door in a ruffled shirt and velvet tux, with thick hair mousse and Michael Jackson–style makeup. Feldman, who didn't look too different than he had six years earlier, when he'd done a Jackson imitation as part of Allan Carr's "Stars of Tomorrow" number, had an animated conversation at the sign-in table for presenters and performers, though he was neither.

Nicholson walked by again, heading the other direction. "Just wandering around," he announced. "No logic to it."

A stagehand watched him pass. "He's so fucking cool," he said.

Paul Newman arrived and came down the steps on the arms of two young women. "We're carrying him," one of them announced. "He's weak." Newman grinned and let his legs buckle.

In the orchestra section of the Shrine, an elderly man grabbed anyone with a production pass. "Do you have anything to do with seating?" he asked, pointing to a large camera. "I'm not paying five hundred bucks to sit behind *that* fucking thing."

6:00 P.M., PACIFIC DAYLIGHT TIME: *"The Academy of Motion Picture Arts and Sciences presents the 67th annual Academy Awards."*

Oscar announcer Randy Thomas stood in her sound booth in a truck behind the Shrine. Thomas was one of the only women to have served as the voice of Oscar, which she'd done in 1993, Cates's year for saluting women in film. (Warned by ABC that sponsors would never accept a female announcer, Cates hired Thomas quietly and kept her hiring a secret; afterward, no one complained.) Thomas was also the voice of the Hooked on Phonics learning system, which Letterman often mocked on his show, and she'd been waiting all week for somebody to apprise Letterman of that fact. If Dave knew, Thomas was sure he'd make a joke about it. But either nobody told Letterman or he passed up the chance to mention it, because the host had yet to say a word about Thomas.

In her hands, Thomas held a stack of index cards with the names and brief descriptions of two dozen movie stars. These were the stars who had been filmed arriving at the Shrine and edited into the montage that would open the show. To the network, this opening was five of the most important minutes of the Academy Awards—because if viewers weren't drawn to the Oscar races themselves, they needed to be quickly reassured that they'd be seeing all their favorite stars over the course of the show.

Thomas couldn't watch her monitor and read the cards at the same time, so another staffer stood behind her, tapping her on the shoulder every time the picture on the screen changed. When Thomas felt the tap, she flipped to the next card and read the ID: "Nominee tonight for best actor, Hollywood legend John Travolta . . . nominee for best actress, double Oscar winner Jodie Foster . . . worldwide box-office favorite Arnold Schwarzenegger, with his wife, Maria Shriver . . ." Tim Allen was not included.

Out in the lobby of the Shrine, latecomers filled the lobby and rushed toward the doors, trying to get in before the cameras were turned on the audience. *Pulp Fiction* star Samuel L. Jackson, nominated for best supporting actor, was one of the last to make it in before the doors from the lobby to the theater were closed. "Samuel! Samuel!" yelled people in the lobby as ABC pages pulled him through the crowd. He turned, waved, and signed one quick autograph before making it into the hall and into his front-row seat.

In his truck, Margolis scanned the monitors in front of him as his cameramen roamed the audience, zeroing in on famous faces. Assistant directors and video technicians surrounded Margolis; behind him, sitting in a row of chairs at the rear of the truck, were Cates, Seligman, and Hamlin. Before Letterman's monologue got under way, Dency Nelson radioed Margolis. "Make sure you have cameras ready for Uma Thurman and Oprah Winfrey," Nelson warned the director.

"I've been dying to do something all day," said Letterman, "and I think maybe we can take care of this." He walked to his left and pointed into the audience. "Oprah." He walked to his right. "Uma. Uuuuma, Ooooprah." Inside the Shrine, the joke fell completely flat. Listening to the silence from his spot in the wings, Nelson grimaced and fervently hoped that he wasn't the only one who'd encouraged Letterman to use the gag.

Scanning his monitors during the monologue, Margolis looked for reaction shots. Susan Sarandon laughed. "Six!" he shouted. Jodie Foster grinned. "Four!" For much of the monologue, camera ten was fixed on Winona Ryder—but she wasn't laughing, so Margolis never called for her.

"Forrest Gump said, 'Life is like a box of chocolates—you never know what you're gonna get,'" continued Letterman. "Unless, of course, you're sitting next to Roger Ebert, and then you know you're not gonna get any." One of the cameras was aimed at Sally Field, who played Forrest Gump's mother. But Field just rolled her eyes, so Margolis chose not to go to her.

"Oprah, Uma. Uma, Oprah," said Letterman a minute later. "It's gonna be one of those things I won't be able to stop doing all night long." Next to Margolis, Acey scanned her script to identify the subjects of the next joke. "Schwarzenegger and Shriver are next," she said into her headset. Camera four went to them.

"One of the pictures nominated tonight for best foreign film is *Eat Drink*

Man Woman," said Letterman. "Coincidentally, as I understand it, this is also how Arnold Schwarzenegger asked Maria Shriver out on their first date." Margolis cut to camera four just in time to catch Schwarzenegger's good-natured laugh, and Shriver's considerably more exuberant one.

Almost half an hour into the show, Tommy Lee Jones handed out the first Oscar of the evening, for best supporting actress. The preshow favorite in most Oscar pools, Dianne Wiest in Woody Allen's *Bullets Over Broadway*, won. "You did good," said Cates, patting Margolis on the shoulder as the show broke for its first commercial. Cates then left the truck, followed quickly by an L.A.P.D. officer who'd been standing nearby and was assigned to shadow the producer during the show.

With the Stupid Pet Trick coming up in the next act, there was a brief moment of panic backstage. Letterman had been planning to ask for Paul Newman's help on the bit, but Newman was no longer in his seat. A stage manager was dispatched to the green room to find him, but Newman wasn't there either. (He was in the bar in the lobby of the Shrine.) Staffers scanned the crowd, looking for a star who was seated close to the stage and might be agreeable. Just before he took the stage, Letterman got his new assignment: "Pick Tom Hanks!"

Hanks looked shell-shocked when Letterman asked him for help, but he gamely played along, helping the host unroll a carpet before the dog came onstage. The audience clapped obediently, Sadie spun frantically, and Winona Ryder laughed and clapped her hands. "Ten!" shouted Margolis.

A few minutes later, Martin Landau won the best supporting actor award for *Ed Wood*. Thirty-one seconds into his speech, the sixty-three-year-old actor threw down a gauntlet of sorts. "Gil Cates, don't put music on," he warned. " 'Cause if it's the *Mission: Impossible* theme, I'll get very angry." Back in the truck, Cates immediately stood up; he knew that long speeches were most troubling early in the show, because they set a bad precedent.

Forging ahead, Landau thanked *Ed Wood* director Tim Burton, Disney, Johnny Depp, his makeup artists, the press . . .

"Come *on*," said Margolis urgently.

. . . his agents, his daughter, his best friend . . .

"Is the clock up?" asked an agitated Cates. Not only was Landau running long, but he was delivering the bane of any Oscar producer: the list of names. "Put the clock up." By this point, if Landau looked toward the TelePrompTer, he could see a flashing red background, and block letters that read PLEASE WRAP UP. But he went on, thanking his sister, then the entire Academy, then the actors' branch of the Academy.

Cates stepped forward, until he was right over Margolis's shoulder. There was an unspoken but undeniable double standard when it came to Oscar speeches: actors were always granted more leeway than unknowns. But this actor was showing no signs of stopping.

Two minutes and seven seconds into his speech, after plugging the NEA, Laudau stopped to take a breath.

"*Music!*" yelled Cates angrily. "Fuck him!" Margolis gave Conti the cue, and the music started.

Onstage, Landau yelled "*No!*" just as cameras cut to Matt Dillon, who stood on the other side of the stage and looked awkwardly toward Landau. Stage manager Jason Seligman cued Dillon to begin reading from the TelePrompTer.

In the doorway to Margolis's truck, the officer assigned to Cates quickly got on his walkie-talkie to a cop stationed inside the house. "Did he clear the stage?" he asked nervously. Told that Landau had finally gone into the wings, he relaxed. The Academy Awards had security measures designed to deal with gate-crashers and overzealous winners who wouldn't relinquish the stage—measures that began with blinding spotlights aimed at the stage and went as far as rubber bullets—but nobody wanted to use them on a sexagenarian Oscar winner. (In fact, none of the measures had ever been used.)

Ninety minutes into the show, Paul Newman surfaced to give the cinematography award to John Toll for *The Legends of the Fall*. On his way across the stage with Toll, with whom he was supposed to go to the press rooms, Newman suddenly stopped. He stared into the rafters above the stage, where Jamie Lee Curtis, clad in a short, impossibly tight black dress, hung from a prop helicopter, ready to make a dramatic entrance to present the sci-tech awards. As she was lowered to the stage in an homage to a scene from the movie *True Lies*, a grinning Newman ran back to catch up with Toll. "Sorry," he said. "Did I leave ya? I just had to see that. Now where do we go?"

A few minutes later, Cates left the truck and came into the wings in search of Tim Robbins and Susan Sarandon. The producer had booked them on the show despite his anger two years earlier when they'd departed from their script to plead the case of a boatload of HIV-positive Haitian refugees. Cates found the couple waiting to go onstage, and quietly urged them to stick to their script rather than mentioning any political causes.

Sitting in a small, curtained enclosure on the other side of the stage, Letterman was not enjoying himself. "Is it over yet?" he kept asking. To cheer him up, stage managers Dency Nelson and Debbie Williams began to approach every star who came through the wings, asking if they'd like to say hello to Dave. Steve Martin, Jack Nicholson, and almost everyone else did so; Sally Field declined, explaining that she had to focus on her job introducing the *Forrest Gump* film clip.

Letterman's Oscar Top Ten List turned out to be "Top Ten Signs the Movie You're Watching Will Not Win an Academy Award." The biggest hand was reserved for number six: "It's a beautifully made documentary about two kids in the inner city trying to realize their dream of playing professional basketball." Number one, "Four words: Dom DeLuise is Ghandi!" was not a particular favorite, and didn't even spell *Gandhi* correctly.

Backstage, tensions rose as Elton John's performance of "Can You Feel the Love Tonight" neared. Nobody wanted a reprise of the spinning dog, but not once during rehearsals had the crew been able to set up John's equipment quick enough to prevent that. But just before John was due to perform, the Russian film *Burnt by the Sun* won the Oscar for best foreign film. Its director, Nikita Mikhalkov, came to the stage accompanied by his daughter Nadezhda, one of the stars of the film. His speech was emotional but also long and rambling. Even after it hit the two-minute mark, though, Conti and his orchestra remained silent. For once, Cates and Margolis didn't mind a long speech, because every minute Mikhalkov spoke gave John's crew more time to finish its setup.

By the time Mikhalkov finished, John was ready. Sadie, who'd been led into the wings just in case, returned to her dressing room. In the press tent, meanwhile, Jack Nicholson broke with Oscar protocol: rather than accompanying honorary Oscar winner Michelangelo Antonioni only through the two photo rooms, Nicholson stuck with the eighty-two-year-old Italian director through the two interview rooms as well. There, he artfully deflected questions that dealt with Nicholson rather than Antonioni.

In a small space between the print and television rooms, Antonioni stopped to blow his nose. "God, he looks tremendous," said one onlooker.

Nicholson grinned slyly, and leaned toward the director. "Not as good as *me*," he whispered to Antonioni. "But tremendous."

Leaving the press area, Nicholson congratulated a dazed Elton John, who was carrying the best-song Oscar he'd just won for "Can You Feel the Love Tonight." Nearby, a security supervisor looked at the growing crowd outside the green room. "The exits are not secure, there are too many people here, and I'm not happy," he told his men.

At 8:45, Al Pacino and Robert DeNiro arrived together in a limo and made a beeline for the green room, where DeNiro huddled with Antonioni.

In the wings of the stage, Clint Eastwood waited for his cue. Letterman walked offstage. "Hi, Clint," he said.

"Hi," said Eastwood. "Hey, I know your people have been calling about getting me on the show."

"Yeah, I know we're always bugging you about that," said Letterman. He grimaced; it was bad enough that he was suffering through the Oscar show, but now he had to hear about his staff harassing famous people on his behalf.

"Well, I think it might be fun," Eastwood assured him.

Letterman shrugged. "I don't know if it'd be fun for you," he said, "but it'd sure be a thrill for *us*."

Eastwood chuckled and changed the subject. "How are you feeling?" he asked.

Dave sighed. "I feel like going home," he said.

Eastwood quickly looked over at the host. "*What?*"

"I feel," said Letterman quietly, "like I sort of want to go home."

Within forty minutes, it was mercifully over for Letterman. Tom Hanks presented the best-actress award to Jessica Lange for *Blue Sky*, then won the best-actor award himself for *Forrest Gump*. Robert Zemeckis won the best-director award for that same film, and then *Gump* completed its sweep over *Pulp Fiction* with a best-picture win. (The only category in which *Pulp* won, best original screenplay, was one in which *Gump* was not eligible.)

Onstage, Letterman looked into the audience one last time. "Ladies and gentlemen, congratulations to everyone," he said. "I've had a lovely evening, thank you very much for inviting me. Good night, folks."

As the credits ran to end the three-hour-and-thirty-two-minute show, an anxious Rob Burnett approached Seligman by the production trailers. "What'd you think?" he asked, frowning.

"What'd I think?" repeated Seligman. "I think you guys did great." A pause. "I'm being honest. I think you should be proud."

In his dressing room, Letterman was downcast. Debbie Williams and Dency Nelson stopped by and told him that he'd done a great job, but the host shook his head. "No, I didn't," he said.

"No, Dave, you were great," they insisted.

"Do you know what Gil said to me?" the famously insecure Letterman replied. "He walked by me after the show and said, 'See you sometime, somewhere.' "

At the Governors Ball, which for the first time was being catered by Wolfgang Puck, Arthur Hiller gave a speech. "I think this was the best Oscar show," he said, "since . . . last year." Stars schmoozed, ate, networked, and headed off to other parties around town. Letterman didn't show his face; instead of making an appearance at the ball, he headed for the airport to go on vacation.

By midnight, the party was emptying. On the steps outside the artists' entrance, Morgan Freeman sat with his wife and daughter, waiting for his limo, and waiting for somebody in charge to explain why his driver had been denied entrance to the parking lot.

There were no more than a dozen people standing around when Sadie, The Dog That Spins When You Applaud, was led out the door, down the steps, and along the red carpet. Seeing one of the stars of the Oscar show, the bystanders broke into a round of unthinking applause. And Sadie of course started spinning for all she was worth. The Oscars were history, the final strains of "Stardust" were drifting out from the party that was winding down inside—and out in the parking lot, a crazy dog twirled wildly as she headed down the red carpet and into the night.

JUDGING BY THE NUMBERS, the 67th Academy Awards show was a huge success. Curiosity over Letterman, together with the fact that a couple of big-grossing movies were in contention, helped give the show its best ratings in a dozen years. The audience was mostly male; in New York City, the ratings were huge.

This did not, however, mean that the show was an unqualified hit in other ways. Reviews for the show were mixed, as always, but generally unkind to Letterman. Even on the Internet, comments from the host's usual rabid fans ranged from "Well, that was painful to watch" to "I think his entire performance was an inspired breath of fresh air into an otherwise archaic and stodgy institution." From inside the Academy, though, the outcry was louder and more negative than at any time since the Allan Carr show.

And from the sound of things, Dave might even have agreed with his critics. A week after the Oscar show, Letterman did his first new *Late Night* broadcast. The Top Ten List was "Top Ten Complaints About the Academy Awards"; number one was "Letterman." By the end of the year, Letterman would regularly trail Jay Leno in the ratings. Leno's resurgence was often tied to the publicity he gained in June, when actor Hugh Grant used *The Tonight Show* for his first public appearance since his arrest for soliciting a prostitute in Los Angeles. Some observers, though, thought that Letterman's decline began with the Oscars.

More than a decade later, some show staffers were still baffled. "Letterman loved Carson, and Letterman wanted to be as good as Carson was on the show," said Seligman, who worked on all five of Carson's Oscar shows. "The difference is that Carson was the host of the Oscars. Letterman didn't do the Oscars, he did the Letterman show."

Added Chuck Workman, whose opening collaboration with Debbie Allen was always awkward and confusing, "The Letterman show was a mess for everybody. My piece didn't work, I was not at my best, and it's the only piece of mine that I regret doing."

The results of the 67th Oscar show also impacted the Academy in ways that had nothing to do with Letterman. Hans Zimmer's win for *The Lion King* in the best original score category was in many ways the final straw for the music branch. The win marked the fourth time in six years that an animated Disney film had won in both the expected category, best song, and also in the best-score category. (Disney didn't release major animated musicals the other two years.) While the wins in the song category could be defended, the branch found it harder to stomach the fact that legendary film composers like John Williams, Ennio Morricone, Jerry Goldsmith, and John Barry, along with hot newcomers like Elliot Goldenthal and Thomas Newman, were being beaten by the music used to link cartoon songs together.

The branch took one of its few available options: it split the award for best original score into two separate awards, one for musical or comedy score, the other for dramatic score. (Technically, the musical or comedy award replaced the Oscar for original song score, a category that hadn't been used in a decade.) The move put the music branch at odds with the rest of the Academy, which never separated categories by genre—but it was, perhaps, a more politic action than the alternative, which would have been to send the members guidelines that read, "Stop voting for animated movies with lots of songs in the original score category."

The Academy also added a new branch, Visual Effects, bringing to thirteen its number of branches.

The chief fallout from the show, though, had to do with the documentary branch of the Academy, and its failure to nominate *Hoop Dreams*. In June, after a three-month review of the documentary screening committee's procedures, the Academy revised its rules for the documentary feature category. The committee was split into two groups, one based in Los Angeles and the other in New York. Rather than a single committee screening sixty-five films, the eligible documentaries would be divided between the two; finalists selected by the L.A. committee would then be screened by the New Yorkers, and vice versa. No longer would a show of flashlights be enough to end a movie prematurely, and no longer would committee members be allowed to hold discussions before voting.

Just as crucially—though its importance was not apparent to those who didn't know that *Hoop Dreams* had lost a nomination largely because of a handful of zero scores—the scoring system was brought in line with other

Oscar categories. In the future, voters would score each documentary on a scale of six to ten, reducing the damage a small group of voters could do to any film. "I don't know," insisted Hiller, "that any of these changes would have made any difference at all in the outcome of nominations voting this year."

For Gil Cates, meanwhile, his sixth Oscar show had not been an easy one. Not only had Letterman proved to be a disappointment, but Cates had started to feel increasing interference from the Academy and the network. In the summer, after Arthur Hiller was reelected to his third term as the president of the Academy, Cates let Hiller know that he would not be available to produce the next Oscars.

A Change Is Gonna Come

The 68th Academy Awards

ON THE CALENDAR of Academy Awards–related events, the Oscar Fashion Show was one of the more useless entries. It was, essentially, a big photo opportunity designed to remind people that the show was coming. Models paraded through the lobby of the Academy's Beverly Hills offices wearing clothes that the show's official fashion coordinator, Beverly Hills clothier Fred Hayman, would like stars to wear on Oscar night. Hayman provided commentary, and a small audience clapped politely. No nominees or presenters showed up to get ideas; that battle was already being waged in private, as top designers courted nominees and presenters with phone calls, letters, freebies, and invitations to hotel suites where the latest, chicest creations were laid out.

At the Oscar Fashion Show, things were ceremonial. The press got to interview the show's producer, down some free coffee and bagels, ogle a few models. And the Academy got a quick, relatively inexpensive blast of publicity to keep itself in the news during the downtime between nominations announcement and the nominees' luncheon.

At least, that's the way it once was. Then came Quincy Jones, executive producer of the Academy Awards show in 1996.

Officially—and to a large extent truthfully—Gil Cates's decision not to return as producer was blamed on his schedule as the producing director of the Geffen Playhouse, a refurbished five-hundred-seat theater near the UCLA campus. With Cates out of the picture, Arthur Hiller opted for the sixty-three-year-old musician and producer Jones, the previous year's recipient of the Jean Hersholt Humanitarian Award. A jazz trumpeter who'd turned to record production and film composing in the 1960s, Jones had made his name, and his fortune, shepherding the likes of Michael Jackson, James Ingram, and Chaka Khan in the recording studio, winning multiple Grammy awards for albums like Jackson's *Thriller* and his own *The Dude*.

In the 1980s, Jones moved into film producing, helping to bring Alice Walker's book *The Color Purple* to the screen with director Steven Spielberg. That movie became one of the biggest losers in Oscar history in March 1986, when it won not a single one of its eleven nominations. (Eight years earlier, *The Turning Point* had attained the same 0-for-11 record.)

No sooner had Jones accepted the gig than he and his business partner of three years, David Salzman, announced that they planned to change *everything* about the Academy Awards. And on March 7, perhaps to persuade those who wondered just how much they could do within given the constraints of an Oscar broadcast, they turned the once-sedate fashion show into a statement of purpose.

For starters, the producers ran up a reported $40,000 tab installing a stage, a full sound system, a checkerboard runway, and a huge lighting rig in the lobby of the Academy building. They brought in choreographer Toni Basil (who, in another incarnation, had the 1980 pop hit "Mickey") to work with the models. They turned on a smoke machine, turned down the lights—and when the lobby was sufficiently dusky, Hayman intoned, "Let the show begin."

It did so not with the usual procession of Oscar-worthy gowns, but with a sultry male model, his black hair slicked back severely and his dark skin gleaming, tap dancing across the stage clad in the kind of outfit that might well get him turned away at the door of the Dorothy Chandler Pavilion: a white silk tuxedo shirt that was not only untucked but also wholly unbuttoned, its shirttails flapping freely around his thighs. When he dropped back into the shadows, a procession of models strode to the runaway and tried their best to look mysterious. They moved quickly, turned suddenly, glanced around the room furtively. They adjusted their shades and fingered their jewelry and conspiratorially struck poses. One strode down the runway leading a pair of Russian wolfhounds.

The music boomed around them: dramatic orchestral passages, hip-hop beats, Booker T and the MGs, flamenco, salsa, forbidding twentieth-century chamber music, Beethoven's Fifth. The outfits were insane. There was a Paco Rabane chain-mail jumpsuit, an Issaye Miyake dress that looked as if it could have been made of Saran wrap, and an iridescent silver shirt with a huge collar that would have looked at home on retro-rocker Lenny Kravitz. One model sported a tuxedo that resembled nothing so much as an electric blue version of the shiny gold lamé suit Elvis Presley wore on the cover of the 1957 album best known as *50,000,000 Elvis Fans Can't Be Wrong*.

In the audience, Bruce Davis looked on impassively. Jeff Margolis beamed. Danette Herman boogied in her seat.

Then Jones and Salzman strutted down the runaway clad in Versace and Donna Karan, respectively. "I bet you thought you were gonna see your usual pre-Oscar fashion show," Quincy said. "The many firsts you saw today were just a little preview of the many firsts you'll see at the show. The evening's story will still be the winners, but just wait until you see what else happens."

Near the rear of the room, longtime Oscar publicity staffer John Pavlik laughed and shook his head. "I'll be curious to see," he said, "if this generates more press than we used to get with a piano and sixty bucks."

IT HAD NOT been a good year for movies—at least, not for major studio movies that might reasonably be expected to compete for Oscars. The year's top-grossing films were *Batman Forever*, the third and definitely not the best of the recent Batman movies, and *Toy Story*, an animated picture made by a relatively young company called Pixar and released by Disney, which to its astonishment watched the entirely computer-animated film make its own large-scale animated effort, *Pocahontas*, look old-fashioned and bland.

A more typical Oscar entry was Mel Gibson's *Braveheart*. Released during the summer, the violent and rousing, if historically suspect, bio of Scottish freedom fighter William Wallace was greeted with respectful but mixed reviews, and only adequate business at the box office. Ron Howard's *Apollo 13*, a look at the ill-fated moon mission that nearly ended in tragedy in 1970, was one of the stronger candidates to come from the major studios, though again it prompted more respect than rapture from critics. And Chinese director Ang Lee, little known in the United States, turned to a quintessentially English story with surprisingly persuasive results when he filmed Jane Austen's *Sense and Sensibility* from a script by actress Emma Thompson.

The year's best-reviewed films, in many cases, came from smaller, independent companies: the harrowing *Leaving Las Vegas*, in which Nicolas Cage drank himself to death while a sympathetic hooker played by Elisabeth Shue watched; actor/director Tim Robbins's *Dead Man Walking*, a grim examination of murder, retribution, and the death penalty, with striking lead performances from Sean Penn and Susan Sarandon; and the Italian film *Il Postino*, the tale of a postman from a small village who's smitten by the power of verse while delivering mail to poet Pablo Neruda. Miramax had picked up this last film for distribution, and the company, always adept at Oscar campaigning, quickly played up the tragic true story behind the film: its star, Massimo Troisi, made the film while seriously ill with a heart condition, and died the day after his final scene.

When the nominations were announced, *Braveheart* and *Apollo 13* were the two leaders, with ten and nine nominations, respectively. *Sense and Sensibility*, *Il Postino*, and *Babe* were the other three best-picture nominees; *Leaving Las Vegas* and *Dead Man Walking* were left out of the top category, but each film scored acting nominations for its two leads, as well as best-director nods for Mike Figgis and Tim Robbins. To fit Figgis and Robbins on the ballot, Ron Howard and Ang Lee were passed over despite the fact that their movies were in the running for best picture.

"IT'S FAST-PACED, peppy, very very different," said Danette Herman. She managed a small smile. "It'll be a lot of fun."

A soft-spoken redhead who always knew more than she let on, Herman had been an Oscar regular for almost two decades. She worked her first show while still attending college in 1968, the year the Oscars were postponed for two days after the assassination of Martin Luther King, Jr. Several years later, Herman began a steady run on the show, booking and dealing with talent during a time when the grand old Hollywood stars gradually yielded to younger faces. "Those were shows that Cary Grant came to," she said, "and Katharine Hepburn and Gregory Peck, Burt Lancaster, Kirk Douglas, Audrey Hepburn. There's always a constant shift going on with the stars, but in the eighties the names were more consistent for a longer period of time. And they weren't asked to do fifty awards shows a year."

Herman still loved classic Hollywood—her favorite Oscar moments centered around names like Greer Garson, Luise Rainer, and Federico Fellini—but she also adored the likes of Liam Neeson, Emma Thompson, and John Travolta. She was known to be fiercely protective of the stars who came on her show: open and kind one moment, she could just as easily slip on a tight frown and assume a kind of tunnel vision, closing out all but the matter that occupied her at the moment. Chuck Warn called it "the Danette face."

As she sat in the production office on a Friday morning just a few days before the production team would move its offices to the Dorothy Chandler Pavilion, it wasn't yet time for the Danette face. Still, with ten days to go until the show, Herman was dealing with the usual myriad of small details and last-minute glitches. The publicist for best-song nominee Bruce Springsteen, for instance, called to ask if Springsteen could once again use Warn as his escort if he won and had to make the trip through the press rooms; Herman had to tell the publicist, Seth Cohen, that Warn worked for Gil Cates. "Chuck's not on the show this year," she told Cohen. "The escorts they have are all publicists from the studios."

No sooner had Herman hung up than she got a call from David Salzman's assistant, Mary Aymar, passing on a message about presenter Nicole Kidman. "She's approved her dialogue," Aymar said, "but she wants us to know that she's blind, so she needs it in really large print."

As she looked from her office window across the garden level of a new (and, except for the Oscar staff, completely unoccupied) office building in

Beverly Hills, Herman had another, bigger worry: the show had yet to be fully booked. "There are still a couple of slots to fill," she said, "which is very unusual for this time of year."

Those decisions were long overdue, but they couldn't be made without Jones, who hadn't yet appeared in the office. As the clock inched closer to 1 p.m., Herman got antsier; she was hoping to meet with Jones and get some answers before one, when she knew he was scheduled to sit for three hours of TV interviews.

As they'd promised, Jones and Salzman had tried to change countless aspects of the Oscar show. Rather than using clips from the nominated performances, they commissioned mini-filmographies incorporating three separate films from each of the acting nominees; when Doug Stewart suggested that they were ordering an enormous amount of work for a feature that might well be cut for time if the show was running long, Salzman insisted, "We're committed to this." But the producers did want to save time, and they hated how long it took for nominees to get to the stage in the craft categories. They floated the idea of moving each category's nominees into the front row when it came time for the category, or running the Oscar and a microphone into the audience so that winners could make speeches without leaving their seats. At one point, they considered putting all the nominees onstage before opening the envelope. "Some of their ideas were just . . . *amazing*," said one Oscar vet carefully.

"Change is good, adjustments are good, but you can't turn the Academy Awards into the MTV Music Awards," said Jeff Margolis. "Some of their ideas were just logistically impossible, and some were good ideas but not for the Academy Awards." Margolis felt that Jones was sensible while Salzman was too determined to change things, so he tried to deal mostly with Q, as everyone called the producer. Others grumbled that Margolis himself was making a power play by separating the two producers.

A few minutes before 1 p.m., Salzman emerged from his office with Alec Berg and Jeff Schaffer, a pair of writers from the *Seinfeld* TV show who'd been hired to punch up the script. "Were they good?" Aymar asked after Salzman showed the writers to the elevator. "I haven't seen that look on your face in a long time."

"Yeah, they were great," he said.

"Just let me ask you a couple of questions," she said.

"Okay, but ask me quick." Then he glanced toward the elevator, and saw that Jones had just arrived. "Wait just a minute," he told Aymar. "While Quincy's not talking, I've got to grab him."

The two men went into Salzman's office, where Herman quickly joined them. She walked over to the bulletin board where the show was laid out, pulled off a small card with the name Hugh Grant on it, and tore it in half. Salzman looked confused. "I thought he was dying to do it," he said.

"He was dying to do it," said Herman. "But he's doing a movie, and they can't change the schedule."

"Who else can we get?" said Salzman.

"Annette Bening?" suggested Herman. "Goldie Hawn? It would be good to get a woman in that slot."

"I prefer Annette Bening," said Salzman. "Now, have we figured out if we're getting Kevin Costner?"

"Quincy, you need to call him today," said Herman. "If we can't get him, I'll go to Jack Lemmon and Walter Matthau. Do we have any word from Dustin Hoffman?"

Jones shook his head. "I don't want to talk about people we don't know if we can get," he said. "I want names up there that we can really get."

Herman sighed. "We should have had this conversation at eight o'clock this morning," she said. "We have five slots open, and we need to fill them *today*."

Salzman looked at the board and frowned. "Is Schwarzenegger willing to introduce the best-picture clip for *Braveheart?*" he said. "Or is he going to insist on presenting an award?"

"We don't know yet," said Herman.

"If he has to give an award, we can give him editing and move Anthony Hopkins to screenplay."

"I'm trying to find out," Herman said, "but I haven't gotten an answer yet from his publicist."

"Forget that," said Jones. "I'll call Maria. Forget about all this other crap. If she likes the idea she'll *make* him do it."

"What about Steven Seagal?" asked Salzman. "He doesn't really want to give out sound. He's thinking about it, but he'd rather do best foreign film."

"Pretend he never existed," Jones snapped. "He was begging for a slot on the show, and then we give him one and he has to *think* about it?"

AS OSCAR NIGHT APPROACHED, the consensus in Hollywood was that the best-picture race was wide open and unpredictable. While even Harvey Weinstein had to realize that *Il Postino* probably fell into the it's-an-honor-just-to-be-nominated category, that didn't stop him from pulling out the stops: Miramax's mailing to Academy members included the video, a CD of celebrities reading the poems of Pablo Neruda, and the original novel by Antonio Skármeta. The Academy found the package unseemly, and took away two of Miramax's tickets to the show.

Meanwhile, cases could be made for any of the other four best-picture nominees. *Sense and Sensibility* was classy and high-toned and had won the Golden Globe for best drama, but Ang Lee's failure to be nominated for best director suggested that his film wasn't embraced by the entire Academy. *Apollo 13* was the kind of serious, inspirational mainstream movie often honored by the Academy, and the fact that director Ron Howard had also been overlooked was partly offset when the Directors Guild, usually a reliable indicator of Academy support, gave him its top award. *Braveheart* hadn't picked up any big critics or guild awards—but with actors making up by far the biggest branch of the Academy, it was foolish to underestimate the appeal of a big, rousing epic directed by an actor. (Kevin Costner's *Dances with Wolves*, after all, had beaten Martin Scorsese's *GoodFellas*, and a decade earlier Robert Redford's *Ordinary People* had beaten Scorsese's *Raging Bull*.)

Still, there was no question which of the nominated films garnered the most affection. As a sweet, funny fable about a talking pig, *Babe* may not have been typical Oscar fare, but its charm and ingenuity had won it a legion of admirers. As the show approached, sentiment began to shift. *Apollo 13* may have been a narrow favorite in the minds of most Oscar forecasters, with *Braveheart* in the running as well—but the momentum, it seemed, was with the little pig.

Jones and Salzman took note of the affection surrounding *Babe*, and decided to incorporate its star into their show. (It didn't hurt that the movie was also a particular favorite of their host, Whoopi Goldberg.) But Babe and the Oscars were an uneasy fit. Where the animators at Pixar eagerly got to work on a segment in which the *Toy Story* characters Woody and Buzz would interact with an Oscar statue (a *talking* Oscar statue—another first, as Salzman proudly pointed out), the creators of *Babe* were more cautious.

Jones and Salzman had decided to include a mock "satellite link" between Goldberg, on the stage of the Dorothy Chandler Pavilion, and Babe, back home on the farm. But the producers could only obtain an unused three-second clip of the piglet, so their plan was to incorporate another famous swine, Miss Piggy. "We have to somehow disguise the fact that we only have three seconds of Babe," said Daniel Salzman, who'd been hired by his father to oversee several segments of the show. "We're doing lots of cuts to Whoopi and to Miss Piggy, and we'll pretend that the satellite is going out." Frank Oz, who operated and supplied the voice for Miss Piggy, would be on hand to help the porcine diva do her bit live, while the voice of Babe, Christine Cavanaugh, would record new voiceovers.

But George Miller, a physician-turned-filmmaker who had directed *The Witches of Eastwick* and the three *Mad Max* movies before producing *Babe*, was fiercely protective of both the movie and the character. He agreed to participate and he supplied the three-second clip, but didn't like the initial script, in which his farm-bred hero evinced too much familiarity with things like box-office returns and Oscar acceptance speeches. "He wants something that preserves Babe's innocence and naïveté," said Daniel Salzman.

David Salzman sighed. "And our script doesn't? 'I'd like to thank all the little people, all of whom are bigger than me'?"

"His point," said Daniel, "is that Babe wouldn't know about acceptance speech clichés."

At 3 p.m., David Salzman picked up the phone and prepared to call Miller, who was working on a film in South Africa. "Okay," he said, "let's do the root canal." As he dialed, he shrugged. "George is a delightful guy and a great artist. He's just trying to protect his project." Daniel Salzman walked around the desk and took a position over his father's left shoulder, ready to listen in and offer suggestions.

"George, I hear that you have some questions and concerns, and I don't want you to have any," Salzman said when he reached Miller. "We just want to do a sweet piece."

Miller told Salzman that he didn't think the script was true to the essential innocence of his little pig, who wouldn't know anything about satellite hookups or the Academy Awards.

"I totally understand what you're saying, George," Salzman said. "This is still an innocent little piglet who's unaffected by all of this. We'll make changes to reflect that." He listened to Miller some more. "Yes, Miss Piggy does have a lot of lines," he said. "You're right about that." He paused. "Yeah, we'll probably cut out a joke or two of hers to tighten it up."

Daniel Salzman grinned. "He's coming around," he whispered.

Miller then suggested a new ending to the piece, one that replaced Babe's "acceptance speech" with a nod to actor James Cromwell, who played the kindly farmer who watches over (and profits from) the little pig.

"That's good, George," said Salzman. "That's good. That's a nice three-beat." Salzman hung up the phone and let out a relieved sigh. He read Miller's new lines to his son: "Babe will say, 'Give my regards to the boss,' and Whoopi will say, 'Oh, you're a Springsteen fan?' And he'll say, 'Farmer Hoggett, silly!' This is a great ending that he wrote for us."

At 3:30, Herman marched into Salzman's office, a determined look on her face. "Quincy's out of his interviews now," she said. "We have *got* to converse. The sun is going down, and we have to know who we're asking to do sound, who's doing screenplay . . ."

HOLLYWOOD BLACKOUT, read the headline on the March 18 issue of *People* magazine. The issue detailed what the magazine said was "a shocking level of minority exclusion" in the movie business. The article did not charge that the Academy Awards were in any way responsible for that exclusion, simply that the lack of African American nominees—only one, it said, out of 166— was a timely symptom of the problem.

Seizing on the magazine story, Jesse Jackson decided to use the scarcity of black Oscar nominees as the focal point of an organized protest by his Rainbow Coalition. Jones, who agreed with many of the points in the *People* article—though he thought the magazine was "thirty-five years too late"— tried to convince Jackson that it might be misguided to protest an Oscar ceremony produced by and hosted by African Americans, and one with a distinctly multiracial lineup of presenters and performers. In an attempt to avoid a swarm of protesters in front of the Chandler, Arthur Hiller contacted Jackson to work out a compromise.

While the Academy president worked that front, Quincy Jones walked into the Dorothy Chandler Pavilion. "The set is screamin'," he said, looking at the stage. "Screamin'."

The Chandler stage was dominated by massive white columns, by sail-shaped pieces hanging over the stage, and by video monitors in gold gilt frames. As production designer Ray Klausen directed placement of the columns and video screens, Jones stood in the aisle watching. "It's got so many looks," said Jones as he gazed at the stage. "The graphics are constantly changing, the Oscars are constantly moving, the screens come down with the names of the categories and the nominees on them . . ."

Backstage, reviews were less generous. Many of the same crew members worked on the show year after year, as well as on other awards shows; they were practical people who knew their jobs, did them well, and were neither starstruck nor dazzled by glitz. Some of them had to move the talent in and out quickly and efficiently; others had to make sure the set changes worked. They knew how to ignore the occasional odd sight backstage: Audrey Hepburn in her slip, ironing her own gown just before going onstage; an unconcerned but stark naked Sigourney Weaver undergoing a last-minute fitting in a dressing room just off the stage. And they knew that no matter how screamin' a set might be, its pieces needed to move in and out quickly and quietly.

On this last count, things were not gelling. "The set is overdesigned," said one. "It's too big, it's got too many moving parts, and it doesn't work. It's a nightmare."

For Jeff Margolis, the biggest problem was that when the set was in place, it left little room for presenters to make their entrances. "Ray Klausen is a brilliant production designer," he said. "But when we got to the theater, it wasn't the same as it was on paper. Whatever the hell happened, there were no entrances. Everybody just had to come around a corner, and that made me nuts."

The crew tried to make it work, a task that involved ditching parts of the set and rearranging others. As they did so, other technical tests continued.

Thursday morning, a stagehand read into Goldberg's microphone in order for the sound crew to set levels and balance the sound. Given the previous year's rocky Oscar show, his choice of reading material was nervy: a book of David Letterman's Top Ten Lists. "Top Ten ways the Dalai Lama is going to spend his Nobel Prize money," the stagehand read. The list included "New kitchen cabinets for Mrs. Lama," "Give Cadillacs to Sonny and Red," and "One seriously large order of McDonald's french fries," but the stagehand didn't get far enough into it to draw a laugh. No sooner had he read "one seriously large—" than stage manager David Wader walked to the podium and interrupted him.

"ABC/Cap Cities says you cannot read that," Wader announced. "You have to read this." He handed over a considerably drier text: "Health and Safety Standards for the Academy Awards."

BY THE MORNING OF SATURDAY, March 23, things were well behind schedule. Of the sixteen awards that were slated to have been rehearsed using stand-ins between 8:30 and 10:00, only six were completed; the others fell victim to unusually long set changes. At 10:15, with a long day of music rehearsals looming and no time to catch up, many of the stand-ins were sent home. "Am I going to see you tomorrow?" asked one stand-in to a friend who was packing up and heading for his car.

"I don't know," came the reply. "They haven't told me yet. I don't think they have any idea."

That afternoon, the stage was awash in dancers, some of them dressed in full flamenco gear, others a mixture of crop tops, spandex, and spike heels. Behind them was an elaborate set that reproduced a Spanish courtyard. In their midst was room for a rock band and for the thirty-six-year-old Canadian rock star Bryan Adams, the singer and one of the writers of "Have You Ever Really Loved a Woman." The film from which his song came, *Don Juan DeMarco*, was only modestly successful, but the lavish, romantic ballad was the biggest hit of the nominated songs, a number-one record for five weeks.

The Canadian singer had made his name as a derivative, commercial,

Springsteen-lite rock 'n' roller, but many of his biggest hits in recent years had been lush love songs drawn from movie soundtracks. His last real rock hit had come in 1987; since then, he'd scored with the hugely successful ballads "(Everything I Do) I Do It for You" from *Robin Hood: Prince of Thieves* and "All for Love" from *The Three Musketeers*. Adams always denied that he was bothered by the dichotomy between his hard-rocking roots and his treacly pop hits, but those close to the singer would occasionally admit that it rankled him.

The scene on the stage of the Chandler—the lavish courtyard setting, the dancers, and several new musicians in addition to Adams's usual band—was one that might also be expected to annoy Adams, who sometimes wore his tough-guy exterior as a badge of honor. But Adams wasn't there to complain: he'd skipped this rehearsal, and his stand-in was undoubtedly more patient than he would have been. "We hear that he's not thrilled with the idea of dancers," said Daniel Salzman as he watched. "But he didn't make it to rehearsal, so too bad."

Outside the theater, a rock star who did make it to rehearsal sat in his trailer waiting his turn. When he got the nomination for writing the title song to *Dead Man Walking*, Bruce Springsteen was just about to begin a solo acoustic tour of Europe—but he rescheduled dates at the Royal Albert Hall in London in order to come to the Oscars. "I just felt like if my song was going to be on the show, I should be the one singing it," he said.

When Springsteen took the stage to rehearse, Daniel Salzman, fresh from cadging an introduction to the Boss from his dad, plopped down between the seat cards for Mel Gibson and Tim Robbins. "I've never had front-row seats for a Bruce concert before," he said.

Springsteen ran through the song twice, while Margolis directed the cameramen to focus tightly on his face. Between takes, Springsteen's manager, Jon Landau, talked on the phone to the director. Though the song ended with a close-up far closer than you usually see on television, Landau wanted it even closer. The lighting was darker than usual for TV, but Landau wanted it darker still. As he'd done two years earlier when Springsteen had performed "Streets of Philadelphia," Landau pushed the crew to forget their usual ways of doing things.

"These are the best people at what they do," explained Landau afterward. "Jeff is the best television director anywhere. What we're trying to do is take the television out of him."

ALL DAY LONG, the mantra continued: *change, change, change* . . . "They told me," said one puzzled member of Springsteen's crew, "that the whole idea was to change every single thing about the show: the way nominees are announced, the way they give out awards in the smaller categories . . . I said, 'Well, Quincy, the statue looks the same.' And he said, 'We're *tryin'*, baby.' "

The biggest change was on display after dinner, when the parade of singers was interrupted by an invasion of six-foot, hundred-pound women with perfect cheekbones, and sculpted hunks with washboard abs and immaculate stubble. In an outgrowth of the Oscar Fashion Show, the producers had decided to showcase the clothing nominated for best costume design not with the traditional sketches or film clips, but with a mock fashion show. Supermodels would strut down a runway erected on the Oscar stage; they'd be surrounded by dancers portraying both photographers and rabid fans, and accompanied by loud music and a barrage of flashbulbs and strobe lights. Photographer Matthew Rolston directed the show, which was to be introduced by actor Pierce Brosnan, flanked by übermodels Claudia Schiffer and Naomi Campbell.

The original plan, though, had been to use a different star. "It was going to be Jack Nicholson with Claudia Schiffer on one arm and Naomi Campbell on the other," ABC's John Hamlin told a colleague in the audience. But Nicholson declined, so the current James Bond was deemed stylish enough for the gig. "Pierce Brosnan *looks* terrific," Hamlin said, "but you need somebody who really has a twinkle."

Loud, glitzy, and more than a little silly, the segment was slated to be the first award of the evening. And if that didn't make a clear enough statement, the copy written for Brosnan and crew spelled it out even further. Within the space of three sentences, it used the phrases "in a totally new way," "as you've never seen them before," and "trust me, as never before."

The rehearsal progressed in an old-fashioned way: slowly and with great difficulty. The models, who included Tyra Banks, Marcus Schenkenberg, Veronica Webb, and Tyson Beckford, didn't have a true runway on which to work; they were restricted to striking quick, pouty poses on a small ramp, most of them inexplicably sucking on lollipops as they did so.

For one take, the voiceover announcer, Les Marshak, was out of sync with the models when he introduced them as they took the stage. Before the next take, a female voice from behind the curtain yelled, "Say my name sexier, please." Stationed in a truck outside the Chandler, Marshak couldn't hear her.

Progress was painstaking, and changes were frequently made to tighten up the awkward segment. After a few run-throughs, Margolis announced, "We're taking a five-minute break here. Five minutes." Backstage, Schiffer went into Jones's and Salzman's office, followed a few minutes later by Campbell. Bruce Vilanch quickly grabbed his copy of the script and joined them, as did writer Stephen Pouliot. The office door closed; a minute later it opened, and David Salzman thrust a couple of script pages at production coordinator Benn Fleishman. "I need five copies, *quickly*," he said.

Danette Herman turned the corner, walking fast. "I need two bottles of water," she said. "How hard can that be?"

As the atmosphere grew tenser, supermodel Tyra Banks walked up the stairs, approached Jones's office door, and looked around. "Somebody said they had an extra burger," she said.

"An extra burger? I don't think they've arrived yet," a staffer told her.

Banks wasn't backing down. "They said there was an extra burger in Quincy's office," she insisted.

"Why don't you let us look into it?"

"Okay," she said. "I'll be sitting out there."

The door to Jones's office opened, and Vilanch walked out. "Welcome," he said, "to *Prêt-à-Porter*."

AT NOON ON SUNDAY, Jones and Salzman gave a press conference outside the Chandler. At least three-quarters of the questions dealt with Jesse Jackson, who had announced that he planned to lead a picket line during the Oscar show. (Out of respect for Jones, the protest would take place not at the Music Center, but at the ABC Prospect lot.) After a few minutes of facing questions about Jackson, Salzman got testy. "Too bad you didn't ask about the exciting races or the new things we're doing this year," he said. "We'd have a lot to say about it, but since you didn't ask, bye."

All afternoon, stars ran through their lines in front of an audience of friends, family, and a few Academy guests. When Sidney Poitier rehearsed his category, best picture, the winner (FOR THIS REHEARSAL ONLY, of course) was *Sense and Sensibility*. Immediately, ABC publicist Dan Doran phoned his sister Lindsay, the film's producer. "Just wanted to let you know that at rehearsal, you won," he told her. Writer Anthony Lane, who was allowed to observe part of the rehearsal for a story in *The New Yorker*, overheard Doran and decided that he was making a consolation call. Because a winner at rehearsal "bears no relation to the name of the eventual victor," he later wrote in an inexplicable leap of logic, the opening of a dummy envelope "therefore cuts one horse out of the field."

In fact, the rehearsal winners were chosen mostly at random. Price Waterhouse made five complete sets of rehearsal envelopes, including every possible winner in each category. Unless the crew needed to test a certain camera move, pure chance determined which films won. The envelopes opened were not, as Lane apparently assumed, the leftovers in a pile from which Price Waterhouse had already removed the true winners.

The atmosphere in and around the green room, where stars could socialize, snack, and watch monitors, was relaxed—though Sharon Stone spent a lot of time complaining about the press, and in particular about a recent *New Yorker* story that painted her as demanding and difficult. "It's always taken out of context, it's always distorted," she said. "I'd say that story was sixty percent fabricated. And the Mark Rydell quotes, he says he didn't say anything like that." She went on a while longer, then shook her head. "The thing to do," she announced, "is *never* do interviews. You just can't do them."

Stone spotted Angela Bassett and gave her a big hug. "How are you?" said Bassett. "Well, you know what it's like," sighed Stone. "I don't know how many dresses I've tried on this week, and they all suck."

In another corner of the room, Steven Seagal cornered Michael Seligman. "I feel like the TelePrompTer guy got a little bit lost when I ad-libbed," Seagal said. "So maybe if I tell him what I'm going to say, he can be ready for it. How would I do that?"

In one corner of the green room, five Oscar posters were laid across a table. Each star was asked to sign all five. The first four were earmarked for Jones, Salzman, Hiller, and Margolis; the fifth, explained a woman at the table, was for Christopher Reeve, who had yet to appear in public following a fall from a horse that had left him paralyzed ten months earlier. Most of the stars quickly autographed the first four, then stopped to write messages on Reeve's.

If the mood was largely good-natured around the green room, it was much tenser down the hall, outside the producers' offices. Jones's door remained shut, guarded by a longtime aide who kept his hand on the doorknob at all times. Occasionally Jones and Salzman emerged, always unsmiling, and hurried away. "They're getting harried," said Arnold Robinson, one of Jones's publicists. "They just want to get the show done."

Getting the show done, though, was proving to be complicated. The set was still causing problems, to the point where some crew members had begun suggesting alternative entrances to Margolis when the planned moves were impossible to implement. At one point, stagehands trying to move the enormous Spanish courtyard set out of the way inadvertently pushed it off the loading dock, where it crashed to the ground. Midafternoon on Sunday, Richard Dreyfuss was standing in the wings with stage manager Debbie Williams when they heard a crash from across the stage.

"What was that?" asked Dreyfuss.

"I don't know," said Williams. "But did you ever see *Naked Gun 33 1/3*?"

"Yeah," said the actor, who was familiar with the comedy that climaxed with an Academy Awards ceremony degenerating into complete chaos.

"Well," she said, "if ever that was going to happen, this would be the year."

DRESS REHEARSAL began at 7:35 with the usual red carpet montage. It was followed by a sequence reminiscent of the recent Michael Jackson video

"Black or White," in which the faces of different movie stars morphed into each other. Backstage, Goldberg tried to watch on a monitor as she waited for her cue—but she had trouble seeing because Claudia Schiffer and Naomi Campbell had planted themselves in front of her monitor and were chatting away, oblivious. "Excuse me," the host said. "*Excuuuuse* me." Finally, they turned, and Goldberg pointed at the TV screen. "My monitor," she pointed out. "Could you move?"

As usual, the rehearsal had its rough spots. Singer Gloria Estefan's voice faltered as she navigated a small stairway, always the bane of female singers in long gowns. Randy Newman's piano was never in sync with the orchestra. An hour into the rehearsal, during what was supposed to be a short commercial break following "You've Got a Friend in Me," the show simply stopped dead. Newman and singer Lyle Lovett remained onstage, crew members made small adjustments, and musical director Tom Scott was hastily summoned over the P.A. system.

Some ninety minutes into the rehearsal, the percussive dance troupe Stomp, which specialized in pounding on any and all available surfaces, delivered a rousing performance. Their moves were synced to film clips, which tenuously tied the routine to the world of movie sound effects. Then things came to a halt once more. Jones ambled onstage and talked to Stomp leader Luke Creswell; Quincy's personal photographer followed and took pictures as they conversed.

By 10:30, three hours in, the show was only about half over and the crowd was thinning out. The "satellite link" between Goldberg, Miss Piggy, and Babe was rough and awkward, and Babe's participation was so minimal that it was hard to figure out the point of the whole thing. Afterward, Goldberg frowned. "I love that pig," she said, "but my whole career's riding on this."

After the latest in a long line of "five-minute" breaks that ended up lasting ten or fifteen, Bryan Adams was introduced. He wasn't ready. Either unaware of or unconcerned with the niceties of dress rehearsal, he continued tuning his guitar when he should have been singing. Then he stepped to the microphone and said, "Could I have a little less vibrato on my voice, Mikey? Are you with me, Mikey?"

Margolis stopped the run-through and waited for Adams to get ready. Then he started again. "Here we go," he said. "Five, four . . ."

"What?" Behind the curtain, Adams was confused. "Aren't they opening the curtain before we start singing?"

A stagehand quickly filled Adams in on what he missed during the previous day's rehearsal: he would begin the song behind the curtain, while dancers cavorted in front of it; then the curtain would part to reveal the band and the Spanish courtyard tableau.

Adams finally got it straight and performed the song—but when it was over, he remained in place. "Where's that stage manager?" he said. "Can we do that again?"

After a minute's hesitation, Jeff Margolis stopped the rehearsal and gave Adams more time. "Well," said a disgusted Vilanch at the production table, "Mr. Adams decided to rehearse." Nearby, Salzman got a neck massage.

At 11:35, Adams was finally done. The show lurched onward with its most mysterious segment, a tribute to the way Hollywood covers social and political issues. It was introduced by someone referred to in the script and in all production materials simply as "special presenter." A stand-in walked onstage to the theme music from *Superman*, and delivered lines that sounded preachy, simplistic, and like a defensive reaction to Jesse Jackson: "Hollywood needs to do more . . . Let's work together . . . There is no challenge that we can't meet."

By 11:55, the rehearsal had been going on for nearly four and a half hours, but two of the show's twelve segments remained unrehearsed. Best actor, best actress, and best picture all had yet to be presented. Rather than incur union penalties, Jones and Salzman called it a night. "That is a wrap," announced Margolis. "We'll see you here tomorrow at 8 a.m."

Staffers started to gather up their belongings. "That was a very good first run-though," added Margolis. Not a person in the building believed him.

AT 10 A.M., Margolis stood onstage, waiting to begin a rehearsal with Robin Williams. A stagehand greeted the director. "You probably got about three hours sleep, huh?"

Margolis looked at him incredulously. "*Three hours?*" he said. "I *wish* I got three hours."

In a backstage hallway, Michael Seligman said he had been at the Chandler until 2:30 a.m. "We had a very rough run-through last night," he admitted. "Very rough. It was the first time in nine years we didn't finish the show. Bryan Adams screwed us up, and we had some real rough spots. But I think we'll be okay."

Nearby, David Salzman tried to remain optimistic as well. "It ran long, so we just tried to shorten a couple of segments," he said. "It wasn't that bad."

Outside the executive suite, though, it was impossible to miss the chorus of grumbles. A stage manager: "This was not a good way to do things this year. This was a terrible way to do it."

One stand-in: "This is ridiculous."

Another: "The whole thing's out of control."

A manager: "The sense I get is that the whole thing is sort of rudderless. They're trying too hard to be different, and doing it on the most superficial level. And every time you talk to Quincy, it's just 'me me me.' All he wants to do is tell you how he's changed everything about the show."

At noon, there was one last rehearsal. This one was smoother than the previous night, though few staffers remained in the audience to watch, and the energy level was low; people were exhausted, or maybe defeated.

Salzman watched from the production table, while Jones stood backstage for most of the rehearsal, chatting with friends outside his office. Some segments had been shortened and streamlined; many of the film packages were trimmed as well. And Doug Stewart, it turned out, had been right to be worried about all the work he'd put into researching and assembling the mini-filmographies earmarked for the acting nominees: overnight, those montages were scrapped in favor of the old standby, single clips from the nominated performances.

In the green room, Springsteen's keyboardist, Roy Bittan, watched the show on a monitor. "It looks like every other Academy Awards show," he said. "What's so different about it?" He grinned. "Okay, they got Tom Scott instead of Bill Conti. What a difference."

Just inside the green room door, four baskets were filled with different-colored ribbons. Near the baskets, a sign read "Ribbon du jour" and decoded the palette: pink for breast cancer awareness, red for AIDS, green for the environment, rainbow for Jesse Jackson's Rainbow Coalition. In the lobby of the theater, ushers carried trays of Jackson's ribbons.

Outside the Chandler, helicopters began to circle the block, and streets around the Music Center were shut down. Though they weren't allowed near the red carpet, demonstrators for a variety of causes—but not Jesse Jackson's crew—began to appear on nearby street corners. One veteran security guard took in the increasingly feverish activity and explained what was about to happen to a pair of new recruits. "It'll get closer to six," he said. "The traffic will get worse, and Edy Williams will show up."

6:00 P.M., PACIFIC DAYLIGHT TIME: *"From Los Angeles, it's the 68th annual Academy Awards."*

The show kicked off with the usual arrivals montage, though this year there was a difference: Oprah Winfrey had been working the red carpet, so the shots of arriving stars were punctuated by a handful of quick, stilted interviews.

Oprah: "To die for, that's what you look like tonight!"

Nicole Kidman: "So do you!"

Oprah: "You're presenting tonight?"

Nicole: "Yes."

Oprah: "Oh, my goodness!"

When the cameras moved inside the Chandler, Goldberg was introduced by the morphing sequence: Elizabeth Taylor morphed into Michelle Pfeiffer, who morphed into Natalie Wood, then Meryl Streep, then Faye Dunaway, then Jerry Lewis. Once again, Claudia Schiffer and Naomi Campbell stood squarely in front of Goldberg's monitor, blind to the host's needs. The supermodels were finally shooed away in time for Goldberg to see the sequence's biggest laugh, which came when a chimpanzee from *Planet of the Apes* morphed into Arnold Schwarzenegger. At the end, Judy Garland's Dorothy morphed into an Oscar statue, which dissolved into Goldberg. "So," she said, after she walked on. "Did you miss me?"

Immediately, the host turned political. "I want to say something to all the folks who brought me ribbons to wear," she said. "You don't tell a black woman to buy an expensive dress and then cover it with ribbons. You don't. I'm sorry. But I got them all, so here it goes. I got a red ribbon for AIDS awareness. Done. I got a purple ribbon for breast cancer. Done. I got a yellow ribbon for the troops in Bosnia. Done. I got a green ribbon to free the Chinese dissidents. Done. I got a milky white ribbon for mad cow disease. Done. I got a rainbow ribbon for gay rights disease. Done, done, done again. I got a fake-fur ribbon for animal rights. Done. I got a wet white ribbon to end Whitewater. Done. A seersucker ribbon to let Martin Landau finish his speech from last year. Done. A plaid ribbon that Mel Gibson wore instead of pants in *Braveheart*. Done. And a blue ribbon that somebody swiped off of Babe. Done. Enough with the ribbons."

In the green room, Alicia Silverstone watched a monitor and nervously adjusted her pale blue boa. Kelly Preston and John Travolta stood nearby. Sandra Bullock, one of the few stars to arrive via the loading dock rather than the red carpet, walked in accompanied by a stern security guard. Kurt Russell and Goldie Hawn hovered near the doorway. Except for Preston, who was accompanying her husband, Travolta, all were due onstage during the first half of the show; in most cases, stars were escorted backstage two commercial breaks before their appearance, and waited in the green room for the summons.

Oscar staffers grew to know the look of terror in many stars' eyes when it was time—and they also grew adept at dispensing last-minute pep talks and reassurances. One of the most frequent questions from females on their way to the stage, laughed vets of the process, was "Are my nipples even?"

Awaiting their cues, the stars gathered around a skimpy buffet table and eyed several TV monitors scattered throughout the small room. "Oscar is sixty-eight—younger than Bob Dole," Goldberg said on the screen. "And I'm glad that it looks like Bob's gonna get that nomination, honey, 'cause it means he'll be too damn busy to go to the movies."

Kurt Russell, a die-hard Republican, shook his head at this jibe at the GOP candidate known for his Hollywood-bashing. "I wish somebody had the balls to make a joke about this idiot of a president we have," he said.

But Goldberg had already changed the subject to *Showgirls*, the disastrous Paul Verhoeven potboiler about cutthroat Vegas strippers. "I haven't seen that many poles mistreated since World War II," she snapped. When the host came into the wings after her monologue, said Dency Nelson, "she was almost floating, she was in such a Zen state."

Less than fifteen minutes into the show, the supermodels strutted down their miniature runway to the beat of tepid but pounding techno music. Watching a pouting Trya Banks show off a gown and tiara from *Sense and Sensibility*, Emma Thompson laughed, then shattered the silence of the green room. "That's my crown!" she shouted at the screen. "Get it *off*, Tyra!"

The glitzy number was met with polite applause, and a few minutes later Goldberg returned to the microphone. "Why do supermodels have that look on their face all the time?" she wondered. "They're getting ten grand an hour, they still look pissed off." The joke quickly took away some of the bad taste left by the fashion show, which was all but forgotten a minute later when Kevin Spacey won the best supporting actor award for *The Usual Suspects*, and followed his extremely popular win with a graceful and emotional speech.

Forty minutes into the show, Robin Williams presented an honorary award to Chuck Jones, one of the pioneers from the glory days of Warner Bros.' Looney Tunes cartoons. "I have a jones for the work of Chuck Jones!" Williams said. "He worked on Bugs, Daffy . . . He has raised speech impediments to an art form!"

On a backstage monitor, Steven Seagal watched Williams. "He's *animated* tonight," he said, grinning from ear to ear. Then he looked over to make sure his publicist, Paul Bloch, got the joke.

Seagal was the only star hanging out with his publicist backstage, and he was only doing so because of a loophole. Personal publicists, once ubiquitous backstage, had been barred from the premises by order of the Academy's Public Relations Coordinating Committee. But Jones himself was represented by the Rogers and Cowan publicity firm; his publicist, Arnold Robinson, was always on hand, as was Robinson's boss, Bloch—who also happened to be Seagal's publicist. When Seagal showed up, Bloch stuck close by.

On the green room monitors, Robin Williams was still on a roll. "Now if Chuck could only animate Bob Dole," he said, "we could have an interesting campaign."

Seagal looked back at Bloch. "Who's Chuck Jones?" he said.

When Randy Newman and Lyle Lovett performed their *Toy Story* song, "You've Got a Friend in Me," Martin Landau unself-consciously clapped along in the green room. At the same time, Sandra Bullock and a friend headed for the door. "We're going to the girls' room," they told her security guard. For once, he didn't follow.

Close to the ninety-minute mark, the second award for a supporting performance turned out to be even more emotional than the first. In something of an upset over the likes of *Nixon*'s Joan Allen, *Sense and Sensibility*'s Kate Winslet, and *Apollo 13*'s Kathleen Quinlan, Mira Sorvino won the best supporting actress award for portraying a squeaky-voiced hooker in Woody Allen's *Mighty Aphrodite*. A stunned Sorvino, who had been the subject of such an aggressive Miramax campaign that some of her supporters had worried about a backlash, gave particular thanks to her father, actor Paul Sorvino. Margolis's cameras caught him sobbing in his front-row seat. "I *love* this show!" the director shouted as he went to commercial.

Backstage, honorary Oscar recipient Kirk Douglas, suffering from the effects of a recent stroke, arrived at the artists' entrance and was immediately ushered into Jones's and Salzman's office. A few minutes later he was joined by Steven Spielberg, who'd never worked with Douglas but had agreed to present the award after Douglas specifically asked for him. (Jones had figured that Michael Douglas should do the honors, but the elder Douglas wanted to keep it out of the family.)

In the green room, Winona Ryder fretted over her upcoming trip across the stage to introduce Springsteen. "My hands are freezing, and I'm still shaking from that walk down the red carpet," she told Goldie Hawn. "I'd never done that walk before."

"You know how to handle the red carpet?" asked Hawn. "Just turn your head and smile, but don't stop. *Never* stop."

Sitting on a cream-colored couch across the room, Angelica Huston overheard Ryder and got up. "You look *so* fabulous," Huston said, nodding at Ryder's beaded, low-cut Badgley Mischka gown and old-fashioned, marcelled hairstyle. "You have nothing to be nervous about."

Springsteen and his wife, Patti Scialfa, approached Ryder. "Hey, thanks for doing my intro," said Springsteen.

"Oh, no, it's my pleasure," said Ryder. "I love that song *so* much."

Springsteen looked around the room and spotted a friend nearby. He'd taken a couple of steps in that direction when the show went to a commercial. "Next," announced Marshak, "Jim Carrey, Winona Ryder, Richard Dreyfuss, Goldie Hawn, Kurt Russell, and Bruce Springsteen."

Springsteen stopped. "Oops," he said. "That's me. I better get ready." He made a U-turn and left the room.

Near the two-hour mark, *One Survivor Remembers*, the story of a Holocaust survivor, won the Oscar for documentary short. Director Kary Antholis came to the stage accompanied by Gerda Weissmann Klein, the subject of his film. Antholis gave a fifty-five-second speech, ten seconds over the limit. When he stepped back from the microphone, Margolis gave Tom Scott the music cue, and the orchestra began to play. But Klein had stepped to the microphone, and she refused to be played offstage or escorted into the wings by trophy lady Traci McGlover. "After what this woman had been through in her life," Margolis said, "I couldn't do it to her." The director told Scott to stop the music.

"I [was] in a place for six incredible years, where winning meant a crust of bread and to live another day," said Klein. She spoke to the hushed crowd for a minute and a half. "Thank you for honoring this memory," she said before walking off.

In the producer's office, Steven Spielberg and Kirk Douglas watched the show with Jones. Jones and Salzman were beginning to feel relief: on the technical side things were running smoothly, and several of the speeches had been genuinely emotional and moving. After the young dancer Savion Glover performed an affecting tribute to the recently deceased Gene Kelly, Douglas clapped. "That was great," he said.

A few minutes later, Douglas was escorted into the wings of the stage to await his cue. "Whether . . . on-screen, or dealing with the all-too-real effects of a recent stroke, courage remains Kirk Douglas's personal and professional hallmark," Spielberg said by way of introduction.

As highlights of Douglas's career played on the large screen, Douglas turned to Debbie Williams. "I hope the words come out of my mouth," he said to her. Then he walked onstage and gave a short speech, struggling to enunciate clearly. "I see my four boys," he said, looking into the audience.

"They are proud of the old man. And I am proud, too." The crowd was tremendously moved, not so much by his simple words, but by his dignity in appearing onstage in his frail condition.

Afterward, Douglas was spared the usual press gauntlet. Where most winners were taken upstairs to the four different press rooms, Douglas was led to a makeshift backdrop erected outside Jones's office. There, an Academy photographer took pictures of Douglas and Spielberg. Then Douglas was escorted to a waiting elevator that went down to the exit, not up to the press rooms. Backstage, Michael Douglas approached Jones and Salzman. "Thank you," he said. "My dad has never been treated with this much respect and honor." He also sought out Mike Shapiro, who'd put together the film clips honoring Douglas.

After accepting Douglas's thanks, Jones had another job to do as Sharon Stone's copresenter in the two film-score categories. When he walked onstage, Jones carried with him the envelope for the musical or comedy score category; while a short film showed the nominees, Price Waterhouse managing partner Frank Johnson came out of the wings and handed a second envelope, for the best dramatic score category, to Stone. Normally, the second envelope would have been carried to the stage by the trophy lady when she brought out statuettes for the first set of winners, but this time the accounting firm had argued for a different method.

Predictably, the award for musical or comedy score went to Alan Mencken and Stephen Schwartz, who wrote the music for the animated Disney film *Pocahontas*. The custom was to give the envelope to the winner along with the Oscar statuette—but as Mencken and Schwartz walked to the stage, Jones put it on the podium in front of him. The trophy lady then gave Jones and Stone Oscar statuettes to present to Mencken and Schwartz. Stone handed her Oscar to Schwartz, but she also mistakenly gave him the unopened envelope for the next category.

Mencken thanked a laundry list of colleagues and supporters, and then picked up the opened envelope bearing his and Schwartz's names as he left the podium. Schwartz nodded his thanks, and walked off not only with his Oscar, but also with the envelope for the next category.

Stone and Jones looked at the TelePrompTer and read the nominees for best dramatic score. Then Stone looked around. "Now, I don't have the thing," she said. Jones made a beeline for the wings, looking for one of the Price Waterhouse reps who had all the winners' names memorized; a stage manager realized what had happened and tried to chase down Schwartz, but he was already in the elevator on his way to the press rooms. "I don't have the envelope," repeated Stone, "so I'd like us all to have a psychic moment. Let's just concentrate." She paused. "It's coming to me." A longer pause. "Oh, you can do better than that."

In the wings, Johnson told Jones that *Il Postino* had won. (To make the task manageable, he memorized the names of the winning films, rather than the names of the winners themselves, in all but the acting categories.) Jones walked back onstage, and whispered the name to Stone. "Oh, my God," she said. "It's *Il Postino*."

In the green room a few minutes later, Stone was still baffled. "When I went to present the award, there was nothing there," she said. "No envelope, nothing." She looked at the skimpy buffet, then turned to an aide. "Is there anything here that'll help me get through tonight?" she asked. The aide started to leave to look for different food. "I'm okay," insisted Stone. "You don't have to go." The aide left anyway, returning a few minutes later with a plate of melon.

At 8:48 p.m., the "special presenter" made his appearance. "Ladies and gentlemen," said Marshak, "Christopher Reeve." The curtain rose to reveal Reeve sitting in his wheelchair center stage. The orchestra remained silent, the *Superman* overture having been vetoed since rehearsal. After a prolonged ovation, the crowd grew still. "What you probably don't know," said Reeve, "is that I left New York last September, and I just arrived here this morning." Margolis cut to several teary-eyed stars; the green room, whose occupants usually only paid partial attention to the monitors, grew very attentive.

In the wings, a nurse was standing by; if Reeve began to have spasms, a real possibility, the plan was for Margolis to immediately cut to the audience while the nurse attended to Reeve. (A few minutes earlier, just before she escorted the actor onstage, Debbie Williams had been told by one of Reeve's companions that if she wanted to touch him, she could do so on the left shoulder. When she told Reeve that his cue would come in thirty seconds, she did just that—only to be stopped cold when he hissed, "Don't do that, I might spasm.")

Reeve was collected and controlled as he introduced a montage of clips from such socially conscious films as *Boyz N the Hood, Philadelphia, In Cold Blood, In the Heat of the Night, The Grapes of Wrath, Silkwood,* and *Schindler's List.* While the film played, Williams stood onstage directly in front of Reeve, purposefully blocking the audience's view so they'd watch the film rather than stare at him.

When the film ended, Reeve spoke again. "Let's continue to take risks," he said. "Let's tackle the issues. In many ways, our film community can do it better than anyone else." Lines that sounded clichéd when read by an able-bodied stand-in were no longer so trite. "There is no challenge, artistic or otherwise, that we can't meet." In the green room, the speech received a rare round of applause, and prompted quite a few tears. Sharon Stone left the room to compose herself. In Jones's office, Spielberg cried.

At the show's three-hour mark, Mencken and Schwartz won the best-song award for "Colors of the Wind" from *Pocahontas.* In the audience, an audible groan, followed by tepid applause, greeted the news that yet another Disney cartoon song had bested the likes of Springsteen and Newman.

But the rest of the show ran smoothly: Mel Gibson was charming and amusing while accepting the best-director award for *Braveheart,* which had begun to steamroll everything else in its path. Susan Sarandon and Nicolas Cage were both popular if predictable winners in the actor and actress categories.

In a hallway backstage, Jones rounded a corner, saw Salzman, and wrapped him in a bear hug. "I'm glad it worked, man," said a friend with audible relief.

Braveheart capped the evening by winning best picture. "Well, we've stomped our way through another Oscar show," said Goldberg. "And if you said three hours and thirty-five minutes, you won the pool."

In his office, Jones dispensed hugs and high fives. "God was with us tonight," he said. The consensus was that it worked, thanks to the genuine emotion of moments like Sorvino's, Douglas's, and Reeve's. Even those who'd been critical of Jones a few hours earlier conceded that things somehow came together. The supermodel fashion show didn't have many fans, but it came early in the evening and was quickly forgotten. "It was just what we wanted," Jones said. "Different, fast, emotional."

Near the musicians' trailers outside the Shrine, Jon Landau and Bruce Allen commiserated over the fact that the artists they managed, Springsteen and Adams, respectively, had lost to a Disney song. The two men posed for a photo together, and Landau commented, "It'll be in *Billboard* next week—a new partnership."

"Yeah," laughed Allen. "And the caption will be, 'Two Losers.'"

Jones and Salzman walked by, heading for the Governors Ball with an entourage that included Oprah Winfrey. "You were great," Jones said to Oprah. "You were like . . . What's that big rock over in Europe?"

"The Rock of Gibraltar?" she said.

"Yeah," he said. "The Rock of Gibraltar."

In the Governors Ball, the biggest crowd gathered around Christopher Reeve's table. Danette Herman stood by proudly. "We've been working on getting Chris here since December," she said. "He wanted to do it, but they had to figure out if he could travel, the doctor had to check out our facilities . . . It was very complicated." The few production staffers who knew about the booking used code names for Reeve, she added; most of the staff didn't know about it.

At the ball, Jones and Salzman basked in congratulations. But the two men also knew that the experience had been a rough one, and not one they were inclined to repeat. "It was nice working with you," Jones told Mike Shapiro. "I'd say let's work together again, but I'm never doing this show again as long as I live."

AFTER THE SHOW, Jesse Jackson announced that his protests and his ongoing dialogue with Hollywood executives were having positive results. He also insisted that the fact that Goldberg joked about his campaign on the show was good, because it meant she was addressing the serious issue, albeit with humor.

The ratings did not keep pace with the upward trend of the past few years: it was the lowest-rated Oscar telecast in four years, with the biggest one-year drop-off since 1985. For the first time since 1987, ABC did not finish atop the Nielsen ratings for the week in the eighteen-to-nineteen demographic, though it did win the week overall. Still, the show was the highest-rated entertainment program since the previous Oscar show, and the 30.3 rating was higher than that of seven out of the past ten shows.

In addition, the show picked up some of the best reviews of any Academy Awards show in years. Though some of the praise was due to the fresh approach of Jones and Salzman—the appearance of Stomp foremost—much of it was due not to their attempted overhaul of the show, but to the emotional moments that no Oscar producer can truly plan. Appearing before the Academy's review committee, Jones deflected some of the credit and suggested that the Oscar vets, primarily Margolis, deserved the kudos.

4

===

Secrets and Lies

The 69th Academy Awards

HE AMBLED THROUGH THE DOOR just before noon on February 24, 1997, one month to the day before the 69th Academy Awards. Casually dressed in blue jeans, a gray sweater, and sneakers, Billy Crystal stuck his hands in his pockets as he wandered through the nondescript office suite that was serving as a temporary home to the Oscar production staff. Crystal and his manager, a rumpled, curly haired man named David Steinberg, had come to meet with Gil Cates, but for a few seconds they stopped, looked around, and seemed lost. The hallway was nearly deserted, and no nameplates adorned the office doors in the plain high-rise building on Wilshire Boulevard in the Westwood section of Los Angeles.

But when Crystal and Steinberg turned a corner, they spotted a group of faces familiar from Crystal's four previous gigs as the Oscar host. Danette Herman immediately broke into a broad grin. "Nice to see you," she said softly. "*Really* nice to see you." She stepped back, and her smile got bigger and her voice louder. "*Really* nice to see you! *We missed you!*"

Oscar himself had missed Billy Crystal. His stint as host of the show, from 1990 to 1993, had garnered impressive ratings and almost unanimous acclaim. In that stretch, Crystal had staked his claim as the heir to Johnny Carson and Bob Hope, the ideal man for a demanding, tricky, and in some ways thankless job. Able to work a room and a television camera, both undercutting and celebrating the pomp of the occasion, he had delivered several of the time-capsule moments for which the Oscars are most often remembered. There was the entrance he made strapped to a gurney, a leather mask across his face, in homage to Anthony Hopkins's role as the homicidal Hannibal Lecter in *The Silence of the Lambs*; his running string of jokes after seventy-three-year-old Jack Palance celebrated his best supporting actor win by dropping to the stage for some one-handed push-ups; and his ad-lib when one-hundred-year-old Hal Roach decided to make a speech from his seat, without the benefit of a microphone to make his words audible. "I think that's fitting," said Crystal, "because Mr. Roach started in silent films."

But those highlights all came in 1992—and Crystal, not wanting to run his familiar bits into the ground, had walked away from the Oscar assignment following an anticlimactic show the following year. After two years off, he thought about returning to the Oscars—but that was the year Quincy Jones took the reins, and Jones went straight to Whoopi Goldberg without asking Crystal.

But Gil Cates was back the following year; after dealing with Jones, the Academy appreciated the steadier hand of the six-time producer. When Cates agreed to return, he immediately put a call in to Crystal. With a new movie, *Father's Day*, due out a few weeks after the show, Crystal was up for another turn as host.

Crystal had been in touch with Cates since he took the gig, tossing out ideas, particularly about a top-secret film he wanted to show before taking the stage. But he hadn't been by the office, and much of the Oscar production staff hadn't spoken to him in four years.

So when Crystal and Steinberg stopped outside Cates's office and waited for the producer to get off the phone, the group of staffers that had gathered nearby quickly surrounded the comic and welcomed him back. While Bill Conti and Robert Z. Shapiro shook Crystal's hand, a broad grin never left Herman's face.

Secrets and Lies

"How have you been, Billy?" asked Herman. "You know," she repeated one final time, "we really missed you."

IF EVER the Academy Awards needed a host who could energize the show and draw viewers, 1997 was the year. The biggest movies of the previous season were popcorn blockbusters without a chance of winning Oscars in any but the technical categories: *Independence Day*, *Twister*, and *Mission: Impossible* were effective thrill rides for viewers who didn't mind checking their brains at the door, but they were hardly what the Academy was looking for. The films that dominated the year-end critics' polls, instead, were smaller independent films: Joel and Ethan Coen's wry *Fargo*, British director Mike Leigh's largely improvised *Secrets & Lies*, Dane Lars Von Trier's stark *Breaking the Waves*, Arkansas-born actor-director-writer Billy Bob Thornton's southern gothic *Sling Blade*. Scattered support also went to *The English Patient*, a languid romantic epic set during World War II and directed by Anthony Minghella, an Englishman whose two previous films had not been successes. *The English Patient* was supposed to have been made by 20th Century-Fox, but the studio got cold feet over money issues, and pulled out just before production was due to start. Miramax stepped in and bought the film at a cut-rate price.

When nominations were announced on February 11, indie films dominated. In the best-picture race, there was precisely one major studio movie that Middle America had been paying to see: *Jerry Maguire*, director Cameron Crowe's look at a sports agent in crisis, starring Tom Cruise and newcomers Renée Zellweger and Cuba Gooding, Jr. But the rest of the slate was filled with independent films and art movies: *Secrets & Lies*, *Fargo*, *The English Patient*, and *Shine*. The last film, released by Fine Line, was directed by a young Australian named Scott Hicks, and told the story of piano prodigy David Helfgott's lifelong battle with mental illness. The degree to which the movie followed the actual events of Helfgott's life was a matter of considerable debate, but most agreed that British actor Noah Taylor and Australian Geoffrey Rush did fine jobs portraying the tortured pianist as an adolescent and an adult, respectively.

In the acting categories, it was again a heyday for independents and unknowns. In the best-actress category, there was young Welsh actress Emily Watson versus middle-aged British actress Brenda Blethyn, neither of them familiar in the United States. For best actor, the obscure Australian Geoffrey Rush versus the obscure Arkansan Billy Bob Thornton. For best supporting actor, Armin Mueller-Stahl versus William H. Macy. For best supporting actress, Marianne-Jean Baptiste versus Juliette Binoche. In that last category, some old Hollywood glamour was provided by Lauren Bacall, who appeared in Barbra Streisand's otherwise overlooked *The Mirror Has Two Faces*, though Bacall didn't mean much to viewers under thirty.

For those concerned about television ratings—which is to say, everyone at ABC, at the Academy, and on the production team—the nominations were not good news. Viewers tuned in to the Oscars for lots of reasons—for the stars, the fashions, the host, the performers, or simply because everybody else watches—but if they didn't have a rooting interest in the races, the ratings invariably suffered.

As he looked over the nominations in his office a couple of hours after the announcement, Cates knew the show would be a tough sell. "We've got our work cut out for us, getting folks in Middle America to watch this," he said, looking over the bulletin board where he'd posted the nominations. "Thank God Tom Cruise got nominated."

Herman laughed, and went lowbrow to counter all the art-movie names on the board in front of her. "Calling Chris Farley," she said.

"IT'S BEEN A VERY BIZARRE YEAR," said Cates to three dozen staffers sitting in the production office at ten tables arranged into an enormous square. "Things have been a little bit off-kilter for these kinds of shows this year."

With the previous year's Oscar show suffering a drop in the ratings, the lackluster business done by other recent awards shows was a bigger concern than it might otherwise have been. As the staff took notes and examined the schedules and rundowns in front of them, Cates ran through his plans to keep people watching.

"To begin the show, Chuck Workman's doing a thing with clips from the big films of 1996," he said. "Because so many of the [nominated] films this year were ones that many people haven't seen, the idea is to put in scenes from *Independence Day* and *Twister* and *The Rock*, and movies that people did see. We want to get those things at the top of the show."

There was, he added, another option. "Billy might be doing something where he's in film clips from some of the nominated films. If we do that, Act two will begin with Chuck's thing."

On the musical front, Cates told the staff that Madonna would be performing the nominated song "You Must Love Me," from *Evita*. There'd been some question about this, because the singer had been considered a serious best-actress candidate for her performance in that movie's title role. Passed over by Oscar voters, she thought about it for a couple of weeks before agreeing to perform the number, her movie's one new song and a tune written by Andrew Lloyd Webber and Tim Rice specifically to secure a nomination for their otherwise ineligible music.

Another pop diva, Barbra Streisand, was in a similar situation. Streisand had received a best-song nomination for cowriting "I Finally Found Someone," from *The Mirror Has Two Faces*, but otherwise she'd been bypassed for her work directing and starring in the movie. "Barbra may or may not do it," Cates said. "If she does it, she'll obviously do it with Bryan Adams, the way she does in the movie. If not, we've discussed some alternatives."

What went unspoken was Streisand's troubled history with the Oscars. Once, the relationship had been a good one: the singer-turned-actress was allowed to join the Academy in 1967, before her first film, *Funny Girl*, was even released. Though the organization's rules dictated that membership should be granted only after an impressive body of work, Academy president Gregory Peck explained the waiver: "When an actress has played a great role on the stage, and is coming into films for what will obviously be an important career, it is ridiculous to make her wait two or three years for membership." That year's best-actress vote ended in a tie between Streisand and Katharine Hepburn. If Streisand voted for herself, she owed her Oscar to the Academy's early admittance policy.

In subsequent years, though, the Academy was not so generous with Streisand, and the singer was not so enamored with the Academy. Nominated for best actress for the 1973 romance *The Way We Were*, she agreed to attend the ceremony—but, she told Academy president Walter Mirisch, she didn't want people to know she was there unless she won, so she spent the entire ceremony in seclusion backstage. (She didn't win.) In 1984, Academy members voted five nominations for *Yentl*, but none of them went to Streisand, who'd directed and starred in the movie. Seven years later, her film *The Prince of Tides* won seven nominations, including best picture—but once again, she herself was overlooked in the best-director and best-actress categories. *The Mirror Has Two Faces* was also largely overlooked: it had picked up a pair of nominations, a supporting-actress nod for screen legend Lauren Bacall, who'd never won an Oscar, and a song nomination for "I Finally Found Someone."

"She says she'll let us know today," Cates told the staff. "It's a fifty-fifty chance."

ON MARCH 3, the publicity department of the Academy issued a press release: "Chris Farley and David Spade will be presenters at this year's Oscar telecast, producer Gilbert Cates announced today. This is the first appearance on an Academy Awards show for either of them."

WITH TWO WEEKS TO GO until show time, the second-floor lobby of the Shrine Auditorium was filled with dozens of folding chairs. At the end of the lobby, facing the chairs, was a long table. Cates, Seligman, Herman, and choreographer Otis Sallid took seats at the table. So did production designer Roy Christopher and the new director of the Oscar show, Louis J. Horvitz.

Christopher showed off a scale model of his set, which bedecked the wide stage in dozens of off-white, forty-foot-tall louvers, and topped it with a movable ceiling piece that could descend all the way to the floor. "We're trying to go for a very simple, elegant, classic look this year," he said.

"It looks inexpensive," shouted a staffer from the back of the room.

"It is inexpensive," said Christopher with a grin. "And very easy to build."

Horvitz leaned toward his microphone. "He means the model," he said. "The model was inexpensive and easy to build."

Horvitz was one of the few new faces among the show's senior staffers. The forty-nine-year-old director had been working in television, first as a cameraman and then as a director, for more than a decade. He'd spent eight years directing the music variety show *Solid Gold*, and had moved into live events with the *Live Aid* benefit concert in 1985. In recent years, Horvitz had directed music shows that included Paul Simon in Central Park, the Rolling Stones' Steel Wheels tour, and the Judds' farewell concert; he'd done Super Bowl halftime shows and the Emmy Awards. The world of televised awards shows was a fairly small, insular one, in which everyone knew everyone else, and Cates had been watching Horvitz.

Jeff Margolis had directed eight consecutive Oscar shows, but tension between him and Cates had been slowly building. Perhaps Margolis was a threat because he'd been given too much credit; perhaps he was a distraction because he'd tried to take too much control. Whatever the reasons, when Margolis showed up at the Emmy Awards in the fall of 1996, a nominee for directing the Quincy Jones Oscar show, he learned that Cates was also there—not in the audience but in the control truck, watching Horvitz direct. "I knew that Gil was there, but I didn't know why," said Margolis, who was devastated to lose the Oscar job. "I didn't know, but I did. I just didn't *want* to know." To add insult to injury, Margolis lost that night to Horvitz's direction of the 1995 Kennedy Center Honors. Cates suggested that Margolis take a year off from directing the Oscars—but when the director made it clear just how deeply the change hurt him, the rift widened further.

The new director was demanding, a perfectionist who treated his agenda as if it were a battle plan straight out of *Patton*. He had a meticulous approach and sharp visual sense—but when things didn't go right, Louis J., as he was known, could blister underlings with torrents of abuse and profanity. "I don't know why," he conceded, "but I've got a sailor's mouth."

At his first major Oscar production meeting, though, Horvitz was on his best behavior. "When Gil and I first sat down for lunch in January," said Horvitz, "he said, 'You have never in your life been through something like this.' I said, 'Well, I don't know . . .' And he said, 'Trust me. *Never.*'"

The director then led a more detailed discussion of the show. "We want to make everybody feel that one of the last places you can be part of a community is sitting in a movie house," Horvitz said, making explicit the vague and largely unpublicized theme that Cates had chosen for the show.

"We'll have sixteen cameras inside the Shrine," he added. "I think that's a couple more than last year. The idea is to add a little more variety during the three hours and ten minutes, which is the length the show is going to run this year. Right, Gil?"

Cates smiled. "Ho-ho," he said.

"EVERYBODY ELSE IS TENSE," said Otis Sallid. "*This* is where the fun happens."

On Stage 57 at ABC Prospect, the new Oscar choreographer was leading his crew through a rehearsal of a lighthearted pop-rock ditty called "That Thing You Do!" With Cates's much-maligned favorite, Debbie Allen, unavailable, the producer had turned to Sallid, who'd staged dance sequences in such films as *Do the Right Thing* and *Sister Act*. Sallid, though, didn't have much to work with in the crop of nominated songs, and although Herman had also booked Irish American dancer Michael Flatley's "Lord of the Dance" troupe, Sallid would have no hand in the choreography. "That Thing You Do!" had become the young choreographer's sole number.

A slight, peppy, and irresistible sixties-rock pastiche, "That Thing You Do!" was the only up-tempo tune among the five nominated songs. But it was not a case where the Oscars could simply book the original performers. The title song from the movie that marked Tom Hanks's directorial debut, "That Thing You Do!" was supposed to be the one hit enjoyed by a 1960s garage band, the Wonders, before success and excess drove the members apart. In the movie, actors mimed and lip-synched the song, which had been written by Adam Schlesinger (from the pop-rock band the Fountains of Wayne) and recorded by anonymous musicians who'd since become disgruntled at the lack of recognition.

Initially, Hanks and his music supervisor, Gary Goetzman, had offered Cates the services of original actors Jonathan Schaech, Steve Zahn, Ethan Embry, and Tom Everett Scott. The actors were all experts at lip-syncing, said Goetzman, who added that Cates and Sallid could surround the band with whatever kind of choreography and staging they desired.

Sallid mapped out a frenzied, sixties-style dance routine that would follow the rise of the Wonders from a garage to clubs to stardom. But to tell that story required more time and space than the two-and-a-half-minute song provided, so Bill Conti wrote an expanded arrangement that included a midsong instrumental break designed for dancing, and replete with classic rock 'n' roll riffs that had little to do with "That Thing You Do!" Hanks and Goetzman balked at asking the actors to go along with a completely new version of the song. "Bill Conti decided he would be Mr. Rock 'n' Roll, and now it's going to turn into one of those anachronistic Academy Awards production numbers," grumbled one executive with the film.

Sallid knew that he'd be dealing with anonymous lip-syncers in place of the film's actors, but that just gave him more freedom to control the number. On the rehearsal stage, silliness reigned: befitting the catchy song and the sock-hop choreography, the dancers were exuberant, playful, and giddy between takes. Their motto, they announced repeatedly to anyone who would listen, was "Happy to be here! Easy to work with!"

Sallid was dressed mostly in black—slacks, a turtleneck sweater, a baseball cap, along with a long gray trench coat and a silver watch on a chain around his neck. On a nearby stand sat a lyric sheet for "That Thing You Do!" along with the sheet music for the tune. The paper bearing the lyrics was folded so that only the first, second, and final verses were visible; the sheet music was punctuated with boxes describing the onstage action at various points in the song: PAPARAZZI, AUDITORIUM, RADIOS . . . During a break, the dancers stood around a microphone and recorded screams, hand claps, and applause that would later be mixed into the track.

A few minutes later, the dancers began going through their number, an athletic workout that required the predominantly female cast to do a lot of running from one side of the stage to the other. The women wore a variety of sweatpants, shorts, Danskins, and tank tops, and all but one wore sports bras beneath their tops. The one who didn't, Melissa Hurley, a thin brunette who had been briefly engaged to David Bowie a couple of years earlier, grabbed her black halter top as she bopped in place. "Ooh," she said with a sheepish grin. "I gotta hold my little titties."

Watching the rehearsal, Sallid grinned. "For me, working with these people is like driving a Rolls-Royce," he said. "These are the best bodies in the world."

OF THE FIVE NOMINEES, only one had the feel of a best-picture winner. *The English Patient* was far from the most critically acclaimed of the batch, but it was grandiose, epic, and romantic, reeking of seriousness and flaunting the literary pedigree it took from its source novel by Michael Ondaatje. If it was also slow, at times ponderous, and melodramatic—well, that hadn't hurt *Out of Africa*, or *Dances with Wolves*, or *The Last Emperor*, or plenty of other winners over the years. The film had been released by Miramax after 20th Century-Fox had backed out, but it wasn't nearly as quirky or offbeat as indie nominees like *Fargo* and *Secrets & Lies*.

In the past, the power of the major studios to wield blocks of votes would certainly have thrown the race to *Jerry Maguire*, the one nonindie entry. But Academy voters had become a more independent lot, and they knew that giving the prize to the sole studio production in a year that belonged to the independents would make the Academy look positively medieval. Miramax, meanwhile, worked aggressively on behalf of *Sling Blade*'s writer and star, Billy Bob Thornton, but the company's real muscle went behind *The English Patient*, the independent film that didn't look, sound, or feel like an independent film.

IN A TRAILER behind the Shrine, Julie Faust shook her head. On the desk in front of her was a hefty Oscar script; next to it was a phone that kept ringing with phone calls from publicists and agents. "There's a typo on almost every page," said Faust, one of Cates's assistants. "Don't they look at this before it goes out? I have to send this to lots of pissy movie stars!"

It was Friday, March 21, three days before the broadcast and the time when Oscar rehearsals got very serious. Billy Crystal, Madonna, and Michael Flatley were all due in. Potential trouble spots were numerous. All morning, staffers were on edge.

Crystal was the first up, arriving at the Shrine shortly after lunch. The hall was quietly cleared of stand-ins and other observers, while the staffers that were allowed to remain watched intently as the lights dimmed. On the huge center screen, a film began to play. This, everybody knew, would be the top-secret movie Crystal had shot to precede his entrance, the one only a tiny handful had yet seen. But fascination turned to befuddlement when the eagerly awaited movie turned out to be incomprehensible, an odd mélange of people wandering through the desert in an apparent takeoff on the opening scene of *Jesus Christ Superstar*.

"What is *that?*" asked Carrie Fisher, who slipped into a seat near the production table just before Crystal's entrance. "I thought it was going to be Billy going down in a plane piloted by David Letterman."

An actress, writer, and enormously well-compensated Hollywood script doctor, Fisher had been caught by surprise when Cates asked her to join the Oscar team of writers. The money was significantly less than she was accustomed to making, but Fisher was intrigued enough by the offer to accept, joining show vets Buz Kohan and Hal Kanter in writing patter for presenters, performers, and participants—in general, everybody except for Crystal, who relied on a separate team of six writers. Taking the job, she admitted, had brought her some flack from cynical friends who professed to hate the Academy Awards. "Fran Lebowitz yelled at me yesterday for doing this show," Fisher said. "She's not the only friend of mine who's done that."

As they watched the confounding movie play inside the Shrine, Fisher and everybody else in the theater slowly realized that they weren't watching Crystal's real movie. Instead, this was a dummy clip designed to do nothing more than take up the same amount of time. This came as a relief to Chuck Workman, whose montage saluting the popular films of 1996 had been dropped from the show because, he was told, it covered much of the same ground as Crystal's movie. "Well, I'm glad that wasn't his real movie," said Workman. "I'd hate to think that my film was pulled for *that*."

While Crystal went through a low-key rehearsal, Fisher approached Cates. "How are you?" she asked.

"Good," Cates assured her.

"Good," she said, "because Courtney Love isn't."

Love, the former punk singer and widow of Nirvana singer/songwriter

Kurt Cobain, was scheduled to present the Oscar for makeup—a curious category for someone whose look was not exactly Estée Lauder, though a better match than her original slot introducing Kenny Loggins. Her appearance was designed to help the show attract a younger audience, but it also solidified the acceptance the controversial Love had received in Hollywood after her creditable turn as *Hustler* publisher Larry Flynt's tortured wife, Althea, in Milos Forman's film *The People vs. Larry Flynt*.

Love, though, objected to the lines Fisher had written for her. The script began with Love talking about how actresses have to arrive for makeup early in the morning, and how if one is lucky, "she can get an extra hour's sleep while the makeup artists perform their magic, allowing her to nod out plain and wake up pretty." Not only did the lines contain what could be construed as a self-deprecating joke ("Not all of us are lucky enough to wake up pretty"), but they also included a thinly veiled reference to Love's widely publicized substance-abuse problems. One line described seeing what the makeup artists could do as "a fully sobering experience, let me tell you."

" 'Sobering experience' was the first thing to go," Fisher told Cates. But that change wasn't enough to satisfy the rock diva. "She doesn't like the jokes. She wants to be dignified. She sees this as her chance to do a makeover on her reputation."

To Fisher, this was a dubious strategy at best. "It doesn't matter what you do, how long you wait—those things will always be with you," said Fisher, whose own drug-fueled escapades formed the basis for her book *Postcards from the Edge*, which was subsequently made into a movie starring Meryl Streep. "They never left me." She paused and grinned. "Granted, I wrote a book and a movie about it."

DANETTE HERMAN stood by the artists' entrance looking anxious. At 3:45 in the afternoon, Herman's walkie-talkie crackled. "They have arrived," said a voice. "They're heading toward parking." *They*, in this case, meant Madonna and her entourage of about half a dozen, including a nanny for Madonna's five-month-old daughter, Lourdes.

There was reason for the concern that swept through the crew, because

Madonna's history at the Oscars was brief but stormy. She'd appeared on the show in 1991, singing a nominated song from *Dick Tracy*. Before rehearsals began that year, Madonna worked out on her own for weeks, practicing for hours every day with her own choreographer. She had her own costume people work on clothes, and insisted that the production install a sound system identical to the Shrine's in the rehearsal hall she was using on Vine Street in Hollywood. (That building was later purchased by the Academy, and now houses their film archives.)

During rehearsals with the Oscar orchestra, she had been as painstaking and demanding with the musicians as she had been with herself. "She was determined," said Seligman, "that it was going to be perfect."

She also took to showing up at the Shrine at odd hours. "She rehearsed her number, when we got to the Shrine, more than anybody had ever rehearsed a musical number in the history of the Oscars," said Margolis.

"We'd get a call saying, 'Madonna's here,' " remembered stage manager Debbie Williams. "We'd look at the schedule and she wouldn't be listed, but we'd have to find the time to fit her in." Once, the singer arrived late at night wearing slippers and a nightgown, determined to squeeze in a final rehearsal before bedtime. Another time, she was due to rehearse just after a female camera operator had fallen backward off the stage and into the orchestra pit, seriously injuring herself. While the crew waited for paramedics to arrive, Madonna walked onstage. Told of the delay, she looked puzzled. "But she's just lying there," Madonna said of the injured camerawoman. "Can't we do this?"

In her number, Madonna's every move had been carefully choreographed, and her entrance was to be particularly dramatic. She'd rise from beneath the stage through a trapdoor, all blond and glittering, then slink a few steps across the bare stage before turning her back on the audience and the camera. At exactly the right moment, she'd move to the side to reveal a pop-up microphone that had risen into place while she was blocking the audience's view.

"The elevator guy had to push a button at exactly the right bar of music," said Margolis, "and when she hit the floor I went to a head-to-toe shot of her looking sexy, from down low because that makes everybody look taller and it showed off the slit in her dress. After so many bars she'd start walking forward and I'd cut to a high shot. The speed of the microphone had been timed exactly with her walk. The timing was critical."

The night of the show, Madonna was nervous as she waited to perform. Stage manager Rac Clark, who was waiting with her below the stage, gave her a glass of champagne to calm her. But as the song neared, staffers found they couldn't communicate with the technician who was positioned in a small box halfway up the wall in the wings of the theater. His sole job was to activate Madonna's pop-up mike at just the right moment—but sitting in his lonely perch above the Shrine stage, the man had fallen asleep. He didn't hear the frantic attempts to rouse him over his headset, nor respond when stage manager Garry Hood shouted and threw things at him from below.

With no time to spare, Margolis made a quick decision. "Put a stand mike out there!" he ordered. It fell to Clark to tell the singer that her beloved pop-up mike wouldn't be making its dramatically choreographed appearance; instead, she'd be rising onto a stage where a mike stand already waited for her, in full view of the audience and directly between her fabulous gown and Margolis's camera. Clark, the son of TV personality and producer Dick Clark, broke the bad news only seconds before the song was due to begin.

Madonna did not take it well. *"Fucking asshole!"* she screamed at the messenger, launching into an astonishingly profane tirade, despite the fact that the area below the stage was also occupied by a group of children who'd be performing later in the show. Furious, she grabbed Clark around the neck and lifted him bodily off the ground, not relinquishing her grip until the trapdoor opened and she began to rise. The agitation was written on her face as she stumbled through the song she'd been sweating over for weeks. (The napping crew member was subsequently drummed out of the union.)

When Madonna returned to the Oscars six years later, she made it clear that she hadn't forgotten. "I don't have good feelings about this show," she said. Meanwhile, the staff went to great lengths to make her as comfortable as possible. Inside the Shrine, publicists Chuck Warn and Nicole Von Ruden did a sweep of the hall, throwing out most of the bystanders. One of those Von Ruden attempted to eject was Bryan Lourd, Madonna's agent and also Carrie Fisher's ex-boyfriend. When Von Ruden told Fisher about this later,

Fisher was delighted. "You don't wish your ex ill," she said, "but you don't necessarily wish them well, either." Seligman, meanwhile, caught a wire reporter sneaking into the rehearsal, and had the man escorted out of the building.

Using a regular handheld microphone rather than a pop-up, Madonna ran through her song once, then frowned. "I just want to make sure I'm not singing too loud," she said. The orchestra, still warming up, played a snippet of "Mission: Impossible." Madonna looked into the orchestra pit. "Is that a comment on this rehearsal?" she said.

As the rehearsal continued, a security guard spotted a French reporter sitting near the rear of the Shrine with a tape recorder. The woman insisted that she was not taping the rehearsal—but Warn discovered otherwise when he went to the security office and listened to her tape. Though the reporter had traveled from France to cover the show, her credentials were taken away.

For the next couple of takes, Madonna couldn't figure out if the sound was right. "Does it sound better in the house?" she asked, looking out at the sparse crowd. "Everybody who liked it, raise their hands." Then she looked over to where her daughter sat in the fifth row. "Did Baby Pumpkin like it?" she asked, then laughed. "She's sleeping. Oh, that's a good indication."

During a pause between takes, Horvitz's voice came over the P.A. system. "We're going to bring the dress onstage," he said.

"It's not a dress," Madonna snapped. "It's a pantsuit, *okay?*"

"Okay," Horvitz said.

An aide brought out the pantsuit Madonna planned to wear on the show, and the singer held it up for the director to see. "Notice how it picks up the art deco motif?" she said, pointing from the dress to Roy Christopher's set.

"I do," said Horvitz. "Thank you for being thematic."

"Would you like to see the shoes?"

"If you want to show me," said Horvitz. "They're thematic, too, aren't they?"

After take five, Madonna went into Horvitz's trailer to watch a playback. A few minutes later, she returned to the stage in her deco pantsuit. "Is there any way you guys can make me look taller?" she said.

"Sure," said Horvitz.

"I want to look taller and prettier," she added. Then she got serious. "As far as lighting goes, think drama. Drama, and reveal."

"Got it, babe."

Lourdes started crying. Madonna did the song again. Then the crew broke for dinner and Madonna went home. The schedule called for her to rehearse for another hour and a half after the break, but she didn't need it. At dinner, the sense of relief was palpable.

AT 7:15, as the dinner break neared its end, walkie-talkies sprang to life. "The Lord," a voice announced, "needs a towel."

Michael Flatley had arrived. The thirty-eight-year-old Irish American dancer had made his name in the original production of *Riverdance*, a high-tech, high-stepping exhibition of Irish dance set to an amped-up version of traditional Celtic music. After starring in the original production in Dublin and London in 1995, Flatley left the show in a dispute over credit. As the main male dancer in the show—and, he claimed, the originator of much of his own choreography—Flatley felt that he should be credited, and paid, as a cocreator of the show; when that credit and remuneration was denied, he created his own *Riverdance*-style extravaganza, which he modestly dubbed *The Lord of the Dance*.

The show had been a hit on its North American tour of sports arenas, and Herman—a big fan of *Riverdance*—booked him to give the Oscars a jolt of adrenaline. Flatley's reputation for being temperamental preceded him, and heads turned when he entered the Shrine with his troupe of three dozen young dancers. Wearing a black leather jacket with a high collar, black jeans, black boots, and a studded belt, Flatley didn't stand, he posed; he didn't walk, he strutted. "He's like Siegfried and Roy's cousin," whispered Von Ruden.

Flatley and company ran through their routine, while staffers watched and wondered what all this supercharged high-stepping and synchronized clog dancing had to do with film editing. To answer that entirely reasonable question, Fisher was drafted to write an intro saying that film editing, like dance, is all about rhythm. And Workman took Flatley's music and put together a film package that was ostensibly a tribute to the art of film editing—although of the hundreds of edits in the piece, all but four or five were made by Workman, not the original editors that were theoretically being saluted.

"They say it's a tribute to the editors, but it's really a tribute to *me* as an editor," said Workman as he stood in the aisle and watched Flatley rehearse. His film played on a screen behind Flatley, while Horvitz cut between the film and the live performance. While the theater audience saw it all, achieving the right balance for viewers proved to be more difficult. Some of Workman's more ingenious cuts were lost when the camera focused on Flatley and crew, while too much emphasis on the film distracted from the live performance. After one rehearsal, Flatley's agent complained to Cates that his client was being overshadowed by the film. Later, Workman watched on a monitor and was dissatisfied as well. "They're not showing enough of the screens," he said.

After the final run-through, Cates spoke on the phone to Horvitz, then approached Workman in the aisle. "It's great," he said. "And we'll put more screen in."

"Good," said Workman. "Because I was just complaining about that."

"It's a tricky balance," said Cates, "but Lou says he'll get it. And I was worried that our friend would complain about being upstaged, but he was fine."

STANDING IN the center orchestra section of the Shrine, Seligman frowned as he looked at a group of guests sitting behind the ABC table. "Folks, you have to clear the hall for the next half hour," he yelled to them, then turned to one of the two security guards who were helping him make a sweep of the room. "If they're not working a camera," he said, "they can't be here. We've got to get this room cleared."

Working his twentieth Academy Awards, Seligman usually had weightier matters to contend with than throwing people out of the auditorium. But Cates wanted this show to include several big surprises, from Crystal's opening film to the Lord of the Dance. For weeks, the staff had refused to confirm any information about many of the show's bookings, occasionally just lying outright—or, more often, having the press reps lie. The previous day, flamboyant basketball star Dennis Rodman had spoiled one surprise when he told a Chicago sports columnist that he was appearing in a *Brady Bunch*–themed segment of Crystal's film; afterward, everyone was on edge, worried about further leaks. "It's a difficult year," said Seligman as he watched guards attempt to clear the Shrine. "We've got a lot of secrets this year. That makes it hard."

At 10:30 a.m. on Saturday, two days before the Oscar show, the biggest secret was standing behind the theater. Most of the show's production schedules and rundowns made no mention of him; the few that did called him "Scott Murray." Some of the crew, who weren't supposed to speak his name (or even know it, really), dubbed him "Piano Boy"—or, less charitably, "Wacko." A thin, gray-haired man with a nervous manner and a penchant for hugging anyone with whom he was familiar, he was David Helfgott, the Australian pianist whose struggle with mental illness was the subject of *Shine*. Since he was in town for a recital at the nearby Dorothy Chandler Pavilion the night after the Oscars, his presence at the Shrine had been widely rumored—and just as widely denied by Cates.

The producer knew this booking was a gamble: as *Shine* made clear, Helfgott had frozen or fallen apart in public situations before. In recent years, though, he had clearly become more reliable and better able to cope with the pressures of performance. Still, his brief concert tour, designed to capitalize on his new visibility via the movie, drew scathing reviews from many music critics who felt he was at best an uncertain, amateurish pianist, and at worst the victim of exploitation.

The staff knew that Helfgott had to be handled with kid gloves. No stand-ins were allowed to remain in the theater, while the tables usually populated with network executives and members of the set design team were likewise cleared. Cates and Herman remained out back, chatting with Helfgott and his wife and not asking the pianist to come to the stage until they were certain everything was ready. When it was, they led Helfgott into the wings, and then Herman brought the pianist's wife and some friends into the hall. The few people who remained were told to sit toward the back of the floor, and to keep their heads low.

At 10:50 a.m., a stage manager walked to the microphone. "Ladies and gentlemen," she said, "please welcome Scott Murray." Without looking at the tiny audience, Helfgott walked onstage, ran up the few steps to his piano, bounced up and down on his heels a couple of times, then sat down. Immediately, he launched into a nervous, kinetic version of Rimsky-Korsakov's "The Flight of the Bumblebee." When it ended he stood up, bowed, then immediately sat down and played the piece again. Horvitz, who normally spoke to performers over the P.A. system, kept quiet.

When Helfgott finished, Cates left his seat and walked onto the stage shouting, "Bravo!" He showed Helfgott where to stand for his bows. Helfgott hugged Seligman once, then twice. Then he hugged Cates. By 10:55, he was gone.

At noon the next day, Cates, Horvitz, and Arthur Hiller appeared at a press conference outside the Shrine. At the end of the short Q&A session, they asked for questions from the fans who'd already begun to gather in the bleachers. "Is David Helfgott going to perform?" one woman yelled.

"No," said Cates. "Not unless you know something I don't know."

AFTER THE PRESS CONFERENCE, stars began arriving in earnest: Mel Gibson, then Nicolas Cage, then Jim Carrey. Publicist Pat Kingsley lurked by the back door, keeping an eye out for clients. "So," Tommy Lee Jones asked her, "have you seen your entire client list come through here today?"

"Not quite," she said. "But we have eighteen presenters."

In the audience, George Plimpton watched. Interviewing staff members for a piece in *The New Yorker*, he asked a lot of questions about security and seating arrangements; the writer was especially interested in the seat-fillers. "Have there been any interlopers who've gotten onto the stage since the streaker?" he asked intently. Sitting in a sixth-row seat and watching stand-ins take the stage, accept phony wooden Oscar statues, and make mock acceptance speeches, the writer confided that his intentions were not entirely honorable.

"My goal is to get onstage during the show," said Plimpton, who made his name with such participatory stunts as playing quarterback for the Detroit Lions and getting in the ring with boxer Archie Moore. "They're getting me a seat for the show, and I think my best chance will come if *When We Were Kings* wins. I'm in the movie, so they probably won't stop me if I run up to the stage quickly."

Courtney Love arrived in midafternoon. After having *Larry Flynt* director Milos Forman make several calls to Cates and Fisher on her behalf, she brought along an Emily Dickinson poem that she wanted to read in lieu of her speech. "Then sunrise kissed my chrysalis / And I stood up and lived," read the final couplet.

"I told her that you can't say 'kissed my chrysalis,' " Fisher said to the other writers at the production table. "People will think it's sexual. They'll think it's *clitoris*."

Bruce Vilanch nodded. "It's a little vaginal," he said, "coming from a woman who named her band Hole."

In the Shrine lobby, the Pinkerton guards who were providing Oscar security grabbed a man in a tuxedo and held him in an alcove near the Governors Ball until Academy officials could arrive. The man, Scott Kerman, had been spotted and recognized outside the Shrine; he was the author of a book called *No Ticket? No Problem! How to Sneak into Sporting Events and Concerts*. The Pinkertons tailed Kerman until he trespassed, then arrested him. As he was handcuffed and led away, Kerman spotted Plimpton, who'd heard about the gate-crasher and had come to investigate. "Hey, George, you're my hero!" yelled Kerman.

A police officer immediately went to Cates's trailer to tell him of the arrest. Sigourney Weaver was sitting in the outer lobby with Julie Faust. Weaver had her hair piled haphazardly atop her head, and was dressed casually in a brown, long-sleeved T-shirt and tan pants; Faust, on the other hand, was wearing a more tailored blouse and slacks. The cop looked at the two women, took Weaver for the receptionist, and asked, "Is he busy?"

Without waiting for a reply, he headed down the hall toward Cates's desk. "Gil," yelled Weaver, "there's a guy coming to see you. And he's got a gun."

Back inside the Shrine, Plimpton was a little shaken. "The guy said I was his hero," he said, shaking his head. "Maybe this isn't such a good idea."

A few minutes later, Plimpton asked stage manager Garry Hood if he could take the place of a stand-in and accept a dummy Oscar during rehearsal. Hood agreed. When *Hamlet* won the rehearsal Oscar for best score, the writer loped to the stage and cradled the phony statue in his hands. "I'd like to thank Mr. Shakespeare and Mrs. Shakespeare," he said. "All of us down at the Old Globe Theatre are very happy."

"SO," SAID BILLY CRYSTAL, "I'm off to the Governors Ball. It's my eighth one. I've seen more of the Governors Balls than Paula Jones." To the laughter of the few staffers in the hall, he shrugged. "Should I do it?"

The off-color joke wasn't on the TelePrompTer—but as the Saturday evening dress rehearsal began, Crystal was mostly ignoring the actual jokes he'd planned for his monologue. He also withheld his opening film, lest anyone leak its contents to a media outlet with a late deadline. The host did perform his typical opening number "It's a Wonderful Night for Oscar," a medley of song parodies keyed to the best-picture nominees.

Crystal ran through the medley twice, stopping to ask Conti to increase the tempo. "All right," he said after the second take. "Close enough." Then staffers and stand-ins were let back into the hall for the full rehearsal— where, over the next four hours, it was revealed that Madonna had acquired a new outfit since the previous day (a gown rather than a pantsuit), that Piano Boy would sit out this run-through, and that Natalie Cole, who was booked to perform "I Finally Found Someone" when Streisand declined, was sick and couldn't make it. Céline Dion sat in the audience and watched the entire rehearsal, even after performing her song "Because You Loved Me."

The rehearsal ended around 11 p.m. "Thank you very much, everybody," said Horvitz. Most of the staff went home. Dion stayed, as did trumpeter Arturo Sandoval. A music stand was brought to the stage.

Cates went to Horvitz's trailer to go over a few notes on the rehearsal. Then he made a quick stop in his own trailer, where he sighed and explained that the evening was not over yet.

"Natalie Cole is not going to be on the show," he said, shaking his head. "She's been sick all week, and she canceled last night." Initially, he added, he thought about not even looking for a replacement. "I considered dropping the song entirely, but that has ramifications. I looked to see how the song is used in the movie, because I thought I might be able to just play the recording and show a clip. I thought about calling Bonnie Raitt. But I went home without really deciding what I was going to do."

Sunday morning, he added, he got a call from Céline Dion's manager, Rene Angelil. "He said, 'We heard about your problem. And if you need us, we'll help you.' So Céline's going to do Barbra's song."

The last-minute substitution, though, was not without complications. Not only did Angelil hear that Cole had canceled, but so did Marty Erlichman, Streisand's manager. Erlichman phoned Cates as well, claiming that he was calling without Streisand's knowledge. Some who heard about the call were convinced that Streisand was listening in on another line when Erlichman put a question to Cates: If Barbra was willing to do the song after all, would the show be able to clear enough rehearsal time for her? Every minute of rehearsal had long since been allotted, so Cates told an incredulous Erlichman that he'd have to pass. He was going to stick with Dion, the lesser star but by far the lower-maintenance performer.

"This is costing us a fortune," said Cates as he slid into his seat at the production table in the Shrine just after midnight. Less than eighteen hours before the Oscar show would begin, Dion sat on a stool, looked down at the sheet music, and sang "I Finally Found Someone" for the first time. After Dion belted out the song, there were whoops from the staffers, as well as a shout of "*Barbra who?*" Dion's rehearsal was quick and painless; Cates gave her a hug, and she left.

Then Cates huddled with Susan Futterman, who had a couple of problems with the show, beginning with Jim Carrey's use of the word *pissed*. "It has real implications," Futterman said. "It means I have to go to them and say I'm changing the rating. *Bugged* is fine. *Teed off* is fine. *Pissed*, I have to go to a TV-PG14."

"We'll look at it, Susan," Cates said. "I don't see where it's that bad, but we'll look at it."

"The other problem," she continued, "is Jim talking out of his butt. That puts it on a different level. It changes what we'll have to say in the future to Whoopi, to David . . . They'll think, if this guy can cross the line, why can't we?"

ABOVE: *Ben Affleck and Jennifer Lopez hugged, kissed, and canoodled their way through an afternoon run-through in 2003. Behind them, far right, talent executive Danette Herman watched protectively over the celebrated lovebirds.*

BELOW: *Three generations of the Douglas family showed up at the Kodak Theatre for rehearsals in 2003. From left to right: Michael's son Dylan, 2; Michael, 58; and Kirk, 86.*

LEFT: *Cameron Diaz with a plaster rehearsal Oscar stowed between her legs during the run-throughs in 2002*

Jennifer Lopez stood at the side of the Shrine Auditorium stage, awaiting her cue, during 2001 rehearsals.

ART STREIBER

ABOVE: *The most low-maintenance host imaginable, Steve Martin sat in the audience and watched many of the 2003 rehearsals.*
BELOW: *Before taking the stage to rehearse in 2001, Winona Ryder snuck a peek into the audience.*

ART STREIBER

ART STREIBER

Minutes after declining to use the dramatic staircase entrance he'd planned for her in 2004, Julia Roberts made nice with Oscar producer Joe Roth.

The man who transformed Oscar campaigning, Miramax's Harvey Weinstein was a common presence in and around the green room. In 2004, he held court with Jim Carrey outside the Kodak Theatre's backstage restrooms.

Producer Laura Ziskin's big coup in 2002 was persuading the notorious Oscar-phobe Woody Allen to show up. Allen introduced a clip saluting New York City, then left the stage, pulled off his bow tie, and headed for the exit. In the background, Ziskin (blond hair, black suit) celebrated by high-fiving a pal.

TOP: *Before winning the best-actress award in 2004, Charlize Theron waited in the wings to present the award for foreign language film. To her left was a fellow presenter, Jude Law; to her right was PricewaterhouseCoopers partner Greg Garrison, one of the two keepers of the Oscar envelopes.*

BOTTOM: The Lord of the Rings: The Return of the King *director Peter Jackson and his partner, writer-producer Fran Walsh, took a breather between sweeping the Oscars and hitting the parties in 2004.*

TOP: *As best-actress winner Julia Roberts walked by the green room in 2001, a worker prepared to pull down some draperies. With the show running surprisingly ahead of schedule, backstage finery had to be dismantled to make room for the Governors Ball.*

BOTTOM: *In 2002, the stunned best-actress winner, Halle Berry, brought then husband Eric Benet along as she negotiated the hallways that led from the Kodak Theatre to the press area in the adjoining Hollywood Renaissance Hotel.*

ABOVE: *Tom Hanks used a prerogative open only to star participants: rather than wait in the long line out front, Hanks and his son Truman entered the 2001 Governors Ball directly from the backstage area.*
BELOW: *Fresh from being booed by some in the audience in 2003, filmmaker Michael Moore walked into the wings to the derision of a few union stagehands but the approval of his presenter, actress Diane Lane. "That was very inspirational," she told him of his incendiary speech.*

ABOVE: *In one of the meetings that are an integral part of rehearsals the day before every Oscar show, producer Gil Cates went over the 1997 script with presenter Sigourney Weaver.*
BELOW: *At the time Hollywood's most glamorous young couple, Brad Pitt and Gwyneth Paltrow waded through the red-carpet crowd as they entered the Dorothy Chandler Pavilion in 1996. Four years later, she'd be ducking her head to avoid him at rehearsal.*

After the show in 2002, Nicole Kidman hung out in the front row, posed for pictures with the Oscar stage crew, and was among the last to leave the Kodak.

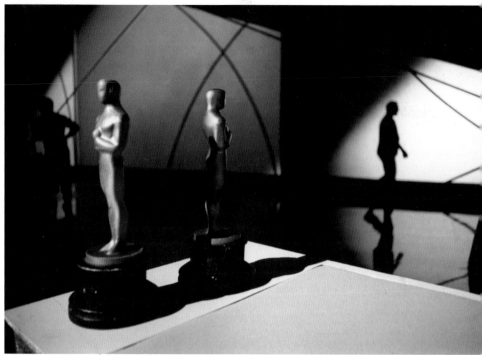

TOP: *All that glitters is not gold: dummy Oscar statuettes, made of plaster and painted to look like the real thing, sat on a backstage table for use by stars and stand-ins during rehearsals in 1994.*
BOTTOM: *Producer Gil Cates looked over the top-secret board bearing the names of possible presenters and performers in 1994. Color-coded dots indicated who was in, who was out, and who was still under consideration.*

ABOVE: *Host David Letterman—unshaven, casual, and out-of-place—tried out a Stupid Pet Trick during rehearsals in 1995. To Letterman's immediate right was Sadie, the Dog That Spins When You Applaud.*
BELOW: *Arnold Schwarzenegger rehearsed his presentation of the Irving Thalberg Award to Clint Eastwood in 1995. On the screen behind Arnold was a scene from* Bronco Billy, *not necessarily one of the honoree's finer moments.*

ABOVE: *Antonio Banderas picked up his lavish gift basket as he left rehearsal in 1994. Within a couple of years, the baskets would be too big and unwieldy for a single person to carry.*
BELOW: *In 1996, the big Oscar recipient was Mel Gibson, who directed and produced the best-picture winner,* Braveheart. *When the show ended, Gibson used an equipment case as a seat and rested with his twin Oscars in a hallway outside the press rooms.*

TOP: *In 1997, a year after winning the supporting-actress Oscar, Mira Sorvino returned to hand the supporting-actor award to Cuba Gooding, Jr. She then accompanied the exuberant winner as he cooled down in a hallway between the Shrine Auditorium and the press tent.*

BOTTOM: *The aftermath of the Oscar show in 1995: a messy production office and an exhausted staffer, all dressed up with, apparently, no place to go. The Governors Ball was getting under way downstairs, but few of those who worked on the show were invited.*

Host Whoopi Goldberg tried to survive an awkward 1996 skit that found her chatting with Miss Piggy and with the porcine star of Babe.

Oscar statuettes arrived at the Dorothy Chandler Pavilion the morning of the 1994 show, several hours before they'd be needed. To keep them secure and out of sight, the Oscars were stashed in a small kitchen just off the Chandler stage and watched over by the building's longtime propmaster, Carmine Marinelli

Chris Farley was booked to help lure Middle American viewers to the Oscars in 1997, a year when art movies and obscure actors captured most of the nominations. The tactic didn't work—it was the lowest-rated Oscar show in eleven years—but it did give Farley a chance to clown around with a mirror ball destined for the after party.

LARA JO REGAN

BELOW: *Director Renny Harlin accompanied his then wife, Geena Davis, to rehearsal at the Dorothy Chandler Pavilion in 1994. While she ran through her lines, he tried out the seat he'd have on Oscar night.*

LARA JO REGAN

In a quiet backstage corrid
in 1996, best-actor winn
Nicolas Cage grabbed a mome
with his then wife, Patricia Arquett

Wearing the lavender silk chiffon
evening dress that helped put Prada on
Hollywood's radar screen, Uma Thurman
ducked behind the Shrine Auditorium for
a smoke after losing best supporting
actress in 1995.

Futterman and Cates hashed it out for a few minutes longer. "Gil," she said, "I don't want to put the show on a delay, but . . ."

"Susan, that's bullshit and you know it."

When Cates left the Shrine after 1 a.m., nothing was resolved with Futterman.

"OKAY, SUSAN," said Cates the next morning. "*Pissed* is out. But Jim Carrey's ass is none of your business."

It had been a busy morning. After her offer to sing "I Finally Found Someone" was declined, Barbra Streisand suddenly decided that she ought to attend the Academy Awards after all. The Academy gave her Natalie Cole's tickets.

Michael Flatley, meanwhile, asked for more credentials so that he could station a few extra staffers in the wings to attend to his needs during his number. He was granted one wardrobe person to hand him his jacket.

The producer's office had also received a flurry of phone calls from Al Pacino's publicist, Pat Kingsley, and his girlfriend, actress Beverly D'Angelo. Pacino, who hadn't come to rehearsal, wanted to make sure that it was okay to cut his lines to the bare minimum and simply announce, "The nominees for best picture are . . ." Cates okayed the change.

In the morning, David Helfgott's record company, BMG, put out a press release announcing that he was on the show. "Shit," said Cates when he found out.

At noon, the final rehearsal began. For the first time, Crystal showed his opening film, which placed him in scenes from many of the nominated movies. Its climax came when the pilot of a crashing airplane from *The English Patient* turned out to be a kamikaze David Letterman, shouting out hosting advice to Crystal as he went down in flames: "Introduce Uma to Oprah, and Oprah to Uma, and then Uma to Oprah, and then do it again! Uma, Oprah, Oprah, Uma . . . !"

In the audience, Vilanch laughed. "Letterman really wanted to do this," he said. "He kept saying, 'I want to be the dumb guy.' "

At the end of the movie, Crystal made his entrance by jumping through a slit in the big movie screen that sat center stage. But as he jumped through the screen, Crystal tripped and fell, hard, on his elbow. He lay on the ground for a few minutes, then climbed to his feet. "It's too high," he said, wincing. "Damn, it's so high."

Garry Hood approached the host. "Do you need a doctor?"

"No," said Crystal, in obvious pain. "Let's get through this." He turned to the sparse audience. "Make me feel better," he said. They responded with big cheers. "A funny thing happened to me on the way to the theater," Crystal said to open his monologue. "I broke my elbow." He got through his song, holding his elbow at an awkward angle; during the first break, his arm was examined by a doctor, wrapped, and put on ice. A stand-in read Crystal's lines for the rest of the rehearsal.

In the command truck two hours later, Horvitz watched as the stage crew failed to reset the stage in time for Céline Dion's second song. The director put his head in his hands. "We're going down in flames here," he said. "Are we gonna make it tonight?"

"Yes," said an assistant director.

Horvitz sighed, then feigned collapsing on his desk. "They never told me it would be this many hours," he said.

Seligman, sitting in a row of chairs behind the director, leaned forward. "*I* told you," he said.

At 3:00, the rehearsal ended. Half an hour later, as the crew ate lunch, Crystal walked onstage in sweats and sneakers. He stood with his hands in his pockets, looking out at the seats for a long time. Then he ran through some of his lines and some of his opening song. Unmiked, he was almost inaudible. A handful of workers remained in the Shrine, but nobody paid him any attention.

6:00 P.M. PACIFIC DAYLIGHT TIME: *"Live, from Los Angeles, California, the 69th annual Academy Awards."*

Barbra Streisand, who had arrived just before show time and stopped along the red carpet to tell a couple of interviewers how the show had turned down her offer to perform, entered the Shrine at 6:04. The usher stationed at a door that led from the lobby into the theater said she couldn't go in until the first commercial break. She and James Brolin waited in the lobby surrounded by an entourage of seventeen, most of them men in dark suits.

After a welcoming speech from Arthur Hiller, Crystal's movie played on a large screen that covered the center of the stage. The audience cheered to find the host speaking to Yoda in *The Empire Strikes Back* (then in rerelease in theaters), then discussing his return to the Oscars with Tom Cruise's *Jerry Maguire*, as well as with characters from *Secrets & Lies*, *Shine*, *Fargo*, and *The English Patient*. When Letterman appeared piloting the doomed airplane from that last film, the crowd inside the Shrine erupted. Onstage, Crystal stood in the darkness behind the screen, listening to the screams of laughter. How, he thought, will I ever be able to follow *this?*

In his ensuing monologue, he quickly summed up the year in Hollywood. "New faces among the nominees," he said. "*Really* new faces. Who *are* you people?"

During Crystal's monologue and opening song, six cameramen roamed the audience, aware of what jokes were coming next and ready to focus on the stars mentioned in those jokes. When Crystal mentioned Billy Bob Thornton, the picture cut to him. When the next line mentioned Edward Norton, Horvitz cut to Norton. When Lauren Bacall was mentioned, though, the camera stayed on Crystal, because a seat-filler was occupying Bacall's seat. The actress had also arrived late and was standing in the lobby having a lively conversation with Streisand.

The first award, best supporting actor, went to Cuba Gooding, Jr., for *Jerry Maguire*. Gooding leapt to his feet, rushed to the stage, talked for about twenty-five seconds, then stopped to take a breath. In the truck, Cates and Horvitz thought Gooding was finished. "Go to music," said Cates. "Music!" shouted Horvitz. Conti's orchestra started playing.

But Gooding wasn't finished and wasn't about to relinquish his moment in the spotlight. As the music got louder, so did his speech; he thanked everybody, he danced, and the crowd roared. In the wings just off the stage, Sandra Bullock laughed, then clapped her hands, then threw her head back and whooped. In the trailer, Horvitz and Cates laughed and applauded as well; the moment may have made them look trigger-happy, but they knew it made for entertaining TV.

Thirty-five minutes into the show, Crystal introduced Madonna. "I think it's really classy," he said, "that Madonna showed up to sing her song." In the control trailer, Horvitz cut to camera nine. It showed an unsmiling Streisand.

This time, Madonna's mike worked, though her voice still sounded tentative. As the singer made her way back to her dressing room after her performance, Courtney Love presented the award for makeup. "The makeup artists have the power to transform us," she said, "from the cocoon of the dressing room to the butterfly of the film." There was nothing in her speech about substance abuse, and nothing about the sunrise kissing anybody's chrysalis. The winners were Rick Baker and David Leroy Anderson for *The Nutty Professor*, but Love forgot to read Baker's name. Leaving the stage with the winners, she apologized. "I fucked up," she said as they came into the wings. "I'm so fucking sorry, you guys." Then she brightened. "Well, it was just human error," she said. "It wasn't like adultery or something."

A few minutes later, Carrie Fisher grabbed Love, who was standing outside the green room. "C'mon," Fisher said. "We gotta go." As they walked toward the artists' entrance, Fisher turned to Love. "You were great," she said. "You were great." New comrades-in-arms at the end of a tough couple of days, the two women spent the next twenty minutes outside the Shrine, smoking cigarettes and chatting animatedly.

At the one-hour mark, Kevin Spacey presented the Oscar for best supporting actress. Though the seventy-two-year-old Lauren Bacall was considered a near shoo-in, she lost to an actress thirty-nine years her junior: Juliette Binoche, from *The English Patient*. It was not clear whether the win was part of an *English Patient* groundswell (the film having already won in the art direction and costume design categories) or another symptom of the Academy's apparent distaste for all things Streisand-related; Binoche, though, was as surprised as everyone else in the room. "I thought Lauren was going to get it," she said, seemingly dazed. "And I think she deserves it."

Shortly after "That Thing You Do!"—which despite Sallid's best efforts came across as downright dumb—Chris Farley and David Spade took the stage. "Maybe there was some kind of a mix-up," said Spade, "and right now Jeremy Irons is performing at the Improv and Daniel Day-Lewis is at a fat camp in Hilton Head."

Behind the Shrine, Fisher and Love continued to smoke, chat, and ignore the rest of the event. Their tête-à-tête broke up just about the time that Céline Dion sang "I Finally Found Someone," some ninety minutes into the show. Streisand was not in her seat, so Horvitz's camera could not capture her reaction. The next day, her publicist explained that Streisand had left her seat to go to the bathroom, not knowing that her song was up next. But six minutes later, when *Breathing Lessons* won the award for best documentary short and director Jessica Wu commented, "You know you've entered new territory when you realize your outfit cost more than your film," Streisand was standing in a darkened hallway at the back of the Shrine, watching from a vantage point well out of camera range. If the ushers in the lobby were following orders (the way they were when Streisand arrived late at the Shrine), Streisand could not be in the hallway watching Wu unless she had also been there watching Dion.

Two minutes later, *When We Were Kings* won the award for best documentary feature. Muhammad Ali and George Foreman both took the stage. George Plimpton did not.

During the ensuing commercial, Steve Martin left his front-row seat and went back a few rows to where Juliette Binoche sat. "I just wanted to say congratulations," he told her.

A couple of rows farther up, a teenage boy approached Kurt Russell. "I don't know if you remember me," he said. "I was in *Captain Ron*."

"Sure," said Russell. "How are you doing?"

As the show neared its third hour, Nicole Kidman took the stage and donned a pair of glasses. "Editing provides the rhythm and pace of the movie," she read. "In many ways, it's like the dance, moving back and forth at a particular pace, always pushing deftly and percussively toward its climax." Her words served to introduce Michael Flatley, who ripped across the stage sporting red and black leather, and for the second half of the number showing off a bare, oiled chest. At one point, Flatley whacked into a cameraman who didn't get out of the way quickly enough.

A short time later, David Helfgott was introduced, for the first time, by his real name. Sitting behind Horvitz in the control trailer, Cates suddenly got to his feet and pointed at the screen, where flashes of light were briefly washing out Horvitz's carefully composed shots. Immediately, Cates's security guard got on a walkie-talkie to a guard stationed inside the Shrine. "There's still more flash cameras," he said. "It's affecting what's going out, and Gil's getting upset. They're on the main floor. See if you can find them. And try to get the names."

When Helfgott finished, Horvitz let out a sigh and sank back in his chair. "Good stuff," he said quietly. "Good stuff."

In the last half hour of the show, the big awards piled up. First, Frances McDormand won the best-actress Oscar for *Fargo*. On her way to the press tent, McDormand stopped and used a cell phone to call her son. "Did you see it?" she said excitedly. "Here's Daddy!" She handed the phone to Joel Coen.

A few minutes later, Susan Sarandon presented the best-actor award to Geoffrey Rush for *Shine*. Then Pacino walked to the stage. "Bye," shouted Sarandon.

"We've come to the part of the show, now, that you've all been waiting for," Pacino said onstage. "It's the halfway mark." The audience laughed. "Thought I'd try that," he said with a slight grin.

Not having rehearsed (and apparently not having paid much attention to the show, during which *The English Patient* had already won eight awards and producer Saul Zaentz had been thanked several times, in addition to winning the Irving Thalberg award), Pacino mispronounced Zaentz's name. The insult was eased somewhat when he gave the producer the Academy Award for best picture.

When Zaentz finished his speech, Crystal said good night. In the nearby Governors Ball, the band was already playing. Pacino walked off the stage, out the back door, down the red carpet, and into a waiting limo. Sarandon and Robbins followed, as did Streisand and Brolin.

On the stage, the crew gathered and poured champagne into plastic glasses. At the front of the stage, an agitated woman approached a security guard. "My friend had his camera taken away," she complained. "Where can we go to get it back?"

"They'll have it tomorrow at the Academy," the guard explained. "He can pick it up then, after they've destroyed the film."

IN THE YEAR of the independent film, the big winners were the indie movie that looked most like a regular studio production, and the indie company owned by Disney. Miramax wound up with a dozen Oscars, including the nine for *The English Patient* and a best adapted screenplay win for Billy Bob Thornton for *Sling Blade*. The company celebrated with such fervor that its post-Oscar party, held at the trendy Sky Bar inside the Mondrian Hotel in West Hollywood, was temporarily shut down by the Los Angeles County Fire Department.

For the most part, reaction to the return of Billy Crystal was positive, with his opening film (and particularly David Letterman's cameo) singled out for particular praise. In fact, the kudos for Crystal's performance were for the most part enough to obscure the more questionable elements of the broadcast, from the lamentable attempts to play younger and more mainstream (Farley and Spade, Beavis and Butthead) to the mind-boggling production numbers from the Lord of the Dance and the "That Thing You Do!" crew.

When the ratings came in, though, the lesson was clear: *Saturday Night Live* comics, animated MTV characters, and even a best-actor nomination for Tom Cruise were not enough to get people to watch an Oscar show if they didn't care about or know about the movies in contention. As the network, the Academy, and the production team had feared all along, viewership took another hit, falling 10 percent from the previous year. The average rating, 27.4, was the second lowest in Oscar history, besting only the 1986 show at which another pretty, languid epic, *Out of Africa*, steamrollered *The Color Purple*.

Barbara Walters's Oscar special also took a hit, drawing the worst ratings ever for her annual round of interviews with select nominees. On the other hand, E! Entertainment Television garnered the best ratings in its seven-year history for its two-hour preshow broadcast, which starred Joan Rivers and her daughter, Melissa.

Scott Kerman, the gate-crasher who'd been arrested trying to sneak into rehearsals, sued Pinkerton and the Academy, claiming that the organizations had subjected him to ridicule. Over the next two and a half years, all of Kerman's claims were thrown out of court.

After the show, the Academy heard complaints about the Shrine Auditorium from many members. The main problem wasn't the traffic jam on surrounding streets—the city had waived $100,000 in traffic-control costs to keep things moving—but rather traffic inside the building, specifically the logjam that developed as some guests tried to make their way from the theater into the Shrine Exhibition Hall for the Governors Ball, and others tried to exit the theater.

Publicly, the Academy remained committed to keeping the show at the Shrine and the Dorothy Chandler Pavilion. But Academy officials knew that the Shrine was less elegant than they'd like, while the Chandler, which served as home to the Los Angeles Philharmonic and the L.A. Opera, was too busy to give them an ideal amount of rehearsal time. They quietly considered alternate venues, though all seemed to have insurmountable problems, being too old (the Pantages Theatre in Hollywood), too big (a new hockey and basketball arena being built in downtown Los Angeles), or too far away from the home of the movie business (several new theaters and arenas in Orange County, an hour south of L.A.).

Soon after the show, though, Bruce Davis was approached by David Malmuth, senior vice president of the TrizecHahn development firm. The company, which had helped with the revitalization (and, some said, Disneyfication) of New York City's Forty-second Street, was working on an upscale shopping and entertainment center in the heart of Hollywood. Located at the intersection of Hollywood Boulevard and Highland Avenue, it was next to the old Grauman's Chinese Theatre and a block away from the Hollywood Roosevelt Hotel, where the first Oscar ceremony had taken place in 1929.

Malmuth had heard that the Academy was interested in opening a film museum, an idea that had indeed been discussed by the board. But Davis had other ideas. "I suggested that if he really wanted an Academy presence, what he needed to do was build a theater large enough to hold the Oscars," said Davis. "He went away for about two weeks and came back with plans that were suspiciously far along." By August, Academy president Robert Rehme had appointed a committee of governors to study TrizecHahn's proposal.

5

≡

Size Matters

The 70th Academy Awards

THE FIRST FEW TIMES he designed sets for the Shrine Auditorium, the theater scared Roy Christopher. It was simply too big, with a stage nearly a hundred feet wide and a proscenium arch that rose a good eighty feet above it. So when he designed Academy Awards shows at the Shrine in 1995 and 1997, Christopher used tricks to reduce the size of the stage and make things more manageable. Once he'd used vertical panels to focus attention inward, and once he'd created a smaller inner proscenium modeled after the iris of a camera.

But in March 1998, Christopher stood about five rows deep in the orchestra section of the Shrine and looked at the first stage he'd ever designed that used all of the theater. In fact, his set *embraced* its size, with enormous open spaces broken only by huge Oscar statues enclosed in shimmering wraparound cones. Gold mosaic and silver leaf adorned most surfaces, while drapes of crushed velvet hung from rods high above the stage. Across the entire back expanse of the stage, a white, vaguely nautical riser had room for the fifty-piece Academy Awards orchestra, a group usually tucked out of sight in the orchestra pit. The overall effect was bold, flashy, over-sized. Titanic, you might say.

"I wanted something big and glamorous," said Christopher as he watched stagehands struggle with the enormous pieces of the set. "It just didn't seem like the year for modesty and understatement."

In 1998, Christopher's attitude made sense. Even more so than in previous years, this one had to be big. For starters, it was an anniversary show, Oscar's seventieth, always a reason to go bigger and bolder than usual.

Then there were the nominations. The previous year, ratings had suffered when the Academy membership nominated a lineup of independent movies Middle America didn't know much about. But the seventieth Oscars were a completely different story. Among the actors nominated were big movie stars like Jack Nicholson, Robin Williams, and Anthony Hopkins, young heartthrobs like Matt Damon and Ben Affleck, crossover TV stars like Helen Hunt. The best-picture nominees included the $100 million–plus hits *As Good as It Gets* and *Good Will Hunting*. The token "little movie" nominated for best picture, *The Full Monty*, also happened to be the biggest-grossing British movie in history. And nearly overshadowing them all, with fourteen nominations, was The Biggest Movie Ever Made, director James Cameron's *Titanic*, well on its way to a staggering gross on the high side of $600 million.

As Christopher said, it was not a year for understatement. Producer Gil Cates once again signed up Billy Crystal, the consensus choice for the show's ideal host. Then, to commemorate the anniversary, he and Danette Herman put in calls to movie stars and icons, legends and up-and-comers. In addition to assembling the usual lineup of presenters and musical performers (the latter group including a couple of masters of stentorian musical overstatement, Céline Dion and Michael Bolton), they sent letters to every living person who'd ever received an Oscar for acting, inviting them to appear onstage.

With Christopher watching from the audience, stagehands set the scenery so that director Lou Horvitz could try out a dramatic tracking shot. Three huge panels, a good twenty feet on each side, were pushed to the center of the stage; in the center of each panel was a cutout in the shape of an Oscar statuette. Interior edges of the cutouts glistened in gold leaf. A stand-in emerged from the darkness at the rear of the stage, walking through the panels and toward the audience, while a handheld camera followed her as she moved. Lighting designer Robert Dickinson's stark backlighting cast dramatic shadows around her.

It made for one hell of an entrance, but it wasn't even for one of the half dozen biggest awards of the night. The setup was for Sharon Stone, who'd be presenting the Oscar for best foreign film. Presenters for the awards that would follow Stone—best actor and actress, best director, best picture—were getting bigger, grander entrances.

At the production table a few rows behind Christopher, writer Bruce Vilanch took a seat, looked at the stage, and quickly punctured a little of the afternoon's pomposity. "Look!" he cried, pointing at the twenty-foot statues wrapped in glittering mesh. "It's Oscar in a pita! Oscar wrap!"

TITANIC HAD THE INSIDE TRACK; that much was a given. Sure, some people hated it, thought it was too big, too corny, too dumb. But those opinions were all but drowned out as the *Titanic* juggernaut rolled on. The movie monopolized the number-one spot at the box office through January, through February, into March. It set a new Golden Globes record with eight nominations, and won four.

Other films, meanwhile, jockeyed to see who could do the best job of being the thinking voter's alternative. *The Full Monty* certainly qualified: it was low budget, small scale, thoroughly British, the charming tale of a group of working-class blokes who tried to improve their dismal financial situation by putting on a strip show. *L.A. Confidential*, director Curtis Hanson's dense, smart remake of the grim James Ellroy novel about corruption and moral decay in the Los Angeles of the 1940s, was a strong alternative as well: it was tough where *Titanic* was soft, cynical where Cameron's epic was sentimental. It was possibly too tough and too cynical to win over enough Academy voters, but it nonetheless wound up as the most favorably reviewed movie of the year. And *Good Will Hunting* was Miramax's big entry, which meant it'd be foolish to count out the story of Boston friends, one a troubled math genius mentored by a kindly shrink played by Robin Williams. With *Good Will Hunting*, Miramax also had a good behind-the-cameras story to run with: the movie's writers were a pair of struggling actors, Matt Damon and Ben Affleck, who'd written the script to create the kind of good parts nobody else would give them, and who stubbornly refused to sell the screenplay unless they could play the lead roles.

"If Jim Cameron is saying size matters, then we at Miramax are saying less is more," Harvey Weinstein insisted in an interview with CNN. A couple of weeks after he made the comment, *Titanic* broke a record by holding the number-one spot for the fourteenth consecutive weekend.

"LOU?" said Billy Crystal nervously. "As soon as the curtain opens, bring the ship down. *As soon as it opens.*"

Crystal was standing near the back of the Shrine stage, gripping the railing of a small platform attached to a hydraulic lift. With *Titanic* so dominant, the host's all-important entrance clearly had to be themed to Cameron's film—so with the help of the lift and a drape painted to look like the prow of an ocean liner, Crystal planned to make his initial appearance atop a mock ship some twenty feet above the stage. The lift would descend and the ship would appear to sink, whereupon Crystal would hop off the boat and onto the stage.

That, at least, was the plan. At the moment, though, three days before the Oscar show, the plan was complicated by the fact that the host was terrified of starting his entrance from such a lofty perch.

"It's *really* high," he said, stepping away from the lift and eyeing it nervously. "Oy."

On the more familiar terra firma of the stage, though, Crystal relaxed and began to run through his traditional medley, "It's a Wonderful Night for Oscar," in which five familiar songs were given new lyrics that poked fun at the five best-picture nominees. Crystal had done this number every year he'd hosted the Oscars; it was his replacement, he said when he introduced it for the first time in 1990, for "that big, terrible number that usually opens the Oscars."

According to Marc Shaiman, who had provided musical accompaniment for Crystal since the comic's days on *Saturday Night Live*, the routine began with a simple question. "We just thought, how can we make fun of those

Oscar production numbers?" said Shaiman. "We decided to stick lyrics about the movies into songs that were never meant to be like that. And since then, it's just become a chance to do an entertaining musical number that has that cushion of irony so needed for the modern world to accept anything musical."

Over the years, Shaiman and Crystal had encountered a few problems getting permission to parody certain songs, though that often had more to do with the movies involved than the songs themselves. The 1991 Oliver Stone film *JFK*, for instance, set off alarms with the publishers who held the rights to music from *Fiddler on the Roof*; they didn't want that musical turned into *Gunman on the Knoll*, with "Tradition" recast as "Suspicion." Crystal's second choice, also vetoed, was to adapt "Trouble" from *The Music Man*: "You've got trouble my friends, right here in Dallas / With a capital D and that rhymes with G and that stands for Gun . . ." Crystal finally got an okay from the publishers of "Three Coins in the Fountain," which became "Three Shots in the Plaza."

Eventually, Crystal and Shaiman learned that they got better results if they cut the lawyers out of the equation and made the appeals themselves. "If Billy Crystal's on the phone," said Shaiman, "people are a little starstruck." In 1998, their medley kicked off with a *Titanic* spoof delivered to the tune of the theme from *Gilligan's Island*. It also included a riff on the relationships in *As Good as It Gets* set to "Let's Call the Whole Thing Off," a parody of "Night and Day" retitled "Matt and Ben," "Fascinating Rhythm" recast as "L.A. Confidential," and a salute to *The Full Monty* à la "Hello Dolly."

Wearing blue jeans with a black shirt and black blazer, Crystal first ran through the medley a capella and unmiked, and then to the accompaniment of Conti's orchestra. As he sang, he eyed the seat cards that showed where the stars would be sitting Oscar night. He didn't like what he saw. Jack Nicholson and Helen Hunt were situated in the first row toward the left side of the orchestra section, and Crystal wanted to come into the audience to sing part of his song directly to Nicholson. But in the medley, "As Good as It Gets" was followed by "Matt and Ben," and Damon and Affleck were on the far side of the Shrine. Crystal wanted to be standing in front of them when he sang, "Your script was tight / And damnit, so are your buns"—but given the size of the theater, that required a long dash that might leave him winded.

"Is there any way to move them closer together?" he asked. "I don't think I can get across there fast enough."

"No," explained Horvitz over the P.A. "We're locked into a nomination situation. It would have serious ramifications."

ONE OF THE INDISPENSABLE ELEMENTS of each Oscar show was the montage alternately called In Memoriam, the Late Show, or the Necrology. A roundup of about two dozen notables who'd died since the previous year's show, the montage always drew the attention of staffers the first few times it was shown during rehearsals; as it ran, crew members would invariably murmur, "I didn't know *he* died" as faces appeared on-screen.

Jimmy Stewart, Lloyd Bridges, Red Skelton, Toshiro Mifune, Chris Farley, J. T. Walsh, and Robert Mitchum were among those featured in the In Memoriam package when it screened inside the Shrine on the Friday before the show. "They had to deal with some *big* controversies this year," said Mike Shapiro, who put the montage together. "If people's family members or friends aren't included, they get very upset."

The segment hadn't always been so popular. "When I first told Gil I wanted to do the clip about people who'd died," said Shapiro, "his eyes rolled back in his head and he said, 'Oh, Christ, we tried that and it was deadly.' I told him I wanted to do it not like an obituary, but more as a celebration, and a sentimental opportunity to say good-bye to these people we've spent our whole lives with." Cates remembers the conversation differently, and says he fought for the In Memoriam piece from the beginning; both men agree that the producer had a tough job selling the concept to a reluctant Bruce Davis at the Academy, and then to a reluctant John Hamlin at ABC.

Shapiro worked at assembling clips of stars and other film notables looking their best, and setting them to a piece of music with, he said, "the right balance of celebration and sentiment." Over the years, he'd used film scores from composers like Alan Silvestri and James Horner; movies about dogs, it turned out, were often appropriate. "Some of the best stuff," he said with a laugh, "comes from scenes where the dog is finally reunited with his family and all the puppies."

The sequence had become a popular part of the Oscar show, but also a contentious one. "It is a beloved segment, but I would much prefer we didn't do it," said Bruce Davis, who often dealt with the calls from friends and relatives demanding to know why their dear departed wasn't included. "It's awful, just awful," he said. "We can only do about two dozen people, and when you sit down to do the list, the last fifteen or twenty cuts you make are people with substantial careers. You just feel like *shit* for days afterwards. And there is *nothing* you can say to somebody's wife or daughter about why they didn't make it into the sequence."

Davis shook his head as he thought about the misery the sequence caused him. "I have had a person, in midsummer, call me from the hospital to say, 'My father just died, what do I do to get him in the sequence?' " he said. "This was not a person I'd ever heard of, and I think I'm fairly knowledgeable about the industry."

Davis still had to write conciliatory letters to some whose loved ones hadn't made the cut, but as rehearsal moved on that duty wasn't exactly pressing. Instead, the biggest fuss of the afternoon was for someone known, in virtually all the production materials, as Special Guest. A list of guidelines had been issued detailing the precautions that needed to be taken when the guest appeared: "No eating or drinking around Special Guest, because he will want to share . . . Women should not wear perfume around Special Guest . . . Women on their menses should take care around Special Guest . . ."

As a joke, Vilanch rewrote the guidelines using "Miss Gabor" in place of every mention of "Special Guest." But Cates's big surprise turned out to be Bart the Bear, the fourteen-hundred-pound ursine star of the recent film *The Edge*, as well as ten other movies. Although Bart's favorite movie stars were reportedly Brad Pitt and Anthony Hopkins, Mike Myers had drawn the task of receiving the envelope from Bart in the sound effects editing category.

A forklift operator carefully lifted Bart's small, steel-lined enclosure, which had been concealed in the Shrine's parking lot for several days while the bear became acclimated to Los Angeles weather. The cage was towed into the theater and backed into the wings of the stage. There, a small railing, only a foot high, was erected to create a pen of sorts. Before the door to Bart's cage was opened, the railing was electrified. "Oh, that's *cheating*," said one stagehand. "Step over it, Bart!"

"Folks, you've got to keep this a secret," Cates said before the bear made his appearance. "No one knows about it. Talk about it, and we'll feed you to the bear." (This was not a pleasant thought: Bart stood ten feet tall when fully upright, and his daily meal generally consisted of twenty four-pound chickens, a five-pound bucket of carrots, and another bucket of apples.)

Carefully, Bart was led out of the cage by his trainer, Doug Seus, who was himself a big, bearish man. Seus slowly walked Bart around the stage on a leash, then took the bear through his paces. He got Bart to sit up, to hold a dummy Oscar envelope, to clap, and to bow to the crowd. When he complied, Bart was rewarded by having cans of Hawaiian Punch poured down his throat.

In the wings stood a man with a gun. Close by, a stagehand waited with a broom and dustpan. "Is this big enough?" he said, pointing to his dustpan.

Seus laughed. "Just wait," he said. "Just wait."

Chuck Warn watched the whole thing from a safe distance, and chuckled. "A lot of special preparations," he said. "But nowhere near Streisand."

THE NEXT MORNING, Chuck Workman approached Cates at the production table. Workman had been hired to do a fast-paced montage celebrating seventy years of Academy Awards shows—"sort of an Oscars greatest hits," he said. Though Workman's montage was finished—without, he was proud to say, using Sally Field's "You really like me!" line—he came to Cates with the offer of a last-minute addition. "I can put together a new version," he said, "that would include a shot of the bear."

"How can you do that?" said Cates, intrigued.

"I can take a video-only shot of the bear holding the envelope from dress rehearsal," said Workman, "and cut into the piece. You can have both versions in the system, and then it'll be your call which one to use."

"Well, we'd use the one with the bear, of course," said Cates. "Why wouldn't we use that?"

"Maybe the bear will run amok or something."

"Oh, great," moaned Cates. "What a thing to bring up."

"I'm not saying it'll happen," insisted Workman. "I'm just trying to be prepared."

Michael Seligman laughed. "Why don't you prepare us for a plague of locusts while you're at it?" he said.

For twenty-one consecutive years, Seligman had been the moneyman for the Academy Awards. He was the guy who negotiated everybody's contracts, came up with a budget for the show, and ran interference on all matters financial.

The job could be complicated, because for years the Academy had divided the cost of producing the Oscar show with ABC. Anything that was deemed necessary to physically stage the show for a live audience was considered to be an Academy expense, while costs related to the broadcast of that show fell under ABC's purview. For instance, explained Seligman, the total cost of lighting the Oscar stage might run around $300,000. But the vast majority of those lights were needed for the TV cameras, not the audience inside the theater; if the show weren't televised, it could be lit for about $5,000. In that case, the Academy would pay $5,000 for lighting, and ABC would chip in the remaining $295,000.

The split made for some tricky financial arrangements: even some executives' salaries were paid partly by the network, partly by the Academy. (Most of the Academy money, of course, came from the fee that ABC paid to broadcast the show.) But the union crews that worked on the broadcast, from the National Association of Broadcast Employees & Technicians, were hired and paid by ABC.

In January 1998, though, that changed. Shortly after the previous year's Oscar show, the contract NABET had with the network expired, and a new pact had yet to be signed. In November 1997, New York NABET workers walked off the job for twenty-four hours, forcing the network to cancel coverage of one round of a golf tournament. The union also made threats to disrupt the coverage of football games and other sporting events.

Knowing that Oscar night could be an irresistible target for the union, the Academy decided to make its own deal with the union and produce the show itself. "ABC now gives us a package price, and we do everything ourselves," said Seligman. "We use the same union people we always used, but we've made our own deals with them. And even though it's all the Academy's money, we still separate what would be Academy expenses and what would be ABC, in case anything ever changes."

AS A GROUP OF DANCERS stretched on the stage of the Shrine, Danette Herman came up to Cates in the aisle, a grim frown on her face. She leaned toward Cates and spoke to him softly and quickly. "Shit," said Cates. "Fuck," he added.

Cates sat down at the production table next to his wife, Judith Reichman. "We just lost Juliette Binoche," he said of the previous year's best supporting actress winner, who was slated to present the award for supporting actor. "She broke her foot doing a play in London."

While Herman tried to wrangle a replacement, Cates turned his attention back to the stage. There, the forty-one-year-old, Los Angeles–born dancer and choreographer Daniel Ezralow was readying his troupe for a segment that appeared every few years on the Academy Awards: a dance number performed to the music of the nominated film scores.

With Debbie Allen otherwise engaged, Cates had turned to the younger choreographer, who had performed with the modern dance companies Momix, Pilobolus, and one he cofounded, ISO Dance. He'd also choreographed music videos and worked on a handful of movies and TV shows.

With a mop of curly hair and a taut dancer's body, Ezralow found a few admirers in the Oscar audience. One was Judith Reichman, who smiled as she watched Ezralow take his dancers through their paces. "He's a dancer, he's talented, and he's Jewish," said Reichman, laughing. "If I were younger and not married, he'd be my ideal man!"

Reichman was best known as a physician, a gynecologist to the stars, an author, and an expert on women's health issues for the *Today* show. But she had a dance background, and often stopped by Oscar rehearsals to see the dance numbers take shape. She watched eagerly as Ezralow worked with his dancers on a mostly lighthearted routine set to music from the nominated comedy or musical scores: *The Full Monty*, *As Good as It Gets*, *My Best Friend's Wedding*, *Anastasia*, and *Men in Black*. In most cases, he tried to play off the movie itself: there was a mock love triangle to go with the *Wedding* music, a line of gyrating men for *Monty*, and a row of black suits and shades for *Men in Black*.

This last segment featured a series of synchronized, high-stepping moves done by five men joined to each other by thick black bands linking their ankles. As she watched, Reichman shook her head. "That doesn't look right," she said. "They should lose the straps around their ankles."

During a break, she walked over to assistant choreographer Susan Lonergan and told her as much. "I agree," said Lonergan. "Why don't you see if Gil will talk to Daniel about it?"

Reichman did so, and Cates went onstage to speak with Ezralow. A minute later, he returned to the production table. "They're going to try it without the bands," he said. During the next rehearsal, the men in black danced unfettered. Everyone agreed it looked better.

Dr. Reichman beamed. "The power of the bed," she said.

DIANNE WIEST had just walked in the back door of the Shrine when she found that her way was blocked by a man in chinos, a white T-shirt, and a blazer. He quickly dropped to his knees, bowed in front of her, and kissed her hand. Wiest grinned as she looked down at Warren Beatty. "Are you the welcoming committee?" she said.

In a way, he was. Beatty was at the Shrine to rehearse handing out the best-director award, but he'd stuck around for the POWs. The acronym stood for "past Oscar winners," and there were almost six dozen of them, recipients of acting Oscars who'd been summoned to help celebrate the show's seventieth birthday.

At first, the plan had been vague. "We wanted to do something to mark the seventieth, and we had this idea of inviting back past winners," said Herman. "We knew it was a little early, that we should wait for the seventy-fifth to do it. But I also thought we should do it while those people were still around, because you never know how long we'll have them." Cates lobbied to include directors, but in the end it seemed cleaner and easier to restrict it to those who'd won acting awards, and actors who'd been given honorary

Oscars. (If directors had made the cut, Beatty would have been included alongside Dianne Wiest: though he'd been nominated for four acting awards, he'd won his only Oscar for directing *Reds*.)

As RSVPs came in, the number of past winners fluctuated. It got to seventy, the number Herman "thought would be cool," then as high as seventy-eight. "It was up and down," she said. "It was seventy-two, it was sixty-eight, it was sixty-nine. And I was thinking, there's no way I'm going to have sixty-nine. It's *got* to be seventy." As the stars showed up for rehearsal two days before the show, the number stood at seventy-one.

Mindful of the insulting way that screen legends had been plopped into the production number that opened Allan Carr's Oscar show, or left to mingle aimlessly onstage at the beginning of the fiftieth-anniversary show in 1978, Cates and Herman had promised the winners individual introductions. But there was no way to move them on and off stage quickly and with dignity. The solution was to reveal them all sitting onstage together, then pan across the group while introducing the POWs one at a time.

To do that, a four-level riser was erected on the stage, with seventeen or eighteen chairs on each of the four tiers. The camera would pan down each row, introducing the past winners in alphabetical order while superimposed film clips showed their Oscar-winning performances. Not only would the stars, many of them elderly, have to get up the stairs and into their places quickly, but if they weren't in exactly the right order, the film clips wouldn't match.

Not all the POWs could make it to rehearsal, so stage manager Debbie Williams rounded up stand-ins and assigned them to play the part of those missing in action. "He's too tall to be Dustin Hoffman," she said, appraising one stand-in. "He can be Charlton Heston."

The Irish actress Brenda Fricker, wearing jeans and a sweatshirt, was one of the first to come through a metal detector at the end of a small red carpet behind the artists' entrance. She was followed, in short order, by Celeste Holm, then Susan Sarandon, Joel Grey, Ernest Borgnine, Rod Steiger, Karl Malden, Ben Kingsley, Rita Moreno, and Martin Landau. Anna Paquin, who won for her first movie, *The Piano*, at age eleven, signed in just as a car pulled up bearing Kirk Douglas, who after more than seventy movies finally won an honorary award when he was seventy-nine. Marlee Matlin (*Children of a Lesser God*) and Angelica Huston (*Prizzi's Honor*) both set off the metal detector, but nobody stopped them. Gregory Peck and his wife walked by, each carrying a black bag containing a small Pekingese dog.

After signing in, the stars were greeted by Herman, then led to what had been dubbed the POW Room, a large space enclosed by curtains and containing a few couches, lots of director's chairs, television monitors, and a huge sign that read WELCOME BACK OSCAR WINNERS. Borgnine walked into the room, took one look at the assembled star power, and exclaimed, "Oh, my God!"

In the POW Room, many of the stars gathered around eighty-nine-year-old Luise Rainer, who won in 1936 and 1937 for *The Great Ziegfeld* and *The Good Earth* and then left Hollywood, disappointed by the lack of opportunities she was given. Elsewhere, Red Buttons chatted amiably with Peck and Landau, and Jon Voight spent his time talking to a stand-in who wore a sign around his neck reading DENZEL WASHINGTON. Susan Sarandon grabbed Voight. "Have you spoken to Wayne Wang?" said Sarandon, who was about to begin shooting the film *Anywhere But Here* with the Hong Kong–born director of *The Joy Luck Club*. "Because he mentioned you to me as a possibility."

Debbie Williams, who was in charge of making sure the segment came off cleanly, led the stars to the stage, explaining that on Oscar night they'd need to form four alphabetical lines. For the first rehearsal, though, they simply milled about on the stage, then took their seats in the risers as Williams called their names.

As the stars sat in their assigned places, new conversations started up. Holly Hunter leaned across Patricia Neal and Jack Nicholson to greet her *Piano* costar Paquin, while a pair of African American juniors, Cuba Gooding, Jr., and Louis Gossett, Jr., laughed together. Marlee Matlin had an enthusiastic conversation with Karl Malden, aided by a sign-language interpreter who stood nearby, signing Malden's words to the hearing-impaired actress.

To move down any aisle of chairs was to get a jumbled, chaotic overview of film history. There was the workaholic British actor Michael Caine sitting next to George Chakiris, who was younger than Caine but had rarely been seen on screen since winning for *West Side Story* in 1961 . . . then Cher, the flamboyant singer who had to struggle to be taken seriously as an actress . . . then Julie Christie, the stunning British actress whose career, and her devotion to the movie business, seemed to fade after she made her mark in the sixties and early seventies . . . then the indefatigable Scotsman Sean Connery, equally well known as the original James Bond and as a tireless worker who was known to make his share of foolish choices . . . then the former model Geena Davis, a surprise best supporting actress winner in 1988 for *The Accidental Tourist* . . . then Robert DeNiro, about whom the only surprise was why he'd won just two Oscars after thirty years of startling performances.

You could quibble with some of Oscar's choices, and with many of those who'd been ignored. But on Saturday afternoon at the Shrine, the parade of legendary faces was too impressive a lesson in cinema history for anyone to worry about who did or didn't deserve to be included. "I'm trembling," said Roy Christopher as he and other crew members stood by and watched. Though the warm interaction between the past winners was thrilling to many of the staffers on hand, Cates had nixed the idea of having a documentary crew film the historic gathering, feeling that cameras would interfere with the winners' enjoyment of the experience.

Once everyone was seated, Cates picked up a microphone. "Ladies and gentlemen," he said, "I just want to say you're a splendid-looking group." After Cates and Herman thanked them for coming, Horvitz ran through the segment once, showing film clips as the camera panned from one star to the next. "I hope that when people see this on TV," said Christopher as he watched the dry, straightforward run-through, "they get some sense of the joy and the camaraderie we're seeing here."

Afterward, the departing POWs were given Oscar sweatshirts and hats as they left the Shrine. Jack Palance, though, didn't notice the freebie table; instead, he headed straight out the back door. Faye Dunaway noticed, and chased him down. "Did you get a gift, Jack?" she asked.

"No," he said.

"Come with me." She grabbed him by the hand and led him back to the POW Room for his loot.

As the stars departed, Michael Caine, Ben Kingsley, and Martin Landau stood outside the room, saying good-bye to everyone. Louise Fletcher walked out, shaking her head. "They must have started to do this a *long* time ago, to pull all of this together," she said.

Joel Grey complimented Williams on how well organized it was. "The night of the show," he said, "do you want my help?"

ELLIOTT SMITH could be forgiven for wondering how he got himself into this mess. A slight, dour-looking man clad in jeans and yellow T-shirt, with a wool cap pulled down low over his mop of lank brown hair, Smith was a reluctant émigré from the world of alternative rock music. He was far more comfortable on the stages of small rock clubs than swankier joints like the Shrine.

But in addition to being one of the more acclaimed of the morosely talented singer-songwriters on the ferociously hip Portland, Oregon–based independent label Kill Rock Stars, Smith was also an Academy Award nominee. Director Gus Van Sant, who came from the ranks of independent film, had seen Smith perform in Portland coffeehouses and drafted him to add several songs to the soundtrack of *Good Will Hunting*. When that movie became a hit, it gave the soundtrack enough visibility that "Miss Misery," which Smith had written specifically for the film, won a nomination.

A mournful little ditty that captured some of the self-destructive bent of the character played in the film by Matt Damon—its opening line was "I'll fake it through the day / With some help from Johnny Walker Red"—"Miss Misery" was the most unexpected of the five nominated songs, and Smith was clearly the odd man out among a lineup of musical performers that included Céline Dion, Michael Bolton, Trisha Yearwood, and Aaliyah.

Dion was a French Canadian pop diva known for thumping her chest and engaging in elaborate emotional histrionics, Bolton a gut-busting former (and failed) rock 'n' roller who took his extravagant ballads to gravel-voiced extremes. Yearwood, generally more tasteful than those two, was a country singer with a powerful voice, while Aaliyah was a young soul diva about to launch an acting career.

For the most part, their songs were big, dramatic, and more than a little overblown: Aaliyah's pop-soul manifesto "Journey to the Past," Bolton's bombastic "Go the Distance," Yearwood's power ballad "How Can I Live," and, of course, Dion's "My Heart Will Go On," a monster hit from the *Titanic* soundtrack. Against those other songs, Smith's spare, melancholy "Miss Misery" sounded downright malnourished—not a bad thing for fans of intelligent, understated pop music, but not exactly the way to hold your own sandwiched between Yearwood and Dion. And sandwiched between those two women was exactly where Smith was: to save a little time, Cates had decided to put the five songs into two medleys. (Initially, a plan had been floated to cut all the nominated songs except for "My Heart Will Go On" down to ninety seconds, but the idea didn't get far; even though the Dion song was by far the biggest hit and an almost certain winner, that kind of favoritism wouldn't fly on the Oscars.)

When Smith shuffled into the Shrine for rehearsal, stagehands directed him to a spot near the rear of the stage, just in front of the orchestra riser. Smith strummed his acoustic guitar, sang a few tentative lines, and frowned his way through a take, plainly irritated. When the song ended, he walked to the front of the stage, sat down on the steps that led to the audience, and played the song again. Then he stood up and walked to the microphone.

"I can't do it back there," he said, an edge of quiet anger in his voice. "Because the monitors are, like, forty feet away from where I'm sitting, and I can't sing like that." He pointed to the front of the stage. "What I want to do is sit in a chair right here. 'Cause that's what I do. But for some reason, I can't."

Rehearsal ground to a halt, as Cates, Horvitz, and Christopher discussed a move. The singer stood a few feet away from them, alone, his head down, a hand in his pocket. Within a few minutes, a stagehand brought out a stool, and set it near the front of the stage. Smith sang a few lines from his new location, then stopped. "It's woofy and weird," he said of the sound mix. "I can't sing on key up here if I can't hear the note I'm singing. I just need to hear myself better."

The sound mix was adjusted, and Smith tried again. "Is that better?" asked a stage manager.

"Yeah, I guess," he said, still frowning. "There's no way we could just get one monitor right here, is there?" He pointed to the floor directly in front of him.

Christopher shook his head, knowing that a clunky black monitor sitting center stage would look terrible with the clean lines of the set. Less than five minutes later, though, a soundman came out with a monitor, and stuck it at Smith's feet. The singer ran through his song one more time. He still sounded miserable—but this time it had to do with the song, not the setting.

In the audience, Michael Davies, ABC's new executive vice president of alternative series and specials, watched the rehearsal from a seat near Cates. At one point, the producer leafed through the show rundowns in front of him. Knowing that there was no way to prevent it from being a very long telecast, Cates turned to Davies. "Are you comfortable with a three-and-a-half-hour show?" he asked.

Davies laughed. One of the open secrets about the Academy Awards was that the network didn't really mind if the show ran overtime. Certainly, it wasn't ideal to go well past midnight and risk losing a chunk of the East Coast audience; the final rating established for the show was an average of the ratings for each half hour, so a drop in viewership could drag it down overall. Still, even if the Oscars lost viewers when it passed three hours, the broadcast drew significantly higher ratings than whatever else ABC might be airing. And the show delivered such a large audience, in such a desirable demographic, that ratings points had relatively little effect on ad rates.

"Gil," said Davies, "I'd be happy if the show lasted for a month."

TITANIC may have turned Leonardo DiCaprio into Hollywood's reigning heartthrob, at least among teenage girls whose repeated viewings of the movie were helping fuel the record grosses. But the Academy didn't entirely cooperate with DiCaprio's coronation as the man of the hour. Although he'd been nominated for best supporting actor for *What's Eating Gilbert Grape* in 1994, before his twentieth birthday, DiCaprio was passed over for *Titanic*, though his leading lady, Kate Winslet, and costar Gloria Stuart were nominated. He'd also turned down an invitation to appear on the show, but word of that apparently hadn't reached the throngs of young women who filled the bleachers in front of the Shrine, many of them toting homemade signs that sang his praises.

With DiCaprio out, the show's staff had to turn elsewhere for participants who might appeal to the marginally postpubescent set. That they succeeded was clear on Sunday afternoon, when the crush of youngsters around the artists' entrance reached epic proportions just as Ben Affleck and Matt Damon were arriving.

Affleck and Damon, twenty-six and twenty-eight, respectively, were childhood friends from Boston. Struggling actors until *Good Will Hunting* put them on the map and won them Oscar nominations for their original screenplay, the two arrived at the Shrine together, an hour earlier than their call time. They were accompanied by Affleck's mother, Chris, who asked if she could take a few photos inside the Shrine. Publicist Eva Demirjian ran the request by the longtime Oscar security chief, Jerry Moon, who agreed to rescind the ban on cameras just for Mrs. Affleck.

After they'd rehearsed, the two actors walked out the rear artists' entrance. A handful of teenagers, most of them the children of show staffers, worked the sign-in table there, handing out hats and sweatshirts along with the elaborate Oscar gift baskets. For the most part, the kids politely took turns dispensing the swag, but every year there were a few exceptions. When everybody wanted to do the honors, when the usually retiring volunteers fought over who got to hand over the sweatshirt and hat, you knew that the Oscars had booked somebody hot.

In 1998, the clear favorites were Damon and Affleck. Rather than pushing through the crowd and heading for their car, though, the two happily worked the room. They stood by the sign-in table for a good twenty minutes, chatting with the kids and posing for photos. At one point, Danny Shapiro, the eleven-year-old son of Robert Z. Shapiro, whispered to Affleck, "Kick *Titanic*'s ass."

Affleck broke into a huge grin and gave Shapiro a hug. "You're gonna go far in this life, kid," he said. "You speak your mind."

When they finally headed for their car, Affleck and Damon ran into Bruce Vilanch. "It's just gonna be all *Titanic* jokes, isn't it?" Affleck asked.

"No," Vilanch insisted. "We're egalitarian."

Watching Affleck and Damon charm the crowd, one veteran staffer smiled. "Everybody's so on their best behavior when they first come here," she said. "I call it the three-year plan. The first time they're nominated and they come here, they're totally nice, just taking it all in. But it only takes them three years to come back and be an entirely different human being. That's when you look at them and think, Oh, my God."

As Affleck and Damon chatted with Vilanch, a pair of pages stood by with two gargantuan gift baskets. An Oscar tradition for several years, the baskets had been steadily growing in both size and value. "Originally, we did it because we'd been having trouble getting the younger stars to show up," said Seligman. "So I said, 'Let's give them something. Let's create a little gift basket.' I called some people around town, and suddenly *everybody* wanted to be in the basket."

Perfumes, jewelry, and electronic devices were mainstays in the basket in early years; over time, the value increased dramatically as the baskets grew to include spa memberships, restaurant vouchers, hotel stays (airfare usually not included), United Airlines upgrades, and the free use of luxury automobiles. By 1998, the value was nearing $20,000, and the Academy was beginning to get a little nervous about the attention the baskets garnered. "What they don't tell you is that all the gift certificates have deadlines," laughed one Oscar participant who had received several of them. "To use everything in that basket, you'd have to make it your full-time job."

"LADIES AND GENTLEMEN," announced stage manager Garry Hood from the stage of the Shrine, "we need to clear the house for the next twenty minutes. There are no exceptions. We need to clear it for twenty minutes, and then we'll let you all back in."

With dress rehearsal about to begin, Hood's entreaties meant one thing: as usual, Billy Crystal wanted to keep secret his entrance, his opening film, his monologue, and his medley. So even though Crystal wasn't even going to show his real film, even though he wasn't going to be using many of the real jokes in his monologue, and even though he'd rehearsed his entrance and his medley two days earlier without clearing the house, Hood stood firm. "Guests, stand-ins, anybody who is not *working* personnel, we need to clear you," he said. "Security, please help me with this. Make sure everybody is out, and close the front entrances, side entrances, balcony entrances, outhouse entrances . . ."

At the artists' entrance to the Shrine, one guard took his new responsibilities a little too seriously. "Wait a minute, he doesn't have a pass," he barked, stopping stage manager Rita Cossette as she walked through the door with a companion. Cossette looked at the guard incredulously. "He's okay," she said, pointing to Billy Crystal, whom she was escorting to the stage.

The dress rehearsal began in front of a near-empty house that included Academy president Robert Rehme and director/choreographer Stanley Donen, who was to receive an honorary Oscar. Crystal ran through his song twice, then walked to the podium. "I will do the rest of the rehearsal as Jerry Weintraub," he said, switching into the croaky, gravelly voice of the longtime producer and manager. "Okay, to throw out the first fuckin' Oscar is a guy . . ."

The only star presenter required for this run-through was Mike Myers, who had the tricky task of working with Bart the bear. Myers and his wife arrived in a white stretch limo, inexplicably sent by the company hired to provide less ostentatious town cars for the presenters. "We went to the prom first," Myers jokingly said to Herman after he got out of the car. "We opened up the top and stuck our heads out all the way down Sunset."

When Myers walked to the stage, Herman immediately got on her walkie-talkie. "Get in touch with the limo company," she said, "and tell them that white stretch limos are *not* acceptable."

Myers got through his routine with the bear without incident. As planned, the curtains opened to reveal the bear sitting up and holding the envelope, with his trainer just out of sight in the wings. Myers went over to the edge of the electrified fence, gingerly took the envelope from Bart, and then returned to his podium to read it. Chuck Workman got a shot to quickly edit into his montage.

During the next commercial break, Myers came into the audience. "Mike!" yelled Cates. "Great job!"

"Thanks," said Myers. "I was good, if I can admit it myself."

"It was great," agreed Cates. "The only thing is that the trainer will not be there tomorrow."

"Are you serious?" said Myers slowly, looking as if he might believe the producer. Then he broke into a grin as Cates laughed. "Now I need to change my pants," Myers said. "You'll get my dry-cleaning bill."

Myers grinned. "No, he's a sweet bear," he said. "A sweet puppy."

"Actually," said Seligman, "he *eats* puppies."

Myers walked a couple of rows away and talked to friends. "I admit, I'm nervous," he told them. "Don't think I haven't figured out an escape route: down the steps, past Brenda Fricker . . ."

After the break, Crystal returned to the podium. "The answer is, a bear doesn't shit in the woods," he said. "He does it in the green room."

The rehearsal finally ended about 11:30 p.m. At midnight, ABC's Susan Futterman informed Seligman that one of Julianne Moore's nipples was visible through her sheer blouse in a film clip from the movie *Boogie Nights*. "Who the fuck cares?" he replied. "*Billy's* nipples are bigger than hers." Futterman didn't buy the logic. Edits were ordered.

FOUR PARALLEL ROWS OF TAPE ran along the floor outside the POW Room. At the end of each row was the name of the Oscar winner who'd be leading a line of stars onto the stage: Robert Duvall, Shirley Jones, Joe Pesci, and Teresa Wright. "When we get to that part of the show, I'll have six minutes to get them from here onto the stage and into their seats before the curtain opens," said Debbie Williams. "I think it took about seven minutes at rehearsal on Saturday, and then I was able to spread them out over the whole stage. It's going to be *very* tight."

Outside, on the red carpet, a huge bottleneck developed as guests tried to make their way through six metal detectors, three for stars who'd be working the press line and three for regular guests who'd be bypassing the press. Sean Connery and Neve Campbell took the latter route.

Backstage, Jon Voight sat by himself in the POW Room, studying the script to *Varsity Blues*, a high school drama he was about to start shooting. "They gave me two tickets, but I'd really rather use the time to go over this script," he said. "Do you know anybody who needs seats up front?" Just before the show began, two seat-fillers slipped into Voight's seats, and got to stay in them all night long.

With thirty seconds to show time, actor Robert Forster, a supporting-actor nominee for the Quentin Tarantino movie *Jackie Brown*, came into the auditorium. An usher told him he'd have to wait until the first commercial break, some twenty-three minutes away, before taking his seat. "I'm a nominee," he said, "and I'm in the first row." The usher let him in just as the orchestra began to play a new fanfare composed specially for the Oscars by Jerry Goldsmith.

6:00 P.M., PACIFIC DAYLIGHT TIME: *"Live from Los Angeles, California, the 70th anniversary Academy Awards."*

Backstage, Billy Crystal moved into position as a large movie screen descended from the rafters. As he stepped onto the platform of the hydraulic lift, Crystal's opening movie began to play. As it had the previous year, his entrance film used newly shot footage to integrate Crystal into scenes from many of the year's biggest movies, beginning and ending with *Titanic*. At the end of the clip, Crystal was dangling from the prow of James Cameron's ship as it began to sink. "I can't imagine a worse disaster!" he cried.

"Oh yeah?" shouted Kevin Costner, the star and director of the year's most notable flop, *The Postman*. "Well, *I* can!" As the audience roared at the sight of Costner engaging in the same kind of self-mockery that David Letterman had done the previous year, the hydraulic lift began to rise. As it went up, Crystal grabbed the railing and gripped it tightly.

A few jokes and five quick songs later, Crystal turned the stage over to the preceding year's hyperkinetic winner for best supporting actor, Cuba Gooding, Jr. Gooding read his lines, then tossed in an ad-lib. "One quick word of advice," he shouted. "The lady that graces this stage this evening, while you're giving your acceptance speech, take your time! Don't listen to the music! Do your *thing*, please!" An astonished Kim Basinger won, thanked "everybody I've ever met in my entire life," and wrapped up her speech in an un-Cuba-like fifty-six seconds, only eleven over the allotted limit.

Backstage, Basinger spotted Danette Herman. "I can't believe it, I can't believe it, I don't believe it!" she screamed. Herman screamed, too. Basinger turned the corner by the green room, saw Cates, screamed again, and hugged him. "I can't believe it, I'm still staring at it," she said, holding the Oscar. "Oh, my God. Oh, my God."

Gooding joined Basinger at Cates's side. "Thank you," Cates said, giving Gooding a hug. "But I didn't like that advice you gave."

"Sorry," said Gooding, who didn't appear to be.

Half an hour into the show, a visibly nervous Neve Campbell introduced Aaliyah and Michael Bolton to perform the first of the song medleys. As Aaliyah sang, the bear's trailer was slowly backed into the wings of the stage. The armed guard watched. When Aaliyah finished her song, she stood in the wings and watched Bolton on a monitor, unaware that Bart, still in his trailer, was about three feet away from her.

Bart's preparations were proceeding slowly—the fence erected and electrified, the door to his cage unlatched—while Mira Sorvino announced the winner for best supporting actor: Robin Williams for *Good Will Hunting*. In the audience there was an immediate scream, and a standing ovation. "Oh man," Williams said. "This might be the one time I'm speechless." Behind him, obscured by a curtain, Doug Seus led Bart out of his cage and onto the stage.

As the curtain opened to reveal the bear, Bart dropped the envelope. Seus darted into the enclosure, picked up the envelope, and handed it back to Bart in time for Mike Myers to take it from his fourteen-hundred-pound copresenter. As Myers walked back to the podium, the curtain closed and Bart was quickly led to his trailer. "Good boy, good boy, good boy," said Seus. By the time the sound effects technicians for *Titanic* finished their acceptance speech, Bart was in the parking lot of the Shrine; by the time the next commercial break ended, Seus was at the wardrobe room below the stage, turning in his tux and following Bart out the door.

"We had a little problem backstage," Crystal said as the broadcast resumed. "You know that old joke: does a bear —— in the woods?" He shook his head. "In the green room."

In the wings of the stage, Affleck and Damon awaited their cue. Dency Nelson, who was responsible for getting them into position, approached the pair singing Crystal's parody song, "Matt and Ben." They laughed. "Wonderful," said Affleck.

"Okay, guys, follow me," said Nelson. Affleck reached into his pocket, pulled out a set of car keys, and dropped them on the director's chair behind him. "You watch these?" he said to a guard, adding, "The car is not that nice, and the phone, you gotta punch a code in." As the pair took the stage, Robin Williams rushed back into the wings after his run through the press rooms. He waited for Damon and Affleck to come offstage, then gave long, fervent hugs to the men who wrote his Oscar-winning part. A few minutes later, Helen Hunt won the Oscar for best actress. The giddy Williams stayed in the wings, waited for her, and gave her a big hug, too. "Now I can go back to comedy," he said.

A few feet away, in a curtained-off hallway just outside the green room, Sharon Stone stood in front of one of a pair of makeup tables. A makeup artist retouched Stone's face, while a second staffer adjusted the wrap-around Vera Wang skirt that Stone had paired with one of her husband's white dress shirts. At the table next to her, Ashley Judd touched up her own makeup. Nobody bothered to inspect Judd's off-white Richard Tyler dress, which was slit to the top of her thigh. But when Judd walked across the stage a few minutes later, she immediately ignited a debate about what she was wearing beneath that skirt. (The consensus: nothing.)

At the show's two-hour mark, Madonna came into the wings and settled into a director's chair to await her turn onstage. A makeup artist touched her up while she watched on a monitor as director Stanley Donen received an honorary Oscar and incorporated a delightful song and dance into his acceptance speech. Watching the seventy-three-year-old Donen effortlessly serenade his statuette with "Cheek to Cheek," Madonna laughed and broke into applause. Behind the Shrine, *My Cousin Vinny* stars Marisa Tomei and Joe Pesci chatted while Pesci smoked a cigar.

During the commercial break after "My Heart Will Go On" won the Oscar for best song, dozens of pages swept through the hall, pulling past Oscar winners out of their seats and leading them to the POW Room. There, a large crowd gathered around a TV monitor as Robin Williams introduced Workman's film of highlights from past Oscar shows. Robert DeNiro got up, walked over to a monitor, and turned up the volume. Tomei, Pesci, Voight, and Landau watched with him.

A few minutes later, Frances McDormand read the nominees for best actor, and clips from each of the nominated performances were shown. When a scene of Dustin Hoffman's work in *Wag the Dog* included a quick shot of DeNiro, Rita Moreno spoke up. "Didn't you just *love* DeNiro in that?" she said to the group of POWs around her. A couple of feet in front of her, DeNiro turned around and smiled. "Oh," she said, laughing, "I didn't know it was *you!*"

Jack Nicholson won the award, completing a sweep for the lead actors in *As Good as It Gets*. After rambling for about a minute, Nicholson looked into the orchestra pit at Bill Conti. "I know Gil Cates is starting to sweat back there now, isn't he, Bill?" he said. When Nicholson finished, Horvitz cut to a shot of Judith Reichman applauding.

L.A. Confidential and *Good Will Hunting* picked up the screenplay awards, with the latter win confirming a trend that had also seen Emma Thompson (*Sense and Sensibility*) and Billy Bob Thornton (*Sling Blade*) winning in recent years. When actors wrote their own screenplays, they often won Academy Awards, no doubt courtesy of support from the large actors' branch.

In the POW Room backstage, Debbie Williams got on a microphone and directed the stars out the door and into four lines. "Mr. Robert Duvall," she said. "Mr. Duvall. Miss Faye Dunaway. Miss Faye Dunaway is after Robert Duvall. Richard Dreyfuss is after Faye Dunaway . . . Mr. DeNiro, are you coming? Okay, I hear you . . ." Obedient and orderly, the celebrities formed lines. There were exactly seventy of them, Dianne Wiest having failed to make it because of a limo mix-up. Slowly, keeping the lines together, they walked around the corner and toward the stage. Instantly, stagehands started dismantling the POW Room to make more room for the Governors Ball.

Onstage, Denzel Washington handed out yet another Oscar to *Titanic*. While cinematographer Russell Carpenter spoke, the POWs began filing into their chairs. A large curtain behind Carpenter remained closed. Williams tried to direct traffic and keep things moving without her voice carrying beyond the curtain.

Three of the night's four new Oscar winners in the acting categories— Kim Basinger, Robin Williams, and Helen Hunt—were led into the wings; the fourth, Jack Nicholson, was already part of the segment as a previous winner.

With some of the past winners still finding their seats, Susan Sarandon took the stage. She spoke very slowly and deliberately. "In celebration of this year's anniversary, the Academy invited all those who have been honored with leading, supporting, honorary, or juvenile awards for acting over the three score and ten years of Academy history," she said, pausing frequently. "And I think they're still getting in their places." She took a breath. "Ladies and gentlemen"—a pause—"Oscar's"—she brought up both hands, her fingers crossed—"family album."

The curtain opened, and the POWs appeared on-screen—all in place, in the right seats. In the wings, Williams yelled "Yaaaay!" In the seats, a camera caught Alec Baldwin mouthing "My God" as he looked at the array of winners. For the next fifteen minutes, announcer Norman Rose read the names of the seventy winners, as the camera panned from one to another. At the end, the night's newest winners were introduced.

Afterward, twenty-six pages descended upon the wings, each assigned to lead two or three POWs back to their seats. Robin Williams was a priority, because the next award was for best director—and in the unlikely event that *Good Will Hunting* director Gus Van Sant won, Horvitz wanted a reaction shot of Williams.

In the wings on the side of the stage, seven Oscars remained on a double-decker cart that had carried more than four dozen statuettes three hours earlier. With only two awards left, and none of the best-picture nominees sporting more than two producers, a maximum of three statuettes would be needed. A guard collected four of the Oscars and took them away.

To the surprise of no one, James Cameron won for best director, the tenth *Titanic* win of the night. "I don't know about you," he said, "but I'm having a really good time." He thanked his fellow producers, his family, his parents. "There is no way to express to you how I feel right now," he said. "My heart is bursting. Except to say—I'm the *king of the world*!" After this quote from his own movie, he whooped, threw his arm in the air, and walked off the stage. From the wings he was taken straight back down the steps and to his seat, to await the final category.

He didn't stay there for long. Opening the envelope containing the name of the best-picture winner, Sean Connery feigned a double take, then read the name: "*Titanic*." Producer Jon Landau spoke first, reading four dozen names in a rapid-fire minute and a half. Then Cameron took over for another two minutes, including a moment of silence for those who died on the *Titanic*. "Thank you very much," he said after sixteen quiet seconds had passed. "That's about as much as I'm sure Gil Cates can stand. All right, you really made this a night to remember in every way. Now let's go party till dawn!"

Backstage, Cameron headed not for the party, but for the press tent. "It's been a great night, we're all tired," said Crystal. "Matt Damon just hit on Shirley Temple. Good night everybody, see you next year."

It ended at 9:45, the longest Oscar show in history. Among the production staff, the consensus was that despite the length, the show was exhilarating—and regardless, everybody involved knew it was going to be long.

Guests moved on to the Governors Ball or to other parties, or simply headed out front to pick up their cars. Limo drivers returned to their vehicles and awaited orders. On the first floor of a parking structure adjacent to the Shrine Exhibition Hall, the tables where the drivers had been fed during the show were deserted. The catering crew had moved on as well, but they'd left behind an enormous pile of ice, slowly melting into the gutter outside the theater. For those who didn't mind stretching for cheap metaphors, the message was clear: this time, the boat won and the ice didn't stand a chance.

THE LESSON TAUGHT by the Academy Awards show in 1997—that the show's ratings were determined to a large degree by public interest in the competing movies—was reinforced in 1998. Despite the fact that the show contained little suspense and was of record length, it drew its biggest ratings in thirteen years, and its largest American audience ever at eighty-seven million viewers.

Though it hardly needed the extra publicity it picked up by winning eleven awards—which put it in a tie with *Ben-Hur* for the most Oscar wins ever—*Titanic* kept on rolling at the box office. It passed the $500 million mark the week of the Oscars, and by the end of the summer it had topped $600 million, making it the top-grossing movie in history. Worldwide, it topped the $1 billion mark.

After the Oscars, *Titanic* added one more week to its record-setting dominance of the box-office charts. The first weekend in April, however, its fifteen-week run at the top was finally ended by the big-screen version of the 1960s television series *Lost in Space*; although the movie was almost universally panned, it had a $20 million opening weekend that knocked *Titanic* out of the number-one spot.

Later that month, the Motion Picture Association of America's anti-piracy unit said that tapes of *Titanic* sent to Academy members had been used as the source for pirated copies of the movie, which had become a hot seller on the black market.

The film's reputation began to sink soon after the Oscars, helped along by viewers who found Cameron's acceptance-speech grandstanding to be more than a touch egomaniacal. In 2003, viewers of a BBC television show in England would vote it the worst movie of all time.

On the heels of the blockbuster ratings, the Academy had significant leverage when it opened negotiations for a new television contract. Rather than simply re-signing with ABC, the organization entertained proposals from other channels, including an extraordinarily lucrative offer to move the show to a cable outlet. It would have meant more money but a smaller audience, so the board voted to stick with the alphabet network.

In an attempt to keep viewership high in subsequent years, the Academy decided to move upcoming Oscar shows to Sunday, the one day on which the show had never taken place. (Monday and Thursday were the most popular.) In the past, the Academy had stayed away from Sunday because of a deal made in the 1950s to placate movie theater owners who were worried that a televised Oscar show might hurt theater attendance. But nearly half a century later, given the unrivaled power of television to hype movies, an agreement to avoid weekend Oscar shows no longer made much sense.

The move also enabled the network to start the show half an hour earlier, at five-thirty instead of six. Not only would West Coast viewers not be racing home from work to catch the show, but also those on the East Coast stood a better chance of seeing the best-picture winner before midnight.

During the summer, the Academy's longtime accounting firm, Price Waterhouse, merged with another company, Coopers & Lybrand, and the company name was changed to PricewaterhouseCoopers.

When Emmy nominations were announced during the summer, the Oscar show picked up eight. Most years, the Oscars would receive seven, eight, or nine nominations, and then win a single award. This time, though, it won in five of the eight categories, including direction, lighting direction, music direction, sound mixing, and performance (for Billy Crystal). No Oscar show had ever before won more than three.

A few days after the seventieth show, the Academy formally agreed to use the proposed theater in the Hollywood & Highland complex for upcoming Oscar shows. The organization signed a twenty-year lease with TrizecHahn, though the contract also included escape clauses that could be invoked after ten years. In October, TrizecHahn held a groundbreaking ceremony at the site. Quincy Jones hosted the event, and announced that the complex would include Q's Jook Joint, a restaurant and nightclub. TrizecHahn said that the first Oscar show would take place in the new venue in March 2001, and that the entrance to the theater would be dramatic. "It won't be a mall," developer David Malmuth told *Daily Variety*. "The Academy said, 'We don't want to be part of a mall.' "

6

≡

Sunday Bloody Sunday

The 71st Academy Awards

AS ONE OF THE BIGGEST MOVIE THEATERS in Los Angeles, the 1,012-seat Samuel Goldwyn Theater was normally filled only for premieres or the hottest screenings, and rarely before sunset. But in the chilly predawn hours one morning a year, all that changed—which is why, at 5 a.m. on Tuesday, February 9, 1999, the theater inside the Academy's Beverly Hills headquarters was jammed with folks who would not normally be up at such an ungodly hour. Nominations for the 71st Academy Awards were being announced at precisely 5:38 and thirty seconds, so the Goldwyn teemed with cameras, cameramen, reporters, publicists, studio executives, Academy staffers, and the assorted flotsam and jetsam of the movie industry.

Louis Horvitz was directing the brief but momentous telecast. He sat in front of three monitors as he waited for the clock to count down to the moment when Academy president Bob Rehme and Oscar-winning actor Kevin Spacey would read the nominations. In the audience, more than 550 reporters readied their cameras and their notebooks. Throughout the hall, television reporters had final touchups done to their makeup.

Sunday Bloody Sunday

Near the back of the theater, producer Gil Cates took in the entire pageant. Cates had already been working on the show for a couple of months, enlisting Whoopi Goldberg to return as host, hiring the key staff members, commissioning packages of film clips. As the clock edged past 5:30, he was one of the handful of people in the room who knew what Pricewaterhouse-Coopers executives had divulged to top Academy staffers several hours earlier: that *Shakespeare in Love* and *Saving Private Ryan* would lead the pack with thirteen and eleven nominations, respectively, and that the acting field would include stars like Tom Hanks and Meryl Streep alongside the lesser-known likes of Ian McKellen, Cate Blanchett, and Fernanda Montenegro. Waiting for everyone else to hear the news, Cates stuck his hands into the pockets of his gray slacks, looked around, and shook his head.

"What a zoo," he said with a chuckle. "What a zoo."

In a nearby aisle stood Doug Stewart, whose company, DMS, was responsible for the slides that would appear on screens behind Rehme and Spacey. Stewart had been in the building all night, after spending the past few weeks collecting photos and logos of every film and every actor he thought might have a chance at a nomination. The idea was not to be caught unprepared by any long shots—although on the occasions when that did happen, Stewart had ways to play catch-up, even at midnight in Beverly Hills. The Academy library on nearby La Cienega Boulevard, for example, was kept open all night, with a small crew of staffers ready to scour magazines and promo materials if need be.

For Stewart, a more pressing problem was locating photos that met his needs without appearing to play favorites. "Getting good material is very tricky," he said, "because the Academy does not want to give the slightest impression that they have any inkling who will be nominated." Stewart had, in fact, run afoul of the organization just a few days earlier, when Dream-Works sent him *Saving Private Ryan* materials that were oriented vertically; the screens he'd be using were better suited to horizontal images.

"I called the DreamWorks publicity people and said, 'Hey, could you make these horizontal, instead of vertical?' They said, 'Sure, no problem.' Well, it wasn't too long after that that I got a call from the Academy saying, 'It's really problematic when you do that. Please don't do it again.' "

Stewart laughed. "I have to be kept on a very short leash," he said. "And rightly so."

FOR MUCH OF THE YEAR, *Saving Private Ryan* was the clear Oscar front-runner. A World War II epic from director Steven Spielberg, *Private Ryan* opened with a twenty-minute depiction of the invasion of Normandy on D-Day that was startling in its virtuosity and in the relentless nature of its carnage. And Spielberg wasn't alone in exploring the war: the legendary but reclusive Terrence Malick, who hadn't directed a movie in twenty years, made *The Thin Red Line*, a brutally rhapsodic war movie set on the Pacific island of Guadalcanal during World War II. Even Roberto Benigni, an Italian comic known mostly for his frenetic mugging, had the nerve to make *Life Is Beautiful*, in which he played an Italian Jew who during the war is sent to a concentration camp, where he convinces his young son that it's all an elaborate game.

But 1998 also had its share of movies that weren't loud, testosterone-laden, or filled with weaponry. *Shakespeare in Love*, a Miramax film that starred Harvey Weinstein's favorite leading lady, Gwyneth Paltrow, was a lark that in its charming but insistent way tried to make much of the similarities between Elizabethan England and modern Hollywood. And if Spielberg's film had been the favorite ever since its summer release, Miramax knew how to play the underdog. When *Shakespeare* came out of early screenings with a good buzz, the company quickly went to work. Miramax did what most studios did—it hired outside consultants, sent out videocassettes, courted journalists, and spent lavishly on ads in the Hollywood trade papers—but it seemed to do so more aggressively and feverishly than others. When *Saving Private Ryan* found itself losing occasional guild or critics' awards to the likes of *Shakespeare*, *The Thin Red Line*, and writer-director Bill Condon's *Gods and Monsters*, the Oscar race suddenly seemed closer and more competitive than anyone would have predicted.

"WELCOME TO CAMP OSCAR," said Bob Rehme, as he looked around the awfully luxurious campground: an elegant conference room at the swanky

Century Plaza Hotel in Century City. The walls were a soft peach color, a crystal chandelier hung from the ceiling, and tables laden with coffee, Danish pastries, and fruit juices awaited any of the several dozen Oscar staffers who might have been looking for a quick breakfast before a 10 a.m. production meeting.

Cates then looked around the room. "Let's see, who is here?" he asked, and then grinned. "Fuck." When the producer start spewing unprompted obscenities, longtime insiders knew it meant only one thing: "Oh, yes," said Cates. "Susan Futterman." From her seat, ABC's director of broadcast standards for comedy/variety grinned and waved. After years of waging battles large and small, she was used to this kind of shit from Cates. Futterman also knew that she had her work cut out for her: while Whoopi Goldberg talked as if she were an unpredictable wild card but then behaved once the cameras were on during her first go-around as host of the Oscars, she'd been far looser and less predictable on her return engagement. Now that Goldberg was back for number three, Futterman expected the host to push things even further.

When the staffers present had all introduced themselves, Cates removed the black cloth that had been draped over a bulletin board at the front of the room. On the board was a breakdown of the entire show, though the names of most of the presenters had been omitted. "Please, please, please, let's keep this in the room," Cates implored. "The press loves to give away our secrets. That's why most of the stars' names aren't up here. When you look at the board in my office, it has such stars and glitter. This is just the bare bones."

In fact, as Cates took staffers through the show itself, his rundown was infuriatingly vague. "Then a star comes out," he said. Later: "A very funny star." Later: "A big, beautiful, wonderful star comes out and introduces the *Life Is Beautiful* clip."

With seven nominations, *Life Is Beautiful* had set a record for a foreign film. Three days earlier, the movie's director and star had been named best actor at the Screen Actors Guild ceremony, and had responded with a delirious, lengthy speech in broken English. Remembering that, Cates laughed. "And if Roberto Benigni wins," he said, "be prepared for a *very* long show."

Finally, Cates arrived at what could become a defining moment of the seventy-first Oscars: the honorary Academy Award presentation to director Elia Kazan. "There will probably be a standing ovation," Cates predicted. "Some people probably won't stand, and some people probably won't clap. Whatever happens, happens. And we'll show whatever happens."

HONORARY ACADEMY AWARDS had been stirring up controversy for decades. From the first Academy Awards in 1929, when *The Jazz Singer* was declared ineligible for the real awards but then given a special Oscar for revolutionizing the industry, the honorary Oscars were often used to correct oversights and balance the inequities of the voting. If Alfred Hitchcock, one of the premier filmmakers of the century, somehow made it into his sixties without winning an Oscar despite half a dozen nominations, the solution, in 1967, was to give him the Irving Thalberg Award, the Oscar presented to a producer for his body of work. If Paul Newman's wins-to-nominations ratio was 0-for-6 after a splendid thirty-year career, the answer was to give the reluctant actor an honorary Oscar in 1983. (He won best actor the following year.) Harold Lloyd, Buster Keaton, Groucho Marx, Cary Gant, Greta Garbo, Edward G. Robinson, Kirk Douglas, Fred Astaire, Steven Spielberg—the list of those who'd been given an honorary Oscar or a Thalberg after years of being snubbed by the voters cut across the history of film.

But the special awards—which, besides the regular honorary Oscar and the Thalberg, grew to include the Jean Hersholt Humanitarian Award and, for a brief time, special juvenile awards—were not always doled out to right wrongs. They'd also rewarded friends of Oscar like Bob Hope. They'd gone to people of power within the organization: Darryl F. Zanuck, for instance, won three. And they'd been used to honor foreign filmmakers like Akira Kurosawa, Federico Fellini, and Michelangelo Antonioni, who otherwise would have little chance outside the foreign film category. The awards were usually proposed by members, partly because the board tended to ignore lobbying from outside the Academy. "If we made decisions based on public proposals," said Bruce Davis, "all of the Three Stooges would have honorary awards."

That Elia Kazan's relatively brief film career had been influential was not in question. When he made the move into films after an acclaimed career in theater, his performers—fresh, rough faces like Marlon Brando and Karl Malden, many of them trained in what would become known as Method Acting—brought a startling level of intensity and realism to the screen. Kazan was known as an actor's director, and his actors helped revolutionize the craft. Between *A Tree Grows in Brooklyn* in 1945 and *America, America* eighteen years later, actors in his movies won two dozen Oscar nominations, and took home nine statuettes.

In those years, Kazan himself was nominated for best director five times, winning for *Gentleman's Agreement* in 1947 and *On the Waterfront* seven years later. But from the early sixties on, he rarely worked in Hollywood, making only *The Arrangement* in 1969, *The Visitors* in 1972, and *The Last Tycoon* in 1976. None was particularly successful.

Still, those who objected to giving Kazan an honorary Oscar didn't do so simply because his career had tailed off after an early period for which the Academy had already rewarded him. Instead, they attacked the director, and the Academy, because in 1952, Kazan had gone before the House Un-American Activities Committee and named names.

During the 1930s, some in the creative community, Kazan among them, had embraced communism as a utopian economic philosophy and a system they felt was more equitable than unchecked capitalism. Some remained Communists, while many others walked away when Soviet dictator Josef Stalin's abuses and ambitions came to light, and when it became obvious that the philosophy laid out by Karl Marx and Friedrich Engels was being used for destructive ends. But the House Un-American Activities Committee, chaired by Senator Joseph McCarthy, reduced the complex situation to a single question: "Are you now, or have you ever been, a member of the Communist Party?"

In 1952, Kazan was not, but twenty years earlier he had been. When the committee asked him to name others who were once Communists, he complied. Kazan had not initially intended to name names; he did so, he claimed in his autobiography, only after a crisis of conscience in which he decided that the secretive nature of Communist Party membership was proof that the party really was trying to infiltrate and subvert the movie industry, just as McCarthy had charged.

Of the many industry figures called to testify, those who refused were blacklisted from further employment in Hollywood, as were those identified as Communists. And although McCarthy was publicly humiliated during a hearing in 1954, the blacklist affected a group of screenwriters—the so-called "Hollywood ten"—for years afterward. It wasn't until the 1960s, after people like Kirk Douglas and Otto Preminger began to hire and give screen credit to banned writers like Dalton Trumbo, that the blacklist lost its force.

While the blacklist was in effect, several Academy Awards for screenwriting went to people who had little or nothing to do with the scripts for which they won; the winners were fronts for the otherwise unemployable true writers. Worse, the Academy dishonored itself by adopting a rule that stripped Oscar eligibility from anyone who'd been a member of the Communist Party, or had refused to testify before a congressional committee. But that rule was quickly rescinded, and in the 1970s the Academy began to set the record straight and give Oscars—often as not posthumously—to the blacklisted writers who had earned them.

For decades, the chances of the Academy giving any further awards to Kazan seemed remote. But Karl Malden, a past president of the Academy and a man with clout on the board, was an avid supporter of the director who'd guided him to the only two Oscar nominations of his career. (Malden won for *A Streetcar Named Desire* and was also nominated for *On the Waterfront*.) In January 1999, at a board meeting devoted to the awarding of honorary Oscars, Malden stood and made his case.

Ordinarily, a nominating speech would have been followed by other governors speaking out on behalf of their candidates. Several rounds of voting then would narrow the field to a single candidate, whereupon the governors would vote one more time; if two-thirds of the board approved the selection, an award would be bestowed. The process could be repeated up to two more times with additional candidates.

In Kazan's case, though, Malden's speech was so persuasive that the governors voted immediately, with a show of hands rather than by secret ballot. One participant at the meeting recalled that two members of the board abstained, but otherwise the vote was unanimous. "It was a really good speech, and it came at a time when a lot of the old wounds had healed," said Bruce Davis, who attended the meeting. "I think it's a legitimate question: are we about morality or are we about art? Because if we start factoring in morality, there's a lot of people who might not be eligible."

When Kazan's award was announced, the criticism started. Abraham Polonsky, who'd been blacklisted and couldn't write anything under his own name for more than a decade, called Kazan "a creep" and bluntly declared, "I'll be watching, hoping somebody shoots him." Kazan's detractors asked those attending the awards to remain seated and not applaud when he came onstage.

The man at the middle of the controversy remained quiet. Kazan's third wife, Frances Kazan, did grant a rare interview to *Los Angeles Times* columnist Patrick Goldstein, who reminded her that some might be watching to see if Kazan would apologize for his actions.

"Too fucking bad," Mrs. Kazan said. "It's not going to happen."

BY THURSDAY of Oscar week, crews were crawling over the stage and backstage areas at the Dorothy Chandler Pavilion. In the middle of the stage sat an enormous white rotunda, the central element in an old-fashioned, classically ornate set that most staffers thought was Roy Christopher's best Oscar set ever.

"It's the last Oscars of the twentieth century, so I was looking for something classic yet forward-looking to end the millennium," explained Christopher. "And I was sort of at a loss until I saw a sixteenth-century drawing of an Italian rotunda in forced perspective." In front of the designer was a bag full of supplies that might prove vital as he did eleventh-hour touch-ups: fifteen rolls of Venetian Gold Plastifoil, a glittery cover-up for surfaces that might require some flash.

Outside the Chandler, the Academy held a noon press conference with Rehme, Cates, and Horvitz. One reporter asked about the size of the Oscar viewership. "We don't know the exact number," said Rehme, "but it's in the hundreds of millions."

This marked a significant change from what had for years been the Academy's and the network's standard line, that the Oscars were watched by a billion people. "We decided to drop the one billion figure," confessed ABC publicist Dan Doran as he watched the press conference. "It got ridiculous when the Grammys started claiming a billion six, even though they're on in fewer countries than we are. When we heard that, we thought, We can't get into this game with them. So now the official figure is hundreds of millions."

Bruce Davis was even blunter. "There has never been a television event in the history of the world that had a billion viewers," he said. "It's a handy number to throw around, but it's not true. I don't mind a little showmanship, but when you look at the domestic audience of around seventy-five million, that's a *long* way from a billion."

In much of the world, the Oscars were not broadcast live—or if they were, they were shown in the middle of the night, a dismal time for big TV ratings. Even in England, most of the viewers shunned the 2 a.m. live broadcast in favor of an edited version prepared by the BBC for airing the following night, by which time the results were known. "If you already know who's going to win," Davis said, "then you're left wondering if somebody will say something funny, or if somebody will cry. Which is not uninteresting, but the essence of the experience has evaporated at that point."

At the press conference, Cates also handled what had become an annual question: how long is the show going to be? "It's like the Super Bowl," he said, trotting out the analogy he would come to use at every opportunity. "It'll take as long as it takes."

Backstage, the consensus was that it would take a long time. For one thing, the show featured a dance number, an appearance by the grandson of Roy Rogers's famous horse, Trigger, and a large number of film packages, beginning with Mike Shapiro's usual In Memoriam package. But Frank Sinatra and Stanley Kubrick, both of whom had died since the last show, were being given separate tributes of their own. Cates had also ordered film salutes to cowboy stars, and to real-life heroes depicted on-screen. The producer knew that he had overloaded the show, but he had done so for a reason: afraid that the Kazan award would cast a pall over the entire night, he'd gone out of his way to lighten the show with additional entertainment.

The last of these elements was a five-minute Chuck Workman piece to open the evening. By the standards of Oscar film montages, five minutes was an eternity—but Cates wanted Workman's piece to cover a century of film, so he made room. "Since this is the last Oscar show of the twentieth century, they wanted to show what Academy members think are the best film moments of the century," said Workman. "So they had little postcards that they sent out, along with a very official-looking letter asking everybody to vote for their three favorite moments."

About 1,700 of the Academy's 5,500 voters had returned ballots. Workman took the top 350 vote-getters, added another 150 scenes of his own choosing, and then narrowed his choice down to the 250 clips that made up the final package. "What surprised me," he said, "was how many people voted for themselves. Val Kilmer nominated three of his own movies, including *Batman Forever*, and apologized for it in the postcard. He said, 'I can't help it, these are my three favorite movies.' And then a lot of people called me afterwards and said, 'You are going to include my scenes, aren't you?'" The top four vote-getters were the final scenes of *Citizen Kane*, *Casablanca*, and *Sunset Boulevard*, and the sequence from *When Harry Met Sally* in which Meg Ryan loudly faked an orgasm while dining with Billy Crystal at the Carnegie Deli.

Late in the afternoon, Debbie Allen made her return to the Academy Awards after a three-year absence. Rather than recruit a large cast, the way she usually did, Allen had opted for a more serious, intimate presentation of dances to accompany the five nominated film scores. She chose five dancers: the Spanish flamenco sensation Joaquin Cortez; eighteen-year-old Rasta Thomas, a San Francisco–born dancer who was studying at the Kirov Academy; New York–bred ballerina Tai Jimenez, the only woman of the group; Desmond Richardson, a member of the American Ballet Theater who had worked extensively on Broadway; and the twenty-five-year-old tap dancer Savion Glover, who'd performed on the Oscars three years earlier and had also made an appearance in 1989 as the youngest and most talented of Allan Carr's "stars of tomorrow."

Allen had choreographed a series of solos, duets, and group scenes set to snippets of music from *Life Is Beautiful*, *Saving Private Ryan*, *Elizabeth*, *Pleasantville*, and *The Thin Red Line*. As usual for Allen's Oscar routines, the sheer athleticism and grace of the dancers proved far more persuasive up close and live than it did on the television screen, where questions tended to arise about such issues as whether it was appropriate to salute the bloody World War II epic *Saving Private Ryan* with a tap dance from Glover.

At the Chandler, of course, it was far too late to ask those kinds of questions. Allen arranged her dancers across the stage, and then lectured them like she was a schoolmarm and they were unruly fifth graders. "Child, be a gentleman, don't paw her," she said to Thomas, who had idly placed his hand on Jimenez's back. Then she turned to the whole group. "Once you're in place, you must not fidget," she said sternly. "Lights are all around you, and you never know when he's going to focus on you. You must be *still*."

The dancers ran through the number a couple of times in low gear, taking it easy on the most physical aspects, the lifts and leaps. "Okay, guys," Allen said finally. "I need you to do it full out this time. Please? Otherwise we don't know what we've got." The next time through, some of the crew members who were watching cheered at the sheer virtuosity of the dancers—particularly Thomas, as word swept through the Chandler that he was still a teenager.

NORMALLY, recipients of honorary Oscars gave their speeches to the Academy ahead of time, so that their lines could be placed on the TelePromp Ter. But Elia Kazan did not do that. When he made his first appearance at the Chandler on Friday morning, tensions were running high and nobody knew what he was going to say.

Walking slowly, flanked by his wife, Frances, and by several security guards, Kazan looked frail, tentative, and a little confused. At first, Cates walked him through the rehearsal, with stand-ins taking the place of Robert DeNiro and Martin Scorsese, who would give Kazan his award. But when one of the stand-ins said, "Ladies and gentlemen, Mr. Elia Kazan," and then handed over the plaster Oscar statuette used for rehearsals, Kazan studied it, a quizzical look on his face.

"Say something, Elia," said Frances.

"Here's where you say thank you," added Cates.

"That's it?" said Kazan. "And go home?" He frowned. "Where does Bobby stand?"

Cates pointed to the stand-ins. "Bobby will be right there, and so will Martin."

For the second rehearsal, Kazan was led to the back of the stage, where he waited while the tribute film played on a large screen center stage. As he waited, Frances coached him. "After they give you the Oscar, just say thank you," she said. "That's *all* you have to say."

The second time through, Kazan took the dummy Oscar, looked into the audience, and delivered a two-word speech: "Thank you." Then he walked off. The brevity of his remarks stunned staffers who'd wondered if he would use the occasion to answer his critics or acknowledge the controversy.

But Kazan was unconcerned with whatever furor he may have caused; he simply walked into the wings, sat in a chair, and watched the rehearsal on a nearby monitor. The film critic and historian Richard Schickel, who put together the tribute saluting Kazan, came up to say hello. "This must be fun for you, being on a set again," he said.

"Yeah," said Kazan. "I've never seen a show like this."

As the two men chatted, stagehands wrestled with a huge Oscar statue that had been positioned under the rotunda. On the monitor, Anne Heche ran through her lines; backstage, Renée Zellweger waited for her cue to do the same.

"Where are you going from here, Richard?" asked Kazan. "Are you going to write another book?"

"I might write a book about *you*, Elia," said Schickel. "What do you think of that?"

"I think there's too much talk about me," said Kazan wearily. "I'm just another Joe."

"STAND BY, boys and girls, or dysfunctional children," Lou Horvitz announced over the P.A. system as lunchtime ended. "Daddy's home."

Daddy, in the person of Horvitz, could be a stern taskmaster—as well as a world-class screamer whose tirades were already legendary by his third year with the Oscars. "I don't have a big patience level," he conceded. "The team I put around me are all A players, so I have incredibly high expectations of them not to drop the ball. I'm not in it to be a nice guy, and I'm not going to win a popularity contest. But I feel that I'm fair, and I feel that I'm damn humorous."

Horvitz had also won kudos for his ability to react quickly, and for the meticulous way he planned the show—from seeing the shots in his head before he ever got to the theater to laying out "relationship charts" identifying where each nominee's loved ones and costars would be sitting, in order to get quick reaction shots. "If a winner's third-grade teacher is sitting in the balcony, Lou knows about it," said Garry Hood.

Still, other staffers found the level of Horvitz's preparation—the scripts he sent out two weeks before the show, laying out every single camera move and cutaway—to be stifling. Confided one veteran staffer, "The show's not as much *fun* as it used to be."

Fun was on the afternoon agenda, though, because Aerosmith was in the house. Formed in Boston in 1970, Aerosmith was a hard-rock band that modeled itself after the Rolling Stones, both in the raucous, blues-based music, and in the offstage excesses. By the beginning of the 1980s, the band had fought, broken up, and reunited; just because they could get the band back together, though, didn't mean they could get themselves together. "There's nothing to do on the road but take drugs and fuck," lead singer Steven Tyler declared during an attempted comeback in 1984, shortly before showing for a concert in such an altered state that he fell off the stage.

The old Aerosmith would never have been booked to perform on the Academy Awards—but then, that Aerosmith wouldn't have recorded "I Don't Want to Miss a Thing," a big, generic hard-rock ballad written by Dianne Warren for director Michael Bay's big, generic hard-rock movie *Armageddon*. But Aerosmith had cleaned up and had a string of hits that included "Love in an Elevator" and "Dude (Looks Like a Lady)." The latter-day Aerosmith was calmer, its music slicker. Tyler even had a movie star daughter, Liv Tyler, who played Ben Affleck's love interest in *Armageddon*.

Still, even the new Aerosmith was an uneasy fit for the Oscars. Before the band rehearsed, Cates and Conti met with them backstage. The recorded version of "I Don't Want to Miss a Thing" featured an orchestra, but the difficulties in balancing the rock band and the orchestra were formidable. Cates, who appreciated Bruce Springsteen and loved Céline Dion but was assuredly not a rock fan, gave the boys a pep talk. "You don't need the orchestra!" he told them. "You're a *band*!"

A few minutes later, Aerosmith took the stage and ran through the song for the first time. Though it was only a casual rehearsal, Tyler gave the kind of full-out, theatrical, scarf-flinging performance for which he had become known. The second rehearsal included two columns of flame at the rear of the stage, plus an explosion and a shower of sparks. Undeniably entertaining, it was massively louder than anything else on this or maybe any other Academy Awards show.

As the band got ready to leave, show publicist Eva Dimergian returned from its dressing room. "They're really worried about their drummer, Joey Kramer," she said. "I guess he *never* gets dressed up." She laughed, and thought of the dress code that applied to stagehands. "And I don't know how they're going to get some of those roadies into tuxes."

THE FIRST TIME that Whoopi Goldberg hosted the Oscars, it was the year of *Schindler's List*; the second time, Jesse Jackson led a protest against the paltry extent of African American representation in Hollywood. And when she took the job in 1999, Goldberg was once again dismayed at what she saw as the limited opportunities for jokes provided by nominated films like *Saving Private Ryan*. But when she and Bruce Vilanch noticed that two different women had been nominated for playing Queen Elizabeth—Cate Blanchett in *Elizabeth* and Judi Dench in *Shakespeare in Love*—they decided that it might be fun for Goldberg herself to enter dressed as the queen.

"The idea sort of grew from there, because we're always looking for things that Whoopi can do during the show," said Vilanch. "And eventually we thought, Why doesn't she wear clothes from the five films nominated for costume design, and then give out that award?"

The decision to turn Goldberg into a fashion model had a twofold effect: it forced the host to spend much of her time backstage doing eleven frantic costume changes, and it made her rehearsals top secret. The theater was cleared of all guests before Goldberg's Friday afternoon rehearsal, which began when she took the stage dressed in a hugely elaborate Queen Elizabeth costume, including full whiteface. "Good evening," she said. "I am the African Queen."

Goldberg ran through her lines quietly, almost unintelligibly; the main reason for this rehearsal wasn't to test the jokes, but to see if she could make her costume changes quickly enough. When she changed into the fifties-style suburban frock from *Pleasantville*, she mispronounced the name of costume designer Judianna Makovsky. "I think you'd better spell it phonetically for the colored girl, 'cause we don't have names like that," she told the TelePrompTer operator. "We have names like Jackson, Jones . . . Anyway, the bitch made some cool costumes." Sitting in the second row in front of Goldberg, Susan Futterman laughed and shook her head.

Goldberg's ensuing costume changes put her into slave rags from *Beloved*, a glam-rock outfit from *Velvet Goldmine*, an Old Globe actor's getup from *Shakespeare in Love*, and a return to full Elizabethan garb, this time a man's outfit that included a beard, from *Elizabeth*. This last costume prompted a number of off-color gags, beginning when Goldberg stroked the beard and commented, "I feel like Ellen DeGeneres." When the audience groaned again, she snapped, "You think this is easy? I haven't taken my dress off so many times since my first audition."

A minute later, she read her intro to John Travolta, whose recent movies had included *Primary Colors* and *A Civil Action*. "Our next presenter played a politician and a personal injury lawyer, and we still like him," she said, and then paused. "Bruce?" she said, looking for Vilanch. "Did I miss the joke? It's just that I'm standing up here with my panties down, and I want to know why. So I don't fuck up the joke."

With the small audience in stitches at her gleeful, good-natured profanity, Goldberg stoked the fires even further. When it was time for her to open the envelope and present the award for costume design, the TelePrompTer flashed the word ENVELOPE. Goldberg looked at it, annoyed. "Quit flashing ENVELOPE at me," she said, holding up the dummy Oscar. "I've been here before. I *got* one of these motherfuckers."

She looked toward Futterman. "Is Susan still breathing?"

AEROSMITH'S SONG may have been the biggest change of pace from the usual Oscar fare, but it was far from the trickiest of the nominated tunes. That distinction had to go to "When You Believe" from the animated DreamWorks film *The Prince of Egypt*. In the film, the song existed in two different versions. The first was sung by Michelle Pfeiffer, who supplied the voice for one of the lead characters, and also by Sally Dworsky, who provided the singing voice for a character played by Sandra Bullock. But to run over the final credits—and, crucially, to score a pop hit that would help sell the movie—a second version of the song was recorded by the prolific pop/soul singer and producer Kenneth "Babyface" Edmonds.

Edmonds refashioned some of the music to make the song more commercial, wrote a new bridge, took a cowriting credit, and brought in Whitney Houston, Mariah Carey, and a gospel choir, the last in place of the children's chorus that sang in Hebrew in the original song. While Schwartz's song was called "When You Believe," the Babyface revision bore the title "The Prince of Egypt (When You Believe)."

Schwartz's version was the one nominated for an Oscar—the songwriter had seen to that when he declined to give Edmonds a writing credit in forms submitted to the Academy. After Houston and Carey were booked to perform on the Oscar show, the Academy insisted that they'd be performing the original song, rather than the pop version with which the singers were more familiar.

Conti wrote an arrangement that added a few pop touches to Schwartz's original song. It seemed crucial that Houston and Carey have enough rehearsal time to work on this hybrid—but at the last minute, Houston called to say she wouldn't be able to join Carey at the Friday night rehearsal.

Among the crew, there was some uncertainty about her excuse. "She missed her plane, or she has an ear condition, or some other bullshit story," snapped one top executive. And when Carey arrived and learned that her fellow diva wouldn't be showing up, her immediate reaction was to leave as well, though she eventually reconsidered.

Another drama, meanwhile, was playing out among the stand-ins. Early in the day, stand-in Janis Uhley had done a creditable job singing Céline Dion's part at a rehearsal of the Dion–Andrea Bocelli duet "The Prayer." (Bocelli's part had been handled by a young singer named Josh Groban, a protégé of songwriter and producer David Foster.) Uhley, who'd once worked as Horvitz's assistant, wanted to sing Houston's part as well, but some stage managers thought she wasn't the right choice for the job; in this situation, they needed somebody who'd blend in and stay out of Carey's way. ("Janis likes to sing too much," explained one.) Uhley went over their heads to plead her case, and word came down from Horvitz to let her sing.

At about 8:30, the members of a gospel choir took their places on a large pyramid that sat at the rear of the stage. After the choir rehearsed the song a couple of times, with Debbie Allen directing the singers in where to stand and how to wave their arms, Carey walked onstage in tight black capri pants and a snug white spaghetti-strap shirt. Allen showed her the flight of stairs she'd be walking down at the beginning of the song, and Carey laughed. "Maybe someday," she sighed, "awards shows will have escalators."

On the first run-through, Carey looked nervous and unsteady, and she couldn't remember all of the lyrics. Stand-in Uhley didn't have any such problem; in fact, she sang with a theatricality and gusto that seemed more than a little inappropriate, and even unnerving. In the audience, a few staffers exchanged glances as Carey laid back and let Uhley belt out the song. Afterward, Carey's reps spoke quickly and urgently to the production crew. "Their basic message," said one crew member, "was 'Get her off the stage.'" The next time through, a different, more subdued stand-in took over.

Sitting at the production table during the late-night rehearsal, Michael Seligman looked over his shoulder and saw Susan Futterman still sitting a few rows back. "Hey, Futterman," he yelled, "isn't it past your bedtime?"

"Have you fixed the piano yet?" she yelled back.

Seligman flinched. A few hours earlier, Futterman had informed him that the Steinway and Sons logo visible on Randy Newman's piano would have to be covered, because Steinway wasn't paying for product placement. Seligman hadn't taken care of the offending logo yet, so he cupped his hands over his ears and played deaf.

"What?" he said.

"Have you fixed the piano yet?"

"*What???*"

After Futterman gave up, Seligman shook his head. "I was in the middle of dealing with a big problem this afternoon," he said, "when Susan called me to tell me that something in the script didn't read right, because a comma was in the wrong place." He sighed. "I said, Susan, take your fuckin' comma . . ."

SATURDAY AFTERNOON, Elia Kazan returned to the Chandler for another rehearsal. Again, he was accompanied by his wife and by several security guards. This time, Kazan's speech was marginally longer. "Thanks to the Academy," he said, "for its good heart and its generosity. Thank you all." He walked off, went straight into the wings, grabbed a chair, and sat down where he could watch rehearsals on a monitor.

For the next hour, Liv Tyler struggled to read the TelePrompTer, Gwyneth Paltrow laughed out loud when she realized how extensive the ritual was with the stand-ins, and Catherine Zeta-Jones rehearsed while stagehands tried to secure a loose pipe high on a side wall in the wings. Nearby, another crew member used black paint to cover the Steinway and Sons logo on Randy Newman's piano.

Kazan, meanwhile, sat calmly in his director's chair, occasionally talking to staffers about his days in live television.

Eventually, Frances Kazan approached her husband. "I'm tired," she said. "I want to go lie down."

"Lie down in the green room," he said.

"But I want to go home."

Kazan wasn't moving. "Go ahead and go," he said.

"But you have the limo."

"Then take a taxi."

Giving up, she left Kazan in the company of his bodyguards. He remained in the wings, a slight smile on his face as he took in the activity around him. "Elia's our new mascot," Debbie Williams told Cates when the producer walked by.

Cates looked at Kazan and nodded. "It's his last hurrah," he suggested gently. "And he knows it."

DRESS REHEARSAL ran smoothly, though Goldberg continued to take particular delight in tweaking the ABC censor. Reading her introduction of the Irish actor Liam Neeson, the host began slowly and suggestively stroking the microphone stand in front of her. The audience howled with laughter at the completely inappropriate bit—particularly, it seemed, Judith Reichman, Cates's wife and, coincidentally, Futterman's gynecologist. During a break,

Reichman approached Futterman to plead that she not cut the sight gag. When Futterman said she was more concerned with Goldberg's suggestive beard jokes, Reichman quickly brokered a deal: let Whoopi stroke the mike stand and she'll keep quiet about the beard. "Every woman in America will love it," Reichman promised.

The rehearsal made it clear that it was going to be a very long show. Cates knew that the show had gotten away from him, but he tried to shrug it off. "The ironic thing," he told Rehme, "is that if you make the show shorter, it'll be more boring. If you take away what makes it long, then there'll be no entertainment."

Vilanch dropped by the production table to say that lots of jokes about the show's length had been prepared. "There's, 'While you've been watching the show, another century has passed. Get ready for Y3K.' And, 'For those of you who were upset that the show was moved from Monday night, guess what? It's Monday night!' "

As soon as the dress rehearsal ended, stagehands pulled an enormous Oscar statue off the stage and rolled in staircases for Mariah Carey and Whitney Houston. Houston had finally arrived a few hours earlier for the dress run-through, but her unfamiliarity with the song's new arrangement had left her begging for more rehearsal time. Though it meant paying overtime, Cates had quickly agreed to give the divas an additional run-through once the main rehearsal ended.

The pair returned to the stage around eleven p.m., Houston's arm around Carey's shoulders. Houston wore a tailored black suit that hung on her stylishly; Carey was squeezed into impossibly tight blue jeans and a low-cut T-shirt.

"I love divas," said Vilanch. "I live for divas."

As Bill Conti played his arrangement of the song, Houston shook her head, tried briefly to adapt, and then stopped singing altogether. "I'm sorry, Bill," she said. "We're just used to the recorded version, and it's freaking us out, man."

Over and over, Houston returned to the same complaint. "Is it okay to do it how they originally had it?" she asked, referring not to the original, nominated version of the song, but to the Babyface revision to which Schwartz had denied the nomination. "This is a totally different count. I want what was on the record, and this ain't it." She shook her head in frustration. "I'm incapable of expressing it. You know what I'm talking about?"

Finally, after about forty minutes of tinkering, Conti crafted an arrangement close enough to the Babyface version to satisfy Houston (and Carey, who'd been letting her partner take the lead). "Whoo!" shouted Houston when Conti delayed a crucial chord change just long enough. "Hallelujah, darling!"

Carey nodded. "We got it now," she said.

"Thank you, everybody," added Houston, "and God bless you."

At 11:40, the cameramen were sent home. Houston and Carey headed into the wings together, decided they didn't want to wait for the elevator, and walked up a flight of stairs to their dressing rooms. Trailed by two large entourages, they walked arm in arm, harmonizing on "When You Believe" all the way up the stairs.

AT 2:15 on the day of the show, walkie-talkies crackled backstage. "We have a request," said a voice, "for some pizzas for Aerosmith."

A minute later came the reply. "That's an okay on those pizzas."

A few minutes later, the best-picture award at the final rehearsal went to *Shakespeare in Love.* The choice was random but intriguing, because many Oscar handicappers felt that Miramax's romantic comedy had been picking up momentum in recent weeks. The company's strategy was clear. To many people, *Saving Private Ryan* did not resonate the way Spielberg's *Schindler's List* had done five years earlier. Some Academy members admired the film but couldn't embrace it; *Ryan* was too long, too violent, a return to an area the director had covered with more feeling and sensitivity. Surely some voters were ready for a lighter, wittier alternative; the trick was to make sure that they thought of *Shakespeare in Love* as that alternative.

A handful of critics' awards and a win over *Private Ryan* at the Writers Guild awards helped *Shakespeare*'s cause, and Miramax kept up the pressure with so many trade ads that DreamWorks publicly complained about having to step up its own ad campaign to keep pace. "There is no question that the aggressiveness of the extraordinary campaign Miramax has run in support of 'Shakespeare' has caused us to do more on behalf of 'Ryan' than we had initially planned," DreamWorks cochairman Jeffrey Katzenberg told the *Los Angeles Times*. *New York* magazine suggested that Harvey Weinstein was privately bashing Spielberg's movie, while others insisted that Weinstein wasn't, but that DreamWorks was trying to spread the word that he was. Campaign spending by one or both companies was estimated to be as high as $15 million.

All those charges were hotly denied, but bad blood and ill will hung in the air. By the week of the Oscars, asking who would win best picture had, in Hollywood at least, become tantamount to asking if Miramax's *Shakespeare* campaign had worked, or if the studio had gone too far and created a fatal backlash.

The Academy, for its part, was not pleased with the emphasis on campaigning. "Miramax has gone at the whole idea of campaigning in a way that just hadn't been seen before," said Bruce Davis. "They see it as a competitive sport, and look for every edge, every angle. And they're not the only ones responsible, because the others have felt the need to step up and match them."

OSCAR CAMPAIGNS weren't the only area that had been heating up. For years, ABC and the Academy had been watching as the hoopla surrounding all aspects of the Oscars grew. The growth was accelerated by outlets like *Entertainment Tonight*, the syndicated entertainment news show that began in 1981; the similarly focused *Access Hollywood*, which started thirteen years later; and E! Entertainment Television, a cable network devoted entirely to the entertainment industry.

For these outlets, the Oscars were the Super Bowl and Election Day combined; simply covering the results wasn't enough. There had to be daily Oscar updates, "backstage at the Oscars" features, and of course "countdown to the Oscars" preshows. E! enjoyed its highest ratings of the year by parking comedian Joan Rivers and her daughter, Melissa, on the red carpet, where they sucked up to celebrities' faces but lambasted their fashion choices once the stars had moved on. The ABC affiliate in Los Angeles, KABC, syndicated its preshow coverage, making it the station's most profitable show.

With the move to Sunday at 5:30, the Academy decided to produce its own half-hour preshow. During that final thirty minutes, other crews would not be allowed to broadcast live from the red carpet. "It was such an odd thing that we were doing this show and allowing six or seven other entities to do a show right ahead of our show, on our turf," said Bruce Davis. "We wanted to claim that turf, at least for the half hour."

Cates was nominally in charge of the preshow as well. But since he had his hands full with what quickly came to be called "the big show," he hired Dennis Doty to oversee the preshow. Doty, a longtime producer of made-for-television movies, was not only a good friend of Cates's, but also his partner in Cates-Doty Productions.

Promising looks into areas of the show that viewers had never seen, Doty and his crew prepared a variety of features, including the history of Oscar fashions and the making of Oscar statuettes. He also hired a pair of hosts, CNN reporter Jim Moret and actress Geena Davis, and set up bases along the red carpet and in the Founders Room, an elaborate private room on the mezzanine level of the Dorothy Chandler Pavilion.

Since it would have been folly to rely on the right people to be on the red carpet at the right time, Doty planned to pretape several of Moret's and Davis's interviews. (Home viewers wouldn't be apprised of this.) At 4 p.m. in the Founders Room, Davis prepared for one of those interviews. Standing on a small circular stage in front of an elaborate backdrop, the actress looked over cue cards bearing questions for the nominated Australian actor Geoffrey Rush. Besides the camera crew, about a dozen other staffers and bystanders stood around, watching.

"I'll ask him about Australia first, and then *Shine*," Davis said. "And then I should just pick one of those other questions. I think the one about costume design is more interesting."

A few minutes later, Rush showed up. At first, he spoke so softly that the interview had to be halted in order that a staffer could reposition Rush's microphone closer to his mouth. Then Davis tried again. "Seven of your fellow Australians," she began. "And yourself, of course." She stopped. "Can I start that again?" She tried again, and flubbed the opening question again.

When she finally finished the interview, an aide informed her that it was thirty seconds too long for the slot where they'd be using it. "When you ask me that last question about the costumes," suggested Rush, "I'll just say, 'Yes, I liked the costumes,' and end it at that."

After a few more false starts, Davis completed the interview to everyone's satisfaction. Then she looked around the room. "Could there be more people watching?" she said, mildly annoyed. "Actually, I wouldn't mind if we cleared the room."

What Davis didn't know was that the entire episode—the false starts, the flubbed lines, the muttered conversations between takes—continued to be shown, unedited, on monitors throughout the backstage area. It also played on a pair of monitors at opposite ends of the Dorothy Chandler Pavilion lobby, where the crowd had already begun to arrive.

"I'm such a novice," Davis sighed, as Academy guests and staffers listened in.

An hour later, home viewers saw the completed version of the interview, along with a breathless but tepid collection of other interviews and clips. At the end of the preshow broadcast, cameras inside the command truck showed Cates standing behind Horvitz. "Two minutes to air, ladies and gentlemen, to over a billion people watching," Horvitz said. "Have fun."

5:30 P.M., PACIFIC DAYLIGHT TIME: *"Live from the Dorothy Chandler Pavilion in Los Angeles, California, the 71st annual Academy Awards."*

As the traditional montage of arriving stars played, best supporting actress nominee Judi Dench rushed through the lobby and arrived at a door into the hall moments after it had been shut. "I'm sorry," said an usher. "You'll have to wait until the first commercial break."

"No, we have to get her inside!" yelled a stage manager who was scanning the latecomers. "Lou wants her in the audience for Whoopi's entrance!" Dench was quickly and quietly whisked to her third-row aisle seat.

At the same time, several guards brought Whitney Houston into the backstage area through a small hallway. Grasping the folds of her dress in one hand and her young daughter in the other, Houston looked at the pages and guards who had been stationed in that area. "Who *are* these people?" she snapped impatiently.

An usher watched the diva and her entourage sweep past. "Some people," the usher muttered under her breath.

As Houston fled to her dressing room, Goldberg walked onstage as Queen Elizabeth, wearing whiteface and an enormous gown and wig. Horvitz cut to Judi Dench, who was laughing. "Good evening, loyal subjects," Goldberg said. "I am the African Queen. Some of you may know me as the virgin queen, but I can't imagine who."

Then she tried to head a few critics off at the pass. "This will be a long show," she said, "so we don't want to read about how damn long it was. We know it's long. Tough." She brought out Bob Rehme, and as soon as the Academy president took the stage Goldberg rushed offstage and hurried through a black curtain in the wings. She headed to her left down a short, heavily guarded corridor, made a quick right, ducked into her dressing room, and ripped off the heavy gown.

As Chuck Workman's film of memorable movie moments played, stage manager Dency Nelson led Kim Basinger out of the wings and into position behind an enormous Oscar statue that sat center stage. Behind the statue was a stool for Basinger to sit on, but she didn't use it.

Goldberg returned to the stage in a less ostentatious gown, wiping the last of the white makeup off her face. With Basinger and Nelson hidden behind the huge Oscar statue, all eyes were on Goldberg as she ran through a seven-minute monologue. "I thought the blacklist was me and Hattie McDaniel, shit," she said, muttering the last word softly but clearly. About twenty feet behind Goldberg, Basinger swayed back and forth. Hidden from the audience, she bounced on her heels and took occasional sips from a bottle of water she then placed on the base of the giant Oscar statue. Nelson sat on the floor behind her, consulting his notes.

"Armageddon ready to hand out some little bald boys," cracked Goldberg. "Our first presenter went home last year with two of the best-looking men in Hollywood: Oscar and Alec Baldwin," said Goldberg. "Lucky girl." From her hiding place behind the statue, Basinger grinned. Nelson got up off the floor and cued Basinger, who presented James Coburn with the best supporting actor award for *Affliction*.

"I finally got one right, I guess," said Coburn, a veteran of more than seventy films. As he talked, five handheld cameras remained focused on the other nominees, in case he decided to say something about them. Coburn went well over the suggested forty-five-second limit, ignoring the TelePrompTer, which was flashing PLEASE WRAP UP! against a red background. A minute and a half into Coburn's speech, Horvitz cued Conti to begin playing music. "Wait a minute, *wait a minute!*" Coburn shouted. "I've gotta say something else here!" The orchestra continued playing, but softly, as Coburn finished his remarks.

At 5:55, the show cut to its first commercial break. Upon its return, members of the gospel choir took their places on the stage. At the same time, Mariah Carey and Whitney Houston stood in the wings stage right and left, respectively. Houston dabbed at her nose and mouth with a tissue.

As the two divas sang "When You Believe," Matt Damon, Ben Affleck, Edward Norton, and Billy Bob Thornton stepped outside the theater for some fresh air.

An hour into the show, Goldberg came onstage in her *Pleasantville* frock. "Good evening, I'm Marilyn Quayle," she said. She described the movie's clothes as being "inspired by those memorable black-and-white television series of long ago. More white than black, as I recall. But let's just leave that to beaver." A pause. "I didn't say whose." She grinned wider. "You know, I may not be doing this show ever again. So let's just go right to the edge and go over, what do you say?"

When Robin Williams took the stage to present the best supporting actress Oscar, Damon, Affleck, Norton, and Thornton headed back into the lobby to watch a monitor. As they went through the door, a catering employee dashed toward them, shouting "Mr. Norton!" Norton stopped. "I just wanted to say hi," she told him—violating the first rule of working at the Oscars, which was "Don't bother the stars."

"Thank you," Norton said politely. The catering employee headed back to her coworkers, who greeted her with whoops. Damon, Affleck, Norton, and Thornton watched as Williams made a suggestion. "In terms of the Kazan controversy," he said, "let Lainie sing!" Then he gave the supporting-actress award to Judi Dench for *Shakespeare in Love*. In the lobby, Damon clapped.

During a commercial break after the award, the aisles were clogged with stars coming and going. Coburn returned to his seat, where he was congratulated by his *Affliction* costar Nick Nolte. A few seats away, Emily Watson hugged Rachel Griffiths, her costar in (and fellow nominee for) *Hillary and Jackie*. Robin Williams headed in a side door, walked over to Norton, and shook his hand. "Powerful stuff," he said to the star of *American History X*. Jack Nicholson left his seat and made his way toward the exit, pausing to shake Damon's hand. As Nicholson went out the door, Harvey Weinstein stopped him to say hello. Aerosmith's roadies, wearing everything from tuxes to black T-shirts, set up the band's equipment as Conti's orchestra played "Over the Rainbow."

Back from the commercial break, Goldberg spotted Goldie Hawn and Kurt Russell standing in the aisle, pointing at the seat-fillers who'd taken their seats. "Hi, Goldie," she said. "Siddown. Shiiiii . . ." She trailed off before supplying the final consonant. The seat-fillers quickly vacated Kurt's and Goldie's seats.

As Chris Rock presented the award for sound effects editing, the members of Aerosmith took their places behind a screen that hid them from the audience. Drummer Joey Kramer was wearing a gold lamé suit. "It's a big, controversial night," said Rock as the band members picked up instruments. "I saw DeNiro backstage. You better get Kazan away from DeNiro, 'cause you know he hates rats." There were audible groans from the crowd. "Now, somebody has a death wish if they wanted me to come up here," said Rock.

After Rock's introduction, a short film spotlighting the nominees played on the screen in front of Aerosmith. During the few seconds when the home audience could only hear that film's soundtrack, the band members quickly tested their instruments. Hearing the rock 'n' roll riffs blasting from behind the curtain, a few audience members hooted. As the film ended, a stage manager cued the band to stop playing and wait for their introduction from Liv Tyler. The group's performance was typically spirited; leaving the stage, Steven Tyler high-fived his huge bodyguard, who was waiting for him in the wings.

In the green room, Nicolas Cage talked to a page. Andie MacDowell watched the show on a monitor. Outside the room, Bruce Vilanch smiled. "Two *shits* and one *beaver* so far," he said. "I'm counting. And Chris Rock took care of Kazan for us." He looked pleased. "Susan Futterman keeps putting little notes on the mirror in Whoopi's dressing room: DON'T GO THERE; NO MORE SHIT; THIS IS SUSAN: WATCH YOUR MOUTH, GIRL."

Cheers sounded in the green room as *Life Is Beautiful* won the award for best foreign-language film. As expected, Roberto Benigni went crazy, walking on seat backs and rambling through an exuberant two-and-a-half-minute speech in amusingly broken English. "I feel like now to dive into this ocean of generosity," he said.

Immediately afterward, John Travolta introduced a tribute to Frank Sinatra. In the west lobby, a huge group of seat-fillers stood around the monitor, watching. Just outside the lobby, in a secluded area by some of the control trailers, Nick Nolte stood by himself, hands in his pockets. Behind a black drape not far from Nolte, Val Kilmer was led through a stage door and into the wings. He was followed quickly by Triggerson, the grandson of Roy Rogers's famous steed. As the trainer held Triggerson, Kilmer walked around the horse, petting and talking to him.

On the stage, Goldberg introduced Liam Neeson, stroking the microphone stand as she spoke. The audience tittered. Backstage, Triggerson started stomping his foot, a trick for which he was usually rewarded with a treat. (To ensure he didn't leave an unsightly souvenir onstage, the horse's feeding schedule had been changed.) Though the trainer tried to calm Triggerson, Kilmer didn't feel comfortable trying to ride the skittish horse—so when he took the stage to introduce a tribute to cowboy actors, he was beside Triggerson rather than astride him. The horse walked in circles and resisted Kilmer's attempts to control him. "Debbie Allen didn't choreograph this part," Kilmer said.

A few minutes later, Helen Hunt read the nominees for best actor. Peter Gabriel and Randy Newman stood in the wings, waiting for their turn to perform. Roberto Benigni won, in a huge upset over Ian McKellen's remarkable performance in *Gods and Monsters*. "This is a terrible mistake because I used up all my English!" Benigni shouted. "My body is in tumult! I would like to be Jupiter and kidnap everybody and lie down in the firmament making love to everybody . . ."

Newman and Gabriel, due up next, watched the spectacle from the side of the stage. "It'll be like following an animal act," said Newman as Benigni went on and on.

After a minute and a half, the music came up to play off Benigni, and the show cut to a commercial. During the break, three of the best-actor nominees—Nolte, Norton, and McKellen—ran into each other in the bar and teased one another about losing to the hyperactive Italian.

Paltrow, meanwhile, stepped outside for a smoke. Danette Herman stuck her head into Cates's office, where Elia and Frances Kazan sat with Scorsese and DeNiro. "One more segment," she said, "and then it'll be time." It was already eight o'clock, two and a half hours into the show. "It's Sunday *and* Monday at the Oscars," Herman said apologetically.

When the word spread backstage that the upcoming segment would include the award to Kazan, there was a sudden flurry of activity. Damon and Affleck, who were presenting the award immediately before Kazan's, asked Debbie Williams if there was any way they could get back to their seats to see the honorary award. "I'm sorry," she told them, "but there's no time to reseat you."

With thirty seconds left before the commercial ended, a page approached stage manager Rita Cossette. "Val Kilmer would like to return to his seat to see the Kazan award," she said. "Is that possible?"

"I can do it," said Cossette. "Where is he?" She rushed to the green room, but returned a minute later shaking her head. "He's got his girlfriend with him, and they're three seats in from the aisle," she said. "It'd be impossible."

The act began with Goldberg wearing a glittery silver glam-rock ensemble from *Velvet Goldmine*; bedecked with feathered plumes, she tottered on massive platform boots. After introducing Lisa Kudrow, Goldberg dashed into the wings and headed for her dressing room to change into a costume from *Shakespeare in Love*. Garry Hood saw the look on her face as she passed, and thought the host was probably regretting her decision to wear so many outfits.

While she was changing, Scorsese and DeNiro began to speak about Kazan. The green room got very quiet. A huge crowd also gathered around another backstage monitor, this one hanging just above the stage door. Nicolas Cage stood about two feet from the monitor, watching intently. Kudrow and Renée Zellweger hurried to the monitor in Horvitz's office.

In the theater lobby, Geoffrey Rush and David Geffen were among those gathered around a different monitor. "What about all the movies that didn't get made because of what he did?" Geffen was overheard asking, rhetorically.

In the hall, reaction to Kazan was sharply divided. Applause was steady but subdued; the standing ovation was spotty, and some of it was made up of seat-fillers, who were always told to stand for the honorary Oscar winners. Horvitz cut to shots of Karl Malden standing and applauding, then to Warren Beatty doing the same, then to Spielberg clapping from his seat, then to Ed Harris and Amy Madigan sitting silently, arms in front of them and frowns on their faces.

"Thank you very much," said Kazan. "I really like to hear that. And I want to thank the Academy for its courage, generosity, and I want to tell you that I've been a member of the Academy, on and off, for I don't know how many years. So I'm pleased to say what's best about them, they're damn good to work with. I also want to thank . . ." He stopped, and looked around. "Marty, where are you?" he said. "Hiding behind me? C'mon here." Scorsese walked up to Kazan, who hugged him. "Thank you all very much," he concluded. "I think I can just slip away."

After leaving the stage, Kazan headed into Cates's office. "I need to use the bathroom," he said.

Affleck and Damon walked through the backstage area. "Whew," said Affleck, shaking his head.

The show had already passed the three-hour mark by the time Annette Bening introduced the In Memoriam package, which included footage of such notables as E. G. Marshall, director Alan J. Pakula, Maureen O'Sullivan, Phil Hartman, Akira Kurosawa, and Roddy McDowall. Goldberg watched it from the wings. When Bowery Boy Huntz Hall appeared on the screen, she sighed. "Oh, Huntz," she said.

In the green room, a very slinky tête-à-tête was taking place: Geena Davis, Uma Thurman, and Goldie Hawn, all in long gowns, stood around a silver tray laden with strawberries.

A few minutes later, Thurman was led into the wings. A stagehand going the other direction stepped on the full skirt of her Chanel couture gown, bringing her to an abrupt, jarring halt. "You okay?" asked Debbie Williams.

"Yeah," said Thurman uneasily. "He nearly pulled my dress off. That would have been unfortunate." She paused. "For me."

Three and a half hours in, Gwyneth Paltrow won the best-actress award, the fifth win of the night for *Shakespeare in Love*. She immediately broke down, delivering a teary two-and-a-half-minute acceptance speech. In the green room, Harrison Ford and Kevin Costner watched stoically, sitting side by side. Eyeing the same monitor from a nearby seat, Renée Zellweger got a little misty-eyed. Geena Davis applauded. On the fourth floor, in the general photo room, half a dozen weary photographers started heckling the monitor. An Academy publicist warned them to keep it down.

Ten minutes later, with four awards yet to be handed out, Robert Shapiro stepped outside the Chandler. "What do you think?" he asked. "Longest show ever?"

A security guard looked at his watch. "Oh, yeah," he said. "You're in the record book."

"All *right*," said Shapiro.

Ten minutes later, Kevin Costner walked out to give the best-director award. "They say the show's running a little long," said the star of the epic films *Dances with Wolves*, *The Postman*, and *Waterworld*. "I like things that run long."

The winner was Spielberg, who received a standing ovation. "Am I allowed to say I really wanted this?" he asked. After the award, Spielberg was rushed straight back to his seat to await the best-picture category. As Spielberg sat back down, Harrison Ford paced backstage. In his right hand, Ford carried a piece of paper that contained his lines. In his left, he held the night's final envelope.

When Ford opened that envelope onstage, a brief flicker of dismay seemed to cross his face. "The Oscar goes to *Shakespeare in Love*," he said. To huge cheers from the Miramax contingent and gasps from other sections of the audience, the film's five producers came to the stage—including Harvey Weinstein, who pulled a sheet of paper from his jacket pocket as he walked up the steps to the stage. After Donna Gigliotti and David Parfitt spoke, the pale, hefty Miramax chief leaned toward the microphone. "This was an ensemble film, and it took an ensemble team to make it," said Weinstein, who thanked Michael Eisner and Joe Roth at Disney, then moved to the Miramax staff, then to his "loving wife," his "two rotten kids," his two nieces, and his mother. At this point, Cates had heard enough. For the first time in memory, the orchestra played off a best-picture winner.

When the credits finally ended, Seligman checked his watch. "4:02," he said. The show was, officially and irrevocably, the longest Academy Awards telecast in history.

Backstage, Roberto Benigni headed for the elevator, only to be chased down by Goldie Hawn. "Thank you," she said, "for your great heart."

A few minutes later, Elia and Frances Kazan left Cates's office. In the hallway, they ran into Warren Beatty and Annette Bening. Beatty wrapped Kazan, who had directed him in *Splendor in the Grass* in 1961, in a big hug. "Warren," said Kazan. "I'm so glad to see you! I haven't seen you in so long! And now you're a producer and a director. I haven't seen your movie yet, but I'm going to."

"*Bulworth?*" said Beatty. "It's funny." The couples chatted awhile longer. Then Beatty asked Kazan, "Are you going to the ball?"

"I don't know," said Kazan. He pointed to his wife. "She's telling me what to do tonight."

Beatty laughed. "So is mine," he said.

Upstairs in the press rooms, Paltrow began to do interviews. One reporter told her that many people in the room cried during her acceptance speech.

"Come on, you are all a bunch of hardened, cynical journalists," said Paltrow. "Don't try to pull that on me."

While guests began to filter into the Governors Ball, crew members gathered onstage, tried to shoot the corks from a few bottles of Moët & Chandon champagne off the head of a giant Oscar statue, and cut a cake decorated with a picture of the set.

Amid the hugs and thank-yous and snapshots, Whoopi Goldberg was presented with a souvenir that had been fashioned backstage since the dress rehearsal: an ample, hand-carved, polished wooden dildo. She laughed at the gift, and then—at the urging of just about everyone who'd worked on the show—marched across the stage and bestowed the item on Susan Futterman.

Sunday Bloody Sunday

And as the Oscar seventy-one crew hooted and hollered and the host beamed, ABC's Madame Censor Lady broke into a big grin, grabbed hold of her new dildo, and began stroking.

BACKSTAGE after his big win, Harvey Weinstein claimed that he'd talked to Warren Beatty, who'd spoken to Jeffrey Katzenberg, who'd admitted that DreamWorks spent more on the *Saving Private Ryan* campaign than Miramax spent on *Shakespeare in Love*.

The move to Sunday couldn't stop a nearly inevitable ratings skid after the previous year's record-setting mark. The show was down 18 percent over those titanic numbers—while, to use a fairer comparison, it improved on the dismal figures from two years earlier by a paltry 4 percent.

The preshow was widely panned. The show itself received the usual range of reviews, with Benigni receiving a mixture of approval and ridicule, and reaction to Debbie Allen's dance number leaning toward the latter.

A few days after the show, Roy Christopher got a call from a friend who worked at the Metropolitan Opera. "When I started doing the Oscars, I didn't put much value on it," said Christopher. "I wanted to do opera, I wanted to do something meaningful, something beautiful, something amazing. But this friend called me after seeing the show, and he said, 'Let me tell you something. You may think that you're not doing art, but you would never get the opportunity at the Met to do anything that beautiful. So you might as well shut up and appreciate it.' "

After four years of separate awards for dramatic and comedy scores— years in which, crucially, animated Disney films were beaten by the music for *Emma* and for *Shakespeare in Love*—the music branch went back to a single award for best score. Unwilling to completely relinquish a category, the branch reinstated the award for best song score, though it wouldn't be given out unless enough films qualified during the year.

In June, the board of governors also voted to change the rule governing the best-picture award. In the future, it announced, no more than three producers could be awarded Oscars in the best-picture category. The Academy did not say that the rule change was due to the five people who trooped to the stage on behalf of *Shakespeare in Love*, and then spoke until the orchestra stopped them—but considering that it had been twenty years since a best-picture winner had more than three producers, it was impossible not to lay this one at the feet of Harvey Weinstein and crew.

The young singer who'd served as Andrea Bocelli's stand-in, Josh Groban, signed a recording contract with Warner Bros. before the year was over and began recording with producer David Foster. When his debut album came out in November 2001, it contained a version of "The Prayer," the song he'd sung at Oscar rehearsals.

By the end of the year, on the corner of Hollywood Boulevard and Highland Avenue in the heart of Hollywood, construction was under way on the entertainment complex that would house the new, permanent home of the Academy Awards. The initial plan was to have the theater ready in time for the Oscar show in 2001—but that was beginning to seem unlikely, considering that the property was little more than a hole in the ground, surrounded by fences bedecked with murals advertising *Toy Story 2* and *The Tigger Movie*. Quincy Jones, meanwhile, had changed his mind about opening a nightclub in the new complex.

Two blocks away, in a sleepy shopping center that sat between a multiplex theater and the Hollywood Museum (an attempted tourist attraction usually devoid of tourists), the Tower Records chain had opened a video clearance outlet. As the next Oscar season began to heat up, a big table near the entrance to the Tower outlet was piled high with *Oscar's Greatest Moments* videocassettes, which were selling for ninety-nine cents each.

1

Everybody's Talkin'

The 72nd Academy Awards

SITTING ACROSS THE TABLE from Richard and Lili Fini Zanuck, Lou Horvitz couldn't figure it out. The couple, he knew, was Hollywood royalty—particularly Richard, a small, trim, white-haired man of sixty-five whose father, the legendary Darryl F. Zanuck, had cofounded 20th Century-Fox studios and helped create the Hollywood studio system. Richard Zanuck himself ran Fox for a spell, then formed his own company and produced such films as *Jaws*, *The Verdict*, *Cocoon*, and *Driving Miss Daisy*. For that last film, he and Lili Zanuck, his third wife and a producer and director in her own right, received best-picture Oscars.

But now the couple had agreed to produce the 72nd Academy Awards show, which is why they were meeting with Horvitz. To the three-time Oscar director, though, their decision didn't make sense. Of course it was a prestige gig, but what's left to prove when you've already won the Thalberg and a best-picture award?

"I was sitting in front of people whose careers I'd really studied, and they were asking me questions about how the show worked," remembered

Horvitz. "I just stopped and said, 'Can I ask something? You have Oscars, Thalbergs . . . Why would you possibly want to produce the Oscars?' "

Richard Zanuck's reply came quickly. "I don't," he told Horvitz. Then he nodded toward his wife. "She does."

Months later, Lili Zanuck laughed about how she'd essentially forced her husband to produce the Academy Awards. "From the time we said yes, which I think was in September or October," she said, "I always knew there was going to be this moment when my husband was going to say, 'I never wanted to do this, you're the one that wanted to do it.' I thought that moment was going to come around February. But actually, he said it the very next day."

RICHARD ZANUCK may not have wanted the job, but when he and his wife took it they were ready to change the face of Oscar. "The minute we said yes, we had ideas for every single thing," said Lili Zanuck. "We wanted to revamp it as much as we could, because we thought for years it had had a similar look."

In certain ways, Gil Cates had created the template for the modern Oscars. His shows differed from year to year, but they all relied on a familiar blend of film clips, musical numbers, and dance routines that sometimes struggled to find a connection with the movies. They'd also been growing steadily longer, from three and a half hours or less in the early 1990s to more than four hours in 1999. Bob Rehme thought it was time to bring in new producers—and when he called on the Zanucks, the couple had some immediate priorities: "We wanted to freshen it up a bit, make the pace faster, make the show shorter," said Richard.

As the Zanucks got to work from production offices in the heart of Beverly Hills, they made plans and they made promises. They immediately announced that the show would not include any dance numbers, and that it would be far shorter than other recent Oscar shows. In some of the interviews they gave, the Zanucks promised to bring in the show at three hours and fifteen minutes; in other conversations, Lili hinted at hitting the seemingly unattainable mark of three hours.

Their new vision involved elaborate changes. They hired art director

Bob Keene to design a set that featured towers of high-tech video screens, along with a stage floor that was lit from beneath. They booked actor and commercial voiceover artist Peter Coyote to be the voice of Oscar, and to appear on-screen when Horvitz's cameras ventured into the wings. And Lili Zanuck had ideas for a dramatically different use of music, incorporating a pit band led by pop-rock producer Don Was and another combo under the direction of legendary songwriter Burt Bacharach.

When Michael Seligman heard the new producers' plans, he knew the Academy was going to have to write some big checks. The usual Oscar show was budgeted at about $10 million, but the longtime associate producer quickly realized that the Zanucks' plans were far more extravagant. Seligman listened, took notes, ran the numbers, and reported to the Academy that the show would cost significantly more than the usual Oscar telecast. Not wanting to rein in the new producers, the Academy agreed to the largest budget in Oscar history.

ON VALENTINE'S DAY, 2000, on the eve of Oscar nominations, the Internet struck in the familiar form of Harry Knowles. An overweight twenty-eight-year-old with flaming red hair, Knowles ran a Web site called Ain't It Cool News out of his father's house in Austin, Texas. AICN was respected in some quarters and tolerated in others, but it occasionally infuriated Hollywood studios with inside news, gossip, and particularly reports from what were supposed to be confidential test screenings of upcoming movies. The Web site spread positive word-of-mouth about films like *Titanic*, but it also broke the bad news after its spies infiltrated screenings of *Batman and Robin*.

Knowles relied on a network of informants and insiders, and tried his best to determine which of them could be trusted. The day before the Oscar nominations were announced, he trumpeted a major scoop. "From Deep Within the Halls of The Academy of Motion Pictures Arts & Sciences [*sic*] comes the list," he wrote, claiming to have obtained "the list that they narrow down from." It consisted of eight potential nominees in seventeen different Oscar categories.

The fact that the Academy never had such a list didn't deter Knowles, who reported that for best picture, the top eight vote-getters were British theater director Sam Mendes's twisted drama *American Beauty*; *The Green Mile*, another Stephen King adaptation from Frank Darabont, director of *The Shawshank Redemption*; *The Insider*, director Michael Mann's look at a tobacco industry whistle-blower; Indian-born writer-director M. Night Shyamalan's blockbuster thriller *The Sixth Sense*; Anthony Minghella's stylish and morally ambiguous *The Talented Mr. Ripley*; Neil Jordan's World War II romance *The End of the Affair*; Mike Leigh's Gilbert and Sullivan story *Topsy-Turvy*; and Norman Jewison's biography of imprisoned boxer Ruben Carter, *The Hurricane*.

As soon as the list hit the Internet, other media outlets jumped on it, spreading the information that Ain't It Cool News had somehow hacked into the Academy's computers.

EARLY THE NEXT MORNING, the Samuel Goldwyn Theater once again filled with reporters, publicists, and studio reps anxious to see just how accurate Ain't It Cool News had been. In an aisle seat near the back of the theater was Tony Angelotti, a publicist and awards consultant who had helped run campaigns for such films as *The English Patient*, *Shakespeare in Love*, and *Pulp Fiction*, and was considered one of the savviest Oscar predictors in town. "*Toy Story 2* has no chance for a best-picture nomination," said Angelotti to those around him. "It won't happen. First of all, it had three directors, so the directors' branch isn't going to vote for it. You don't see the actors in it, so it won't get support from the actors' branch . . ."

"What about Hilary Swank?" asked someone sitting near Angelotti. Swank, best known for a stint on the TV show *Beverly Hills, 90210*, had won raves and critics' awards for *Boys Don't Cry*, in which she played a true-life teenage girl who passed herself off as a boy and was raped and murdered when her ruse was discovered.

"She might get a nomination," Angelotti announced, "but she can't win. She came out of nowhere, and the movie wasn't successful. The Academy likes to give the supporting-actress award to unknowns, but never best actress. If she wins, she'll be the first unknown actress since World War II to win for a movie that wasn't a big hit. Marlee Matlin was an unknown when she won, but she was in a big movie from Paramount, *Children of a Lesser God. Boys Don't Cry* is a small movie from Fox Searchlight. She can't win."

A few minutes later, Angelotti and the rest of the room learned that Swank had indeed been nominated—and that the Miramax movie on whose behalf he was working, Swedish director Lasse Hallström's *The Cider House Rules*, had won seven nominations, the same as *The Insider* and one less than the year's leader, *American Beauty*.

Ain't It Cool News, it turned out, had missed the best-picture and best-director nods for *Cider House*, even though its list contained eight contenders instead of five. It also erred on a few other crucial nominations, such as the best-director citation for Spike Jonze, a former video director who'd made the delightfully twisted *Being John Malkovich*.

But proving Ain't It Cool wrong wasn't the biggest treat for the Academy's staff, which had known all along that the Internet list couldn't possibly be accurate. Instead, Bruce Davis was more delighted to find relatively little overlap with the Golden Globe Awards, which reveled in its widely disseminated reputation as the harbinger of the Oscars. It had long grated on Davis that an organization made up of around eighty reporters for foreign newspapers and magazines, a group widely considered susceptible to being wined, dined, and flattered, was thought to have any impact on the votes of the Academy.

"The thing that bothers me, and it's not just with the Golden Globes but with all the other shows and the guilds, is this fallacy that because one thing follows another, the first thing was the cause of the second," Davis said. "Our members do not need the Hollywood Foreign Press to show them what a good movie is."

It was true that the nominees and winners for the Oscars and the Globes often did coincide—but to a large degree, the overlap was based on a statistical quirk. The Globes split their main awards into separate categories for drama and musical or comedy, which meant that it named ten best-picture nominees each year. With twice the number as the Academy, that usually made it a safe bet that the films nominated for the best-picture Oscar had already been up for Golden Globes.

But that wasn't the case in 2000. "Even with ten slots," a delighted Davis said to executive administrator Ric Robertson, "they only got two of our best-picture nominations." (The two were *American Beauty* and *The Insider*, which were nominated along with *Cider House*, *The Sixth Sense*, and *The Green Mile*.)

Standing in the rear of the theater with Davis, Danette Herman was particularly interested in the five nominees for best song. She'd expected four of the nominations: the title song to *Music of My Heart*, written by Diane Warren and sung in the film by Gloria Estefan and the up-and-coming boy band 'N Sync; "Save Me" from *Magnolia*, written by alternative-rock singer-songwriter Aimee Mann; "When She Loved Me" from *Toy Story 2*, written by thirteen-time nominee Randy Newman but sung by the Canadian singer Sarah McLachlan; and "You'll Be in My Heart" from the Disney film *Tarzan*, written and sung by Phil Collins.

Herman had figured that the fifth nominee would probably be "Beautiful Stranger," a new Madonna song written for *Austin Powers: The Spy Who Shagged Me*. Though few staffers relished the idea of telling the pop diva that she'd have to cut her song down to a minute and a half to fit into the medley the Zanucks had envisioned, Madonna was the kind of big name that ABC loved.

Her name, though, was nowhere on the list of nominees. Instead, the fifth slot went to "Blame Canada," from the gleefully but astonishingly profane animated film *South Park: Bigger, Longer and Uncut*. The movie, based on the series that had brought the Comedy Central cable network its highest ratings ever, took vicious swipes at society's tendency to look for pop-culture scapegoats; along the way, according to one count, it contained more foul language per minute than any movie ever made. The two masterminds behind *South Park*, Trey Parker and Matt Stone, fought Paramount Pictures over the editing and marketing of their movie, and waged a lengthy and bitter battle with the MPAA to keep it from being rated NC-17.

South Park: Bigger, Longer and Uncut was a very funny movie, and a full-fledged musical that not only mocked the conventions of Disney-style animated musicals, but worked extraordinarily well on its own terms. In addition to being a foul-mouthed malcontent who hated the movie business, Parker was also a fanatic devotee of Broadway musical theater. Together with Marc Shaiman he came up with the richest song score in years, one that would have been a shoo-in in the recently restored category of best song score had 1999 seen the release of enough musicals for the category to be implemented.

Of course, the *South Park* songs included lyrics like "Shut your fucking face, Uncle Fucka / You're a boner-biting bastard, Uncle Fucka," lines completely unsuitable for the Oscars. So Paramount put a small push behind "Blame Canada," a song in which a group of mothers, concerned over the foul language their kids pick up at a movie starring a pair of Canadian comedians, decide that the fault lies with the country to our north. Parker, who six years earlier had won a student Academy Award and, he claimed, stiffed the Academy for his bar tab, was astonished when the song was nominated.

So was Herman. "Who sings 'Blame Canada'?" she said with a frown.

Told that some of the voices were done by Parker and Stone themselves, along with voiceover artist Mary Kay Bergman, who had committed suicide two months earlier, Herman shook her head. "Trey Parker?" she said, envisioning how that name would go over with the network and its advertisers. "Oh, great."

"I know," said Ric Robertson, who was standing nearby. "Let's get Ann Reinking to sing it."

Herman laughed at the idea of inviting the Broadway star Reinking, who had famously butchered Phil Collins's song "Against All Odds" in 1985, while an appalled Collins sat in the audience and watched. "Well," she said, "I'm sure we'll work something out."

THE NEXT DAY, a chastened Harry Knowles admitted that the Oscar nominations made him look "like a complete moron." After complaining about reporters who'd written that he'd hacked the Academy's computers—"I wouldn't even begin to know how to do any hacking," he said—Knowles explained that the trouble began two days earlier, when he received an e-mail from a source who claimed to have found the preliminary list of nominees in an unprotected FileMaker database on an Academy computer.

Knowles said he immediately began double-checking the names on the list to make sure they were all eligible for nominations, and he looked up past articles about the nomination process. Knowles then had a more tech-savvy friend check the Internet address from which the material had supposedly come. The friend suggested, wrongly, that it had indeed come from an Academy computer.

After more correspondence with the original source, who said that the files were a database earmarked for the Oscar.com webmaster, Knowles decided that the material was legitimate. It wasn't until the real nominations were released that he was able to figure out the truth, which was that his list was simply the best guesses of a staffer for ABC.com, who didn't realize that his cable modem allowed outside computers access to his files.

On AICN, Knowles apologized to the Academy, blamed "faulty research" for the confusion, and added, "[T]here never was an attempt on an Academy computer. The nominations were never in any danger. And both Price Waterhouse [*sic*] and the Academy can sleep well at night knowing that at no point was there any failure in their security."

AS FAR as the Zanucks were concerned, the big musical number of the 72nd Academy Awards was going to be Burt Bacharach's medley of past Oscar-nominated songs. But they still had to deal with the five new songs. Calls went out to Randy Newman, Aimee Mann, Phil Collins, Gloria Estefan, and 'N Sync, all of whom agreed to perform and, reluctantly, to cut their songs to ninety seconds.

But dealing with the disgruntled likes of Newman and Mann—and they were indeed disgruntled at the prospect of cutting their songs in half—was nowhere near as tricky as figuring out what to do with "Blame Canada." Not only were the song's original performers either dead (Mary Kay Bergman) or unknown and unpredictable (Trey Parker and Matt Stone), but the song itself made little sense to people who hadn't seen the movie. In addition, the lyrics called Canadian singer Anne Murray "that bitch," took a swipe at perennial Oscar favorite Céline Dion, used the word *fart*, and included the immortal couplet "My boy Eric used to have my picture on his shelf / But now when he sees me he tells me to fuck myself."

The Zanucks approached "Blame Canada" songwriters Parker and Shaiman for ideas. "The first big kick in the balls we got," said Parker, "was that they were going to do all the songs together as a medley. And another part of their master plan was to get rid of the orchestra and let it be Don Was and a couple of synthesizers. And we were like, 'You've got to be kidding. These are Broadway-type songs, and they should be done in Broadway fashion.' They were like, 'No, this is young and hip and cool, let's get Jewel to come out and do it with a guitar.' "

Parker and Shaiman fought for an orchestra and a chorus. Shaiman, who for years had cowritten Billy Crystal's "It's a Wonderful Night for Oscar" medley, used the clout he'd accumulated to plead his case. "Billy's medley is totally in the Rat Pack style of big band and strings," he said, "and 'Blame Canada' is a big musical comedy number. As the composer, I didn't want my songs to be on the grandest of presentations with, like, a synthesizer playing trumpet and trombone parts, not to mention oboe parts and bassoon parts and piccolo parts."

Initially, Shaiman took his case to the laid-back Was—whose response, he said, was, "Hey, man, whatever. Call Burt Bacharach." The call to Bacharach was not a pleasant one: "It's like going to Olympus and speaking to the gods, and yet having to have this sort of antagonistic conversation with him. And he didn't want to be bothered. I felt terrible having to piss off Burt Bacharach, but it was the Academy Awards, and I was going to really fight for an orchestra."

At the same time, ABC's standards and practices department had more bad news for Parker and Shaiman. The word *fuck* was out, of course, but so was *fart*. So was calling Anne Murray a bitch—because, they reasoned, she might sue.

ON WEDNESDAY, March 1, the Academy staged its annual ballot-mailing photo op for the Oscar-hungry press. Afterward, staffers from Pricewater-houseCoopers took the ten bags, which contained forty-two hundred ballots going to Academy members in California, and left them on the loading dock at the Beverly Hills post office. (Out-of-state ballots had already been mailed.) The bags, though, were mislabeled third class and sent to a routing center in the industrial town of Bell, twenty miles southeast of Beverly Hills.

On Saturday night, March 4, at the annual Scientific and Technical Awards ceremony, Academy officials began to hear from anxious members who had yet to receive their ballots. The problem was tracked down, new ballots were mailed, and the deadline for returning them was extended for two days, from March 21 to March 23, just three days before the ceremony.

Two days after the Sci-Tech dinner, a shipment of Oscar statuettes from Chicago arrived at a loading dock that was coincidentally also in Bell. Six boxes, weighing 470 pounds and containing fifty-five Oscars, disappeared. Still reeling from the embarrassment of the mislabeled ballots, the Academy decided to keep quiet about this new loss.

WHILE THE ZANUCKS struggled with "Blame Canada" and the Academy tried to track down ballots and statuettes, the battle over best picture began to resemble nothing so much as the previous year's fracas between *Saving Private Ryan* and *Shakespeare in Love*. Again, on one side was DreamWorks, with a film generally acknowledged to be the front-runner; on the other side was Miramax, trying its best to turn a one-time dark horse into an upset victor.

This time, DreamWorks had *American Beauty*, stage director Sam Mendes's caustic look at anomie, voyeurism, pedophilia, homosexuality, and other undercurrents running through American suburbia. One of the best-reviewed movies of the year, it was tough stuff, narrated from beyond the grave by Kevin Spacey's malcontent suburban dad, who began the movie masturbating in the shower and ended it dead on the garage floor. The movie wasn't for everybody, but it won most of the major critics' awards, and led the Oscar nominations with eight.

The Miramax entry was *The Cider House Rules*, Lasse Hallström's adaptation of the John Irving novel about a beloved small-town physician. Dr. Wilbur Larch, played by Michael Caine, watched over generations of orphans and, on the side, had a thriving business performing illegal abortions. Somewhere along the way, he'd also become addicted to sniffing ether. Gorgeously shot, languid, and unabashedly sentimental at times, the film picked up mixed reviews and didn't win any major awards—but Miramax saw a chance to position it as the perfect choice with voters for whom *American Beauty* was too dark. On their side was the fact that brilliant but risky movies usually won the screenplay award but lost in the best-picture race to safer fare: *Forrest Gump* over *Pulp Fiction*, *The English Patient* over *Fargo*. If *American Beauty* was the liberal choice, *Cider House* could be the conservative alternative. Of course, to position it as such required emphasizing the romantic, feel-good side of *Cider House*, and ignoring the fact that it dealt with drug addiction and incest, and at heart was a fairly passionate defense of the right to abortion. Miramax's ad campaign, almost as lavish as the one the company had mounted the year before on behalf of *Shakespeare in Love*, emphasized the love affair between characters played by Tobey Maguire and Charlize Theron, the kindhearted benevolence of Doc Larch, and the lush visuals. To look at the ads, on television and in newspapers and in the trades, you'd never guess that the philosophical heart of the movie might offend hard-right conservatives as much as the perversion on display in *American Beauty*.

At first, Miramax's strategy appeared to be paying dividends. Prognosticators routinely referred to the best-picture competition as a two-horse race, and the consensus was that *Cider House* was picking up momentum. Even Trent Lott, the conservative Senate majority leader from Mississippi, weighed in with the news that *The Cider House Rules* was his favorite movie—though when *Entertainment Weekly* pressed a Lott staffer as to why the senator liked such a prochoice movie, the spokesperson grew evasive.

At the same time, though, distaste for the misleading ad campaign began to surface—actively encouraged, suggested many, by DreamWorks, which was determined not to see its Oscar favorite lose to Miramax two years in a row. Meanwhile, *American Beauty* continued to win awards: best dramatic film at the Golden Globes, best actor and actress at the Screen Actors Guild Awards, plus top honors from the Directors Guild and Producers Guild. As the Oscar show neared, most insiders felt that *The Cider House Rules* was losing momentum, and that for a change Miramax might have been out-campaigned.

The battleground even moved to the Oscar show itself. Chuck Workman was supervising all the film clips that would run during the show, including clips of the best-picture nominees. But the piece he'd put together saluting *The Cider House Rules* was, he said, too true to the movie—and as such, it flew in the face of a studio marketing campaign that was misrepresenting the film as a feel-good love story.

"Miramax hated what I did, and they screamed at me that it wasn't the way they wanted us to present the film," said Workman. "They said, 'The movie's about the relationship between the young man and the doctor, and about the love story between Tobey Maguire and Charlize Theron. You can't use any shots of Delroy Lindo,' " who played the boss on the farm where Maguire worked picking apples.

Workman's argument was simple: "It's my job to show people why the movie was nominated," he said. "The movie is called *The Cider House Rules*, and we need to show the Cider House. But they didn't care about that— they just wanted us to help their marketing."

It was not, he added, the first time Miramax had caused problems with Oscar clips. "They push the rules as far as possible to sell their movies," he said, "and no one ever tells them that the way they do business is reprehensible."

TREY PARKER had spent the weekend in Las Vegas, one of the favorite haunts of a thirty-year-old with lots of new money and a zest for partying. But on the morning of March 12, Parker returned from his two-day binge in time for a more sedate soiree, the Oscar nominees' luncheon.

Standing by the bar before the lunch got under way, Parker looked around; nearby were Tom Cruise, Annette Bening, and Warren Beatty. He laughed at the incongruity of the setting. "I was in a strip club in Vegas at four o'clock this morning," he said. "I was pretty fucked up, but I do remember looking up at a stripper and yelling, 'Hey, you wanna go with me to the Academy Awards nominees' lunch tomorrow?' And she looked down and yelled, 'Sure!' "

In the end, Parker left his stripper friend back in Vegas and came to the luncheon with his more presentable assistant, Jennifer Howell. He was still amazed at the furor "Blame Canada" had caused. "They say you can't say the word *fart* on TV," he said, baffled. "I don't believe it. That really shows where America is at."

The producers, he added, still hadn't booked a singer. "I don't know what we're going to do," he said. "They want Bette Midler or somebody, they want one vocalist. We said, 'No, we need a chorus,' and they said, 'No, we're not doing that this year.' It's like, goddamnit, we're pulling our hair out trying to get them to see that this has to be a *big* number."

When the hundred-or-so Oscar nominees were seated, Bob Rehme welcomed them. "I had a speech prepared," he said, "but the Beverly Hills post office lost it." He didn't mention the missing statuettes, still a secret outside the L.A.P.D. and the Academy. But later in the week, the Academy decided that publicity was its ally and announced that the statuettes had been stolen.

At a press conference, Bruce Davis noted the coincidence that both the missing ballots and the statuettes had passed through the town of Bell. "We have told Billy Crystal not to go anywhere near Bell," he said. Privately, Crystal and his writers were asked not to prepare too many jokes about the theft.

FOR WEEKS, concerns about the extraordinarily complex stage had been growing. Particularly troublesome were the tower units, thirty-five-foot columns designed to spin and slide. Together, the towers made up a wall of video screens that could show individual images, or come together to display one large image. "It was a kluge of every piece of equipment that existed in the world," said Lou Horvitz. "There were twenty-two video sources, all these graphic playbacks. Lili would say, 'Oh, this is great,' but every day we just kept getting in deeper and deeper."

In addition, the stage floor had to be raised so that it could be lit from beneath, but the heat from those lights threatened to buckle it. A cooling system was implemented to pump in cold air as a countermeasure, but that caused sound problems. The only way to make sure it would all work, that the towers wouldn't topple and the images could be synced, was to build and set everything up and try it out.

The entire stage was erected on a soundstage at ABC Prospect, and rehearsals were held using stand-ins. The towers remained upright and the digital projections were sharp. "There was a tremendous amount of choreography that had to go into it, but it worked," said a relieved Richard Zanuck. After an initial bit of panic while Keene tried to find a route that didn't pass under any low bridges, the stage was moved to downtown Los Angeles and the entire operation shifted to the Shrine Auditorium.

Horvitz, meanwhile, struggled to mark his script with everything that was needed. Normally, he'd use the script to indicate cuts, camera moves, and cues for video packages—but this time, he realized as he started working on it, the video towers alone complicated his task enormously. "It took me almost an hour and a half to write the first cue, out of twenty-six," he said. "It was 'Tower one shows this, tower two, tower three, tower four . . .' After I wrote that first page, I looked in the mirror and went, 'Louis J., what the fuck did you do?' "

As the production relocated, a sixty-one-year-old junk scavenger named Willie Fulgear found all but three of the missing Oscar statuettes behind a drugstore in the Koreatown neighborhood of Los Angeles. A Roadway employee admitted involvement and implicated a fellow driver. The two men were arrested. Although Roadway wanted to wait until he'd been officially cleared of any involvement by the police, the Academy quickly gave Fulgear tickets to the Oscar show, and encouraged the shipping company to give him the $50,000 reward it had offered.

INSIDE THE SHRINE, the Zanucks were a study in contrasts. Richard was low key, dressed Beverly Hills casual: sports coats, slacks, and dress shirts. Lili was more energetic—as one staffer put it, she was "an unassuming-looking fireball" in tattered jeans and untucked men's shirts.

"She is a pistol," said stage manager Garry Hood. "She speaks her mind and she *goes*. Richard's more the old Hollywood-style producer and mogul type. He just sits back and puts in his two cents. But she just goes all over the place, and there is such great energy that it's great fun."

Still, even crew members who admired and liked the couple were confused as the week wore on. Instead of spending Tuesday and Wednesday doing lighting and camera tests, and then bringing in the stand-ins to begin proper rehearsals, the schedule bogged down with an unusual number of camera tests, film tests, music tests . . .

By now the Zanucks knew that three hours and fifteen minutes was a lost cause. Instead, they cautiously mentioned three and a half hours as a goal. But besides Bacharach's lengthy medley and several packages of film clips (including a baffling six-minute montage presenting the history of the world as seen through Hollywood movies), the show contained many small elements that could slow it down. Categories that had often been handled by a single presenter, like the two documentary or short-subject categories, were being presented separately, while an unusually large number of awards were being handed out by multiple presenters, necessitating the kind of chitchat the producers once seemed eager to cut.

"It's going to be a very long show, and we all know it," said one crew member. "But I don't see Lili and Dick worrying about that. They just keep doing all these tests. That's what you do when you're making a movie, but you don't have time for that stuff on live TV. They're just not on terra firma anymore."

IN DOWNTOWN LOS ANGELES, the crew at the Shrine Auditorium was getting ready for a day devoted largely to rehearsing the Oscar show's musical numbers. Across town, in Pacific Palisades, Randy Newman sat in his backyard and looked out toward the Pacific Ocean. He was due at Oscar rehearsals in a couple of hours, but first he spent a few minutes mulling over his experiences with the Academy Awards.

"You know, I've been seeing these shows for fifty years," said Newman, whose uncles Alfred and Lionel had each conducted the Oscar orchestra. "As a little boy I remember looking at them. And they said the same thing every year: 'This year it's going to be better than a really bad vaudeville show.'" He shrugged. "Billy Crystal's funny, but I don't know if there's any such thing as a good Oscar show."

Newman thought back to the previous year, and Savion Glover's tap dance set to music from *Saving Private Ryan*. "I will miss the dances," he said with a grin. "I mean, that evocation of World War II was one of the most unbelievable things I've ever seen. I had my mouth open when I saw that at rehearsal."

Newman, one of the smartest but toughest songwriters in pop music and a man who freely described himself as "an old crock," also took issue with the musical choices the Zanucks had made. "They wanted the show to be entertaining," he said, "so they cut Sarah McLachlan, Phil Collins, Robin Williams, and Gloria Estefan. And it really is ludicrous how they cut the orchestra. I like to hear the band hacking away at *American Beauty* or whatever."

One could, of course, accuse Newman of a modicum of sour grapes—after all, his nomination for the song "When She Loved Me" was his thirteenth without a single win. The previous year he'd scored a rare trifecta with nominations for best song ("That'll Do" from *Babe: Pig in the City*), best dramatic score (*Pleasantville*), and best musical or comedy score (*A Bug's Life*), only to lose to music from *The Prince of Egypt*, *Life Is Beautiful*, and *Shakespeare in Love*, respectively.

"Always, the nomination really is what matters," he insisted. "Because it's musicians voting. But in the final voting . . ." He paused, looked down at his ensemble of Hawaiian shirt and rumpled chinos, and laughed. "I mean, why should I be able to vote for costume design? *Look* at me. Or makeup. What the hell do I know about it? I sort of liked *The Talented Mr. Ripley*, so I voted for the makeup of Jude Law, but who the hell knows if the makeup of Jude Law was really any good. And the same is true of music. People think they know—they say, 'I like that little tune in *Il Postino*,' or whatever beat me that year—but they don't really know. There have been scores lately that actually hurt the movie, that slowed it down, but they won."

Newman stopped and chuckled. "I hear myself complain, and I think, it's a wonder I ever get a job," he said.

"THIS," said Don Was, "is a ritual at the foot of a modern Mount Olympus."

Was, born Donald Fagenson in Detroit, cut an unusual figure on a show that usually turned to the old-school likes of Bill Conti for its musical director. The forty-eight-year-old musician wore his hair in dreadlocks and favored sweatpants and sandals regardless of the occasion. The onetime leader of an adventurous rock/dance group called Was (Not Was), whose biggest hit was the novelty tune "Walk the Dinosaur," Was had become well known as a producer, engineering the remarkable comeback of singer Bonnie Raitt and producing hits for everyone from the Rolling Stones to the B-52's.

Was had also assembled and led versatile bands for the Grammys, among other shows, which is why Lili Zanuck hired him to be one of the two Oscar bandleaders and threw him into what had become a complicated and unprecedented musical setup. By this point, there were four separate bands performing on the show—including the Oscar orchestra, which the Zanucks had reluctantly agreed to reinstate. Don Was's eight-piece band, which occupied the orchestra pit stage left, included three synthesizer players and one deejay; they played music for entrances and exits. Bacharach's ten-piece combo, which included three singers, sat in the pit stage right to handle entertainment during commercial breaks. The orchestra, forty-eight players strong, was ensconced in a room on the third floor of the Shrine. And a nine-piece onstage band combined members of all three groups to perform Bacharach's medley.

It was, as one staffer put it, "an audio nightmare"—not to mention the fact that orchestral musicians accustomed to sitting in the pit were not happy about being exiled upstairs and out of sight. Still, the orchestra *was* in the building, a tribute to the persistence of Marc Shaiman and Trey Parker, who insisted that "Blame Canada" just wasn't the type of song you could toss off unobtrusively.

"We decided to highlight the whole piece, instead of hiding it," explained Richard Zanuck. "It wasn't the most exciting song, but we made a big, colorful number out of it." To do so, the Zanucks brought in a large group of background singers and dancers. This was a curious move on a show that up to then had so avidly proclaimed "no dance numbers," but it wasn't technically a violation of the producers' promise; "Blame Canada" was simply a nominated song that would include dancers, not a dance number per se.

Partly, the more extravagant staging came about because Shaiman had persuaded Robin Williams, a fan of *South Park*, to perform the song. "Once Robin was in, it changed everything," said Parker. "That's what you learn about the Academy Awards: all they're trying to do is get ratings. They're selling fucking dish soap, and once Robin Williams was on, it was like, 'Great, we're gonna sell more dish soap.' "

Richard Zanuck had also talked the network into relenting and allowing Williams to say *fart*. Anne Murray sent word that it was fine to call her a bitch, and Williams promised to neither say nor mouth the word *fuck*.

The presence of an orchestra, meanwhile, had repercussions that Don

Was hadn't anticipated. Even though the orchestra was only being used for Billy Crystal's medley, "Blame Canada," and an overture that Bacharach had written, union regulations for the American Federation of Musicians required that they be paid for all the music played on the show.

"You can't just say, 'Okay, you're hired for this hour,' " said Was. "I'm using some drum loops and samples from a record I made in 1992 that was never released—and even though it was recorded in '92, it was deemed to be done for the Oscars, because that'll be the first public performance. It's costing $30,000, because every member of the orchestra has to be paid for something I did seven years ago."

Was had already run afoul of many Oscar music vets. One of his first ideas had been to do away with the traditional way of bringing winners and presenters onstage, which was for the orchestra to perform a snippet of the score from the film with which they had won, or the film with which they were most closely identified. In an attempt to modernize the tradition without completely junking it, Was decided that his band would bring people onstage to some sort of steady groove or drum pattern—but at the same time, the deejay in the orchestra pit would layer in recorded samples from the appropriate film score. The music director was particularly proud of the intro he'd worked up for Steven Spielberg: the theme from *Jaws* sawing away while a thudding groove kept the beat.

To Was, using recorded samples of the original scores was a matter of respecting the original composers. Since, say, John Williams had recorded the score to *Angela's Ashes* with a large orchestra, Was felt the composer would be better served by his original orchestration than the scaled-down version that would have been necessitated by the smaller Oscar forces. But orchestral musicians and the support staff that surrounded them didn't agree. "There's an infrastructure that doesn't have anything to do with the people producing the show," said Was. "It's a permanent bureaucracy of copyists and contractors and rehearsal studios, and I think everyone's just freaked out that they're not going to be part of the proceedings. I don't get a whole lot of help from them. I get a lot of hostility."

At rehearsal on Friday, Was also got lots of advice about how to deal with the hot boy band 'N Sync, which would be performing with Gloria Estefan on "Music of My Heart." Warned that the group was used to lip-syncing onstage and probably couldn't cut it vocally in live performance, Was recorded their harmony parts and sampled them so that they could be triggered by his keyboard player. But when Estefan first rehearsed, the tempo required by the samples seemed sluggish.

So Was approached Justin Timberlake, Lance Bass, and the other band members. "You guys can sing live, right?" he said. "Forget about the samples, let's try it." On the next take, the group nailed the harmonies. Afterward, Was felt vindicated. " 'N Sync can absolutely sing," he said. "People talk about how these boy bands can't perform live, but maybe it's because nobody gives them a chance."

BURT BACHARACH had spent months painstakingly crafting his big number. When the composer and performer signed on late in 1999, Lili Zanuck sent him a list of every song that had been nominated for an Oscar, highlighting about thirty of her favorites.

Bacharach chose the tunes he wanted to use in an extended medley; through January and February, the medley was his passion, and his obsession. He carefully dovetailed more than a dozen songs, plotting the dynamics and keying everything to the singers who'd agreed to perform: Ray Charles, Garth Brooks, Queen Latifah, Isaac Hayes, Dionne Warwick, Whitney Houston, and Bacharach himself. Early versions of the medley were more than twelve minutes long, far too lengthy for the show. Bacharach slowly and deliberately trimmed it, until he had it down to about eight minutes: "We fought for every bar," said Was.

Bacharach had been involved with the Oscars on and off over the years, presenting the best-song award a few times and winning three Oscars himself, most recently in 1982 for the song "Arthur's Theme (Best That You Can Do)," from the film *Arthur*. The writer of dozens of stylish pop hits in the 1960s and 1970s, including the movie themes "The Man Who Shot Liberty Valance," "What's New Pussycat?" and "Alfie," he hadn't been a steady presence on the pop charts for more than a decade. But he'd always had admirers in the world of rock 'n' roll, including the acclaimed singer-songwriter Elvis Costello. Bacharach's hip cachet was unassailable, as was his reputation as a brilliant, painstaking, and demanding bandleader and arranger. Bacharach was not a strong singer—he had a thin, breathy voice without much range—but he knew exactly what he wanted, and his musicians knew that he would instantly hear every flat note or missed cue.

Early the week of the show, Bacharach rehearsed his medley in studios at Paramount Pictures, running through the number with all of the singers except Whitney Houston, who failed to show up. A remarkable singer and sometime actress who'd had a string of number-one hits in the 1980s and one of the biggest singles of all time with "I Will Always Love You" (from the movie *The Bodyguard*) in 1993, Houston had once been considered demanding but professional. In recent years, though, she'd become increasingly erratic, unreliable, and disruptive. Rumors had long been rampant of drug use by Houston and her husband, R&B singer Bobby Brown, though Houston always denied them. She faced a charge of drug possession in January 2000 when a guard at an airport in Hawaii allegedly found marijuana in her purse, though the charges were later dropped.

Still, the rail-thin thirty-six-year-old was capable of turning in stunning performances, and Bacharach knew her well. In the sixties he'd often worked with her mother, gospel singer and background vocalist Cissy Houston, and he'd written and produced a dozen top-twenty hits for her aunt, Dionne Warwick.

At the Shrine, rehearsals for the medley took place on Friday night, in front of a small, tense group of staffers. Most of the medley's singers were in good spirits and good voice—Garth Brooks being a particular favorite among the stagehands—but from the start it was clear that Houston wasn't at her best. She looked puffy and a little disoriented; watching her stumble as she tried to navigate the stairs onstage, staffers described her in terms that ranged from "out of it" to "completely fucked up."

Houston was assigned two songs, the *Wizard of Oz* standard "Over the Rainbow" and the Barbra Streisand chestnut "The Way We Were." She wasn't happy with the keys in which Bacharach was asking her to sing, but he'd arranged the medley to build in a specific way, and he wasn't about to change that for Houston. During an early run-through, Bacharach played the introductory music to "Over the Rainbow" as Houston gingerly walked down the stairs. When she got to the bottom, she began singing "The Way We Were."

Bacharach immediately stopped the music and tried to tactfully point out her mistake. "Gosh," he said gently, "I love that song, but . . ."

Houston looked at him, realizing what was wrong. "Oh, yeah," she said, vaguely. "I don't know why I sang that."

For the next few minutes, Bacharach tried again. But Houston's voice was shaky, she seemed distracted and jittery, and her attitude was casual, almost defiant. Finally, Bacharach slumped over the piano, his head down on the keys. "I thought he was having a coronary," said Was.

During a break, Bacharach huddled with the Zanucks. He told them he didn't think Houston could cut it, that they were taking a big risk if they kept her on the show. Lili Zanuck wasn't necessarily convinced—"Dick and I thought she might have just been walking through rehearsal to save her voice, though nobody else was doing that," she said—but she agreed to back her musical director. "We cued off of Burt," she said. "We told him we'd do whatever he wanted because, quite frankly, it would be so easy for this show to be about something else. We all remember those years. We didn't want to work for six months for this to be a show about how fucked up Whitney Houston was."

Dionne Warwick took Houston's side and argued with the Zanucks. But before they went home for the night, the producers made a decision: Houston was off the show. Richard Zanuck called Houston's agent and manager to break the news, while Lili Zanuck placed a 1 a.m. call to the manager for country singer Faith Hill, for whom Zanuck had directed a music video.

"They absolutely made the right decision," said stage manager Garry Hood, who watched the rehearsal closely. "Sometimes somebody needs to say no instead of continuing to enable a situation, which we all do in this business. You want that name, so you're willing to put up with unfortunate situations. But they said no and they stood by their decision, and that doesn't happen very often."

Don Was, for his part, was not convinced that Houston would have been a liability once show time arrived. "Whitney's personal problems are well documented, but there was a certain amount of protest in her cavalier approach that I thought was not pharmaceutically driven," he said. "Burt deserved to have the medley done properly, and there was reason to question whether she would have done it properly. But if you ask me, I say she'd have come through in the end. I think she was maybe fucking with everybody a little bit. It's not un-diva-like behavior to leave everybody worrying about whether you're going to show up, or you're going to deliver, until the last minute, and then to deliver. But there's no black or white in this, everything's gray. It's hard to say . . ." He trailed off, then shrugged.

"Certainly she was loaded," he said with a smile, "but I wouldn't want to do urinalysis on a number of people involved in the show. Let's leave it at that."

AS USUAL, star day was tightly controlled and chaotic at the same time. Roberto Benigni flirted with the trophy ladies, Gwyneth Paltrow wore shades and nursed a hangover, and Mike Myers discussed the difference between the words *asshole* and *butthead* with an ABC standards and practices rep. When Russell Crowe took the stage to rehearse his lines, he looked into the audience and saw that the seat card marking his chair was one of the few not to include a photo. "What, nobody has a fucking picture of me to put up there?" he asked. As soon as he finished rehearsing, Crowe borrowed a pen and drew a stick figure on his card. Then he did the same with the blank card that marked the seat of *American Beauty* star Wes Bentley. "Okay," Crowe said when he finished. "Now I can go."

But when he walked out the back door of the Shrine to light up a cigarette, Crowe ran straight into Brad Pitt, who was standing near the artists' entrance wearing a powder-blue shirt unbuttoned to the navel. "No way!" shouted Pitt. The two men hugged, then launched into an animated conversation. As they talked, Paltrow rounded the corner and was headed for the back door when she spied Pitt, her old boyfriend, standing in her path. She turned away from him, ducked her head so he couldn't see her, and blew past him quickly.

Later, Keanu Reeves stood by the artists' entrance and watched Myers make a beeline for the green room buffet. "Damn actors, man," he said. "Them and their free lunches." Tommy Lee Jones walked by in a jacket and tie. "Oh, my God," Reeves said. "That's Tommy Lee fucking Jones. He is the *man*." Then Peter Coyote shook Reeves's hand. "My God," said Reeves. "Peter Coyote and Tommy Lee Jones in one day."

In midafternoon, Lili Zanuck huddled with Antonio Banderas and Penélope Cruz, who were giving out the award for foreign film. The odds-on favorite in the category was *All About My Mother*, a film from the flamboyant
Spanish director Pedro Almodóvar, with whom both Cruz and Banderas
had worked. Almodóvar had given an extremely long, meandering, and often incomprehensible acceptance speech a month earlier at the Golden
Globes. At rehearsal, Lili Zanuck pleaded with the presenters to speak to
Almodóvar. "Please tell Pedro that if he wins, we do not want to play him
off," she said. "But we *cannot* afford for him to take five minutes, like he
did at the Golden Globes." Banderas and Cruz assured her that they'd pass
along the message.

Arnold Schwarzenegger arrived late in the afternoon, hours past his
scheduled 9:30 a.m. rehearsal time. He was smoking a cigar, and had two little girls in tow. Onstage, Schwarzenegger had trouble with his introduction
to the visual effects award. After stumbling over his lines, he snapped at the
TelePrompTer operator. "You're running it too fast, too fast," he said.

In the audience, a staffer looked at the testy scene—typical, she thought,
for Schwarzenegger—and rolled her eyes. "And you can't read, okay?" she
muttered under her breath. Richard Zanuck went to the podium and asked
that Schwarzenegger's microphone be turned off. The actor and the producer went over the lines seven or eight times, until Arnold got it right.

"IT'S CHAOS DOWN THERE," yelled stage manager Alissa Levisohn as she
ran up the stairs to the stage level of the Shrine. Dress rehearsal was under
way, and Levisohn had just been to the dressing rooms beneath the stage,
checking on the progress of the singers and dancers who would be needed
shortly for "Blame Canada." What she found, rather than the usual costume
crew moving with dispatch, was the slower, more deliberate pace of a six-
foot-three-inch former model named L'Wren Scott, whom Lili Zanuck had
hired to be the Oscars' "Style Designer."

"The stylist has no idea what it is to get people in and out of makeup,"
complained Levisohn to other stage managers. "She's playing around with
costumes now, and she doesn't understand we have rehearsal." Other staffers were sent downstairs to speed things up.

But costume problems with "Blame Canada" were nothing compared to the trouble that awaited when it was time for Bacharach's medley. Except for Faith Hill, who'd been at the Shrine all afternoon, the singers arrived around 9 p.m., at which point they were quietly informed that Whitney Houston had been replaced.

Garth Brooks heard the news when Lili Zanuck and Danette Herman visited his trailer, but Garth was not in an understanding mood. The singer, by far Nashville's biggest-selling artist for much of the 1980s and '90s, worked hard to sustain his image as a down-to-earth guy—but once his first two albums had sold twenty million copies and he'd been all but anointed the savior of the country music industry, he hadn't been shy about using his clout to get what he wanted.

Brooks was supposed to be the first artist to perform during the medley, kicking things off with the hit song "Everybody's Talkin' " from *Midnight Cowboy*. (Curiously, the song had never been nominated for an Oscar, and shouldn't have even been included.) But when Debbie Williams went to Brooks's trailer to tell him it was time to rehearse, the thirty-eight-year-old Oklahoman wouldn't leave. "You're gonna have to buy some time for me here," he told her. "I need to make some calls."

Garry Hood, who lived in Nashville and knew Brooks from other shows, was sent to talk to the singer; he got nowhere. Brooks punched numbers into his cell phone and paced outside his trailer, furious that Houston had been replaced, that he hadn't been told about the move right away—and, some suggested, that Houston's replacement, Faith Hill, also happened to be a country singer with crossover success.

Lili Zanuck tried to reason with Brooks, as rehearsal ground to a halt. Firing Houston wasn't right, Brooks told Zanuck. It wasn't fair. Whitney had to be reinstated.

Zanuck did not budge. Quietly, a stand-in was told to be ready to take Brooks's place if need be. The other artists stood by and waited.

But after what seemed to be an interminable delay, Brooks suddenly walked back into the Shrine, took his place onstage, and said he was ready. Bacharach's band launched into "Everybody's Talkin'," Brooks crooned the song as he walked down a flight of stairs, and the dress rehearsal resumed.

"Ultimately, he got through to Whitney on the phone, that's why he came back," said Don Was. "Garth was trying to be humanitarian, and he told her, 'If you want to come back, I'm holding out for you.' And Whitney said, 'I'm not going back to that fucking show.' And that was pretty much the end of it."

THE NEXT AFTERNOON, as show time neared, most of the crew changed into tuxedos and formal dresses. An exception was made for stagehands who'd be moving scenery on and off the stage. Because the floor was illuminated from beneath with bright white light, those stagehands were issued white jumpsuits that would allow them to blend in more easily. "They look like a bunch of sperm running around the stage," said one staffer upon first spotting the crew.

By 4:00, when the doors to the Shrine were opened, almost everybody was formally dressed. There were exceptions, though. Lili Zanuck walked around backstage in her usual baggy men's shirt, not changing until almost show time.

Trey Parker and Matt Stone arrived wearing knockoffs of notable awards-show dresses worn by Jennifer Lopez and Gwyneth Paltrow, respectively. They were accompanied by Marc Shaiman, who hadn't been told of their plans far enough in advance to work out his own drag act; if he had, he said he would have gone as Cher the year she wore a towering feathered headdress to the Oscars. Instead of donning a dress, Shaiman huddled quickly with stylist Scott, who helped him work up a garish baby blue outfit complete with fedora and puffy faux fur jacket. On their way down the red carpet Paltrow shot the trio a dirty look. Michael Caine walked over to tell them he loved their outfits. "Awesome," he said.

Inside the theater, Jack Nicholson had no sooner arrived at his front-row seat than he got up and strolled down the aisle that ran across the front of the theater. It surprised nobody that Nicholson was on the move: of all the stars who regularly attended the Academy Awards, he was almost definitely the most fidgety. That's why directors tended to show reaction shots of Nicholson with disturbing frequency. You needed to take advantage of the times you had him in his seat, because you never knew when it would happen again.

At the previous year's Oscar show, Nicholson had been seated in the third row, six seats in from the aisle, which proved to be predictably problematic. When Roberto Benigni started climbing over seat backs or Elia Kazan divided the audience into opposing camps, Jack's sunglassed countenance was backstage, out of camera range. So the following year, Nicholson was back up front, where he'd be more likely to stick around for a few good reaction shots—particularly reactions to Billy Crystal, who *loved* to talk about Jack.

Still, Nicholson had barely arrived before he took a stroll. As he did, he glanced into the orchestra pit, knowing that he'd see the usual complement of forty or fifty tuxedo-clad musicians awaiting a cue from their elegantly attired conductor.

Instead, Nicholson found himself looking down on eight casually clad musicians, three of them standing behind synthesizers and one with a pair of *turntables* in front of him. Nicholson took it all in—the musicians, the electronics, the fact that the guy in charge had dreadlocks and was wearing sandals. He frowned. "What the fuck is *this?*" he said.

5:30 P.M., PACIFIC DAYLIGHT TIME: *"This is the 72nd annual Academy Awards."*

Minutes after preshow cohost Tyra Banks gave a backstage high five to Academy president Bob Rehme, Peter Coyote kicked off the Oscar show from his desk just off the stage. Richard Zanuck sat in the wings near Coyote, ready to greet winners and producers. Lili Zanuck settled into a seat behind Horvitz in the command truck.

Rehme delivered a brief opening speech, and then walked off during Crystal's opening film. In it, the host found himself in a variety of famous movies, from *The Gold Rush* to *Taxi Driver* to *Psycho* to *The Godfather*. In this last clip, he asked for advice from Marlon Brando's Don Corleone: "Godfather, I don't know what to do . . . These producers, they're movie people. They've never done the Oscars. They don't want to have a dance number!" Crystal kept up the no-dancing theme when he segued into a scene from *West Side Story*, where he was serenaded by an angry musical gang: "The Jets ain't gonna get their chance tonight / They're telling us that we can't dance tonight . . ." Crystal broke into a rendition of one of that musical's signature songs, "Tonight": "Tonight, tonight / Please Billy, make it tight / Cut the clips, cut the jokes, cut the songs . . ."

Backstage, it seemed to some crew members as if babies were everywhere, courtesy of an unusually large number of new mothers. A trailer just outside the artists' entrance was turned into a center for nannies and breastfeeding moms. Another facility, nearer to the stage, was earmarked for the nine-months-pregnant Annette Bening. The crew called it "the Sinatra Bathroom," in honor of the facility that had to be kept in the wings during Frank Sinatra's final shows.

From the stage, Crystal introduced Willie Fulgear, who'd found the missing statuettes. "Willie got $50,000 for finding the fifty-two Oscars," said Crystal. "Not a lot of money, when you realize that Miramax and Dream-Works are spending millions of dollars just to get one."

After Crystal's opening, the three stars of *Charlie's Angels*—Cameron Diaz, Drew Barrymore, and Lucy Liu—walked onstage together. To accompany their entrance, Don Was took a sample from the movie's soundtrack, laid a thudding drum loop beneath it, and had his band play over the top of the sample. But while the drum track boomed, the soundtrack sample, which was supposed to be providing the melody on which the band was riffing, was completely inaudible. "It sounded like people were walking on to tribal drums," said Was, who stopped short of saying he was sabotaged but found it astonishing that nobody noticed the missing samples or tried to fix them.

Backstage in the green room during the first commercial break, Erykah Badu's two-year-old son, Seven, banged his head on the corner of a glass coffee table and began screaming. Winona Ryder, James Coburn, and the other stars in the small, tastefully appointed room studiously tried to act as if nothing untoward was happening. But the timing was particularly unfortunate: Badu was due to present an award during the show's next segment, which meant it was time for her to head to the wings. A talent staffer quietly suggested to Badu's nanny that she move the child to the trailer outside, lest he really erupt when his mom was taken away.

At the end of the show's second segment, forty minutes into the broadcast, James Coburn awarded the first major Oscar of the night, best supporting actress, to Angelina Jolie for *Girl, Interrupted*. Afterward, in an Oscar rarity, the cameras followed Jolie offstage, where she hugged Jude Law and Cate Blanchett. During the commercial break after Jolie's win, fellow nominee Chloë Sevigny headed for the lobby. This was typical: the lobby was often crowded with those who didn't win in the last couple of categories.

By the one-hour mark, it was clear that the high-tech video presentation and funkier music had indeed given the show a more modern, accelerated feel—but at the same time, the band had trouble stopping quickly when winners and presenters got to the microphone, and the new trophy ladies, models without awards show experience, didn't always get the winners off-stage quickly. The show felt faster, but in some ways things were moving even more slowly than usual. In the truck, Lili Zanuck checked the time and figured the show was running ahead of schedule.

In the orchestra pit, meanwhile, Don Was didn't know what to think. During rehearsals, Was and his former Was (Not Was) partner David Weiss, who was working the turntables, had looked into the audience and found themselves staring at a field of seat cards bearing famous names: Warren Beatty, Annette Bening, Kevin Spacey, Tom Cruise, Nicole Kidman . . . They'd imagined the electricity that must come from that kind of star power—but when the show started, the musicians quickly realized that the stars inside the Shrine were too distracted, preoccupied, or nervous to give back much energy to the performers onstage or in the pit. "This room," muttered a disappointed Weiss to his partner, "is *smaller* than life."

At about 6:40, LL Cool J and Vanessa Williams introduced Randy Newman and Sarah McLachlan, the first performers in the medley of nominated songs. The five songs made up a twelve-minute medley that was capped by Robin Williams's showstopping romp through "Blame Canada," accompanied for much of the song by two dozen singer-dancers and another two dozen Rockette-style hoofers in Mountie garb.

"Blame Canada" got the biggest reaction, but the best-song Oscar went, as expected, to Phil Collins's Tarzan song, "You'll Be in My Heart." During the ensuing commercial break, nominees Diane Warren and Aimee Mann headed for the lobby. So did Trey Parker and Matt Stone, who stood against a wall accepting congratulations and ignoring stares. "This is cold and uncomfortable," said Stone of his pink spaghetti-strap gown.

"I'm getting sick to my stomach," added Parker. "Everybody up there's just patting themselves on the fucking back. And the last thing these people need is to be patted on the back, because they get it every fucking day." They sent an assistant to fetch the suits they'd brought with them, then changed clothes and left the Shrine. "I never even knew you could do that," laughed Shaiman, who'd also lost during his four previous stints as a nominee.

An hour after Jolie's supporting-actress win, the second major award of the night, best supporting actor, was given to Michael Caine for *The Cider House Rules*. His gracious acceptance speech included nods to his fellow nominees but lasted almost three minutes, the longest of the night so far. When he saw the TelePrompTer flashing PLEASE WRAP UP, Caine frowned. "Well, Dick, I wasn't here last time I won," he said, referring to his no-show when he won for 1986's *Hannah and Her Sisters*. "So give me a bit extra on my speech." Dick Zanuck, though, was sitting in the wings; it was Lili in the control trailer, with the power to tell Horvitz to cue the band and cut off Caine. She didn't.

By this point, Lili realized that the show was falling well behind schedule. She just hoped that people would be entertained.

The next segment, though, was the driest of the night. It started with Jane Fonda presenting a special Oscar to Polish director Andrzej Wajda, who gave a subtitled acceptance speech in Polish. Then came awards for sound effects, followed by a recap of the scientific and technical Oscars, followed by the award for visual effects. *The Matrix* was a popular winner in this last category—but when John Gaeta's acceptance speech passed the one-minute mark with no end in sight, Zanuck reconsidered her unspoken rule not to play winners offstage. Reluctantly, she gave the cue to Horvitz, who yelled "Shut that motherfucker up!" into Was's headphones. Earlier, Was had pretended not to hear a suggestion that his band interrupt the documentary winners, but this time he complied, cutting the speech off as it reached a minute and a half.

In the lobby, Jude Law waited at the bar with a group of friends that included Gwyneth Paltrow. They both ordered Heinekens and drank them straight from the bottle. (Before the show, drinks were free; after 5:30, the bars started charging but the lines stayed long.)

By the two-hour mark, many stars were finding refuge and refreshment in and around the green room. But Crystal had planned a comedy bit in which he would "read the minds" of many of the notables in the audience. For the jokes to work, those actors had to be in their seats. So during a commercial break at 7:35, staffers and pages rounded up the likes of Jack Nicholson and Judi Dench and asked them to please return to their seats. "Why am I going back out there?" asked Dench as a stage manager escorted her into the auditorium. "It's for something Billy is doing," the staffer said vaguely. Nearby, Meryl Streep returned to her own seat, while Brad Pitt and Jennifer Aniston talked to nominee Catherine Keener.

With the stars reseated, Crystal told us what they were thinking. Streep: "The designated hitter rule is ruining baseball." Dench: "This thong is killing me." Michael Clarke Duncan: "I see white people." Russell Crowe: "Boy, I could use a cigarette right around now." Crowe nodded after hearing this line; though the camera had been cutting to him all night, he had yet to crack a visible smile.

Then Bacharach led his medley of past nominated songs. Isaac Hayes was obscured by an overactive fog machine during his rendition of "The Theme from *Shaft*," but otherwise things went without a hitch. As the performers left the stage at the end of the medley, Richard Zanuck made a beeline for Garth Brooks and pumped his hand.

At about 8:00, *All About My Mother* won the Oscar for foreign film. As Lili Zanuck had feared, Pedro Almodóvar began babbling in broken English with no apparent intention of stopping. The band came in after a minute and a half, but that didn't faze the hyperactive Spaniard, who remained at the microphone until Antonio Banderas dragged him off by the arm.

A few minutes after Almodóvar cleared the stage, Edward Norton introduced the In Memoriam film. Besides the usual array of Academy members and Oscar winners, the montage featured several stars with indelible ties to the Oscar ceremony: George C. Scott, who refused to accept the best-actor trophy when he won for *Patton*; Abraham Polonsky, a blacklisted writer and outspoken foe of Elia Kazan who'd helped lead the fight against Kazan's honorary award; Charles "Buddy" Rogers, who'd starred in the first best-picture winner, *Wings*, and sixty years later sat onstage during part of the gruesome production number that kicked off Allan Carr's show; and Carr himself, who'd died the previous June of liver cancer.

As the show hit the three-hour mark—with a full eight awards yet to be handed out—Jack Nicholson came into the wings, ready to give the Irving Thalberg Award to Warren Beatty. He looked at a particularly large stage-hand, clad in the regulation white jumpsuit. "Who are you?" he asked. "The baker?"

Beatty turned out to be a gracious recipient, but also a troublesome honoree late in a show that was already running long. His speech, which he had refused to show to the Zanucks ahead of time, was amusing, but also meandering and very long—almost six minutes, putting it neck-and-neck with Greer Garson's legendary speech in 1943, which was later reputed to have lasted as long as an hour. In fact, Garson had spoken for five and a half minutes—but she did so at the end of a long, slow show, after 1 a.m., when everybody was ready to go home.

By the time Beatty left the stage, the show was already close to the 3:15 mark that was the Zanucks' original goal. At this point, though, the evening was just getting to the prestige awards, the ones that had a bearing on the best-picture race. And clearly, the contingents from DreamWorks and Miramax knew it. When *American Beauty* won for cinematography, a large DreamWorks crowd jumped up as one. When *Cider House Rules* writer John Irving won the adapted-screenplay award a few minutes later—and pointedly referred to the movie as "a film on the abortion subject" at the beginning of his speech—the Miramax crowd did the same. When Alan Ball won the original-screenplay Oscar for *American Beauty*, DreamWorks celebrated anew.

Before cutting to a commercial a few minutes later, the camera focused on Peter Coyote in the wings. "He's back," said Coyote. "Academy Award winner Roberto Benigni presents the best-actress Oscar when the 72nd annual Academy Awards return." Benigni stood a few feet away, out of sight of the camera. "Get in there, get in there!" crew members whispered to him, pushing the actor toward Coyote. Suddenly shy, Benigni protested; when they insisted, he jumped into the frame and mugged with Coyote for a few seconds before the commercial.

During the next segment, Benigni handed the best-actress Oscar to Hilary Swank for *Boys Don't Cry*. When she left the stage, Swank embraced Gwyneth Paltrow, who then presented the best-actor award to Kevin Spacey for *American Beauty*. It was too late for funny intros, so Crystal dropped the joke he'd planned and said simply, "Ladies and gentlemen, Mr. Steven Spielberg." Spielberg walked onstage as Was's band played along with a sample from the *Jaws* soundtrack. As had happened all night, the sample was inaudible.

Spielberg presented the best-director Oscar to *American Beauty*'s Sam Mendes, then Clint Eastwood named that film 1999's best picture. The show finally ended at 9:38 p.m. "I've been told that this is the shortest Oscar show of the century," said Billy Crystal. "So how about that?" Four hours and eight minutes after it began—roughly half an hour of clips, eighty jokes, and sixteen songs after Crystal sang "cut the clips, cut the jokes, cut the songs"—the longest Academy Awards show in history was over.

AT THE GOVERNORS BALL, Lili Zanuck was accosted by an angry Pedro Almodóvar, who said he was offended that he had been played off, and mad at Banderas for grabbing his arm. Then he threw in a few more complaints for the hell of it: he thought it was terrible that a committee voted for the foreign films rather than the entire academy membership, he was mad that foreign nominees weren't invited to the nominees' luncheon . . . "He took me aside for thirty fucking minutes," said Zanuck. "And I thought, God, what if this guy hadn't *won?*"

Across town in West Hollywood, Billy Crystal's daughter was at the *Vanity Fair* party. "I'm so glad it's over," she told a friend. "You have *no idea* what the pressure is like."

In his *Daily Variety* column on Monday morning, Army Archerd reported that during Friday's rehearsal, Bacharach "decided not to go with Whitney Houston and she was taken off the show!" Almost immediately, urgent calls went out from the producers' office to many of those who worked on the show. The story that *must* be used, everyone was told, was that Houston had to drop out because of a sore throat. It would be months before the Zanucks admitted the truth.

Ratings were up by 2 percent over the previous year. Many viewers found the show to be a fresh update over the usual Oscar show, though the use of Peter Coyote was roundly panned. More than a few observers were amused that after the early promises of a shorter show with no dance numbers, the Zanucks produced a show of historic length highlighted by a rendition of "Blame Canada" that featured about forty dancers.

"We made all these pronouncements about how we were going to make it a faster show, and we failed miserably," Lili Zanuck freely admitted a few months later. Still, she said, she wouldn't rule out producing the show again. "It was about as much work as I expected, but it was a lot more fun than I thought it was going to be."

Whitney Houston's rocky year didn't get any better after the Oscars. Just weeks after the show, she was a no-show at the Rock and Roll Hall of Fame ceremony, where she was supposed to help induct Clive Davis, the record executive who'd signed her to Arista Records and guided her career. Not long afterward, she was sued for nonpayment by a company run by her father. Her husband, Bobby Brown, spent two months in jail for parole violations after he tested positive for cocaine. At the end of the year, Houston appeared on ABC's *Primetime*, swearing to interviewer Diane Sawyer that her self-destructive days were over—and adding that contrary to rumors, she'd never smoked crack cocaine. "I make too much money for me to ever smoke crack," she said.

A little more than two months after the Oscar show, Willie Fulgear reported to police that a five-hundred-pound safe, containing what was left of the reward he'd received for finding the Oscar statuettes, had been stolen from his Los Angeles apartment.

The Roadway Express truck driver and loading dock worker arrested in the theft of those statuettes pleaded no contest. The truck driver, Lawrence Ledent, received a six-month jail term, while the dock worker, Anthony Hart, received probation. In October, charges were filed against a third man, John Harris, who was the half-brother of Fulgear. Police admitted they found the relationship suspicious, but Fulgear said he and Harris were estranged, and no charges were filed.

The final three Oscar statuettes were never found.

In the aftermath of what also turned out to be the most expensive Oscar show ever—a show that was reputed to cost half again as much as the usual show—the Academy decided to change the way in which it financed the Oscars. Instead of having Seligman talk to the producers and work up a budget that he'd submit to the Academy for approval, the organization decided that future producers would be given a dollar figure up front and would be expected to stick to it.

In July, the Eastman Kodak Company agreed to pay $75 million for the naming rights to the theater that was being built in the Hollywood & Highland complex.

8

≡

Short Cuts

The 73rd Academy Awards

THE SPEECHES were always a problem. No matter what a producer told the nominees, once they heard their names announced they talked too long, or they pulled out a list and read a bunch of names of people the audience didn't know or care about. Most of them, sad to say, had no idea how witty and entertaining you could be in forty-five seconds. They got in the spotlight, they looked at the famous people in front of them, they froze, and they rattled off names until the orchestra cut them off.

It hadn't always been like that. "The thing that's most striking if you look back at the shows from, say, the early eighties, is that most of the accepters just said, 'Thank you,' " recalled Bruce Davis. "Now everybody makes a speech, everybody has their VCR turned on back at home. People who used to walk up almost embarrassed, grab the statuette and smile and say 'Thanks' and get off, are now giving long speeches."

In the winter of 2001, as Gil Cates prepared to produce his tenth Academy Awards show, he was determined to try to change that. He had to: the last time he'd produced the show, in 1999, he'd been responsible for what had been, for one year, the longest Academy Awards show in history. For years, Cates had been using sports analogies to shrug off questions about the show's length, comparing it to major athletic events: "It'll take as long as it takes." But with the show's overall rating an average of each half-hour segment, the metaphor was no longer working.

"We can't compare it to the Super Bowl anymore," said Davis. "That's too self-indulgent. In fact, we have to get this thing in in three and a half hours or shorter. We've been looking at the breakdowns from ABC, which can give you each city at fifteen-minute intervals. And you can just see the sets clicking off on the East Coast when you run past midnight. It hurts the rating. You're hurting yourself in the second hour if you run into a fourth."

That was one of the reasons the Academy, two years earlier, had moved the show from Monday to Sunday night, and from a 6:00 p.m. start time to 5:30. But while the earlier start time was partly designed to let East Coasters get to bed before midnight, that hadn't happened. In both of the shows since the time change, the final awards weren't handed out until after 12:30 a.m.

So when Cates agreed to take over the seventy-third Oscar show, time was a priority. The producer had certain ideas about how to streamline the show, but none of them meant much if the speeches ran long. The key, he knew, was to convince nominees that he was serious about that forty-five-second limit on acceptance speeches, and serious when he said they should not pull out written lists.

His best chance to make that point came at the nominees' luncheon on March 12, a little less than two weeks before the Oscar show. The room contained about a hundred nominees from all categories, including actors Jeff Bridges, Russell Crowe, Willem Dafoe, Tom Hanks, Ed Harris, Kate Hudson, and eighty-one-year-old producer Dino De Laurentiis, who had been voted the Thalberg Award. As they sat at tables spread out across the grand ballroom of the Beverly Hills Hotel and lunched on sea bass with red pepper coulis and chateaubriand in merlot sauce, Cates walked to a podium at the front of the room and made his plea.

"I've done this every year for ten years," he said. "I've tried to be charming and humorous. I've tried persuasion and bribery. It all comes down to my belief that brevity is next to godliness . . . I just beg you, *please*, keep your speech to forty-five seconds, and don't read off a list of names. Studies have shown that most of those people won't hire you again anyway." As usual, Cates showed a montage of bad acceptance speeches—all of them lists of names—and then a second montage of what he said were good speeches, including Joe Pesci's terse, "It's my privilege, thank you" in 1991 and Alfred Hitchcock's minimalist, "Thank you very much" upon receiving the Irving Thalberg Award in 1968.

He neglected to supply the backstory to both of those speeches. Hitchcock's, for instance, was widely taken to be the normally eloquent sixty-eight-year-old director's slap at the Academy, which had never given him an Oscar despite more than fifty movies, many of them classics. As for Pesci, the supporting-actor winner for *GoodFellas* was so overcome upon winning that he couldn't have said anything more if he'd wanted to: as soon as he got offstage, the actor collapsed in a heap on the floor, right at the feet of the startled British actress Brenda Fricker. "I can't beeeelieve this, I can't beeeelieve this," he kept muttering, crouching on the floor in the dark.

"When you come off the stage," Cates continued, "you can hand us a list of all the people you want to thank, and we'll post it on the Oscar.com Web site right away. It'll be up there that night, and if people ask why you didn't thank them, you can tell them to go to the Web site."

Before he sat down, Cates had a final offer. "As an incentive, the person with the shortest speech gets a special award: a brand-new high-definition TV." At the tables, nominees laughed. Nobody was quite sure if Cates was serious.

FOR NOMINEES, the matter of acceptance speeches had always been a tricky one. To unfold a written speech and a list of names risked incurring the wrath of the producers and earning a rude sendoff from the orchestra. To speak off the cuff, unprepared, was to run the risk of leaving out someone important in the heat of the moment and the glare of the lights. But to have an eloquent speech memorized—well, that could be seen as the height of presumption. The happy medium was to have remarks prepared, but to deliver them in such a way that you appeared to be speaking off the cuff, but that was a tough one to pull off. Still, people tried: even Greer Garson prefaced the most famously lengthy acceptance speech in Oscar history by saying, "I am practically unprepared."

Many winners found the time constraints almost impossible to deal with. "When I watch our acceptance speech now, the panic is written all over us," said Lili Zanuck, who coproduced the 1988 best-picture winner *Driving Miss Daisy* with Richard. Their own acceptance-speech anxiety fueled their desire not to rush winners offstage when they produced the Oscars in 2000. "We know what it's like to go as fast as you can because you're afraid you're going to get played off in forty-five seconds."

Then there was the matter of whom to thank and whom to leave out. While it wasn't as blatant as Oscar campaigning, acceptance-speech campaigning also took place in Hollywood. Virtually every nominee could tell stories about the congratulatory calls he'd received, first after the nominations were announced and then, again and again, in the weeks leading up to the show itself.

Richard Sylbert, the set decorator who was nominated for six Oscars and won for *Who's Afraid of Virginia Woolf?* in 1967 and *Dick Tracy* twenty-four years later, once recalled getting a surprisingly pleasant phone call from Jeffrey Katzenberg, then the chairman of Walt Disney Studios, not long before the Academy Awards in March 1991. Sylbert and Katzenberg were not exactly friends; in fact, many of those associated with *Dick Tracy* were furious at the executive for a twenty-eight-page memo he'd written two months earlier. The so-called "Katzenberg memo," which was supposed to be kept in-house at Disney but was quickly leaked to the press, laid forth Katzenberg's philosophy of low-cost, low-risk moviemaking, and held up Warren Beatty's lavish $100 million salute to the comic strip hero as an example of the kind of movie Disney should no longer make. "As profitable as it was," Katzenberg wrote, "*Dick Tracy* made demands on our time, talent, and treasury that, upon reflection, may not have been worth it."

So when Sylbert got a call from Katzenberg just before the Oscar show, he didn't know what to think. "He said he was calling just to say hello, to see how I was doing," said Sylbert several years before his death in March 2002. "When I hung up I was very confused, so I called Warren and told him about it. And Warren said, 'Don't you know what that call was about?' I said, 'No, I don't.' And he said, 'The little prick wants you to thank him if you win.' " Sylbert did win. He thanked Beatty, but not Katzenberg.

IT WAS A RARITY: a year in which there was no true front-runner in the best-picture competition. *Gladiator* and *Crouching Tiger, Hidden Dragon* received the most nominations, but neither of them was typical Oscar fare: the first, from *Blade Runner* director Ridley Scott, was the kind of violent, big-budget, crowd-pleasing action movie that usually won in the technical categories but nowhere else, while the latter, shot in Mandarin Chinese with subtitles for English-speaking viewers, was director Ang Lee's tribute to the martial arts movies from Hong Kong he'd loved as a child. They may have been expertly crafted films with more depth and resonance than most genre movies—but genre movies, whatever depth and resonance they may have, seldom won many Academy Awards.

Director Steven Soderbergh's *Traffic* was more typical Oscar bait, but the high-minded three-hour film about the drug trade along the U.S./Mexican border was also inconsistent, and Soderbergh's fondness for mixing in grainy film stock and jerky handheld cameras didn't figure to endear him to older Academy voters. In addition, Soderbergh might well split the vote, because he'd also directed another best-picture nominee, *Erin Brockovich*, a more conventional film that had won raves for Julia Roberts's performance as a hell-raising legal assistant.

The fifth nominee was *Chocolat*. The morning that nominations were announced in the Samuel Goldwyn Theater, a slight groan had run through the crowd of reporters, publicists, and studio reps when its name was announced. A trifle from Lasse Hallström, the director of *The Cider House Rules*, *Chocolat* was to most viewers a lesser achievement than, say, Christopher Nolan's intriguing *Memento*, Darren Aronofsky's unrelentingly bleak *Requiem for a Dream*, the Coen Brothers' romp *O Brother, Where Art Thou?* or a number of other movies. *Chocolat*, though, fulfilled the apparent requirement that Miramax must produce one best-picture nominee each year.

Since *Gladiator* received the most nominations, twelve to *Crouching Tiger*'s ten, it began to assume the mantle of a front-runner almost by default. DreamWorks, which had coproduced the film with Universal, used its campaign to play up the movie's heroic, epic qualities rather than its blood and gore. But *Crouching Tiger* remained a sentimental favorite, and USA Films quietly worked to position *Traffic* as not only the best, but also the most important movie of the batch. The best-actor race narrowed to a two-man competition between the always-popular Tom Hanks, who spent most of *Cast Away* acting alongside a volleyball, and *Gladiator* star Russell Crowe, who in the past year had become a world-class movie star, hell-raiser, and tabloid staple via rumored romances with everyone from Meg Ryan (confirmed) to Nicole Kidman (denied). The only sure bet, most observers felt, was in the best-actress category, where it seemed a foregone conclusion that *Erin Brockovich* would bring home the gold for Julia Roberts.

With so many races presumably up for grabs, Oscar campaigns kicked into overdrive, and each move by one studio was countered by another. No sooner had Universal sent a "Making of *Erin Brockovich*" DVD to every *Daily Variety* subscriber than a rival publicist called writers to suggest that the move was a sneaky way to reach Oscar voters by skirting the Academy's rules against such items. DreamWorks rereleased *Gladiator* at a deluxe theater in Century City, and for the first week trotted out Russell Crowe, composer Hans Zimmer, and five other nominees to speak after the screenings—again, a violation of Academy rules if the screenings hadn't been open to the public. Sony Classics, determined to fill the art-movie-with-a-real-chance slot that Miramax usually occupied, sent *Crouching Tiger, Hidden Dragon* to twenty different film locations for special cast-and-crew screenings.

ON THURSDAY, March 22, three days before the seventy-third Oscars show, Steve Martin pulled into the parking lot behind the Shrine Auditorium. Like all presenters, performers, and previous hosts, Martin had been offered the use of a town car and driver at Academy expense—but to the astonishment of Cates and many staffers, Martin turned it down in favor of driving his own Lexus to and from the downtown theater. What's more, he brought his own laptop computer to meetings, and took his own notes.

Martin had appeared on several Oscar shows in the past, and he'd declined one offer from Cates to host the show. But when first-year Academy president Frank Pierson approached Cates in the fall and asked him to over-see the show, the producer knew he wouldn't be able to turn to Billy Crystal. At the September wedding of Crystal's daughter, the comic's manager had already told Cates that his client would be too busy directing the HBO movie *61** to even consider the gig.

"Steve was an easy choice," said Cates, sitting in the lunch area of the Shrine Exhibition Hall and waiting for Martin's first rehearsal. "And this is the Oscars, so you don't have to worry about contracts and negotiations and all that bullshit. I called Steve's agent, Ed Limato, and asked if he thought Steve would be interested. Ed said, 'He might be, why don't you call him?' So I called Steve, asked him if he wanted to host, and he said yes."

By the time he showed up at the Shrine, Martin had already been to the production office several times, testing his monologue before small groups of staffers. The host had also declined suggestions that he incorporate props into his duties: he wanted to keep his initial Oscar stint classy.

Just before 2:30, Martin showed up on the stage and stepped to a micro-phone. "Testing," he said. "Testing, one, two, three." He paused, and looked into the audience. "That's my opening line," he said.

Looking calm and composed, with a pair of glasses hanging around his neck, he peered toward the TelePrompTer. "I'm not going to do the mono-logue, because you'll tell everyone," he said. "So, blah blah blah . . ." Then he stopped. Tired of throwing out nonsense, he looked toward a group of his writers, including Bruce Vilanch, comedian Rita Rudner, and Martin's manager, David Steinberg. "What are some of the jokes we have that we're not going to use?" he asked. "You know, the ones that are too mean."

He thought for a minute, then launched into the first of the rejected jokes. "Michael Douglas this year became a father to Catherine Zeta-Jones," he said. "Wait, did I say *to*? I meant *with*." The audience let out a low groan. "See why we're not going to use it?" Martin said. Then he ran through more of the rejected jokes. "One of the nominees is *Chocolat*, starring Juli-ette Binoche and . . . some guy who gets to touch Juliette Binoche."

He looked back at his writers. "What else?"

"Madonna and Guy Ritchie!" yelled Vilanch.

"Oh, right," said Martin. "Madonna married Guy Ritchie—who before the wedding was known as Guy Poory . . . Any others?"

"Travolta!"

"Our next presenter is John Travolta, who can still wear the suit he wore in *Saturday Night Fever* . . . as a bib."

After this line, ABC's Susan Futterman yelled to the stage, "You should put that back in!"

"Should I?" said Martin. "Isn't it a little mean?"

"No," yelled Futterman. "Use it!"

Martin shrugged, then forged ahead. "Here's another one we're not using. This just in: Erin Brockovich has found toxic mold on Dino De Laurentiis. Or this one: I'm so envious of Russell Crowe, because he's been in some *fabulous* things this year."

After rehearsing for about half an hour, Martin left the stage and chatted with Cates. As they spoke, Martin's publicist, Catherine Olim, approached Vilanch.

"I know you're not using that joke about Russell," she said uneasily. "But as his publicist I have to tell you, they're *just good friends.*"

Vilanch looked confused. "What?" he said. "Russell and who?"

"Nicole Kidman. She's my client, too."

"You have nothing to worry about," Vilanch assured her.

AT THE OSCARS, as in much of the rest of Hollywood, one of the true signs of power was the proximity of one's parking space. At the Shrine Auditorium, the parking lot at the rear of the building was prime but rarefied territory, reserved for the likes of Cates, Horvitz, Herman, Seligman, and a handful of other bigwigs, along with top executives from ABC and the Academy. Those who didn't rate quite so highly parked farther away, with a hundred or so allocated spaces in a parking structure adjacent to the Shrine Exposition Hall.

But out of the fifteen hundred or so workers who came to the Shrine during Oscar week, most were exiled to outlying lots. The bulk of these lots were to the south of the Shrine, past the USC campus, on the outskirts of a large complex of city buildings known as Exposition Park. The area included the Los Angeles Memorial Coliseum, the Sports Arena, and the Museums of Natural History and Science and Industry; it also had abundant parking, and during Oscar week a fleet of shuttle buses made constant trips to and from the Shrine.

On Friday morning, two days before the Oscar show, one of those shuttles had a typical cross-section of riders: a couple of technicians, some office staffers, and one security guard. Most of the bus, though, was occupied by stand-ins, who spent the ride to the Shrine mulling over their version of a typical Oscar question: what should I wear?

For rehearsals, the stand-ins had been separated into two teams, with twenty in each team. The first team was due in the theater at 8:15 in the morning, in order that they could spend the day playing the part of presenters and nominees whenever Horvitz got the chance to run through the show. The second team wasn't due until 8 p.m.; they'd handle the same chores for the night shift. Nobody talked about it out loud, but everyone knew that stand-ins Horvitz liked got the day shift, ones he wasn't so sure about the night.

On the bus, though, they weren't talking about the stand-in hierarchy; after all, this was the day shift, which meant they were all on Horvitz's good side. Instead, they were trying to figure out what to do about a new edict. For dress rehearsal the next night, the stand-ins had been told, Horvitz wanted them to dress as if they were really attending the show.

"How can I dress like that?" complained one woman. "I'm staying at my friend's apartment this week—I didn't bring my best clothes with me."

"Do they expect us to wear our best clothes if we're here all day," griped a man, "or are we supposed to bring them and then change before the dress rehearsal? It's just not practical."

"It's ridiculous," summed up a third stand-in. "We're supposed to dress like the stars, but we don't have their budget."

FRIDAY WAS DEVOTED largely to rehearsing the nominees for best song. The importance of the songs was more pronounced than usual, because the telecast didn't include any medleys of past songs or dance numbers to illustrate sound effects or film editing. (A tentative plan to feature a ballet number themed to the British film *Billy Elliott*, in which a small-town working-class boy yearned to become a dancer, was scotched when that movie received only a single nomination.)

The slate of songs was wildly mixed. It included Randy Newman, now up to fourteen nominations without a win, for a bouncy tune from *Meet the Parents*; the chirpy Icelandic alternative-rock princess Björk, with an atmospheric track from *Dancer in the Dark*; former rock god turned mainstream balladeer Sting with a languid song from the animated Disney film *The Emperor's New Groove*; and writers Jorge Calandrelli, Tan Dun, and James Schamus for a lush ballad sung by Asian star Coco Lee in *Crouching Tiger, Hidden Dragon*.

The last slot was filled by the biggest name of the group, rock legend Bob Dylan, with "Things Have Changed" from *The Wonder Boys*. Once it would have been inconceivable to find the iconoclastic and often perverse Dylan performing on the Academy Awards—and from the moment he received the nomination, serious doubt existed about whether he could be persuaded to appear. Even before the nominations, Dylan had scheduled an Australian tour for the month of March; some suggested that he was well aware of what he was doing when he booked himself on the opposite side of the globe.

Over the ensuing weeks, negotiations took place to secure Dylan's participation on the show. Columbia Records, Dylan's label, offered to buy out the conflicting Australian shows, to pay off promoters and give the singer time to get back to the United States. Dylan refused, meaning the Oscars would need to either find somebody else to sing the song, or set up a remote broadcast.

Remotes were rarely used on the Academy Awards. The last time a nominated song had been performed anywhere but at the show was twenty-five years earlier, when Diana Ross had sung "Theme from *Mahogany* (Do You Know Where You're Going To)" from Amsterdam, lip-syncing the song while riding the streets in a horse-drawn carriage. Nobody wanted a return to that kind of foolishness—but at the same time, nobody wanted to book an inappropriate substitute for a nominated singer, especially one as legendary as Dylan. Besides Ann Reinking's famously awful rendition of "Against All Odds" in 1985, other regrettable choices included a 1984 rendition of "Maniac," Michael Sembello's driving rock song from *Flashdance*, by Herb Alpert and the Tijuana Brass, who at the time hadn't had a hit in twenty years; a stab at the pile driver "The Eye of the Tiger" (from *Rocky III*) by the odd coupling of the action-film actress Sandahl Bergman and the vocal group the Temptations; and Paul McCartney's James Bond theme, "Live and Let Die," entrusted to the actress and one-time teen-pop singer Connie Stevens.

Both options—a satellite link or a different performer—were distasteful. With some inside the production and the Academy adamantly opposed to doing a live remote, a few replacement names were bandied about, among them the gravel-voiced bard Tom Waits. Still, it was hard to take what seemed to be a meaningful, personal song from the greatest songwriter of his generation, and hand it over to somebody else. In the end, Cates decided that it was better to have Dylan from afar than somebody else in person. "If it were anybody but Dylan," said Robert Z. Shapiro, "the decision would have been a lot harder."

On Friday, Björk was the first of the nominees to rehearse, arriving at 8:30 in the morning with her fourteen-year-old son, Sindri, in tow. The singer wore a long, gauzy white dress, and kicked off her shoes as soon as she got to the stage. Her son watched, wearing a black Oscar cap.

In the film, Björk's nominated song, "I've Seen It All," was performed as a duet with Thom Yorke, the leader of Radiohead, the most influential and acclaimed British rock band of the past ten years. Though he tended to be somewhat reclusive and didn't enjoy performing, Yorke had initially agreed to appear on the Oscars with Björk, until the Academy's time constraints quite literally got in the way. "Thom was definitely up for it," said Björk's publicist, Joel Amsterdam, as he stood in the aisle and watched her pace the stage. "But the song's five and a half minutes long, and they told us we had to cut it down to three minutes. There's no time for his part."

Over the course of several rehearsals, Björk slowly became acclimated to the stage. At first she stared at her sheet music as she sang the droning song, which was set to a lurching, mechanical train rhythm. With each take, though, she loosened up a little more, meandering around, then bouncing on her heels, swaying, and turning into an oddly, endearingly magnetic performer.

Over a walkie-talkie, an assistant director radioed one of the stage managers. "This may sound like a weird question," he said, "but you may want to ask Björk if she's going to be wearing the glass dress."

The stage manager looked over at Amsterdam. "Um, is Björk going to be wearing a glass dress?" she asked.

"No," he said, as if the question were a completely normal one. He pointed to a small gym bag sitting on a nearby seat, and grinned. "Her dress is in that bag."

By the end of the day, Randy Newman had also come through, as had Sting and the striking Asian singer Coco Lee. But Cates was most excited about a midafternoon appearance by the classical virtuosos Itzhak Perlman and Yo-Yo Ma, who'd been booked to perform a suite of music from the nominated scores.

"Did you hear the joke that Itzhak told?" Cates asked Seligman a couple of hours after Perlman and Ma had rehearsed. "Jean-Claude Van Damme, Sylvester Stallone, and Arnold Schwarzenegger got together, and they decided to make an action movie about famous composers. Van Damme said, 'I'll be Tchaikovsky.' Stallone said, 'I'll be Mozart.' And then Schwarzenegger said, 'I'll be Bach.'"

Seligman and a handful of staffers laughed politely, and Cates shrugged. "It's not so funny when I tell it," he insisted, "but it's *very* funny when Itzhak Perlman tells it."

AS REHEARSAL WOUND DOWN, a couple of ABC pages got on the shuttle bus that would take them back to the lot where their cars were parked. The pages, most of them men and women in their twenties, were used to escort stars to and from their cars, to stay with them when they were in the Shrine, and to make sure they got their gift baskets and other freebies. Because the stage managers and talent staff had so many stars to deal with, they relied on pages to offer the kind of constant attention the show staff couldn't, both during rehearsals and during the show itself.

On the shuttle bus, the two young men looked over the schedules they'd been given for the next day.

"I have Hilary Swank tomorrow morning at ten," said one.

"How is she?" asked the other.

"She's really nice."

The second page looked at his sheet. "Tomorrow at four I've got Penélope!"

"I've got Kate Hudson at five. I'll trade ya."

"No thanks."

"I thought you liked blondes."

"Yeah, but Penélope's *hot.*"

DURING A NORMAL YEAR, getting stars to the Oscars involved an intricate game of scheduling. Actors with movies in production needed at least a day off if they were nominees, a minimum of two if they were presenters; for those whose films weren't shooting in Southern California, travel time had to be factored in as well. In 2001, though, things were even trickier than usual, because the Screen Actors Guild and the Writers Guild had both threatened to strike in early summer if new contract negotiations weren't concluded. To make sure they'd have enough product to see themselves through the possible strikes, the major studios and production companies rushed films into production, anxious to finish as much as possible by Memorial Day.

"With the strikes coming up, everybody is just fried," said Danette Herman as she stood at the top of the steps overlooking the artists' entrance to the Shrine. It was 9 a.m., and in fifteen minutes a procession of movie stars were due to arrive. "Some people are doing two movies at once," added Herman. "But everybody's going to show up."

As usual, that wasn't quite true: Tom Cruise was skipping rehearsal, per his custom, and so was Julia Roberts. But more than two dozen others, including Michael Douglas, John Travolta, Russell Crowe, Kate Hudson, and Renée Zellweger, were due at the Shrine. On the way to his trailer, Cates stopped for a minute to talk with Herman. "This is a rough morning for me," he said. "I have to sit in my trailer and talk to lots of beautiful women."

First up was the previous year's best-actress winner, Hilary Swank, who arrived early. When she got to the podium for the first time, Swank looked into the audience at the seat cards.

"Oh," she said, "Jeff Bridges has my seat from last year. Anthony Hopkins has Meryl Streep's seat."

Debbie Williams was incredulous. "How do you remember that?" she asked.

"I remember *everything* about last year," said Swank.

The day's rehearsal proceeded uneventfully, with a few exceptions. Russell Crowe, reportedly the object of a recent kidnapping plot, was accompanied by two handlers and a pair of large, stern men in suits. Afterward, a stage manager asked the gum-chewing Crowe to go to the sound truck, where he could record the nominees' names in a voiceover that would run while film clips were being shown. Crowe declined to do so. Cates was summoned to the green room to convince the recalcitrant actor—but once again, Crowe refused. "It's a *live* show," Crowe said. "Why would I do that?"

The other presenter who needed careful handling was Ben Stiller, who was handing out the award for short subjects. Stiller wasn't thrilled with his category—but, as he told the show's writers, "It was either that or some technical award." The actor also didn't care for the copy that had been written for him, so he tried to substitute a bit of his own that drew on the fact that Stiller, Woody Allen, and Martin Scorsese were all short—"but not our private parts." When that line failed to pass muster, Stiller sat at the writers' table and hashed out a new version that was less juvenile, but still phallic: "It's not the length of your film, it's what you do with it." By the time Stiller was finished rewriting his lines, he didn't have time to record his own voiceover.

Outside the hall, Cates left his office and escorted Penélope Cruz to the green room. He waved good-bye to Winona Ryder and Jennifer Lopez as they were leaving, then stopped to say hello to Sigourney Weaver. As they were talking, Kate Hudson dashed in the artists' entrance, ten minutes past her call time. "I'm so sorry I'm late," she said to Cates.

"It's no problem," he told her, giving her his arm. "C'mon, let's go to my office." On the way, he stopped, turned around, and grinned. "Hard job," he said.

BOB DYLAN hadn't been the easiest performer to deal with—and neither had his crew in Australia, key members of which were dubbed "flakes" by Seligman. Staffers at the Shrine were clearly tense as the time approached for an early evening test of the satellite link to Dylan. It was, perhaps, appropriate that to get his song down to the three-minute mark required by the Oscars, Dylan had eliminated the second of the four verses in "Things Have Changed"—the verse that began, "This place ain't doin' me any good / I'm in the wrong place, I should be in Hollywood."

Guitarist Charlie Sexton, eighteen hours ahead and seven thousand five hundred miles from Hollywood, subbed for his boss during the brief rehearsal. Sexton had been playing with Dylan for close to two years, and he even obliged by singing one verse in a creditable Dylanesque drawl that drew hoots of laughter back in Los Angeles. "I've been walkin' forty miles of bad road," snarled the Texas-born guitarist. "If the Bible is right, the world will exploooode." Meanwhile, a beefy, middle-aged, white-haired roadie stood in Sexton's usual spot, absently strumming a nonexistent guitar.

Once they'd rehearsed the song, the next order of business was to practice what would happen if Dylan won—a distinct possibility, since the song was the odds-on favorite. To keep things as simple as possible, presenter Jennifer Lopez was due to open the envelope immediately after Dylan's performance. While the band waited, a stand-in did the honors. "The Oscar goes to Bob Dylan," she announced, whereupon Horvitz cut back to Sexton, who once again was playing the part of his employer.

"Uh, thank you," Sexton mumbled in his best Dylan voice. At the Shrine, many observers figured that Sexton's three-word speech was probably the exact same one they'd hear from Dylan if he received the award.

Cates, though, breathed a sigh of relief when the satellite rehearsal went off without a hitch. "I think if Dylan wins it will actually be an exciting moment," he said to Seligman. "I'm not nearly as worried about it as I was."

STEVE MARTIN didn't seem worried, either. In fact, as the first dress rehearsal neared, the host was to all appearances completely relaxed. While Horvitz counted down the minutes from his truck and Cates settled behind the production table inside the Shrine, Martin wasn't in his dressing room fretting about last-minute changes; instead, the tuxedo-clad host stood in the center aisle, chatting with friends and posing for photos. It wasn't until Bill Conti's orchestra started playing the overture—the Richard Strauss theme from *2001: A Space Odyssey*, which made sense given the year, but had also been used to kick off David Letterman's ill-fated gig at the Oscars six years earlier—that the host left the aisle and ambled onstage.

There, he delivered what was essentially a dummy monologue: a few jokes, some mumbling, and lots of lines like "blah blah blah, I'm so funny now, standing ovation, blah blah blah . . ." After one joke, he listened to the applause—more than ought to be coming from the small group of stand-ins and staffers watching the rehearsal—and shook his head. "Is that sweetening I hear?" he scolded, accurately identifying the canned laughter coming from the P.A. system. "Oh, thanks. That's a real confidence builder."

Martin remained loose and relaxed throughout the rehearsal. Unless he was needed onstage, he watched the show from a seat near his writers, putting his fingers in his ears during every musical performance. The rehearsal ended at the unnervingly early time of 10:46, just a few minutes past the three-hour mark. Stage manager Garry Hood, who was in charge of cuing Martin during the show, was impressed. "There's low-maintenance, there's high-maintenance, and there's Steve Martin: no maintenance," he said. "Normally a host comes off, I hand them their script for the next bit and tell them how long they've got. Steve comes off, and before I can say anything he says, 'I know. Item forty-two, I'm introducing Julia. I'll see you in five minutes.' "

After Martin left, Cates shook his head. "He is a man," he said admiringly, "totally without angst."

ON THE MONITORS in front of Horvitz, Itzhak Perlman and Yo-Yo Ma alternately caressed and ripped into music from the five nominated scores. They sounded great, but Horvitz didn't like what he was seeing during the final rehearsal. The two men sat in chairs that had been placed atop a center-stage platform, while behind them large screens showed footage from the films whose scores they were performing. Horvitz needed to capture both the musicians and the screens—but as the pair ran through their number, he scanned the dozens of monitors in front of him with increasing impatience, nowhere seeing the kind of shots he wanted.

"That's fucked," said Horvitz into his headset. "We need a wider shot somewhere in here. This *has* to be dealt with."

"We can't stop to fix it, right?" an assistant director asked.

"No," the director replied. "We'll have to fix it on the show." He turned and focused on the monitors in front of him. "Ready camera two. Dissolve to three. Dissolve to four." He stopped. "Damnit, Hector, how many fucking times did we do that shot?" He put his head in his hands. "Guys, I gotta have some help here, goddamnit."

Outside the truck, the atmosphere may have been unexpectedly relaxed for an Oscar show; inside, where decisions were made on the fly and there was no such thing as a second take, the usual tensions gripped the crew.

Sitting in a chair behind Horvitz, Cates leaned forward after the Perlman and Ma performance. "By the way," he said, "if they get a standing ovation, you can really milk it. I love those guys."

A COUPLE OF HOURS LATER, Björk returned to the Shrine, turning heads in the dress she'd had stuffed into her gym bag during rehearsal. A swan's head curled around her neck; the swan's body formed a fluffy tutu of sorts. When she arrived backstage in the outfit most people stared, though Anthony Hopkins walked by without noticing.

From the outside, the green room was draped in dramatic red velvet curtains, shielded by an entry corridor that contained two makeup tables. Inside, things were a soothing shade of pale blue, the translucent curtains dotted with small stars. The furniture—a couple of couches and a few chairs arranged around a handful of tables and a small spread of hors d'oeuvres and drinks—was a subdued, quietly tasteful beige. Early arrival Ben Stiller sat in there with his wife, Christine Taylor, while PricewaterhouseCoopers partner Lisa Perozzi held one of the two briefcases that contained complete sets of envelopes announcing the winners. (Her colleague Greg Garrison, stationed on the far side of the stage, had the other set.)

An hour before the show began, Itzhak Perlman entered the auditorium on his motorized cart. He rolled into the backstage area, accompanied by an aide carrying his priceless Stradivarius violin.

"How are you doing?" said a bystander as Perlman passed.

"Just schlepping," replied the virtuoso.

The Oscars themselves were wheeled out of a small, locked room about half an hour before show time, accompanied by a phalanx of guards. Academy historian Patrick Stockstill, wearing white gloves, walked alongside the surprisingly nondescript, even dingy cart on which the gleaming statuettes rested. Stockstill would be the only one to touch the Oscars until he handed them to one of the show's trophy ladies.

5:30 P.M., PACIFIC DAYLIGHT TIME: *"Live from the Shrine Auditorium in Los Angeles, California, the 73rd annual Academy Awards."*

Just outside the artists' entrance at the rear of the Shrine, Michael Douglas and Catherine Zeta-Jones stood in what passed for a smoking section. Between drags on her cigarette, Zeta-Jones studied the lines she'd be reading as the night's first presenter. (Her husband would be the last.) Shortly before a stage manager took her into the wings, Zeta-Jones began fanning herself with her script pages.

On the stage, Steve Martin launched into a monologue that dealt largely with show business—in fact, the subtext of most of it was the venality of the entertainment industry. "Please hold your applause," he said at one point, "until it's for me."

Eighteen minutes into the show, the first major award of the night, best supporting actress, went to Marcia Gay Harden for *Pollock*. When Harden and presenter Nicolas Cage were almost off the stage, a crew member yelled "*Go!*" and stagehands immediately began sliding a large center screen and two huge side panels off the stage. One of the panels almost hit the two actors.

Onstage, Martin mentioned how the phrase "and the winner is . . ." had been changed to "and the Oscar goes to . . ." "Because God forbid anyone should think of this as a competition," he said. "It might make the trade ads seem crass." He introduced Russell Crowe, who gave the editing award to *Traffic* and then immediately headed for the smoking area, trailed by a page, a publicist, and two guards.

A few minutes later, Martin reminded the nominees about Cates's offer of a free TV for the shortest speech, then introduced Ben Stiller. "You loved him in *There's Something About Mary*," he said. "You loved him in *Meet the Parents*. And you were just fine with him in *Mystery Men*." Stiller presented the award for best animated short to Dutch filmmaker Michael Dudok de Wit for *Father and Daughter*. De Wit thanked three people and the Academy, and wrapped up his speech in eighteen seconds.

As the show neared the one-hour mark, Benicio Del Toro won the award for best supporting actor, for *Traffic*. In the wings, Danette Herman let out a whoop. As Del Toro exited, stagehands began to move the huge scenic elements into place for the nominated song from *Crouching Tiger, Hidden Dragon*. "There's gonna be a lot of scenery coming through here, folks," yelled stage manager Peter Margolis. "We need everybody up against the walls."

While the scenery was being set, Mike Myers came onstage to present the awards for sound. "Now, ladies and gentlemen, the award we've all been waiting for," he said in a portentous tone. "Sound and sound editing. Now, I know what you're asking yourself: will the winner this year be Chet Flippy, or Tommy Bloobloo?" As he mocked the anonymity of the nominees, some members of the sound branch began to stew.

When Myers walked offstage and returned to the green room, he passed dozens of waiters and workers in the Governors Ball area. Nearby, Yo-Yo Ma and Itzhak Perlman warmed up in a quiet corner, then headed for the stage. On the way there, Ma spotted a woman walking off the stage with an Oscar in her hand. It was Tracy Seretean, the winner of the award for documentary short. Although he didn't know her, the cellist stopped and congratulated Seretean.

At this point the show was flowing easily; on backstage monitors, a countdown clock had it coming in at almost exactly three and a half hours. During a break, Cates left his usual post in the command truck. Trailed by a security guard, the producer walked past the green room and into the wings of the stage, where he greeted writer Buz Kohan.

"How's it playing out here?" said Cates.

"Good," Kohan assured him. "It's playing really well."

Cates nodded. "It's light, airy, pizzicato," he said. "And we'll be at three and a half hours, unless somebody does something stupid." Then he smiled, and his smile was informed by the experience of producing ten Academy Awards shows. "Which they may."

On the stage, Randy Newman and Bangles singer Susanna Hoffs performed "A Fool in Love." In the wings, Perlman slowly climbed up a set of steps to the platform on which he and Ma would perform. Ma followed. Casually, unheard by anyone except those nearby, Perlman and Ma began to play along with Newman's song.

While they played, a visibly nervous Renée Zellweger came into the wings, where she chatted with Goldie Hawn. "I'm going to trip over my dress, I know it," Zellweger fretted.

Cates walked over to greet the women, but he refrained from offering hugs. "He's done this for so long," said Zellweger, "he knows better than to wrap his arms around us."

After Newman's performance, Steve Martin returned to the stage. "The FBI has just announced a suspect in the plot to kidnap Russell Crowe," he said. "And all I can say is, Tom Hanks, you should be ashamed of yourself." The camera caught a priceless reaction from Hanks, who looked chastened and guilty. Behind Martin, the wings of the stage were plunged into chaos: Newman's bandstand and grand piano had to come off the stage and out of the way so that Perlman and Ma's platform could be pushed into place, but other scenery initially blocked the way. Stagehands rushed around trying to maneuver the huge set pieces. Hawn and Zellweger stood nearby and chatted, while Winona Ryder tried to stay out of the way.

When Perlman and Ma began their own performance a few minutes later, Julia Roberts took up residence in a corner of the Governors Ball, away from the hubbub of the green room. Accompanied by her boyfriend, Benjamin Bratt, and a group of about eight friends, she ate from a plate of sushi that Bratt had brought to her.

Behind the theater, the crowd steadily grew as some people stepped outside to smoke, others to escape the congestion in the green room. One woman approached Kevin Spacey and Ben Affleck. The two men were hanging out together, Spacey with a drink in his hand, Affleck with a cigarette.

"Do you mind if my boyfriend takes a picture of me with the two of you?" she asked.

"No problem," said Affleck. Then he pointed to Spacey. "You know, he *won* last year." When Penélope Cruz walked by, Affleck quickly left Spacey for a whispered conversation with the Spanish actress.

Closer to the back door, Winona Ryder nursed a cigarette. Goldie Hawn, who'd introduced Perlman and Ma, stepped outside for a smoke as well. Zellweger and John Travolta immediately rushed over to Hawn. "How did it go?" asked Zellweger. "We can't see anything out here."

"That's not true," joked Travolta. "We saw it, and you were *shit*." Then he laughed. "No, no. You look fabulous tonight, Goldie." He paused, and leaned forward intently. "And it's not just the dress," he added. "It's you."

Zellweger sighed. "He knows just the right words," she said.

As Winona Ryder was escorted to the stage to introduce Björk, Hilary Swank rushed out the back door, holding up her dress. "Hurry hurry hurry," she said, making a beeline for the women's room. A minute later, Julie Andrews headed in the same direction.

Two and a half hours into the show, the satellite link to Sydney went off smoothly. As Bob Dylan performed "Things Have Changed," Horvitz kept the singer in extreme close-up on a big screen that sat center stage. The idea was for Dylan's image to be big enough that shots from the back of the theater could show both the live audience and Dylan's facial expressions— though it meant that guests at the show found themselves staring at the enormous, grizzled visage of the fifty-nine-year-old Dylan, who sported a pencil-thin mustache and piercing blue eyes.

His head cocked to the side, Dylan drawled and snarled his way through a strange, riveting performance. Ang Lee watched from the wings, holding the best foreign film Oscar he'd just won for *Crouching Tiger*. Jennifer Lopez stood nearby, accompanied by the night's largest security guard. In midsong, an audience shot caught Danny DeVito munching on a carrot stick. From the booth where they were watching the show, Martin and Vilanch noticed this, and sent a staffer into a nearby hospitality room to fetch some dip.

Dylan won the Oscar and gave a surprisingly long speech that ended, "I want to thank the members of the Academy, who were bold enough to give me this award for . . . a song that doesn't pussyfoot around nor turn a blind eye to human nature. God bless you all with peace, tranquillity, and good will."

Outside the green room, a minor brouhaha developed when stagehands, trying to make room for the Governors Ball, began taking down the drapes covering one side of the room. Seligman chewed out a supervisor—but the Governors Ball organizers were scrambling, because the show was actually running ahead of schedule.

The next time he took the stage, Steve Martin walked into the audience and gave a bowl of dip to DeVito.

A few minutes later, Russell Crowe won the best-actor award for *Gladiator*. But when Crowe took his Oscar and headed out the back door, he didn't follow the usual winners' path toward the press tent; instead, he turned the other way and hung out in the smoking area with a few buddies.

While Crowe stood there, security guards suddenly asked guests and bystanders around the artists' entrance to clear the area. Despite three days of star comings-and-goings, this was a first, and it puzzled credentialed guests who wondered why the guards were suddenly so paranoid. The answer came a minute later, when a limo pulled up to the end of the red carpet and Tom Cruise got out, accompanied by a friend and by publicist Pat Kingsley.

Wearing a suit instead of a tux, with no tie and an unbuttoned blue shirt, Cruise had arrived less than half an hour before he was due onstage. While security guards tried to keep people away from him, Cruise hustled down the red carpet. He was almost in the back door when he spotted the newly crowned best actor lingering by the entrance. "Russell!" he shouted. "You won!"

The two men spent a few minutes embracing, laughing, and doing some mild but manly head- and fist-butting. Then Cruise ducked into the green room and Crowe went back to his seat—though he was temporarily blocked by a carpet sweeper cleaning the corner of the Governors Ball.

As the show neared the three-hour mark, Julia Roberts was named best actress. Deliriously giddy, she gave a three-and-a-half-minute speech that began, "I have a television, so I'm going to spend some time here to tell you some things." Besides being studded with cries like "I love it up here!" and whoops of delight, her speech was also full of warnings to Conti—"stickman," she called him—not to start the music. In truth, she was in no danger; one reason for the forty-five-second rule was so that at the end of the night, big stars like Roberts could have all the time they needed.

As the orchestra played the music from *2001* for the sixth time (but not for the last), Roberts came into the wings, hanging on to presenter and past winner Kevin Spacey. "Oh, my *God*," she said, hugging him. "My knees are weak."

"I know," Spacey said. "You need to sit down, you need to have a drink." He looked at the staffers around them and took charge. "Julia needs a drink," he announced. Then he turned to Roberts. "What would you like to drink?"

"Champagne?"

"Okay," Spacey said. "Julia needs champagne."

A staffer pointed to the nearby watercooler. "We have water right there."

"No," said Spacey quickly. "Only champagne will do. You have to understand."

Debbie Williams ran through the wings and into the Governors Ball, which was in the final stages of preparation. "I need a bottle of champagne!" she shouted to the bartender.

He shook his head. "I can't give it to you," he said.

"Julia Roberts just won," insisted Williams, "and she wants champagne!" The bartender promptly passed her a bottle. Williams grabbed two glasses, and back in the wings Roberts and Spacey shared a toast and quietly talked for a few more minutes. "I really see why they have the tradition of previous winners giving out the awards," he said. "You need somebody who understands what you're going through."

Roberts hugged Spacey a few more times, took some sips from her champagne glass, looked at her Oscar, and shook her head. "I know that everybody was writing about how I was going to win," she said, "but I didn't believe the stuff I read in the papers." She looked down again at the statuette in her hand. "My God," she said with a huge grin, "I just won an Oscar!"

Spacey turned to Roberts's publicist. "You'll be hearing that a lot for the next couple of weeks," he said.

Onstage, Martin introduced Tom Hanks, who himself introduced Arthur C. Clarke, the writer of *2001: A Space Odyssey*, to hand out the adapted screenplay award from Clarke's home in Sri Lanka. The segment was pretaped; Clarke had done five different takes, one for each of the nominees. Greg Garrison left his spot in the wings and went to the truck, where he told Horvitz which clip to run.

As Julia Roberts finally headed back to her seat, the two screenwriting winners—Stephen Gaghan for *Traffic* and Cameron Crowe for *Almost Famous*—stood in the wings talking to Hanks. "This," said Crowe, "is a psychedelic experience."

Up to this point, awards had been split fairly evenly between *Gladiator*, *Traffic*, and *Crouching Tiger, Hidden Dragon*, which had four, three, and three wins, respectively. In something of an upset, the best-director Oscar then went to Soderbergh for *Traffic*, confounding handicappers who figured that his dual nominations for that film and *Erin Brockovich* would split the vote. "Suddenly, going to work tomorrow doesn't seem like such a good idea," said Soderbergh, who was shooting *Ocean's Eleven* in Las Vegas.

When he came offstage, Soderbergh waited in the wings to see the best-picture winner. Though at this point the race suddenly seemed to be wide open, the winner was the preshow favorite, *Gladiator*. All the night's big winners were quickly herded backstage for commemorative photos. Russell Crowe finally headed for the press rooms, where he greeted the assembled scribes by saying, "Ask me questions that I can answer yes or no to, and we'll all get along really well."

At about 8:55 Pacific time, the show ended—less than three and a half hours after it began, forty minutes shorter than the previous year. Afterward, the show's staff gathered on the stage to share cake and champagne as usual, and the stage managers posed for a photo with Julia Roberts. "I see you guys more often than my family," said Roberts, who'd been hitting the awards show circuit hard.

The Governors Ball had taken over much of the backstage area, and the party was just beginning. But the green room still sat in its corner; no longer protected by thick drapes or a shielded entryway, it was still a place of

n amid the debris of setup, Oscar exerted a powerful lure. Days before the show in 1998, a local television reporter found herself irresistibly drawn to the big guy outside the Shrine.

gest and potentially the deadliest Oscar presenter in 1998, Bart the Bear wandered inside an electrified n the Shrine Auditorium stage, watched closely by an armed guard and some curious stagehands.

ABOVE: *Before rehearsing in 1998, presenter Sean Connery waited in the wings with a stage manager. Behind him, another crew member moved a panel to reveal the orchestra riser at the rear of the nautical-themed stage, an appropriate look in the year of* Titanic.
BELOW: *The same year, Matt Damon would win an Oscar for co-writing* Good Will Hunting. *The day before the show, Damon was escorted through the artists' entrance behind the Shrine by stage manager Rita Cossette. Damon arrived at rehearsal with pal Ben Affleck and Affleck's mother; the next day, Damon brought his own mom to the Oscar show.*

TOP: *Elia Kaʒan, whose presence dominated the show in 1999, practiced his succinct, unapologetic acceptance speech on the stage of the Chandler. Behind him, between a stage manager and a stand-in, stood director Martin Scorsese and Kaʒan's wife, Frances.*
BOTTOM: *The Kaʒan year also marked the first time the Academy produced its own pre-show. To prepare for that broadcast, stand-ins gathered outside the Shrine and donned name tags.*

ABOVE: *In 1999, stage manager Jason Seligman signaled host Whoopi Goldberg and the presenters when to read from the TelePrompTer. He wore white gloves to make his gestures easily visible from the stage.* BELOW: *Dame Judi Dench took home the supporting-actress Oscar that same year for her six-minute role* in Shakespeare in Love. *After winning, she waited with an escort on the fourth floor of the Dorothy Chandler Pavilion.*

Adjusting Oscar outside the Shrine Auditorium, 2000

ART STREIBER

In 2000, Cameron Diaz couldn't keep her hands off the hair of her Charlie's Angels *costar, Lucy Liu*

Sitting at the podium where, in 2000, he would serve as the first on-camera voice of Oscar, actor Peter Coyote was flanked by stage manager Dency Nelson, left, and soon-to-be best-actor winner Kevin Spacey, right.

*Prepping for a 2000 show whose producers had proudly boasted of no dance numbers, Robin Williams l[...]
a line of hoofers through the profane and problematic song "Blame Canada."*

refuge. Before gearing up for the press and the parties, Roberts went in and flopped down on the couch. Kate Hudson and Goldie Hawn followed her in—and Hudson, relieved that the big night was coming to an end, whipped out a cigarette. "Okay," she yelled, "let's light up!"

From her couch, the new best actress looked up and broke into a huge grin. "Honey," she said, "*it's that time!*"

FOR THE MOST PART, reviewers found the slimmed-down Oscar show to be a welcome change. "Neat and clean, tasty and cheery," *Daily Variety* said the next day. But the numbers were not as favorable: the show drew the second-lowest number of viewers in ten years, and its lowest rating and share ever.

Dutch filmmaker Michael Dudok de Wit, who took home the Oscar for animated short, won the television set Cates had promised for the shortest speech. But de Wit said he was giving the set to a children's charity. "I did not write the shortest speech to win the television set," he said. "I have many television sets."

The day after the show, the Academy heard from members of the sound branch, who were not amused to hear Mike Myers making fun of the nominees in their category. Bob Rehme wrote the branch a formal letter of apology.

In June, the Academy announced that the Kodak Theatre would be ready in time for the seventy-fourth Oscar show.

The same month, the board of governors voted to tighten the rules regarding eligible producers of the best-picture nominees. The number of producers eligible had been reduced to three the previous year, but the board went further, pointing out that the Academy "shall not be bound by any contract or agreement relating to the sharing or giving of credit." Aimed principally at studio executives and personal managers who had increasingly negotiated for producer credit regardless of their actual day-to-day input during production of the movie, the new guidelines made it harder for managers or studio bosses—say, for instance, Harvey Weinstein—to go home with an Oscar.

The governors also approved the rules for the new category of animated feature film, specifying that it would be given out anytime at least eight eligible films were released. The award, the board said, would go to "the key creative talent most clearly responsible" for the film, usually a single person and never more than two people.

In July, the fourteenth branch of the Academy, the documentary branch, elected its first governor.

In August, with Bob Rehme's tenure ended, the board of governors chose screenwriter and director Frank Pierson as the new president of the Academy. Pierson, best known for writing *Cat Ballou*, *Cool Hand Luke*, *Dog Day Afternoon*, and the 1976 Barbra Streisand remake of *A Star Is Born*, had served as president of the Writers Guild twice, once in the early 1980s and again a decade later. His first WGA tenure coincided with Gil Cates's election to the presidency of the Directors Guild. As leaders of the two famously combative guilds—among other things, the writers were still upset that directors had seized the "a film by" possessory credit—Pierson and Cates had not gotten along especially well.

Work proceeded on what was now called the Kodak Theatre, and on the Hollywood & Highland complex. Academy officials and key members of the Oscar production crew were consulted about what they needed to make the theater an ideal home for their show. In addition, the Academy was given veto power over the other tenants in the center. That stretch of Hollywood Boulevard may have been home to lots of discount electronics shops, T-shirt emporiums, and cheesy souvenir shops, but Oscar's immediate neighborhood had to be classier.

"From the beginning," said Bruce Davis, "we made it clear that there was not going to be an Oscar Drugstore or an Academy Awards Haberdashery, or whatever. We had a whole list: there could be no T-shirt shops within the mall, that kind of thing. There would be a dignity about the place. And we also told them, 'Look, whether you guys admit this or not, this is a mall. You're asking us to do our show in the middle of a shopping center, so you're going to have to shut down your mall and clear those businesses out for the day of the show and a portion of the night previous.' "

Quickly, TrizecHahn agreed to the stipulations. "Even though we would only be there one month out of the year, we were a very large gorilla," said Davis. "So they gave us a lot of control."

9

≡

Movin' on Up

The 74th Academy Awards

"AS A LITTLE GIRL, I dreamed that I produced the Academy Awards," Laura Ziskin told Bruce Vilanch in one of their first meetings. "Now I think I've gone insane."

From the early September day when Frank Pierson had asked Ziskin to produce the seventy-fourth Oscars, her life had been tumultuous. Ziskin was a movie producer whose films included *To Die For* and *What About Bob?*, a Hollywood vet of more than twenty years who'd gotten her start as an assistant to the fiery producer Jon Peters. Pierson had met Ziskin in 1975, when he was directing the remake of *A Star Is Born* and she was working with Peters and Barbra Streisand. She also lived with screenwriter Alvin Sargent, an old friend of Pierson's—and though Ziskin's only experience with live television had come on the George Clooney project *Fail Safe*, which ran on CBS in April 2000, the Academy president knew that she was interested in the Oscar job.

Before accepting his offer, though, Ziskin told Pierson some of her ideas. She wanted an orchestra conducted by film composer John Williams.

She wanted to hire a production designer who usually worked in film. She wanted to commission notable filmmakers to put together the show's film packages. And she didn't want to open with the traditional arrivals montage from the red carpet, since that was a reprise of what viewers had just seen on the preshow. Pierson signed off on all the ideas and Ziskin took the job, even though she was already producing *Spider-Man*, which she'd be delivering to Sony Pictures right around Oscar time.

A few days after she accepted Pierson's offer, terrorists flew passenger planes into the World Trade Center and the Pentagon. "I don't know exactly how it's going to affect us, but those events are going to resonate forever," she said a few weeks later. "I think everybody in the movie business has started to think, God, what we do is all so insignificant. And then another part of me takes over and says, No, it's significant. Movies are really powerful, they're a big part of people's lives, they give us solace and stimulation and they provoke us. Those things are important."

Still, Ziskin knew her concerns would have to be openly addressed on Oscar night. "I feel an obligation at the top of the show to say what is really in my head," she said. "The world is a tricky and dangerous and serious place, and we're gonna sit there and congratulate ourselves. Is that a lot of bullshit?"

IN NOVEMBER, the Kodak Theatre opened with a gala concert featuring tenor Russell Watson. Designed like a European opera house, the inside of the Kodak was lush and dramatic. Opera boxes lined the walls, rich cherry-wood surfaces ran throughout the theater, and three balconies rose toward the "corona," a large oval ring that hung eight stories above the orchestra seats.

But the theater was not without problems—and the Academy, admitted Bruce Davis, was "sweating bullets." In the fall, TrizecHahn had sent the organization a letter that appeared to renege on previous agreements to close all of Hollywood & Highland's shops on Oscar day, and to secure nearby space for production and satellite trucks. Both items were deal-breakers to the Academy, but after a few tense meetings and some posturing in the press, TrizecHahn agreed to abide by the original agreement.

Still to be settled, though, were issues of traffic control and security. The

Kodak was situated at one of the busiest intersections in Hollywood, an area jammed with cars on a good day. In addition, a subway stop sat directly beneath Hollywood & Highland. Not only had the problem of securing the entire area added more than a million dollars to the security costs of the show, but Los Angeles's Metropolitan Transit Authority had yet to agree to close the subway stop during the Awards.

"Particularly in light of recent events, we are determined that the MTA skip that stop for a few hours that evening," said Davis. "Basically, the entrance is within our security perimeter, so it's not a good idea to have crowds come up those stairs and be inside our security line."

As the show approached, the board of governors took an additional, unprecedented step. Mindful of the unstable world situation, they paid a million dollars for a catastrophe insurance policy that would pay off in case of a terrorist attack that delayed, disrupted, or canceled the Oscar show.

TO ENTER the Samuel Goldwyn Theater required walking a security gauntlet unprecedented at previous nominations announcements. Invited guests with laminated passes had to pass security guards, submit to scanners, and walk through metal detectors. "What's with all the security?" asked one studio rep as he settled into a seat in the Goldwyn Theater. "Like they're gonna blow up a room full of publicists?"

In fact, things didn't really get ugly until after the nominations were announced. To go by the numbers, the race was dominated by *The Lord of the Rings: The Fellowship of the Ring*, the first of director Peter Jackson's trilogy based on the classic fantasy epic by J.R.R. Tolkien. But while it received thirteen nominations, five more than any other film, Jackson's movie was the kind of special effects–laden extravaganza that rarely won major Oscars; many of its nominations were in the technical categories. In the best-picture race, front-runner status gravitated instead toward Ron Howard's *A Beautiful Mind*, the kind of high-minded, serious film the Academy usually loved. Baz Luhrmann's delirious musical *Moulin Rouge!* also picked up eight, while veteran director Robert Altman's witty drawing room comedy *Gosford Park* was surprisingly strong with seven; the French romance *Amélie* and the intense low-budget drama *In the Bedroom* received five each.

In the best-actor category, the strongest contenders appeared to be Denzel Washington for his explosive role in *Training Day*, along with two actors playing real people: Will Smith as the flamboyant boxer Muhammad Ali in *Ali*, and Russell Crowe as troubled mathematician John Nash in *A Beautiful Mind*. In the labyrinthine logic of Oscar calculations, though, Crowe's chances were thought to be hurt by his win the year before for glowering and fighting his way through *Gladiator*—an award that was in itself partly attributed to Academy remorse over not giving him the Oscar the year before that for *The Insider*. In best actress, the front-runners were actresses from three smaller movies: Sissy Spacek from *In the Bedroom*, Judi Dench from *Iris*, and Halle Berry from *Monster's Ball*.

To become an Oscar front-runner, though, was to become an immediate target. Working on information from unidentified sources, Internet reporter Matt Drudge had already lit into *A Beautiful Mind* for omitting any mention of Nash's alleged homosexual encounters, and after the nominations he stepped up his attacks. The film, he charged, whitewashed Nash's life, leaving out anti-Semitic statements made in the grip of his schizophrenia and idealizing Nash's marriage when in fact he and his wife, Alicia (played as a long-suffering supporter and muse by Jennifer Connelly), were divorced, and Nash had fathered a child with another woman.

The whispering campaign against *A Beautiful Mind* continued, though nobody could pin down who was behind it. The usual reaction to underhanded campaigning was to blame it on Miramax, but that studio's best-picture nominee, *In the Bedroom*, was such a long shot that many figured that Harvey Weinstein didn't have enough motivation to slander *A Beautiful Mind*. At one point, Universal even took the unusual step of publicly absolving Miramax of responsibility for the attacks. New Line, meanwhile, tried to stay out of that fray and draw voters' attention to the fact that *The Fellowship of the Ring* dealt with the battle between good and evil, a pertinent theme after September 11.

By the time of the nominees' luncheon on March 11, even the normally mild-mannered Ron Howard had heard enough. The campaign to undermine his movie's credibility, he told reporters in the press room, was "an attack strategy" reminiscent of the one the late Republican strategist Lee Atwater had developed during the 1988 presidential campaign, in which

George Bush had defeated Michael Dukakis. Meanwhile, Stacey Snider, the chairman of Universal Pictures, made her own statement. "Lines that should be clear to all of us," she said, "have recklessly been crossed."

THE EIGHT-FOOT OSCAR statue that stood in the lobby of Laura Ziskin's office on the Sony Pictures lot was a loaner from the Academy, a courtesy extended to Oscar producers who wanted a tangible sign of the job. But Ziskin wasn't content to simply stick the giant Oscar in the corner and leave it at that: instead, her statue sported a curly black wig, a pink boa, and a pair of lightly tinted aviator-style sunglasses. A cigarette dangled from the corner of its mouth.

One of Ziskin's requirements when she took the producing job was that she had to keep her office on the Sony lot; otherwise, there was no way she'd be able to work on the show and finish *Spider-Man* at the same time. Her first-floor office suite, tucked into a corner of the lot not far from the main gate, was decorated with posters from the films she'd worked on—*No Way Out*, *Murphy's Romance*, *Hero*—as well as a signed photo of actress Drew Barrymore and a ticket stub from the 1998 World Series at San Diego's Qualcomm Stadium, signed by record-breaking St. Louis Cardinals slugger Mark McGwire (whose team didn't play in that series).

The Monday before the Oscar show, Ziskin welcomed preshow host Leeza Gibbons to the office. Gibbons, the former host of *Entertainment Tonight* who had moved to the competing show *Extra*, arrived bearing a lavish basket of beauty products for Ziskin. The producer responded with a gift of her own: a small, sterling silver egg timer with exactly forty-five seconds' worth of sand inside it. "I gave these to all the nominees at the luncheon," she told Gibbons, "just to encourage them to keep their speeches short."

"Oh, my gosh, that's adorable," said Gibbons. "I feel very inside."

Gibbons took a seat on Ziskin's brown leather couch, while other members of the preshow production team arranged themselves around a low, rectangular coffee table covered in dark fabric. The meeting included Ziskin, preshow director Bruce Gowers, producer Pamela Oas Williams, and researcher Simbiat Hall, as well as producer Marty Pasetta, Jr., the man whose father had directed seventeen Oscar shows before his unceremonious departure in 1988. (It was hardly unusual for the children of awards-show vets to follow their fathers into the business: the sons of Michael Seligman and Jeff Margolis worked the awards circuit as well.) As the staff took seats, Ziskin set Gibbons's gift basket behind her desk, near two Spider-Man action figures and a copy of the book *Inside Oscar*.

"Tentatively, we've planned that your first interview will be live with Julia Roberts, and all the rest of your interviews will be pretapes," Williams told Gibbons. "But we're throwing in a few live segments, to give the illusion that the whole thing is live."

Gibbons looked at the script, which included introductions to and possible questions for the people she'd be interviewing. "Can I be more casual with this intro?" she asked.

"Of course," said Ziskin. "In terms of dialogue, feel free to rewrite it and make it comfortable for you."

"Of these questions for Julia, I feel like the question about George Clooney and the rat pack has been asked so many times before," Gibbons said. "I'd rather talk about the year since she won, what the differences have been."

"Fine," said Ziskin with a quick laugh. "More than that, George Clooney isn't coming to the show. So screw him."

For the next twenty minutes, they mulled over the best questions to ask several of the stars on the preshow. The freshest approach for Ian McKellen, they decided, would be to ask him about hosting *Saturday Night Live*, though Gibbons was also inclined to ask the openly gay McKellen about his thoughts on John Nash's sexuality, or on the ugliness of the Oscar campaigns. For Cameron Diaz, they decided to focus on future projects, though Ziskin was also fascinated by the fact that Diaz didn't use a stylist. "Even the seat-fillers have stylists," she said.

Finally, they discussed the end of the preshow, and Gibbons's interaction with her two cohosts, talk show host Ananda Lewis and veteran movie reporter Chris Connelly. "We'll start with a shot of Ananda on the red carpet," said Williams, "and then she'll throw it to you at the bottom of the stairs. You have your last words, and then you throw it to Chris at the top of the stairs."

Gibbons frowned. "Why can't I be where Chris is?" she said.

"It's easier to light at the bottom of the stairs," explained Gowers. "Chris will be walking to the door of the theater, and that's an awkward walk for a lady to do, because we can't light it. At the bottom of the stairs, you'll be completely gorgeous all the time."

"I understand," she said, pouting a little. "But that's the big ending, there at the top."

"Also," said Ziskin quickly, "the opening of the show is going to be seeing the stars in the theater, not on the red carpet. So when we go to you at the bottom of the stairs, it'll be an exciting shot—there will be a lot of activity behind you as we get the stars into the theater."

"Okay," Gibbons said, clearly trying to show—or at least feign—some enthusiasm. "I'm so excited about it. It's going to be a blast. And I love the people I'm going to talk to."

Gowers sighed. "If you really want to be at the top of the stairs . . ."

"Only because that's the ultimate shot," said Gibbons. "But it's okay, really." She chuckled. "Who's sleeping with Chris?"

At the end of the meeting, Ziskin walked Gibbons to the door. After Ziskin returned, Pasetta looked at her. "Leeza's going to be at the top of the stairs," he predicted.

BY THE MIDDLE OF THE WEEK, the Kodak Theatre was tightly secured. The system of passes was more extensive and complex than ever before, with seven different levels of access and seventeen different ways to classify each staffer, from ACADEMY and PRODUCTION to BLEACHER CREW, SEAT-FILLER, and BODYGUARD. Passes were scanned each time an employee came onto the property, to make sure the bearer matched the picture stored in the system's memory; metal detectors also stood at each entrance to the grounds. When staffers applied for passes, their names and stats were fed into a computer that flagged possible security risks—including one Governors Ball staffer whose pass was voided when he turned out to have the same name as someone who'd been detained by the L.A.P.D.

Outside, Hollywood Boulevard had been shut down in front of the Hollywood & Highland complex. Workers erected scaffolding, laid the red carpet, and went to great expense to disguise the mall. One by one, storefronts were obscured by hanging banners or hidden by platforms; even a huge Kodak Theatre sign, which sat atop an enormous arch through which every guest would pass, was painstakingly covered by a framework that held an ACADEMY AWARDS banner.

Inside the theater, staffers who'd been consulted by the builders were surprised at what they found. For starters, the wings of the stage were far smaller than at the Shrine Auditorium—particularly stage left, where there was almost no room at all. There was a spacious green room, but in an unusable location: a couple of hallways and one flight of stairs below the stage itself. And the backstage rest rooms were woefully inadequate.

"Plenty of thought and planning went into it, and a lot of good stuff ended up being in there," said Horvitz. "But it was not what we thought it would be. It started out to be bigger and wider, but then retail came in and retail was very important. And suddenly it's a vertical house, and it seems my stage left was now the Krispy Kreme Donuts store." (This was not technically correct: stage left was truncated to leave room for a driveway between the Kodak and the Orchid Suites Motel. Krispy Kreme was farther away, out in the mall.)

While Horvitz tried to figure out how to shoot a vertical theater in TV's horizontal aspect ratio, a small hallway near the stage was commandeered to serve as the new green room. Production designer J. Michael Riva's staff transformed the space, which was fifty feet long but less than fifteen feet wide, using lots of red velvet drapery, tiger-print carpet, and black deco furniture. Clearly influenced by the look of *Moulin Rouge!*, the new green room was variously and affectionately compared to both a train car and a bordello. The rear door of the room led onto the loading dock, to a small patch of carpet designed to serve as the stars' smoking section. A fire marshal set the capacity of the new room at twenty-five, less than a third of the capacity of the room downstairs.

Along a hallway that led from the Kodak's lower lobby to the backstage area were offices for Ziskin, Seligman, Horvitz, and host Whoopi Goldberg. At the rear of the stage were large doors to the loading dock, where Horvitz's command truck was parked. Dressing rooms, the main production office, and offices for Herman and her staff were located one floor below the stage. Other offices, including the three press rooms, were located in the Renaissance Hollywood Hotel, which was connected to the Kodak by a rather complicated and lengthy series of hallways.

Production designer Riva, a veteran art director whose films included *The Color Purple*, *Lethal Weapon*, and *Charlie's Angels* (and who was the grandson of Marlene Dietrich), had spent much of his budget on an enormous art deco proscenium arch that framed the Kodak stage; the idea was to create the look of a vintage movie palace.

As workmen positioned the arch during one of the days devoted to loading in the set, the Kodak's sensitive alarm was triggered by stray smoke somewhere in the building. The system had been designed to suck smoke (or, given the times, poison gas) out of the building in a matter of seconds, using huge fans concealed behind panels in the ceiling. But with the doors between the stage and the loading dock wide open for the load-in, the fans sucked air in the back door and blew it out the ceiling with such force that stagehands struggled to keep the unsecured proscenium from toppling onto the orchestra seats.

Determined to make sure the system wouldn't be triggered again, supervising producer Seligman met with building supervisors, who assured him that the automatic sensors would be switched off.

"WE KNOW it's going to be longer than four hours," said Bruce Vilanch. "We're blaming that on the fact that we've got a new award, animated film, plus three honorary awards."

Standing backstage three days before the show, Vilanch shrugged as he considered what had become the only real question among Oscar staffers: would it simply be one of the longest Oscar shows, or would it beat the Zanucks' show to become *the* longest?

"Laura seems convinced that Lili's show was 4:20," said Vilanch. "But I think it was more like 4:11." In fact, the 2000 show was a mere 4:08.

The dilemma, clearly, was that Ziskin had lots of ideas—and since this was her first and perhaps only time producing the Oscars, she was determined to use them all. There were five film packages, an orchestral medley, a circus performance, long introductions . . . When the board of governors voted in January to give three honorary awards, she knew she should probably jettison something, but she couldn't bring herself to do it.

"All of her concepts were really quite good, and everything had a tremendous impact," said Horvitz. "But it's like going to a baseball game that goes into extra innings. After a while you're going, 'Somebody please break this up so I can go home.' "

According to several participants, Ziskin hadn't wanted to hire Horvitz; she'd heard about his temper and preferred somebody less volatile. But Horvitz had prominent supporters within the Academy and the production, who persuaded the first-time producer that she needed an experienced hand in the director's seat. She found out just how tricky the job was at a large production meeting, when Horvitz took his turn at the mike.

"We talked about the profiles, we talked about the floor, we talked about the aspect ratio," said Horvitz. "Then we talked about getting the big screen out, the stair unit, the new theater, this and that, item after item, department after department. And finally she turns to me and she goes, 'You are *really* underpaid.' She said, 'Directors don't do this in film.' And I said, 'Well, we do here.' "

Ziskin was one of the few who liked the way Peter Coyote had served as the voice of Oscar in 2000, so she took Lili Zanuck's idea one step further. She hired two actors, Glenn Close and Donald Sutherland, both of whom had thriving careers doing voiceovers.

Close arrived for a Thursday afternoon rehearsal wearing an open-necked white blouse under a black blazer, while Sutherland was clad in a dark suit and tie, with a heavy muffler wrapped around his neck. They sat at a black, deco-style table in the wings, stage right; behind them were a video monitor and three shelves that would bear Oscar statuettes.

At first, they ran through their copy simultaneously, testing different pronunciations. "Mar-eesa Tomei," said Sutherland. "Mar-issa Tomei."

Next to him, Close read the names of the stars she'd be identifying during the show's opening segment. "Dame Judi Dench, Dame Maggie Smith, Sir Ian McKellen, Sir Ben Kingsley." She went back over the lines. "Dame Judi Dench, Dame Maggie Smith, Dame Ian McKellen, Dame Ben Kingsley . . ."

For much of the rehearsal, the voices of Oscar kept things light and playful. Close joked with everyone around her, while Sutherland affected a grave, deadpan manner that didn't obscure a dry wit.

During a short break, he suddenly turned to Close. "Glenn, do you like sushi?" he asked, apropos of nothing in their conversation.

"Yes," she said, a little confused. "Is that what we're having for dinner?"

"No, I'm not having dinner tonight," he said. "I just wanted to let you know that the best sushi restaurant in town is on Sawtelle, between Olympic and Pico."

A minute later, stage manager John Best pointed to a hardcover book sitting in front of Sutherland. "Can I move that over here?" he said, pointing to a nearby shelf.

"No, you may not," said Sutherland solemnly. "I think I'll put it here in my pocket." He paused. "Do you want to see what it is?"

"Okay," said Best.

Sutherland held up the book: *Cod*, by Mark Kurlansky. "What do you think it's about?" Sutherland asked.

"Uh . . . fish?"

"Yes," said Sutherland. "It's about the fishing industry. The author has another book called *Salt*. You know, you can't understand salt until you understand the history of refrigeration."

About an hour into the rehearsal, Sutherland suddenly closed his script and got out of his chair. "Somebody is smoking," he said. "I can't stay here if people are smoking." He turned and headed for his dressing room downstairs.

The offending smoker, it turned out, was in a designated smoking area on the loading dock, a good 125 feet away from Sutherland. "I'm sorry he's smelling smoke, but that's the way it goes," snapped one stagehand as the doors to the loading dock were closed. "I can't load the goddamn set if I have to close the door."

Ziskin and Seligman came into the wings, and new edicts came down: don't smoke on the loading dock, and keep the doors closed as much as possible. With large pieces of the set coming in and out through those doors, this last order would clearly be problematic. Making matters worse, the smoking area attached to the green room was located just outside those doors.

"What can we do?" Ziskin asked Debbie Williams and Rita Cossette.

"We really can't do anything," said Williams, who knew full well that the smoking area was often the most crowded area backstage. "All the talent is going to be out there smoking."

"Well, let's keep this door closed for now, and we'll have to figure something out," said Ziskin. Then she spotted a crew member with a cigarette on the loading dock. "You can't smoke here," she yelled. "Please go as far away from the door as possible!"

EVERY OSCAR PRODUCER knew that one of the trickiest parts of the job was keeping the branches happy. The Academy was made up of fourteen different branches, and invariably most of them were unhappy about the fact that come Oscar time, their members weren't lavished with quite as much attention and love as were the members of the actors' branch.

Over the years, changes had been made to appease various branches. Nominated writers got their pictures on-screen during the show, then had their categories added to the list of those read at the nominations announcement. Bowing to a request from Oscar show producer Howard Koch, in 1997 Gil Cates added photos of the nominated producers to the package when best-picture nominees were read.

Bruce Davis always tried to look over Oscar scripts and identify potential trouble spots: a common one, he said, was when a star presenting the award for cinematography would applaud the nominees and their fellow directors of photography for putting actors in a flattering light. "They *hate* to have their art form reduced to making the star look good," he said. "That is one thing that just drives them up the wall, but the actors all think it's a great and original joke. Every time it happens, there's an uprising in the cinematography branch."

Through no fault of her own, Ziskin had stepped into a major brouhaha started the year before by Mike Myers's cavalier introduction of the acting categories. When Ziskin was hired, she received a letter from Don Rogers, one of the governors of the sound branch, reiterating the members' concern. "Don't worry," she told Rogers. "I'm going to do something great for you."

Originally, Ziskin's plan was to bring back Myers and have him tortured by foley artists, who create sound effects in a variety of unusual—and in this case, presumably punishing—ways. But she jettisoned that idea early on, and instead went looking for a screenwriter who could honor the category.

Ziskin had already farmed out much of the script to a group of noted screenwriters. She'd asked David Mamet to write about editing, Buck Henry to explain makeup, James Cameron to rhapsodize on visual effects, Joel and Ethan Coen to explicate art direction. She also asked William Goldman, an Oscar winner for *Butch Cassidy and the Sundance Kid* and *All the President's Men*, to write about sound, but he declined, saying he didn't know anything about it.

Vilanch suggested songwriters (and Academy governors) Alan and Marilyn Bergman. His logic was twofold: songwriters might know about sound, and the Bergmans' positions on the Academy board might make it harder for touchy soundmen to criticize them. The couple came up with a lengthy introduction that scanned like a song lyric—"Sound is the sensation that is due to stimulation / It's transmitted by vibration to the centers of the brain"—and included a long list of noises: "A smack, a whack, a quack / A creak, a squeak, a shriek / A punch, a crunch, a munch / a breeze, a wheeze, a sneeze . . ." In the right hands, it might work—but on paper, it also seemed light, frivolous, and maybe even silly. As soon as the script was distributed to show participants, Ziskin got a call from Frank Pierson, who didn't like the copy and had written an alternative introduction himself. Ziskin said she'd look at it, but she encouraged Pierson to keep an open mind.

Friday morning, Pierson arrived early to watch Halle Berry rehearse the sound awards. With the Academy president sitting in the third row and a rep from the sound branch lurking nearby, the Bergmans sat with Ziskin and Vilanch at the production table. Berry walked onstage wearing a black cap, a long-sleeved pink T-shirt, and beige pants with silk piping and a dangling drawstring. She delivered the intro with flair, turning the Bergmans' lines into a surprisingly charming ode to the art of sound. When she finished, Marilyn Bergman clapped heartily. Her husband looked over at Pierson, who smiled and gave a thumbs-up sign.

"She is darling," said Marilyn Bergman. "*Darling*."

For her part, Berry was relieved to have a task that took her mind off her best-actress nomination. "This is great for me," she said after going over the lines. "It gives me something to think about. I won't be so nervous about the award if I'm concentrating on this."

BACK IN THE FALL, Ziskin had spent weeks obsessively watching past Oscar shows, taking notes and looking for inspiration. She'd been most impressed by the shows that departed most drastically from the template, by Quincy Jones's Oscars in 1996 and the Zanucks' marathon four years later. Uncomfortable with dance numbers but determined to give her show a shot of adrenaline around the halfway mark, she was particularly fascinated by Jones's booking of the percussion troupe Stomp. That, she decided, was precisely what she needed: "some wham-bam entertainment in the middle, 'cause that's usually when the show sags."

Doug Stewart, who'd known Ziskin since their days at USC film school, suggested she look into the bizarre but frequently hilarious Blue Man Group. But at the top of Ziskin's wish list was Cirque du Soleil, the arty French-Canadian circus troupe. When they surprised her by agreeing to appear on the Oscars, Ziskin gave Stewart the task of finding a connection between the circus performers and the movies. He responded by putting together a split-screen video that put Cirque acts side-by-side with movie special effects they seemed to echo. Using Stewart's as the model, Cirque choreographer Debra Brown then prepared her own film to run on screens behind the performers.

On Friday night, the result was showcased for staffers and a handful of guests inside the Kodak. Wholly different from anything seen on the Oscars before, twenty-nine performers (recruited from five different Cirque shows around North America) ran through a four-minute act that incorporated acrobats, trapeze artists hanging high above the stage, and a few of the inexplicable but artsy touches for which the troupe was known, including a headless giant toting an umbrella.

As a woman onstage spun four hula hoops around her body, a screen at the rear of the stage showed a figure enclosed in rings of electricity in Fritz Lang's 1927 classic *Metropolis*. As a powerfully built performer twirled a flaming ball and chain around him in a large circle, the screen showed the ring of power from *The Lord of the Rings*, gleaming with fiery light. The film also showcased visual effects from movies like *The Wizard of Oz*, *E.T.*, *Star Wars*, and *Royal Wedding*, in which Fred Astaire appeared to dance on the walls and ceiling of a room.

Despite the stylish juxtapositions, though, the Cirque number was a virtuoso exhibition by a company whose work never really had anything to do with motion pictures. As the performers were warming up, a Cirque vice president, Roslyn Heward, approached Seligman. "We made a few cuts," she said, holding the script page that bore Maggie Smith and Ian McKellen's introduction. "I took out that part about how much we were influenced by the movies. Because we weren't."

The most dangerous part of the act was the ring of flames. For the first few run-throughs, the troupe did the number without fire. Then, while three fire marshals watched attentively, Cirque performer Mike Brown lit a heavy round torch that was attached to a long chain. Grabbing the end of the chain, he spun the flaming ball in circles around him, just a few inches off the ground. But when he finished, the stage continued to burn for several seconds before going out, leaving a scorched ring some twenty feet in diameter.

A crowd gathered and tallied up the damage: seventeen of the shiny blue tiles that covered the stage would have to be replaced. "Just a little pyro thing, man, nothing could possibly go wrong," said one technician with a rueful grin. "Isn't that what they said?"

"Well, we were going to repaint that floor anyway," said another, well aware that the burn went deeper than one level of paint.

Stage manager Garry Hood shook his head. "Well, we're not gonna do *that*," he said.

Seligman walked around the stage and surveyed the damage. He didn't say a word. When he returned to the production table, Horvitz's voice came over the P.A. system. "Michael Seligman, your insurance broker on line one," he said. "Michael Seligman, line one."

At the production table, Heward quickly conferred with Ziskin, Seligman, and Riva. "I've never seen that happen," she insisted.

"I don't want to lose the fire, but we can't have them burning our stage," said Ziskin. "What do we do about this?"

"In our other shows, there's a lot of other martial arts stuff with fire that doesn't touch the ground," Heward suggested. "I could bring in a different fire act."

Heward walked away, punching the buttons on her cell phone. A minute later, she returned. "Okay, we're calling the Mystère guy," she said, referring to a Cirque show in Las Vegas. "Mystère uses fire, but it doesn't have to touch the floor." She turned to Riva. "We talked to your pyro guy," she said, "and apparently you use something in your paint."

"Yeah," he snapped. "It's called lacquer."

When Heward left, Riva turned to Ziskin. "You know, we sent them a sample of this floor weeks ago," he said.

Over the next hour, the plan changed constantly. Ziskin considered dropping the fire segment from the performance, but that entailed cuts in the backing film and the music as well. The technical director and one of the performers from Mystère agreed to make the five-hour drive to Los Angeles first thing Saturday morning—but the clip from *The Lord of the Rings* was designed to go not with just any fire performance, but with a ring of fire. Seligman suggested laying a false floor over the real floor and letting that burn, but the stage crew doubted it could get a phony floor on and off in time, and Riva resisted the idea of putting something on top of his floor.

They continued rehearsing the performance without the fire, making additional changes and struggling to get everything finished by eleven o'clock. Aerialist Yuri Maiorov had to scale down a stunt that had him soaring in circles above the audience, but landing far too hard in the vicinity of Nicole Kidman's seat. Across the Kodak, another performer flung hula hoops into the audience, where Nathan Henderson, an acrobat with his hair teased into devil horns, was supposed to catch them. During one of the final rehearsals, the last of the hoops landed squarely on Julia Roberts's seat card. Afterward,

Henderson was defiant. "If Julia Roberts was sitting there," he insisted, "I *definitely* would have caught it."

As they struggled to get the twelve different acts in sync, Seligman came up to Heward. "We're gonna do this three or four more times," he said. "We're gonna go past eleven, so we can get it right." He paused, and grinned. "And you can write me a check."

At the production table, Ziskin put her head in her hands and sighed. "Whose idea was this?" she asked.

"Yours, thank you very much," said Riva.

As the chaotic rehearsal wound down, Ziskin left the Kodak and went to her room at the adjoining Renaissance Hotel. She called Alvin Sargent and bemoaned how she'd tried to cram more stuff—more junk, more crap— into the Oscar show than it could possibly accommodate. "I feel suicidal," she told him.

IT HAD BEEN A LONG WEEK for the stand-ins, too. The gig looked easy— read from the TelePrompTer, walk to the stage, pretend you've just won an Oscar, collect your twenty-three dollars an hour—but it was full of unexpected land mines. Even when they were sitting around waiting to see if they'd be needed, stand-ins needed to be alert: reading the newspaper while on the clock, for example, was definitely out. (At the American Music Awards or other shows produced by Dick Clark, so was chewing gum.)

Mock acceptance speeches, too, were trickier than they looked. There were unwritten rules about what should and shouldn't be done when a stand-in took the stage and received a dummy Oscar statue. Thanking the Academy, of course, was a must. But thanking other stand-ins was a definite mistake; people had been fired for that. A good speech was unobtrusive but not completely generic, with enough detail to suggest that the stand-in took this job seriously. Sometimes, if the mood was right in the theater and in the truck, jokes and a bit of frivolity were acceptable; other times the production staff might be getting tense, and it was best to get on and off without any silliness.

When movie stars were in the house, the job was even more delicate. Stand-ins were expected to treat the stars with respect, to give them space, but not to fawn. The important thing was to help the star do his or her job, without overstepping the bounds of the job. A star might ask a stand-in what was happening with a certain entrance or bit of staging; in those cases, it was always best to defer to the director or stage manager.

Boyce Miller was one of twenty-three stand-ins who had the day shift, and by Saturday afternoon he was exhausted. Miller had his SAG and AFTRA cards, did some acting, and also worked as a freelance writer; he'd been doing stand-in jobs for more than fifteen years. On Saturday, Miller was assigned to stand in for nominees. As a succession of stars arrived to rehearse their lines, he'd check his script for each item; if he had an assignment for whatever award the star was rehearsing, he'd move into the seat that would be occupied by one of the nominees. If his nominee won, he'd go onstage and make an acceptance speech; if not, he'd check his script to see whose seat he'd be occupying next.

Before Will Smith took the stage to practice presenting the award for cinematography, Miller checked his script. He was assigned to be Pietro Scalia, who'd been nominated for *Black Hawk Down*. Scalia was sitting in the sixth row of section C, way off to the side of the theater; if he won, he'd have the longest walk of any of the nominees. Miller settled into his seat and hoped he didn't win.

Smith walked onstage wearing a black T-shirt emblazoned with the Batman logo. He read his lines, watched snippets from the nominees' work play behind him, then opened the dummy envelope. "For this rehearsal only," he read, "the Oscar goes to Pietro Scalia for *Black Hawk Down*."

Miller stood up and walked toward the stage, trying to figure out what to say when he got there. He'd seen *Black Hawk Down*, which helped. When he got to the stage, Smith smiled, handed over the phony Oscar, offered insincere congratulations; like many stars, he was amused by how elaborate the whole ritual was. Just as Miller was about to start speaking, Smith interrupted.

"You ain't no Pietro Scalia," he said.

Miller turned to look at Smith, and the words just came out. "And you ain't no Ali," he said.

Smith burst out laughing, while Miller thought to himself, I am *so* fired. Quickly, the stand-in tried to repair the damage: "But you *could* be," he added. Smith, still laughing, drew his arm back as if to throw a punch. When Miller finished his acceptance speech and the two men walked off, Smith kept bumping into the stand-in, nudging him closer to the lip of the stage and the fifteen-foot drop into the orchestra pit.

"We came offstage and people were howling," said Miller. "And Debbie Williams, God bless her, said very loudly, 'Best line by a stand-in this year: Boyce Miller.' And I thought, Well, thank you, dear, but maybe you shouldn't have announced exactly who I was." When he showed up at the Kodak the next morning, Miller was still wondering if he'd be fired. Instead, Garry Hood handed him a videocassette of the previous day's rehearsal. "Here's your Oscar moment," Hood said. "Congratulations."

WHOOPI GOLDBERG hadn't been the first choice to host the Oscar show—except for the Quincy Jones year, she never was, a fact that didn't seem to bother her. And as the dress rehearsal began, Goldberg made the sort of showstopping entrance that the acrophobic Billy Crystal or the studiously tasteful Steve Martin would never have considered: clad in an outlandish collection of glitter and feathers, she descended, Moulin Rouge style, from a swing that hung from the rafters eight stories high. "She's fearless," laughed Vilanch. "She won't fly in a plane, but she'll hang on a trapeze."

"I'm the original sexy beast," Goldberg said as she took the stage. That line had been deemed a more seemly beginning than the runner-up, which was, "Welcome to the vagina monologues."

Ziskin watched the rehearsal from the production table in the middle of the house, drinking from a can of caffeine-free Diet Coke and making an occasional note on her laptop computer. At times the producer looked lively and energized; other times she appeared drawn and weary, her mouth pursed into a slight frown.

Early in the show, Goldberg introduced a stand-in for director Nora Ephron, who according to the show's lineups was going to introduce her own film paying tribute to New York City. By now, everyone on the crew knew that Ephron's name was a phony, put into the lineup simply to hide the identity of a top-secret guest. Somebody else—a bigger name closely associated with New York City, the reasoning went—would in fact be introduc-

ing Ephron's film. But few staffers had any idea who that might be. Speculation centered on politicians like Hillary Clinton and Rudy Giuliani. Word
spread that the guest would come in through the loading dock and spend the
show in Seligman's or Ziskin's office.

Ziskin and Herman knew the guest would be Woody Allen, who was
legendary for never showing up at the Oscars; Ziskin had been working to
get Allen since *Premiere* magazine's Women in Film luncheon the previous
October, when she'd pitched DreamWorks cochairman Jeffrey Katzenberg
on the idea and he'd promised to make it happen. But she'd shared that information with almost nobody except, reluctantly, ABC consultant John
Hamlin, who'd stormed into Ziskin's office in the middle of rehearsals
wielding a rundown and demanding to know why she was wasting so much
time on Ephron.

At the dress rehearsal, when Ephron's film finished, Ziskin and Herman
shared a smile. "I think that's my favorite thing on the show," said Herman.

Almost two hours into the rehearsal, Cirque du Soleil's performance ran
smoothly. Michael Riva had broken down and bought rolls of the material
that Cirque used for its performances, covering the center of the stage with
a round mat that could burn without damaging the tiles beneath it. Everything was synced to the film clips, and when the performance ended it drew
an immediate and enthusiastic standing ovation from the staff. Ziskin
jumped to her feet, thrust her right arm high in the air, and gave Seligman
a resounding high five. Then she slumped back into her seat, exhausted.

A few minutes later, Goldberg introduced a stand-in for Denzel Washington, one of the presenters of Sidney Poitier's honorary Oscar. When a
white stand-in walked onto the stage to read Washington's lines, she returned to the microphone. "Don't tell me we ran out of black people already!" she shouted. "Even here, when we ain't gettin' no goddamn Oscars,
we don't have enough black people!" Tired and more than a little punch-
drunk, the small audience went into hysterics.

Two and a half hours into the rehearsal, Goldberg walked through the
wings with a friend. "It's endless," she said. "There's another fucking
hour." Nearby, the show's "trophy boy," Silas Gaither, gave a neck massage
to Kimberly Painter. Gaither, the first male to serve in that capacity since

the Allan Carr show, had been a contestant on the popular CBS reality series *Survivor*. On that show, he seemed to be one of the more clueless contestants—but when he appeared on a special *Survivor*-themed week of the game show *Hollywood Squares*, panelist and head writer Vilanch had found him "adorable" and convinced Ziskin to hire him. "Maybe we'll get a few more fourteen-year-old girls to watch," said Vilanch.

For his part, Gaither was anxious to become something other than a Survivor who didn't survive. Among the crew he quickly became known for hitting on every woman backstage, and for the goofy grin that rarely left his face. He took the gig seriously, though: when a reporter asked to interview him, Gaither said he'd talk only if the story didn't mention *Survivor*. Deprived of the only reason people might want to read about the guy, the reporter declined.

While Gaither sat in the wings, Ziskin remained at the production table as the show ground on. Past the three-hour mark, at about 10:15, she turned to Riva. "At this time tomorrow night," she said, "we'll be drunk. *Soused*."

Rehearsal ended a few minutes after eleven, some three hours and fifty minutes after it started. After going over her notes with the staff, Ziskin finally walked back to her hotel. But when she got in bed, the producer couldn't sleep. Hour after hour, all night long, the Oscar show played in her head. Around 5 a.m., with dawn breaking over the mountains to the east of downtown Los Angeles, she finally slipped into about forty-five minutes of slumber. Then she got up, threw on blue jeans and a sleeveless T-shirt, and walked over to the Kodak Theatre to put on a show.

ZISKIN HAD only been back in the theater for a couple of hours when disaster struck once more. Early in the final rehearsal, a huge gust of wind suddenly rushed into the theater, sucking dust and debris into the Kodak and threatening to topple the large panels onstage. Near the back door to the loading dock, a heavy tool kit began sliding across the floor toward the stage. Glenn Close ducked her head and grimaced, while Donald Sutherland immediately grabbed a piece of cardboard and held it up in front of his face.

After a moment of sheer panic at the production table, Ziskin and Seligman looked up and saw that emergency panels had once again opened in the roof of the theater. The fans mounted up there were sucking air through the loading dock, into the theater, and then out the roof.

Immediately, Seligman ran backstage and confronted a building supervisor. "Do we know what happened, and how to prevent it tonight?" he asked.

"We have a technician in the elevator room working on it," she told him.

"So we don't know yet."

"No."

"Tell me when you find out."

Slowly, details emerged: smoke in one elevator shaft had triggered the automatic response. "Apparently," the building supervisor reported to Seligman, "there was a legitimate smoke reading in one shaft. So it's a real call, and we can't disconnect the system without disabling the elevators."

"Well, we need to figure this out," said Seligman. "Those are the elevators that lead to the winners' walk, and we need them."

He turned to Kirk Smith, an L.A.P.D. officer who was serving as the head of security at the Oscars. "If we can't get these elevators running again, we'll need to find a different way to get the winners to the hotel," he said. "That'll probably involve using the escalators in the mall, but we'll need more people from you to keep things clear out there."

"No, you won't," said Smith. "Once the show starts, we seal everything off in the mall. There won't be anybody else out there."

"Well, let's keep that as an option," said Seligman.

As building officials tried to figure out what triggered the alarm—speculation centering on the smoke machines at the rear of the stage, which ran continuously so that the lighting effects would look more dramatic—others studied just how much of the system could be shut down to prevent a mid-show recurrence. Within a few minutes, Smith's security team presented Seligman with four alternate routes for getting winners to the press rooms without using the elevators.

Ziskin, meanwhile, walked into the lower lobby of the Kodak, and noticed that the air appeared to be full of particles of some sort. "This is hellish," she said, heading for her office.

In the hallway, Danette Herman tried to find a silver lining. "Well," she offered, "thank God the sprinklers didn't go on."

As rehearsal started up again, two violinists from John Williams's orchestra were walking down a hallway beneath the stage. Suddenly they stopped and stared at a fifty-nine-year-old man with messy brown hair standing in the doorway of a dressing room. "Oh, my God," said one of the women. "It's—"

Before she could finish the sentence, the man looked over at her and grinned. "Yes!" he said brightly. "It's Paul McCartney!"

The ex-Beatle, who'd written the title song to the Cameron Crowe movie *Vanilla Sky*, was one of the performers in a medley of best-song nominees. Sting, Faith Hill, Enya, and Randy Newman (with John Goodman) were the others, but none of them had the star power of McCartney, who arrived at the Kodak midmorning and quickly got a tour of the premises from Debbie Williams.

Along the way, Williams told him that she'd seen the Beatles' final concert at Candlestick Park in 1965, when she was fourteen.

"Could you see me?" he asked.

"No, not really," she confessed.

"Could you hear me?"

"Not very well."

McCartney grinned. "It was a double," he confided.

"What do you mean?"

"It was a double," he repeated solemnly. "The crowds were so far away and the girls were all screaming so loud that it didn't matter if it was us or not. We used doubles sometimes, and nobody ever noticed. It wasn't me at Candlestick."

Williams stared at him incredulously. "The biggest moment of my life," she moaned, "and you're telling me it wasn't you?"

McCartney laughed. "Gotcha," he said. "Just joking. It was me."

On the side of the stage, McCartney waited for his turn to perform. "I'm not going to win," he told Williams. "It's taken me twenty-eight years to get back here"—his previous nomination having come for the title song to the James Bond movie *Live and Let Die* in 1974—"and it'll probably take me that long to get back again." He shrugged. "Randy Newman's going to win." Newman had sixteen nominations without a single win, making McCartney's prediction something of a long shot.

McCartney rehearsed "Vanilla Sky" a couple of times, drawing big cheers from the small audience. He grinned, threw his left fist in the air, and affected a surprisingly persuasive Elvis drawl as he spit out the first line of "Blue Suede Shoes": "Well, it's one for the money . . ."

The crowd went wild, but McCartney stopped and shook his head. Then the cheers continued, mixed with a few shouts of "Yes!" and "Do it!" McCartney grinned, leaned back toward the microphone, and continued. "Two for the show, three to get ready, now *go cat go!*"

AS SHOW TIME APPROACHED, the biggest worry had to do with the show's opening. Normally, footage shot on the red carpet was edited into an opening montage, but Ziskin was determined to show the stars—twenty-two of them, if possible—sitting in their seats inside the theater. That meant they all had to be seated before 5:30, something that almost never happened.

But concerns about the Hollywood traffic, along with incessant urging from Ziskin's office, had its effect. By 5:00, most of the stars had in fact arrived; by 5:15, all but one were inside the theater.

Staffers were not surprised to learn who the latecomer was. The day before, a few crew members had flipped a coin to see who'd be saddled with escorting the three most demanding stars: Barbra Streisand, Jennifer Lopez, and Kevin Spacey. But coming up fast on that list was Russell Crowe. The Australian actor was the only star who'd been downright unpleasant to Ziskin when she outlined the new regulations against smoking on the loading dock; in addition, he'd refused to record a voiceover the previous day, and had purposely mixed up the names of the best-actress nominees when he rehearsed.

Crowe finally arrived at the door of the Kodak just as Donald Sutherland announced, "Five minutes to show time." A stage manager and an ABC page met him at the door and offered to whisk Crowe and girlfriend Danielle Spencer to their seats. He refused. "I can find my own way, thank you very much," he said gruffly, and headed for the men's room.

"He is *such* an asshole," muttered one staffer under her breath.

From the stage, Ziskin saw that virtually all the stars had arrived—but most of them were standing in the aisles talking, not sitting in their seats. She walked down the stairs and began to make personal appeals. "Julia, I've got to start the show, could you please sit down?" she said to Julia Roberts, who was standing in the aisle chatting with Hugh Grant.

"Oh, yeah, okay," said Roberts. When Ziskin walked away, Roberts and Grant resumed their conversation.

Ziskin went up to Ron Howard. She nodded toward Russell Crowe, who was finally near his seat but not in it. "Please make your actor take his seat," she said to Howard.

Finally, Ziskin threw up her hands, went onstage, and took the microphone from Garry Hood. "I'm here as a stage manager, not as the producer," she told the audience. "*We need you all to please take your seats.*"

Outside, the preshow was ending. Ananda Lewis, who stood at the bottom of the stairs leading into the Kodak, threw it to Chris Connelly and Leeza Gibbons, who stood together at the top of the stairs. "We better get going!" shouted Connelly as the two hosts ran toward the doors of the Kodak.

In the wings of the stage, Bruce Vilanch talked to Tom Cruise, who had just come in through the loading dock. Goldberg walked by in a glittery, spangled outfit, plumes of feathers sticking out behind her. "*Moulin Rouge?*" asked Cruise with a grin.

"Yeah," said Vilanch. "Either that, or it's show time at the Apollo."

6:00 P.M., PACIFIC DAYLIGHT TIME: "*Tonight, the highest award in film-making will be awarded to one of these motion pictures.*"

As Sutherland and Close read their opening lines, Horvitz's cameras captured nominees, presenters, and notables, all of them safely in their seats. The camera trained on supporting-actor nominee Ethan Hawke also had a bird's-eye view into the voluminous cleavage sported by Hawke's wife, Uma Thurman. A chorus of whoops erupted in the wings. "Uma's frisky tonight!" shouted one writer.

After the opening, Tom Cruise delivered a speech written for him by

Cameron Crowe, and designed to answer the question of why the Oscars remained important in the aftermath of September 11. "What of a night like tonight?" intoned the bestubbled Cruise. "Should we celebrate the joy and magic that movies bring?" He paused dramatically. "Well, dare I say it: more than ever." The remarks quoted director Billy Wilder, who was watching the show from his home, and introduced a delightful film by documentarian Errol Morris (modeled on an earlier one by Chuck Workman), in which First Lady Laura Bush, rock stars Lou Reed and Iggy Pop, composer Philip Glass, writer Fran Lebowitz, and a host of lesser knowns rhapsodized about movies from *The Wizard of Oz* to *Godzilla vs. Mothra*, *The Bicycle Thief* to *Ernest Goes to Jail*. Backstage, Dency Nelson brought Benicio Del Toro into the wings to watch on a monitor. Del Toro moved as far to the side as he could, so as not to block anybody else's view.

Ten minutes into the show, Whoopi Goldberg descended on her swing, singing a rewritten version of "Diamonds Are a Girl's Best Friend" and shouting Nicole Kidman's signature line from *Moulin Rouge!*: "Come and get me, boys!" As Goldberg walked to the stage, Horvitz cut to a shot of an amused Russell Crowe—perhaps the first reaction shot of the actor laughing in the history of the Oscars. "So much mud has been thrown this year," said Goldberg when she got to the stage, "all the nominees look black." She scanned the front row. "Oh, look, the Smith family are seated together," she said. "Will, Jada, and Maggie Smith."

Del Toro presented the first award of the night, best supporting actress, to *A Beautiful Mind*'s Jennifer Connelly. "This is Jennifer Connelly's first Academy Award nomination," Glenn Close read as Connelly walked to the stage. "She made her screen debut at the age of eleven in Sergio Leone's *Once Upon a Time in America*." Factoids about the other four nominees occupied the same page in her script, but they went unread.

During the first commercial break, Owen Wilson entered the green room, followed a minute later by Jodie Foster. Ryan O'Neal and Ali MacGraw entered the building via the loading dock.

Early in the next act, husband and wife Reese Witherspoon and Ryan Phillippe read the nominees for best makeup. "Can I open it?" Witherspoon asked when Phillippe held up the envelope.

"Go ahead," he said. "You make more money than I do." The line wasn't on the TelePrompTer, but Witherspoon and Phillippe had tried it out earlier during an interview on the red carpet.

Backstage, Will Smith posed for a photo with a security guard. Then he spotted the Academy president outside the green room. "Frank Pierson!" he yelled to the staffers standing around. "Everybody get to work!"

Smith approached a talent coordinator. "I need, like, an inside connection that can get me some *stuff*," he said conspiratorially.

"There's food in the green room, Will," said Debbie Williams, who brought him a martini glass filled with strawberries and cream. Smith beamed, but asked for a couple more glasses. "We'll eat 'em real fast in the commercial, and then hand 'em off," he promised. Finally, he went into the green room himself, where he filled two more glasses with strawberries and loaded a small plate with sushi.

Shortly after 6 p.m., the door to Ziskin's office opened. *"Woody's here!"* whispered a friend to Julia Roberts outside the green room.

Staffers stared, incredulous, as Allen made his way down the hallway and into the wings of the stage. "That is *much* cooler than any of the people we were guessing," said one.

The atmosphere changed as another special guest made her entrance. Barbra Streisand came in from the loading dock, walking through the backstage area accompanied by James Brolin and a phalanx of staffers and security guards. Streisand looked to be wearing no makeup; she walked fast, pulling a red coat up tight around her neck and barely glancing at staffers and bystanders. When a page showed her the location of the green room, Streisand didn't even look up; instead, she ducked into a waiting elevator and went to her dressing room beneath the stage.

"Ladies and gentlemen," said Goldberg as Streisand was on her way downstairs, "it is my pleasure and my honor to introduce Mr. Woody Allen."

Allen took the stage to a standing ovation. "Thank you very much," he said. "That makes up for the strip search." Watching on a monitor in the truck, Ziskin had no idea what he was going to say; all she knew was what Allen had told DreamWorks marketing chief Terry Press—that when he practiced his speech in the shower, it lasted two minutes. Onstage, stretched by two standing ovations and frequent gales of laughter, the delightful monologue took four.

When Allen left the stage, Ziskin bolted from the truck and caught up with him in the hall. "Thank you!" she said.

Danette Herman ran to Ziskin, and the two women exchanged an enthusiastic high five. "I was crying," said Herman.

Ziskin turned to head back to the trailer and stepped squarely on the dress of Catherine Martin, who was holding the Oscar she'd just won for costume design for *Moulin Rouge!* Ziskin apologized, straightened Martin's dress, and went back outside.

Backstage about an hour into the show, Susan Futterman left the control truck and ran into Vilanch. "I was just on a nipple check," she said. The nipples in question, it turned out, belonged to Cameron Diaz. "She's wearing a beautiful dress," said Futterman, "but under the lights . . ." With her fingers, she outlined a pair of areolas.

In the trailer, Futterman had suggested to Ziskin and Horvitz that they show Diaz from the shoulders up. Horvitz complied most of the time, though he did occasionally cut to a shot that was framed in such a way that the offending nipples were visible—barely, and only if you looked very closely.

While Horvitz dealt with Diaz's nipples, Julia Roberts wandered around the loading dock in search of the smoking section, which was largely obscured by plants and equipment cases. (Prohibited during rehearsal, smoking had been restored to a small area of the dock.) As Roberts gave up and turned to go back inside the Kodak, Kate Winslet spotted her and yelled, "Julia!"

"Darling!" shouted Roberts, running to Winslet for a long, lingering embrace. Then she lit up a cigarette. Jennifer Lopez and Harvey Weinstein also puffed away. The large doors from the loading dock to the stage remained closed, shielding Donald Sutherland from the smoke. A minute later, Woody Allen and his wife, Soon-Yi Previn, left the theater via the loading dock, unnoticed by any of the smokers.

A few minutes before seven, Catherine Martin won her second Oscar of the night, for the art direction of *Moulin Rouge!* During the next commercial, director Baz Luhrmann accepted congratulations on Martin's two wins as he stood in an aisle. "Can you believe it?" he said. "It's all downhill from here."

When the show returned from the commercial, twelve empty seats were noticeable in the first three rows. In the truck, Ziskin, who had considered doing away with the seat-fillers but in the end had chosen to simply cut their numbers, realized how bad the vacancies looked. She also knew that Cirque du Soleil was due up shortly, and she wanted lots of famous people applauding. Ziskin went into the wings and corralled Herman. "I want them back in their seats," she said. "Get Julia back to her seat!"

In the next act, Cirque du Soleil performed and won a rousing standing ovation—including cheers from Roberts, who had been coaxed back into the auditorium. When the performance ended, whoops and hollers resounded through the backstage area. A stagehand sighed. "Fuck, it's over," he said. "Time for a deep breath and a big cocktail."

During the ensuing break, the large doors that led from the stage to the loading dock were opened wide in order for Cirque du Soleil's props to be moved out and the four bandstands rolled in. Almost miraculously, the smoking section outside the green room was deserted.

After presenting the Oscar for best score to Howard Shore for *The Lord of the Rings*, Sandra Bullock and Hugh Grant left the stage. Costars in *Two Weeks Notice* and a rumored real-life couple, the pair stopped in the hallway outside the green room.

"How much time is left in the show?" Grant asked.

"An hour," guessed an aide.

A stagehand looked at a show rundown. "An hour and a half," she said, generously.

Grant grimaced. "An hour and a half?" He turned to Bullock. "What do you want to do now?" he asked. "We can sit, or we can go to the bar."

"I don't know," said Bullock. "Do you want to sit in the audience? We can't sit down until the next break. Do you want to go to the bar?"

Grant shrugged. "We can go to the bar, or we can go to the green room . . ."

They stood in the hallway dithering for a few more minutes. "I don't care what we do," Bullock finally said with a faintly exasperated sigh. "I just want you to make a *decision*." He did, and they headed for the bar.

As the two-and-a-half-hour mark approached, Sidney Poitier received standing ovations both before and after his eloquent five-minute speech. He left the stage to a round of applause from stagehands and bystanders, and was about to leave the wings when Nelson ran up. "Sidney!" he yelled. "Sidney, wait for a minute! Whoopi wants to see you, Whoopi's running this way." Poitier turned around and waited for the show's host, who ran up to offer her congratulations.

Outside the green room, Paul McCartney talked to Carrie Fisher, a member of the writing team Vilanch had assembled. Kevin Spacey stood near them, staring at McCartney and looking for all the world like an enraptured fan.

A few minutes later, after the medley of song nominees, Sting and Randy Newman were led away from the monitor where they'd been watching the other performers and positioned closer to the stage. On the other side of the stage, McCartney and Enya took a similar position. The move was designed to more quickly catch the winner's reaction. In a huge upset, Newman won. "I told you so," said McCartney to Williams.

Newman walked onstage to a healthy round of applause. "Randy Newman has sixteen Academy Award nominations," read Close, "and now the Oscar." Throughout the hall, people who'd been sitting and applauding got to their feet.

Newman looked out into the audience, stunned. "I don't want your pity," he said, before thanking the music branch "for giving me so many chances to be humiliated over the years." When the TelePrompTer began flashing numbers, indicating the time left before his forty-five seconds were up, Newman stared into the orchestra pit, which was filled with musicians he'd hired to play on his film scores over the years. "Are you really gonna play in four seconds?" he asked. "Don't play." They didn't.

During the next commercial break, Gwyneth Paltrow came into the wings to present the screenwriting awards with Ethan Hawke. Before going on, she took out her chewing gum and put it into a ball of tissue. Nelson took the tissue from her and threw it in a nearby trash can. Paltrow's top was more transparent than Cameron Diaz's had been, and Futterman had ordered Horvitz to frame her tightly—but since she was copresenting with Hawke, the director needed a wider shot to show both stars. As Paltrow and

Hawke presented the adapted-screenplay award to Akiva Goldsman for *A Beautiful Mind*, Robert Redford paced outside the green room. He walked slowly back and forth, hands in his pockets, opening and closing his mouth and rolling his tongue around, clearing his throat and stretching his mouth for his upcoming speech.

When Redford walked onstage to accept his honorary Oscar, a page approached Debbie Williams in the wings. Visibly shaking, the page told Williams that Will Smith's daughter had just been taken to the hospital with an ear infection and Smith and his wife had left the theater to be with her. Smith did, however, leave a cell phone number so that he could be called if he won.

The show reached the three-and-a-half-hour mark with the four major awards still to come. Waiting in the wings to present the first of them, best actress, Russell Crowe turned to Garry Hood. "I want to thank you for being so good to work with," said Crowe, who then praised the Kodak. "This is the best place I've ever been for actually watching a show." Crowe proceeded to mispronounce Sissy Spacek's name as he read the nominees.

Halle Berry won for *Monster's Ball*, marking the first best-actress win for an African American. The stunned winner delivered an impassioned four-minute speech that began, "This moment is so much bigger than me." Choking back sobs, she continued: "This moment is for Dorothy Dandridge, Lena Horne, Diahann Carroll. It's for the women that stand beside me: Jada Pinkett, Angela Bassett, Viveca Fox. And it's for every nameless, faceless woman of color that now has a chance, because this door tonight has been opened." Three minutes later, the tearful Berry got around to thanking her agent and lawyer.

Inside Whoopi Goldberg's waiting room in the wings, Vilanch and the other writers quickly came up with a variety of punch lines. Just as quickly, they decided that the moment was too big to joke about. The next time she took the stage, Goldberg simply said, "First of all, I would like to congratulate Miss Halle Berry."

Backstage, a shell-shocked Berry was still making her way behind the stage, where a small walkway led to the path to the press rooms. As she headed down that hallway, her mother and husband were hustled through the wings to catch up with her. They did so on the far side of the stage, where the best-actress winner and her family shared some long, tearful embraces.

While Berry was navigating the passageway known as "winners' walk," Julia Roberts presented the best-actor award to Denzel Washington, completing a historic and unprecedented sweep of the top acting categories by African Americans. In his speech, Washington bowed to one of the night's honorary recipients, Poitier. "I'm proud to follow in your footsteps, Sidney," he declared.

In the wings, Mel Gibson and then Tom Hanks came up to Washington to offer congratulations. An ecstatic Roberts hung on to Washington the whole time. Gibson, about to present the award for best director, approached Rita Cossette. "Is my collar flipping up?" he said. She assured him it wasn't.

Four hours and seven minutes into the show—in other words, the point when the credits were rolling during what had previously been the longest Oscar show ever—Gibson presented the directing Oscar to Ron Howard for *A Beautiful Mind*. Howard came offstage with his Oscar, but he was held in the wings close to the stage, because he'd need to go back out if his movie also won for best picture. It did, and Howard returned to the stage to accept the final Oscar of the night from Tom Hanks.

As the credits began to roll, Hanks put his arm around Howard in the wings. "You got *two!*" said Hanks, who won his two Oscars in different years. "I had to split 'em up, but you got two."

A huge crowd gathered around Howard and his producer, Brian Grazer. Hanks laughed again. "Now I'll need a string of new anecdotes about the two of you," said Hanks, who had been directed by Howard in *Splash* and *Apollo 13*. "I'll have to do more interviews about you now." Photographers gathered to snap the winners, and Hanks looked at them and quoted the title of the low-budget 1976 movie Howard had acted in for producer Roger Corman, who in return gave him a chance to direct his first film. "Ron Howard says, 'Eat My Dust!'"

Four hours and twenty minutes after the show began, Donald Sutherland read the voting rules to cap off the longest Oscar telecast ever. Glenn Close came out from behind the announcers' table and hugged Mel Gibson. Ziskin ran into the wings and kissed Howard and Grazer, then hugged

Sutherland and Close. Hanks's wife, Rita Wilson, hugged Howard. The *Beautiful Mind* winners lingered on the stage, mingling with the staff and crew. The stage crew pulled Nicole Kidman out of the audience and posed for photos with her. Michael Riva's cell phone rang. "Wasn't it wonderful?" he said.

"I DID ABOUT 75 PERCENT of what I wanted to do, and I never get that percentage on anything I do," said Ziskin a few days after the show. "I did what I wanted, it was a historic night, and I was lucky to have that happen on my watch."

The show received mostly positive reviews, as did the Kodak Theatre. The ratings, though, were another matter: continuing the downward trend, the number of viewers was the lowest in five years. The average rating, dragged down by the loss of viewers in the show's final hour, was the lowest ever.

In Laura Ziskin's office on the Sony lot, it was easy to ignore that bad news amid the congratulatory messages that poured in. Harvey Weinstein, for instance, sent over a bottle of Cristal champagne along with a note. "Dear Laura," it read, "You can print this: 'This was the best Oscar show in ten years.' You did a brilliant job." Other letters came in from Marilyn and Alan Bergman, Jenna Elfman, Hugh Jackman, and many others.

In a way, Ziskin's favorite was the one she received from Sidney Lumet, the veteran director whose films included *Dog Day Afternoon*, *Network*, and *The Verdict*. "We don't know each other," Lumet wrote, "but I must tell you it was the best Oscar show ever. It was moving, funny, dramatic—all good words. I'm sure they'll give you a hard time about the length. Don't even think twice about it. That's what the evening was for. All those people bubbling over to a point where they were uncontrollable. It was terrific."

Three days after watching a show that had begun with a speech that quoted him, Billy Wilder died.

In the aftermath of the show, the Academy's review committee was left facing one inescapable fact: the broadcast had gotten to be too long. With the three longest shows in history all occurring in the last four years (the exception being Cates's relatively breezy three-and-a-half-hour show in 2001), the committee and the board of governors grappled with ideas for making things shorter.

The In Memoriam segment, always a bone of contention, was considered a candidate for elimination, though this was not simply because of the length of the show. The segment had caused an uproar by omitting actress Dorothy McGuire, whose near-fifty-year career had included an Oscar nomination for 1947's best-picture winner, *Gentleman's Agreement*. Some insiders insisted that the Academy, Ziskin, and segment directors Gary Ross and Michael Johnson simply forgot about McGuire, though the official explanation was that she was duly considered.

"There was this wave of criticism," said Bruce Davis. "And it wasn't just family, it was fans and a lot of other people. There were a couple of people in the segment who had much less extensive careers, and the board just thought, this seems to be hurting as many feelings as it's making people happy. Why are we doing this? So they decided to drop it."

That decision later changed—in part, said Davis, because the following year would provide the opportunity to salute such notables as Wilder, Milton Berle, Lew Wasserman, Rod Steiger, Richard Harris, and James Coburn.

At its monthly meeting in July, the board of governors tightened up the rules for giving honorary awards. In the futurehe, the first awards—be it a Thalberg, a Hersholt, or an honorary Oscar statuette—would require a two-thirds vote of the governors; the second would require a three-fourths majority. After two consecutive years in which three honorary awards were bestowed, a new rule stipulated that no more than two would ever be allowed in a single year.

In addition, new guidelines were formulated to tighten the Academy's financial oversight of the Oscar show. "Because Gil had been doing the show so consistently, it had not been necessary to really look at the process," said Frank Pierson. "Everything was done by estimate and guesstimate, and there was no procedure so that you knew when you were beginning to go over and you could cut back. That was okay because we were in good hands when Gil was the one who was estimating and improvising. But Laura went spectacularly over budget and overtime because she and I were both doing it for the first time." Cates helped formulate the new procedures, which included an auditor to constantly track the production; the Academy president also took over some responsibility for eliminating elements when a show was running overtime, so that the show's producer wouldn't have to spend valuable time explaining to a star why he'd been cut from the show.

Still, Pierson avidly defended Ziskin's show. "She bit off an awful lot, but I personally loved the show," he said. "The only thing I think was a mistake was the Cirque du Soleil sequence. It was beautiful, it was wonderful in the theater, but it meant nothing on the tube. And it was lengthy, and very, very expensive."

Ziskin's Oscar show received seven Emmy nominations. It won in one category, choreography. The award went to Debra Brown, who designed the Cirque du Soleil number.

10

War Games

The 75th Academy Awards

GIL CATES liked to say that the Academy Awards always reflected the year in which they took place. As the seventy-fifth Oscar show approached in early 2003, that was not necessarily a good thing.

For months, the administration of George W. Bush had been talking about removing Iraqi dictator Saddam Hussein from power. The president spoke of ties between Hussein and the Al Qaeda terrorist organization, responsible for the September 11 attacks on America, of the dictator's record of brutality and violence within his own country, of the likelihood that he had or was preparing weapons of mass destruction. By January, military action against Iraq seemed likely, perhaps inevitable.

If not for the threat of war, Cates would have been focusing on celebrating Oscar's seventy-fifth anniversary, while at the same time keeping the show to a reasonable length. The past four years had seen three Oscar shows of record-breaking length; ratings had continued to decline, and the Academy knew it needed to hand out the final awards before TV sets up and down the East Coast were switched off. Given that priority, the obvious choice as producer was Cates, who'd brought in the 2001 show at an elegant three hours and twenty-five minutes, and who didn't feel the need to stick every one of his ideas into the show. After all, he'd already done it ten times and figured to do a few more before he was through.

Still, Pierson felt the need to put a little extra pressure on his producer. Before the nominations were announced on February 11, the Academy president went to Cates and said he'd like to publicly promise that the best-picture winner would be revealed before midnight, East Coast time.

Cates considered the request. He knew Pierson's scenario had happened only once in the past twenty-five years, and that the final winner wasn't usually revealed until after 12:30 a.m. He knew that an Oscar show stripped of everything—no film packages, no dance numbers, nothing but two dozen awards, five songs, and half an hour of commercials—would still take three hours. He thought about it all, and he agreed. Make your promise, he told Pierson, and I'll give you a three-and-a-half-hour Oscar show.

Just past 5:30 a.m., Pierson and Marisa Tomei read the names of the year's nominees. "And for those of you on the East Coast," concluded Pierson, "here's a presidential promise: you'll know the best-picture winner before the clock strikes twelve."

At the back of the hall, executive consultant Robert Z. Shapiro shrugged off the pressure. "Actually," he pointed out, "all we have to do is give out best picture first."

IF YOU JUST WENT by the numbers, the year's nominations were a triumph for director Rob Marshall's musical *Chicago*, which led all films with thirteen nominations. Also for Martin Scorsese's *Gangs of New York*, which had ten, for British director Stephen Daldry's adaptation of the Michael Cunningham novel *The Hours*, with nine, and for fugitive director Roman Polanski, whose Holocaust-themed drama *The Pianist* won seven nominations, including nods for best director, actor, and screenplay.

Inside the film industry, though, the nominations were not simply seen as a victory for *Chicago* or *Gangs of New York* or *The Pianist*, but as a triumph for Harvey Weinstein.

It had been a rough few months for the bellicose and controversial Miramax chief, the subject of a scathing profile in *The New Yorker* the previous December. The piece went into great detail about the bullying manner Weinstein was known to employ, delighting Harvey-bashers and infuriating his supporters. The nominations, though, played as vindication: the Miramax releases *Chicago*, *Gangs of New York*, and *Frida* accounted for twenty-nine nominations, plus one for *The Quiet American* and another for the Chinese film *Hero*. (Miramax also held some foreign rights to *The Hours*, while Harvey and Bob Weinstein received executive producer credit on another multiple nominee, *The Lord of the Rings: The Two Towers*, though their credit was simply a condition of the deal made when Miramax sold the property to New Line.) Miramax's total far outstripped the combined nominations for Warner Bros., Universal, Disney, 20th Century-Fox, and Sony.

Of the Miramax films, *Chicago* seemed the best bet for a serious Oscar haul. Weinstein, though, made no secret that he was playing favorites in one of the categories. Martin Scorsese, the director of *Gangs of New York*, had never won an Oscar despite having one of the most distinguished careers of the past three decades. Twice, he had lost in the best-director and best-picture competitions to films that, in retrospect, seemed markedly inferior to his: the first time in 1980 when his brutal masterpiece *Raging Bull* lost to actor Robert Redford's directorial debut, *Ordinary People*, then again ten years later when his *GoodFellas* was beaten by the first directing job of another actor, this time Kevin Costner with *Dances with Wolves*.

Weinstein wanted badly to be the man who finally brought home an Oscar for Scorsese—and he didn't care who knew it, even if that meant alienating *Chicago* director Rob Marshall. If *Gangs of New York* was far from Scorsese's best work, that was okay: Miramax would subtly play up the idea of a directing Oscar as a de facto lifetime achievement award for Scorsese by suggesting, vociferously if a bit foolishly, that *Gangs* was in some way a summation of the director's craft and style.

Another best-director nominee, Roman Polanski, was not available for campaigning. The director had fled the United States in 1978 after pleading guilty to the statutory rape of a thirteen-year-old girl, and couldn't enter the country without exposing himself to possible arrest. Actor Adrien Brody, the largely unknown star of the film, handled many of the promotional chores in Polanski's stead. But the focus kept slipping back to the director's legal troubles: the girl with whom he'd had consensual sex emerged to say that Polanski should be judged solely on his work, and then a transcript from his court case showed up on the Web site thesmokinggun.com. Suspicions grew that a rival studio had actually put the girl up to it—not to support Polanski, but to remind voters of his crime. Focus Features, the small company that had distributed *The Pianist*, kept up a low-key campaign and hoped that Miramax's relentless politicking on behalf of *Chicago* and *Gangs* would prove to be off-putting to Academy members.

ON MARCH 6, President Bush gave a press conference in which he pushed for a United Nations vote authorizing the use of force to remove Saddam Hussein from power. "Iraq is a country that has got terrorist ties," he said. "It's a country with wealth, it's a country that trains terrorists, a country that could arm terrorists. And our fellow Americans must understand, in this new war against terror, that we not only must chase down Al Qaeda terrorists, we must deal with weapons of mass destruction."

The same day, about a hundred crew members gathered in the lower lobby of the Kodak Theatre for a production meeting. At the meeting, Cates spent some time discussing the most problematic and surprising of the best-song nominees. The troubled but charismatic young rapper Eminem had been nominated for the song "Lose Yourself" from *8 Mile*, a film from director Curtis Hanson in which Eminem played a character loosely based on himself. The song was a hit, an assured, tough-minded statement of purpose, and more central to its movie than any of the other nominees—but it was also a rap song, the first the Academy had ever nominated. And for every person who saw Eminem as a conflicted but brilliant young writer and performer, others simply viewed him as a sullen, foul-mouthed thug.

When he'd performed "Lose Yourself" on the Grammys a month earlier, Eminem had refused to clean up the song's language; ABC had simply bleeped out the two *motherfuckers* and three *shits*. To do that on the Oscars meant going to a delay, something the producers had been fighting for years. But handing the song to a different, more compliant performer ran the risk of offending the nominee and making the Academy look stodgy.

"We don't know if Eminem will do it," said Cates at the production meeting. "But we're auditioning in the back of the room if any of you have a feeling for it."

At the end of his talk, Cates made one final point. "The question has been asked about security, and what happens if we go to war," he said. "The thing is, we're going to do the show on the twenty-third. If a war happens, it'll probably be a week before or a week after. We have several contingency plans in place, so I think we'll be okay."

Then the Oscars' security chief, Kirk Smith, had some final advice. "Security will be tighter than ever this year," he said. "We ask that you tell your folks, please empty out your trunks before you come to the theater. We will be searching cars, and we don't want to have to go through your vacation stuff every time you drive into the building."

For its part, the Academy's board of governors decided not to renew the $1 million catastrophe insurance policy it'd bought the previous year. "If we decide to postpone because of the war, our contract with ABC says we'll still get paid," said Bruce Davis. "And if there's some terrible terrorist thing that happens in the auditorium, a million dollars' worth of insurance isn't going to cover your losses anyway." Some board members made it clear that they thought the decision was foolhardy.

LOUIS J. HORVITZ couldn't help but get a special kick out of auditioning trophy ladies. Years earlier, when he was working for Dick Clark's company, the director had met his wife, a statuesque blonde named Steffanee Leaming, at one such audition.

"I went to Dick Clark's, I was a little late, I'd been playing tennis, I walk in and there's a whole room of models," he remembered. "Some new faces, some who'd auditioned before. I looked across the room and I saw Steffanee, and she looked at me and my heart started palpitating and I thought, Oh, God, no, I don't want to be in love." When he told producer Al Schwartz that he wanted Leaming in addition to the two women who'd already been hired, Schwartz knew something was up. "He said, 'Do you want her for the show, or do you want to date her?' And I said, 'I'll marry her if I can.'"

A month shy of Horvitz and Leaming's seventh wedding anniversary, another lobby full of beautiful women waited for him and Cates. The two men sat in Cates's small corner office on the twelfth floor of a building on the eastern edge of Century City. The producer sat in a black plastic chair behind a modest natural wood desk, while Horvitz took a spot on the small couch. The board laying out the Oscar show dominated one wall, but a white shade had been pulled down to cover the privileged information.

When each prospective trophy lady entered his office, Cates greeted her, glanced at her eight-by-ten glossies, made small talk, and got through the interview quickly. He'd ask if she'd done a show like the Oscars before; most had. He'd inquire where she was from, drawing answers as diverse as Michigan, Connecticut, Mexico, and Austria. He'd ask if an audience of a billion people intimidated her, and she'd assure him that it didn't. He'd wonder about her career goals, and she'd tell him she wanted to act.

"Well," he'd say after less than ten minutes, "you're a beautiful woman, you're great, nice to meet you, and I don't have anything else."

Horvitz occasionally took the interviews a step further. "Do you feel comfortable onstage?" he asked a tall brunette from New England wearing a low-cut, long black dress.

"Oh, yes," she said. "I've done theater."

"Could you stand up and do your runway walk for us?" he said.

She walked across the small office, through the door into an adjoining conference room, then back.

"Okay, good," said Horvitz. "You'd get onstage and stand there . . ."

She stood there, smiling.

". . . and if people give a speech you listen to them, and if they're funny, laugh . . ."

She giggled, just a little.

". . . and then escort them off."

She walked toward the office door.

"Well, listen, you're a terrific, wonderful woman," said Cates. "And we'll get back to you when we decide."

The next model, a blonde named Joanna Krupa, got an even more comprehensive audition. Horvitz asked his assistant, Deborah Read, to bring in a candy dish with the standing figure of a cat on it. Then he had Krupa take the dish as if it were an Oscar, do her walk, hand the dish to Read, and stand by smiling while Read made a mock acceptance speech.

When she left, Cates sighed. "You don't even recognize it when it's happening," he said, shaking his head. "But it's terrible to realize you've gotten older and turned into a dirty old man."

ROBERT Z. SHAPIRO walked into Cates's office. In his hand, he held a piece of paper.

"Gil," he said, "look at this."

"What is it?" said Cates, taking the paper.

"The show's running time."

Cates looked at the page and frowned. The listed time was three hours, fifty-five minutes, and forty seconds.

"Who came up with this?" he said.

"The script department."

Cates turned away and walked to his desk. "Jesus fucking Christ," he muttered under his breath.

AT THE NOMINEES' LUNCHEON on March 10, Cates made his usual welcoming speech, showed his usual film of good and bad acceptance speeches, and delivered his usual spiel about keeping the speeches under forty-five seconds. To Adrien Brody, Chris Cooper, John C. Reilly, Salma Hayek, Diane Lane, Queen Latifah, and others, this was something new; to Nicolas Cage and Julianne Moore, it was old hat.

Then the producer veered into uncharted territory. "To make sure that the show doesn't run long, we have two new rules this year," he said. "If you pull out a list, you're done. The orchestra is going to play you off. Even if you don't have a list, if you start naming names, you can thank five people. When you mention the sixth, you're done. The music is coming in."

Nominees looked at each other nervously, silently counting up the people they knew they'd *have* to thank. "These are harsh measures, but necessary," Cates insisted. "We'll have Bill Conti, our music director—or stickman, as Julia Roberts so eloquently called him—play you off."

In the pressroom outside the main ballroom, reporters asked the nominees if they thought the Oscars would be appropriate if a war was taking place. "It would seem obscene if we were seen bouncing up the red carpet grinning when people are dying," said Daniel Day-Lewis. "It's going to be very difficult to find a way to do this."

THE SAME DAY as the nominees' luncheon, a full-page ad ran in the Hollywood trade papers. The ad reprinted an article that had run a few days earlier in the *Los Angeles Times*, as well as other local papers. The piece bore the byline of Robert Wise, the eighty-eight-year-old director of *The Sound of Music* and *West Side Story*, and a past president of the Academy. Wise lavished praise on Martin Scorsese and *Gangs of New York*, calling it "a summation of his entire body of work." Miramax headlined the ad "Two-time Academy Award–winner Robert Wise declares Scorsese deserves the Oscar for 'Gangs of New York.' "

Miramax competitors and some neutral observers cried foul, particularly with regard to Wise's suggestion that Scorsese deserved the Oscar because *Gangs* summed up his entire career. In an ideal world, of course, a director's body of work was not supposed to enter into a voter's judgment of a specific film; more grievously to the Academy, Wise's article violated an unspoken Academy rule that members were not to publicly reveal their votes to anyone.

In its defense, Miramax said that it was simply answering an opinion piece that had run in *Daily Variety* the previous month. In that article, Oscar-winning screenwriter William Goldman bluntly stated that Scorsese did not deserve to win the best-director Oscar. "*Gangs of New York* is a mess," he declared. While eviscerating Scorsese's epic, Goldman also detoured to point out that he would never forgive Miramax "for hyping the Oscar to Roberto Benigni, the scummiest award in the Academy's history."

When the firestorm hit, Wise admitted that he'd signed the ad at the urging of Miramax, but denied having written it. (Privately, a source close to the director said that Wise didn't really like *Gangs* very much, but was a fan and friend of Scorsese.) Wise credited the piece to Mike Thomas, who had done some ghostwriting for Wise in the past, and who'd also worked as Cates's publicist on the Oscar show two years earlier. Thomas denied having anything to do with the ad. On Friday the fourteenth, Murray Weissman, a publicist hired by Miramax to work on the studio's Oscar campaign (and a member of the executive committee of the Academy's public relations branch), admitted having written the article. Some Academy members, furious at the underhanded way Miramax had used Wise, asked for their ballots to be returned so they could change their votes. PricewaterhouseCoopers refused. According to people close to *Chicago* director Rob Marshall, the ads sent Marshall over the edge as well; he angrily confronted Weinstein about playing favorites so blatantly.

The Academy was furious at Miramax, but it didn't feel that it could punish the studio by taking away any of its tickets. The problem, said Bruce Davis, was that the previous year the Academy had taken no action when 20th Century-Fox took out an ad in which Robert Wise voiced his support of *Moulin Rouge!* (another movie, said a source close to Wise, with which the director was not particularly enamored). If Miramax was punished for doing the same thing Fox had done the year before, Weinstein could have made a strong case that he was being unjustly persecuted.

"We didn't do anything last year, and we should have," conceded Davis. "You have to hand it to Harvey. He knows every angle, and he knows *exactly* how much he can get away with."

ON THURSDAY, March 13, Chuck Warn and Toni Thompson looked at a calendar that covered the wall of a room in ABC's Burbank headquarters. Warn, the press rep for Cates, pointed to Friday the fourteenth. "Bush is scheduled to speak here," he said. "Then we'll know more about what's going on in the war. The beginning of next week I'll go back to Larry King and see if he wants to devote a show to something lighter."

Thompson, a publicist for the Academy, pointed to the following week, the seven days leading up to the show on March 23. "We have to feed the monster every day," she said. "We already have two things for Friday, but we need something Thursday. Is just letting them into the theater enough?"

"Yeah, that's enough," said Warn. "They'll be happy to just get in the building."

As Warn and Thompson plotted strategy, Cates walked out of the room where he and Bruce Vilanch had been doing radio interviews to promote the show. "What do you think is going to happen with the war?" an ABC staffer asked the producer.

"I think we're going to war," said Cates, sighing. "I only hope—and I know this sounds awful—I hope it either starts Monday the seventeenth, or March 24. If it starts anytime between the twentieth and the twenty-third, we're fucked. *We are fucked.*"

ST. PATRICK'S DAY was Monday, March 17, the last day off the union crew would enjoy before the Oscar show. In the Kodak Theatre, the stage sat empty and unattended. The doors between the stage and the loading dock remained closed. In the production office, TV monitors were turned to CNN. SHOWDOWN IRAQ, read the on-screen graphics.

Fears grew that if the war began Thursday or later, blanket news coverage would make televising the show impossible. Although the Academy's contract with ABC obligated the network to broadcast the ceremony, nobody thought it'd be a good idea to force ABC's hand during wartime. Besides, said Warn, "if a war starts two days before the show, celebrities are going to start pulling out, and we won't have a show anymore."

On a less serious front, the staff was still struggling to wrestle the show down to three and a half hours. On the previous day's run-through, the show had timed out to three hours and fifty-six minutes, with the best-picture presentation not slated to occur until 12:19 a.m., East Coast time. The latest round of cuts, one of which moved a Penelope Spheeris film of past Oscar hosts into the preshow, reduced the running time by six minutes.

That night, George W. Bush addressed the nation. He gave Saddam Hussein forty-eight hours to relinquish power and leave Iraq. Tuesday, Hussein rejected Bush's ultimatum. CNN changed its graphic to THE BRINK OF WAR: FINAL PREPARATIONS.

At the Kodak, though, it was starting to look like the Oscars. Seat cards were in place in the orchestra section of the theater. Roy Christopher watched the crew make adjustments to his set, which was dominated by a giant white latticework, shaped like a champagne flute, at the rear of the stage. Above the stage hung a huge ball, fourteen feet in diameter and encircled around its equator by four-foot letters that spelled out 75TH ANNUAL ACADEMY AWARDS as they slowly spun. The piece was a clear homage to the historic spinning-globe logo of Universal Pictures—and, said Christopher, the kind of nod to the past that he'd only do in an anniversary year.

Working in the Kodak for the first time, the designer wondered what had happened to the notes he'd given the builders while the theater was in the planning stages. "Gil and I, and Louis J., and Bob Dickinson spent hours poring over these plans they sent us," he said, exasperated. "We made our notes, we had our meetings, and not one thing we suggested was processed. It was essentially a charade. They used all of us as consultants, but they didn't do anything we asked them to do."

Still, Christopher didn't have to worry about turning a dingy hallway into the green room, the way Michael Riva had done the previous year. *Architectural Digest* had made a deal to underwrite and assist with the room; it was located in the same place it had been in 2002, but there was more space and more money to work with.

Down a long hallway from the green room, a sign had been posted on the door to Cates's office. WHEN THIS DOOR IS CLOSED, it read, IT MEANS PLEASE DO NOT COME IN.

Danette Herman posted a different sign on her door. THE BUNKER, it read. Will Smith's publicist called to say that the actor no longer felt it was appropriate for him to be on the show. Herman quickly replaced Smith with Brendan Fraser. Increasingly, Cates and Herman fielded phone calls from reps for actors who were uncertain about walking the red carpet, who said they'd rather quietly slip in the back way. Warren Beatty, whose wife, Annette Bening, was booked to be a presenter, ran into Cates's wife and told her he thought the show should be canceled.

For days, the staff had also been under pressure from executives at ABC, which was pushing not to cancel but to delay the show. Cates and Pierson repeatedly discussed the ramifications of various delays: with a one-day postponement, the show might lose a few stars, but most people would stick around; a delay of four or five days or a week would require buying out the run of a Scooby-Doo musical coming into the Kodak Theatre, an expensive proposition, and would probably wreak havoc with the lineup of presenters and performers; beyond that, they'd have to look into changing venues, which could become enormously expensive, particularly given the Academy's lack of insurance.

ABC kept arguing for a one-week delay, while Cates remained adamant that a seven-day postponement wouldn't solve anything and could be catastrophic for the show. He was supported by staffers who'd worked on the fall 2001 Emmy Awards, which were postponed after September 11, postponed a second time after military action began in Afghanistan, and finally took place almost two months later in a smaller theater with a different producer and a scaled-down presentation. For his part, Pierson was also determined that the show take place on time—particularly, he thought, since it would be shown on aircraft carriers and in other places where American troops could watch.

At lunch on Tuesday, a group of production and Academy staffers met at the Grill, a restaurant in the Hollywood & Highland complex. After reiterating his desire for the show to proceed as planned, Cates proposed doing away with the bleachers of fans along the red carpet, suggesting that it wouldn't be appropriate for celebrities to run that shrieking gauntlet. Warn pointed out that if the Academy took that step, the press that lined the other side of the carpet would just keep asking questions about the absence of fans.

"Well," said Cates, "then maybe we should get rid of the press, too."

At four o'clock, in the main Oscar press room at the Renaissance Hotel, Cates and Pierson took their places at a small table and faced several dozen reporters and camera crews.

"For some months now, Gil and his crew have been preparing for our show on Sunday while the clouds of war were gathering around us," read Pierson from a page in front of him. "We always knew there were some changes we would make if we needed to . . . We need the show to reflect a kind of soberness and seriousness we are all confronted with."

Cates then announced that the portion of the red carpet that ran along Hollywood Boulevard, between bleachers filled with fans and the press, would be eliminated. Interviews on the red carpet would not be permitted, and only a few crews would be allowed to photograph arriving stars. The preshow broadcast would be scaled back, and its tone changed to reflect events in the world.

"Is there a consideration for canceling the show?" asked a reporter.

"We're not prepared to address that question now," said Pierson.

"Have you been in touch with Washington?"

"No."

"Are the changes in the arrival area related to security?"

"No," said Cates. "Just the concerns of the celebrities."

"Do you plan to shorten the show at all?"

"That's a question we get every year," said Cates, allowing himself a slight smile.

Afterward, Cates headed back to his office. "Tough day, eh?" asked a bystander.

"Fuckin' A," said Cates. Then he smiled and shrugged. "It's exciting. It'll be great."

"YOU KNOW there's no red carpet?" David Jones said. "Photographers are going to be *pissed*."

Sitting behind a console at the Capitol Recording Studios in Hollywood on Tuesday night, Jones's sister laughed. "Oh, poor photographers," said Catherine Zeta-Jones, who was embroiled in a lawsuit against a British paper that published unauthorized wedding photographs. "I feel *so* sorry for them."

Due to have her first child in two weeks, Zeta-Jones was wearing black stretch pants and a black-and-white-print shirt. Her hair was tied back and she wasn't wearing makeup. She'd come to the studio to record vocals to the nominated *Chicago* song "I Move On," this prerecord being an Oscar tradition designed as insurance in the event of last-minute attacks of nerves or laryngitis.

In the movie, Zeta-Jones performed the song with her fellow nominee Renée Zellweger. But Zellweger didn't feel comfortable performing live, so another *Chicago* star, Queen Latifah, was booked instead. The Academy deliberately didn't announce that news until after the polls had closed, for fear that it might reflect poorly on Zellweger while voters still had their ballots.

While she waited for Latifah and for *Chicago* director Rob Marshall, Zeta-Jones grilled her brother and her publicist about the afternoon's press conference. "There's no chance it'll be canceled, right?" she asked.

"Oh, no," said David Jones. "They won't cancel."

"Actually, there is a small chance," said Zeta-Jones's publicist. "If the war starts Saturday, it might be postponed a couple of days."

Zeta-Jones looked at her bulging belly. "Oh, no," she moaned. "What am I going to do?"

ON WEDNESDAY MORNING, five laminated, blown-up pages had been affixed to the wall next to the entrance to the production office inside the Kodak. Three dealt with the protocol on handling bomb threats, two with suspicious mail. During the day, Jim Carrey and Cate Blanchett pulled out of their spots as presenters. Blanchett said she didn't want to leave her family in London. Angelina Jolie canceled as well.

On Thursday, March 20, ABC anchorman Peter Jennings made an announcement. "The war has begun in earnest," he said, "if not in full."

At 8:30, a few key staff members met for what had become the first order of business every morning: a security meeting that covered everything from terrorist threats to gate-crashers.

Small cuts, meanwhile, had been made throughout the script. Now the show was down to three hours and thirty-eight minutes—still too long, but closer to Pierson's goal. A major savings came with the decision to drop "Lose Yourself" from the show, Eminem having sent word that he didn't want to do it but didn't feel comfortable with anybody else taking the song, either. (That hadn't stopped Cates from asking actor Patrick Stewart to consider reciting the song; Stewart came to the studio and rehearsed what witnesses say was a creditable version of the song, but afterward the classically trained actor said he wasn't comfortable with the material.)

At lunch, Cates sat at a table with Warn, Seligman, John Hamlin, and a few others. The conversation turned to *Are You Hot?*, ABC's appalling reality show in which a panel of judges rated the physical characteristics of wannabe sex symbols. Cates laughed at the idea of the network that put it on the air telling him what was and wasn't acceptable on the Oscars.

"Susan Futterman was in Australia when it aired," said Hamlin. "She said she'd never have let Lorenzo Lamas point at a woman with his laser pointer and say something like, 'Your titties are too small.' "

"Well, if Susan gives me any shit," said Cates, "I'm just going to say, 'You can't talk to me about standards and practices, because ABC doesn't have any standards or practices anymore.' "

In the middle of the discussion, Cates's cell phone rang. He had a quick conversation and then hung up. "My wife says she was talking to a detective who said he heard from a friend of his that the Oscars were canceled," said Cates. "She said, 'Oh, I'll have to let my husband know.' "

He frowned. "Fucking rumors," he said.

"WERE THERE ANY JOKES you didn't like?" Steve Martin looked around the room at a group of Oscar staffers who'd just heard his opening monologue. "Anything I should take out? If there are, let me know and I'll meet with the writers."

Nobody responded. "Okay, good," said Martin. "Now, remember your vow: not a word."

Martin was standing one floor below the stage, in the Kodak Theatre's main green room. He'd taken over the space to try out his monologue in a controlled setting, asking that the audience be made up of staffers who hadn't heard the material during the few times he'd tested it in the production office. About two dozen of them had been recruited. With a TV monitor in the corner serving as a makeshift TelePrompTer, the host ran through the whole monologue with casual élan, and drew an enthusiastic reaction.

Cates, who'd come in late with Shapiro and Seligman, hugged Martin as the gathering broke up. "It was great," he said. "Thank you."

"You missed the beginning," said Martin. "I said, 'You'll notice that there was no red carpet tonight. Boy, *that'll* send a message.' " Shapiro and Seligman laughed, and Cates nodded. "Also, I had another one: 'Saddam, if you're watching, I hope your communications are knocked out just before best picture.' "

Cates frowned. "Let's see what happens before we use that one," he said. "He could be dead by then."

"If he's dead," Martin promised, "I'll cut it."

As the afternoon wore on, things were quiet. There were no big meetings, no press conferences, no emergencies. Martin's well-received appearance, both in the green room and later on the stage, seemed to have reassured the staff that it was okay to proceed as if it were business as usual—to take note of the situation in Iraq, but then move forward and put on a show.

Still, it was impossible to ignore the war for long—especially for Cates, who was asked to participate in constant conference calls with ABC about the network's options for canceling or postponing the show. Just after 7 p.m., as the orchestra settled into the pit and the stage was reset to rehearse a song from *Frida*, Cates walked to the production table and sat down with a sigh.

"It's been a very strange year," he said softly. "Very strange. I was literally on the phone with Annette Bening, I hung up, and the second I hung up the phone it rang again, and somebody was calling me to say, 'Did you hear Annette Bening canceled?' I do not know where the rumors come from, but you *cannot* control them. And eventually, it makes you wonder—is somebody spreading these things deliberately?"

He shrugged. "We've lost people, sure. We always lose people at the last minute. We'll probably lose more than usual this year, because people are afraid to travel. But we're back up to full strength now, and we'll be at full strength Sunday night."

FRIDAY MORNING, Cates had his usual conference call with ABC executives. The network, which was showing war coverage around the clock, continued to push for a one-week postponement; Cates and Pierson continued to lobby for a less glitzy, more appropriate Oscar ceremony taking place as scheduled. Alex Wallau, the president of ABC networks, wanted the

Oscar crew to plan for and have answers to all possible situations that might arise, from a dramatic escalation in the war to an abrupt end to hostilities. Cates argued that they simply couldn't plan for everything, and would have to deal with some eventualities only if and when they occurred. When Cates got off the phone, he sighed, "We're doing it," and then repeated the phrase as if to convince himself. "We're doing it. We're doing it."

At noon, on what would have been the red carpet along Hollywood Boulevard, Cates, Horvitz, and Pierson held a press conference. This Q&A session took place every year, and had been on the schedule well before any questions of cancellation or postponement arose. In front of dozens of reporters, many of them still smarting over the fact that they'd lost access to the red carpet, the three men reiterated that the show would go on. Cates admitted that "one or two" presenters had dropped out, said that some "flippant stuff" had been taken out of the script, and added that he anticipated some speeches to acknowledge the war.

When the press conference ended, a large group that included Cates, Horvitz, Warn, Bruce Davis, Ric Robertson, and others headed for the producer's office. On the way, a man approached Cates's assistant, Capucine Lyons, and began babbling about tickets, asking her if she wanted to go to the show with him.

When she got back to her desk, Lyons called the security staff. A few minutes later, they called her back. "They arrested him," Lyons said when she hung up the phone. "They found crystal meth on him." She smiled sweetly. "That's the second person I've had arrested in the last two days."

FIVE YEARS EARLIER, when seventy Academy Award recipients gathered at the Shrine Auditorium to celebrate another anniversary, the past Oscar winners had been referred to by their acronym: POWs. Cates and Herman had decided to have a similar segment on the seventy-fifth show—but this time, given the events in Iraq, the acronym went unused.

Sixty-three Oscar winners had originally agreed to participate, but by Friday afternoon the number was down to sixty-one. The winners straggled in over the course of an hour, starting with Ernest Borgnine, Teresa Wright, Kathy Bates, and Shirley Jones.

The stars filled up several rows in the parterre, the Kodak's name for a raised rear section of orchestra seats. Nicolas Cage, looking very Elvis-like in a white shirt and blue blazer, sat near Jon Voight and Martin Landau. Sean Connery showed up, hugged Michael Caine, and shook hands with Ben Kingsley, Landau, and Voight. Cage leaned over a row to greet Caine. "Hello, sir," Cage said. "Nice to see you again."

Cuba Gooding, Jr., walked up the aisle looking tentative, then brightened when he spotted Lou Gossett, Jr., who sat next to him at the reunion five years earlier. Mira Sorvino, stunning in a simple black miniskirt, sat by herself, the most glamorous wallflower in town.

When the past winners had all taken seats, Cates and Herman welcomed them. Then stage manager Peter Margolis took over. "Okay," he said, "I am going to give everybody a number. Julie Andrews, you are number one. Kathy Bates, number two . . ."

Margolis went through the entire list, assigning numbers to each of the stars. When Connery received number ten, Jon Voight turned to him. "Can you remember that?" he said.

In groups of seventeen, winners walked backstage and took their places in long lines outside the green room. Everyone navigated the stairs and hallways easily except for ninety-three-year-old Luise Rainer. The actress had already informed the Academy that she didn't like her hotel room and that as the oldest of the past winners, she expected special treatment. Moving from her seat to the aisle, she stumbled and grabbed her thigh. "My leg, my leg!" she yelled, before resuming a fast hobble.

Backstage, the winners formed two long lines, with stand-ins taking the place of those who couldn't make it to rehearsal. Enthusiastic conversations sprang up between Oscar recipients who found themselves next to each other: Louise Fletcher and Eva Marie Saint here, Sean Connery and Tatum O'Neal there. When Mickey Rooney showed up late, cheers erupted all the way down the lines. "Mickey la Rooney la Rooney la Mickey!" shouted Red Buttons.

Watching the tableau, Herman smiled. "The last couple of days have been horrible," she said. "But today is much better. There's been all this talk about people canceling, but we have five wonderful, courageous women who have flown a long way to get here. Olivia de Havilland from France,

Luise Rainer from London, Brenda Fricker from Ireland, Teresa Wright from New York, and Celeste Holm from Hong Kong. This reminds me why we love the movies, why we do this show. My heart is full."

LATE FRIDAY NIGHT, Bono paced the stage of the Kodak, gazing at the opera boxes lining the walls. Then he turned and eyed the giant, translucent, fluted panel that dominated the rear of the stage. Around him, the other three members of U2 settled into their places. "I just realized that we've never performed this song before," said Bono, who was wearing a backward cap and a loose brown jacket over a green V-neck sweater, along with black cargo pants and clunky black shoes. "So anything can happen."

U2, the Irish quartet that over the past fifteen years had become the biggest and most successful rock 'n' roll band in the world, had been nominated for the song "The Hands That Built America" from *Gangs of New York*. A brooding, conflicted look at a journey many of the Irish had made, it built from an acoustic opening to a near-psychedelic middle section featuring Bono's distorted, wordless moans. The last verse was spare and intimate as it lamented the destruction of September 11: "It's early fall / There's a cloud on the New York skyline / Innocence dragged across a yellow line . . ."

For the first couple of takes, the band, and particularly its famously intense and combative lead singer, seemed ill at ease. During the third run-through, Bono stopped singing altogether, walked down the steps into the audience, took Catherine Zeta-Jones's seat card out of her front-row seat, and slouched down in her spot to listen to the band. Then he turned to Hal Wilner, a music producer who had accompanied the band to rehearsal.

"I'm not really enjoying it right now," Bono said.

"What do we need?" asked Wilner.

"I don't know," said Bono. "Talent?"

He looked back at the stage, where the flute glowed with white light, and grimaced. Then he picked up the wireless microphone he'd carried with him and spoke into it. "This time, whoever's doing the lighting, I'd like to try it without the crystal lit," he said. "I'd like to see what it looks like with darkness." He waited for a minute, but nothing changed. "If anybody didn't understand that last comment, feel free to ask me about it."

Slowly, the band began to get a handle on the song. As the balance between U2 and the orchestra improved, Bono pushed himself harder, though he never approached the kind of intensity he was capable of displaying onstage. Screens behind the band showed vintage black-and-white photos of workers building New York's skyscrapers, images the band had requested. "Thanks a lot," Bono said after the final run-through. Then he turned and looked at the image frozen on the video screens: a row of workmen sitting on a beam high over New York City, their backs to the camera. "That's a great shot," he said. "That's a great ending."

Afterward, Bono went into the control truck and watched a playback with Cates and Horvitz. At midnight, he stood in a hallway outside his dressing room. "The room is shit," he said bluntly. "I fucking *hate* the room. We're singing a song about poverty underneath a huge fucking Waterford crystal. But it doesn't look like that on TV, and the director, Lou, has none of the ego that directors can have. I just have to forget the room and let it go."

From behind his lightly tinted bubble glasses, Bono looked determined. "We know what to do," he said. "I haven't found a way yet, but I will."

BEN AFFLECK and Jennifer Lopez stood on the edge of the Kodak stage, their arms around each other. Looking into the audience, Affleck pointed out Harvey Weinstein's seat card, which identified the Miramax chief as one of the producers of *Gangs of New York*. "He was listed as a producer on *Shakespeare in Love*," said Affleck, who'd made *Good Will Hunting* for Miramax. "He puts his name on movies he doesn't produce."

By Saturday, focus inside the Kodak had shifted to the day's parade of stars: to Affleck and Lopez, who barely left each other's sight and rarely kept their hands off each other; to a disconcertingly effervescent Renée Zellweger, who kept up a steady line of chatter the entire time she was in the building; to the young Mexican star Gael García Bernal, who left a trail of giddy women in his wake.

So did the Irish actor Colin Farrell, who arrived sporting a blue knit cap and a T-shirt that read YOU OUGHT TO BE IN PICTURES, BECAUSE EVERY-THING YOU DO IS A BIG PRODUCTION. Farrell's copresenter was the star of *Frida*, Salma Hayek, who was similarly dressed down in a long-sleeved T-shirt and charcoal sweatpants. As she stood in the wings waiting for her turn onstage, Hayek picked up one of the dummy Oscar statues and examined it closely. "He doesn't have a penis," she said.

"He does," insisted stage manager Dency Nelson, "but it's hidden behind his sword."

Sitting in the third row of the Kodak, Capucine Lyons had a big grin on her face. "You know who the sexiest man alive is?" said Cates's young assistant. "Colin Farrell. Every woman in the office got weak in the knees when he came in. And he stopped in midsentence to say hello to me."

Near the green room, Herman was similarly stricken. "I have a new favorite," the veteran talent booker admitted. "Colin Farrell. He's a sweetheart, in addition to being *adorable*."

In Iraq, bombs continued to drop, and most of the networks kept up their nonstop coverage of the hostilities. But in the Kodak, with star day winding down and dress rehearsal looming, some of the monitors that had been showing combat footage were switched to a golf tournament. Staffers no longer gathered to watch CNN and see if events would affect the show; instead, they glanced at it as they worked, assuming that the Oscars would take place as scheduled. The show was being played out against a backdrop of rumors, and with the constant adjustments that needed to be made as presenters and reunion talent dropped out, but it had gathered what seemed to be an inexorable momentum.

BEFORE DRESS REHEARSAL, Cates took part in a conference call with ABC executives to discuss how to handle the war coverage during the Oscars. ABC's news division asked for four minutes of time in the show, to update viewers on any developments from Iraq. This, of course, meant that Cates had to shorten the show even more if he wanted to hand out the best-picture award before midnight. In addition, Alex Wallau wanted a hotline phone installed at his seat in the twelfth row of the Kodak, so that he could be notified in the case of events so momentous that the show would have to be taken off the air. The production staff was becoming increasingly frustrated with the network's demands, but they acquiesced.

Early in the rehearsal, Cates spotted *Chicago* director Rob Marshall, who was on hand to stage the musical number from his movie. The producer pulled a seat card from one of the chairs in the Kodak, went over to Marshall, and said, "Here, Rob, this'll make you feel better." He turned the card over and set it in front of Marshall. On it was the smiling face of Harvey Weinstein. Marshall grimaced and threw up his hands in mock horror.

Half an hour later, Julie Taymor and Elliot Goldenthal arrived. Taymor was the director of *Frida*; Goldenthal, her partner, was a double nominee for writing the score to that movie, and for cowriting the song "Burn It Blue." "Did you go to the party?" Cates asked them.

"Yeah, we were at the Miramax party," Taymor said. "It was boring. We did 'Burn It Blue.' We were the life of the party."

Cates laughed. "Harvey wanted to come to rehearsal," he said. "I told him no."

This was not the first time Weinstein had made a fuss over access to the Oscars. Miramax initially made a splash at the show in 1990, when Daniel Day-Lewis won the best-actor award for *My Left Foot*, Brenda Fricker won the supporting-actress Oscar for the same film, and *Cinema Paradiso* picked up best foreign film. That year, Day-Lewis had given his extra front-row ticket to Alison Brantley, who worked in acquisitions for Miramax—but according to Peter Biskind's book *Down and Dirty Movies*, Harvey and Bob Weinstein had tried everything possible to wrest the prime seat from Brantley so that Harvey could use it.

This time, Harvey already had a good seat—fourth row, on the center aisle, right behind Scorsese and across the aisle from Marshall. But in his year of Oscar triumph, Weinstein also wanted to drop in on rehearsals. He'd had assistants call on his behalf, then made a personal appeal to Cates, who explained that the policy was not to allow studio heads at rehearsal. Weinstein didn't back down until Cates suggested that it wouldn't look good for Weinstein to be granted special access, given the furor over Robert Wise's Miramax-ghosted endorsement of Scorsese.

Late in the rehearsal, Steve Martin took the stage to test a new joke. "We just realized something about that," he said, pointing at the giant globe that was hanging, and slowly rotating, above the seats where the biggest stars in Hollywood would be sitting. "It's not supposed to spin," said Martin in mock concern. "We think it's *unscrewing*."

During the next break, Cates approached his host with a big grin. "That's the best joke of the show," he said. "The audience is going to be aware of the globe spinning up there all night long, and then you'll say it's unscrewing . . ." He grinned. "It'll be a great moment."

After the reunion of past winners, Martin returned to the stage and told the audience how thrilling the segment had been—"though backstage smells a little like Grandma's house," he added.

In the audience, some staffers and guests groaned. Martin stopped. "Yea or nay?" he said. "Let's see a show of hands."

He proceeded to poll the crowd. "Yea?"

Big applause.

"Nay?"

Silence.

"Oh, you're just afraid," scoffed Martin.

By the end of the dress rehearsal, the mood was one of exhaustion, mixed with irritation. Still, Bruce Davis proclaimed himself happy. "I'm tremendously relieved," he said. "We just have to be aware that ABC News has the option of taking four minutes of news promo time—and you know they're going to take the whole fucking thing. That's $5 million worth of promotion, and Peter Jennings is not going to give it up."

Cates then headed to the control truck, where Seligman, Horvitz, and Hamlin were waiting. "It's coming along," said Seligman. "3:26:30 is what I timed it at, and that includes people speaking in every category."

SUNDAY MORNING, some top Oscar staffers received calls alerting them to a tug-of-war still taking place within ABC. According to the caller, Michael Eisner, head of the network's parent company, the Walt Disney Company, had been golfing that morning with his chief operating officer, Robert Iger; during the round, Eisner announced that he wanted the Oscars canceled. Iger reportedly talked his boss out of it.

Frank Pierson, meanwhile, heard from Warren Beatty. "He called me and said he'd consulted with a number of his friends, including Jack Nicholson," said Pierson. "He said, 'Do you really think we should go ahead with this?' And I said, 'Yes, I don't see any reason not to.'" But Pierson was also feeling pressure from circles far to the east of Beverly Hills, from no less than George W. Bush's chief political strategist. "I do know," he said flatly, "that Karl Rove was calling from the White House to some people, pushing for us to cancel."

Determined to ignore those urgings, the production crew pressed on with rehearsal.

During the second full run-through on Sunday afternoon, Martin sat in the audience with his writers when he wasn't onstage. At one point, he turned to Dave Barry, Rita Rudner, and Andy Breckman. "Gil has made a case for cutting 'Grandma's house,'" he said.

When Martin left, Breckman turned to Barry and complained, "There's no edge at all to this show."

In the truck, Horvitz guided the final stages of the rehearsal. "With a little bit of luck," Cates said to Seligman as the rehearsal wound down, "this show could be something like 3:25. Which would be fucking fantastic."

"It would be great," agreed Seligman.

"If nothing else," said Cates, "it would make sure we got hired another year."

As the crew reset for the past winners' segment, Cates looked at the CNN monitor. "What's going on in the war?" he asked. He put on a headset connected to the news channel, listened for a few minutes, and then took off the headphones. "It's all babble," he said. "It's fucking babble."

He turned to Horvitz. "Just one comment," he said. "If someone makes a speech that's very political, cover both sides. Like you did with Elia Kazan, so we don't get accused of favoring one side. If somebody says something political, show both sides."

UPSTAIRS IN THE LUNCH AREA half an hour later, Cates allowed himself a few minutes to relax. "The only way I'd call it off now," he said, "is if a nuke goes off."

With the war temporarily restricted to the background, the producer began to speculate about the night's winners. "I'm sensing a lot of support for Roman Polanski," he said.

"You don't think it'll be all *Chicago?*" asked Vilanch.

"I don't know," said Cates. "Lately, it seems like everybody I've talked to has told me they voted for Polanski. I think *Chicago*'s still going to win best picture, but it wouldn't surprise me if Polanski wins best director."

As show time approached, John Travolta and Robert Duvall discussed diets in the green room. Jack Nicholson and Nicolas Cage stepped out the back door onto the loading dock for a cigarette. Renée Zellweger joined them, but didn't smoke. A semicircle of crew members stood about fifteen feet away, just watching.

With five minutes to go, Zellweger left the loading dock and headed for her seat. Just before she went through the final door into the Kodak, she stopped. "Wait!" she said to the page escorting her. "Do I have time to call my mom?" Without waiting for an answer, she pulled out a cell phone and dialed. "Hi, we're just about to go in," she said into the phone. "I just wanted to call to tell you how much I love you!" She paused. "Thanks, Mom! Thanks, Dad! Okay, we have to go in now!"

5:30 P.M., PACIFIC STANDARD TIME: *"Since 1928, the Hollywood community has gathered together to honor the finest motion picture achievements of the year."*

The show began not with the usual red-carpet recap, but with a shot inside the theater. A boom camera panned past the giant globe—which, during the opening fanfare, had suddenly stopped turning. The letters that spelled out OSCAR 75 were on the opposite side from Horvitz's camera. Almost immediately, the staff realized that there'd be no way to fix the problem during the show.

"Well," said Martin, looking around the theater, "I'm glad they cut back on all the glitz." The audience laughed nervously. "By the way," he added, "the proceeds from tonight's telecast—and I think this is so great—will be divvied up between huge corporations." This time, the laughter was heartier.

"This year, some people in Hollywood were insulted by the use of the term *gay mafia*," said Martin. "And I say to them . . ." Before the host could get to his punch line, a crew member stationed in the rafters high above the stage brushed up against a railing, dislodging a small two-way radio clipped to his belt. The radio fell to the back of the stage and noisily broke into pieces, one of which ricocheted toward Martin. The host stopped and looked back. "They seem to be *extremely* upset," he said. "And I say to them, 'Hey, fellas, don't get your thongs in a knot.' " Laughter was tepid at best. "Well, there's a lesson for you," Martin said. "It's not a good idea to throw a cell phone in the middle of a joke."

In the Kodak, the audience slowly loosened up during the monologue, as Martin moved from current events to the movie business. In the wings, Cameron Diaz watched on a monitor and laughed uproariously. "He is one funny motherfucker," she said.

As the show approached the half-hour mark, Jennifer Connelly introduced the nominees for best supporting actor. Warming up in the wings, the dancers in the *Chicago* number—many of whom had appeared in the movie—clapped for that film's John C. Reilly. The winner, though, was Chris Cooper for *Adaptation*. As he thanked his wife about forty-five seconds into his speech, Cooper began to tear up. "In light of all the troubles in this world," he said, "I wish us all *peace*."

When Cooper and Connelly left the stage, she declined to follow protocol and accompany him to the press rooms. Instead, she headed back to the green room. "That wasn't too bad," Connelly told a friend. "Painless."

As the show cut to a commercial, the TV audience saw a close-up of the globe. It was spinning, because this time they were viewing bumper footage shot the previous day.

At 6:10, ABC News cut away from the Oscars for a two-minute newsbreak. Peter Jennings said that American forces were less than one hundred miles from Baghdad but were experiencing heavy resistance, and that fifteen U.S. soldiers were believed to have been killed during the day. "I'm Peter Jennings," he concluded. "Back to the Oscars."

A few minutes later, Catherine Zeta-Jones won the best supporting actress Oscar for *Chicago*, that film's third win of the night. "My hormones are just too way out of control to be dealing with this," she said.

Leaving the stage with her Oscar, Zeta-Jones ran into Zellweger in the hallway. "Way to go, baby!" shouted Zellweger. "Well done!" Zeta-Jones was hustled toward the elevator that would take her to her dressing room on the lower floor, unaware that her husband was in a rest room only a few feet away.

In the green room, Julia Roberts told staffers that she didn't want to read the introduction that had been written for the cinematography category. To be sure, her lines were lengthy and a bit florid: they began with "Cinematography is the art and science of putting the moving in moving pictures," and included the notion that the job involved "the art of lighting shadows and shadowing lights." Roberts said she preferred to simply read the list of nominees. Cates huddled with Kohan in the wings, and then sent the writer into the green room to speak with Roberts.

Onstage, Gael García Bernal introduced the performance of "Burn It Blue" with some lines that weren't on the TelePrompTer. "The necessity for peace in the world is not a dream, it is a reality, and we are not alone," he said. "If Frida was alive, she would be on our side, against war."

Outside the green room, Diane Lane retouched her makeup, then joined Zellweger in line outside the rest rooms. A minute later, Hilary Swank walked up. "Is this a line?" she asked.

"We're the line, honey!" said Lane.

The rest room door opened and Julie Andrews walked out. Zellweger, Lane, and Swank burst out laughing.

"Yes," said Andrews, "Mary Poppins really does go to the bathroom."

An hour after its first newsbreak, ABC News took a second. This one was less than one minute long, and repetitive: a hundred miles from Baghdad, heavy resistance, fifteen dead. "The war grinds on," said Jennings.

Back at the Kodak, Zellweger was still outside the rest rooms when Julianne Moore came offstage. "Is there somewhere I can get a drink?" she asked the page who was escorting her.

"You can go to the green room," said the page.

"No, I don't think they have real drinks," said Moore. "I think they just have water. I want a beer or something."

"My girlfriend brought cans of malt liquor," offered Zellweger.

"I'm right there with her," said Moore with a laugh.

"She's my most white trash girlfriend," said Zellweger. "She goes to all these events and wears a dress and carries a can of malt liquor."

The show approached the two-hour mark without much in the way of political speechmaking, but Michael Moore changed all that when he won the feature documentary award for his incendiary *Bowling for Columbine*. As Moore walked to the stage accompanied by all the other nominees in his category, the audience greeted the filmmaker with a standing ovation. Moore told the audience that the other nominees "are here in solidarity with me," and then launched into a denunciation of the U.S. policy in Iraq. "We like nonfiction," he said, "and we live in fictitious times. We live in a time when we have fictitious election results that elects a fictitious president."

Cheers for Moore continued, but one audience member shouted, "No!" and a smattering of boos began to come from the back of the theater.

"We have a man sending us to war for fictitious reasons!" Moore shouted, as the boos grew to about the same volume as the cheers. "We are against the war, Mr. Bush! Shame on you, Mr. Bush!"

In the wings of the stage, stagehands began shouting at Moore. "That's bullshit!" yelled one.

"Get him *off*!" shouted another.

Vilanch, who'd been standing in the wings stage right, looked at the angry stagehands and made an immediate beeline for the other side of the stage.

In the truck, Horvitz cut to a line of stars, most of whom were reacting with stone faces as the boos grew louder. Worried about the growing tension in the hall, Cates ordered Horvitz to cue the orchestra.

As the music began to play, Moore shouted out one more line. "Anytime you've got the pope and the Dixie Chicks against you, your time is up!" he yelled, before leaving the stage to a mixture of applause and derision.

Before Moore could go to the press rooms, Diane Lane pulled the director aside. "That was very inspirational," she said. "Thank you."

A few minutes later, Steve Martin returned to the stage with the line that had just been crafted by his team of writers in the wings. "It was so sweet backstage, you should see it," he said. "The teamsters are helping Michael Moore into the trunk of his limo."

Martin then introduced Julia Roberts. "It is my honor to present the Academy Award for cinematography," Roberts said, before heading straight for the area that most infuriated the cinematographers' branch: "I find this a personally fantastic award, because I happen to know what I look like at five o'clock in the morning when I go to work."

During a commercial break at 7:30, the members of U2 walked through the wings on their way to the stage. Bono spotted Roberts, grabbed her arm, and began nuzzling her neck. She beamed. On the other side of the stage door, many of the past Oscar winners began to gather.

When U2 performed "The Hands That Built America," Bono changed the lines that had initially dealt with September 11. Instead of "a dark cloud on the New York skyline," he introduced a timelier image. "Late in spring," he sang softly. "Yellow cloud on a desert skyline / Some father's son / Is it his or is it mine?"

After U2, Susan Sarandon took the stage to introduce the In Memoriam segment. On her way to the podium, she flashed a peace sign. Backstage, Peter O'Toole walked into the green room. Mickey Rooney jumped up and stuck out his hand. "I've wanted to meet you for years," Rooney said. A timer in the wings indicated that the goal of a three-and-a-half hour show was within reach.

In an upset that drew an immediate standing ovation from the crowd, Adrien Brody won the best-actor award for *The Pianist*. He seized presenter Halle Berry in a passionate embrace and kiss, and then faced the audience, dazed. "There comes a time in life when everything seems to make sense," he said. "This is not one of those times."

Two and a half minutes into Brody's speech, Conti's orchestra began to play. "One second, one second, one second, please," Brody implored. "Cut it out." In the truck, Cates told Horvitz to stop the music, and Brody went on to decry "the sadness and the dehumanization" of war. "Whether you believe in God or Allah, may he watch over you, and let's pray for a peaceful and swift resolution," he said.

Immediately after Brody left the stage, Dustin Hoffman introduced a film clip from *The Pianist*. Outside the green room, Julia Roberts looked at all the past winners who had gathered there. "I'm overwhelmed," she said softly to Louise Fletcher and Eva Marie Saint.

Onstage, Barbra Streisand awarded the best-song Oscar to the one nomi-
inee who had neither performed nor attended, Eminem. "This all goes to
Marshall," said cowriter Luis Resto, who was wearing a long jacket over
a Detroit Pistons basketball jersey. "He's a good man, good heart."

As he spoke, Peter Margolis addressed the past winners backstage.
"Could everybody line up on your numbers, please?" he said. They began
to form long rows.

Adrien Brody came out of the green room. The past winners saw him
and began applauding. "Bravo!" shouted Karl Malden. "Welcome to the
club, Brody!"

During the next commercial break, the doors to the loading dock were
opened and the three large risers for the past winners were pushed to the
stage. "Okay," said Margolis to Herman, "now the last people get pulled,
and then we walk."

The last arrivals were Daniel Day-Lewis, Jennifer Connelly, Jack
Nicholson, Kathy Bates, Sean Connery, and Nicolas Cage. Meryl Streep
waited in line outside the bathroom. When the door opened, Brody
emerged. Streep screamed, opened her arms wide, and embraced him.
"Yeahhh!" she yelled. "It was wonderful!"

As Herman ran back and forth, checking the line and helping round up
new winners, Denzel Washington gave Nicole Kidman the best-actress Oscar. "Why do you come to the Academy Awards when the world is in such
turmoil?" said a teary Kidman. "Because art is important, and because you
believe in what you do and you want to honor that."

In the wings, the past winners began to walk to the stage. Luise Rainer
moved very slowly. Julia Roberts stopped, held her hand, and walked with
her every step of the way.

Kidman came into the wings, dazed. "I don't know what I said," she
she said.

"Congratulations," Dency Nelson told her. "Now stay right here. As a
winner tonight, you get to join this group." He pointed to the past winners.
"So stay right here, collect yourself, and enjoy."

Onstage, Olivia de Havilland introduced the group of fifty-nine past
Oscar winners. As the camera panned from one face to another, time
seemed suspended in the truck. "Lose it," Horvitz said. "Pan. Announce

roll. And lose it. Pan. Announce roll . . ." The cadences went on and on for more than eight minutes, but it seemed much longer.

In the wings, Kidman walked in small circles, fanning herself with the envelope that bore her name. She hugged Zeta-Jones, then Brody, losing an earring in the process. Brody dropped to his hands and knees, retrieved it, and handed it back to her. She put it on, then poked Zeta-Jones in the stomach. "Oscar baby," she said. A few feet away, the night's other acting winner, Chris Cooper, stood by himself quietly.

A timer now estimated that the show wouldn't end until 12:06 a.m., East Coast time.

When the roll call of past winners finally ended, Horvitz sighed. "That's a Zen moment, let me tell you," he said. "It'll lull you right out of it if you're not careful."

In the middle of the next act, Martin introduced Marcia Gay Harden. Then he walked into the wings. It was 8:39. Garry Hood approached Martin, a show rundown in hand. "You're not going to believe this," he told the host, "but your next item is good nights."

With twenty-one minutes left until midnight on the East Coast, four awards and six minutes of commercials remained. In the truck, thoughts of the war had been banished; the struggle to find an appropriate tone for the show was forgotten. One thing mattered: handing out that last award before midnight.

First, Marcia Gay Harden gave the award for adapted screenplay to Ronald Harwood for *The Pianist*. "Roman Polanski deserves this," said Harwood, to a huge round of applause.

In a small foyer stage left, Peter O'Toole waited for an elevator to take him to the press rooms. He spotted a bucket full of water bottles and frowned. "Any booze?" he asked.

"There's some in the press room, sir," his escort said.

A minute later, Pedro Almodóvar won the original-screenplay Oscar for *Talk to Her*. The Spanish director, who three years earlier had been furious at Lili Zanuck for cutting off his three-minute speech when he won for best foreign film, this time spoke for only one minute. He dedicated the award to "all the people that are raising their voices in favor of peace, respect of human rights, democracy, and international legality," then apologized for going overtime.

During the last commercial break, it was 8:51. For the show to come in at less than three and a half hours, the final act would have to be a short one. In the truck, Cates leaned forward. "Whatever you can do to hustle it would be good," he told Horvitz.

When the break ended, Harrison Ford took the stage to hand out the best-director award. Horvitz whipped through his changes, stopping the music quickly and cuing Ford to read the nominees. An assistant director leaned to a microphone and reminded the cameramen, "One no-show in this, Roman Polanski."

Ford opened the envelope. "And the Oscar goes to Roman Polanski for *The Pianist*," he said.

"Wow," said John Hamlin, who was sitting in the truck. Cates nodded and smiled. No acceptance speech meant he had his three-and-a-half-hour show.

As the audience stood and cheered for the exiled director, Horvitz shouted cues for reaction shots at breakneck speed. "Ready twelve, twelve! Ready eleven, eleven! Ready ten, ten! Read it, Harrison! Show it to him!"

"Roman Polanski cannot be here tonight," read Ford off the TelePrompTer, "but the Academy congratulates him and accepts this award on his behalf."

"Music!" shouted Horvitz. Cates grinned and gave two thumbs-ups.

When Kirk and Michael Douglas took the stage for the final award, the elder Douglas began talking in a slow, halting manner. "It's okay," Cates said to Horvitz. "We're fine on time."

Kirk Douglas opened the final envelope and saw that the best-picture winner was *Chicago*. He ripped the card in two and handed half to his son. They'd rehearsed this the day before, though they planned to do it only if the right movie—the one that featured Michael's wife and Kirk's daughter-in-law—won. The two men put the pieces together, and then shouted, in unison, *"Chicago!"*

"Fantastic!" Horvitz yelled.

Producer Martin Richards, a seventy-one-year-old veteran of the

Broadway stage, took the final Oscar and began to speak. Horvitz directed his cameramen to get reaction shots. "Camera twelve," he said, "get Harvey!" When Richards thanked Weinstein, Horvitz cut to the beaming Miramax chief.

After stumbling through a minute and a half of thank-yous, Richards stopped. "God, I'm forgetting someone," he said.

In the truck, Cates grew impatient. "Oh, come on, you old fart," he said. He leaned toward Horvitz. "Start a little music, quietly," he said.

"Oh, yes, one thing!" said Richards.

"Stop," said Cates quickly. "No music."

"I couldn't end it without thanks to my two angels who sat on my shoulders all the time," said Richards, who didn't name those angels. He ended his speech without music, then walked off.

At one minute to midnight on the East Coast, Steve Martin returned to the stage. "To our young men and women who are watching overseas, we are thinking of you," he said. "We hope you enjoyed the show, it was for you."

As the credits rolled, applause ran through the truck. Cheers rang out when Cates's and Horvitz's names appeared on the screen. Bob Dickinson shook Cates's hand. "Congratulations," he said. "I was proud to be here. And I think it was great live television."

Leaving the auditorium, Pierson found himself walking alongside Michael Moore. "Did I make an ass out of myself up there?" asked Moore.

"No, Michael," said Pierson to the normally rumpled filmmaker, who'd actually worn a tux for the occasion. "I want to thank you for coming—and I particularly want to thank you for wearing a tie."

AT THE GOVERNORS BALL, Pierson thanked Martin and Cates. Then he tried out a variation on his line to Moore, this time thanking the Oscar winner "for wearing a suit." A few partygoers booed.

The next day, police said they had arrested twelve people at both pro- and antiwar demonstrations on the streets surrounding Hollywood & Highland.

That same day, Barbra Streisand gave *Daily Variety* a copy of the speech she said she would have liked to deliver at the Oscar show—but didn't, said the paper, because she was "respecting the wishes of the producers of the Oscar ceremony." Her remarks offered prayers for American servicemen, faulted the Bush administration for its failed attempts at diplomacy, and celebrated the freedom to offer dissenting views.

"It was a very powerful night," said Danette Herman afterward. "There was a very interesting connection that happened. Steve gave people permission to feel comfortable about being at the show, and everybody that was there had a sense of purpose about being there."

While reviews were split on the balancing act of a wartime Oscars, the choices of Academy voters grabbed attention from the show itself. Belying the organization's image as a stodgy, conservative institution, Oscar voters had made unexpectedly daring choices in several categories. Adrien Brody for best actor, Roman Polanski for best director, Pedro Almodóvar for best original screenplay (for a script that wasn't written in English!), Eminem for best song, even the stylish piece of Japanese anime *Spirited Away* over the homegrown major studio films *Ice Age* and *Lilo & Stitch* in the animated-film category. The fact that in many cases these were probably the correct choices did not lessen the surprise.

The ratings, though, were not good. With an average viewership of just over thirty-three million—a drop-off of more than 20 percent over the previous year's lackluster totals—it was the smallest audience ever recorded for an Oscar show. Few blamed the Academy or the producer for the numbers: the war had given CNN and Fox News almost four times their usual number of viewers.

In previous years, even when its ratings fell the Oscar show had still been the most-watched entertainment program of the year. In 2003, however, it couldn't even beat the numbers from the final episode of Fox's tawdry reality show *Joe Millionaire*.

Michael Moore received much attention in the weeks following the show. The filmmaker published his own version of the night's events on his Web site, claiming that everyone down front was clapping, and that all the boos came from the Kodak's balconies. The Oscar review committee did not agree with Moore, but it also realized that the television broadcast didn't accurately capture the sound of the audience. At future Oscar shows, the committee decided, a microphone should be mounted in a position that would allow it to accurately capture crowd noise.

In April, the Academy issued its timetable for the Oscar show in 2004—and as expected, the show was moved from late March to February 29. The purpose, essentially, was to boost ratings—both by placing the show into February's Sweeps Month, in which the networks try to attract larger audiences through a variety of special programs and stunts, and by placing the Oscars closer to the year in which the competing movies were released.

"There was a growing feeling that we had been awfully polite waiting until the end of March, while every year it seemed like there was a new set of film awards in ahead of us," said Bruce Davis. "Everybody still concedes that we're the most important show, but in terms of expecting the public to get excited, if you've seen Julia Roberts win that award three other times before Oscar night, it's hard to go 'Wow!' "

The date change was frequently interpreted as an attempt to reduce the length of Oscar campaigns, but Davis insisted that was not a factor. "That literally never came up in the discussion," he said. "And I don't even understand how that was supposed to work. It seems to me to be obvious that it would just start earlier or become more intense while it was going on."

Which is not to say that campaigning wasn't an issue within the Academy as well. "For the past ten years, we've been watching Academy campaign techniques that we felt unleveled the playing field," said former Academy president Richard Kahn, chairman of the Public Relations Branch Executive Committee. "And the seventy-fifth show was the apogee of ruthless Academy campaigning. It was something that appalled us."

Kahn's committee issued new guidelines—which were retitled *regulations* as a statement of purpose—in July, and sent an eight-page booklet summarizing those rules to all Academy members in September. After decrying the very existence of the phrase "Academy campaign," the regulations insisted that ads "be free of endorsements from Academy members," while campaigns "designed to engender sympathy votes on behalf of filmmakers because of the strength of their bodies of work" were deemed inappropriate. Extreme caution was recommended in hosting the ubiquitous Oscar-season parties that had become, the guidelines suggested, "one of the most distasteful aspects of the Awards process."

Elsewhere, the regulations stated that members found to be in violation could be suspended or expelled from the Academy, and that more serious violations could result in films losing their Oscar eligibility. And in a deliberate attempt to prevent zealous campaigners from obeying the letter of the law while flaunting its spirit, a paragraph late in the booklet specifically pointed out that the new rules did not pretend to address every possible infraction.

"Members presumably have their own moral compasses that let them know with reasonable reliability when they are playing Oscar's game fairly," it read. "It is essential for the well-being of our award that we monitor those compasses closely."

Richard Kahn conceded that the Academy's position opened it up to criticism, but he made no apologies. "We do take a rather puritanical view of Academy Awards campaigns," he said. "For years we liked to pretend they didn't exist, and when we found out about them we were like Inspector Renault in *Casablanca*—we were shocked, *shocked* to find it was going on. Now we are accused of being rather haughty, stiff-necked, and arrogant. But that is the stance we choose to take."

11

≡

Young Blood

The 76th Academy Awards

"BEAR WITH ME ON THIS ONE," began Joe Roth, looking across the table at Danette Herman and Michael Seligman. The two Oscar vets, with fifty-three Academy Awards shows between them, exchanged a quick glance, then turned back to the producer who'd just begun to work on his first.

"I know I have lots of crazy ideas, but just listen," continued Roth. The director, producer, and studio chief sketched out his version of a new, im-proved Oscar seating chart: movie stars in the center section, nominees in half of the craft categories in the first couple of rows of the side sections. "When they win," he said, "they can get to the stage more quickly because they're already close to it."

Seligman and Herman nodded slowly, reserving judgment. "So, during one of our four-minute commercials halfway through the show," continued Roth, "we literally take all those people, the nominees in the first categories, and we move them to the back of the house. And we bring up the nominees for the categories we haven't presented yet. I bet you could save fifteen min-utes of shoe leather. And they couldn't complain about having to move back, because if we didn't do that they'd have to sit in the back for the whole show."

Seligman and Herman grimaced at the prospect of reseating close to one hundred sound editors, documentarians, costume designers, and their guests in the middle of a live television show. "I know it'd be a fun break, when we move people from the front to the back," admitted Roth. "That's when I'd go out for a smoke."

"One problem," suggested Herman gently, "is that the winners do press after they win. So when they came back to the theater, they'd have to find a different seat."

"And Lou will go crazy when you mess with his seating chart," added Seligman.

"No," corrected Herman. "He'll go *more* crazy."

"Well, it's something to think about," said Roth. "Let's talk to the Academy about this. Because I don't have the nerve to ask them if we could give out the documentary awards during a commercial break."

JOE ROTH HAD IDEAS, and he had energy, and he certainly had connections. What he didn't have was any experience producing live television—or, for that matter, any desire to produce an Oscar show by all the old rules. But with the show's ratings on a precipitous decline, the Academy was ready for somebody with a new vision, particularly if that person also had the clout to lure stars who might normally avoid the Oscars.

The head of Revolution Studios, the former production head of 20th Century-Fox and Disney Studios, and a producer whose movies ranged from *Bachelor Party* and *Young Guns* in the 1980s to *Mona Lisa Smile* in 2003, Roth was fifty-five, but he looked and acted younger. Well liked by talent, he was a lean, unsentimental man who refused to stand on ceremony. He never wore ties or used e-mail, when necessary delegating the latter chore to an assistant so as to keep his reputation clean.

By early fall Roth was already planning the show, though he couldn't devote full time to it: he was still running Revolution, which had been experiencing a tough year with the monumental Ben Affleck–Jennifer Lopez flop *Gigli*, as well as with the disappointing returns for films like Ron Howard's grim Western *The Missing* and the poorly received buddy cop movie *Hollywood Homicide*.

Revolution's headquarters occupied a modern three-story building on Olympic Boulevard in Santa Monica. On the second floor, a wing that had recently been used for postproduction on the Revolution movie *Peter Pan* was being converted for use by the Oscar production crew. Directly above that space was Roth's office, which occupied a corner of the third floor. It was a comfortable, wood-paneled room well lit by a skylight above his desk and windows that covered most of two walls.

Roth's executive assistant, Angela Pierce, was on hand for a morning meeting; so were Seligman and Herman, the latter of whom had been given the title of coordinating producer after more than two dozen years working talent on the Oscars. Roth looked at the board on which the show had been laid out. "I really want young people," he said. "This may be selfish of me, but this is the only time I'm going to do the show, and I'd love for it to be a show with ten or fifteen really hot young stars."

After he took the job, Roth had asked ABC for a demographic breakdown of the last few Oscar telecasts, and the figures disturbed him. In addition to the fact that the ratings had been in a slow, steady decline for close to a decade—with the exception of a few big shows, the *Titanic* year foremost among them—the audience had been growing older and more female. Roth was determined to change that by making the show younger, faster, and funnier, though he'd also gone back to Billy Crystal, who hadn't hosted the show for four years. "The most important thing is to get a young enough group of presenters," he said, "and to get people like Jack Black for the boys."

The new producer was also determined to revamp the promotion for the show, which in the past had often consisted of ads on ABC, morning show appearances on the same network, and a trailer in movie theaters shortly before the show. At the urging of Roth and some members of the board of governors—including Gil Cates—the Academy spent $1.5 million to buy ad time on a variety of cable channels that had never before run Oscar spots. They also made a deal to run the Oscar trailer in Blockbuster video stores for the first time, and gave Oprah Winfrey access to rehearsals and production meetings for a series on her show.

"I don't want to do all that work and have nobody watch," Roth told Seligman. "I want to know that they've got a whole promo package going to get the demos hipper and younger."

One of the key factors in that promotion was the Oscar trailer. "The Academy sent this over with three different songs attached to it," Roth said as Pierce cued up the tape and turned on a plasma screen monitor.

The trailer consisted of a barrage of familiar Oscar clips, ranging from Billy Crystal's entrance as Hannibal Lecter to Whoopi Goldberg in Queen Elizabeth whiteface. Dropped throughout the barrage of quick clips were phrases like "It's Oscar night," "Anything goes," and the unofficial motto of the show, "Expect the unexpected." The three versions were identical except for the music. One was set to "Hey Ya," a new single from the acclaimed rap group Outkast, one to Madonna's "Hollywood" ("Everybody comes to Hollywood / They're gonna make it in the neighborhood"), and one to Pink's anthem "Get the Party Started," which had been the National Basketball Association's theme song a year earlier.

"I told them," said Roth after the clips ended, "that I love the first song, I'm going to quit the show if they use the second song, and the third song is okay but it's been used ten thousand times. So we're trying to clear the Outkast song."

Seligman and Herman stared, trying to figure out just how serious their new boss was. "You guys haven't worked with me before, but that's the way I am," he laughed. "Like I said, I have lots of crazy ideas."

He turned to Seligman. "I even had a great idea for Billy's entrance, but you shot me down, Michael."

"What did I shoot down?" asked Seligman.

"Well," explained Roth, "remember, Mel Gibson's movie *The Passion* comes out the week of the show. Don't you think it's going to be on everybody's mind?"

Seligman groaned, and Roth forged on. "So I say, bring Billy out in a loin cloth, carried on a cross through the Academy."

THE ACCELERATED OSCAR schedule was already putting a pinch on voters who wanted to see many of the 254 eligible films. With a few exceptions, studios had long been holding their top Oscar contenders for the last few weeks of the year, particularly after past years in which early front-runners like *Saving Private Ryan* had had trouble maintaining momentum. But with nominating ballots due at PricewaterhouseCoopers by January 17, the schedule didn't leave much time for voters to catch up with all the contenders.

Films that in normal years might have been released in late December began to trickle out earlier. Clint Eastwood's grim tragedy *Mystic River*, which drew raves for a cast that included Sean Penn, Tim Robbins, Kevin Bacon, Laura Linney, and Marcia Gay Harden, was released in October, and immediately seized something of a front-runner status. *Lost in Translation*, a quietly unnerving movie from director Francis Ford Coppola's daughter, Sofia, came out in limited release the same month, drawing attention as the film that might finally win an Oscar nomination for the perennially over-looked Bill Murray.

Also in October, Jack Valenti, the president of the Motion Picture Association of America, announced that the MPAA's member studios would no longer send out DVDs or cassettes, dubbed "screeners." The move was designed to combat the proliferation of pirated movies on the black market and on the Internet, where many were routinely available for download before they even hit theaters. But independent studios immediately cried foul, charging that the move was designed less to prevent piracy than to freeze out the smaller films that had been doing surprisingly well at Oscar time. Since at least 1978, when airings of Woody Allen's *Annie Hall* on Los Angeles's Z channel were considered instrumental in that movie's best-picture win, lower-budget films had been relying on alternative avenues to draw the attention of the electorate; in recent years, *The Pianist* and *Monster's Ball* were among the films that had depended heavily on screeners. A slate of prominent directors, including Robert Altman, Robert Redford, Francis Ford Coppola, and Joel Coen, wrote an open letter to Valenti protesting a ban they felt would kill the Oscar chances of independent, risky films.

The Academy originally took no position on the MPAA ban, but Frank Pierson contacted Valenti when he saw that the credibility of the Oscars might be at stake. The men worked out a compromise in which Academy members who signed an agreement to not let the screeners out of their control would receive videocassettes. The deal infuriated members of the various critics' groups and smaller awards shows, all of whom were excluded from receiving screeners. A coalition of independent producers, meanwhile, went to court to end the ban. On Friday, December 5, they succeeded when a federal judge in New York City ruled that the MPAA's ban violated federal antitrust laws.

Still, most observers figured that the odds-on favorite was a film that didn't need any help from screeners, because it stood to be on thousands of screens by Christmas. While the first two movies in New Zealand director Peter Jackson's massive *Lord of the Rings* trilogy, *The Fellowship of the Ring* and *The Two Towers*, had both become blockbusters and received best-picture nominations, the films had won only in the technical categories. The Academy was not usually fond of fantasy films, none of which had ever been named best picture, but Jackson's achievement was hard to ignore—and the conventional wisdom had long been suggesting that Oscar voters were waiting for the final film, *The Lord of the Rings: The Return of the King*, to reward Jackson for the entire series.

But that movie wouldn't be out until mid-December. In the meantime, members made do with videocassette screeners, and with an accelerated slate of advance screenings that swamped L.A.'s prime screening rooms.

One of the few movies that didn't get caught in the crunch was *Seabiscuit*, director Gary Ross's adaptation of the Laura Hillenbrand best-seller about a legendary racehorse in the 1930s. Released into theaters in July and on video in December, *Seabiscuit* was the only top contender widely available on DVD. Universal spent lavishly to keep *Seabiscuit* fresh in voters' minds, and the studio also made the most of the DVD release by throwing a party at the Beverly Hills Hotel's storied Polo Lounge. The Academy had tried to crack down on parties in which lobbying opportunities were disguised as social occasions, but a soiree to celebrate a DVD release was well within its new, stricter guidelines. Even as members waited to see how the screener wars would play out, DVD copies of *Seabiscuit* were available to any voter with $19.99 or a Blockbuster rental card.

"JUST TO TELL YOU, Michael," Roy Christopher said to Seligman, "we got our first bid in on the Oscar statues."

The veteran production designer grinned. He was used to Seligman pushing him to keep costs down—though for the seventy-fifth Oscar show, with its balky spinning globe, his budget had hit the $1 million mark for the first time. The seventy-sixth show figured to be less expensive, but its futuristic collection of panels and platforms was complicated by the use of forced perspective, which meant that seven Oscar statues ranging in height from ten to twenty-two feet had to be specially made.

"They have to be bent a little bit," Christopher said. "The first bid was a quarter of a million dollars."

Seligman didn't say anything, but the stunned look on his face spoke volumes.

"Do you want to sit down, Michael?" asked Roth.

"We're getting other bids," said Christopher quickly.

"Good," said Seligman.

"It's okay," shrugged Roth. "We'll end up doing them in Manila."

By this point, mid-December, some of Roth's ideas had fallen by the wayside as the producer discovered the limitations of the Oscar format. His plan to move nominees midway through the show, for instance, didn't get far: "It turns out," he said, "that it wouldn't have saved much time after all."

But Roth was still determined to make the show young, fast, and funny. Comedians Jack Black and Will Ferrell were among the earliest bookings, and Roth held out a slim hope that Black, star of the rock 'n' roll comedy *School of Rock*, could sing a medley of all five nominated songs. He'd also been avidly but so far fruitlessly pursuing the likes of Orlando Bloom, Keira Knightley, and Johnny Depp to appear on the show.

The task was complicated by the fact that he didn't know what would be nominated, though the board in his office contained some guesses. The board listed *The Return of the King* as a sure nominee, along with *Mystic River* and Peter Weir's seagoing saga, *Master and Commander*. The fourth slot was held for either Miramax's prime Oscar entry, Anthony Minghella's Civil War drama *Cold Mountain*, or *Seabiscuit*. A slate of contenders for the last spot included *Lost in Translation*, the Tom Cruise movie *The Last Samurai*, and the animated *Finding Nemo*. (Two Revolution movies, *Mona Lisa Smile* and *The Missing*, had once been listed as possibilities, but their cards had since been removed from the board.)

"One way to introduce the best pictures," said Roth as he looked at the board, "is to go very straight. Pacino for *Lost in Translation*, Ian McKellen for *Lord of the Rings*, Oprah for *Cold Mountain* or *Seabiscuit* or *Mystic River*."

"Jim Carrey is so clever, he could do one of them," said Herman. "Last year, he wanted to do a picture clip. Depending on what gets nominated, as long as he didn't make fun of it, he could have fun with *Master and Commander*, or *Last Samurai*, or even *Lord of the Rings*."

"It's a bit of a fine line," agreed Roth. "Where could he goof around?"

"He could goof around within reason on all of them," said Herman. "If we put him on *Master and Commander* or *Last Samurai*, who are the directors?"

"Peter Weir and Ed Zwick," said Roth.

"Do either of them have a sense of humor?"

"No," Roth said quickly. "Neither does Minghella, neither does Gary Ross, neither does Eastwood."

Roth stood up, slipped out of his shoes, and walked around the back of his chair, examining the names of the films in contention. "Universal is spending as much money as everybody else combined to get *Seabiscuit* nominated," he said. "And now *Cold Mountain* will start."

That last film had yet to be released, but Miramax was building up word-of-mouth through advance screenings. "Harvey has once again done a brilliant job of waiting for the field to play out," Roth said with a sigh. "He waited until everything else was out, and then he'll put out *Cold Mountain* and grab the momentum. He didn't show it early, he's putting it out on Christmas Day, and they'll go into January as the hot movie. I still think we're looking at a *Lord of the Rings* sweep—but who knows? Maybe he'll steal it again like he stole it with *Shakespeare in Love*."

IN MOST CATEGORIES, Oscar nominations were made by a vote of the members in the appropriate branch. Things were different for foreign films and documentaries, where committees made the choice. And in three categories—visual effects, makeup, and sound editing—the decision came down to a process popularly known as the bakeoff.

The bakeoffs were held the week of January 18 at the Academy's Samuel Goldwyn Theater. On January 21, the visual effects program was due to start at 7:30, but by 7:00 much of the theater was already full; the dominant gender in the room was male, the primary clothing color black. Each of the seven finalists had five minutes to introduce up to fifteen minutes of persuasive film clips, followed by a short Q&A session. The finalists had been chosen from a field of nineteen contenders by an executive committee, which was made up of thirty-four members from the visual effects branch. One of the entries, though, boasted not only the most realistic computer-generated character ever created, but also as many special effects shots as most of the other finalists combined. "Why don't they just give *Lord of the Rings* a special achievement award, and everybody else can go home?" asked one bemused member.

But that wasn't how a bakeoff worked—and within the Academy, everybody knew about movies that had either hurt or helped their chances with bakeoff presentations. The previous year, for instance, *The Planet of the Apes* had been inexplicably passed over for a makeup nomination in favor of *Frida* and *The Time Machine*, movies that reportedly made snappier presentations.

The Pirates of the Caribbean: The Curse of the Black Pearl was up first, with a reel that zipped through the entire movie, cutting from one effects shot to another: Johnny Depp stepping off the mast of his sinking ship, cannons bombarding a city, a pirate with a skeleton hand, a ship in a storm, more ghostly pirates . . . Afterward, Edlund asked the film's special effects coordinator, Terry Frazee, if he had any interesting stories from the production. "No, Richard, no interesting stories," said Frazee. "Just hard work."

For the next two hours, six more films strutted their stuff. The *Master and Commander* crew did an exceptionally good job of pointing out how difficult it was to make a computer-generated ocean seem real, while *The Return of the King*'s reel was predictably overwhelming. *Peter Pan* had the unenviable task of following that epic with its whimsical small-scale effects, which were immediately overshadowed by a presentation that conclusively proved that *Terminator 3* lost virtually nothing in the transition from a two-hour movie to a fifteen-minute special effects reel. *X-2* and *The Hulk* rounded out the night, and then the voters had to work quickly: the PricewaterhouseCoopers reps on hand only stayed for fifteen minutes before collecting the ballots and leaving.

Young Blood

THE DAY AFTER THE BAKEOFF, police arrested Russell Sprague in the Chicago suburb of Homewood, Illinois. For years, investigators said, Sprague had been receiving Oscar screeners from Carmine Caridi, a sixty-nine-year-old character actor who lived in Los Angeles, and uploading those films to the Internet. Sprague was charged with criminal copyright infringement. At the next meeting of the board of governors, Caridi, who claimed he had no idea his friend was pirating the films, was expelled from the Academy.

JOE ROTH got up from his desk, walked across the room, and stuck his head out the door. "Try Jamie Lee," he said to his assistant, Colleen King. "Then Pat Kingsley, then Sean Penn on his cell phone."

Three and a half hours earlier, nominations had been announced. *The Lord of the Rings: The Return of the King* and *Master and Commander: The Far Side of the World* were the big winners, with eleven and ten nominations, respectively; *Mystic River*, *Lost in Translation*, and *Seabiscuit* rounded out the best-picture category. In what was immediately seen as an anti–Harvey Weinstein vote, *Cold Mountain* received nominations for Jude Law and Renée Zellweger, but was shut out of the best-picture and best-director competitions. Bill Murray got his best-actor nomination for *Lost in Translation*—and in an even bigger surprise, Johnny Depp landed one as well for his outrageous comic turn in *Pirates of the Caribbean*. Tom Cruise, considered a top candidate for *The Last Samurai*, was passed over, as was Russell Crowe, who once figured to be a shoo-in for *Master and Commander*. Sean Penn, who had drawn raves for both *Mystic River* and *21 Grams*, received a nomination for the former.

After speaking with Kingsley about Cruise and Depp, Roth reported to Herman, Seligman, Pierce, and musical director Marc Shaiman. "Pat's instinct is that Tom will skip the whole thing," he said. "But she knows we're offering best director, which is the second most prestigious category, so she'll talk to him. Johnny Depp, she said he's got to be there. But if we want him to present, he did it once before and he had a horrible time and said he'd never do it again."

King stuck her head in the office. "Joe, Sean Penn on line one."

Roth picked up the phone to speak to the four-time nominee, who had

363

never before attended the Oscar ceremony. "Sean, congratulations!" he began. "If you ask me, you should have been nominated for two movies, not one, but I guess they don't do that." He listened for a minute, then continued. "So we're hoping that you'll be there, and I'd love to let people know early that you'll be there. I think it'll be good for you *and* me, frankly." The implication was clear: if they knew the sometimes prickly Penn was coming to the show, Academy members might be more inclined to vote for him.

When he hung up, Roth was smiling. "Sean is coming," he announced.

"Yahoo!" said Herman.

"He wants a seat for his mother, and one for his wife. But he's not presenting. He says he thinks he'll be too nervous to do anything but sit there."

"ACT ONE, it's all comedy and sex," Roth told dozens of Oscar staffers who had filled the Kodak's lower lobby for a production meeting. "Act two, still all comedy and sex."

For about fifteen minutes, Roth laid out his vision of the Oscar show: young, fast, funny . . . and pretty long. "Less than four hours," he promised. "More than three."

While Roth was trying to add new wrinkles to the show, ABC had added a first of its own: the network was putting the show on a five-second delay. The move had been prompted by Janet Jackson flashing a breast during the recent Super Bowl halftime show—a bit of allegedly accidental exposure that turned out to be not just another symptom of the coarsening of pop culture, but the watershed moment at which a cross-section of concerned citizens, moral arbiters, and cultural overlords decided that enough was enough.

The board of governors objected to ABC's decision, but decided not to fight it. Roth tried to lobby Disney CEO Michael Eisner, for whom he'd once run the studio, but he found his old boss preoccupied with a takeover bid and a stockholder revolt. "I tried to talk to Michael Eisner this morning to complain about the five-second delay," Roth said at the meeting, "but he's got other things on his mind."

As distressing as Janet Jackson's breast had apparently been to some Super Bowl viewers, so were many of the advertisements that ran during the game itself. There were numerous ads for products that promised to cure erectile dysfunction; there was a Budweiser ad that featured a dog biting a man's crotch, another that centered around a horse farting. These, however, did not concern the Academy. Budweiser may have been a sponsor of the Oscars, but the Academy prescreened every commercial that ran during its show; if the ad didn't pass muster, it didn't air.

The reasons for this had less to do with good taste than with a long-standing attempt to avoid the appearance of favoritism or impropriety. The Academy had long ago taken control of the show's advertising, largely to ban movie ads or spots that featured any of the night's nominated actors. In 1985, the Academy refused to let Coca-Cola run ads that used the nominated song "Ghostbusters" unless they also produced ads featuring the other four nominated songs. Even Disneyland couldn't advertise on the show, because its name contained the name of a movie studio.

"The feeling is that for one night, we are really trying to be about the art of motion pictures, not about the business of motion pictures," said Bruce Davis. "If you're selling them at the same time that you're honoring the art, it blurs the message. We're a little prim about this stuff, but we do maintain a certain amount of decorum." (They also restricted advertising to about half an hour over the course of a three-and-a-half-hour show, significantly less than most other awards shows.)

After the formal meeting ended, Roth stood at the side of the room while staffers broke into smaller groups to go over their plans. ABC was still on his mind, but it wasn't just the delay that bothered him. "The hardest part of this whole thing is the promos," he said. "They only want to show them on ABC, which has half the audience of NBC and CBS. It's like promoting a movie—if I was putting out *Mona Lisa Smile* and I could only advertise on ABC, I'd be dead."

GIVEN THE LARGE NUMBER OF DEATHS in the film community since the last Oscar show, the final round of cuts for the In Memoriam film had been particularly brutal. But the year had also seen the passing of several people who deserved to be singled out at greater length: eighteen-time Oscar host Bob Hope, four-time winner Katharine Hepburn, and two-time winner and past Academy president Gregory Peck.

In December, Roth had mentioned this to the board of governors as a reason for not bestowing any honorary awards. But like other Oscar producers, Roth had no control over the board, as he learned when its members voted an honorary award to Blake Edwards, the director of the *Pink Panther* movies.

Edwards arrived at the Kodak on the Wednesday of Oscar week. Although the honoree was eighty-three years old, Roth was determined that his segment could still be fast and funny. He approached Edwards about a stunt that would take its cue from Peter Sellers's slapstick physical comedy in *The Pink Panther* and its sequels; although he'd recently injured his foot and was getting around by using a wheelchair and a cane, Edwards agreed. With the help of a pretaped segment, a souped-up wheelchair, a breakaway wall, and a stuntman who looked like Edwards, the director would appear to lose control of his wheelchair, shoot across the stage, and crash through a wall on the far side.

The veteran stuntman Mickey Gilbert would do the dirty work. Edwards would be waiting with Roth behind the wall, ready to emerge when presenter Jim Carrey came to get him. "If I had to guess," said Roth as he stood onstage watching preparations, "I'd say that Jim will drag or fireman-carry Blake onto the stage."

The producer dismissed the idea that it might be inappropriate to drag an octogenarian lifetime-achievement winner onto the stage, or to turn an honorary Oscar presentation into a stunt. The crowd that gathered around Edwards as he sat in the wings, meanwhile, just wanted to see something funny. Among the stagehands and bystanders, Jim Carrey and Billy Crystal jockeyed for position.

The stunt would open with a shot of Edwards sitting in his wheelchair in the wings. When Carrey introduced him, he'd push a control button on the armrest and then act shocked as the chair took off with unexpected force. Horvitz wouldn't be shooting that portion until Friday, but on Wednesday the director needed to work out his shots, and Edwards needed to practice looking shocked.

He did so several times, reacting as a stagehand yanked on a cord to pull the wheelchair out of the camera frame. When one take drew an exaggerated but appropriately horrified look from Edwards, the crowd around him burst out laughing.

"That's great!" laughed Carrey.

"That is *so* funny," added Crystal.

Carrey turned and grinned at his fellow funnyman. "We're looking at our future, you know," he said.

THE NEXT DAY, Steven Spielberg stood on the stage of the Kodak, frowning as he looked at the card he'd just pulled out of a rehearsal envelope. In the truck, Horvitz waited for Spielberg to read the name on the card. In the audience, fourteen stand-ins waited to see which of them would be going onstage to pretend he'd just won the Oscar for best picture.

But Spielberg couldn't do it. "You want me to read this?" he said uneasily. "*Really?*"

He showed the card to stage manager Garry Hood, who was standing nearby. FOR THIS REHEARSAL ONLY, it read, THE OSCAR GOES TO *THE LORD OF THE RINGS: THE RETURN OF THE KING.*

"Yeah, just read it," said Hood, who knew that the name was there completely by chance.

Spielberg, though, just couldn't bring himself to bestow any early kudos on the movie that had become a prohibitive Oscar favorite. "It's obvious it's going to win," he muttered. "Should I really?" Then inspiration struck. "The Oscar goes to *Cat on a Hot Tin Roof,*" he said. "Lawrence Weingarten, producer."

In Hollywood, few handicappers would have quarreled with Spielberg's take on the race. Other studios had tried to battle Peter Jackson's monster: for several weeks, TV ads for *Mystic River* featured Clint Eastwood talking about how his movie was "a really fine piece of material for actors, it's not about special effects," which was essentially a quieter way of saying, "Filthy hobbitses, we hates 'em." But Eastwood's film had failed to pick up any momentum through the early rounds of critics' and guild awards. There were still questions in the best-actor category, where Bill Murray was considered a strong bet to knock off front-runner Sean Penn, while Johnny Depp had scored a stunning win at the Screen Actors Guild awards. But aside from the occasional grumble about the twenty minutes of false endings that concluded *The Return of the King*, that movie's preeminence wasn't even threatened by the usual whispering campaigns. *The New York Times* dubbed it "the cleanest, most aboveboard, most decent Oscar race in years," and then added, "and the most boring."

"In a lot of ways, the competition has been a little more gentlemanly this year," agreed Bruce Davis. "Which is good, because the board is in a mood where, if something really underhanded had come up, they were clearly prepared to rule that a picture is not eligible as best picture. And until somebody gets that death penalty, there will be a tendency to push the edges."

The year's most blatant infraction came late in the game from Spielberg's company, DreamWorks. Trade ads on behalf of Shohreh Aghdashloo, a supporting-actress nominee for *House of Sand and Fog*, reprinted features that had run in several magazines, including *Rolling Stone*. "Will win: Renée Zellweger," they read. "Should win: Shohreh Aghdashloo." Miramax, the aggrieved party in an Oscar dispute for once, charged that the ads broke the unwritten rule of never attacking an opposing candidate. DreamWorks immediately apologized and pulled the ads, and the Academy decided not to penalize the company.

Back at the Kodak, Spielberg finished his rehearsal and stood in the wings watching a monitor with Joe Roth. "That's a beautiful set," he said. Then he turned to Roth. "Is there going to be anything on *The Passion of the Christ*?" he asked quietly of the movie that had made a staggering $23.6 million in its first day, while causing an outcry over what some saw as its anti-Semitism.

"Billy might do a couple of jokes," said Roth. "But not much."

Spielberg nodded. "Good," he said. "That's good."

FRIDAY WAS LARGELY devoted to music, which was not necessarily good news for Roth. The nominated songs worried him and put a serious crimp into his plans for nonstop sex and comedy. While the likes of Elton John, Pearl Jam, and Bono had been passed over, the nominees were a largely slow and somber group. Two of them, "The Scarlet Tide" and "You Will Be My Ain True Love," were mournful ballads from *Cold Mountain*. Another, "Into the West," was a stately tune from *The Return of the King*. The fourth song, "A Kiss at the End of the Rainbow," was an intimate, intentionally clichéd love song from the Christopher Guest spoof *A Mighty Wind*; the actors who performed it in the film, Eugene Levy and Catherine O'Hara, planned to do it at the Oscars in character.

The final song was the only up-tempo tune of the bunch, but "Belleville Rendez-Vous" was far from a guaranteed crowd-pleaser. A slight, jazzy ditty from the art-house animated French film *The Triplets of Belleville*, the song had been performed in the movie by a group of unknowns. Roth and Herman tried to interest Destiny's Child in the Andrews Sisters–style tune, then turned to Bette Midler; when those overtures failed, they went with the original performers, songwriter Sylvain Chomet and a French-Canadian chanteuse named Betty (pronounced Be-*tee*.)

If it worked, "Belleville Rendez-Vous" could be fun. More problematic were the *Cold Mountain* songs—old-fashioned ballads written by Sting and by Elvis Costello and T-Bone Burnett, and meant to evoke the Civil War music of the South.

Burnett, a highly respected producer and performer who had also produced the best-selling soundtrack to *O Brother, Where Art Thou?*, was arranging and trimming the songs, and he'd recruited both Sting and Costello to perform them along with Alison Krauss, the young bluegrass singer who handled lead vocals on both.

Roth figured the best way to deal with the two songs was to perform them together, along with the similarly yearning song from *The Return of the King*, which was sung by Annie Lennox. The songs were almost agonizingly deliberate and austere; Sting's in particular was little more than a stylish drone. If Roth's goal was to produce a fast, young, and funny Oscar show, a medley of "You Will Be My Ain True Love" and "The Scarlet Tide" was the antithesis of what he wanted: the songs were slow, they were written to sound 150 years old, and they were dead serious. When the numbers were performed back to back, with a surprisingly lengthy break between them to slightly change the instrumentation and replace Sting with Costello, their stillness and glacial pace caused frowns at the production table.

To give the songs an extra kick, Roth had planned to bring all the participants together for an encore on a short, jubilant gospel song, "Liberty," which would be led by the Sacred Harp Singers from *Cold Mountain*. But at the last minute Lennox decided she didn't want to appear in the encore, making it so unwieldy that Roth decided it should be cut from the show.

As Krauss rehearsed her songs one final time, Jack Black and Will Ferrell arrived for their own late-night rehearsal. Oblivious to the fact that Krauss was onstage, the two comics walked down the front row, checking out seat cards and turning to talk to an MTV film crew that trailed Black. It was an instructive tableau: the singer that Roth was forced to book tried to negotiate her intimate, haunting songs one last time, while the comic he would have preferred wandered in front of her, drawing all the attention as he went.

STAR DAY was ordinarily something of a ritual, but Joe Roth didn't put much stead in rituals. He quickly did away with a couple of the day's more ceremonial aspects: he asked the photographer assigned to shoot him with stars to back off ("What am I going to do, put them on my wall?" he asked, entirely rhetorically), and shunned the usual format in which the producer remained in his office while a procession of stars were taken to see him every fifteen minutes.

"It felt like being sent to the principal's office," he said before taking a seat in the wings with writer Jon Macks and a woman who made changes in the TelePrompTer copy. "I've been sent to the principal's office before, and I see no need to do that to Clint Eastwood." He shrugged. "It's a working session. It shouldn't be ceremonial."

It was also a workday for Susan Futterman, who during the show would be controlling a pair of buttons tied to the five-second delay. One would bleep out any offending words; the other would change to a reverse shot of the audience in the case of any untoward exposure.

When Robin Williams showed up at the Kodak, Futterman grew particularly attentive. Backstage, the hyperkinetic comedian kept up a nonstop comedy routine that veered wildly and unpredictably from *The Passion of the Christ* to Janet Jackson's Super Bowl appearance. When he stopped to take a breath, Futterman stepped in.

"Now Robin," she said, "you have to be good."

"I will," he promised.

"No *Jesus*," she said patiently. "No *Christ*."

"No *Jesus*, no *Christ*," he repeated.

"No *goddamn*. No C-word."

"No C-word?" he said, amazed that she'd bring it up. "No shit."

After Williams left, Futterman hung around to see Jamie Lee Curtis, who took the stage and promised the small audience, "I'm going to look *so* hot. I figure that this is my last shot up here, so I am going to look so fabulous. Every single fashion rule I've ever made for myself, I'm breaking in one night."

When Curtis left the stage, Futterman approached her. "What are you going to wear?" Futterman asked anxiously. "Are your nipples covered?"

"Yes, my nipples are covered," Curtis said incredulously. Then she spotted a nearby camera crew from Oprah Winfrey's show. "Get over here!" she yelled to the crew. When they obliged, Curtis turned to Futterman.

"Ask me again," she commanded.

"Are your nipples covered?" Futterman said obediently.

"Yes, my nipples are covered," Curtis announced.

Reassured, Futterman left. Curtis turned to her assistant. "That was actually scary," she said.

AT THE END OF STAR DAY, while most of the crew was eating dinner and recharging for the dress rehearsal, Roth met with Seligman and Herman in his office. They'd spent a couple of days trimming the script and looking for ways to save time—but after a day of revisions made to satisfy the presenters, things weren't looking good.

"Well, we gained about two and a half minutes during today's rewrites," said Seligman. "Basically, everything we'd taken out is back in. The thing with Ben Stiller and Owen Wilson is longer, John Travolta and Sandy Bullock is longer . . ."

"Yeah, but it's funny," said Roth. "And now we're getting lots of pressure to put the gospel thing back in." He sighed. "Harvey's been pressuring us, I've been getting lots of calls."

"If we cut it," said Herman, "we have to cut it tonight. That's not a decision we can postpone."

"I know," said Roth. "Let's see how it goes tonight. T-Bone has promised to shorten the other songs and speed them up. So we'll see. We'll look at the timings, and then we'll decide."

"We shouldn't wait for the timings to come in," said Herman. "We should decide as quickly as possible after we see the songs."

"We definitely have a time problem," added Seligman. "We're back up over 3:45, close to 3:50."

"I know your opinion, Michael," said Roth.

"I'm not expressing an opinion," insisted Seligman. "I'm just telling you the facts."

AT DRESS REHEARSAL, "You Will Be My Ain True Love" and "The Scarlet Tide" didn't appear to be appreciably faster than before, despite Burnett's promise to "blow the roof off this place." And with Lennox opting out and the encore requiring a complete reset and a new introduction from Liv Tyler, "Liberty" was spirited but jarring.

A few minutes after the songs were performed, John Hamlin walked into Roth's office with Andrea Wong, ABC's senior vice president of alternative programming and specials. When Wong ducked into Roth's rest room, Hamlin sighed. "I knew she'd be upset," he said to Angela Pierce. "But I guess if you've got to do those two songs, it's best to get them over with early in the show."

In the truck, Roth quickly decided that "Liberty" had to be eliminated. Seligman and Herman spoke to Burnett and Costello in the hallway outside the green room, where Costello fought for the gospel tune.

"I'm just making a case for the heart of the show," he insisted. "You're missing the chance to say something important."

"I understand what you're saying," said Seligman, who felt that Costello wanted to retain the song for the political statement he saw in it. "But we're at the point with this show where we just can't spare the time."

"You say you can't spare that thirty seconds, but I'm saying that thirty seconds will be a burst of energy that will impact the whole show."

"I know what the song means to you," said Seligman, "and I apologize."

"You don't have to apologize," said Burnett. "I understand."

"We all understand," said Costello. "But that song is *important*. You could be cutting thirty of the most important seconds of the show."

When Herman and Seligman left, Burnett shook his head at what he saw as the show's typical failure of nerve. "I think that Oscarosis has taken over," he said. "That's what Errol Morris called it at a party the other night: Oscarosis."

When the rehearsal ended, Garry Hood cleared the house so that Billy Crystal could show his opening movie to an audience of top staffers and Academy officials.

As he waited for the film to begin, Bruce Davis thought about the Academy's decision to move the Oscars from March to February. "Not one member has complained about not having enough time to do the initial screening process, which was our big worry," he said. "Harvey kept saying that nobody's going to be able to see all the movies, that it'll cause big problems." He laughed. "He said it so much that I was beginning to believe him."

BEFORE THE REAL STARS ARRIVED, fans in the bleachers along Hollywood Boulevard had to content themselves with the celebrity press. Just after 3:00 the day of the show, fashion guru Steven Cojocaru strutted down the red carpet, drawing a few screams. Preshow host Maria Menounos got a similar reaction for her cleavage. And E!'s Melissa Rivers drew shrieks when she flung a broken shoe into the crowd. (Immediately, bleacher dwellers began taking photos of the woman who'd caught Rivers's shoe.)

By 4:00, the star quotient was rising and Roth had taken up a position near the center of the red carpet. "Anything to pass the time," he said.

Inside the Kodak, Jamie Lee Curtis and Christopher Guest were the first celebrities to head for their seats. As show time approached, Diane Lane worked the front row. "You look *smashing*," she told Curtis, who was clad in a low-cut, strapless aquamarine gown by Monique Lhuillier. Moving down the row, Lane stopped to show Susan Sarandon how to fasten a strap on her shoe, then congratulated Scarlett Johansson.

At 5:10, announcer Andy Geller tried to get the crowd into their seats by telling them that the show would begin in ten minutes. Backstage, preshow cohost Chris Connelly prepared to conduct some live preshow interviews from his spot outside the greenroom. Roth offered to serve as a celebrity wrangler. "How many names do you need?" he asked.

"Less than five," said Connelly.

"Less than five," repeated Roth, who turned, went into the green room, and began grabbing stars. Tom Hanks was the first; as it turned out, Hanks was the only one the preshow had time to use.

In the front row, Renée Zellweger approached thirteen-year-old best-actress nominee Keisha Castle-Hughes. "You were magnificent," she said. *"Magnificent."*

With ten minutes to go, another preshow host, Billy Bush, began broadcasting from the orchestra section of the Kodak. He parroted David Letterman's unfortunate line of nine years earlier ("Uma, Oprah"), plopped into a seat between Zellweger and Nicole Kidman, then pulled Castle-Hughes out of her chair to meet Johnny Depp, on whom she'd admitted a crush. In the wings of the stage, Billy Crystal paced, got loose, and eyed Bush on the monitor. "That is the most annoying man on TV," he said.

5:30 P.M., PACIFIC STANDARD TIME: *"Live from the Kodak Theatre at Hollywood & Highland, welcome to the 76th annual Academy Awards."*

Crystal cleared his throat and walked toward the back of the stage. Jim Carrey was caught on camera as he walked to his seat in the front row, accompanied by a page.

After an introduction by Sean Connery, Billy Crystal's opening film played. Similar to Crystal's previous movies, it featured the comic inserted into scenes from many of the year's prominent movies, from *Terminator 3* to *Cold Mountain*, *Pirates of the Caribbean*, and *Finding Nemo*. By far the biggest reaction came when Michael Moore suddenly appeared during a battle scene from *The Lord of the Rings: The Return of the King*. "Stop this war!" Moore shouted, video camera in hand. "Shame on you hobbits, shame on you! This is a fictitious war!" When Moore was summarily stepped on and crushed by a huge elephant, the audience roared. In the wings, Catherine Zeta-Jones, who would be presenting the first category, watched on a monitor. "That's *so* great," she said to her escort. For the end of the movie, Crystal had tried desperately to recruit Johnny Carson to play the wise wizard Gandalf, but Carson declined and Jack Nicholson did the cameo instead.

As Crystal went into his "Wonderful Night for Oscar" medley, Zeta-Jones took her place at the rear of the stage. When he'd finished, she presented the best supporting actor award to Tim Robbins for *Mystic River*. Despite fears that his outspoken liberal politics might seep into his speech, Robbins simply thanked the cast and crew, his family, and then pleaded with victims of violence and abuse to seek help. As he walked into the wings with his Oscar, Zeta-Jones screamed with delight and grabbed him around the neck from behind.

Just after 6 p.m., *The Lord of the Rings: The Return of the King* won its first Oscar of the night, for art direction. The win drew resounding applause from the audience at the Kodak.

Robin Williams followed, and stayed away from anything Susan Futterman might have to bleep. But as he tore into the envelope containing the name of the best animated feature winner, *Finding Nemo*, Williams ripped so aggressively that he tore off a chunk of the envelope, which fluttered to the ground. On the way off the stage, Williams kept up a running line of jokes as he congratulated winner Andrew Stanton. "Dude! Dude!" he drawled in his best stoner voice. "That's so righteous!"

During the second commercial Renée Zellweger walked into the wings. A page trailed her, holding up the voluminous train of her dress. Zellweger presented the Oscar for costume design to *The Return of the King*, its second win of the night; immediately afterward, during the best-picture clip for *Master and Commander*, she was hustled back to her front-row seat. The aide followed, still carrying her train. "Oh, thanks," said Zellweger. "I could pick up some interesting things back there."

At the same time, Chris Cooper stood in the wings loosening up. Cooper shook his arms and legs, jerked his elbows, did some quick shadow boxing, rolled his neck, and opened and closed his mouth. He made a variety of guttural noises. Then, suddenly, he stopped, stood bolt upright, buttoned his tuxedo jacket, and waited for his cue.

Seven minutes after handing out an Oscar, Zellweger was back onstage to pick one up, this time as the winner in the best supporting actress category. "I am overwhelmed," she said softly, though she'd been the prohibitive favorite in the category. "I am overwhelmed." When she walked offstage, she spotted *Cold Mountain*'s executive music producer towering over the rest of the staffers in the wings. "T-Bone Burnett!" she shouted.

"You did good," Burnett told her quietly, patting her arm. "You did good." Zellweger sighed and leaned into Burnett, who wrapped her in a hug. Nearby, Alison Krauss borrowed her manager's tuxedo jacket to keep warm before going onstage.

At the one-hour mark, Ben Stiller and Owen Wilson handed out the awards for short subjects. The winners for live-action short, Aaron Schneider and Andrew J. Sacks, both brandished sheets of paper as they accepted their Oscars, but only Schneider got to read his. After he'd thanked about three dozen people (including Joe Roth and Marc Shaiman for not interrupting his speech) in a breathless but dull minute and twelve seconds, Horvitz cued conductor Harold Wheeler to start the music. Sacks glared at his partner as they walked away from the microphone. Backstage, Tom Hanks left the Kodak via the loading dock. On his way out, he passed Uma Thurman and John Cusack, the only celebrity occupants of the smoking section outside the green room.

Including the time spent changing sets, the performance of the two *Cold Mountain* songs and "Into the West" took up more than ten minutes; it was, as Roth had feared, austere, ethereal, and *very* slow. In the lower lobby of the Kodak, few people in the bar or lobby paid attention to the monitors. One exception was actress Annette O'Toole, who together with her husband, Michael McKean, had been nominated for writing "A Kiss at the End of the Rainbow." O'Toole stood a few feet from one monitor, eyeing the competition in her category. Sean Penn, who'd gone to acting school with O'Toole, walked by with his wife, Robin Wright Penn. "Do you know Annette O'Toole?" he asked her; when she said she didn't, he brought his wife over to meet his old friend.

After chatting with O'Toole for a few minutes, Robin Wright Penn turned to her husband. "What do you want to do?" she said. "Go back to the seats, or get a smoke?" Penn decided he wanted to go back to his seat, but the doors were closed until the next commercial break, so he joined a large crowd at the end of the hallway that led to the seats.

A few minutes later, Joe Roth joined the crowd as well. During the commercial, he went into the theater to fetch Blake Edwards.

At the end of the break, Catherine Zeta-Jones walked backstage, finding herself behind the mogul who'd pushed her best supporting actress campaign for *Chicago*. "Hi," he said, sticking out his hand. "Harvey Weinstein, Miramax Pictures."

Zeta-Jones laughed. "Nice to meet you," she said.

Then Weinstein shrugged. "Well, at least we bring our girls home," he said. "Catherine one year, Renée the next."

At the hour-and-a-half mark, *The Return of the King* won its third Oscar, this one for visual effects. Jamie Lee Curtis stepped outside the green room, spotted a friend, yanked down the top of her dress, and flashed a breast.

The Blake Edwards stunt went off smoothly. Horvitz ran tape of Edwards sitting in the wings, then cut to Mickey Gilbert speeding across the stage, grabbing the statuette from Carrey, and crashing through the wall. Roth helped Edwards get into place behind the rubble, and the director pretended to be dazed as he followed Carrey to the microphone. "Don't touch my Oscar," he snapped at the comic.

Afterward, Roth approached Edwards and Carrey in the wings. "Great," he said. "Great," he repeated. "Great great great great great great great great great great great great great."

Edwards smiled, but looked unconvinced.

"You got the only standing ovation of the night so far," Roth told him.

"No," Edwards said.

"Yeah," Roth insisted, "you got the only standing ovation."

Outside the stage door, Bill Murray waited for his cue to come to the stage. Behind him, an elevator door opened. Murray nonchalantly stepped backward, into the elevator. The page assigned to escort him hesitated, then stepped in with him.

"Can we go up?" asked Murray, deadpan.

"Yeah, I guess so," she said. Murray rode the elevator up, then down, then back up, killing a couple of minutes before he was due onstage.

While *The Return of the King* was winning Oscars number four and five, for makeup and sound mixing, Dency Nelson spoke urgently to Horvitz on his headset. "Lou, I'm here with Joe," he said. "Julia does not want to use the stairs center. She wants to use the stage-right ramp."

This was a major change—worse, in a way, than the last-minute rewrite Roberts had insisted upon the year before. It meant the large staircase that dominated one of Roy Christopher's most dramatic sets would go unused, that a key look would never be seen, and that two consecutive star entrances would be made in exactly the same way. If Roberts had suggested as much at rehearsal, a lengthy discussion would have ensued—but since she didn't attend rehearsal, since she made the request just before she was due to take the stage, there was no time to talk about it.

Horvitz wasn't surprised. When Roth had told him about the plans to give Roberts a big, grand entrance down the staircase, the director had been skeptical. "My experience with her," he'd told Roth, "is that she does not like to come down stairs." Roth told him not to worry. "I'll get her to do it," he said.

But Roberts wouldn't do it, not even after the entrance had been adjusted so she'd only have to walk down the last couple of steps. Horvitz immediately acquiesced; like everybody else in the crew, he knew that Roberts was a special priority for Roth. Dency Nelson showed Roberts her new, quick entrance. "Oh, thank you so much," she said. She waited in the wings for her cue, speaking quietly with Roth the whole time.

"It's now official," said Billy Crystal onstage. "There is nobody left in New Zealand to thank." He introduced Roberts, who delivered her tribute to Katharine Hepburn, then returned to the wings and watched the ensuing film package with her arm around the producer's shoulder. When the montage ended, Roberts nodded. "That's so nice," she said. She turned, hugged and kissed Roth, and apologized again for changing the entrance.

When Roberts had left, Roth turned toward the back door. "I'm going to walk," he said. But instead of heading back to the truck, he stepped out the door, lit up a cigarette, and hung around with a dozen stagehands in the smoking section. A couple of the crew members grinned and whispered about the bigwig in their midst. When the producer finally got back to the truck, Horvitz greeted him with a smile. "What a surprise," he said. "Julia didn't want to use the stairs."

Roth shrugged. "I tried," he said.

Early in the show's third hour, the Oscar for best documentary feature went to Errol Morris, the filmmaker who'd been overlooked in the past despite acclaimed films like *The Thin Blue Line* and *A Brief History of Time* (and who, according to Burnett, coined the word *Oscarosis*). After winning for *The Fog of War*, his documentary about the Vietnam War and the former secretary of defense Robert McNamara, he began his speech by saying, "I'd like to thank the Academy for finally recognizing my films." A minute later, he turned political. "Forty years ago this country went down a rabbit hole in Vietnam, and millions died. I fear we're going down a rabbit hole once again, and if people can stop and think and reflect on some of the ideas and issues in this movie, perhaps I've done some damn good here."

As Morris left the stage, Frank Pierson introduced the In Memoriam segment. The three-and-a-half minute film honored thirty men and women, from actors Gregory Peck, Hope Lange, Art Carney, Alan Bates, Gregory Hines, Ann Miller, and Donald O'Connor to controversial directors Elia Kazan and Leni Riefenstahl to experimental filmmaker Stan Brakhage and movie trailer pioneer Andrew Kuehn. In the wings, Sting and Phil Collins stood together, watching on a monitor. When composer Michael Kamen, with whom both men had worked, appeared on-screen, Sting clasped his hands together as if in prayer, and extended them toward the screen. Then he turned to Dency Nelson. "Is this show running on time?" he asked.

"We're actually not doing too bad," said Nelson, who checked the time in his rundown. "We're supposed to be at this point in the show at 7:52, and it's 7:54. So we're only two minutes over." He laughed. "Of course, let's look at the total time." He turned a page. "The show's timed at 3:43, and we're two minutes over that."

Sting and Collins presented the Oscar for best score to Howard Shore; it was the sixth win for *The Return of the King*, followed immediately by number seven when the film won the award for editing. "Did you know that people are moving to New Zealand just to be thanked?" asked Crystal.

As Jamie Lee Curtis introduced the songs from *A Mighty Wind* and *The Triplets of Belleville*, Jim Carrey, Will Ferrell, and Jack Black analyzed Oscar swag in the hallway outside Roth's office. "Dude, did you get the gift basket from this thing?" asked Black.

The giveaway had undergone a physical downsizing; where hard goods once filled mammoth baskets, the new one was an elegant valise that contained a plethora of vouchers. It may have lacked the most astonishing offer of the previous year's basket—free Botox injections—but the new one made up for that with lots of travel, including a week in New Zealand, this time with airfare included.

But the vouchers were strictly nontransferable. "There's a lot of great shit that you can't give away, that's the bummer," Black continues. "There's, like, twelve trips . . ."

"All to Mexico," added Ferrell.

"Yeah," said Black. "Trips to Cabo, and you can't give any of 'em away." He turned to Carrey. "Are you going to the ball?" he asked.

"No," said Carrey, laughing. "I'm blowing that shit off."

A little after eight o'clock, Tom Cruise arrived at the loading dock and headed straight to the green room. In the wings, Charlize Theron and Catherine Zeta-Jones checked out each other's outfits: Theron in beaded Gucci, Zeta-Jones in a red silk-chiffon Atelier Versace. "You could *not* be more beautiful," Theron said.

Zeta-Jones laughed, returned the compliment, and then turned the conversation to acting. "I loved you in *Monster*," she said. "It was wonderful."

"Oh, you're more talented than me," said Theron.

"No," demurred Zeta-Jones.

"No, really," insisted Theron. "You do more things really well. You should hear *me* sing."

Zeta-Jones made it back to her seat in time for Black and Ferrell, who sang what they claimed were the lyrics to the song used to play winners off when their speeches run overtime: "No time to thank your parakeet / You're boring / Look at Catherine Zeta-Jones / She's snoring . . ." As Black and Ferrell read the nominees for best song, Catherine O'Hara and Eugene Levy were led toward the stage, where a camera could catch their reaction in the unlikely event that "A Kiss at the End of the Rainbow" won. It didn't: instead, the award went to "Into the West," number eight for *The Return of the King*.

"Awww, it's that *Lord of the Rings* movie," grumbled O'Hara good-naturedly as she walked through the crowd in the wings. "It's a sweep!"

Behind her, Annie Lennox came offstage accompanied by cowriters Fran Walsh and Howard Shore. "This is one hell of a night," said Lennox, who was beaming from ear to ear.

A few minutes later, *The Return of the King* picked up another award, for best adapted screenplay—its ninth out of nine nominations, in a category in which the competition was tough. With only two categories remaining, best director and best picture, the film was suddenly almost a sure thing for an unprecedented eleven-for-eleven sweep.

First, though, Sofia Coppola won the original screenplay award for *Lost in Translation*. When she walked offstage, she became the first winner to receive a round of applause in the wings—an ovation led by Tom Cruise, who greeted her as soon as she left the stage. A minute later, though, Cruise was even more enthusiastic in handing the best-director Oscar to Peter Jackson.

When Jackson came offstage, stage manager Doug Smith told the director about the ending Roth had envisioned: all the night's winners on the stage, mingling as the credits rolled. Because Jackson was nominated for best picture, he couldn't remain backstage with the rest of the winners—and while it was looking like a sure thing that he'd be onstage with the final award of the night, Smith couldn't take any chances.

"At the end of the night," he told Jackson, "if you're still in your seat, we're going to invite you up onstage as a winner."

"Right," said Jackson. "And I'll bring the other Oscars with me."

In a break with tradition, the best-actor and best-actress awards were presented in between best director and best picture. The decision had been made months earlier, when Roth and his staff were considering the effects of a possible *Rings* sweep: "We didn't want to have the same group come to the stage two or three times in a row," he said. "It felt like it would take all the drama out of the end of the show."

The best-actress award came first; as expected, Charlize Theron won. A minute later, Blake Edwards was led into the wings to wait alongside the night's other winners. "Charlize won for *Monster*," his assistant told him.

"Good," said Edwards.

Slowly, the wings grew crowded with men and women toting Oscar statuettes. Theron asked for a tissue, then congratulated Edwards. Howard Shore walked by with a pair of Oscars. "I'm so happy," he sighed.

The final commercial break took place a few minutes before midnight, East Coast time. "When we return, the Oscar for actor in a leading role," said announcer Andy Geller. "And also coming up, Steven Spielberg and the winner for best picture." For Roth, this was a victory: he'd known for days that his show would be longer than three and a half hours, so his goal had been to make sure that announcer Geller could tease the final two awards before midnight in the East.

To begin the show's last act, Sean Penn won the best-actor award and was greeted with a standing ovation. When he left the stage, Nicole Kidman chased him down, shouting, "Sean! Sean! Take this!" She handed over the envelope bearing his name, a souvenir all winners were given along with their statuettes.

Just past midnight, East Coast time, Steven Spielberg opened the night's final envelope. The name inside was the same as in his rehearsal envelope three days earlier, but this time Spielberg didn't balk. "It's a clean sweep!" he announced. "*The Lord of the Rings: The Return of the King.*"

As Peter Jackson dragged ten cast and crew members onto the stage with him, Geller gave the stats: the eleven Oscars tied with *Titanic* and *Ben-Hur* for the most ever won by a movie. The former film, though, lost in three of the categories in which it was nominated, the latter in one; the previous record for a sweep was *Gigi*'s nine-for-nine in 1959.

"Remember," said Billy Crystal at the end of the night, parroting a TV ad campaign for Las Vegas. "What happens at the Oscars, stays at the Oscars." The night's winners, spread out across the back of the stage, stayed in a long line rather than mingling; it wasn't until Horvitz went to the usual package of show highlights that they began to socialize.

Annie Lennox, still beaming, walked across the stage to say hello to the four diminutive actors who played hobbits in Jackson's epic: Elijah Wood, Sean Astin, Billy Boyd, and Dominic Monaghan. Astin spoke into his cell phone, then handed it to Wood. As the hobbits celebrated, Clint Eastwood remained in the aisle near his seat, speaking quietly to a handful of friends.

Backstage, Susan Futterman was all smiles. "Never used the button," she said. "Isn't that wonderful? We were well prepared, but we never used it. That's the way we like it."

As the last stragglers left the Kodak and headed for the parties, the stage was nearly deserted. Downstage center, stuck to the floor, was a shred of the best animated feature envelope; Robin Williams had torn it off when he ripped open the envelope, and it had been there ever since.

Over in the Renaissance Hollywood Hotel, in a foyer outside the press rooms, Sean Penn stood with his wife and his mother and wiped away a few tears. Tim Robbins and Susan Sarandon passed around a cell phone. And Peter Jackson, waiting his turn in front of the cameras, took off his glasses and wiped his forehead with a tuxedo-clad forearm. "I need a Coke," he sighed.

Standing with Jackson, Steven Spielberg laughed. "Oh, it's not over yet," he said to the new Oscar winner. "You know what gets tired? You think it's your legs that'll get tired, but it's not." He nodded toward the glittering statuette clutched in Jackson's sweaty hand. "It's your arm. Your arm gets tired holding it."

THE DAY AFTER THE OSCAR SHOW, South African president Thabo Mbeki officially congratulated Charlize Theron for winning the country's first Academy Award, calling her life and her victory "a grand metaphor of South Africa's move from agony to achievement." In New Zealand, Prime Minister Helen Clark said the *Lord of the Rings* sweep made it "an incredibly proud day to be a New Zealander."

DreamWorks took out a full-page trade ad congratulating Renée Zellweger on her best supporting actress Oscar. Opinions were divided on whether the ad was a good-faith gesture because Zellweger was providing voiceovers for the studio's upcoming animated film *Shark Tale*, or an apology for the Shohreh Aghdashloo ads that had targeted Zellweger.

Ratings for the show were good, almost one-third higher than the previous year's war-deflated numbers, and slightly better than the 2002 figures. The audience was also younger and more male than for the past few Oscar shows.

Joe Roth pronounced himself pleased. "I enjoyed it very much," he said. "The two big challenges were the music, which worked out as well as it could, and the fact that there was a movie that won eleven awards. So the same music was played and the same people were thanked all night." He laughed. "Halfway through, when *Lord of the Rings* clearly was going to sweep, I felt like the producer of a Super Bowl who had a 61–0 score at halftime, trying to figure out how to keep it going."

The most amusing part of the experience, he said, was finding out how many people thought that Blake Edwards himself had crashed through the wall. (In his *Daily Variety* column the next day, Army Archerd called it "the big scare of the night.") "Ninety percent of the people I talked to thought it was Blake in the chair," Roth said. "Even people in the special effects business, which I thought was kind of wild, didn't realize that we had pulled the old bait and switch."

Andrew Sarris, a critic who Roth said was a hero of his, reviewed the show in *The New York Observer* and called it "the funniest and least tedious in memory." After noting that the show had received a considerable number of what he thought were mysteriously negative reviews, Sarris concluded, "As far as this old critic's concerned, Mr. Roth, you did a fine job."

The review committee focused on many of the usual concerns, including the length of the show and the question of whether the In Memoriam segment still made sense at a time when nearly every other awards show also trotted out a similar device. It also focused on the thank-you speeches, always a sore spot. In the past, Pierson had seriously suggested getting thank-you lists from all nominees, and running those lists on a crawl at the bottom of the screen as winners made their way to the stage; this time, he turned his attention to the fact that only about two-thirds of the nominees make it to the nominees' luncheon, and the ones who don't often give the longest speeches. The committee agreed to make a video compiling good and bad acceptance speeches, and send it to all future nominees.

In March, the board of governors voted to stick to the accelerated schedule and hold the 77th Academy Awards on February 27, 2005.

In June, the Academy made public for the first time the roster of those who'd been invited to become new members. Frank Pierson released the list of what he said were 127 "remarkably accomplished" film professionals in an attempt to disprove the widely held view that most Academy members were old and out of touch. The list of actors included recent nominees Shohreh Aghdashloo, Keisha Castle-Hughes, Patricia Clarkson, Scarlett Johansson, Sean Penn, and Ken Watanabe, along with Maggie Gyllenhaal, Viggo Mortensen, and Paul Bettany. Sofia Coppola was invited to join by both the writers' and directors' branches, though Academy rules stipulated that she could only choose one.

The following month, the organization conducted its annual review of the rules governing Oscar campaigning. Citing the relatively genteel nature of the past campaign season, the board introduced only one significant new rule, which prohibited "specific and disparaging references to other pictures or individuals competing in a given category."

Epilogue

The Oscar Gods

"IT'S A STRANGE SHOW," said Frank Pierson slowly. Sitting in his office on the top floor of the Academy headquarters, flanked by framed posters from his films *Cool Hand Luke*, *Cat Ballou*, and *Dog Day Afternoon*, the president of the Academy thought about the three Oscar shows that had taken place during his tenure, and the countless others he'd seen during his forty-six years in the business. "I think that it's gotten better over the years—and if it has, the one who deserves the most credit is Gil because he's really developed the awards show format. But it's strange."

He trailed off, then chuckled. "Mike Nichols and I were going to do the show one year, and we both quit," he said, remembering the forty-second Oscar show, in April 1970, for which he and the noted stage and film director Nichols had originally been hired. "We were still conceptualizing, very early in the process, when we started feeling that we were failing, and that we weren't going to be able to do what we wanted to do."

Pierson grinned. "We couldn't figure out how to do it," he said. "As

Mike said, 'Every time we got a show going, some asshole had to hand out an Oscar.' "

JOE ROTH tried to figure it out. He did what he could to put his stamp on the Academy Awards, to give the evening a shot of adrenaline. He'd booked young comics, pushed hard on the promotional front, even turned the presentation of an honorary Oscar into a sight gag. He'd won over some critics without alienating the stodgier side of the Academy, and gotten through it all in a reasonable amount of time, at least by Oscar standards.

And yet . . .

And yet Roth's Academy Awards looked a lot like Gil Cates's Academy Awards, which looked a lot like Laura Ziskin's Academy Awards, which looked a lot like Richard and Lili Zanuck's and Quincy Jones's Academy Awards. The format was inescapable and to a large degree inalterable: two dozen awards, film clips, five songs you can't choose. Roth thought about it a month later, and conceded the point. "You are constrained somewhat," he said, "by the elements you're given and the things you can't change."

Certainly, the Oscars do change—but more slowly and more incrementally, perhaps, than the pop culture, the media culture, the corporate culture in which they reside. To some, particularly some within the Academy, the deliberate pace with which the show accommodates the world around it is a sign of strength, inviolability, and incorruptibility. It would be unseemly, after all, for the august institution to drop awards, chase demographics, ditch the grand old format in pursuit of this year's model. Better to retain the template, as confining as it may be, and let producers tinker with it, sometimes drastically but more often not.

And yet . . .

And yet the format itself, the Oscar model that had been in place for decades before Gil Cates redefined it in the early 1990s, has been under increasing scrutiny in recent years. In the days after Roth's Oscar show, the two leading Hollywood trade papers, *Daily Variety* and the *Hollywood Reporter*, ran articles suggesting that it might be time to revamp the entire Academy Awards presentation. The *Reporter* article was written by Robert Osborne, who had recently published the Academy's official chronicle,

75 Years of Oscar. His piece, headlined IT'S TIME TO RETHINK OSCAR'S BIG NIGHT, suggested that the Academy consider handing out the awards at a banquet, the way they'd done until World War II (and, though Osborne didn't point it out, the way the Golden Globes did it). In *Variety*, an unsigned editorial lambasted "the predictability of the kudocast," said it was "hobbled by fundamental limitations of format and protocol," and offered a few suggestions: no more awards for shorts, no clips of the best-picture nominees, less shtick from the host.

The Academy has heard the complaints and knows the limitations of its show. The board might someday eliminate some or all of the three awards for short films; they considered that in the past, and almost did it once. But to move any of the other awards into a preshow or to a separate ceremony would be tantamount to admitting that some branches of the Academy are more important than others; that's a step no producer can expect, though many might wish for it.

"Complaints about the format raise a deeper philosophical issue," said Pierson. "Is this simply a show we put on to raise the money to do the good work that the Academy does? If that's the case, then you put on the best show that you possibly can, and anything that doesn't entertain the audience is out the window. If you were going to be hard-headed about the whole thing, you'd say that the documentary shorts and short subjects don't belong on the show, and we should give them along with the scientific and technical awards on another night, or during the commercials. Or are the Oscars our annual tribute to the best work of our members and others around the world in the arts and sciences of motion pictures? If that's what they are, then those other awards absolutely belong."

He shrugged. "It's a question the Academy has yet to clearly answer one way or another. So in the meantime, the show remains something of a hybrid. And, of course, another word for *hybrid* is *mongrel*."

Which leaves the Oscar show as it has been for decades: big, long, sometimes slow, and always reliant on what Cates calls "the Oscar gods."

"As a producer, you're dependent on so much that's beyond your control," says Bruce Davis. "You can script what the presenters are going to say and where the songs are going to go. But what people remember about the evening is what those winners say. And you have no control of how much thought they've given it, whether they're going to say something wonderful or brilliant or funny or heartbreaking. If you get two or three of those moments in the course of that *looong* three-and-a-half-hour epic, people remember it as a great show. If you get just one of those, people say, 'Ah, nothing happened!' And there's nothing the producer can do."

Cates got those moments with Jack Palance and Cuba Gooding, Jr., Quincy Jones got them with Kirk Douglas and Christopher Reeve, Laura Ziskin got them with Denzel Washington and Halle Berry. On those nights, the Oscar gods were in attendance. Other years they went to bed early.

It has now been fifteen years since Allan Carr shook up the Academy Awards and took a big fall. The Academy of Motion Picture Arts and Sciences is in the homestretch of its first hundred years, with lots of money in the bank and plans that reach well beyond the dispensing of gold statuettes. Outside, the battle rages over campaigning, positioning, and cashing in on Academy Awards. Inside, the Academy fine-tunes its rules, imposes the occasional penalty, and holds to its position—its naïve, perhaps foolish, but entirely admirable position—that it's all about the artistry. And somewhere, the man who paved the way for the past decade and a half of Oscar shows has to smile as he sees what has come to pass: amped-up promotion, supermodel fashion shows, trophy boys, green rooms sponsored by *Architectural Digest*, and a theater designed like a European opera house sitting at the back of a Hollywood mall. Occasionally, Carr is even remembered along the way—sometimes as the producer who failed, but once in a while, maybe, as a fabulous showman just a little ahead of his time, the unfortunate victim of what might have been a bad rap.

One such moment of remembrance took place on Saturday, March 25, 1995, two days before the sixty-seventh Oscar show. Gil Cates had been in charge of the ceremony for six years; it was midway between Carr's debacle and his death. David Letterman was hosting the show that year, and earlier in the evening he'd rehearsed much of his material. He'd raffled off a car, showed a film with New York City cab drivers, and presented another in which a series of big stars ran variations on the line "Would you like to buy a monkey?" Plus he'd introduced a Stupid Pet Trick.

At about 11 p.m., Bruce Vilanch walked into the production office upstairs in the Shrine Exhibition Hall. The writer, who'd gotten his Oscar start on a certain show six years earlier, sat down at his desk, shook his head, and broke into a beatific smile.

"Did you like the spinning dog?" he asked. "I want to send a tape of it to Allan Carr, along with a note that says, 'And to think, you got in trouble for Snow White. How times have changed.' "

Acknowledgments

"I'D LIKE TO THANK THE ACADEMY"—isn't that how Oscar thank-yous always begin? And in this case, I certainly would like to thank the Academy. But plenty of others also deserve my gratitude, and since there's no flashing TelePrompTer and no stickman to play me off, I'm going to violate protocol by pulling out a long list.

This book began with Howard Karren, an editor at *Premiere* magazine, who in early 1994 asked if I'd be interested in writing about the inner workings of the Academy Awards show. As I recall, the story was assigned to be five thousand words in length, though Howard and I both knew that if we got the access we wanted, it would end up far longer than that. Six months and about thirty thousand words later, Howard found himself staring at a manuscript considerably heftier than he'd expected, or wanted. But he liked it enough to go to bat for it—and to my surprise and great pleasure, Susan Lyne, the founder and editor-in-chief of *Premiere*, wanted not only to run the story relatively intact, but to turn it into an annual feature. I must start by thanking both Howard and Susan. At *Premiere*, thanks also to Chris

Acknowledgments

Connelly, Anne Thompson, James Meigs, Kathy Heintzelman, Leslie Van Buskirk, Sean Smith, Kristin Lootens, Christine Spines, Charlie Holland, Catriona Ni Aolain and Peter Herbst—plus, of course, the many fact-checkers who every year waded through page after page of indecipherable scrawls from dozens of reporter's notebooks.

The photographers who shot the Oscars for *Premiere* put up with far more restriction and interference than I did, and continually produced remarkable work despite the many obstacles. Thanks to Lara Jo Regan, who inaugurated the assignment and shot the first four years; to David Strick and Antonin Kratochvil, each of whom took over for a year; and to Art Streiber, who adroitly handled the gig for the last five years. Additional thanks to Art's assistant, Armando Gonzalez, and to their intrepid Academy escort, Steve Streich. Several others also helped secure the photographs used in this book: Aaron Roth, Lori Reese, Marion Durand, Helene Lagrange, and Gabriela Kratochvil.

My agent, Sarah Lazin, helped focus my thinking and offered invaluable advice on how to turn a batch of magazine articles into a book. Denise Oswald, my wonderfully sympathetic and supportive editor at Faber and Faber, understood what I wanted to do and kept me on track as I tried to figure out how to do it. Thanks also to Sarah Almond at Faber and Faber.

The Academy of Motion Picture Arts and Sciences did not authorize or approve this book. All the same, I could not have written it without the support and cooperation of the Academy. My thanks go to Academy presidents Arthur Hiller, Robert Rehme, Frank Pierson, and Richard Kahn, to executive director Bruce Davis, and to executive administrator Ric Robertson. Particular thanks are due to John Pavlik, a reliable, honest, and effective supporter of the project for more than a decade. Thanks also to Leslie Unger, Toni Thompson, Kim Tamny, Jane La Bonte, Frank Lieberman, and Bob Werden; I know that many times their publicists' instincts argued against giving a writer the kind of access I had, but they did so anyway. At the Academy's archives, thanks to Jeff Gough and Snowden Becker.

Many of the staff and crew who worked on the Oscars were of invaluable assistance, both by sharing stories and by not kicking me out when I got in the way. They include Louis J. Horvitz, Jeff Margolis, Robert Z. Shapiro, Bruce Vilanch, Buz Kohan, Hal Kanter, Carrie Fisher, Roy Christopher,

Acknowledgments

Robert Dickinson, Chuck Workman, Mike Shapiro, and Douglass M. Stewart. Also Don Was, Boyce Miller, Eva Demergian, Mike Thomas, Anat Reichman, Daniel Salzman, Lynn Padilla, Capucine Lyons, Dina Michelle, Julie Kaneko Hall, Angela Pierce, Colleen King, and many others over the years, a few of whom I'm sure I've forgotten. Special thanks to the stage managers, in whose domain I spent a great deal of time: Garry Hood, Dency Nelson, Rita Cossette, Peter Margolis, and particularly Debbie Williams.

Danette Herman is admirably zealous in protecting the stars who trust and depend on her, but she nonetheless granted me access to her terrain with grace and good humor. Michael Seligman likewise made sure I always had what I needed—this despite the fact that he was inexplicably and unfortunately edited out of my first *Premiere* story back in 1995.

This book could not exist without the cooperation and forbearance of the men and women who have produced the Oscar show: Joe Roth, Laura Ziskin, Quincy Jones and David Salzman, and Richard and Lili Fini Zanuck.

The most essential producer to the project, though, was Gilbert Cates. I met Gil in January 1994, when he was in the midst of producing the sixty-sixth Oscars and I had the task of persuading him to give me unfettered access; after we spoke for about fifteen minutes, he shrugged and said, "Okay, let's do this." From that point on, Gil's commitment was as total as it was crucial. He is a man of integrity and class, without whose help this book would have been impossible. I also owe an enormous debt to Gil's press rep, Chuck Warn, who shepherded me through the complexities of the Oscars with an insight and wit I could not have found elsewhere. If my errors of misinterpretation and indiscretion occasionally made things difficult for Gil and Chuck—and I know that there were times when they did—I can only offer my apologies, and offer profound thanks for making this possible.

Final thanks, of course, have to go to the two people who learned many years ago that they wouldn't be seeing me very much come mid-March (later mid-February)—and that when they did see me, likely as not I'd be distracted by production schedules and unreturned phone calls. This is for my wife, Mary, and my son, Adam.

Index

Carson, Johnny, 28–30, 69, 84, 98, 132, 374
Casablanca, 21, 199, 353
Cast Away, 262
Castle, William, 5
Castle-Hughes, Keisha, 374, 384
Cat Ballou, 282, 385
Cates, Gilbert, 16, 34–38, 74, 92, 105, 134–35, 140, 150, 185, 187, 193–94, 224, 268, 271, 294, 316, 331–32, 339, 356, 385–88; actors and, 182–83, 270, 276; bear act arranged by, 167–69, 180–81; Carr's production critiqued by, 7–8, 10; Crystal and, 36–38, 132, 162; Futterman and, 152–53, 193, 332; dance numbers staged by, 35–36, 38, 44–45, 63, 76, 77, 138–39, 147, 170, 171; Emmy nominations of, 37–38; female announcer hired by, 91; film career of, 34–35; Geffen Playhouse directed by, 102; Goldberg and, 191; at Governors Ball, 66; Helfgott and, 148–49, 157–58; Horvitz and, 136–38, 151, 212; and In Memoriam segment, 166; and Iraq war, 326–30, 333–34, 338, 341–42; Kahn and, 4, 31; and Kazan award, 194, 200, 207, 217, 218; and Kodak Theater, 328; and length of show, 177, 208, 257–59, 275–76, 281, 315, 318–19, 324–25, 341, 349, 350; Letterman and, 68–71, 83, 87–88, 97, 100; Margolis and, 36, 93, 137; Martin and, 262–64, 272, 332–33, 340; and past Oscar winners segment, 171, 174; and Perlman–Ma perfor-
mance, 268, 273; and performances of nominated songs, 42–44, 57, 80, 135–36, 151–52, 176, 202, 267, 271, 321–22, 337; Pierson and, 282, 319; and playing off of winners, 62, 93–94, 155, 220, 325, 345, 346; and preshow, 211; at press conference, 197, 198; promotional interviews with, 49–51, 327; reviews read by, 67; and seating arrangements, 54–55; trophy ladies auditioned by, 323–24; writers and, 141–42, 150
Cat on a Hot Tin Roof, 367
Cavalcade, 20
Cavanaugh, Christine, 109
Chakiris, George, 25, 173
Champion, Gower, 26
Champlin, Charles, 9
Chaplin, Charlie, 18, 27
Charisse, Cyd, 6
Charles, Ray, 241
Charlie's Angels, 249, 291
Chayevsky, Paddy, 28
Cher, 8, 173–74, 247
Chevrolet, 82
Chicago, 319–21, 326, 330–31, 339, 342, 343, 349, 376
Children of a Lesser God, 172–73, 227
Chocolat, 261, 263
Chomet, Sylvain, 369
Chorus Line, A, 31
Christie, Julie, 174
Christopher, Roy, 37, 42–44, 57, 84, 136, 145, 161–63, 174, 176, 197, 221, 328, 359–60, 377
Cider House Rules, The, 227, 228, 232–34, 251, 253, 261

Index

Index

Index

Index

P9-DNV-827

2008 COMMANDER-IN-CHIEF INSTALLATION EXCELLENCE AWARD

DOVER AFB

Port Mortuary

PORT MORTUARY

PATRICIA CORNWELL

G. P. PUTNAM'S SONS

NEW YORK

PUTNAM

G. P. PUTNAM'S SONS

Publishers Since 1838

Published by the Penguin Group

Penguin Group (USA) Inc., 375 Hudson Street, New York, New York 10014, USA · Penguin Group (Canada), 90 Eglinton Avenue East, Suite 700, Toronto, Ontario M4P 2Y3, Canada (a division of Pearson Penguin Canada Inc.) · Penguin Books Ltd, 80 Strand, London WC2R 0RL, England · Penguin Ireland, 25 St Stephen's Green, Dublin 2, Ireland (a division of Penguin Books Ltd) · Penguin Group (Australia), 250 Camberwell Road, Camberwell, Victoria 3124, Australia (a division of Pearson Australia Group Pty Ltd) · Penguin Books India Pvt Ltd, 11 Community Centre, Panchsheel Park, New Delhi–110 017, India · Penguin Group (NZ), 67 Apollo Drive, Rosedale, North Shore 0632, New Zealand (a division of Pearson New Zealand Ltd) · Penguin Books (South Africa) (Pty) Ltd, 24 Sturdee Avenue, Rosebank, Johannesburg 2196, South Africa · Penguin Books Ltd, Registered Offices: 80 Strand, London WC2R 0RL, England

Library of Congress Cataloging-in-Publication Data

Cornwell, Patricia Daniels.
Port mortuary / Patricia Cornwell.
p.   cm.
ISBN 978-0-399-15721-9
1. Scarpetta, Kay (Fictitious character)—Fiction.   2. Medical examiners (Law)—Fiction.
3. Forensic pathologists—Fiction.   4. Women physicians—Fiction.   5. Terrorism—Prevention—Fiction.
6. United States. Dept. of Defense—Fiction.   7. Cambridge (Mass.)—Fiction.   I. Title.
PS3553.O692P575   2010   2010034650
813'.54—dc22

Printed in the United States of America
1   3   5   7   9   10   8   6   4   2

BOOK DESIGN BY CLAIRE NAYLON VACCARO

U.S. Air Force Photograph on endpaper by Jason Minto 436th AW/PA

A Note to My Readers

While this is a work of fiction, it is not science fiction. The medical and forensic procedures, and technologies and weapons, you are about to see exist now, even as you read this work. Some of what you are about to encounter is extremely disturbing. All of it is possible.

Also real and fully operational at this writing are various entities, including the following:

> Port Mortuary at Dover Air Force Base
> Armed Forces Medical Examiner (AFME)
> Armed Forces DNA Identification Laboratory (AFDIL)
> Armed Forces Institute of Pathology (AFIP)
> Department of Defense (DoD)
> Defense Advanced Research Projects Agency (DARPA)
> Royal United Services Institute (RUSI)
> Special Weapons Observation Remote Direct-Action
>   System (SWORDS)

Although completely within the realm of possibility, the Cambridge Forensic Center (CFC), the Georgia Prison for Women, Otwahl Technologies, and the Mortuary Operational Removal Transport (MORT) are creations of the author's imagination, as are all of the characters in this story and the plot itself.

My thanks—

To all the fine men and women of the Armed Forces Medical Examiner System and the Armed Forces Institute of Pathology, who have been kind enough during my career to share their insights and highly advanced knowledge, and to impress me with their discipline, their integrity, and their friendship.

As always, I'm deeply indebted to Dr. Staci Gruber, director of the Cognitive and Clinical Neuroimaging Core, McLean Hospital, and assistant professor, Harvard Medical School, Department of Psychiatry.

And, of course, my gratitude to Dr. Marcella Fierro, former chief medical examiner of Virginia, and Dr. Jamie Downs, medical examiner, Savannah, Georgia, for their expertise in all things pathological.

To Staci

You have to live with me

while I live it—

Port Mortuary

nside the changing room for female staff, I toss soiled scrubs into a biohazard hamper and strip off the rest of my clothes and medical clogs. I wonder if *Col. Scarpetta* stenciled in black on my locker will be removed the minute I return to New England in the morning. The thought hadn't entered my mind before now, and it bothers me. A part of me doesn't want to leave this place.

Life at Dover Air Force Base has its comforts, despite six months of hard training and the bleakness of handling death daily on behalf of the U.S. government. My stay here has been surprisingly uncomplicated. I can even say it's been pleasant. I'm going to miss getting up before dawn in my modest room, dressing in cargo pants, a polo shirt, and boots, and walking in the cold dark across the parking lot to the golf course clubhouse for coffee and something to eat before driving to Port Mortuary, where I'm not in charge. When I'm on duty for the Armed Forces Medical Examiner, the AFME, I'm no longer a chief. In fact, I'm outranked by quite a number of people, and critical decisions aren't mine to make, assuming I'm even asked. Not so when I return to Massachusetts, where I'm depended on by everyone.

It's Monday, February 8. The wall clock above the shiny white sinks reads 16:33 hours, lit up red like a warning. In less than ninety minutes I'm supposed to appear on CNN and explain what a forensic radiologic pathologist, or RadPath, is and why I've become one, and what Dover and the Department of Defense and the White House have to do with it. In other words, I'm not just a medical examiner anymore, I suppose I'll say, and not just a habeas reservist with the AFME, either. Since 9/11, since the United States invaded Iraq, and now the surge of troops in Afghanistan—I rehearse points I should make—the line between the military and civilian worlds has forever faded. An example I might give: This past November during a forty-eight-hour period, thirteen fallen warriors were flown here from the Middle East, and just as many casualties arrived from Fort Hood, Texas. Mass casualty isn't restricted to the battlefield, although I'm no longer sure what constitutes a battlefield. Maybe every place is one, I will say on TV. Our homes, our schools, our churches, commercial aircraft, and where we work, shop, and go on vacation.

I sort through toiletries as I sort through comments I need to make about 3-D imaging radiology, the use of computerized tomography, or CT, scans in the morgue, and I remind myself to emphasize that although my new headquarters in Cambridge, Massachusetts, is the first civilian facility in the United States to do virtual autopsies, Baltimore will be next, and eventually the trend will spread. The traditional postmortem examination of dissect as you go and take photographs after the fact and hope you don't miss something or introduce an artifact can be dramatically improved by technology and made more precise, and it should be.

I'm sorry I'm not doing *World News* tonight, because now that I think of it, I'd rather have this dialogue with Diane Sawyer. The problem with my being a regular on CNN is that familiarity often breeds contempt, and I should have thought about this before now. The interview could get personal, it occurs to me, and I should have mentioned the possibility to General Briggs. I should have told him what happened this morning when the irate mother of a dead soldier ripped into me over the phone, accusing me of hate crimes and threatening to take her complaints to the media.

Metal bangs like a gunshot as I shut my locker door. I pad over tan tile that always feels cool and smooth beneath my bare feet, carrying my plastic basket of olive oil shampoo and conditioner, an exfoliant scrub made of fossilized marine algae, a safety razor, a can of shaving gel for sensitive skin, liquid detergent, a washcloth, mouthwash, a toothbrush, a nail brush, and fragrant Neutrogena oil I'll use when I'm done. Inside an open stall, I neatly arrange my personal effects on the tile ledge and turn on the water as hot as I can stand it, hard spray blasting as I move around to get all of me, then lifting my face up, then looking down at the floor, at my own pale feet. I let water pound the back of my neck and head in hopes that stiff muscles will relax a little as I

3

mentally enter the closet inside my base lodging and explore what to wear.

General Briggs—John, as I refer to him when we're alone—wants me in an airman battle uniform, or better yet, air force blues, and I disagree. I should wear civilian clothes, what people see me in most of the time when I do television interviews, probably a simple dark suit and ivory blouse with a collar, and the understated Breguet watch on a leather strap that my niece, Lucy, gave me. Not the Blancpain with its oversized black face and ceramic bezel, which also is from her, because she's obsessed with timepieces, with anything technically complicated and expensive. Not pants but a skirt and heels, so I come across as nonthreatening and accessible, a trick I learned long ago in court. For some reason, jurors like to see my legs while I describe in graphic anatomical detail fatal wounds and the agonal last moments of a victim's life. Briggs will be displeased with my choice in attire, but I reminded him during the Super Bowl last night when we were having drinks that a man shouldn't tell a woman what to wear unless he's Ralph Lauren.

The steam in my shower stall shifts, disturbed by a draft, and I think I hear someone. Instantly, I'm annoyed. It could be anyone, any military personnel, doctor or otherwise, whoever is authorized to be inside this highly classified facility and in need of a toilet or a disinfecting or a change of clothes. I think about colleagues I was just with in the main autopsy room and have a feeling it's Captain Avallone again. She was an unavoidable presence much of the morning during the CT scan, as if I don't know how to do one after all this, and she drifted like ground fog

4

around my work station the rest of the day. It's probably she who's just come in. Then I'm sure, because it's always her, and I feel a clenching of resentment. *Go away.*

"Dr. Scarpetta?" her familiar voice calls out, a voice that is bland and lacking in passion and seems to follow me everywhere. "You have a phone call."

"I just got in," I shout over the loud spatter of water.

It's my way of telling her to leave me be. *A little privacy, please.* I don't want to see Captain Avallone or anyone right now, and it has nothing to do with being naked.

"Sorry, ma'am. But Pete Marino needs to talk to you." Her unemphatic voice moves closer.

"He'll have to wait," I yell.

"He says it's important."

"Can you ask him what he wants?"

"He just says it's important, ma'am."

I promise to get back to him shortly, and I probably sound rude, but despite my best intentions I can't always be charming. Pete Marino is an investigator I've worked with half my life. I hope nothing terrible has happened back home. No, he would make sure I knew if there was a real emergency, if something was wrong with my husband, Benton; with Lucy; or if there was a major problem at the Cambridge Forensic Center, which I've been appointed to head. Marino would do more than simply ask someone to let me know he's on the phone and it's important. This is nothing more than his usual poor impulse control, I decide. When he thinks a thought, he feels he must share it with me instantly.

I open my mouth wide, rinsing out the taste of decomposing charred human flesh that is trapped in the back of my throat. The stench of what I worked on today rises on swells of steam deep into my sinuses, the molecules of putrid biology in the shower with me. I scrub under my nails with antibacterial soap I squirt from a bottle, the same stuff I use on dishes or to decon my boots at a scene, and brush my teeth, gums, and tongue with Listerine. I wash inside my nostrils as far up as I can reach, scouring every inch of my flesh, then I wash my hair, not once but twice, and the stench is still there. I can't seem to get clean.

The name of the dead soldier I just took care of is Peter Gabriel, like the legendary rock star, only this Peter Gabriel was a private first class in the army and had been in the Badghis Province of Afghanistan not even a month when a roadside bomb improvised from plastic sewer pipe packed with PE-4 and capped with a copper plate punched through the armor of his Humvee, creating a molten firestorm inside it. PFC Gabriel took up most of my last day here at this huge high-tech place where the armed forces pathologists and scientists routinely get involved in cases most members of the public don't associate with us: the assassination of JFK; the recent DNA identifications of the Romanov family and the crew members of the *H.L. Hunley* submarine that sank during the Civil War. We're a noble but little-known organization with roots reaching back to 1862, to the Army Medical Museum, whose surgeons attended to the mortally wounded Abraham Lincoln and performed his autopsy, and I should say all this on CNN. Focus on the positive. Forget what Mrs. Gabriel said. I'm not a monster or a bigot. *You can't blame the poor woman*

for being upset, I tell myself. She just lost her only child. The Ga-
briels are black. *How would you feel, for God's sake? Of course you're
not a racist.*

I sense a presence again. Someone has entered the changing
room, which I've managed to fog up like a steam shower. My
heart is beating hard because of the heat.

"Dr. Scarpetta?" Captain Avallone sounds less tentative, as if
she has news.

I turn off the water and step out of my stall, grabbing a towel
to wrap up in. Captain Avallone is an indistinct presence hovering in haze near the sinks and motion-sensitive hand dryers. All
I can make out is her dark hair and her khaki cargo pants and
black polo shirt with its embroidered AFME gold-and-blue
shield.

"Pete Marino . . ." she starts to say.

"I'll call him in a minute." I snatch another towel off a shelf.

"He's here, ma'am."

"What do you mean *'here'?*" I almost expect him to materialize
in the changing room like some prehistoric creature emerging
from the mist.

"He's waiting for you out back by the bays, ma'am," she informs me. "He'll take you to the Eagle's Rest so you can get your
things." She says it as if I'm being picked up by the FBI, as if I've
been arrested or fired. "My instructions are to take you to him
and assist in any way needed."

Captain Avallone's first name is Sophia. She's army, just out of
her radiology residency, and is always so damn military-correct
and obsequiously polite as she lingers and loiters. Right now is

not the time. I carry my toiletry basket, padding over tile, and she's right behind me.

"I'm not supposed to leave until tomorrow, and going any-where with Marino wasn't part of my travel plans," I tell her.

"I can take care of your vehicle, ma'am. I understand you're not driving. . . ."

"Did you ask him what the hell this is about?" I grab my hairbrush and my deodorant out of my locker.

"I tried, ma'am," she says. "But he wasn't helpful."

A C-5 Galaxy roars overhead, on final for 19. The wind as usual is out of the south.

One of many aeronautical principles I've learned from Lucy, who is a helicopter pilot among other things, is that runway numbers correspond to directions on a compass. Nineteen, for example, is 190 degrees, meaning the opposite end will be 01, oriented that way because of the Bernoulli effect and Newton's laws of motion. It's all about the speed air needs to flow over a wing, about taking off and landing into the wind, which in this part of Delaware blows in from the sea, from high pressure to low, from south to north. Day in and day out, transport planes bring the dead and take them away along a blacktop strip that runs like the River Styx behind Port Mortuary.

The shark-gray Galaxy is the length of a football field, so huge and heavy it seems scarcely to move in a pale sky of feathery clouds that pilots call mare's tails. I would know what type of airlifter it is without looking, can recognize the high pitch of its scream and whistle. By now I know the sound of turbine engines producing a hundred and sixty thousand pounds of thrust, can identify a C-5 or a C-17 when it's miles out, and I know helicopters and tilt rotors, too, can tell a Chinook from a Black Hawk or an Osprey. During nice weather when I have a few moments to spare, I sit on a bench outside my lodgings and watch the flying machines of Dover as if they're exotic creatures, such as manatees or elephants or prehistoric birds. I never tire of their lumbering drama and thundering noise, and the shadows they cast as they pass over.

Wheels touch down in puffs of smoke so close by I feel the rumble in my hollow organs as I walk across the receiving area with its four enormous bays, high privacy wall, and backup generators. I approach a blue van I've never seen before, and Pete Marino makes no move to greet me or open my door, and this bodes nothing one way or another. He doesn't waste his energy on manners, not that being gracious or particularly nice has ever been a priority of his for as long as I can remember. It's been more than twenty years since the time when we first met in Richmond, Virginia, at the morgue. Or maybe it was a homicide scene where I first was confronted with him. I really can't recall.

I climb in and shut the door, stuffing a duffel bag between my boots, my hair still damp from the shower. He thinks I look like hell and is silently judging. I can always tell by his sidelong glances that survey me from head to toe, lingering in certain places that are none of his business. He doesn't like it when I wear my AFME investigative garb, my khaki cargo pants, black polo shirt, and tactical jacket, and the few times he's seen me in uniform I think I scared him.

"Where'd you steal the van?" I ask as he backs up.

"A loaner from Civil Air." His answer at least tells me nothing has happened to Lucy.

The private terminal on the north end of the runway is used by nonmilitary personnel who are authorized to land on the air force base. My niece has flown Marino here, and it crosses my mind they've come as a surprise. They showed up unannounced to spare me from flying commercial in the morning, to escort me home at last. Wishful thinking. That can't be it, and I look for answers in Marino's rough-featured face, taking in his overall appearance rather much the way I do a patient at first glance. Running shoes, jeans, a fleece-lined Harley-Davidson leather coat he's had forever, a Yankees baseball cap he wears at his own peril, considering he now lives in the Republic of the Red Sox, and his unfashionable wire-rim glasses.

I can't tell if his head is shaved smooth of what little gray hair he has left, but he is clean and relatively neat, and he doesn't have a whisky flush or a bloated beer gut. His eyes aren't bloodshot. His hands are steady. I don't smell cigarettes. He's still on the wagon, more than one. Marino has many wagons he is wise to stay on, a train of them working their way through the unsettled territories of his aboriginal inclinations. Sex, booze, drugs, tobacco, food, profanity, bigotry, slothfulness. I probably should add mendacity. When it suits him, he's evasive or outright lies.

"I assume Lucy's with the helicopter . . . ?" I start to say.

"You know how it is around this joint when you're doing a case, worse than the damn CIA," he talks over me as we turn onto Purple Heart Drive. "Your house could be on fire and nobody says shit, and I must have called five times. So I made an executive decision, and Lucy and me headed out."

"It would be helpful if you'd tell me why you're here."

"Nobody would interrupt you while you were doing the soldier from Worcester," he says to my amazement.

PFC Gabriel was from Worcester, Massachusetts, and I can't fathom why Marino would know what case I had here at Dover. No one should have told him. Everything we do at Port Mortuary is extremely discreet, if not strictly classified. I wonder if the slain soldier's mother did what she threatened and called the media. I wonder if she told the press that her son's white female military medical examiner is a racist.

Before I can ask, Marino adds, "Apparently, he's the first war casualty from Worcester, and the local media's all over it. We've gotten some calls, I guess people getting confused and thinking any dead body with a Massachusetts connection ends up with us."

"Reporters assumed we'd done the autopsy in Cambridge?"

"Well, the CFC's a port mortuary, too. Maybe that's why."

"One would think the media certainly knows by now that all casualties in theater come straight here to Dover," I reply. "You're certain about the reason for the media's interest?"

"Why?" He looks at me. "You know some other reason I don't?"

"I'm just asking."

"All I know is there were a few calls and we referred them to Dover. So you were in the middle of taking care of the kid from

Worcester and nobody would get you on the phone, and finally I called General Briggs when we were about twenty minutes out, refueling in Wilmington. He made Captain Do-Bee go find you in the shower. She single, or does she sing in Lucy's choir? Because she's not bad-looking."

"How would you know what she looks like?" I reply, baffled.

"You weren't around when she stopped by the CFC on her way to visit her mother in Maine."

I try to remember if I was ever told this, and at the same time I'm reminded I have no idea what has gone on in the office I'm supposed to run.

"Fielding gave her the royal tour, the host with the most." Marino doesn't like my deputy chief, Jack Fielding. "Point being, I did try to get hold of you. I didn't mean to just show up like this."

Marino is being evasive, and what he's described is a ploy. It's made up. For some reason he felt it necessary to simply appear here without warning. Probably because he wanted to make sure I would go with him without delay. I sense real trouble.

"The Gabriel case can't be why you just showed up, as you put it," I say.

"Afraid not."

"What's happened?"

"We've got a situation." He stares straight ahead. "And I told Fielding and everybody else that no way in hell the body was being examined until you get there."

Jack Fielding is an experienced forensic pathologist who doesn't take orders from Marino. If my deputy chief opted to be hands-off and defer to me, it likely means we've got a case that could have political implications or get us sued. It bothers me considerably that Fielding hasn't tried to call or e-mail me. I check my iPhone again. Nothing from him.

"About three-thirty yesterday afternoon in Cambridge," Marino is saying, and we're on Atlantic Street now, driving slowly through the middle of the base in the near dark. "Norton's Woods on Irving, not even a block from your house. Too damn bad you weren't home. You could have gone to the scene, could have walked there, and maybe things would have turned out different."

"What things?"

"A light-skinned male, possibly in his twenties. Appears he was out walking his dog and dropped dead from a heart attack, right? Wrong," he continues as we pass rows of concrete and metal maintenance facilities, hangars, and other buildings that have numbers instead of names. "It's broad daylight on a Sunday afternoon, plenty of people around because there was an event at whatever that building is, the one with the big green metal roof."

Norton's Woods is the home of the American Academy of Arts and Sciences, a wooded estate with a stunning building of timber and glass that is rented out for special functions. It is several houses down from the one Benton and I moved into last spring so I could be near the CFC and he could enjoy the close proximity of Harvard, where he is on the faculty of the medical school's Department of Psychiatry.

"In other words, eyes and ears," Marino goes on. "A hell of a time and a place to whack somebody."

"I thought you said he was a heart attack. Except if he's that young, you probably mean a cardiac arrhythmia."

"Yeah, that was the assumption. A couple of witnesses saw him suddenly grab his chest and collapse. He was DOA at the scene—supposedly. Was transported directly to our office and spent the night in the cooler."

"What do you mean *'supposedly'*?"

"Early this morning Fielding went into the fridge and noticed blood drips on the floor and a lot of blood in the tray, so he goes and gets Anne and Ollie. The dead guy's got blood coming out of his nose and mouth that wasn't there the afternoon before, when he was pronounced. No blood at the scene, not one drop, and now he's bleeding, and it's not purge fluid, obviously, because he sure as hell isn't decomposing. The sheet he's covered with is bloody, and there's about a liter of blood in the body pouch, and that's fucked up. I've never seen a dead person start bleeding like that. So I said we got a fucking problem and everybody keep your mouth shut."

"What did Jack say? What did he do?"

"You're kidding, right? Some deputy you got. Don't get me started."

"Do we have an identification, and why Norton's Woods? Does he live nearby? Is he a student at Harvard, maybe at the Divinity School?" It's right around the corner from Norton's Woods. "I doubt he was attending whatever this event was. Not if he had his dog with him." I sound much calmer than I feel as we have this conversation in the parking lot of the Eagle's Rest inn.

"We don't have many details yet, but it appears it was a wedding," Marino says.

"On Super Bowl Sunday? Who plans a wedding on the same day as the Super Bowl?"

"Maybe if you don't want anybody to show up. Maybe if you're not American or are un-American. Hell if I know, but I don't think the dead guy was a wedding guest, and not just because of the dog. He had a Glock nine-mil under his jacket. No ID and was listening to a portable satellite radio, so you probably can guess where I'm going with this."

"I probably can't."

"Lucy will tell you more about the satellite-radio part of it, but it appears he was doing surveillance, spying, and maybe whoever he was fucking with decided to return the favor. Bottom line, I'm thinking somebody did something to him, causing an injury that was somehow missed by the EMTs, and the removal service didn't notice anything, either. So he's zipped up in the pouch and starts bleeding during transport. Well, that wouldn't happen unless he had a blood pressure, meaning he was still alive when he was delivered to the morgue and shut inside our damn cooler. Forty-something degrees in there and he would have died from exposure by this morning. Assuming he didn't bleed to death first."

"If he has an injury that would cause him to bleed externally," I reply, "why didn't he bleed at the scene?"

"You tell me."

"How long did they work on him?"

"Fifteen, twenty minutes."

"Possible during resuscitation efforts a blood vessel was somehow punctured?" I ask. "Antemortem and postmortem injuries, if severe enough, can cause significant bleeding. For example, maybe during CPR a rib was fractured and caused a puncture wound or severed an artery? Any reason a chest tube might have been placed presumptively and that caused an injury and the bleeding you've described?"

But I know the answers even as I ask the questions. Marino is a veteran homicide detective and death investigator. He wouldn't have commandeered my niece and her helicopter and come to Dover unannounced if there was a logical explanation or even a plausible one, and certainly Jack Fielding would know a legitimate injury from an accidental artifact. *Why haven't I heard from him?*

"The Cambridge Fire Department's HQ is maybe a mile from Norton's Woods, and the squad got to him within minutes," Marino says.

We are sitting in the van with the engine off. It is almost completely dark, the horizon and the sky melting into each other with only the faintest hint of light to the west. *When has Fielding ever handled a disaster without me? Never.* He absents himself. Leaves his messes for others to clean up. That's why he's not tried to get hold of me. Maybe he's walked off the job again. How many times does he need to do that before I stop hiring him back?

"According to them, he died instantly," Marino adds.

"Unless an IED blows someone into hundreds of pieces, there's really no such thing as dying instantly," I reply, and I hate it when Marino makes glib statements. Dying instantly. Dropping dead. Dead before he hit the ground. Twenty years of these generalities, no matter how many times I've told him that cardiac and respiratory arrests aren't causes of death but symptoms of dying, and clinical death takes minutes at least. It isn't instant. It isn't a simple process. I remind him again of this medical fact because I can't think of anything else to say.

"Well, I'm just reporting what I've been told, and according to them, he couldn't be resuscitated," Marino answers, as if the EMTs know more about death than I do. "Was unresponsive. That's what's on their run sheet."

"You interviewed them?"

"One of them. On the phone this morning. No pulse, no nothing. The guy was dead. Or that's what the paramedic said. But what do you think he's going to say—that they weren't sure but sent him to the morgue anyway?"

"Then you told him why you were asking."

"Hell, no, I'm not retarded. You don't need this on the front page of the *Globe*. This hits the news, I may as well go back to NYPD or maybe get a job with Wackenhut, except no one's hiring."

"What procedure did you follow?"

"I didn't follow shit. It was Fielding. Of course, he says he did everything by the book, says Cambridge PD told him there was nothing suspicious about the scene, an apparent natural death that was witnessed. Fielding gave permission for the body to be transferred to the CFC as long as the cops took custody of the gun and got it to the labs right away so we could find out who it's registered to. A routine case, and not our fault if the EMTs fucked up, or so Fielding says, and you know what I say? It won't matter.

We'll get blamed. The media will go after us like nothing you've ever seen and will say everything should move back to Boston. Imagine that?"

Before the CFC began doing its first cases this past summer, the state medical examiner's office was located in Boston and was besieged by political and economic problems and scandals that were constantly in the news. Bodies were lost or sent to the wrong funeral homes or cremated without a thorough examination, and in at least one suspected child-abuse death the wrong eyeballs were tested. New chiefs came and went, and district offices had to be shut down due to a lack of funding. But nothing negative ever said about that office could compare to what Marino is suggesting about us.

"I'd rather not imagine anything." I open my door. "I'd rather focus on the facts."

"That's a problem, since we don't seem to have any that make much sense."

"And you told Briggs what you just told me?"

"I told him what he needed to know," Marino says.

"The same thing you just told me?" I repeat my question.

"Pretty much."

"You shouldn't have. It was for me to tell. It was for me to decide what he needs to know." I'm sitting with the passenger's door open wide and the wind blowing in. I'm damp from the shower and chilled. "You don't raise things up the chain just because I'm busy."

"Well, you were busy as hell, and I told him."

I climb out of the van and reassure myself that what Marino

has just described can't be accurate. Cambridge EMTs would never make such a disastrous mistake, and I try to conjure up an explanation for why a fatal wound didn't bleed at the scene and then bled profusely, and I contemplate computing time of death or even the cause of it for someone who died inside a morgue refrigerator. I'm confounded. I haven't a clue, and most of all I worry about him, this young man delivered to my door, presumed dead. I envision him wrapped in a sheet and zipped inside a pouch, and it's the stuff of old horrors. Someone coming to inside a casket. Someone buried alive. I've never had such a ghastly thing happen, not even close, not once in my career. I've never known anyone who has.

"At least there's no sign he tried to get out of the body bag." Marino tries to make both of us feel better. "Nothing to indicate he might have been awake at some point and started panicking. You know, like clawing at the zipper or kicking or something. I guess if he struggled he would have been in a weird position on the tray when we found him this morning, or maybe rolled off it. Except I wonder if you would suffocate in one of those bags, now that I think of it. I guess so, since they're supposed to be watertight. Even though they leak. You show me a body bag that doesn't leak. And that's the other thing. Blood drips on the floor leading from the bay to the fridge."

"Why don't we continue this later." It's check-in time. There are plenty of people in the parking lot as we walk toward the inn's modern but plain stucco entrance, and Marino has a big voice that projects as if he's perpetually talking inside an amphitheater.

"I doubt Fielding has bothered to watch the recording," Marino adds anyway. "I doubt he's done a damn thing. I haven't seen or heard from the son of a bitch since first thing this morning. MIA once again, just like he's done before." He opens the glass front door. "I sure as hell hope he doesn't shut us down. Wouldn't that be something? You do him a fucking favor and give him a job after he walked off the last one, and he destroys the CFC before it's even off the ground."

Inside the lobby with its showcases of awards and air force memorabilia, its comfortable chairs and big-screen TV, a sign welcomes guests to the home of the C-5 Galaxy and C-17 Globemaster III. At the front desk I silently wait behind a man in the muted pixilated tiger stripes of the army combat uniform, or ACU, as he buys shaving cream, water, and several mini bottles of Johnnie Walker Scotch. I tell the clerk that I'm checking out earlier than planned, and yes, I'll remember to turn in my keys, and of course I understand I'll be charged the usual government rate of thirty-eight dollars for the day even though I'm not staying the night.

"What is it they say?" Marino goes on. "No good deed goes unpunished."

"Let's try not to be quite so negative."

"You and me both gave up good positions in New York, and we shut down the office in Watertown, and this is what we're left with."

I don't say anything.

"I hope like hell we didn't ruin our careers," he says.

I don't answer him because I've heard enough. Past the business center and vending machines, we take the stairs to the second floor, and it is now that he informs me that Lucy isn't waiting with the helicopter at the Civil Air Terminal. She's in my room. She's packing my belongings, touching them, making decisions about them, emptying my closet, my drawers, disconnecting my laptop, printer, and wireless router. He's waited to tell me because he knows damn well that under ordinary circumstances, this would annoy me beyond measure—doesn't matter if it's my computer-genius, former-federal-law-enforcement niece, whom I've raised like a daughter.

Circumstances are anything but ordinary, and I'm relieved that Marino is here and Lucy is in my room, that they have come for me. I need to get home and fix everything. We follow the long hallway carpeted in deep red, past the balcony arranged with colonial reproductions and an electronic massage chair thoughtfully placed there for weary pilots. I insert my magnetic key card into the lock of my room, and I wonder who let Lucy in, and then I think of Briggs again and I think of CNN. I can't imagine appearing on TV. What if the media has gotten word of what's happened in Cambridge? I would know that by now. Marino would know it. My administrator, Bryce, would know it, and he would tell me right away. Everything is going to be fine.

Lucy is sitting on my neatly made bed, zipping up my cosmetic case, and I detect the clean citrus scent of her shampoo as I hug her and feel how much I've missed her. A black flight suit accentuates her bold green eyes and short rose-gold hair, her sharp features and leanness, and I'm reminded of how stunning she is in an unusual way, boyish but feminine, athletically chiseled but with breasts, and so intense she looks fierce. Doesn't matter if she's being playful or polite, my niece tends to intimidate and has few friends, maybe none except Marino, and her lovers never last. Not even Jaime, although I haven't voiced my suspicions. I haven't asked. But I don't buy Lucy's story that she moved from New York to Boston for financial reasons. Even if her forensic computer investigative company was in a decline, and I don't believe that, either, she was making more in Manhattan than she's now paid by the CFC, which is nothing. My niece works for me pro bono. She doesn't need money.

"What's this about the satellite radio?" I watch her carefully, trying to interpret her signals, which are always subtle and perplexing.

Caplets rattle as she checks how many Advil are in a bottle, deciding not enough to bother with, and she clunks it in the trash. "We've got weather, so I'd like to get out of here." She takes the cap off a bottle of Zantac, tossing that next. "We'll talk as we fly, and I'll need your help copiloting, because it's going to be tricky dodging snow showers and freezing rain en route. We're supposed to get up to a foot at home, starting around ten."

My first thought is Norton's Woods. I need to pay a retrospective visit, but by the time I get there, it will be covered in snow. "That's unfortunate," I comment. "We may have a crime scene that was never worked as one."

"I told Cambridge PD to go back over there this morning." Marino's eyes probe and wander as if it is my quarters that need to be searched. "They didn't find anything."

"Did they ask you why you wanted them to look?" That concern again.

"I said we had questions. I blamed it on the Glock. The serial number's been ground off. Guess I didn't tell you that," he adds as he looks around, looking at everything but me.

"Firearms can try acid on it, see if we can restore the serial number that way. If all else fails, we'll try the large-chamber SEM," I decide. "If there's anything left, we'll find it. And I'll ask Jack to go to Norton's Woods and do a retrospective."

"Right. I'm sure he'll get right on it," Marino says sarcastically.

"He can take photographs before the snow starts," I add. "Or someone can. Whoever's on call—"

"Waste of time," Marino says, cutting me off. "None of us was there yesterday. We don't know the exact damn spot—only that it was near a tree and a green bench. Well, that's a lot of help when you're talking about six acres of trees and green benches."

"What about photographs?" I ask as Lucy continues going through my small pharmacy of ointments, analgesics, antacids, vitamins, eyedrops, and hand sanitizers spread over the bed. "The police must have taken pictures of the body in situ."

"I'm still waiting for the detective to get those to me. The guy who responded to the scene, he brought in the pistol this morning. Lester Law, goes by Les Law, but on the street he's known as Lawless, just like his father and grandfather before him. Cambridge cops going back to the fucking *Mayflower*. I've never met him."

"I think that about does it." Lucy gets up from the bed. "You might want to make sure I didn't miss anything," she says to me.

Wastebaskets are overflowing, and my bags are packed and lined up by a wall, the closet door open wide, nothing inside but empty hangers. Computer equipment, printed files, journal articles, and books are gone from my desk, and there is nothing in the dirty-clothes hamper or bathroom or in the dresser drawers I check. I open the small refrigerator, and it is empty and has been wiped clean. While she and Marino begin carrying my belongings out, I enter Briggs's number into my iPhone. I look out at the three-story stucco building on the other side of the parking lot, at the large plate-glass window in the middle of the third floor. Last night I was in that suite with him and other colleagues, watching the game, and life was good. We cheered for the New Orleans Saints and ourselves, and we toasted the Pentagon and its Defense Advanced Research Projects Agency, DARPA, which had made CT-assisted virtual autopsies possible at Dover and now at the CFC. We celebrated mission accomplished, a job well done—and now this, as if last night wasn't real, as if I dreamed it.

I take a deep breath and press send on my iPhone, going hollow inside. Briggs can't be happy with me. Images flash on the wall-mounted flat-screen TV in his living room, and then he walks past the glass, dressed in the combat uniform of the army, green and sandy brown with a mandarin collar, what he typically wears when he's not in the morgue or at a scene. I watch him answer his phone and return to his big window, where he stands, looking directly at me. From a distance we are face-to-face, an expanse of tarmac and parked cars between the armed forces chief medical examiner and me, as if we're about to have a standoff.

"Colonel." His voice greets me somberly.

"I just heard. And I assure you I'm taking care of this, will be on the helicopter within the hour."

"You know what I always say," his deep, authoritative voice sounds in my earpiece, and I try to detect the degree of his bad mood and what he's going to do. "There's an answer to everything. The problem is finding it and figuring out the best way to do that. The proper and appropriate way to do that." He's cool. He's cautious. He's very serious. "We'll do this another time," he adds.

He means the final briefing we were scheduled to have. I'm sure he also means CNN, and I wonder what Marino told him. What exactly did he say?

"I agree, John. Everything should be canceled."

"It has been."

"Which is smart." I'm matter-of-fact. I won't let him sense my insecurities, and I know he sniffs for them. I know damn well he does. "My first priority is to determine if the information reported to me is correct. Because I don't see how it can be."

"Not a good time for you to go on the air. I don't need Rockman to tell us that."

Rockman is the press secretary. Briggs doesn't need to talk to him because he already has. I'm sure of it.

"I understand," I reply.

"Remarkable timing. If I was paranoid, I might just think someone has orchestrated some sort of bizarre sabotage."

"Based on what I've been told, I don't see how that would be possible."

"I said if I was paranoid," Briggs replies, and from where I stand, I can make out his formidable sturdy shape but can't see the expression on his face. I don't need to see it. He's not smiling. His gray eyes are galvanized steel.

"The timing is either a coincidence or it's not," I say. "The basic tenet in criminal investigations, John. It's always one or the other."

"Let's not trivialize this."

"I'm doing anything but."

"If a living person was put in your damn cooler, I can't think of much worse," he says flatly.

"We don't know—"

"It's just a damn shame after all this." As if everything we've built over the past few years is on the precipice of ruin.

"We don't know that what's been reported is accurate—" I start to say.

"I think it would be best if we bring the body here," he interrupts again. "AFDIL can work on the identification. Rockman will make sure the situation is well contained. We've got everything we need right here."

I'm stunned. Briggs wants to send a plane to Hanscom Field, the air force base affiliated with the CFC. He wants the Armed Forces DNA Identification Lab and probably other military labs and someone other than me to handle whatever has happened, because he doesn't think I'm competent. He doesn't trust me.

"We don't know if we're talking about federal jurisdiction," I remind him. "Unless you know something I don't."

"Look. I'm trying to do what's best for all involved." Briggs has his hands behind his back, his legs slightly spread, staring across the parking lot at me. "I'm suggesting we can dispatch a C-Seventeen to Hanscom. We can have the body here by midnight. The CFC is a port mortuary, too, and that's what port mortuaries do."

"That's not what port mortuaries do. The point isn't for bodies to be received, then transferred elsewhere for autopsies and lab analysis. The CFC was never intended to be a first screening for Dover, a preliminary check before the experts step in. That was never my mandate, and it wasn't the agreement when thirty million dollars was spent on the facility in Cambridge."

"You should just stay at Dover, Kay, and we'll bring the body here."

"I'm requesting you refrain from intervening, John. Right now this case is the jurisdiction of the chief medical examiner of Massachusetts. Please don't challenge me or my authority."

A long pause, then he states rather than asks, "You really want that responsibility."

"It's mine whether I want it or not."

"I'm trying to protect you. I've been trying."

"Don't." That's not what he's trying. He doesn't have confidence in me.

"I can deploy Captain Avallone to help. It's not a bad idea."

I can't believe he would suggest that, either. "That won't be necessary," I reply firmly. "The CFC is perfectly capable of handling this."

"I'm on the record as having offered."

On the record with whom? It occurs to me uncannily that someone else is on the line or within earshot. Briggs is still standing in front of his window. I can't tell if anyone else might be in the suite with him.

"Whatever you decide," he then says. "I'm not going to step on you. Call me as soon as you know something. Wake me up if you have to." He doesn't say good-bye or good luck or it was nice having me here for half a year.

ucy and Marino have left my room. My suitcases, rucksacks, and Bankers Boxes are gone, and there is nothing left. It is as if I was never here, and I feel alone in a way I haven't for years, maybe decades.

I look around one last time, making sure nothing has been forgotten, my attention wandering past the microwave, the small refrigerator-freezer and coffeemaker, the windows with their view of the parking lot and Briggs's lighted suite, and, beyond, the black sky over the void of the empty golf course. Thick clouds pass over the oblong moon, and it glows on and off like a signal lantern, as if telling me what is coming down the tracks and if I should stop or go, and I can't see the stars at all. I worry that the bad weather is moving fast, carried on the same strong south wind that brings in the big planes and their sad cargo. I should hurry, but I'm distracted by the bathroom mirror, by the person in it, and I pause to look at myself in the glare of fluorescent lights. *Who are you now? Who really?*

My blue eyes and short blond hair, the strong shape of my face and figure, aren't so different, I decide, are remarkably the same, considering my age. I have held up well in my windowless places of concrete and stainless steel, and much of it is genetic, an inherited will to thrive in a family as tragic as a Verdi opera. The Scarpettas are from hearty Northern Italian stock, with prominent features, fair skin and hair, and well-defined muscle and bone that stubbornly weather hardship and the abuses of self-indulgence most people wouldn't associate with me. But the inclinations are there, a passion for food, for drink, for all things desired by the flesh, no matter how destructive. I crave beauty and feel deeply, but I'm an aberration, too. I can be unflinching and impervious. I can be immutable and unrelenting, and these behaviors are learned. I believe they are necessary. They aren't natural to me, not to anyone in my volatile, dramatic family, and that much I know is true about what I come from. The rest I'm not so sure about.

My ancestors were farmers and worked for the railroads, but in recent years my mother has added artists, philosophers, martyrs, and God knows what to the mix as she has set about to research our genealogy. According to her, I'm descended from artisans who built the high altar and choir stalls and made the mosaics at Saint Mark's Basilica and created the fresco ceiling of the Chiesa dell'Angelo San Raffaele. Somehow I have a number of friars and monks in my past, and most recently—based on what, I don't know—I share blood with the painter Caravaggio,

who was a murderer, and have some tenuous link to the mathematician and astronomer Giordano Bruno, who was burned at the
stake for heresy during the Roman Inquisition.

My mother still lives in her small house in Miami and is pre-
possessed with her efforts to explain me. I'm the only physician
in the family tree that she knows of, and she doesn't understand
why I've chosen patients who are dead. Neither my mother nor
my only sibling, Dorothy, could possibly fathom that I might be
partly defined by the terrors of a childhood consumed by tending
to my terminally ill father before I became the head of the house-
hold at the age of twelve. By intuition and training, I'm an expert
in violence and death. I'm at war with suffering and pain. Somehow I always end up in charge or to blame. It never fails.

I shut the door on what has been my home not just for six
months but more than that, really. Briggs has managed to remind
me where I'm from and headed. It's a course that was set long
before this past July, as long ago as 1987, when I knew my destiny was public service and didn't know how I could repay my
medical school debt. I allowed something as mundane as money,
something as shameful as ambition, to change everything irrevocably and not in a good way—indeed, in the worst way. But I was
young and idealistic. I was proud and wanted more, not understanding then that more is always less if you can't be sated.

Having gotten full rides through parochial school and Cornell
and Georgetown Law, I could have begun my professional life un-
burdened by the obligations of debt. But I'd turned down Bowman
Gray Medical School because I wanted Johns Hopkins badly. I
wanted it as badly as I'd ever wanted anything, and I went there

without benefit of financial aid, and what I ended up owing was impossible. My only recourse was to accept a military scholarship as some of my peers had done, including Briggs, whom I was acquainted with in the earliest stage of my profession, when I was assigned to the Armed Forces Institute of Pathology, the AFIP, the parent organization of the AFME. A quiet stint of reviewing military autopsy reports at Walter Reed Army Medical Center in Washington, D.C., Briggs led me to believe, and once my debt was paid, I'd move on to a solid position in civilian legal medicine.

What I didn't plan on was South Africa in December of '87, what was summertime on that distant continent. Noonie Pieste and Joanne Rule were filming a documentary and about my same age when they were tied up in chairs, beaten, and hacked, broken bottle glass shoved up their vaginas, their windpipes torn out. Racially motivated crimes against two young Americans. "You're going to Cape Town," Briggs said to me. "To investigate and bring them home." Apartheid propaganda. Lies and more lies. *Why them and why me?*

As I take the stairs down to the lobby, I tell myself not to think about this right now. *Why am I thinking about it at all?* But I know why. I was yelled at over the phone this morning. I was called names, and what happened more than two decades ago is now before me again. I remember autopsy reports that vanished and my luggage gone through. I remember being certain I would turn up dead, a convenient accident or suicide, or staged murder, like those two women I still see in my head. I see them as clearly as I did then, pale and stiff on steel tables, their blood washing through drains in the floor of a morgue so primitive we used handsaws to open their skulls, and there was no x-ray machine, and I had to bring my own camera.

I drop off my key at the front desk and replay the conversation I just had with Briggs, and I have clarity. I don't know why I didn't see the truth instantly, and I think of his remote tone, his chilly deliberateness, as I watched him through glass. I've heard him talk this way before, but usually it is directed at others when there is a problem of a magnitude that places it out of his hands. This is about more than his personal opinion of me. This is about something beyond his typical calculations and our conflicted past.

Someone has gotten to him, and it wasn't the press secretary, not anyone at Dover but higher up than that. I feel certain Briggs conferred with Washington after Marino divulged information, running his mouth and spinning his wild speculations before I'd had the chance to say a word. Marino shouldn't have discussed the Cambridge case or me. He's set something into motion he doesn't understand, because there's a lot he doesn't understand. He's never been military. He's never worked for the federal government and is clueless about international affairs. His idea of bureaucracy and intrigue is local police department policies, what he rubber-stamps as bullshit. He has no concept of power, the kind of power that can tilt a presidential election or start a war.

Briggs would not have suggested sending a military plane to Massachusetts for the transfer of a body to Dover unless he's gotten clearance from the Department of Defense, the DoD—in other words, the Pentagon. A decision has been made and I'm not part of it. Outside, in the parking lot, I climb into the van and won't look at Marino, I'm so angry.

"Tell me more about the satellite radio," I say to Lucy, because I intend to get to the bottom of this. I intend to find out what Briggs knows or has been led to believe.

"A Sirius Stiletto," Lucy says from the dark backseat as I turn up the heat because Marino is always hot while the rest of us freeze. "It's basically nothing more than storage for files, plus a power source. Of course, it also works as a portable XM radio, just as it's designed to, but it's the headphones that are creative. Not ingenious but technically clever."

"They've got a pinhole camera and a microphone built in," Marino offers as he drives. "Which is why I think the dead guy was the one doing the spying. How could he not know he had an audiovisual recording system built into his headphones?"

"He might not have known. It's possible someone was spying on him and he had no idea," Lucy says to me, and I sense she and Marino have been arguing about it. "The pinhole is on top of the headband but in the edge of it and hard to see. Even if you noticed, it wouldn't necessarily cross your mind that built inside is a wireless camera smaller than a grain of rice, an audio transmitter that's no bigger, and a motion sensor that goes to sleep after ninety seconds if nothing's moving. This guy was walking around with a micro-webcam that was recording onto the radio's hard drive and an additional eight-gig SD card. It's too soon for me to tell you if he knew it—in other words, if he rigged this up himself. I know that's what Marino thinks, but I'm not at all sure."

"Does the SD card come with the radio, or was it added aftermarket?" I inquire.

"Added. A lot of storage space, in other words. What I'm

curious about is if the files were periodically downloaded elsewhere, like onto his home computers. If we can get hold of them, we might know what this is about."

Lucy is saying that the video files she has looked at so far don't tell us much. She has reason to suspect the dead man has a home computer, possibly more than one of them, but she hasn't found anything that might tell us where he lived or who he is.

"What's stored on the hard drive and SD card go back only as far as February fifth, this past Friday," she continues. "I don't know if that means the surveillance just started or, more likely, these video files are large and take up a lot of space on the hard drive. They probably get downloaded somewhere, and what's on the hard drive and SD card gets recorded over. So what's here may be just the most recent recordings, but that doesn't mean there aren't others."

"Then these video clips were probably downloaded remotely."

"That's what I would do if it were me doing the spying," Lucy says. "I'd log in to the webcam remotely and download what I wanted."

"What about watching in real time?" I then ask.

"Of course. If he was being spied on, whoever's doing it could log on to the webcam and watch him as it's happening."

"To stalk him, to follow him?"

"That would be a logical reason. Or to gather intelligence, to spy. Like some people do when they suspect their person is cheating on them. Whatever you can imagine, it's possible."

"Then it's possible he inadvertently recorded his own death." I feel a glint of hope and at the same time am deeply disturbed by the thought. "I say 'inadvertently' because we don't know what we're dealing with. For example, we don't know if he intentionally recorded his own death, if he's therefore a suicide, and I'm not ready to rule out anything."

"No way he's a suicide," Marino says.

"At this point, we shouldn't rule out anything," I repeat.

"Like a suicide bomber," Lucy says. "Like Columbine and Fort Hood. Maybe he was going to take out as many people as he could in Norton's Woods and then kill himself, but something happened and he never got the chance."

"We don't know what we're dealing with," I say again.

"The Glock had seventeen rounds in the magazine and one in the chamber," Lucy tells me. "A lot of firepower. You could certainly ruin someone's wedding. We need to know who got married and who attended."

"Most of these people have extra magazines," I reply, and I know all about the shootings at Fort Hood, at Virginia Tech, at far too many places, where assailants open fire without necessarily caring who they kill. "Usually these people have an abundance of ammunition and extra guns if they're planning on mass murder. But I agree with you. The American Academy of Arts and Sciences is a high-profile place, and we should find out who got married there yesterday and who the guests were."

"I figure you're a member," Marino says to me. "Maybe you got a contact for getting a list of members and a schedule of events."

"I'm not a member."

"You're kidding."

I don't offer that I haven't won a Nobel Prize or a Pulitzer and don't have a Ph.D., just an M.D. and a J.D., and they don't count. I could remind him that the Academy may not be relevant anyway, because nonmembers can rent the building. All it takes is connections and money. But I don't feel like giving Marino detailed explanations. He shouldn't have called Briggs.

"Good news and not so good about the recordings." Lucy reaches over the back of the seat and hands me her iPad. "Good news, as I've pointed out, is it doesn't appear anything's been deleted, at least not recently. Which could be an argument in favor of him being the one doing the spying. You might speculate that if someone had him under surveillance and had something to do with his death, that person likely would have logged on to the Web address and scrubbed the hard drive and SD before people like us could look."

"Or how about remove the damn radio and headphones from the damn scene?" Marino says. "If he was being stalked, hunted down, and whoever's doing it whacked him? Well, if it was me, I'd grab the headset and radio and keep walking. So I'm betting he was the one doing the recording. I don't believe for a minute someone else was. And I'm betting this guy was involved in something, and whatever the reason for the spy equipment, he was the only one who knew about it. What sucks is there's no recording of the perp, of whoever whacked him, which is significant. If he was confronted by someone while he was walking his dog, why didn't the headphones record it?"

"The headphones didn't record it because he didn't see the person," Lucy replies. "He wasn't looking at whoever it was."

"Assuming there was a person who somehow caused his death," I remind both of them.

"Right," she says. "The headphones pretty much pick up whatever the wearer is looking at, the camera on the crown of his head, pointing straight out like a third eye."

"Then whoever whacked him came up from behind," Marino states conclusively. "And it happened so fast the victim never even turned around. Either that or it was some kind of sniper attack. Maybe he was shot with something from a distance. Like a dart with poison. Aren't there some poisons that cause hemorrhaging? May sound far-fetched, but shit like this happens. Remember the KGB spy poked with an umbrella that had ricin in the tip? He was waiting at a bus stop, and no one saw a thing."

"It was a Bulgarian dissident who worked for the BBC, and it's not a certainty it was an umbrella, and you're getting deeper into the woods without a map," I tell him.

"Ricin wouldn't drop you in your tracks, anyway," Lucy says. "Most poisons won't. Not even cyanide gas. I don't think he was poisoned."

"This isn't helpful," I answer.

"My map is my experience as a cop," Marino says to me. "I'm using my deductive skills. They don't call me Sherlock for nothing." He taps his baseball cap with a thick index finger.

"They don't call you Sherlock at all." Lucy's voice from the back.

"It's not helpful," I repeat, looking at his big shape as he drives, at his huge hands on the wheel, which rubs against his gut even when he's in what he considers his fighting shape.

"Aren't you the one always telling me to think outside the box?" Defensiveness hardens his tone.

"Guessing isn't helpful. Connecting dots that might be the wrong dots is reckless, and you know it," I say to him.

Marino has always been inclined to jump to conclusions, but it's gotten worse since he took the job in Cambridge, since he went to work for me again. I blame it on a military presence in our lives that is as constant as the massive airlifters flying low over Dover. More directly, I blame it on Briggs. Marino is ridiculously enamored of this powerful male forensic pathologist who is also a general in the army. My connection to the military has never mattered to him or even been acknowledged, not when it was part of my past, not when I was recalled to a special status after 9/11. Marino has always ignored my government affiliations as if they don't exist.

He stares straight ahead, and headlights of an approaching car illuminate his face, touched by disgruntledness and a certain lack of comprehension that is part of who he is. I might feel sorry for him because of the affection I can't deny, but not now. Not under the circumstances. I won't let on that I'm upset.

"What else did you share with Briggs—in addition to your opinions?" I ask Marino.

When he doesn't answer, Lucy does. "Briggs saw the same thing you're about to see," she says. "It wasn't my idea, and I didn't e-mail them, just so we're clear."

"Didn't e-mail what exactly?" But I know what exactly, and my incredulity grows. Marino sent evidence to Briggs. It's my case, and Briggs has been given information first.

"He wanted to know," Marino says, as if that's a good enough reason. "What was I supposed to tell him?"

"You shouldn't have told him anything. You went over my head. It's not his case," I reply.

"Yeah, well, it is," Marino says. "He was appointed by the surgeon general, meaning he basically was hired by the president, so I'd say that means he outranks everyone in this van."

"General Briggs isn't the chief medical examiner of Massachusetts, and you don't work for him. You work for me." I'm careful how I say it. I try to sound reasonable and calm, the way I do when a hostile attorney is trying to dismantle me on the witness stand, the way I do when Marino is about to erupt into an unseemly display of loud profanities and slammed doors. "The CFC has a mixed jurisdiction and can take federal cases in certain situations, and I realize it's confusing. Ours is a joint initiative between the state and federal governments and MIT, Harvard. And I realize that's an unprecedented concept and tricky, which is why you should have let me handle it instead of bypassing me." I try to sound easygoing and matter-of-fact. "The problem about involving General Briggs prematurely, about involving him precipitously, is things can take on a life of their own. But what's done is done."

"What do you mean? 'What's *done*'?" Marino sounds less sure of himself. I detect an anxious note, and I'm not going to help him out. He needs to think about what has been done, because he's the one who did it.

"What's the not-so-good news?" I turn around and ask Lucy.

"Take a look," she says. "It's the last three recordings made, including a minute here and there when the headset was jostled by the EMTs, the cops, and this morning by me when I started looking at it in my lab."

The iPad's display glows brightly, colorfully, in the dark, and I tap on the icon for the first video file she has selected, and it begins to play. I see what the dead man was seeing yesterday at three-oh-four p.m., a black-and-white greyhound curled up on a blue couch in a living room that has a heart-of-pine floor and a blue-and-red rug.

The camera moves as the man moves because he has the headphones on and they are recording: a coffee table covered with books and papers neatly stacked, and what looks like architectural or engineering drafting vellum with a pencil on top; a window with wooden blinds that are closed; a desk with two large flat-screen monitors and two silver MacBooks, a phone plugged into a charger, possibly an iPhone, and an amber glass smoking pipe in an ashtray; a floor lamp with a green shade; a fleece dog bed and scattered toys. I get a glimpse of a door that has a dead bolt and a sliding lock, and on a wall are framed photographs and posters that go by too abruptly for me to see the details. I will wait to study them later.

So far I observe nothing that tells me who the man is or where he lives, but I get the impression of the small apartment or maybe the house of someone who likes animals, is financially comfortable, and is mindful of security and privacy. The man, assuming this is his place and his dog, is highly evolved intellectually and technically, is creative and organized, possibly smokes marijuana, and has chosen a pet that is a needy companion, not a trophy but a creature that has suffered cruelty in a former life and can't possibly fend for itself. I feel upset for the dog and worry about what has happened to it.

Certainly the EMTs, the police, didn't leave a helpless greyhound in Norton's Woods yesterday, lost and alone in the New England weather. Benton told me it was eleven degrees this morning in Cambridge, and before the night is out, it will snow. Maybe the dog is at the fire department's headquarters, well fed and attended to around the clock. Maybe Investigator Law took it home or some other police person did. It's also possible no one realized the dog belonged to the man who died. Dear God, that would be awful.

"What happened to the greyhound?" I have to ask.

"Got no idea," Marino says, to my dismay. "Nobody knew until this morning when Lucy and me saw what you're looking at. The EMTs don't remember seeing a greyhound running loose, not that they were looking, but the gate leading into Norton's Woods was open when they got there. As you probably know, the gate's never locked and is wide open a lot of the time."

"He can't survive in freezing conditions. How could people not notice the poor thing unleashed and running loose? Because

I can't imagine he wasn't running around in the park for at least a few minutes before he ran out of the open gate. Common sense would tell you that when his master collapsed, the dog didn't suddenly flee from the woods and onto the street."

"A lot of people take their dogs off the leashes and let them run loose in the parks like Norton's Woods," Lucy says. "I know I do with Jet Ranger."

Jet Ranger is her ancient bulldog, and he doesn't exactly run.

"So maybe nobody noticed because it didn't look out of the ordinary," she adds.

"Plus, I think everybody was a little preoccupied with some guy dropping dead," Marino states the obvious.

I look out at military housing on a poorly lit road, at aircraft that are bright and big like planets in the overcast dark. I can't make sense of what I'm being told. I'm surprised the greyhound didn't stay close to his master. Maybe the dog panicked or there's some other reason no one noticed him.

"The dog's bound to show up," Marino goes on. "No way people in an area like that are going to ignore a greyhound wandering around by itself. My guess is one of the neighbors or a student has it. Unless it's possible the guy was whacked and the killer took the dog."

"Why?" I puzzle.

"Like you've been saying, we need to keep an open mind," he answers. "How do we know that whoever did it wasn't watching nearby? And then at an opportune moment, took off with the dog, acting like it belonged to him?"

"But why?"

"It could be evidence that would lead to the killer for some reason," he suggests. "Maybe lead to an identification. A game. A thrill. A souvenir. Who the hell knows? But you'll notice from the video clips at one point the leash was taken off him, and guess what? It hasn't showed up. It didn't come in with the headphones or the body."

The dog's name is Sock. On the iPad's display, the man is walking and clucking his tongue, telling Sock it's time to go. *"Let's go, Sock,"* he coaxes in a pleasant baritone voice. *"Come on, you lazy doggie, it's time for a walk and a shit."* I detect a slight accent, possibly British or Australian. It could be South African, which would be weird, a weird coincidence, and I need to get South Africa off my mind. *Focus on what's before you,* I tell myself as Sock jumps off the couch, and I notice he has no collar. Sock— a male, I assume, based on the name—is thin, and his ribs show slightly, which is typical for greyhounds, and he is mature, possibly old, and one of his ears is ragged as if once torn. A rescue retired from the racetrack, I feel sure, and I wonder if he has a microchip. If so and if we can find him, we can trace where he's from and possibly who adopted him.

A pair of hands enters the frame as the man bends over to loop a red slip lead around Sock's long, tapered neck, and I notice a silver metal watch with a tachymeter on the bezel and catch the flash of yellow gold, a signet ring, possibly a college ring. If the ring came in with the body, it might be helpful, because it might be engraved. The hands are delicate, with tapered fingers and light-brown skin, and I get a glimpse of a dark-green jacket and baggy black cargo pants and the toe of a scuffed brown hiking boot.

The camera fixes on the wall over the couch, on wormy chest-nut paneling and the bottom of a metal picture frame, and then a poster or a print rises into view as the man stands up, and I get a close look at a reproduction of a drawing that is familiar. I recognize da Vinci's sixteenth-century sketch of a winged flapping device, a flying machine, and I think back a number of years—when was it exactly? The summer before 9/11. I took Lucy to an exhibition at London's Courtauld Gallery, "Leonardo the Inventor," and we spent many entranced hours listening to lectures by some of the most eminent scientists in the world while studying da Vinci's conceptual drawings of water, land, and war machines: his aerial screw, scuba gear, and parachute, his giant crossbow, self-propelled cart, and robotic knight.

The great Renaissance genius believed that art is science and science is art, and the solutions to all problems can be found in nature if one is meticulous and observant, if one faithfully seeks truth. I have tried to teach my niece these lessons most of her life. I have repeatedly told her we are instructed by what is around us if we are humble and quiet and have courage. The man I am watching on the small device I hold in my hands has the answers I need. *Talk to me. Tell me. Who are you, and what happened?*

He is walking toward the door that is dead-bolted with the slide lock pulled across, and the perspective abruptly shifts, the camera angle changes, and I wonder if he has adjusted the position of the headphones. Maybe he didn't have them completely over his ears and now he's about to turn on music as he heads out. He walks past something mechanical and crude-looking, like a grotesque sculpture made of metal scrap. I pause on the image but can't get a good look at whatever it is, and I decide that when I have the luxury of time I'll replay the clips as often as I want and study every detail carefully, or if need be, get Lucy to forensically enhance the images. But right now I must accompany the man and his dog to the wooded estate not even a block from Benton's and my house. I must witness what happened. In several minutes he will die. *Show me and I'll figure it out. I'll learn the truth. Let me take care of you.*

The man and the dog go down four flights of stairs in a poorly lit stairwell, footsteps sounding light and quick against uncarpeted wood, and the two of them emerge on a loud, busy street. The sun is low, and patches of snow are crusty on top with black dirt, reminding me of crushed Oreo cookies, and whenever the man glances down, I see wet pavers and asphalt, and the sand and salt from snow removal. Cars and people move jerkily and lurch as he turns his head, scanning as he walks, and music plays in the background, Annie Lennox on satellite radio, and I hear only what is audible outside the headphones, what is being picked up by the mike inside the top of the headband. The man must have the volume turned up high, and that's not good, because he might not hear someone come up behind him. If he's worried about his security, so worried that he double-locks his apartment door and carries a gun, why isn't he worried about not hearing what is going on around him?

But people are foolish these days. Even reasonably cautious people multitask ridiculously. They text-message and check e-mail while driving or operating other dangerous machinery or while crossing a busy street. They talk on their cell phones while riding bicycles and while Rollerblading, and even while flying. How often do I tell Lucy not to answer the helicopter phone; doesn't matter that it's Bluetooth-enabled and hands-free. I see what the man sees and recognize where he's walking, on Concord Avenue, moving at a good clip with Sock, past redbrick apartment buildings and the Harvard Police Department and the dark-red awning of the Sheraton Commander Hotel across the street from the Cambridge Common. He lives very near the Common, in an older apartment building that has at least four floors.

I wonder why he doesn't take Sock into the Common. It's a popular park for dogs, but he and his greyhound continue past statues and cannons, lampposts, bare oak trees, benches, and cars parked at meters lining the street. A yellow Lab chases a fat squirrel, and Annie Lennox sings, *"No more 'I love you's' . . . I used to have demons in my room at night . . ."* I am the man's eyes and ears at the time the headphones are recording, and I have no reason to suspect he knows about the hidden camera and mike or that any such thing is on his mind at all.

I don't get the sense he has a dark plan or is spying as he walks his dog. Except that he has a Glock semiautomatic pistol and eighteen rounds of nine-millimeter ammunition under his green jacket. Why? Is he on his way to shoot someone, or is the gun for self-protection, and if so, what did he fear? Maybe it was a habit of his, a normal routine to walk around armed. There are people like that, too. People who don't think twice about it. Why did he grind the serial number off the Glock, or did someone else do it? It enters my mind that the hidden recording devices built into his headphones might be an experiment of his or a research project. Certainly Cambridge and its surrounds are the mecca of technical innovations, which is one of the reasons the DoD, the Commonwealth of Massachusetts, Harvard, and MIT agreed to establish the CFC on the north bank of the Charles River in a biotech building on Memorial Drive. Maybe the man was a graduate student. Maybe he was a computer scientist or an engineer. I watch what is on the iPad's display, abrupt, shaky images of Mather Court apartments, a playground, Garden Street, and the tilted, worn headstones of the Old Burying Ground.

In Harvard Square, his attention fixes on the Crimson Corner newsstand, and he seems to think of walking in that direction, perhaps to buy a paper from the overstocked selection that Benton and I love. This is our neighborhood, where we prowl for coffee and ethnic food, and papers and books, ending up with takeout and armloads of wonderful things to read that we pile on the bed on weekends and holidays when I'm home. The *New York Times* and the *Los Angeles Times,* the *Chicago Tribune,* and the *Wall Street Journal,* and if one doesn't mind news a day or two old, there are fat papers from London, Berlin, and Paris. Sometimes we find *La Nazione* and *L'espresso,* and I read to us about Florence and Rome, and we look at ads for villas to rent and fantasize about living like the locals, about exploring ruins and museums, the Italian countryside and the Amalfi Coast.

The man pauses on the crowded sidewalk and seems to change his mind about something. He and Sock trot across the street, on Massachusetts Avenue now, and I know where they are headed, or I think I do. A left on Quincy Street, and they are walking more briskly, and the man has a plastic bag in his hand, as if Sock isn't going to hold out much longer. Past the modern Lamont

Library and the Georgian Revival brick Harvard Faculty Club and Fogg Museum, and the Gothic stone Church of the New Jerusalem, and they turn right on Kirkland Avenue. It is the three of us, I am with them, cutting over to Irving, turning left on it, minutes from Norton's Woods, minutes from Benton's and my house, listening to Five for Fighting on the satellite radio . . . *"even heroes have the right to bleed . . ."*

I feel a growing sense of urgency with each step as we move closer to the man dying and the dog being lost in the bitter cold, and I desperately don't want it. I'm walking with them as if leading them into it because I know what's ahead and they don't, and I want to stop them and turn them back. Then the house is on our left, three-story, white with black shutters and a slate roof, Federal-style, built in 1824 by a transcendentalist who knew Emerson, Thoreau, and the Norton of *Norton's Anthology* and Norton's Woods. Inside the house, Benton's and my house, are original woodwork and molding, and plaster ceilings with exposed beams, and over the landings of the main staircase are magnificent French stained-glass windows with wildlife scenes that light up like jewels in the sun. A Porsche 911 is in the narrow brick driveway, exhaust fogging out of the chrome tailpipes.

Benton is backing up his sports car, the taillights glowing like fiery eyes as he brakes for a man and his dog walking past, and the man has his headphones turned toward Benton, maybe admiring the Porsche, a black all-wheel-drive Turbo Cabriolet that he keeps as shiny as patent leather. I wonder if he will remember the young man in the bulky green coat and his black-and-white greyhound or if they really registered at the time, but I know Benton.

He'll become obsessed, maybe as obsessed with the man and his dog as I am, and I search my memory for what Benton did yesterday. Late afternoon he dropped by his office at McLean because he'd forgotten to bring home the case file of the patient he was to evaluate today. A few degrees of separation, a young man and his old dog, who are about to be parted forever, and my husband alone in his car heading to the hospital to pick up something he forgot. I'm watching it all unfold as if I'm God, and if this is what it's like to be God, how awful that must be. I know what's going to happen and can't do a thing to stop it.

3

realize the van has stopped and Marino and Lucy are getting out. We are parked in front of the John B. Wallace Civil Air Terminal, and I stay put. I continue to watch what is playing on the iPad as Lucy and Marino begin unloading my belongings.

Cold air rushes in through the open tailgate while I puzzle over the man's decision to walk Sock in Norton's Woods, in what's called Mid-Cambridge, almost in Somerville. Why here? Why not closer to where he lived? Was he meeting someone? A black iron gate fills the display, and it is partially opened and his hand opens it wide, and I realize he has put on thick black gloves, what look like motorcycle gloves. Are his hands cold, or is there another reason? Maybe he does have a sinister plan. Maybe he intends to use the gun. I imagine pulling back the slide of a nine-millimeter pistol and pressing the trigger while wearing bulky gloves, and it seems illogical.

I hear him shake open the plastic bag, and then I see it as he looks down and I catch a glimpse of something else, what looks like a tiny wooden box. *A stash box,* I think. Some of them are made of cedar and even have a tiny hygrometer in them like a humidor, and I recall the amber glass smoking pipe on the desk inside the apartment. Maybe he likes to walk his dog in Norton's Woods because it is remote and usually quite private, and of little interest to the police unless there is a VIP or high-level event that requires security. Maybe he enjoys coming here and smoking weed. He whistles at Sock, bends over, and slips the lead off him, and I can hear him say, *"Hey, boy, do you remember our spot? Show me our spot."* Then he says something that's muffled. I can't quite make it out. *"And for you,"* it sounds like he says, followed by, *"Do you want to send one . . . ?"* Or *"Do you send one . . . ?"* After playing it twice I still can't understand what he is saying, and it may be that he is bent over and talking into his coat collar.

Who is he talking to? I don't see anyone nearby, just the dog and the gloved hands, and then the camera angle shifts up as the man straightens up and I see the park again, a vista of trees and benches, and off to one side a stone walkway near the building with the green metal roof. I catch glimpses of people and conclude by the way they are bundled up for the cold that they aren't wedding guests but most likely are walking in the park just like the man is. Sock trots toward shrubs to leave his deposit, and his master moves deeper into the gracious wooded estate of ancient elms and green benches.

He whistles and says, *"Hey, boy, follow me."*

In shaded areas around thick clumps of rhododendrons the snow is deep and churned up with dead leaves and stones and broken sticks that make me think morbidly of clandestine graves, of sloughed-off skin and weathered bones that have been gnawed on and scattered. He is scanning, looking around, and the hidden camera pauses on the three-tier green metal roof of the glass-and-timber building I can see from the sunporch at Benton's and my house. As the man turns his head, I see a door on the first floor that leads outside, and the camera pauses again on a woman with gray hair standing outside the door. She is dressed in a suit and a long brown leather coat and is talking on her phone.

The man whistles and makes a gritty sound as he walks on the slate gravel path toward Sock, to pick up what the dog has left . . . *"and this emptiness fills my heart . . ."* Peter Gabriel sings. I think of the young soldier with the same name who burned up in his Humvee, and I smell him as though his foul odors are still trapped deep inside my nose. I think of his mother and her grief and anger on the phone when she called me this morning. Forensic pathologists aren't always thanked, and there are times when those left behind act as if I am the reason their loved one is dead, and I try to remember that. *Don't take it personally.*

The gloved hands shake out the rumpled plastic bag again, the type one gets at the market, and then something happens. The man's gloved hand flies up at his head, and I hear the jostle of his hand hitting the headphones as if he's swatting at something, and he exclaims, *"What the . . . ? Hey . . . !"* in a breathy, startled way.

Or maybe it is a cry of pain. But I don't see anything or anyone, just the woods and distant figures in it. I don't see his dog, and I don't see him. I back up the recording and play it again. His black gloved hand suddenly enters the frame, and he blurts out, *"What the . . . ?"* then, *"Hey . . . !"* I decide he sounds stunned and upset, as if something has knocked the wind out of him.

I play it again, listening for anything else, and what I detect in his tone is protest and maybe fear, and, yes, pain, as if someone has elbowed him or bumped him hard on a busy sidewalk. Then the tops of bare trees rush up and around. Chipped bits of slate zoom in and get large as he thuds down on the path, and either he is on his back or the headphones have come off. The screen is fixed on an image of bare branches and gray sky, and then the hem of a long black coat swishes past, flapping as someone walks swiftly, and another loud jostling noise and the picture changes again. Bare branches and a gray sky but different branches showing through the slats of a green bench. It happens so fast, so unbelievably fast, and then the voices and the sounds of people get loud.

"Someone call nine-one-one!"

"I don't think he's breathing."

"I don't have my phone. Call nine-one-one!"

"Hello? There's . . . uh, yeah, in Cambridge. Yes, Massachusetts. *Je-sus!* Hurry, hurry; they fucking have me on hold. Je-sus, hurry! I can't believe this. Yes, yes, a man, he's collapsed and doesn't seem to be breathing . . . Norton's Woods at the corner of Irving and Bryant . . . Yes, someone is trying CPR. I'll stay on . . . I'm staying on. Yes, I mean, I don't . . . She wants to know if he's still not breathing. No, no, he's not breathing! He's not moving. He's not breathing! . . . I didn't really see it, just looked over and noticed he was on the ground, suddenly he was on the ground . . ."

I press pause and get out of the van, and it is cold and very windy as I walk quickly into the terminal. It is small, with restrooms and a sitting area, and an old television is turned on. For a moment I watch Fox News and fast-forward the video on the iPad while Lucy leans against the front desk and pays the landing fee with a credit card. I continue to stare at images of bare branches showing between the slats of green-painted wood, certain now that the headphones ended up under a bench, the camera fixed straight up as the XM radio plays. . . . *"Dark lady laughed and danced . . ."* The music is louder because the headphones aren't pressed against the man's head, and it seems absurdly incongruous to be listening to Cher.

Voices off-camera are urgent and excited, and I hear the sounds of feet and the distant wail of a siren as my niece chats with an older man, a retired fighter pilot now working at Dover part-time as a fixed base operator, he is happy to tell her.

". . . In 'Nam. So that would have been, what, an F-Four?" Lucy chats with him.

"Oh, yeah, and the Tomcat. That was the last one I flew. But Phantoms were still around, you know, as late as the eighties. You build them right and they last like you wouldn't believe. Look how long the C-Five's been around. And still some Phantoms in

Israel, I think. Maybe Iran. Nowadays those left in the U.S., we use them for unmanned targets, as drones. One hell of an aircraft. You ever seen one?"

"In Belle Chasse, Louisiana, at the Naval Air Station. Took my helicopter down there to help with Katrina."

"They've been experimenting with hurricane-busting, using Phantoms to fly into the eye." He nods.

The screen on the iPad goes black. The headphones weren't recording anymore, and I'm convinced that when the man fell to the ground they must have ended up some distance away under a bench. The motion sensor wasn't detecting enough activity to prevent it from dozing, and that's curious to me. How exactly did his headphones get knocked off and end up where they did? Maybe someone kicked them out of the way. It could have been accidental if that's what happened, perhaps by a person trying to help him, or it could have been deliberate by a person who was covertly recording him, stalking him. I think of the hem of the black coat flapping by, and I fast-forward intermittently, looking for the next images, listening for sounds, but nothing until four-thirty-seven p.m., when the woods and the darkening sky swing wildly, and bare hands loom large and paper crackles as the headphones are placed inside a brown bag, and I hear a voice say, ". . . Colts all the way." And another voice says, "Saints are gonna take it. They got . . ." Then murky darkness and muffled voices, and nothing.

Finding the TV remote on the arm of a couch inside the terminal, I switch the channel to CNN and listen to the news and watch the crawl, but not a word about the man on the video clips. I need to ask about Sock again. Where is the dog? It's not acceptable that no one seems to know. I fix on Marino as he enters the sitting area, pretending not to see me because he is sulking, or maybe he regrets what he's done and is embarrassed. I refuse to ask him anything, and it feels as if the missing dog is somehow his fault, as if everything is Marino's fault. I don't want to forgive him for e-mailing the video clips to Briggs, for talking to him first. If I don't forgive Marino for once, maybe he'll learn a lesson for once, but the problem is I'm never quite able to convince myself of any case I make against him, against anyone I care about. Catholic guilt. I don't know what it is, but already I am softening toward him, my resolve getting weaker. I feel it happening as I search channels on the television, looking for news that might damage the CFC, and he walks over to Lucy, keeping his back to me. I don't want to fight with him. I don't want to hurt his feelings.

I walk away from the TV, convinced at least for the moment that the media doesn't know about the body waiting for me in my Cambridge morgue. Something as sensational as that would be a headline, I reason. Messages would be landing nonstop on my iPhone. Briggs would have heard about it and said something. Even Fielding would have alerted me. Except I've heard nothing from Fielding about anything at all, and I try to call him again. He doesn't answer his cell phone, and he's not in his office. Of course not. He never works this late, for God's sake. I try him at his home in Concord and get voicemail again.

"Jack? It's Kay," I leave another message. "We're about to take off from Dover. Maybe you can text or e-mail me an update. Investigator Law hasn't called back, I assume? We're still waiting for photographs, and have you heard anything about a missing dog, a greyhound? The victim's dog, named Sock, last seen in Norton's Woods." My voice has an edge. Fielding is ducking me, and it's not the first time. He's a master at disappearing acts, and he should be. He's staged enough of them. "Well, I'll try you again when we land. I assume you'll meet us at the office, probably sometime between nine-thirty and ten. I've sent messages to Anne and Ollie, and maybe you can make sure they are there. We need to take care of this tonight. Maybe you could check with Cambridge PD about the dog? He might have a microchip. . . ."

It sounds silly to belabor my point about Sock. What the hell would Fielding know about it? He couldn't be bothered to go to the scene, and Marino's right. Someone should have gone.

Lucy's Bell 407 is black with dark tinted glass in back, and she unlocks the doors and baggage compartment as wind buffets the ramp.

A wind sock is stiffly pointed north like a horizontal traffic cone, and that's good and bad. The wind will still be on our tail but so will the storm front, heavy rains mixed with sleet and snow. Marino begins to load my luggage while Lucy walks around the helicopter, checking antennas, static ports, rotor blades, the emergency pop-out floats and the bottles of nitrogen that inflate them, then the aluminum alloy tail boom and its gear box, the hydraulic pump and reservoir.

"If someone was spying on him, covertly recording him, and

realized he was dead, then the person had something to do with it," I say to her, apropos of nothing. "So wouldn't you expect that person to have remotely deleted the video files recorded by the headphones, at least gotten rid of them on the hard drive and SD card? Wouldn't such a person want to make sure we didn't find any recordings or have a clue?"

"Depends." She grabs hold of a handle on the fuselage and inserts the toe of her boot into a built-in step, climbing up.

"If it were you doing it," I ask.

"If it were me?" She opens fasteners and props open a panel of the lightweight aluminum skin. "If I didn't think anything significant or incriminating had been recorded, I wouldn't have deleted them." Using a small but powerful SureFire flashlight, she inspects the engine and its mounts.

"Why not?"

Before she can answer, Marino walks over to me and says to no one in particular, "I got to make a visit. Anybody else needs to, now's the time." As if he's the chief steward and reminding us that there is no restroom on the helicopter. He's trying to make up to me.

"Thanks, I'm fine," I tell him, and he walks off across the dark ramp, back to the terminal.

"If it were me, this is what I'd do after he's dead," Lucy continues as the strong light moves over hoses and tubing, as she makes sure nothing is loose or damaged. "I'd download the video files immediately by logging on to the webcam, and if I didn't see anything that worried me, I'd leave them be."

She climbs up higher to check the main rotor, its mast, its swashplate, and I wait until she is back on the tarmac before I ask, "Why would you leave them be?"

"Think about it."

I follow her around the helicopter so she can climb up and check the other side. She almost seems amused by my questions, as if what I'm asking should be obvious.

"If they're deleted after he's dead, then someone else did it, right?" she says, checking under cowling, the light probing carefully.

Then she drops back down to the ramp.

"Of course he couldn't do it after he was dead." I wait to answer her, because she could get hurt climbing all over her helicopter, especially when she's up around the rotor mast. I don't want her distracted. "So that's why you would leave them if you were the one spying on him and knew he was dead or were the one responsible for his death."

"If I were spying on him, if I followed him so I could kill him, hell, yes, I'd leave the last video recordings made, and I wouldn't grab the headphones from the scene, either." She shines the brilliant light along the fuselage again. "Because if people saw him wearing them out there in the park or on his way to the park, why are they now missing? The headphones are rather beefy and noticeable."

We walk around to the nose of the helicopter.

"And if I take the headphones, I'd have to take his satellite radio, too, dig in his coat pocket and get that out, have to take time to go to all this trouble after he's on the ground, and hope nobody

saw me. And what about earlier files downloaded somewhere, assuming the spying has gone on for a while? How is that explained
if there's no recording device that shows up and we find recordings
on a home computer or server somewhere? You know what they
say." She opens an access panel above the pitot tube and shines the
light in there. "For every crime, there are two—the act itself and
then what you do to cover it up. Be smarter to leave the headphones, the video files, alone, to let cops or someone like you or
me assume he was recording himself, which is what Marino believes, but I doubt it."

She reconnects the battery. Her rationale for disconnecting it
whenever she leaves the helicopter for any period of time is that
if someone manages to get inside the cockpit and is lucky while
fiddling with the throttle and switches, they could accidentally
start the engine. But not if the battery is disconnected. Doesn't
matter her hurry, Lucy always does a thorough preflight, especially if she's left her aircraft unattended, even if it's on a military
base. But it doesn't escape my attention that she is checking everything more thoroughly than usual, as if she suspects something or is uneasy.

"Everything A-okay?" I ask her. "Everything in good shape?"

"Making sure of it," she says, and I feel her distance more
strongly. I sense her secrets.

She trusts no one. She shouldn't. I never should have trusted
some people, either, going back to day one. People who manipulate and lie and claim it is for a cause. The right cause, a godly or
just cause. Noonie Pieste and Joanne Rule were smothered to
death in bed, probably with a pillow. That's why there was no

tissue response to their injuries. The sexual assaults, the hacks with machetes and slashes with broken glass, and even the ligatures binding them when they were tied up in the chairs, all of it postmortem. A godly cause, a just cause, in the minds of those responsible. An unthinkable outrage, and they got away with it. To this day they did. *Don't think about it. Focus on what is before you, not on the past.*

I open the left-front door and climb up on a skid, the wind gusting hard. Maneuvering myself around the collective and cyclic and into the left seat, I fasten my four-point harness as I hear Marino opening the door behind me. He is loud and big, and I feel the helicopter settle from his weight as he climbs into the back, where he always sits. Even when Lucy flies with only him as a passenger, he isn't allowed up front where there are dual controls that he can nudge or bump or use as an armrest because he doesn't think. He just doesn't think.

Lucy gets in and begins another preflight, and I help her by holding the checklist, and together we go through it. I've never had a desire to fly the various aircraft my niece has owned over the years, or to ride her motorcycles or drive her fast Italian cars, but I'm fine to copilot, am handy with maps and avionics. I know how to switch the radios to the necessary frequencies or enter squawks and other information into the transponder or Chelton Flight System. If there was an emergency, I probably could get the helicopter safely to the ground, but it wouldn't be pretty.

". . . Overhead switches in the off position," I continue going down the list.

"Yes."

"Circuit breakers in."

"They are." Lucy's agile fingers touch everything she checks as we go down the plastic-laminated list.

Momentarily, she flips on the boost pumps and rolls the throttle to flight idle.

"Clear to the right." As she looks out her side window.

"Clear to the left." As I look out at the dark ramp, at the small building with its lighted windows and a Piper Cub tied down a safe distance away in the shadows, its tarp shaking in the wind.

Lucy pushes the start switch, and the main rotor blade begins to turn slowly, heavily, thudding faster like a heartbeat, and I think of the man. I think of his fear, of what I detected in those three words he exclaimed.

"What the . . . ? Hey . . . !"

What did he feel? What did he see? The lower part of a black coat, the loose skirt of a black coat swishing past. Whose coat? A wool dress coat or a trench coat? It wasn't fur. Who was wearing the long, black coat? Someone who didn't stop to help him.

"What the . . . ? Hey . . . !" A startled cry of pain.

I replay it in my mind again and again. The camera angle dropping suddenly, then fixing straight up at bare branches and gray sky, then the hem of the long, black coat moving past in the frame for an instant, maybe a second. Who would step around someone in distress as if he was an inanimate object, such as a rock or a log? What kind of human being would ignore someone who grabbed his chest and collapsed? The person who caused it, perhaps. Or someone who didn't want to be involved for some reason. Like witnessing an accident or assault and speeding off so you don't become part of the investigation. A man or a woman? Did I see shoes? No, just the hem or skirt of the coat flapping, and then another jostling sound and the picture was replaced by different bare trees showing through the underside of a green-painted bench. Did the person in the long black coat kick the headphones under the bench there so they didn't record something else that was done?

I need to look at the video clips more closely, but I can't do it now. The iPad is in back, and there isn't time. The blades rapidly beat the air, and the generator is online. Lucy and I put our headsets on. She flips more overhead switches, the avionics master, the flight and navigation instruments. I turn the intercom switch to "crew only" so Marino can't hear us and we can't hear him while Lucy talks to the air traffic controller. The strobes, the pulse and night scanner landing lights, blaze on the tarmac, painting it white as we wait for the tower to clear us for takeoff. Entering destinations in the touch-screen GPS and in the moving map display and the Chelton, I correct the altimeters. I make sure the digital fuel indicator matches the fuel gauge, doing most things at least twice, because Lucy believes in redundancy.

The tower releases us, and we hover-taxi to the runway and climb on course to the northeast, crossing the Delaware River at eleven hundred feet. The water is dark and ruffled by the wind, like molten metal flowing thickly. The lights of land flicker through trees like small fires.

e change our heading, veering toward Philadelphia, because the visibility deteriorates closer to the coast. I flip the intercom switch so we can check on Marino.

"You all right back there?" I'm calmer now, too preoccupied with the long black coat and the man's startled exclamation to be angry with Marino.

"Be quicker to cut through New Jersey," his voice sounds, and he knows where we are, because there is an in-flight map on a video screen inside the rear passenger compartment.

"Fog and freezing rain, IFR conditions in Atlantic City. And it isn't quicker," Lucy replies. "We'll be on 'crew only' most of the time so I can deal with flight following."

Marino is cut out of our conversation again as we are handed off from one tower to the next. The Washington sectional map is open in my lap, and I enter a new GPS destination of Oxford, Connecticut, for an eventual fuel stop, and we monitor weather on the radar, watching blocks of solid green and yellow encroach upon us from the Atlantic. We can outrun, duck, and dodge the storms, Lucy says, as long as we stay inland and the wind continues to favor us, increasing our ground speed to what at this moment is an impressive one hundred and fifty-two knots.

"How are you doing?" I keep up my scan for cell towers and other aircraft.

"Better when we get where we're going. I'm sure we'll be fine and can outrun this mess." She points at what's on the weather radar display. "But if there's a shadow of a doubt, we'll set down."

She wouldn't have come to pick me up if she thought we might have to spend the night in a field somewhere. I'm not worried. Maybe I don't have enough left in me to worry about yet one more thing.

"How about in general? How are you doing?" I say into the mike, touching my lip. "You've been on my mind a lot these past few weeks." I try to draw her out.

"I know how hard it is to keep up with people under the circumstances," she says. "Every time we think you're coming back, something changes, so we've all quit thinking it."

Three times now the completion of my fellowship was delayed by one urgent matter or another. Two helicopters shot down in one day in Iraq with twenty-three killed. The mass murder at Fort Hood, and most recently, the earthquake in Haiti. Armed forces MEs got deployed or none could be spared, and Briggs wouldn't release me from my training program. A few hours ago, he attempted to delay my departure again, suggesting I stay in Dover. As if he doesn't want me to go home.

"I figured we'd get to Dover and find out you had another week, two weeks, a month," Lucy adds. "But you're done."

"Apparently, they're sick of me."

"Let's hope you don't get home only to turn around and go back."

"I passed my boards. I'm done. I've got an office to run."

"Someone needs to run it. That's for sure."

I don't want to hear more damning comments about Jack Fielding.

"And things are fine elsewhere?" I ask.

"They've almost finished the garage, big enough for three cars even with the washing bay. Assuming you tandem park." She starts on a construction update, reminding me how disengaged I've been from what's going on at my own home. "The rubberized flooring is in, but the alarm system isn't ready. They weren't going to bother with glass breakers, and I said they had to. Unfortunately, one of the old wavy-glass windows original to the building didn't survive the upgrade. So you've got a bit of a breeze in the garage at the moment. Did you know all this?"

"Benton's been in charge."

"Well, he's been busy. You got the freq for Millville? I think one-two-three-point-six-five."

I check the sectional and affirm the frequency and enter it into Comm 1. "How are you?" I try again.

I want to know what I'm coming home to in addition to a dead man awaiting me in the morgue cooler. Lucy won't tell me how she is, and now she's accusing Benton of being busy. When she says something like that, she doesn't mean it literally. She's very tense. She's obsessively watching the instruments, the radar screens, and what's outside the cockpit, as if she's expecting to get into a dogfight or to be struck by lightning or to have a mechanical failure. I'm sensing something is off about her, or maybe I'm the one in a mood.

"He has a big case," I add. "An especially bad one."

We both know which one I mean. It's been all over the news about Johnny Donahue, the patient at McLean, a Harvard student who last week confessed to murdering a six-year-old boy with a nail gun. Benton believes the confession is false, and the cops, the DA, are unhappy with him. People want the confession to be genuine, because they don't want to think someone like that might still be loose. I wonder how the evaluation went today, as I envision Benton's black Porsche backing out of our driveway on the video clips I just watched. He was on his way to McLean to pick up Johnny Donahue's case file when a young man and a greyhound walked past our house. Several degrees of separation. The human web connecting all of us, connecting everyone on earth.

"Let's keep one-two-seven-point-three-five on Comm Two so we can monitor Philly," Lucy is saying, "but I'm going to try to stay out of their Class B. I think we can, unless this stuff pushes in any tighter from the coast."

She indicates the green and yellow shapes on the satellite weather radar display that show precipitation moving closer, as if trying to bully us northwest into the bright skyline of downtown Philadelphia, fly us into the high-rises.

"I'm fine," she then says. "Sorry about him, because I can tell you're pissed." She points her thumb toward the back, meaning Marino. "What'd he do besides be his usual self?"

"Were you listening when he talked to Briggs?"

"That was in Wilmington. I was busy paying for fuel."

"He shouldn't have called him."

"Like telling Jet Ranger not to drool when I get out the bag of treats. It's Pavlovian for Marino to shoot off his mouth to Briggs, to show off. Why are you more surprised than usual?" Lucy asks as if she already knows the answer, as if she's probing, looking for something.

"Maybe because it's caused a worse problem than usual." I tell her about Briggs wanting the body transported to Dover.

I tell her that the chief of the Armed Forces Medical Examiners has information he's not sharing, or at least I suspect that he is withholding something important from me. Probably because of Marino, I say. Because of what he's managed to stir up by going over my head.

"I don't think that's all of it by a long shot," Lucy says as her tail number is called out over the air.

She presses the radio switch on her cyclic and answers, and as she talks to flight following, I enter the next frequency. We hopscotch from airspace to airspace, the shapes on the weather radar mostly yellow now and bird-dogging us from the southeast, indicating heavy rains that at this altitude will create hazardous conditions as supercooled water particles hit the leading edges of the rotor blades and freeze. I watch for moisture on the Plexiglas windscreen and don't see anything, not one drop, while I wonder what Lucy is referring to. What's not it by a long shot?

"Did you notice what was in his apartment?" Lucy's voice in my headset, and I assume she means the dead man and what I watched on the video clips recorded by his headphones.

"You said that's not all of it." I go back to that first. "Tell me what you're referring to."

"I'm about to and didn't want to bring it up in front of Marino. He didn't notice, wouldn't know what it was, anyway, and I didn't point it out because I wanted to talk to you and I'm not sure he should know about it, period."

"Didn't point out what?"

"My guess is Briggs didn't need it pointed out," Lucy goes on. "He had a lot more time to look at the video clips than you did, and he or whoever else he's showed them to would have recognized the metal contraption near the door, sort of looks like a six-legged creepy crawler welded together with wires and composite pieces and parts, about the size of a stackable washer and dryer. Picked up by the camera for a second when the man and Sock were on their way out to Norton's Woods. I'm sure it wasn't lost on you, of all people."

"I caught a glimpse of what I thought was a crude metal sculpture." Obviously, I missed a connection she's made. A big one.

"A robot, and not just any robot," Lucy informs me. "A prototype developed for the military, what was supposed to be a tactical packbot for the troops in Iraq, and then another creative purpose was suggested that went over like the proverbial lead balloon."

A glint of recognition, and an ominous feeling begins working its way up from my gut, tightening my chest, creating awareness, then a memory.

"This particular model didn't last long," she continues, and I think I know what she's talking about.

MORT. Mortuary Operational Removal Transport. *Good God.*

"Never made it into service and is obsolete if not silly now, replaced by biologically inspired legged robots that can carry heavy loads over rough or slippery terrain," she says. "Like the quadruped called Big Dog that's all over YouTube. Damn thing can carry hundreds of pounds all day long in the worst conditions imaginable, jumps like a deer and regains its balance if it trips or slips or you kick it."

"MORT," I go ahead and say it. "Why would he have a pack-bot like MORT in his apartment? I think I'm misunderstanding something."

"You ever see it in person back then, when you got into a debate about it on Capitol Hill? And you're not misunderstanding anything. I'm talking about MORT."

"I never saw MORT in person." I saw it on videotaped demonstrations only, and I got into more than one debate, especially with Briggs. "Why would he have something like that?" I ask again about what Lucy claims is in the dead man's apartment.

"Creepy as hell. Like a giant mechanical ant, gas-powered," she says. "Sounds like a chain saw when it's ambulating slowly on its short, clunky legs with two sets of grippers in front like Edward Scissorhands. If you saw it coming at you, you'd run like hell or maybe lob a grenade at it."

"But in his apartment? Why?" I remember demonstrations that I found horrifying, and heated discussions that became nasty skirmishes with colleagues including Briggs at the AFME, at Walter Reed, and in the Russell Senate Office Building.

MORT. The epitome of wrongheaded automation that became the source of a controversy in military and medical intelligence. It wasn't the technology that was such a terrible idea, it was the suggestion of how it should be used. I remember a hot summer morning in Washington, the heat rising off a sidewalk crowded with Boy Scouts touring the capital as Briggs and I argued. We were hot in our uniforms, frustrated and stressed, and I remember walking past the White House, people everywhere, and wondering what would be next. What other inhumanities would be offered by technology? And that was almost a decade ago, almost the Stone Age compared to now.

"I'm pretty sure—in fact, more than pretty sure—that's what's parked inside the guy's apartment," Lucy is saying. "And you don't buy something like that on eBay."

"Maybe it's a model," I suggest. "A facsimile."

"No way. When I zoomed in on it, I could see the composite parts in detail, some wear and tear on it from usage, probably from R-and-D on hard terrain and it got scraped up a little. I could even see the fiber-optic connectors. MORT wasn't wireless, which was just one of a number of things wrong with it. Not like what they're doing today with autonomous robots that have onboard computers and receive information through sensors controlled by man-wearable units instead of lugging around a cumbersome

Pelican case—based one. Like the military guys are doing so their field-embedded operators are hands-free when they're out with their robotic squads. This whole new thing with lightweight rugedized processors that you can wear in your vest, say you're operating an unmanned ground vehicle or the armed robots, the SWORDS unit, the Special Weapons Observation Remote Direct-Action System. A robotic infantry armed with M-two-forty-nine light machine guns. Not something I'm comfortable with, and I know how you feel about that."

"I'm not sure that there are words for how I feel about it," I reply.

"Three SWORDS units so far in Iraq, but they haven't fired their weapons yet. Nobody's sure how to get a robot to have that kind of judgment. Artificial EQ. A rather daunting prospect but I'm sure not impossible."

"Robots should be used for peacekeeping, surveillance, as pack mules."

"That's you but not everyone."

"They should not make decisions about life and death," I go on. "It would be like autopilot deciding whether we should fly through these clouds rolling toward us."

"Autopilot could if my helicopter had moisture and temperature sensors. Throw in force transducers and it will land all by itself as light as a feather. Enough sensors and you don't need me anymore. Climb in and push a button like the Jetsons. Sounds crazy, but the crazier, the better. Just ask DARPA. You got any idea how much money DARPA invests in the Cambridge area?"

Lucy lowers the collective, losing altitude and bleeding off speed as another ghostly patch of clouds rolls toward us in the dark.

"Besides what it's invested in the CFC?" she then says.

Her demeanor is different, even her face is different, and she's no longer trying to hide what has come over her. I know this mood. I know it all too well. It is an old mood I haven't seen in a while, but I know it like I know the symptoms of a disease that has been in remission.

"Computers, robotics, synthetic biology, nanotechnology, the more off the wall, the better," she continues. "Because there's no such thing as mad scientists anymore. I'm not sure there's any such thing as science fiction. Come up with the most extreme invention you can imagine, and it's probably being implemented somewhere. It's probably old news."

"You're suggesting this man who died in Norton's Woods is connected to DARPA."

"Somehow he is, in some capacity. Don't know how directly or indirectly," Lucy answers. "MORT isn't being used anymore, not by the military, not for any purpose, but was *Star Wars* stuff about eight or nine years ago when DARPA stepped up funding for military and intelligence-gathering applications of robotics, bio and computer engineering. And forensics and other applications germane to our war dead, to what happens in combat, in theater."

It was DARPA that funded the research and development of the RadPath technology we use in virtual autopsies at Dover and now at the CFC. DARPA funded my four-month fellowship that turned into six.

"A substantial percentage of research grants are going to Cambridge area labs, to Harvard and MIT," Lucy says. "Remember when everything became about the war?"

It's getting harder to remember a time when that wasn't true. War has become our national industry, like automotives and steel and the railroads once were. That's the dangerous world we live in. I don't believe it can change.

"The brilliant idea that robots like MORT could be utilized in theater to recover casualties so troops didn't risk their lives for a fallen comrade?" Lucy reminds me.

Not a brilliant idea but an unfortunate one. A supremely stupid one, I thought at the time and still do. Briggs and I weren't on the same side about it. He'll never give me credit for saving him from a PR misstep that could have injured him badly.

"The idea was aggressively researched for a while and then got tabled," Lucy adds.

It got tabled because using robots for such a purpose supposes they can decide a fallen soldier, a human being, is fatally injured or dead.

"DoD got a lot of shit for it, at least internally, because it seemed cold-blooded and inhumane," she says.

Deservedly. No one should die in the grippers of something mechanical dragging them off the battlefield or out of a crashed vehicle or from the rubble of a building that has collapsed.

"What I'm getting at is the early generations of this technology have been buried by DoD, relegated to a classified scrap yard or salvaged for pieces and parts," Lucy says. "Yet your guy in the cooler has one in his apartment. Where'd he get it? He's got a connection. He has drafting paper on the coffee table. He's an inventor, an engineer, something like that, and somehow involved in classified projects that require a high level of security clearance, but he's a civilian."

"How can you be so sure he's a civilian?"

"Believe me, I'm sure. He's not experienced or trained, and he sure as hell isn't military intel or a government agent or he wouldn't walk around listening to music turned up loud and armed with an expensive pistol that has the serial number ground off—in other words, he probably bought it on the street. He'd have something that would never be traced to him or anyone, something you use once and toss. . . ."

"We don't know who the gun is traced to?" I want to make sure.

"Not that I know of, not yet, which is ridiculous. This guy isn't undercover. Hell, no. I think what he is is scared," Lucy says as if she knows it for a fact. "Was," she adds. "He *was.* And someone had him under surveillance—my belief, anyway—and now he's dead. In my opinion, it's not a coincidence. I suggest you exercise extreme caution when talking to Marino."

"Sometimes he has terrible judgment, but he's not trying to do me in."

"He's also not medical intel like you are, and his understanding only goes so far as not discussing cases with his buddies at the bowling alley and not talking to reporters. He thinks it's perfectly fine to confide in people like Briggs, because he's got no sense when it comes to military brass." Lucy's demeanor is as uneasy and somber as I've seen her since I can't remember when. "In a case like this one, you talk to me, you talk to Benton."

"Have you told Benton what you just told me?"

"I'll let you explain about MORT, because he's not likely to understand what it is. He wasn't around when you went through all that with the Pentagon. You tell him, and then all of us can talk. You, him, me, and that's it, at least for now, because you don't know who is what, and you damn well better have your facts straight and know who's us and who's them."

"If I can't trust Marino with a case like this, or any case, for that matter, why do I have him?" Defensiveness sharpens my tone, because Marino was her idea, too.

She encouraged me to hire him as CFC's chief of operational investigations, and she talked him into it, too, although it wasn't exactly a hard sell. He'd never admit it, but he doesn't want to be anywhere I'm not, and when he realized I was going to be in Cambridge, he suddenly got disenchanted with the NYPD. He lost interest in Assistant DA Jaime Berger, whose office he was assigned to. He got into a feud with his landlord in the Bronx. He started complaining about New York taxes, even though he'd been paying them for several years. He said it was intolerable having no place to ride a motorcycle and no place to park a truck, even though he owned neither at the time. He said he had to move.

"It's not about trust. It's about acknowledging limitations." It's an uncharacteristically charitable thing for Lucy to say. Usually, people are simply bad or useless and deserve whatever punishment she decides.

She eases up on the collective and makes subtle adjustments with the cyclic, increasing our speed and making sure we don't climb into the clouds. The night around us is impenetrably dark, and there are stretches where I can't see lights on the ground, suggesting we are flying over trees. I enter the frequency for McGuire so we can monitor its airspace while keeping an eye on the Traffic Collision Avoidance System, the TCAS. It is showing no other aircraft anywhere. We might be the only ones flying tonight.

"I don't have the luxury to allow for limitations," I tell my niece. "Meaning I probably made a mistake hiring Marino. I probably made a bigger one hiring Fielding."

"Not probably, and not the first time. Jack walked out on you in Watertown and went to Chicago, and you should have left him there."

"In all fairness, we lost our funding in Watertown. He knew the office was probably going to close, and it did."

"That's not why he left."

I don't respond, because she's right. It isn't why. Fielding wanted to move to Chicago because his wife had been offered a job there. Two years later, he asked if he could come back. He said he missed working for me. He said he missed his family. Lucy, Marino, Benton, and me. One big, happy family.

"It isn't just them. You have a problem with everybody there," Lucy then says.

"So nobody should have been hired. Including you, I suppose."

"Probably not me, either. I'm not exactly a team player." She was fired by the FBI, by ATF. I don't think Lucy can be supervised by anybody, including me.

"Well, this is a nice thing to come home to," I reply.

"That's the danger with a prototype installation that no matter what anyone says is in fact both civilian and military, has both local and federal jurisdiction and also academic ties," Lucy says. "You're neither-nor. Staff members don't exactly know how to act or aren't capable of staying within boundaries, assuming anyone even understands the boundaries. I warned you about that a long time ago."

"I don't remember you warning me. I just remember you pointing it out."

"Let's enter the freq for Lakehurst and squawk VFR, because I'm ditching flight following," she decides. "We get pushed any farther west and we're going to have a crosswind that will slow us down more than twenty knots and we'll be grounded for the night in Harrisburg or Allentown."

nowflakes are crazed like moths in landing lights and the wind of our blades as we set down on the wooden dolly. The skids tentatively touch, then spread heavily as the weight settles, and four sets of headlights begin to move toward us from the security gate near the FBO.

The headlights move slowly across the ramp, illuminating snow that is falling fast, and I recognize the silhouette of Benton's green Porsche SUV. I recognize the Suburban and the Range Rover, both of them black. I don't know the fourth car, a sleek, dark sedan with a chrome mesh grille. Lucy and Marino must have driven here separately today and left their SUVs with the line crew, which makes sense. My niece always arrives at the airport well in advance of everyone else so she can get the helicopter ready, so she can check it from the pitot tube on its nose to the stinger on its tail boom. I haven't seen her like this in a while, and as we wait the two minutes in flight idle before she finishes the shutdown, I try to remember the last time, pinpoint it exactly, in hopes of figuring out what's happening. Because she isn't telling me.

She won't unless it fits into her overall plan, and there is no getting information out of her when she's not ready to offer it, which can be never in extreme situations. Lucy thrives on covert behavior, is far more comfortable being who she's not than who she is, and that's always been the case, going back to her earliest years. She feeds on the power of secrecy and is energized by the drama of risk, of real danger. The more threatening, the better. All she's revealed to me so far is that an obsolete robot in the dead man's apartment is a DARPA-funded packbot called MORT that at one time was intended for mortuary operations in theater, in other words, body removal in war, a mechanical Grim Reaper. MORT was insensitive and inappropriate, and I fought it aggressively years ago, but the peculiarity of the dead man having such a thing in his apartment doesn't explain Lucy's behavior.

When was it that she scared me so badly, not that it's been only once, but the time I thought she might end up in prison? Seven or eight years ago, I decide, when she came back from Poland, where she was involved in a mission that had to do with Interpol, with special ops that to this day I'm unclear about. I'll never know just how much she would tell me if I pushed hard enough, but I won't. I've chosen to remain foggy about what she did over there. What I know is enough. It's more than enough. I would never say that about Lucy's feelings, health, or general well-being, because I care intensely about every molecule of her, but I can say it about some complex and clandestine aspects of the way she has lived. For her own good and mine, there are details I will not ask about. There are stories I don't want to be told.

During the last hour of our flight here to Hanscom Field, she got increasingly preoccupied, impatient, and impossibly vigilant, and it is her vigilance that has a special caliber. That's what I recognize. Vigilance is the weapon she draws when she feels threatened and goes into a certain mode I used to dread. In Oxford, Connecticut, where we stopped for fuel, she wouldn't leave the helicopter unattended, not for a second. She supervised the fuel truck and made me stand guard in the cold while she trotted inside the FBO to pay because she didn't trust Marino with guard duty, as she put it. She told me that when they had refueled in Wilmington, Delaware, earlier today en route to Dover, he was too busy on the phone to care about security or notice what was going on around them.

She said she watched him through the window as he paced on the tarmac, talking and gesturing, no doubt swept up in telling Briggs about the man who allegedly was still alive when he was locked inside my cooler. Not once did Marino look at the helicopter, Lucy reported to me. He was oblivious when another pilot strolled over to check it out, squatting so he could inspect the FLIR, the Nightsun, and peering through Plexiglas into the cabin. It didn't enter Marino's mind that the doors were unlocked, as was the fuel cap, and of course there is no such thing as securing the cowling. One can get to the transmission, the engine, the gear boxes, the vital organs of a helicopter, by the simple release of latches.

All it takes is water in the fuel tank for a flameout in flight, and the engine quits. Or sprinkle a small amount of contaminant into the hydraulic fluid, maybe dirt, oil, or water into the reservoir, and the controls will fail like power steering in a car, but a little more serious when you're two thousand feet in the air. If you really want to create havoc, contaminate both the fuel and the hydraulic fluid so you have a flameout and a hydraulic failure simultaneously, Lucy described in gory detail as we flew with the intercom on "crew only" so Marino couldn't hear. That would be especially unfortunate after dark, she said, when emergency landings, which are difficult enough, are far worse, because you can't see what's under you and had better hope it isn't trees, power lines, or some other obstruction.

Of course, the sabotage she fears most is an explosive device, and she's obsessed in general with explosives and what they're really used for and who is using them against us, including the U.S. government using them against us if it suits certain agendas. So I had to listen to that for a while before she went on to depress me further by explaining how simple it would be to plant such a thing, preferably under luggage or a floor mat in back so that when it detonates it takes out the main fuel tank beneath the rear seats. Then the helicopter turns into a crematorium, she told me, and this made me think of the soldier in the Humvee again and his devastated mother lashing out at me over the phone. I was making unfortunate associations most of the time we were flying, because for better or worse, any disaster described evokes vivid examples from my own cases. I know how people die. I know exactly what will happen to me if I do.

Lucy cuts the throttle and pulls the rotor brake down, and the instant the blades stop turning, the driver's door of Benton's SUV opens. The interior light doesn't go on. It won't in any one of the three SUVs on the ramp, because cops and federal agents, including former ones, have their quirks. They don't sit with their backs to the door. They hate to fasten their seat belts, and they don't like interior lights in their vehicles. They are imprinted to avoid ambushes and restraints that might impede their escape. They resist turning themselves into illuminated targets. They are vigilant but not as vigilant as Lucy has been these past few hours.

Benton walks toward the helicopter and waits near the dolly with his hands in the pockets of an old black shearling coat I gave him many Christmases ago, his silver hair mussed by the wind. He is tall and lean against the snowy night, and his features are keen in the uneven shadow and light. Whenever I see him after a long separation, it is with the eyes of a stranger, and I'm drawn to him all over again, just like the first time long ago in Virginia when I was the new chief, the first woman in America to run such a large medical examiner system, and he was a legend in the FBI, the star profiler and head of what was then the Behavioral Science Unit at Quantico. He walked into my conference room, and I was suddenly unnerved and unsure of myself, and it had nothing to do with the serial murders we were there to discuss.

"You know this guy?" he says into my ear as we hug. He kisses me lightly on the lips, and I smell the woodsy fragrance of his aftershave and feel the soft leather of his coat against my cheek.

I look past him to a man climbing out of the sedan, what I

now can see is a dark-blue or black Bentley that has the throaty purr of a V12 engine. He is big and overweight, with a jowly face and a fringe of thinning hair that flails in the wind. Dressed in a long overcoat, the collar up around his ears, and with gloves on, he stands a polite distance away with the detached demeanor of a limo driver. But I sense his awareness of us. He seems most interested in Benton.

"He must be waiting for someone else," I decide as the man looks at the helicopter, then looks at Benton again. "Or he's mixed up."

"Can I help you?" Benton steps closer to him.

"I'm looking for Dr. Scarpetta?"

"And why might you be looking for Dr. Scarpetta?" Benton is friendly but firm, and he gives nothing away.

"I was sent here with a delivery, and the instructions I got is the party would be on Dr. Scarpetta's helicopter or meeting it. What branch of service you with, or maybe you're Homeland Security? I see it's got a FLIR, a searchlight, a lot of special equipment. Pretty high-tech; how fast does it go?"

"What can I do for you?"

"I'm supposed to give something directly to Dr. Scarpetta. Is that you? I was told to ask for identification." The driver watches Lucy and Marino carry my belongings out of the passenger and baggage compartments. The driver isn't interested in me, not so much as a glance. I'm the wife of the tall, handsome man with silver hair. The driver thinks Benton is Dr. Scarpetta and that the helicopter is his.

"Let's get you out of here before this turns into a blizzard," Benton says, walking toward the Bentley in a way that gives the driver no choice but to follow. "I hear we're getting six to eight inches, but I think we're in for more, like we need it, right? What a winter. Where are you from? Not here. The south somewhere. I'm guessing Tennessee."

"You can tell after twenty-seven years? Guess I need to work on talking Yankee. Nashville. Was stationed here with the Sixty-sixth Air Base Wing and never got around to leaving. I'm not a pilot, but I drive pretty good." He opens the passenger door and leans inside. "You fly that thing yourself? I've never been in one. I knew right away your chopper wasn't air force. I guess if you're CIA, you're not going to tell me. . . ."

Their voices drift back to me as I wait on the ramp where Benton left me. I know better than to follow him to the Bentley but am unwilling to sit inside our car when I have no idea who the man is or what delivery he's talking about or how he knew someone named Scarpetta would be at Hanscom, either on a helicopter or meeting it, and what time it would land. The first person who comes to mind is Jack Fielding. It's likely he knows my itinerary, and I check my iPhone. Anne and Ollie have answered my text messages and are already at the CFC, waiting for us. But nothing from Fielding. *What is going on with him?* Something is, something serious. This can't be nothing more than his usual irresponsibility or indifference or erratic behavior. I hope he's all right, that he's not sick or injured or fighting with his wife, and I watch Benton tuck something into a coat pocket. He heads straight to the SUV, and that's his message to me. Get in and don't ask questions on the ramp. Something just transpired that he doesn't like, despite his relaxed, friendly act with the driver.

"What is it?" I ask him as we shut our doors at the same time Marino opens the back and starts shoving in my boxes and bags.

Benton turns up the heat and doesn't answer as more of my belongings are loaded, and then Marino comes around to my door. He raps a knuckle on the glass.

"Who the hell was that?" He stares off in the direction of the Bentley, and snow is falling thick and hard, frosting the bill of his baseball cap and melting on his glasses.

"Did many people know you and Lucy were heading out to Dover today?" Benton leans his shoulder against me as he talks to him.

"The general. And Captain What's-her-name, Avallone, when I called trying to get a message to the Doc. And certain people at our office knew. Why?"

"Nobody else? Maybe a mention in passing to the EMTs, to Cambridge police?"

Marino pauses, thinking, and a look passes over his face. He's not sure whom he told. He's trying to remember, and he's calculating. If he did something foolish, he won't want to admit it, has heard quite enough about how indiscreet he is. He doesn't intend to be chastised yet again, although, to be fair, he wouldn't have had a reason to behave as if it was classified information that he and Lucy were flying to Delaware to pick me up. It's not a state secret where I've been, only why I've been there, and I was supposed to come home tomorrow, anyway.

"No big deal if you did." Benton seems to be thinking the same thing I am. "I'm just trying to figure out how a messenger knew to meet the helicopter here, that's all."

"What kind of messenger drives a Bentley?" Marino says to him.

"Apparently, the kind who's been told your itinerary, including the helicopter's tail number," Benton replies.

"Goddamn Fielding. What the hell's he doing? He's fucking lost it, that's what." Marino takes off his glasses and then has nothing to wipe them with, and his face looks naked and strange without his old wire-rims. "I mentioned to a few people that you were probably coming back today instead of tomorrow. I mean, obviously certain people knew because of the problem we have with the dead guy bleeding and everything else." He directs this at me. "But Fielding's the one who knew exactly what you were doing, and he sure as hell knows Lucy's helicopter, since he's been in it before. Shit, you don't know the half of it," he adds darkly.

"We'll talk at the office." Benton wants him to shut up.

"What the hell do we really know about him? What the fuck's he up to? It's damn time to quit protecting him. He's sure as hell not protecting you," he says to me.

"Let's talk about this later," Benton replies with a warning in his tone.

"Setting you up somehow," Marino says to me.

"Now's not the time to get into it." Benton's voice flattens out.

"He wants your job. Or maybe he just doesn't want you to have it." Marino looks at me as he digs his hands into the pockets of his leather jacket and steps away from my window. "Welcome home, Doc." Flakes of snow blowing into the car are cold and wet on my face and neck. "Good to be reminded who you can really trust, right?" He stares at me as I roll up the glass.

Anticollision beacons flash red and white on the wingtips of parked jets as we drive slowly across the ramp toward the security gate, which has just swung open.

The Bentley drives through, and we are right behind it, and I notice its Massachusetts plate doesn't have *livery* stamped on it, suggesting the car isn't owned by a limousine company. I'm not surprised. Bentleys are unusual, especially around here, where people are understated and conservation-minded, even those who fly private. I seldom see Bentleys or Rolls-Royces, mostly Toyotas or Saabs. We pass the FBO for Signature, one of several flight services on the civilian side of the airfield, and I place my hand on the soft suede of Benton's coat pocket without touching the creamy white envelope barely protruding from it.

"Would you like to tell me what just happened?" It appears he was given a letter.

"Nobody should know you just flew here or that you might be here, shouldn't know anything about you personally or your whereabouts, period," Benton says, and his face and voice are hard. "Obviously, she called the CFC and Jack told her. She's certainly called there before, and who else but Jack?"

He says it as if it's really not a question, and I have no idea what he is referring to.

"I can't understand why he or anyone would talk to her, for

Christ's sake," Benton goes on, but I don't believe he doesn't understand whatever it is he's talking about. His tone says something else entirely. I don't sense that he's even surprised.

"Who?" Because I have no idea. "Who's called the CFC?"

"Johnny Donahue's mother. Apparently, that's her driver." Indicating the car up ahead.

The windshield wipers make a loud rubbery sound as they drag across the glass, pushing away snow that is turning to slush as it hits. I look at the taillights of the Bentley in front of us and try to make sense of what Benton is telling me.

"We should look at whatever it is." I mean the envelope in his pocket.

"It's evidence. It should be looked at in the labs," he says.

"I should know what it is."

"I finished evaluating Johnny this morning," Benton then reminds me. "I know his mother has called the CFC several times."

"How do you know?"

"Johnny told me."

"A psychiatric patient told you. And that's reliable information."

"I've spent a total of almost seven hours with him since he was admitted. I don't believe he killed anyone. There are a lot of things I don't believe. But I do believe his mother would call the CFC, based on what I know," Benton says.

"She can't really think we would discuss the Mark Bishop case with her."

"These days people think everything is public information, that they're entitled," he says, and it's not like him to make assumptions and to indulge in generalities. His statement strikes me as glib and evasive. "And Mrs. Donahue has a problem with Jack," Benton adds, and that comment strikes me as genuine.

"Johnny's told you his mother has a problem with Jack. And why would she have an opinion about him?"

"Some of this I can't get into." He stares straight ahead as he drives on the snowy road, and the snow is falling faster and slashes through the headlights and clicks against glass.

I know when Benton is keeping things from me. Usually, I'm fine with it. Right now I'm not. I'm tempted to slide the envelope out of his pocket and look at what someone, presumably Mrs. Donahue, wants me to see.

"Have you met her, talked to her?" I ask him.

"I've managed to avoid that so far, although she's called the hospital, trying to track me down, called several times since he was admitted. But it's not appropriate for me to talk to her. It's not appropriate for me to talk about a lot of things, and I know you understand."

"If Jack or anyone has divulged details about Mark Bishop to her, that's about as serious as it gets," I reply. "And I do understand your reticence, or I think I do, but I have a right to know if he's done that."

"I don't know what you know. If Jack's said anything to you," he says.

"About what specifically?"

I don't want to admit to Benton and most of all to myself that I can't remember precisely when I talked to Fielding last. Our conversations, when we've had them, have been perfunctory and brief, and I didn't see him at all when I was home for several days over the holidays. He had gone somewhere, presumably taken his family somewhere, but I'm not sure. Long months ago, Fielding quit sharing the details of his personal life with me.

"Specifically, this case, the Mark Bishop case," Benton says. "When it happened, for example, did Jack discuss it with you?"

Saturday, January 30, six-year-old Mark Bishop was playing in his backyard, about an hour from here in Salem, when someone hammered nails into his head.

"No," I answer. "Jack hasn't talked about it with me."

I was in Dover when the boy was murdered, and Fielding took the case, which was extraordinarily out of character, and I thought so then. He's never been able to deal with children but for some reason decided to deal with this one, and it shocked me. In the past, if the body of a child was en route to the morgue, Fielding absented himself. It made no sense at all that Fielding would take the Mark Bishop case, and I'm sorry I didn't return home, because that was my first impulse. I should have acted on it, but I didn't want to do to my second in command what Briggs just did to me. I didn't want to show a lack of faith.

"I've reviewed it thoroughly, but Jack and I haven't discussed it, although I certainly indicated I would make myself available if there was a need." I feel myself getting defensive and hate it when I get that way. "Technically, it's his case. Technically, I wasn't here." I can't stop myself, and I know it sounds weak, like I'm making excuses, and I feel annoyed with myself.

"In other words, Jack hasn't tried to share the details. I should say he's not shared his details," Benton says.

"Consider where I've been and what I've been doing," I remind him.

"I'm not saying it's your fault, Kay."

"What's my fault? And what do you mean, *'his'* details?"

"I'm asking if you've asked Jack about it. If maybe he's avoided discussing it with you."

"You know how he is when it's kids. At the time, I left him a message that one of the other medical examiners could handle it, but Jack took care of it. I was surprised he did, but that's how it went. As I've said, I've reviewed all of the records. His, the police, the lab reports, et cetera."

"So you really don't know what's going on with it."

"It seems you're saying I don't."

Benton is silent.

"Know what's going on in addition to the latest? The confession made by the Donahue boy?" I try again. "Certainly I know what's been in the news, and a Harvard student confessing to such a thing has been all over it. Obviously, what you're getting at is there are details I've not been told."

Again Benton doesn't answer. I imagine Fielding talking to Johnny Donahue's mother. It's possible Fielding gave her details about where I would be tonight, and she sent her driver to deliver an envelope to me, although the driver didn't seem to know Dr. Scarpetta was a woman. I look at Benton's black shearling coat. In the dark, I can make out the vague white edge of the envelope in his pocket.

"Why would anyone from your office talk to the mother of the person who's confessed to the crime?" Benton's question sounds more like a statement. It sounds rhetorical. "We absolutely sure nothing was leaked to the media about your leaving Dover today, maybe because of this case?" He means the man who collapsed in Norton's Woods. "Maybe there's a logical explanation for how she knew. A logical explanation other than Jack. I'm trying to be open-minded."

It doesn't sound like he's trying to be open-minded at all. It sounds like he believes Fielding told Mrs. Donahue for a reason, one I can't begin to fathom. Unless it's what Marino said minutes ago, that Fielding wants me to lose my job.

"You and I both know the answer." I hear the conviction in my tone and realize how certain I am of what Jack Fielding could be capable of. "Nothing's been in the news that I'm aware of. And even if Mrs. Donahue found out that way, it doesn't explain her knowing the tail number of Lucy's helicopter. It doesn't explain how she knew I was arriving by helicopter or would land at Hanscom or at what time."

Benton drives toward Cambridge, and the snow is a blizzard of flakes that are getting smaller. The wind is beating the SUV, gusting and shoving, the night volatile and treacherous.

"Except the driver thought you were me," I add. "I could tell by the way he was dealing with you. He thinks you're Dr. Scarpetta, and Johnny Donahue's mother certainly must know I'm not a man."

"Hard to say what she knows," Benton answers. "Fielding's the medical examiner in this case, not you. As you said, technically you have nothing to do with it. Technically, you're not responsible."

"I'm the chief and ultimately responsible. At the end of the day, all ME cases in Massachusetts are mine. I do have something to do with it."

"It's not what I meant, but I'm glad to hear you say it."

Of course it's not what he meant. I don't want to think about what he meant. I've been gone. Somehow I was supposed to be at Dover and at the same time get the CFC up and running without me. Maybe it was too much to ask. Maybe I've been deliberately set up for failure.

"I'm saying that since the CFC opened, you've been invisible," Benton says. "Lost in a news blackout."

"By design," I reply. "The AFME doesn't court publicity."

"Of course it's by design. I'm not blaming you."

"Briggs's design." I give voice to what I suspect Benton is getting at.

He doesn't trust Briggs. He never has. I've always chalked it up to jealousy. Briggs is a very powerful and threatening man, and Benton hasn't felt powerful or threatening since he left the FBI, and then there is a past Briggs and I share. He is one of very few people still in my life who predates Benton. It feels as if I was barely grown up when I first met John Briggs.

"The AFME didn't want you giving interviews about the CFC or publicly talking about anything relating to Dover until the CFC was set up and you were finished with your training," Benton goes on. "That's kept you out of the limelight for quite a while. I'm trying to remember the last time you were on CNN. At least a year ago."

"And coincidentally, I was supposed to step back into the limelight tonight. And coincidentally, CNN was canceled. The third time it's been canceled, as my return here was delayed and delayed."

"Yes. Coincidentally. A lot of coincidences," Benton says.

Maybe Briggs has compromised me and done so intentionally. How brilliant it would be to groom me for a bigger job, the biggest job so far, while systematically making me less visible. To silence me. Ultimately, to get rid of me. The idea of it is shocking. I don't believe it.

"Whose coincidences, that's what you would need to know," Benton then says. "And I'm not stating as fact that Briggs did anything Machiavellian. He's not the entire Pentagon. He's just one gear in a very big machine."

"I know how much you dislike him."

"It's the machine I don't like. It's always going to be there. Just make sure you understand it so you don't get chewed up by it."

Snow clicks and bounces against glass as we pass stretches of open fields and dense woods, and a creek runs hard against the guardrail to our right as we pass over a bridge. The air must be colder here, the snow small and icy as we drive in and out of pockets of changing weather that I find unsettling.

"Mrs. Donahue knows that the chief medical examiner and director of the CFC, someone named Dr. Scarpetta, is Jack's boss," Benton then says. "She had to know that if she went to the trouble to have something delivered to you. But maybe that's all she knows," he summarizes, offering an explanation for what just happened at the airport.

"Let's look at whatever it is." I want the envelope.

"It should go to the labs."

"She knows I'm Jack's boss but doesn't know I'm a woman." It seems preposterous, but it's possible. "Even though all she had to do was Google me."

"Not everybody Googles."

I'm reminded of how easy it is for me to forget that there are still technically unsophisticated people in the world, including someone who might have a chauffeur and a Bentley. Its taillights are far ahead of us now on the narrow two-lane road, getting smaller and more distant as the car drives too fast for the conditions.

"Did you show the driver your identification?" I ask.

"What do you think?"

Of course Benton wouldn't. "So he didn't realize you're not me."

"Not from anything I did or said."

"I guess Mrs. Donahue will continue to think Jack works for a man. Strange that Jack would tell her how to find me and not indicate how her driver might recognize me, at least indicate I'm not a man. Not even use pronouns that might indicate it. Strange. I don't know." I'm not convinced of what we're conjecturing. It doesn't feel right.

"I wasn't aware you were having so many doubts about Jack. Not that they aren't warranted." Benton is trying to draw me out. The FBI agent in him. I've not seen it in a while.

"Just don't say I'm twice bitten or thrice bitten or whatever. Please," I say with feeling. "I've heard it enough today."

"I'm saying I wasn't aware."

"And all I've been aware of is my usual misgivings and denials about him," I reply. "I've not had sufficient information to be more concerned than usual." My way of asking Benton to give me sufficient information if he has it, to not act like a cop or a mental-health practitioner. *Don't hold back,* I'm telling him.

But he does hold back. He doesn't say a word. His attention is fixed straight ahead, his profile sharp in the low illumination of the dashboard lights. This is the way it's always been with us. We step around confidential and privileged information. We dance around secrets. At times we lie. In the beginning, we cheated, because Benton was married to someone else. Both of us know how to deceive. It isn't something I'm proud of, and I wish it didn't continue to be necessary professionally. Especially right this minute. Benton is dancing around secrets, and I want the truth. I need it.

"Look, we both know what he's like, and yes, I've been invisible since the CFC opened," I continue. "I've been in a vacuum, doing the best I can to handle things long distance while working eighteen-hour days, not even time to talk to my staff by phone. Everything's been electronic, mostly e-mails and PDFs. I've hardly seen anyone. I should never have placed Jack in charge under the circumstances. When I hired him yet again and rode out of town, I set everyone up for exactly what's happened. And you did tell me so, and you aren't the only one."

"You've never wanted to believe you've got a serious problem with him," Benton says in a way that unsteadies me further. "Even if you've had plenty of them. Sometimes there's simply no sufficient evidence that will make us accept a truth we can't bear to believe. You can't be objective when it comes to him, Kay. I'm not sure I've ever understood the reason."

"You're right, and I hate it." I clear my throat and calm my voice. "And I'm sorry."

"I just don't know if I'll ever figure it out." He glances over at me, both hands on the wheel, and we're alone on a snow-blown road that is poorly lit, driving through a snowy darkness. The Bentley is no longer visible up ahead. "I'm not judging you."

"He wrecks his life and needs me again."

"It's not your fault he wrecks his life unless you haven't told me something. Actually, no matter what, it wouldn't be your fault. People wreck their own lives. They don't need others to do it."

"That's not entirely true. He didn't choose what happened to him as a child."

"And that's not your fault, either," Benton says, as if he knows more about Fielding's past than I've ever told him, what few details I have. I've always been careful not to probe my staff, especially not to probe Fielding. I know enough about his early tragedies to be mindful of what he might not want to talk about.

"Of course it sounds stupid," I add.

"Not stupid. Just a drama that will always end the same way. I've never completely understood why you feel the need to act it out with him. I feel like something happened. Something you've not told me."

"I tell you everything."

"We both know that's not true about either of us."

"Maybe I should just stick with dead people." I hear the bitterness in my tone, the resentment seeping through barriers I've carefully constructed most of my life. Maybe I don't know how to live without them anymore. "I know how to handle dead people just fine."

"Don't talk like that," Benton says quietly.

It's because I'm tired, I tell myself. It's because of what happened this morning when the black mother of a dead black soldier disparaged me over the phone and called me names, referred to my following not the Golden Rule but the *White Rule.* Then Briggs tried to override my authority. It's possible I've been set up by him. It's possible he wants me to fail.

"It's such a goddamn stereotype," Benton then says.

"Funny thing about stereotypes. They're usually based on something."

"Don't say things like that."

"There won't be any more problems with Jack. The drama will end, I promise. Assuming he hasn't already ended it, hasn't walked off the job. He's certainly done that before. He has to be fired."

"He's not you, never was or could be, and he's not your damn child." Benton thinks it is as simple as that, but it isn't.

"He has to be let go," I answer.

"He's a forty-six-year-old forensic pathologist who's never earned the trust you show him or anything the hell you do for him."

"I'm done with him."

"You are done with him. I'm afraid that's true and you're going to have to let him go," Benton says, as if a decision was made already, as if it isn't up to me. "What is it you feel so guilty about?" There's something in his tone, something about his demeanor. I can't put my finger on what it is. "Way back in your Richmond days when you were just getting started with him. Why the guilt?"

"I'm sorry I've caused so many problems." I evade his question. "I feel I'm the one who's let everybody down. I'm sorry I've not been here. I can't begin to express how sorry I am. I take responsibility for Jack, but I won't allow it anymore."

"Some things you can't take responsibility for. Some things aren't your fault, and I'm going to keep reminding you of that, and you'll probably keep believing it's your fault, anyway," my husband the psychologist says.

I'm not going to discuss what is my fault and what isn't, because I can't talk about why I've always been irrationally loyal to Jack Fielding. I came back from South Africa, and my penance was Fielding. He was my public service, what I sentenced myself to as punishment. I was desperate to do right by him because I was convinced I'd wronged everyone else.

"I'm taking a look." I mean at what is in Benton's coat pocket. "I know how to look at a letter without compromising it, and I need to see what Mrs. Donahue wrote to me."

I slide the envelope out, holding it lightly by its edges, and discover the flap is sealed with gray duct tape that partially covers an address engraved in an old-style serif typeface. I recognize the street as one in Boston's Beacon Hill, near the Public Garden, very close to where Benton used to own a brownstone that was in his family for generations. On the front of the envelope is *Dr. Kay Scarpetta: Confidential* written elaborately with a fountain pen, and I'm careful about touching anything else with bare hands, especially the tape. It is a good source for fingerprints, for DNA and microscopic materials. Latent prints can be developed on porous surfaces such as paper by using a reagent such as ninhydrin, I calculate.

"Maybe you've got a knife handy." I place the envelope in my lap. "And I need to borrow your gloves."

Benton reaches across me and opens the glove box, and inside is a Leatherman multi-tool knife, a flashlight, a stack of napkins. He pulls a pair of deerskin gloves out of his coat pockets, and my hands are lost in them, but I don't want to leave my fingerprints or eradicate those of someone else. I don't turn on the map-reading light, because the visibility is bad and getting worse. Illuminating what I'm doing with the flashlight, I slip a small blade into a corner of the envelope.

I slit it along the top and slide out two folded sheets of creamy stationery that are of heavy stock with a watermark I can't make out clearly, what looks like some type of emblazonment or family crest. The letterhead is the same Beacon Hill address, and the two pages are typed with a typewriter that has a cursive typeface, which is something I haven't seen in many years, maybe a decade at least. I read out loud:

Dear Dr. Scarpetta,

I hope you will excuse what I'm sure must seem an inappropriate and presumptuous gesture on my part. But I am a mother as desperate as a mother could possibly be.

My son Johnny has confessed to a crime I know he did not commit and could not have committed. Certainly he's had difficulties of late that resulted in our seeking treatment for him, but even so, he's never demonstrated any serious behavior problems, not even when he began Harvard as a withdrawn and bullied fifteen-year-old. If he was going to have a breakdown, I should think it would have been then, having left home for the first time and not possessing the normal skills for interacting with others and making friends. He did remarkably well until this past fall semester of his senior year, when his personality became alarmingly altered. <u>But he did not kill anyone!</u>

Dr. Benton Wesley, a consultant for the FBI and a member of the McLean Hospital staff, knows quite a lot about my son's background and developmental obstacles, and perhaps he is at liberty to discuss these details with you, since he hasn't seemed inclined to discuss them with your assistant, Dr. Fielding. Johnny's is a long, complex story, and I need you to hear it. Suffice it to say that when he was admitted at McLean last Monday, it was because he was deemed to be a danger to himself. He had not harmed anybody else or so much as intimated that he might. Then suddenly out of the blue he confessed to such a vicious and horrible crime, and in short order was transferred to a locked ward for the criminally insane. I ask you, how is it possible the authorities have been so quick to believe his ludicrous and deluded tales?

I must talk to you, Dr. Scarpetta. I know your office performed the autopsy on the little boy who died in Salem, and I believe it is reasonable to request a second opinion.

Of course you know Dr. Fielding's conclusion—that the murder was premeditated, carefully planned, a cold-blooded execution that was an initiation for a satanic cult. Something as monstrous as that is absolutely inconsistent with anything my son could do to anyone, and he has never had anything to do with cults of any description. It is outrageous to assume that his fondness for books and films with a horror or supernatural or violent theme might have influenced him to "act out."

Johnny suffers from Asperger's syndrome. He is spectacularly gifted in some areas and completely incompetent in others. He has very rigid habits and routines that he is obsessive about, and on January 30, he was eating brunch at The Biscuit with the person he is closest to, a supremely gifted graduate student named Dawn Kincaid, just as they do every Saturday morning from ten a.m. until one p.m. He could not, therefore, have been in Salem when the little boy was killed mid-afternoon.

Johnny has the remarkable ability to remember and parrot the most obscure details, and it is clear to me that what he has said to the authorities has come straight from what he's been told about the case and what's been in the news. He truly does seem to believe he is guilty (for reasons I can't begin to comprehend), and even claims that a "puncture wound" to his left hand was from the nail gun misfiring when he used it on the boy, which is fabricated. The wound is self-inflicted, a stab wound from a steak knife, and one of the many reasons we took him to McLean to begin with. My son seems determined to be severely punished for a crime he didn't commit, and the way things are going, he will get his wish.

Below are numbers to contact me. I hope you will have compassion and that I hear from you soon.

Sincerely,

Erica

Erica Donahue

6

return the sheets of heavy, stiff stationery to their envelope, then wrap the letter in napkins from the glove box to protect it as much as possible inside the zip-up compartment of my shoulder bag. If I have learned nothing else, it is that you can't go back. Once potential evidence has been cut through, contaminated, or lost, it's like an archaeologist's trowel shattering an ancient treasure.

"She doesn't seem to know you and I are married," I comment as trees thrash in the wind along the roadside, snow swirling whitely.

"She might not," Benton replies.

"Does her son know?"

"I don't discuss you or my personal life with patients."

"Then she may not know much about me."

I try to work out how it might be possible that Erica Donahue wouldn't tell her driver that the person he was to deliver the letter to is a small blonde woman, not a tall man with silver hair.

"She uses a typewriter, assuming she typed this herself," I continue to deduce. "And anyone who would go to so much trouble taping up the envelope to ensure confidentiality probably isn't going to let someone else type the letter. If she still uses a typewriter, it's unlikely she goes on the Internet and Googles. The watermarked engraved stationery, the fountain pen, the cursive typeface, possibly a purist, someone very precise, who has a very certain and set way of doing things."

"She's an artist," Benton says. "A classical pianist who doesn't share the same high-tech interests as the rest of her family. Husband's a nuclear physicist. Older son's an engineer at Langley. And Johnny, as she pointed out, is incredibly gifted. In math, science. Writing that letter won't help him. I wish she hadn't."

"You seem very invested in him."

"I hate it when people who are vulnerable are an easy out. Because someone is different and doesn't act like the rest of us, he must be guilty of something."

"I'm sure the Essex County prosecutor wouldn't be happy to hear you say that." I've assumed that's who hired Benton to evaluate Johnny Donahue, but Benton isn't acting like a consultant, certainly not like one for the DA's office. He's acting like something else.

"Misleading statements, lack of eye contact, false confessions. A kid with Asperger's and his never-ending isolation and search for friends," Benton says. "It's not uncommon for such a person to be overly influenced."

"Why would someone want to influence Johnny to take the blame for a violent crime?"

"All it takes is the suggestion of something suspicious, such as what a weird coincidence that you were talking crazy about going to Salem, and then that little boy was murdered there. Are you sure you hurt your hand when you stuck it in a drawer and got stabbed by a steak knife, or did it happen some other way and you don't remember? People see guilt, and then Johnny sees it. He's led to say what he thinks people want to hear and to believe what he thinks people want to believe. He has no understanding of the consequences of his behavior. People with Asperger's syndrome, especially teenagers, are statistically overrepresented among innocent people who are arrested and convicted of crimes."

Snowflakes are suddenly large and blowing wildly like white dogwood petals in a violent wind. Benton downshifts the Tiptronic transmission and lightly touches the brakes.

"Maybe we should pull over." I can't see the road as the headlights bounce off whiteness swarming all around us.

"Some freakish storm cell, like a microburst." He leans close to the steering wheel, peering straight ahead, as angry gusts of wind buffet us. "I think the best thing is to drive out of it."

"Maybe we should stop."

"We're on pavement. I can see which lane we're in. Nothing's coming." He looks in the mirrors. "Nothing's behind us."

"I hope you're right." I'm not just talking about the snow. Everything seems ominous, as if sinister forces surround us, as if we're being warned.

"It wasn't a smart thing for her to do. An emotional thing, maybe even a well-intended thing, but not smart." Benton drives very slowly through chaotic whiteness. "It's hearsay, but it won't be helpful. It's best you don't call her."

"I'll need to show the letter to the police," I reply. "Or at least tell them about it, so they can decide what they want to do."

"She's just made things worse." He says it as if he's the one deciding things. "Don't get mixed up in this by calling her."

"Other than her trying to influence the medical examiner's office, how has she made things worse?" I ask.

"Several key points she incorrectly makes. Johnny doesn't read horror or supernatural or violent fiction or go to movies like that, at least not that I'm aware of, and that detail won't help him. Also, Mark Bishop wasn't murdered mid-afternoon. It was closer to four. Mrs. Donahue may not realize what she just implied about her son," Benton says as the white squall ends as suddenly as it began.

Flakes are small and icy again, swirling like sand over pavement and accumulating in shallow drifts on the roadsides.

"Johnny was at The Biscuit with his friend, that's true," Benton continues, "but according to him, he was there until two, not one. Apparently, he and his friend had been there numerous times, but I'm not aware of him having some rigid regimen of being there every Saturday with her from ten to one."

The Biscuit is on Washington Street, barely a fifteen-minute walk from our house in Cambridge, and I think of Saturdays when I've been home, when Benton and I have wandered into the small café with its chalkboard menu and wooden benches. I wonder if Johnny and his friend were ever in there when we were.

"What does his friend say about what time they left the café?" I ask.

"She claims she got up from the table around one p.m. and left him sitting there because he was acting strange and refused to leave with her. According to her statement to the police, Johnny was talking about going to Salem to get his fortune read, was talking wildly about that, and was still at the table when she walked out the door."

I find it interesting that Benton would have looked at a police statement or know the details of what a witness said. His role isn't to determine guilt or innocence or even to care but to evaluate if the patient is telling the truth or malingering and is competent to stand trial.

"Someone with Asperger's would have a hard time with the concept of a fortune being read or cards being read or anything of that nature," Benton is saying, and the more he tells me, the more perplexed I am.

He's talking to me as if he's a detective and we're working the case together, yet he's cryptic when it comes to Jack Fielding. There's nothing accidental about it. My husband rarely lets information slip, even if he gives the appearance otherwise. When he thinks I should know information he can't tell me, he finds a way for me to figure it out. If he decides it's best I don't know, he won't help me. It's the frustrating way we live, and at least I can say I'm never bored with him.

"Johnny can't think abstractly, can't comprehend metaphors. He's very concrete," Benton is saying.

"What about other people inside the café?" I ask. "Could anybody in the café verify what the friend said or what Johnny claims?"

"Nothing more definitive than he and Dawn Kincaid were in there that Saturday morning," Benton says, and I don't remember when I've seen him so disturbed by someone he has evaluated. "Don't know about it being a weekly routine, and by the time Johnny confessed, several days had passed. Amazing what shitty memories people have, and then they start guessing."

"Then all you have is what Johnny says and now what his mother says in this letter," I reiterate what I'm hearing. "He says he left The Biscuit at two, which might not have given him enough time to get to Salem and commit the murder at around four. And his mother is saying he left at one, which could have given him enough time to do it."

"As I said, it's not helpful. What's in his mother's letter is quite bad for him. So far the only real alibi anyone can offer that might show his confession is bullshit is a problematic timeline. But an hour makes all the difference, or it could."

I imagine Johnny getting up from his table at The Biscuit at around one p.m. and heading to Salem. Depending on traffic and when he was actually out of Cambridge or Somerville and heading north on I-95, he could have been at the Bishops' house in the historic district by two or two-thirty.

"Does he have a car?" I ask.

"He doesn't drive."

"A taxi, the train? Not a ferry this time of year. They don't start running again until spring, and he would have had to board it in Boston. But you're right. Without a car, it would have taken him longer to get there. An hour would make a difference for someone who had to find transportation."

"I just don't understand where she got that detail," Benton says. "Well, maybe from him. Maybe he's changed his story yet again. Johnny said he left The Biscuit at two, not one, but maybe he's changed that rather critical detail because he thinks it's what someone wants to hear. However, it would be unusual, very unusual."

"You were just with him this morning."

"I'm not the one who would influence him to change a detail."

Benton is saying that the detail is new and he doesn't believe that Johnny has changed his story about what time he left the café. It would seem Mrs. Donahue simply made a mistake, but when I try to imagine that, something feels wrong.

"How would he have gotten to Salem at all?" I ask.

"He could have taken a taxi or a train, but there's no evidence he did either. No sightings of him, no receipts found, nothing to prove he was ever in Salem or had any connection with the Bishop family. Nothing except his confession," Benton says as his eyes cut to the rearview mirror. "And what's important about that is his story is exactly what's been in the news, and he changes the details as news accounts and theories change. That part of his mother's letter is accurate. He parrots details word for word. Including if somebody suggests a scenario or information—leads him, in other words. Suggestibility, vulnerable to manipulation, acting in a way that generates suspicion, hallmark signs in Asperger's." He glances in the mirror again. "And attention to detail, to minutiae that can seem bizarre to others. Like what time it is. He's always maintained he left The Biscuit at two p.m. Three minutes past two, to be exact. You ask Johnny what time it is or what time he did something, and he'll tell you practically to the second."

"So why would he change that detail?"

"In my opinion, he wouldn't."

"Seems like he'd be better off saying he left earlier if he really wants people to believe he murdered Mark Bishop."

"It's not that he wants people to believe it. It's that he believes it. Not because of what he remembers but because of what he doesn't remember and because of what's been suggested to him."

"By whom? Sounds like he confessed before he was ever a suspect and interrogated. So he wasn't enticed into a false confession by the police, for example."

"He doesn't remember. He's convinced he suffered a dissociative episode after he left The Biscuit at two p.m., somehow got to Salem and killed a boy with a nail gun—"

"He didn't," I interrupt. "That much I can tell you with certainty. He didn't kill Mark Bishop with a nail gun. Nobody did."

Benton doesn't say anything as he speeds up, the snowflakes small again and sounding like grit hitting the car.

"Mrs. Donahue's also clearly misunderstood Jack's medical opinion." I talk with conviction as another part of me won't stop worrying about how I should handle her. I consider doing what Benton said and not calling her. I'll have my administrative assistant, Bryce, contact her instead, first thing in the morning, and say I'm sorry but I'm not able to discuss the Mark Bishop case or any case. It's important Bryce not give the impression that I'm too busy, that I'm unmoved by Mrs. Donahue's distress, and that makes me think of PFC Gabriel's mother again, of the painful things she said to me this morning at Dover. "I assume you've reviewed the autopsy report," I say to Benton.

"Yes."

"Then you know there is nothing in Jack's report that mentions a nail gun, only that injuries caused by nails penetrating the brain were the cause of death." I decide I can't possibly let Bryce make such a call on my behalf. I'll do it myself and ask Mrs. Donahue not to contact me again. I'll emphasize it's for her own protection. Then I'm filled with doubt, going back and forth on what to do with her, no longer so sure of myself. I've always had confidence in my ability to handle devastated people, bereft and enraged people, but I don't understand what happened this morning. Mrs. Gabriel called me a bigot. No one has ever called me a bigot before.

"A nail gun hasn't been ruled out by the people who count," Benton informs me. "Including Jack."

"I find that almost impossible to believe."

"He's been saying it."

"First I've heard of it."

"He's been saying it to whoever will listen. I don't care what's in his written report, the paperwork you've seen," Benton repeats as he looks in the rearview mirror.

"Why would he say something contrary to lab reports?"

"I'm simply relaying to you what I know for a fact that he's been saying about a nail gun being the weapon."

"Saying a nail gun was used is absolutely contrary to scientific and medical fact." In my sideview mirror I see headlights far behind us. "A nail gun leaves tool marks consistent with a single mechanized blow, similar to a firing-pin impression on a cartridge case. Instead, what we have in this instance are tool marks on nails that are consistent with a handheld hammer, and there were hammer marks on the boy's scalp and skull and underlying pattern contusions. Nail guns often leave a primer residue similar to gunshot residue, but Mark Bishop's wounds were negative for lead, for barium. A nail gun wasn't used, and I'm frankly amazed if what you're implying is that the police, the prosecutor, believe otherwise."

"Not hard to understand a number of things people choose to believe in this case," Benton says, and he's sped up, driving the speed limit.

I look in my sideview mirror again, and the headlights are much closer. Bright bluish-white lights blaze in the mirror. A large SUV with xenon headlights and fog lamps. *Marino,* I think. And behind him, I hope, is Lucy.

"Wanting to believe that Johnny's confession is true, as I've said," Benton continues. "Wanting to think that it had to be a blitz attack, that Mark Bishop couldn't have seen it coming or he would have struggled like hell. No one wants to think a child was held down and knew what was about to happen to him as someone drove nails into his skull with a hammer, for Christ's sake."

"He had no defense injuries, no evidence of a struggle, no evidence of being held down. It's in Jack's report. I'm sure you've seen it, and I'm sure he explained all this to the prosecutor, to the police."

"I wish you'd done the damn autopsy." Benton cuts his eyes to his mirrors.

"What exactly has Jack been saying beyond what I've read in his paperwork? Besides the possibility of a nail gun."

Benton doesn't answer me.

"Maybe you don't know," I then say, but I believe he does.

"He said he couldn't rule out a nail gun," Benton replies. "He said it isn't possible to tell definitively. He said this after he was asked because of what Johnny claimed in his confession. Jack was specifically and directly asked if a nail gun could have been used."

"The answer's definitively no."

"He would debate that with you. He said it isn't possible to tell definitively in this case. He said it's possible it was a nail gun."

"I'm telling you it's not possible, and it is possible to tell definitively," I reply. "And this is the first I've heard about a nail gun except for what's been on the Internet, which I have dismissed, since I dismiss most things in the news unless I am certain of the sources."

"He suggested if you pressed a nail gun against someone's head, you'd get what's similar to the muzzle mark made by a contact gunshot wound. And it's possible that's what we're seeing on the scalp and underlying tissue. And that's why there's no evidence of a struggle or that the boy knew what was happening."

"You wouldn't get a muzzle mark similar to a contact gunshot wound, and it's not possible," I reply. "The injuries I saw in photographs are hammer marks, and just because there was no evidence of a struggle doesn't mean the boy wasn't somehow coerced or coaxed or manipulated into cooperating. It sounds to me as if certain parties are choosing to ignore the facts of the case because of what they want to believe. That's extremely dangerous."

"I think Fielding is the one who might be ignoring the facts of the case. Maybe intentionally."

"Good God, Benton. He might be a lot of things . . ."

"Or it's negligence. It's one or the other," Benton says, and he has something in mind, I believe he does. "Listen. You did the best you could these past six months."

"What's that supposed to mean?" I know what it means. It means exactly what I've feared every single day that I've been gone.

"Remember when he was your fellow in the dark ages, in Richmond?" Benton is getting close to an area that is off-limits, even though he couldn't possibly know it. "From day one, he couldn't stand doing kids, that's absolutely true, as you've pointed out. If a kid was coming in, he'd run like hell, sometimes disappearing days at a time. And you'd drive around, trying to find him, going to his house, his favorite bar, the damn gym or tae kwon do, drinking himself into a stupor or kicking the shit out of someone. Not that any of us like dealing with dead children, for Christ's sake, but he's got a real problem."

I should have encouraged Fielding to go into surgical pathology, to work in a hospital lab, looking at biopsies. Instead, I mentored and encouraged him.

"But he took the Mark Bishop case," Benton says. "He could have passed him off to one of your other docs. I just hope he didn't lie; I sure as hell hope he didn't do that on top of everything else." But Benton thinks Fielding is lying. I can tell.

"On top of what else?" I ask as I look into my sideview mirror, wondering why Marino is on our bumper.

"I hope someone didn't encourage him to suggest the possibility of a nail gun even if he knows better." Benton has a way of looking in his mirrors without moving his head. All his years of undercover work, of watching his back because he really had to. Some habits never die.

"Who?" I ask.

"I don't know."

"You sound like you do know. You're not going to tell me." It is useless to push him. If he's not telling me, it's because he can't. Twenty years of the dance and it never gets easier.

"The cops want this case solved, that's for damn sure," Benton says. "They want a nail gun to be the weapon, because it's what Johnny has confessed to and because the thought is easier to deal with than a hammer. It concerns me that someone has influenced Jack."

"Someone has? Or you're just guessing that someone has."

"It concerns me that it might be Jack who is influencing people," Benton says next, and that's what he really thinks.

"I wish Marino would get off our bumper. He's blinding me with his damn lights. What's he doing?"

"It's not Marino," Benton says. "His Suburban doesn't have lights like that, and he has a front plate. This one doesn't. It's from out of state, a state that doesn't require a front plate, or it's been removed or is covered with something."

I turn around to look and the lights hurt my eyes. The SUV is only a few car lengths behind us.

"Maybe someone trying to pass us," I wonder aloud.

"Well, let's see, but I don't think so." Benton slows down, and so does the SUV. "I'll make you pass us, how about that," and he's talking to the driver behind us. "Grab the number from the rear plate as he goes by," Benton says to me.

We are almost stopped in the road, and the SUV stops, too. It backs up quickly and makes a U-turn, going the other way, fishtailing as it speeds off in the snowy night on the snowy road. I can't make out the plate on its rear bumper or any detail about the SUV except that it is dark and large.

"Why would someone be following us?" I say to Benton as if he might know.

"I have no idea what that was," Benton says.

"Someone was following us. That's what that was. Staying too close because of the weather, because visibility is so bad you would have to stay close or you could easily lose the person if they turned off."

"Some jerk," Benton says. "Nobody sophisticated. Unless he deliberately wanted us to know he was back there or thought we wouldn't notice."

"How's it even possible? We just drove through a blizzard. Where the hell did it come from? Out of nowhere?"

Benton picks up his phone and enters a number.

"Where are you?" he says to whoever answers, and after a pause he adds, "A large SUV with fog lights, xenons, no front plate, on our ass. That's right. Made a U-turn and sped off the other way. Yes, on Route Two. Anything like that just pass you? Well, that's weird. Must have turned off. Well, if . . . Yes. Thanks."

Benton places his phone back on the console and explains, "Marino's a few minutes behind us, and Lucy's right behind him. The SUV's vanished. If someone's stupid enough to follow us, he'll try again and we'll figure it out. If the point was to intimidate, then whoever it is doesn't know his target."

"Now we're a target."

"Anyone who knows wouldn't try it."

"Because of you."

Benton doesn't answer. But what I said is true. Anyone who knows anything about Benton would be aware of how foolhardy it is to think he can be intimidated. I feel his hard edge, his steely aura. I know what he can do if threatened. He and Lucy are similar if confronted. They welcome it. Benton's simply cooler, more calculating and restrained than my niece will ever be.

"Erica Donahue." That's the first thought to come to mind. "She's already sent one person to intercept us, and I doubt she realizes how dangerous her son's charming, handsome Harvard psychologist is."

Benton doesn't smile. "Wouldn't make sense."

"How many people know our whereabouts?" There is no point in trying to lighten the mood, which is unrelentingly intense. Benton has his own caliber of vigilance. It is different from Lucy's, and he is far better at concealing it. "Or my whereabouts. How many people know?" I go on. "Not just the mother or the driver. What did Jack do?"

Benton speeds up again and doesn't answer me.

"You're not thinking Jack has some reason to intimidate us. Or try," I then say.

Benton doesn't reply, and we drive in silence and there is no sign of the SUV with the fog lamps and xenon headlights.

"Lucy suspects he's drinking a lot." Benton finally starts talking again. "But you should get that from her. And from Marino." His tone is flat, and I hear the unforgiveness in it. He has nothing but disdain for Fielding, even if he is silent about it most of the time.

"Why would Jack lie? Why would he try to influence anyone?" I'm back to that.

"Apparently, he's been coming in late and disappearing, and he's having his skin problems again." Benton doesn't answer my question. "I hope to hell he's not doing steroids on top of everything else, especially at his age."

I resist the usual defense that when Fielding is acutely stressed, he has problems with eczema, with alopecia, and that he can't help it. He's always been obsessed with his body, is a classic case of megarexia or muscle dysmorphia, and most likely this can be attributed to the sexual abuse he suffered as a young boy. It would sound absurd to go down the list, and I'm not going to do it this time. For once, I won't. I continue checking my sideview mirror. But the xenon headlights and fog lamps are gone.

"Why would he lie about this case?" I ask again. "Why would he want to influence anybody about it?"

"I can't imagine how you could make a kid stay still for that," Benton says, and he's thinking about Mark Bishop's death. "The family was inside the house and claim they didn't hear screams, didn't hear anything. They claim that Mark was playing one minute and the next he was facedown in the yard. I'm trying to envision what happened and can't."

"All right. We'll talk about that, since you're not going to answer my question."

"I've tried to picture it, to reconstruct it, and draw a blank. The family was home. It's not a big yard. How is it possible no one saw someone or heard anything?"

His face is somber as we drive past Lanes & Games, where Marino bowls in a league. What is the name of his team? *Spare None.* His new buddies, law enforcement and military people.

"I thought I'd seen it all, but I just can't picture how it happened," Benton again says, because he can't or won't tell me what is really on his mind about Fielding.

"A person who knew exactly what he was doing." I can envision it. I can imagine in painful detail what the killer did. "Someone who was able to put the boy at ease, perhaps lure him into doing what he was told. Maybe Mark thought it was part of a game, a fantasy."

"A stranger showed up in his yard and got him to play a game that involved having nails hammered into his head—or pretending to, which is more likely," Benton considers. "Maybe. But a stranger? I don't know about that. I've missed talking to you."

"It wasn't a stranger, or at least didn't seem like one to Mark. I suspect it was someone he had no reason to distrust—no matter what he was asked to do." I base this on what I know about his injuries or lack of them. "The body showed no signs that he was terrified and panicky, someone trying to fight or escape. I think it's likely he was familiar with the killer or felt inclined to cooperate for some reason. I've missed talking to you, but I'm here now and you're not talking to me."

"I am talking to you."

"One of these days I'm going to slip Sodium Pentothal into your drink. And find out everything you've never told me."

"If only it worked, I would reciprocate. But then we'd both be in serious trouble. You don't want to know everything. Or you shouldn't. And I probably shouldn't, either."

"Four p.m. on January thirtieth." I'm thinking about how dark it would have been when Mark was murdered. "What time did the sun set that day? What was the weather?"

"Completely dark at four-thirty, cold, overcast," says Benton, who would have found out those details first thing if he was the one investigating the case.

"I'm trying to remember if there was snow on the ground."

"Not in Salem. A lot of rain because of the harbor. The water warms up the air."

"So no footprints were recovered in the Bishops' yard."

"No. And at four it was getting dark and the backyard was in shadows because of shrubbery and trees," Benton says, as if he's the detective on the case. "According to the family, Mrs. Bishop, the mother, went out at four-twenty to make Mark come into the house, and she found him facedown in the leaves."

"Why are we assuming he had just been killed when she found him? Certainly his physical findings would never allow us to pinpoint his time of death to exactly four p.m."

"The fact that the parents recall looking out the window at

approximately a quarter of four and seeing Mark playing," Benton says.

"'Playing'? What does that mean exactly? What kind of playing?"

"Don't know exactly." Benton and his evasiveness again. "I'd like to talk to the family." I suspect he's already talked to them. "There are a lot of missing details. But he was playing by himself in the yard, and when his mother looked out the window at around four-fifteen, she didn't see him. So she went out to make him come into the house and found him, tried to rouse him, and picked him up and rushed him inside. She called nine-one-one at exactly four-twenty-three p.m., was hysterical, said that her son wasn't moving or breathing, that she was worried he had choked on something."

"Why would she think he might have choked?"

"Apparently, before he went out to play, he'd put some leftover Christmas candy into his pocket. Hard candies, and the last thing she said to him as he was going out the door was not to suck on candy while he was running or jumping."

I can't help but think that this is the sort of detail Benton would have gotten from the Bishops in person. I feel he has talked to them.

"And we don't know what kind of playing he was doing? He's by himself, running and jumping?" I ask.

"I just got involved in this case after Johnny confessed to it." Benton is evasive again. For some reason, he doesn't want to talk about what Mark was doing in his backyard. "Mrs. Bishop later told police she didn't see anybody in the area, that there was no sign of anybody having been on their property, and she didn't know until Mark got to the emergency room that he'd been murdered. The nails had been hammered in all the way, and his hair hid them, and there was no blood. And his shoes were missing. He was wearing a pair of Adidas while playing in the yard, and they were gone and haven't shown up."

"A boy playing in his yard in the near dark. Again, hard to imagine he would cooperate with a stranger. Unless it was someone who represented something he instinctively trusted." I continue making that point.

"A fireman. A cop. The guy who drives the ice-cream truck. That sort of thing," Benton considers easily, as if this is safe to talk about. "Or worse. A member of his own family."

"A member of his family would kill him in such a sadistic, hideous fashion and then take his shoes? Taking the shoes sounds like a souvenir."

"Or supposed to look like one," Benton says.

"I'm no forensic psychologist," I then say. "I'm playing your role, and I shouldn't. I'd like to see where it happened. Jack never went to the scene, and he should have made a retrospective visit." My mood settles lower as I say that. He didn't go to Mark Bishop's scene, and he didn't go to Norton's Woods.

"Or another kid. Kids playing a game that turned deadly," Benton says.

"If it was another kid," I reply, "he was remarkably well informed anatomically."

I envision the autopsy photographs, the boy's head with his

scalp reflected back. I envision the CT scans, three-dimensional images of four two-inch iron nails penetrating the brain.

"Whoever did it couldn't have picked more lethal locations to drive the nails," I explain. "Three went through the temporal bone above the left ear and penetrated the pons. One was nailed into the back of the skull, directed upward, so it damaged the cervico-medullary junction, or upper cervical spinal cord."

"How fast would that have killed him?"

"Almost instantaneously. The nail to the back of the head alone could have killed him in minutes, as little time as it takes to die after you can no longer breathe. Injury at the C-one and C-two levels of the spinal cord interferes with breathing. The police, the prosecutor, a jury, for that matter, would have a hard time believing another child could have done that. It seems that causing death, almost immediate death, was the intention, and it was premeditated, unless the hammer and nails were at the scene, in the yard or house, and by all accounts they weren't. Correct?"

"A hammer, yes. But what house doesn't have a hammer? And the tool marks don't match. But you know that from lab reports. No nails like the ones that killed him. Those weren't found at the family's home, and no nail gun," Benton says.

"These were L-head nails, typically used in flooring."

"According to the police, no nails like that were found at the residence," he repeats.

"Iron, not stainless steel." I continue with details from photographs, from lab reports, and all the while I hear myself, I'm aware that I'm going over the case with Benton as if it's mine. As if it's his. As if we are working it the way we used to work cases in our early days together. "With traces of rust despite their protective zinc coating, which suggests they weren't just purchased," I go on. "That maybe they'd been lying around somewhere and exposed to moisture, possibly saltwater."

"Nothing like that at the scene. No L-head flooring nails, no iron nails at all," Benton says. "The father's been spreading the rumor about a nail gun, at least publicly."

"Publicly. Meaning he told the media," I assume.

"Yes."

"But when? He told the media when? That's the important question. Where did the rumor come from and when? Do we know for a fact it started with the father, because if it did, that's significant. It could mean he's offering an alibi, suggesting a weapon he doesn't have, that's he trying to lead the police in the wrong direction."

"We're thinking the same thing," Benton says. "Mr. Bishop might have suggested it to the media, but the question is, did someone suggest it to him first?"

I detect more subtleties. It occurs to me that Benton knows how the rumor about a nail gun started. He knows who started it, and it's not difficult to guess what he's implying. Jack Fielding is trying to influence what people think about this case. Maybe Fielding is the one behind the rumor that is now all over the news.

"We should do a retrospective. I'm trying to remember the name of the Salem detective." There's so much to do, so much I've missed. I hardly know where to start.

"Saint Hilaire. First name James."

"Don't know him." I'm a stranger to my own life.

"He's convinced of Johnny Donahue's guilt, and I'm really concerned it's just a matter of time before he's charged with first-degree murder. We have to move fast. When Saint Hilaire reads what Mrs. Donahue just wrote to you, it will be worse. He'll be more convinced. We have to do something quickly," Benton says. "I'm not supposed to give a damn, but I do because Johnny didn't do it and no jury is going to like him. He's inappropriate. He misreads people, and they misread him. They think he's callous and arrogant. He laughs and giggles when something isn't funny. He's rude and blunt and has no idea. The whole thing is absurd. A travesty. Probably one of the most classic examples of false confessions I've ever seen."

"Then why is he still on a locked unit at McLean?"

"He needs psychiatric treatment, but no, he shouldn't be locked up on a unit with psychotic patients. That's my opinion, but no one's listening. Maybe you can talk to Renaud and Saint Hilaire and they'll listen to you. We'll go to Salem and review the case with them. While we're there, we'll look around."

"And Johnny's breakdown?" I ask. "If his mother is to be believed, he was fine his first three years at Harvard and suddenly has to be hospitalized? He's how old?"

"Eighteen. He returned to Harvard last fall to begin his senior year and was noticeably altered," Benton said. "Aggressive verbally and sexually, and increasingly agitated and paranoid. Disordered thinking and distorted perceptions. Symptoms similar to schizophrenia."

"Drugs?"

"No evidence whatsoever. Submitted to testing when he confessed to the murder and was negative; even his hair was negative for drugs, for alcohol. His grad-school friend Dawn Kincaid is at MIT, and she and Johnny were working together on a project. She became so concerned about him she finally called his family. This was in December. Then a week ago, Johnny was admitted to McLean with a stab wound to his hand and told his psychiatrist that he'd murdered Mark Bishop, claiming he took the train to Salem and had a nail gun in a backpack, said he needed a human sacrifice to rid him of an evil entity that had taken over his life."

"Why nails? Why not some other weapon?"

"Something to do with the magical powers of iron. And most of this has been in the news."

I recall seeing something on the Internet about devil's bone, and I mention that.

"Exactly. What iron was called in ancient Egypt," Benton replies. "They sell devil's bone in some of the shops in Salem."

"Lashed together in an X that you carry in a red satin pouch. I've seen them in some of the witcheries. But not the same type of nails. The ones in the witcheries are more like spikes, are supposed to look antique. And I doubt they're treated with zinc, that they're galvanized."

"Supposedly, iron protects against malevolent spirits, and thus the explanation for Johnny using iron nails. That's his explanation. And his story's completely unoriginal; as you just pointed out, it was one of the theories all over the news the days before he confessed to the murder." Benton pauses, then adds, "Your own office has suggested black magic as a motive, presumably because of the Salem connection."

"It's not our job to offer theories. Our job is to be impartial and objective, so I don't know what you mean when you say we suggested such a thing."

"I'm just telling you it's been discussed."

"With whom?" But I know.

"Jack's always been a loose cannon. But he seems to have lost what little impulse control he had," Benton says.

"I think we've established that Jack is a problem I can no longer attempt to solve. What project?" I go back to what Benton mentioned about Johnny Donahue's female MIT friend. "And what's Johnny's major?"

"Computer science. Since early last summer, he was interning at Otwahl Technologies in Cambridge. As his mother pointed out, he's unusually gifted in some areas. . . ."

"Doing what? What was he doing there?" I envision the solid façade of precast rising up like the Hoover Dam not far from where we just drove past, the part of Cambridge where the SUV with xenon lights was following us before it vanished.

"Software engineering for UGVs and related technologies," Benton says, as if it is no great matter because he doesn't know what I do about UGVs.

Unmanned ground vehicles. Military robots like the prototype MORT in the dead man's apartment.

"What's going on here, Benton?" I say with feeling. "What in God's name is going on?"

The storm has settled in, the wind much calmer now, and the snow is already several inches deep. Traffic is steady on Memorial Drive, the weather of little consequence to people used to New England winters.

The rooftops of MIT fraternity houses and playing fields are solid white on the left side of the road, and on the other side the snow drifts like smoke over the bike path and the boathouse and vanishes into the icy blackness of the Charles. Farther east, where the river empties into the harbor, the Boston skyline is ghostly rectangular shapes and smudges of light in the milky night, and there is no air traffic over Logan, not a single plane in sight.

"We should meet with Renaud as soon as possible—the sooner, the better." Benton thinks Essex County District Attorney Paul Renaud should know that there may be something more to Johnny Donahue's confession, that somehow the Harvard senior and a dead man in my cooler could be connected. "But if this involves DARPA?" Benton adds.

"Otwahl gets DARPA funding. But it isn't DARPA, isn't DoD. It's civilian, an international private industry," I reply. "But certainly it's closely tied to government through substantial grants, tens of millions, maybe a lot more than that, since their rather clumsy invention of MORT."

"The question is what else they're focused on. What are they focused on now that could have significance in all this?"

"I honestly can't say, not for a fact. But you know the obvious just by looking at the place." Were we to drive back toward Hanscom, we would pass within a mile of Otwahl Technologies and its adjoining superconducting test facility, a massive self-contained complex with its own private police force. "Neutron science, most likely, because of materials science and how it applies to new technologies."

"Robotics," Benton says.

"Robots, nanotechnology, software engineering, synthetic biology. Lucy knows something about it."

"Probably more than something."

"Knowing her, yes. A lot more than something."

"They're probably making damn humanoids so we never run out of soldiers."

"They might be." I'm not joking.

"And Briggs would know about the robot in this guy's apartment." Benton means the dead man's apartment. "Because of video clips? What else about that? I wonder if he said something to Jack about it, called and alerted him by asking questions."

I explain it further, giving a more detailed account of the man and the recordings Lucy discovered—recordings that Marino inappropriately e-mailed to Briggs before I had a chance to review them first, and when I did get a chance to see them, it was only superficially, en route to the Civil Air Terminal in Dover. I tell Benton all about the ill-fated six-legged robot, the Mortuary Operational Removal Transport, known as MORT, that is parked inside the apartment near the door, and I remind him of the controversies, of the disagreements I had with certain politicians and especially with Briggs over using a machine to recover casualties in theater or anywhere.

I describe the heartlessness, the horror, of a gas-powered metal construction that sounded like a chain saw lurching across the earth to recover wounded or dead human beings by grasping them in grippers that looked like the mandibles of a bull ant. "Think of the message it sends if you're dying on the battlefield and this is what your comrades send for you," I say to Benton. "What kind of message does it send to the victim's loved ones if they see it on the news?"

"You used inflammatory language like that when you testified before a defense appropriations Senate subcommittee," Benton assumes.

"I don't remember what I said verbatim."

"I'm sure you didn't make any friends at Otwahl. You probably made enemies you have no idea about."

"It wasn't about Otwahl or any other technology company. All Otwahl did was create an unmanned robotic vehicle. It was people at the Pentagon that came up with its so-called useful purpose. I think originally MORT was supposed to be a packbot, nothing more. I didn't even remember Otwahl was the company until tonight. They were never a preoccupation of mine. My disagreement was with the Pentagon, and I was going to stand my ground." I almost say *this time*. But I catch myself. Benton doesn't know about the time I didn't stand my ground.

"Enemies who haven't forgotten. Those kinds of enemies never forget. I'm sorry I wasn't privy to all this when it was going on," Benton says, because he wasn't around when I was making enemies on Capitol Hill. He was in a protective witness program and not exactly in a position to give me advice or counsel or even assure me that he wasn't dead. "You must have files on it, records from back then."

"Why?"

"I'd like to take a look, get up to speed. It might explain a few things."

"What things?"

"I'd like to look at what you have from back then," Benton says.

Transcripts from my testimony, video recordings of the segments aired on C-SPAN: What I have would be in my safe in our Cambridge basement—along with certain items I don't want him to see. A thick gray accordion file and photographs I took with my own camera. Bloodstained squares of white cardboard improvised before the days of FTA DNA collection kits, because if blood is air-dried it can last forever, and I knew where technology was headed. Plain white envelopes with fingernail cuttings and pubic combings and head hair. Oral, anal, and vaginal swabs, and cut and torn bloody underpants. An empty Chablis bottle, a beer can. Materials I smuggled from a dark continent half a world away more than two decades ago, evidence I shouldn't have had, items I shouldn't have had privately tested, but I did. I seriously consider that if Benton was aware of the Cape Town cases, he might not feel the same about me.

"You know the old saying, revenge is best served cold," he goes on. "You fucked a huge multimillion-dollar project, a joint venture between DoD and Otwahl Technologies, and stepped on toes, and although a number of years have passed, I suspect there are people out there who haven't forgotten, even if you have. And now here you are, working with DoD in Otwahl's backyard. A perfect opportunity to calculate revenge, to pay you back."

"Pay me back? A man dropping dead in Norton's Woods is payback?"

"I just think we should know the cast of characters."

Then we stop talking about it, because we have reached the girder bridge that connects Cambridge to Boston, the Mass Ave Bridge, or what the locals refer to as the Harvard Bridge or MIT Bridge, depending on their loyalties. Just ahead, my headquarters rises like a lighthouse, silo-shaped with a glass dome on top, seven stories sided in titanium and reinforced with steel. The first time Marino saw the CFC he decided it looked like a dum-dum bullet, and in the snowy dark, I suppose it does.

Turning off Memorial Drive, away from the river, we take the first left into the parking area, illuminated by solar security lights and surrounded by a black PVC-coated fence that can't be climbed or cut. I dig a remote control out of my bag and push a button to open the tall gate, and we drive over tire tracks that are almost completely covered in fresh white powder. Anne and Ollie's cars are here, parked near the CFC's all-wheel-drive cargo vans and SUVs, and I notice one is missing, one of the SUVs. There should be four, but one of them is gone and has been since before it began to snow, probably the on-call medicolegal investigator.

I wonder who is on duty tonight and why that person is out in one of our vehicles. At a scene, or is the person at home, and I look around as if I've never been here before. Above the fence on two sides are lab buildings that belong to MIT, glass and brick, with antennas and radar dishes on the roofs, the windows dark except for a random few glowing dimly, as if someone left a desk light or a lamp on. Snow streaks the night and is loud like a brittle rain as Benton pulls close to my building, into the space designated for the director, next to Fielding's spot, which is empty and smooth with snow.

"We could put it in the bay," Benton says hopefully.

"That would be a little spoiled, since no one else can," I reply. "And it's unauthorized, anyway. For pickups and deliveries only."

"Dover's worn off on you. Am I going to have to salute?"

"Only at home."

We climb out, and the snow is up to the ankles of my boots and doesn't pack under them because it is too cold, the flakes tiny and icy. I enter a code in a keypad next to a shut bay door that begins to retract loudly as Marino and Lucy drive into the lot. The receiving bay looks like a small hangar sealed with white epoxy paint, and mounted in the ceiling is a monorail crane, a motorized lifter for moving bodies too large for manual handling. There is a ramp inside leading to a metal door, and parked off to

the side is our white van-body truck, what at Dover we refer to
as a bread truck, designed to transport up to six bodies on stretch-
ers or in transfer cases and to serve as a mobile crime scene lab
when needed.

As I wait for Marino and Lucy, I'm reminded I'm not dressed
for New England. My tactical jacket was perfectly adequate in
Delaware, but now I'm thoroughly chilled. I try not to think
about how good it would be to sit in front of the fire with a
single-malt Scotch or small-batch bourbon, to catch up with Benton about things other than tragedy and betrayal and enemies
with long memories, to get away from everyone. I want to drink
and talk honestly with my husband, to put aside games and sub-
terfuge and not wonder what he knows. I crave a normal time
with him, but we don't know what that is. Even when we make
love we have our secrets and nothing is normal.

"No updates except Lawless." Marino answers a question no
one asked as the bay door clanks down behind us. "He e-mailed
scene photographs—finally. But says no luck with the dog. No
one's called to report a lost greyhound."

"What greyhound?" Benton asks.

I was too busy describing MORT and didn't mention much
else I saw on the video clips. I feel foolish. "Norton's Woods," I
reply. "A black-and-white greyhound named Sock that apparently ran off while the EMTs were busy with our case."

"How do you know his name is Sock?"

I explain it to him as I hold my thumb over the glass sensor
of the biometric lock so it can scan my print. Opening the door
that leads into the lower level of the building, I mention that the

dog might have a microchip that could supply useful information about the owner's identification. Some rescue groups automatically microchip former racing greyhounds before putting them up for adoption, I add.

"That's interesting," Benton says. "I think I saw them."

"He stared right at you as you were pulling out of the driveway in your sports car about three-fifteen yesterday afternoon," Lucy tells him as we enter the processing area, an open space with a security office, a digital floor scale, and a wall of massive stainless-steel doors that open into cooler rooms and a walk-in freezer.

"What are you talking about?" Benton asks my niece.

"All that time in the car driving through a blizzard and you didn't catch him up on things?" Lucy says to me, and she's not easy to be around when she gets like this.

I feel a prick of annoyance even though she's right. *She knows you, too,* enters my mind. *She knows you just as well as you know her.* She knows damn well when something is bothering me that I stubbornly keep to myself, and I've been bothered and feeling stubborn since I left Dover. It was stupid of me not to go into the sort of detail that Benton can do something with. I don't know of anyone more psychologically astute, and he would have plenty to say about the minutiae picked up by the recorders concealed inside the dead man's headphones.

Instead, I obsessed about DARPA because I was really obsessing about Briggs. I can't get past what happened earlier today, about what happened decades ago, about how what he caused never seems to end. He knows about that dark place in my past, a place I take no one, and a part of me will never forgive him for creating that place. It was his idea for me to go to Cape Town. It was his goddamn brilliant plan.

"He and the greyhound walked right past your driveway just minutes before he died," Lucy is telling Benton, but her gaze is steady on me. "If you hadn't left, you would have heard the sirens. You probably would have headed over there to see what was going on and maybe would have some useful information for us."

She looks at me as if she is looking at the dark place. It's not possible she could know about it, I reassure myself. I've never told her, never told Benton or Marino or anyone. The documents were destroyed except for what I have. Briggs promised that decades ago when I left the AFIP and moved to Virginia, and I already knew reports were missing without being told. Lucy doesn't have the combination to my safe, I remind myself. Benton doesn't. No one does.

"If you drop by my lab," Lucy is saying to Benton, "I'll show the video clips to you."

"You haven't seen them," I say to Benton, because I'm not sure. He's acting as if he hasn't seen them, but I don't know if it's just more of the same, more secrets.

"I haven't," he answers, and it sounds like the truth. "But I want to, and I will."

"Weird you're in them," Lucy says to him. "Your house is in them. Really weird. Sort of freaked me out when I saw it."

The night security guard sits behind his glass window, and he nods at us but doesn't get up from his desk. His name is Ron, a big, muscular dark-skinned man with closely shorn hair and unfriendly eyes. He seems afraid of me or skeptical, and it's obvious he's been instructed to maintain his post, not to be sociable, no matter who it is. I can only imagine the stories he's heard, and Fielding enters my thoughts again. What has happened to him? What trouble has he caused? How much has he hurt this place?

I walk over to the security guard's window and check the sign-in log. Since three p.m., three bodies have come in: a motor-vehicle fatality, a gunshot homicide, and an asphyxiation by plastic bag that is undetermined.

"Is Dr. Fielding here?" I ask Ron.

Retired marine corps military police, he is always neat and proud in his midnight-blue uniform with American flag and AFME patches on the shoulders and a brass CFC security shield pinned to his shirt. His face is wary and not the least bit warm behind his glass partition as he answers that he hasn't seen Fielding. He tells me that Anne and Ollie are here but no one else. Not even the on-call death investigator is in. Randy, he informs me in a monotone, and every other word is *ma'am,* and I'm reminded of how cold and condescending *ma'am* this and *ma'am* that can sound and how tired I got of hearing it at Dover. Randy is working from home because of the weather, Ron reports. Apparently, Fielding told him that was okay, even though it's not. That is against the rules I established. On-call investigators don't work from home.

"We'll be in the x-ray room," I inform Ron. "If anybody else shows up, you can find us in there. But unless it's Dr. Fielding, I need to know who it is and give clearance. Actually, I probably should know if Dr. Fielding shows up, too. You know what, no matter who it is, I need to know."

"If Dr. Fielding comes in you want me to call, ma'am. To alert you," Ron repeats, as if he's not sure that's what I meant, or maybe he's arguing.

"Affirmative," I make myself clear. "No one should just walk in, doesn't matter if they work here. Until I tell you otherwise. I want everything airtight right now."

"I understand, ma'am."

"Any calls from the media? Any sign of them?"

"I keep looking, ma'am." Mounted on three walls are monitors, each split into quadrants that are constantly rotating images picked up by security cameras outside the building and in strategic areas such as the bays, corridors, elevators, lobby, and all doors leading into the building. "I know there's some concern about the man found in the park." Ron looks past me at Marino, as if the two of them have an understanding.

"Well, you know where we'll be for now." I open another door. "Thank you."

A long white hallway with a gray tile floor leads to a series of rooms located in a logical order that facilitates the flow of our work. The first stop is ID, where bodies are photographed and fingerprinted and personal effects not taken by the police are removed and secured in lockers. Next is large-scale x-ray, which includes the CT scanner, and beyond that are the autopsy room, the soiled room, the anteroom, the changing rooms, the locker rooms, the anthropology lab, the Bio4 containment lab reserved for suspected infectious or contaminated cases. The corridor wraps around in a circle that ends where it began, at the receiving bay.

"What does security know about our patient from Norton's Woods?" I ask Marino. "Why does Ron think there's a concern?"

"I didn't tell him anything."

"I'm asking what he knows."

"He wasn't on duty when we left earlier. I haven't seen him today."

"I'm wondering what he's been told," I repeat patiently, because I don't want to squabble with Marino in front of the others. "Obviously, this is a very sensitive situation."

"I gave an order before I left that everyone needed to be on the lookout for the media," Marino says, taking off his leather jacket as we reach the x-ray room, where the red light above the door indicates that the scanner is in use. Anne and Ollie won't have started without me, but it's their habit to deter people from walking into an area where there are levels of radiation much higher than are safe for living patients. "Wasn't my idea for Randy or the others to work from home, either," Marino adds.

I don't ask how long that's been going on or who the "others" are. Who else has been working from home? This is a state government facility, a paramilitary installation, not a cottage industry, I feel like saying.

"Damn Fielding," Marino then mutters. "He's fucking up everything."

I don't answer. Now is not the time to discuss how fucked up everything is.

"You know where I'll be." Lucy walks off toward the elevator, and with an elbow pushes a hands-free oversized button. She disappears behind sliding steel doors as I pass my thumb over another biometric sensor and the lock clicks free.

Inside the control room, forensic radiologist Dr. Oliver Hess is seated at a work station behind lead-lined glass, his gray hair unruly, his face sleepy, as if I got him out of bed. Past him, through an open door, I can see the eggshell-white Siemens Somatom Sensation and hear the fan of its water-cooled system. The scanner is a modified version of the one used at Dover, equipped with a custom head holder and safety straps, its wiring subsurface, its parameter sealed, its table covered by a heavy vinyl slicker to protect the multimillion-dollar system from contaminants such as body fluids. Slightly angled down toward the door to facilitate sliding bodies on and off, the scanner is in the ready status, and technologist Anne Mahoney is placing radio-opaque CT skin markers on the dead man from Norton's Woods. I get a strange feeling as I walk in. He is familiar, although I've never seen him before, only parts of him on recordings I watched on an iPad.

I recognize the tint of his light-brown skin and his tapered hands, which are by his sides on top of a disposable blue sheet, his long, slender fingers slightly curled and stiff with rigor.

In the video clips I heard his voice and saw glimpses of his hands, his boots, his clothing, but I did not see his face. I'm not sure what I imagined but am vaguely disturbed by his delicate features and long, curly brown hair, by the spray of light freckles across his smooth cheeks. I pull the sheet back, and he is very thin, about five-foot-eight and at most one hundred and thirty pounds, I deduce, with very little body hair. He could easily pass for sixteen, and I'm reminded of Johnny Donahue, who isn't much older. Kids. Could that be a common denominator? Or is it Otwahl Technologies?

"Anything?" I ask Anne, a plain-looking woman in her thirties with shaggy brown hair and sensitive hazel eyes. She's probably the best person on my staff, can do anything, whether it is different types of radiographic imaging or helping in the morgue or at crime scenes. She is always willing.

"This. Which I noticed when I undressed him." Her latex-sheathed hands grip the body at the waist and hip, pulling it over so I can see a tiny defect on the left side of the back at the level of the kidneys. "Obviously missed at the scene because it didn't bleed out, at least not much. You know about his bleeding, which I witnessed with my own two eyes when I was going to scan him early this morning? That he bled profusely from his nose and mouth after he was bagged and transported?"

"That's why I'm here." I open a drawer to retrieve a hand lens, and then Benton is by my side in a surgical mask and gown and gloves. "He's got some sort of injury," I say to him as I lean close to the body and magnify an irregular wound that looks like a small buttonhole. "Definitely not a gunshot entrance. A stab wound made by a very narrow blade, like a boning knife but with two edges. Something like a stiletto."

"A stiletto in his back would drop him in his tracks?" Benton's eyes are skeptical above his mask.

"No. Not unless he was stabbed at the base of his skull and it severed his spinal cord." I think of Mark Bishop and the nails that killed him.

"Like I said at Dover, maybe something was injected," Marino offers as he walks in covered from head to foot with personal protective clothing, including a face shield and hair cover, as if he's worried about airborne pathogens or deadly spores, such as anthrax. "Maybe some kind of anesthesia. A lethal injection, in other words. That could sure as hell drop you in your tracks."

"In the first place, an anesthesia like sodium thiopental is injected into a vein, as are pancuronium bromide or potassium chloride." I pull on a pair of examination gloves. "They aren't injected into the person's back. Same thing with mivacurium, with succinylcholine. You want to kill somebody decisively and quickly with a neuromuscular blocker, you'd better inject it intravenously."

"But if they were injected into a muscle, it would still kill you, right?" Marino opens a cabinet and gets out a camera. He rummages in a drawer and finds a plastic six-inch ruler for size reference. "During executions, sometimes the injection misses the vein and goes into the muscle, and the inmate still dies."

"A slow and very painful death," I reply. "By all accounts, this man's death wasn't slow, and this injury wasn't made by a needle."

"I won't say the prison techs do it on purpose, but it happens. Well, it's probably on purpose. Just like some of them chill the cocktail, making sure the dirtbag feels it hit, the ice-cold hand of death," Marino says for Anne's benefit, because she is passionately anti–capital punishment. His way of flirting is to offend her whenever he can.

"That's disgusting," she says.

"Hey. It's not like they cared about the people they whacked, right? Like they cared if they suffered, right? What goes around comes around. Who hid the damn label maker?"

"I did. I lie awake at night figuring out ways to get you back."

"Oh, yeah? For what?"

"For just being you."

Marino digs in another drawer, finds the label maker. "He looks a hell of a lot younger than what the EMTs said. Anybody notice that besides me? Don't you think he looks younger than his twenties?" Marino asks Anne. "Looks like a damn kid."

"Barely pubescent," she agrees. "But then, all college kids are starting to look like that to me. They look like babies."

"We don't know if he was a college student," I remind everyone.

Marino peels the backing off a label printed with the date and case number, and sticks it on the plastic ruler. "I'll canvas the area over there by the common, see if any supers in apartment buildings recognize him, just do it my damn self to keep the rumor mill quiet. If he lives around there, and it sure seems like it, based on what's on the videos, someone's got to remember him and his greyhound. Sock. What kind of name is that for a dog?"

"Probably not his full name," Anne says. "Race dogs have these rather elaborate registered kennel names, like Sock It to Me or Darned Sock or Sock Hop."

"I keep telling her she should go on *Jeopardy*," Marino says.

"It's possible his name might be in a registry," I comment. "Something with Sock in it, assuming we have no luck with a microchip."

"Assuming you find the damn dog," Marino says.

"We're running his prints, his DNA. Right away, I hope?" Benton stares intently at the body, as if he's talking to it.

"I printed him this morning and no luck, nothing in IAFIS. Nothing in the National Missing and Unidentified Persons Sys-

tem. We'll have his DNA tomorrow and run it through CODIS."
Marino's big gloved hands place the ruler under the man's chin.
"It's kind of strange about the dog, though. Someone's got to have
him. I'm thinking we should put out info for the media about a
lost greyhound and a number people can call."

"Nothing from us," I reply. "Right now we're staying away
from the media."

"Exactly," Benton says. "We don't want the bad guys knowing
we're even aware of the dog, much less looking for it."

"'Bad guys'?" Anne says.

"What else?" I walk around the table, doing what Lucy calls
a "high recon," looking carefully at the body from head to toe.

Marino is taking photographs, and he says, "Before we put him
back in the fridge this morning, I checked his hands for trace,
collected anything preliminarily, including personal effects."

"You didn't tell me about personal effects. Just that he didn't
seem to have any," I reply.

"A ring with a crest on it, a steel Casio watch. A couple keys
on a keychain. Let's see, what else? A twenty-dollar bill. A little
wooden stash box, empty, but I swabbed it for drugs. The stash
box on the video clip. For a second you could see him holding it
right after he got to Norton's Woods."

"Where was it recovered?" I ask.

"In his pocket. That's where I found it."

"So he took it out of his pocket at the park and then put it
back in his pocket before his terminal event." I remember what
I watched on the iPad, the small box held in the black glove.

"I'd say we should be looking for the snorting or smoking variety," Marino says. "I'm betting weed. Don't know if you noticed," he says to me, "but he had a glass pipe in an ashtray on his desk."

"We'll see what shows up on tox," I reply. "We'll do a STAT alcohol and expedite a drug screen. How backed up are they up there?"

"I'll tell Joe to move it to the head of the line," Anne refers to the chief toxicologist, whom I brought with me from New York, rather shamelessly stole him from the NYPD crime labs. "You're the boss. All you've got to do is ask." She meets my eyes. "Welcome back."

"What kind of crest, and what does the keychain look like?" Benton asks Marino.

"A coat of arms, an open book with three crowns," he says, and I can tell he enjoys having Benton at a disadvantage. The CFC is Marino's turf. "No writing on it, no phrase in Latin, nothing like that. I don't know what the crests for MIT and Harvard are."

"Not what you described," Benton answers. "Okay if I use this?" He indicates a computer on the counter.

"The keychain is one of those steel rings attached to a leather loop, like you'd snap around your belt," Marino goes on. "And as we all know, no wallet, not even a cell phone, and I think that's unusual. Who walks around with no cell phone?"

"He was taking his dog out and listening to music. Maybe he wasn't planning to be out very long and didn't want to talk on the phone," Benton says as he types in search words.

I pull the body over on its right side and look at Marino. "You want to help me with this?"

"Three crowns and an open book," Benton says. "City University of San Francisco." He types some more. "An online university specializing in health sciences. Would an online university have class rings?"

"And his personal effects are in which locker?" I ask Marino.

"*Numero uno.* I got the key if you want it."

"I would. Anything the labs need to check?"

"Can't see why."

"Then we'll keep his personal effects until they go to a funeral home or to his family, when we figure out who he is," I reply.

"And then there's Oxford," Benton says next, still searching the Internet. "But if the ring he had on was Oxford, it would have *Oxford University* on it, and you said it didn't have any writing or motto."

"It didn't," Marino replies. "But it looks like someone had it made, you know, plain gold and engraved with the crest, so maybe it wouldn't be as official as what you order from a school and wouldn't have a motto or writing."

"Maybe," Benton says. "But if the ring was made, I have a hard time imagining it's for Oxford University, would be more inclined to think if someone went to an online college he might have a ring made because maybe there's no other way to get one, assuming you want to tell the world you're an alum of an online college. This is the City University of San Francisco coat of arms." Benton moves to one side so Marino can see what's on the computer screen, an elaborate crest with blue-and-gold mantling, and a gold owl on top with three gold fleur-de-lis, then below three gold crowns, and in the middle an open book.

Marino is holding the body on its side, and he squints at the computer screen from where he's standing and shrugs. "Maybe. If it was engraved, you know, if the person had it made for him, maybe it wouldn't be that detailed. That could be it."

"I'll look at the ring," I promise as I examine the body externally and make notes on a clipboard.

"No reason to think he was in a struggle, and we might get a perp's DNA or something off the watch or whatever. But you know me." Marino resumes what he was saying to me about processing the dead man's personal effects. "I swabbed everything anyway. Nothing struck me as unusual except that his watch had quit, one of those self-winding kind that Lucy likes, a chronograph."

"What time did it stop?"

"I got it written down. Sometime after four a.m. About twelve hours after he died. So he's got a nine-mil with eighteen rounds but no phone," he then says. "Okay. I guess so, unless he didn't leave it at home and in fact somebody took it. Maybe took the dog, too. That's what I keep wondering."

"There was a phone on a desk in the video clips I saw," I remind him. "Plugged into a charger near one of the laptops, I believe. Near the glass smoking pipe you mentioned."

"We couldn't see everything he did in there before he left. I figured he might have grabbed his phone on his way out," Marino supposes. "Or he might have more than one. Who the hell knows?"

"We'll know when we find his apartment," Benton says as he

prints what he's found on the Internet. "I'd like to see the scene photos."

"You mean when I find the apartment." Marino puts the camera down on a countertop. "Because it's going to be me poking around. Cops gossip worse than old women. I find where the guy lives, then I'll ask for help."

8

n a body diagram, I note that at eleven-fifteen p.m. the dead man is fully rigorous and refrigerated cold. He has a pattern of dark-red discoloration and positional blanching that indicates he was flat on his back with his arms straight by his sides, palms down, fully clothed, and wearing a watch on his left wrist and a ring on his left little finger for at least twelve hours after he died.

Postmortem hypostasis, better known as lividity or livor mortis, is one of my pet tattletales, although it is often misinterpreted even by those who should know better. It can look like bruising due to trauma when in fact it is caused by the mundane physiological phenomenon of noncirculating blood pooling into small vessels due to gravity. Lividity is a dusky red or can be purplish with lighter areas of blanching where areas of the body rested against a firm surface, and no matter what I'm told about the circumstances of a death, the body itself doesn't lie.

"No secondary livor pattern that might indicate the body moved while livor was still forming," I observe. "Everything I'm seeing is consistent with him being zipped up inside a pouch and placed on a body tray and not moving." I attach a body diagram to a clipboard and sketch impressions made by a waistband, a belt, jewelry, shoes and socks, pale areas on the skin that show the shape of elastic or a buckle or fabric or a weave pattern.

"Certainly suggests he didn't even move his arms, didn't thrash around, so that's good," Anne decides.

"Exactly. If he'd come to, he would have at least moved his arms. So that's real good," Marino agrees, keys clicking as an image fills the screen of the computer terminal on a countertop.

I make a note that the man has no body piercings or tattoos, and is clean, with neatly trimmed nails and the smooth skin of one who doesn't do manual labor or engage in any physical activity that might cause calluses on his hands or feet. I palpate his head, feeling for defects, such as fractures or other injuries, and find nothing.

"Question is whether he was facedown when he fell." Marino is looking at what Investigator Lester Law e-mailed to him. "Or is he on his back in these pictures because the EMTs turned him over?"

"To do CPR they would have had to turn him faceup." I move closer to look.

Marino clicks through several photos, all of them the same but from different perspectives: the man on his back, his dark-green jacket and denim shirt open, his head turned to one side, eyes partly closed; a close-up of his face, debris clinging to his lips, what looks like particles of dead leaves and grass and grit.

"Zoom in on that," I tell Marino, and with a click of the mouse, the image is larger, the man's boyish face filling the screen.

I return to the body behind me and check for injuries of his face and head, noting an abrasion on the underside of the chin. I pull down the lower lip and find a small laceration, likely made by his lower teeth when he fell and hit his face on the gravel path.

"Couldn't possibly account for all the blood I saw," Anne says.

"No, it couldn't," I agree. "But it suggests he hit the ground face-first, which also suggests he dropped like a shot, didn't even stumble or try to break his fall. Where's the pouch he came in?"

"I spread it out on a table in the autopsy room, figured you'd want to have a look," Anne tells me. "And his clothes are air-drying in there. When I undressed him, I put everything in the cabinet by your station. Station one."

"Good. Thank you."

"Maybe somebody punched him," Marino offers. "Maybe distracted him by punching or elbowing him in the face, then stabbed him in the back. Except that probably would have been recorded, would be on the video clips."

"He would have more than just this laceration if someone punched him in the mouth. If you look at the debris on his face and the location of the headphones"—I'm back at the computer, clicking on images to show them—"it appears he fell facedown. The headphones are way over here, what looks like at least six feet away under a bench, indicating to me that he fell with sufficient force to knock them a fair distance and disconnect them from the satellite radio, which I believe was in a pocket."

"Unless someone moved the phones, perhaps kicked them out of the way," Benton says.

"That was my other thought," I reply.

"You mean like somebody who tried to help him," Marino says. "People crowding around him and the headphones ended up under a bench."

"Or someone did it deliberately."

There is something else I notice. Clicking through the slide-show, I stop on a photograph of his left wrist. I zoom in on the steel tachymeter watch, move in close on its carbon-fiber face. The time stamp on the photograph is five-seventeen p.m., which is when the police officer took it, yet the time on the watch is ten-fourteen, five hours later than that.

"When you collected the watch this morning"—I direct this to Marino—"you said it appeared to have stopped. You sure it wasn't simply that the time was different than our local time?"

"Nope, it was stopped," he says. "Like I said, one of those self-winding watches, and it quit at some point early in the morning, like around four a.m."

"Seems it might have been set five hours later than Eastern Standard Time." I point out what I'm seeing in the photograph.

"Okay. Then it must have stopped around eleven p.m. our time," Marino says. "So it was set wrong to begin with and then it quit."

"Maybe he was on another time zone because he'd just flown in from overseas," Benton suggests.

"Soon as we finish up here, I got to find his apartment," Marino says.

I check the quality-control numbers in the quality-control log, making sure standard deviation is zero and the noise level of the system or variation is within normal limits.

"We ready?" I say to everyone.

I'm eager to do the scan. I want to see what is inside this man.

"We'll do a topogram, then collect the data set before going to three-D recon with at least fifty percent overlapping," I tell Anne as she presses a button to slide the table into the scanner. "But we'll change the protocol and start with the thorax, not the head, except, of course, for using the glabella as our reference."

I refer to the space between the eyebrows above the nose that we use for spatial orientation.

"A cross-sectional of the chest exactly correlating with the region of interest you've marked." I go down the list as we return to the control room. "An in situ localization of the wound; we'll isolate that area and any associated injury, any clues in the wound track."

I seat myself between Ollie and Anne, and then Marino and Benton pull up chairs behind us. Through the glass window I can see the man's bare feet in the opening of the scanner's bore.

"Auto and smart MT, noise index eighteen. Point-five segment rotation, point-six-two-five detector configuration," I instruct. "Very thin slice ultra-high resolution. Ten-millimeter collimation."

I can hear the electronic pulsing sounds as detectors begin rotating inside the x-ray tube. The first scan lasts sixty seconds. I watch in real time on a computer screen, not sure what I'm seeing, but it shouldn't be this. It occurs to me the scanner is malfunctioning or that some other patient's scan is displayed, the wrong file accessed. *What am I looking at?*

"Jesus," Ollie says under his breath, frowning at images in a grid, strange images that must be a mistake.

"Orient in time and space, and let's line up the wound back to front, left to right, and upward," I direct. "Connect points to get the penetration of the wound track, well, such as it is. There is a wound track and then it disappears? I don't know what this is."

"What the hell am I looking at?" Marino asks, baffled.

"Nothing I've ever seen before, certainly not in a stabbing," I reply.

"Well, for one thing, air," Ollie announces. "We're seeing a hell of a lot of air."

"These dark areas here and here and here." I show Marino and Benton. "On CT, air looks dark. As opposed to the brighter white areas, which show higher density. Bone and calcification are bright. You can get a pretty good idea of what something is by the density of the pixels."

I reach for the mouse and move the cursor over a rib so they can see what I mean.

"CT number is one thousand one hundred and fifty one. Whereas this not-so-bright area here"—I move the cursor over an area of lung—"is forty. That's going to be blood. These dullish dark areas you're seeing are hemorrhage."

I'm reminded of high-velocity gunshots that cause tremendous crushing and tearing of tissue, similar to injury caused by the blast wave from an explosion. But this isn't a gunshot case. This isn't from a detonated explosive device. I don't see how either could be true.

"Some kind of wound that travels through the left kidney, superiorly through the diaphragm and into the heart, causing profound devastation along the way. And all this." I point to murky areas around internal organs that are displaced and sheared. "More subcutaneous air. Air in the paraspinal musculature. Retroperitoneal air. How did all this air get inside of him? And here and here. Injury to bone. Rib fracture. Fracture of a transverse process. Hemopneumothorax, lung contusion, hemopericardium. And more air. Here and here and here." I touch the screen. "Air surrounding the heart and in the cardiac chambers, as well as in the pulmonary arteries and veins."

"And you've never seen anything like this?" Benton asks me.

"Yes and no. Similar devastation caused by military rifles, antitank cannons, some semiautomatics using extreme shock-fragmenting high-velocity ammunition, for example. The higher the velocity, the greater the kinetic energy dissipates at impact and the greater the damage, especially to hollow organs, such as bowel and lungs, and nonelastic tissue, such as the liver, the kidneys. But in a case like that, you expect a clear wound track and a missile or fragments of one. Which we aren't seeing."

"What about air?" Benton asks. "Do you see these pockets of air in cases like that?"

"Not exactly," I reply. "A blast wave can create air emboli by forcing air across the air-blood barrier, such as out of the lungs. In other words, air ends up where it doesn't belong, but this is a lot of air."

"A hell of a lot," Ollie concurs. "And how do you get a blast wave from a stabbing?"

"Do a slice right through those coordinates," I say to him, indicating the region of interest marked by a bright white bead— the radio-opaque CT skin marker that was placed next to the wound on the left side of the man's back. "Start here and keep moving down five millimeters above and below the region of interest specified by the markers. That cut. Yes, that's the one. And let's reformat into virtual three-D volume rendering from inside out. Thin, thin cuts, one millimeter, and the increment between them? What do you think?"

"Point-seventy-five by point-five will do it."

"Okay, fine. Let's see what it looks like if we virtually follow the track, what track there is."

Bones are as vivid as if they are laid bare before us, and organs and other internal structures are well defined in shades of gray as the dead man's upper body, his thorax, begins to rotate slowly in three-dimension on the video display. Using modified software originally developed for virtual colonoscopies, we enter the body through the tiny buttonhole wound, traveling with a virtual camera as if we are in a microscopic spaceship slowly flying through murky grayish clouds of tissue, past a left kidney blown apart like an asteroid.

A ragged opening yawns before us, and we pass through a large hole in the diaphragm. Beyond is shattering, shearing, and contusion. *What happened to you? What did this?* I don't have a clue. It's a helpless feeling to find physical damage that seems to defy physics, an effect without a cause. There's no projectile. There's no frag, nothing metal I can see. There's no exit wound, only the buttonhole entrance on the left side of his back. I'm thinking out loud, repeating important points, making sure everyone understands what is incomprehensible.

"I keep forgetting nothing works down here," Benton comments distractedly as he looks at his iPhone.

"Nothing exited, and nothing is lighting up." I calculate what must be done next. "No sign of anything ferrous, but we need to be sure."

"Absolutely no idea what could have done this," Benton states rather than asks as he gets up from his chair, making rustling sounds as he unties his disposable gown. "You know the old saying, nothing new under the sun. I guess like a lot of old sayings, it's not true."

"This is new. At least to me," I reply.

He bends over and pulls off his shoe covers. "No question he's a homicide."

"Unless he ate some really bad Mexican food," Marino says.

It vaguely drifts through my thoughts that Benton is acting suspiciously.

"Like a high-velocity projectile, but there's no projectile, and if it exited the body, where's the exit wound?" I keep saying the same thing. "Where the hell's the metal? What the hell could he have been shot with? An ice bullet?"

"I saw a thing about that on *MythBusters*. They proved it's impossible because of heat," Marino says, as if I'm serious. "I don't know, though. Wonder what would happen if you loaded the gun and kept it in the freezer until you were ready to fire it."

"Maybe if you're a sniper in the interior of Antarctica," Ollie says. "Where'd that idea come from, anyway? *Dick Tracy*? I'm asking for real."

"I thought it was James Bond. I forget which movie."

"Maybe the exit wound isn't obvious," Anne says to me. "Remember that time the guy was shot in the jaw and it exited through his nostril?"

"Then where's the wound track?" I reply. "We need better contrast between tissues, need to be damn sure there's nothing we're missing before I open him up."

"If you need my help with that, I can call the hospital," Benton says as he opens the door. I can tell he's in a hurry, but I'm not sure why.

It's not his case.

"Otherwise, I'll check on what Lucy's found," Benton says. "Take a look at the video clips. Check on a couple other things. You don't mind if I use a phone up there."

"I'll make the call," Anne says to him as he leaves. "I'll get it arranged with McLean and take care of the scan."

It's been a theoretical possibility this day would come, and we are cleared with the Board of Health, and with Harvard and its affiliate McLean Hospital, which has four magnets ranging in strength from 1.5 to 9 Tesla. Long ago I made sure the protocols were in place to do MRIs on dead bodies in McLean's neuroimaging lab, where Anne works as a part-time MR tech for psychiatric research studies. That's how I got her. Benton knew her first and recommended her. He picks well, is a fine judge of character. I should let him hire my damn staff. I wonder whom he is going to call. I'm not sure why he is here at all.

"If that's what you want, we can do it right now," Anne is saying to me. "There shouldn't be a problem, won't be anyone around. We'll just go right up to the front door and get him in and out."

At this hour, psychiatric patients at McLean won't be wandering around the campus. There's little risk of them happening upon a dead body being carried in or out of a lab.

"What if someone shot him with a water cannon?" Marino stares as if transfixed at the rotating torso on the video screen, the ribs curving and gleaming whitely in 3-D. "Seriously. I've always heard that's the perfect crime. You fill a shotgun shell with water, and it's like a bullet when it goes through the body. But it doesn't leave a trace."

"I've not had a case like that," I reply.

"But it could happen," Marino says.

"Theoretically. However, the entrance wound wouldn't be like this one," I reply. "Let's get going. I want him posted and safely out of sight before everyone starts arriving for work." It's almost midnight.

Anne clicks on the icon for *Tools* to take measurements and informs me the width of the wound track before it blows through the diaphragm is .77 to 1.59 millimeters at a depth of 4.2 millimeters.

"So what that tells me . . ." I start to say.

"How about inches," Marino complains.

"Some type of double-edged object or blade that doesn't get much wider than half an inch," I explain. "And once it penetrated the body up to an approximate depth of two inches, something else happened that caused profound internal damage."

"What I'm wondering is how much of this abnormality we're seeing is iatrogenic," Ollie says. "Caused by the EMTs working on him for twenty minutes. That's probably the first question we'll get asked. We have to keep an open mind."

"No way. Not unless King Kong did CPR," I reply. "It appears this man was stabbed with something that caused tremendous pressure in his chest and a large air embolus. He would have had severe pain and been dead within minutes, which is consistent with what's been described by witnesses, that he clutched his chest and collapsed."

"Then why all the blood after the fact?" Marino says. "Why wouldn't he have been hemorrhaging instantly? How the hell's it possible he didn't start bleeding until after he was pronounced and on his way here?"

"I don't know the answer, but he didn't die in our cooler." I am at least sure of that. "He was dead before he got here, would have been dead at the scene."

"But we got to prove he started bleeding after he was dead. And dead people don't start bleeding like a damn stuck pig. So how do we prove he was dead before he got here?" Marino persists.

"Who do we need to prove it to?" I look at him.

"I don't know who Fielding's told since we don't even know where the hell he is. What if he's told somebody?"

Like you did, I think, but I don't say it. "That's why one should be careful about divulging details when we don't have all the information." I couldn't sound more reasonable.

"We got no choice about it." Marino won't let it go. "We have to prove why a dead person started bleeding."

I collect my jacket and tell Anne, "A head and full-body CT scan first. And on MR, full-body coil, every inch of him, and upload what you find. I'll want to see it right away."

"I'm driving," Marino says to her.

"Well, pull it into the bay to warm it up. One of the vans."

"We don't want him warming up. Matter of fact, think I'll put the AC on full-blast."

"Then you can ride just the two of you. I'll meet you there."

"Seriously. He warms up, he might start bleeding again."

"You've been watching too much *Saturday Night Live.*"

"Dan Aykroyd doing Julia Child? Remember that? *'You'll need a knife, a very, very sharp knife.'* And blood spurting everywhere."

The three of them bantering.

"That was so funny."

"The old ones were better."

"No kidding. Roseanne Roseannadanna."

"Oh, God, I love her."

"I've got them all on DVD."

I hear them laughing as I walk away.

Scanning my thumb, I let myself into the area that is the first stop after Receiving, where we do identifications, a white room with gray countertops that we simply call ID.

Built into a wall are gray metal evidence lockers, each of them numbered, and I use the key Marino gave me to open the top one on the left, where the dead man's personal effects have been safely stored until we receipt them to a funeral home or to a family when we finally know who he is and who should claim him. Inside are paper bags and envelopes neatly labeled, and attached to each are forms Marino has filled out and initialed to maintain chain of custody. I find the small manila envelope containing the signet ring, and initial the form and put down the time I removed it from the locker. At a computer station I pull up a log and enter the same information, and then I think about the dead man's clothes.

I should look at them while I'm down here, not wait until I do the autopsy, which will be hours from now. I want to see the hole made by the blade that penetrated the man's lower back and created such havoc inside him. I want to see how much he might have bled from that wound, and I leave ID and walk along the gray tile corridor, backtracking. I pass the x-ray room, and through its open door I catch a glimpse of Marino, Anne, and Ollie, still in there, getting the body ready for transport to McLean, joking and laughing. I quickly go past without them noticing, and I open the double steel doors leading into the autopsy room.

It is a vast open space of white epoxy paint and white tile and exposed shiny steel tracks with cool filtered lighting running horizontally along the length of the white ceiling. Eleven steel tables are parked by wall-mounted steel sinks, each with a foot-operated faucet control, a high-pressure spray hose, a commercial disposal, a specimen rinse basket, and a sharps container. The stations I carefully researched and had installed are mini-modular operating theaters with down-draft ventilation systems that exchange air every five minutes, and there are computers, fume hoods, carts of surgical instruments, halogen lights on flexible arms, dissecting surfaces with cutting boards, containers of formalin with spigots, and test-tube racks and plastic jars for histology and toxicology.

My station, the chief's station, is the first one, and it occurs to me that someone has been using it, and then I feel ridiculous for thinking it. Of course people would have been using it while I've been gone. Of course Fielding probably did. *It doesn't matter, and why should I care?* I tell myself as I notice that the surgical instruments on the cart aren't neatly lined up the way I would leave them. They are haphazardly placed on a large white polyethylene dissecting board as if someone rinsed them and didn't do it thoroughly. I grab a pair of latex gloves out of a box and pull them on because I don't want to touch anything with my bare hands.

Normally, I don't worry about it, not as much as I should, I suppose, because I come from an old school of forensic pathologists who were stoical and battle-scarred and took perverse pride in not being afraid of or repulsed by anything. Not maggots or purge fluid or putrefying flesh that is bloated and turning green and slipping, not even AIDS, at least not the worries we have now when we live with phobias and federal regulations about absolutely everything. I remember when I walked around without protective clothing on, smoking, drinking coffee, and touching dead patients as any doctor would, my bare skin against theirs as I examined a wound or looked at a contusion or took a measurement. But I was never sloppy with my work station or my surgical instruments. I was never careless.

I would never return so much as a teasing needle to a surgical cart without first washing it with hot, soapy water, and the drumming of hot water into deep metal sinks was a pervasive sound in the morgues of my past. As far back as my Richmond days—even earlier, when I was just starting at Walter Reed—I knew about DNA and that it was about to be admissible in court and become the forensic gold standard, and from that point forward, everything we did at crime scenes and in the autopsy suite and in the labs would be questioned on the witness stand. Contamination was about to become the ultimate nemesis, and although we don't make a routine of autoclaving our surgical instruments at the CFC, we certainly don't give them a cursory splash under the faucet and then toss them onto a cutting board that isn't clean, either.

I pick up an eighteen-inch dissecting knife and notice a trace of dried blood in the scored stainless-steel handle and that the steel blade is scratched and pitted along the edge and spotted instead of razor-sharp and as bright as polished silver. I notice blood in the serrated blade of a bone saw and dried bloodstains on a spool of waxed five-cord thread and on a double-curved needle. I pick up forceps, scissors, rib shears, a chisel, a flexible probe, and am dismayed by the poor condition everything is in.

I will send Anne a message to hose down my station and wash all of its instruments before we autopsy the man from Norton's Woods. I will have this entire goddamn autopsy room cleaned from the ceiling to the floor. I will have all of its systems inspected before my first week home has passed, I decide, as I pull on a fresh pair of gloves and walk to a countertop where a large roll of white paper—what we call butcher paper—is attached to a wall-mounted dispenser. Paper makes a loud ripping sound as I tear off a section and cover an autopsy table midway down the room, a table that looks cleaner than mine.

I cover my AFME field clothes with a disposable gown, not bothering with the long ties in back, then return to my messy station. Against the wall is a large white polypropylene drying cabinet on hard rubber casters with a double clear acrylic door, which I unlock by entering a code in a digital keypad. Hanging inside are a sage-green nylon jacket with a black fleece collar, a blue denim shirt, black cargo pants, and a pair of boxer briefs, each on its own stainless-steel hanger, and on the tray at the bottom are a pair of scuffed brown leather boots, and next to them, a pair of gray wool socks. I recognize some of the clothing from the video clips I saw, and it gives me an unsettled feeling to look at it now. The cabinet's centrifugal fan and HEPA exhaust filters make their low whirring sound as I look at the boots and the socks by picking them up one by one, finding nothing remarkable. The boxer briefs are white cotton with a crossover fly and elastic waistband, and I note nothing unusual, no stains or defects.

Spreading the coat open on the butcher paper–covered table, I slip my hands into the pockets, making sure nothing has been left in them, and I collect a clothing diagram and a clipboard and begin to make notes. The collar is a deep-pile synthetic fur and covered with dirt and sand and pieces of dry brown leaves that adhered to it when the man collapsed to the ground, and the heavy knit cuffs are dirty, too. The sage nylon shell is a very tough material, which appears to be tear-resistant and waterproof with a black fiberfill insulation, none of it easily penetrable unless the blade was strong and very sharp. I find no evidence of blood inside the liner of the coat, not even around the small slit in the back of it, but the areas of the outer shell, the shoulders, the sleeves, the back, are blackened and stiff with blood that collected in the bottom of the body pouch after the man was zipped inside it and then was transported to the CFC.

I don't know how long he might have bled out while he was inside the bag and then the cooler, but he didn't bleed from his wound. When I spread open the denim shirt, long-sleeved, a men's size small, which still smells faintly of a cologne or an after-shave, I find only a spot of dark blood that has dried stiffly around the slit made by the blade. What Marino and Anne have reported seems to be accurate, that the man began bleeding from his nose and mouth while he was fully clothed inside the body bag, his head turned to the side, probably the same side it was turned to when I examined him in the x-ray room a little while ago. Blood must have dripped steadily from his face into the bag, pooling in it and leaking from it, and I can see that easily when I look at it next, an adult-size cadaver pouch, typical of ones used by removal services, black with a nylon zipper. On the sides are webbing handles attached with rivets, and that's often where the problem with leakage occurs, assuming the bag is intact with no tears or flaws in the heat-sealed seams. Blood seeps through rivets, especially if the pouch is really cheap, and this one is about twenty-five dollars' worth of heavy-duty PVC, likely purchased by the case.

As I imagine what I just saw on the CT scan and realize how quickly the damage occurred in what clearly was a blitz attack, the bleeding makes no sense at all. It makes even less sense than it did when Marino first told me about it in Dover. The massive destruction to the man's internal organs would have resulted in pulmonary hemorrhage that would have caused blood to drain out of the nose and mouth. But it should have happened almost instantly. I don't understand why he didn't bleed at the scene. When the paramedics were working to resuscitate him, he should have been bleeding from his face, and this would have been a clear indication that he hadn't dropped dead from an arrhythmia.

As I leave the autopsy room to go upstairs, I envision the video clips again and remember my wondering about his black gloves and why he put them on when he entered the park. Where are they? I haven't seen a pair of gloves. They weren't in the evidence locker or in the drying cabinet, and I checked the pockets of the coat and didn't find them. Based on what I saw in the recordings covertly made by the man's headphones, he had the gloves on when he died, and I envision what I saw on Lucy's iPad when I was riding in the van to the Civil Air Terminal. A black-gloved hand entered the frame as if the man was swatting at something and there was a jostling sound as his hand hit the headphones while his voice blurted out, *"What the . . . ? Hey . . . !"* Then bare trees rushing up and around, then chipped bits of slate looming large on the ground and the thud of him hitting, and then the hem of a long black coat flapping past. Then silence, then the voices of people surrounding him and exclaiming that he wasn't breathing.

The x-ray room door is closed when I get to it, and I check inside, but everyone is gone, the control room empty and quiet, the CT scanner glowing white in the low lights on the other side of the lead-lined glass. I pause to try the phone in there, hoping Anne might answer her cell, but if she's already at McLean and in the neuroimaging lab, it will be impossible to reach her through the thick concrete walls of that place. I am surprised when she answers.

"Where are you?" I ask, and I can hear music in the background.

"Pulling up now," she says, and she must be inside the van with Marino driving and the radio on.

"When you removed his clothing," I say, "did you see a pair of black gloves? He may have been wearing a pair of thick black gloves."

A pause, and I hear her say something to Marino and then I hear his voice, but I can't make out what they're saying to each other. Then she tells me, "No. And Marino says when he had the body in ID first thing, there were no gloves. He doesn't remember gloves."

"Tell me exactly what happened yesterday morning."

"Just sit right here for a minute," I hear her say to Marino. "No, not there yet or they'll come out. The security guys will. Just wait here," she says to him. "Okay," she says to me. "A little bit after seven yesterday morning, Dr. Fielding came to x-ray. As you know, Ollie and I are always in early, by seven, and anyway, he was concerned because of the blood. He'd noticed blood drips on the floor outside the cooler and also inside it, and that the body was bleeding or had bled. A lot of blood in the pouch."

"The body was still fully clothed."

"Yes. The coat was unzipped and the shirt was cut open, the EMTs did that, but he was clothed when he came in and nothing was done until Dr. Fielding went in there to get him ready for us."

"What do you mean, 'to get him ready'?"

I've never known Fielding to get a body ready for autopsy, to actually go to the trouble to move it out of the refrigerator and into x-ray or the autopsy room, at least not since the old days when he was in training. He leaves what he considers mundane tasks to those whom he still calls *dieners* and whom I call autopsy technicians.

"I only know he found the blood and then hurried to get us because he took the call from Cambridge PD, and as you know, it was assumed the guy was a sudden death that was natural, like an arrhythmia or a berry aneurysm or something."

"Then what?"

"Then Ollie and I looked at the body, and we called Marino and he came and looked, and it was decided not to scan him or do the post yet."

"He was left in the cooler?"

"No. Marino wanted to process him in ID first, to get his prints, swabs, so we could get started with IAFIS and DNA, with anything that might help us figure out who he is. The important point is there were no gloves at that time, because Marino would have had to take them off the body so he could print him."

"Then where are they?"

"He doesn't know, and I don't, either."

"Can you put him on, please?"

I hear her hand him the phone, and he says, "Yeah. I unzipped the pouch but didn't take him out of it, and there was a lot of blood in it, like you know."

"And you did what, exactly?"

"I printed him while he was in the pouch, and if there had been gloves, I sure as hell would have seen them."

"Possible the squad removed the gloves at the scene and put them inside the pouch and you didn't notice? And then they got misplaced somehow?"

"Nope. I looked for any personal effects, like I told you. The watch, ring, keychain, the stash box, the twenty-dollar bill. Took everything out of his pockets, and I always look inside the pouch for the very reason you just said. In case the squad or the removal service tucks something in there, like a hat or sunglasses or whatever. The headphones, too. And the satellite radio. They were in a paper bag and came in with the body."

"What about Cambridge PD? I know Investigator Lawless brought in the Glock."

"He receipted it to the firearms lab around ten a.m. That was all he brought in."

"And when Anne put his clothing inside the drying cabinet, well, obviously she didn't have the gloves if you say they weren't there in the first place."

I hear him say something, and then Anne is back on the phone, saying, "No. I didn't see gloves when I put everything else in the cabinet. That was around nine p.m., almost four hours ago, when I undressed the body to get it ready for the scan, not long before you got to the CFC. I cleaned the cabinet to make sure it was sterile before I put his other clothing in there."

"I'm glad something's sterile. We need to clean my station."

"Okay, okay," she says, but not to me. "Wait. Jesus, Pete. Hold on."

And then Marino's voice in my ear: "There were other cases."

"I beg your pardon?"

"We had other cases yesterday morning. So maybe someone removed the gloves, but I got no friggin' idea why. Unless they maybe got picked up by mistake."

"Who did the cases?"

"Dr. Lambotte, Dr. Booker."

"What about Jack?"

"Two cases in addition to the guy from Norton's Woods," Marino says. "A woman who got hit by a train and an old guy who wasn't under the care of a physician. Jack didn't do shit, was gone with the wind," Marino says. "He doesn't bother with the scene, and so we get a body that starts bleeding in the fridge and now we got to prove the guy was dead."

he directorate of what officially is called the Cambridge Forensic Center and Port Mortuary is on the top floor, and I have discovered that it is difficult to tell people how to find me when a building is round.

The best I've been able to do on the infrequent occasions I've been here is to instruct visitors to get off the elevator on the seventh floor, take a left, and look for number 111. It's only one door down from 101, and to comprehend that 101 is the lowest room number on this floor and 111 is the highest requires some imagination. My office suite, therefore, would occupy a corner at the end of a long hallway if there were corners and long hallways, but there aren't. Up here there is just one big circle with six offices, a large conference room, the reading room for voice-recognition dictation, the library, the break room, and in the center a windowless bunker where Lucy chose to put the computer and questioned documents lab.

Walking past Marino's office, I stop outside 111, what he calls CENTCOM, for Central Command. I'm sure Marino came up with the pretentious appellation all on his own, not because he thinks of me as his commander but rather he's come to think of himself as answering to a higher patriotic order that is close to a religious calling. His worship of all things military is new. It's just one more thing that is paradoxical about him, as if Peter Rocco Marino needs yet another paradox to define his inconsistent and conflicted self.

I need to calm down about him, I say to myself as I unlock my heavy door with its titanium veneer. He isn't so bad and didn't do anything so terrible. He's predictable, and I shouldn't be surprised in the least. After all, who understands him better than I do? The Rosetta stone to Marino isn't Bayonne, New Jersey, where he grew up a street fighter who became a boxer and then a cop. The key to him isn't even his worthless alcoholic father. Marino can be explained by his mother first and foremost, and then his childhood sweetheart Doris, now his ex-wife, both women seemingly docile and subservient and sweet but not harmless. Not hardly.

I push buttons to turn on the flush-mount lighting built into the struts of the geodesic glass dome that is energy-efficient and reminds me of Buckminster Fuller every time I look up. Were the famed architect-inventor still among the living, he would approve of my building and possibly of me but not of our morbid raison d'être, I suspect, although at this stage of things I would have a few quibbles with him, too. For example, I don't agree with his belief that technology can save us. Certainly, it isn't making us more civilized, and I actually think the opposite is true.

I pause on gunmetal-gray carpet just inside my doorway as if waiting for permission to enter, or maybe I'm hesitant because to appropriate this space is to embrace a life I've rather much put off for the better part of two years. If I'm honest about it I should say I've put it off for decades, since my earliest days at Walter Reed, where I was minding my own business in a cramped, windowless room of AFIP headquarters when Briggs walked in without knocking and dropped an eight-by-eleven gray envelope on my desk with *CLASSIFIED* stamped on it.

December 4, 1987. I remember it so vividly I can describe what I was wearing and the weather and what I ate. I know I smoked a lot that day and had several straight Scotches at the end of it because I was excited and horrified. The case of all cases, and the DoD wanted me, picked me over all others. Or more accurately, Briggs did. By spring of the following year, I was discharged from the air force early, not on good behavior but because the Reagan administration wanted me gone, and I left under certain conditions that are shameful and cause pain even now. It is karmic that I find myself in a building of circles. Nothing has ended or begun in my life. What was far away is right next to me. Somehow it's all the same.

The most blatant sign of my six-month absence from a position I've yet to really fill is that Bryce's adjoining administrative office is comfortably cluttered while mine is empty and stark. It feels forlorn and lonely in here, my small conference table of brushed steel bare, not even a potted plant on it, and when I inhabit a space there are always plants. Orchids, gardenias, succulents, and indoor trees, such as areca and sago palms, because I want life and fragrances. But what I had in here when I moved in is gone and has been gone, overwatered and too much fertilizer. I gave Bryce detailed instructions and three months to kill everything. It took him less than two.

There is virtually nothing on my desk, a bow-shaped modular work station constructed of twenty-two-gauge steel with a black laminate surface and a matching hutch of file drawers and open shelves between expansive windows overlooking the Charles and the Boston skyline. A black granite countertop behind my Aeron chair runs the length of the wall and is home to my Leica Laser Microdissection System and its video displays and accoutrements, and nearby is my faithful backup Leica for daily use, a more basic laboratory research microscope that I can operate with one hand and without software or a training seminar. There isn't much else, no case files in sight, no death certificates or other paperwork for me to review and initial, no mail, and very few personal effects. I decide it's not a good thing to have such a perfectly arranged, immaculate office. I'd rather have a landfill. It's peculiar that being faced with an empty work space should make me feel so overwhelmed, and as I seal Erica Donahue's letter in a plastic bag I finally realize why I'm not a fan of a world that is fast becoming paperless. I like to see the enemy, stacks of what I must conquer, and I take comfort in reams of friends.

I'm locking the letter in a cabinet when Lucy silently appears like an apparition in a voluminous white lab coat she wears for its warmth and what she can conceal beneath it, and she's also fond of big pockets. The oversized coat makes her seem deceptively nonthreatening and much younger than her years, in her low thirties is the way she puts it, but she'll forever be a little girl to me. I wonder if mothers always feel that way about their daughters, even when the daughters are mothers themselves, or in Lucy's case, armed and dangerous.

She probably has a pistol tucked into the back waistband of her cargo pants, and I realize how selfishly happy I am that she's home. She's back in my life, not in Florida or with people I have to force myself to like. Manhattan prosecutor Jaime Berger is included in this mix. As I look at my niece, my surrogate only child, walking into my office, I can't avoid a truth I won't tell her. I'm glad if she and Jaime have called it quits. That's really why I haven't asked about it.

"Is Benton still with you?" I inquire.

"He's on the phone." She shuts the door behind her.

"Who's he talking to at this hour?"

Lucy takes a chair, pulling her legs up on the seat, crossing them at the ankles. "Some of his people," she says, as if to imply he's talking to colleagues at McLean, but that's not it. Anne is handling the hospital, and she and Marino are there and getting started on the scan. Why would Benton be talking to them or anyone else at McLean?

"It's just the three of us, then," I comment pointedly. "Except for Ron, I assume. But if you want the door shut, I suppose that's fine." It's my way of letting her know that her hypervigilant and secretive behavior isn't lost on me and I wish she would explain it. I wish she would explain why she feels it necessary to be evasive if not blatantly untruthful to me, her aunt, her almost-mother, and now her boss.

"I know." She slides a small evidence pillbox out of her lab coat pocket.

"You know? What do you know?"

"That Anne and Marino went to McLean because you want an MRI. Benton filled me in. Why didn't you go?"

"I'm not needed and wouldn't be particularly helpful, since MR scans aren't my specialty." There is no MRI scanner at Dover's port mortuary, where most bodies are war casualties and are going to have metal in them. "I thought I'd take care of a few things, and when I'm satisfied I know what I'm looking for, I'll get started on the autopsy."

"Kind of a backward way to look at things, when you stop to think about it," Lucy muses, her eyes green and intensely fixed on me. "It used to be you did the autopsy so you knew what you were looking for. Now it's just a confirmation of what you already know and a means of collecting evidence."

"Not exactly. I still get surprises. What's in the box?"

"Speaking of." She slides the small white box across the unobstructed surface of my ridiculously clean desk. "You can take it out and don't need gloves. But be careful with it."

Inside the box on a bed of cotton is what looks like the wing of an insect, possibly a fly.

"Go ahead, touch it," Lucy encourages, leaning forward in her chair, her face bright with excitement, as if she's watching me open a gift.

I feel the stiffness of wire struts and a thin transparent membrane, something like plastic. "Artificial. Interesting. What is this exactly, and where did you get it?"

"You familiar with the holy grail of flybots?"

"I confess I'm drawing a blank."

"Years and years of research. Millions and millions of research dollars spent on building the perfect flybot."

"Not intimately aware of it. Actually, I don't think I know what you're talking about."

"Equipped with micro-cameras and transmitters for covert surveillance, literally for bugging people. Or for detecting chemicals or explosives or possibly even biological hazards. The work's been going on at Harvard, MIT, Berkeley, a number of places here and overseas, even before cyborgs, those insects with embedded micro-electromechanical systems, machine-insect interfaces. Which then spread to doing shit like that to other living creatures, like turtles, dolphins. Not DARPA's finest moments, you ask me."

I place the wing back on the square of cotton. "Let's back up. Start with where you got this."

"I'm worried."

"You and me both."

"When Marino had him in ID this morning"—Lucy means the dead man from Norton's Woods—"I wanted to tell him about the recording system I discovered in the headphones, so I go downstairs. He's fingerprinting the body, and I notice what at a glance looks like a fly wing stuck to the guy's coat collar along with some other debris, like dirt and pieces of dead leaves from his being on the ground."

"It didn't get dislodged by the EMTs," I comment. "When they opened his coat."

"Obviously, it didn't. Was snagged on the fur, the fake-fur collar," Lucy says. "Something struck me about it, you know, I got a funny feeling and I took a closer look."

I get a hand lens out of my desk drawer and turn on an examination light, and in the bright illumination the magnified wing doesn't look natural anymore. What one would assume is the base of the wing, where it attaches to the body, is actually some sort of flexure joint, and the veins running through the wing tissue are shiny like wires.

"Probably a carbon composite, and there are fifteen joints in each wing drive, which is pretty amazing." Lucy describes what I'm seeing. "The wing itself is an electroactive polymer frame, which responds to electrical signals, causing the fanfold wings to flap as fast as the real deal, your everyday housefly. Historically, a flybot takes off vertically like a helicopter and flies like an angel, which has been one of its major design obstacles. That and coming up with something micromechanical that's autonomous but not bulky—in other words, biologically inspired so it has the necessary power to move around freely in whatever environment you put it in."

"Biologically inspired, like da Vinci's conceptualized inventions." I wonder if she is reminded of the exhibition I took her to in London and if she noticed the poster in the living room of the dead man's apartment. Of course she noticed. Lucy notices everything.

"The poster over the couch," she says.

"Yes, I saw it."

"In one of the video clips, when he was putting the leash on his dog. How creepy is that?" Lucy says.

"I'm not sure I know why it's creepy."

"Well, I had the luxury of looking at the recordings more carefully than you did." Lucy's demeanor again, the nuances I've come to recognize as surely as I detect the subtle changes in tissue under the microscope. "It's for the same exhibition you took me to at the Courtauld, has the date on it for that same summer," she says calmly and with a certain goal in mind. "We might have been there when he was, assuming he went."

That's the goal. This is what Lucy thinks. A connection between the dead man and us.

"Having the poster doesn't mean he did," she goes on. "I realize that. It doesn't mean it in a way that would hold up in court," she adds with a hint of irony, as if she's making a dig at Jaime Berger, the prosecutor I'm increasingly suspicious she's no longer with.

"Lucy, do you have some idea of who this man is?" I go ahead and ask.

"I just think it's bizarre to consider he might have been at that gallery when we were. But I'm certainly not saying he was. Not at all."

It's not what she really thinks. I can see it in her eyes and hear it in her voice. She suspects he might have been there when we were. How could she begin to conclude such a thing about a dead man whose name we don't know?

"You're not hacking again," I say bluntly, as if I'm asking about smoking or drinking or some other habit that could be bad for her health.

I've thought more than once that Lucy might have found a way to trace the covertly recorded video files to a personal computer or server somewhere. To her, a firewall and other security measures to protect proprietary data are nothing more than a speed bump on the road to getting what she wants.

"I'm not a hacker," she says simply.

That's not an answer, I think but don't say.

"I just find it an unusual coincidence that he might have been at the Courtauld when we were," she goes on. "And I think it's likely he has that poster because he has some connection to that exhibit. You can't buy them now. I checked. Who would have one unless they went or someone close to them did?"

"Unless he's much older than he looks, he would have been a child then," I point out. "That was in the summer of 2001."

I'm reminded that the time on his watch was five hours ahead of what it should have been for this part of the world. It was set for the United Kingdom's time zone, and the exhibition was in London. That proves nothing. *A consistency but not evidence,* I tell myself.

"That exhibit was exactly the kind of thing a precocious little inventor in the making would love," Lucy says.

"The same way you did," I reply. "I think you walked through it four times. And you bought the lecture series on CD, you were so enthralled."

"It's quite a thought. A little boy in the gallery at the exact moment we were."

"You say that as if it's a fact." I continue to push the same point.

"And almost a decade later I'm here, you're here, and his dead body is here. Talk about six degrees of separation."

It jolts me to hear her refer to something else I was thinking about earlier. First the London exhibit, now the great web that is all of us, the way lives around the planet somehow interconnect.

"I never really get used to it," she is saying. "Seeing someone and then later they're murdered. Not that I can envision him as a boy at a gallery in London, not that I see some little kid's face in my mind. But I might have been standing next to him or even talked to him. In retrospect it's always hard to comprehend that if you had known what was ahead, maybe you could have changed someone's destiny. Or your own."

"Did Benton tell you the man from Norton's Woods was murdered, or did you get that from someone else?"

"We were catching up."

"And you told him about the flybot while you were just now catching up inside your lab." It's not a question.

I feel sure she's told Benton about the robotic fly wing and whatever else she thinks he should know. She's the one who was emphatic in the helicopter a little while ago that he is the only person she really trusts right now, except for me. Although I don't exactly feel trusted. I sense she is sifting through information and selective about what she offers when I wish she wouldn't hold back. I wish she wouldn't be evasive or lie. But one thing I've learned about Lucy is that wishing makes nothing true. I can wish my life away with her and it won't change her behavior. It won't change what she thinks or does.

I turn off the lamp and return the small white box to her. "What do you mean, 'flies like an angel'?"

"Those artistic renderings of angels hovering. I know you've seen them." Lucy reaches for a pad of call sheets and a pen neatly placed next to the phone. "Their bodies are vertical, like someone with a jet pack on, as opposed to insects and birds, whose bodies are horizontal in flight. These little flybots fly vertically, like angels, and that's been one of their flaws, that and their size. Finding the solution is what I mean by 'holy grail.' It's eluded the best and the brightest."

She sketches something to show me, a stick figure that looks like a cross flying through the air.

"If you want an insect like a common housefly to literally be a fly on the wall conducting covert surveillance," she continues, "it should look like a fly, not like a tiny body that's upright with wings attached. If I were having a meeting in Iran with Ahmadinejad and something flew by vertically and landed vertically on a windowsill like a micro–Tinker Bell, I believe I'd notice it and be slightly suspicious."

"If you were meeting with Ahmadinejad in Iran, I'd be slightly suspicious for a lot of reasons. Forgetting why my patient had the wing of one of these things on his coat, assuming this wing is part of an intact flybot—" I start to say.

"Not exactly a flybot," she interrupts. "Not necessarily a spybot, either. That's what I'm getting to. I think this is the holy grail."

"Then whatever it is, what might it have been used for?"

"Let your imagination be the limit," she answers. "I could make quite a list but can't know definitively, not from one wing, although I can tell a few things that are significant. Unfortunately, I couldn't find the rest of it."

"You mean on the body, on his coat? Find it where?"

"At the scene."

"You went to Norton's Woods."

"Sure," she says. "As soon as I realized what the wing was from. Of course I headed straight there."

"We were together for hours." I remind her that she could have told me before now. "Just you and me in the cockpit all the way here from Dover."

"Funny thing about the intercom. Even when I'm sure it's off in back, I'm still not sure. Not if it's something I can't afford having anyone overhear. Marino shouldn't know about this." She indicates the small white box with the wing in it.

"Why exactly?"

"Believe me, you don't want him to know a damn thing about it. It's a very small piece of something a lot bigger, in more ways than one."

She goes on to assure me that Marino knows nothing about her going to Norton's Woods. He is unaware of the tiny mechanical wing or that it was a motivating factor in her encouraging him to bring me home from Dover early, to safely escort me in her helicopter. She didn't mention any of this to me until now, she continues to explain, because she doesn't trust anyone at the moment. Except Benton, she adds. And me, she adds. And she's very careful where she has certain conversations, and all of us should be careful.

"Unless the area has been cleared," she says, and what she means is swept, and the implication is that my office is safe or we wouldn't be having this conversation inside it.

"You checked my office for surveillance devices?" I'm not shocked. Lucy knows how to sweep an area for hidden recorders because she knows how to spy. The best burglar is a locksmith. "Because you think who might be interested in bugging my office?"

"Not sure who's interested in what or why."

"Not Marino," I then say.

"Well, that would be as obvious as a RadioShack nanny cam if he did it. Of course not. I'm not worried about him doing something like that. I just worry that he can't keep his mouth shut," Lucy replies. "At least not when it comes to certain people."

"You talked about MORT in the helicopter. You weren't worried about the intercom, about Marino, when it came to MORT."

"Not the same thing. Not even close," she says. "Doesn't matter if Marino runs his mouth to certain people about a robot in the guy's apartment. Other people already know about it, you can rest assured of that. I can't have Marino talk about my little friend." She looks at the small white box. "And he wouldn't mean anything bad. But he doesn't understand certain realities about certain people. Especially General Briggs and Captain Avallone."

"I didn't realize you knew anything about her." I've never mentioned Sophia Avallone to Lucy.

"When she was here. Jack showed her around. Marino bought her lunch, was kissing her uniformed ass. He doesn't get it about people like that, about the fucking Pentagon, for that matter, or someone he stupidly assumes is one of us, you know, is safe."

I'm relieved she realizes it, but I don't want to encourage her to distrust Marino, not even slightly. She's been through enough with him and finally they are friends again, close like they were when she was a child and he taught her to drive his truck and to shoot and she aggravated the hell out of him and it was mutual. She gets science from my genetics, but she gets her affinity for cop stuff, as she refers to it, from him. He was the big, tough detective in her life when she was a know-it-all difficult wunder-kind, and he has loved and hated her as many different times as she has loved and hated him. But friends and colleagues now. Whatever it takes to keep it that way. *Be careful what you say,* I tell myself. *Let there be peace.*

"From which I conclude Briggs doesn't know about this." I indicate the small white box on my desk. "And Captain Avallone doesn't."

"I don't see how."

"Is my office bugged right now?"

"Our conversation is completely safe," she replies, and it isn't an answer.

"What about Jack? Possible he knows about the flybot? Well, you didn't tell him."

"No damn way."

"So unless someone's called him looking for it. Or maybe its wing."

"You mean if the killer called here looking for a missing fly-bot," Lucy says. "And I'm just going to call it that for purposes of simplicity, although it's not just a garden-variety flybot. That would be pretty stupid. That would imply the caller had something to do with the guy's homicide."

"We can't rule out anything. Sometimes killers are stupid," I reply. "If they're desperate enough."

ucy gets up and goes into my private bathroom, where there is a single-cup coffeemaker on a counter. I hear her filling the tank with tap water and checking the small refrigerator. It is almost one a.m. and the snow hasn't eased up, is falling hard and fast, and when the small flakes blow against the windows, the sound is like sand blasting the glass.

"Skim milk or cream?" Lucy calls out from what is supposed to be my private changing area, which includes a shower. "Bryce is such a good wife. He stocked your refrigerator."

"I still drink it black." I start opening my desk drawers, not sure what I'm looking for.

I think about my sloppy work station in the autopsy room. I think of people helping themselves to what they shouldn't.

"Yeah, well, then why is there milk and cream?" Lucy's loud voice. "Green Mountain or Black Tiger? There's also hazelnut.

Since when do you drink hazelnut?" The questions are rhetorical. She knows the answers.

"Since never," I mutter, seeing pencils, pens, Post-its, paper clips, and in a bottom drawer, a pack of spearmint gum.

It is half-full, and I don't chew gum. Who likes spearmint gum and would have reason to go into my desk? Not Bryce. He's much too vain to chew gum, and if I caught him doing it, I would disapprove, because I consider it rude to chew gum in front of other people. Besides, Bryce wouldn't root around inside my desk, not without permission. He wouldn't dare.

"Jack likes hazelnut, French vanilla, shit like that, and he drinks it with skim milk unless he's on one of his high-protein, high-fat diets," Lucy continues from inside my bathroom. "Then he uses real cream, heavy cream, like what's in here. I suppose if you had guests, were expecting visitors, you might have cream."

"Nothing flavored, and please make it strong."

"He's a superuser just like you are," Lucy's voice then says. "His fingerprints are stored in every lock in this place just like yours are."

I hear the spewing of hot water shooting through the K-Cup and use it as a welcome interruption. I refuse to engage in the poisonous speculation that Jack Fielding has been in my office during my absence, that maybe he's been helping himself while he drinks coffee, chews gum, or who the hell knows what he's been up to. But as I look around, it doesn't seem possible. My office feels unlived-in. It certainly doesn't appear as if anyone has been working in here, so what would he be doing?

"I went over to Norton's Woods before Cambridge PD did, you

know. Marino asked them to go back because of the serial number being eradicated from the Glock. But I got there first." Lucy talks on loudly from inside the bathroom. "But I had the disadvantage of not knowing exactly where the guy went down, where he was stabbed, we now know. Without the scene photographs, it's impossible to get an exact location, just an approximate one, so I combed every footpath in the park."

She walks out with steaming coffee in black mugs that have the AFME's unusual crest, a five-card poker draw of aces and eights, known as the dead man's hand, what Wild Bill Hickok supposedly was holding when he was shot to death.

"Talk about a needle in a haystack," she continues. "The flybot's probably half the size of a small paper clip, about the size of, well, a housefly. No joy."

"Just because you found a wing doesn't mean the rest of it was ever out there," I remind her as she sets a coffee in front of me.

"If it's out there, it's maimed." Lucy returns to her chair. "Under snow as we speak and missing a wing. But very possibly still alive, especially when it gets exposed to light, assuming it's not further damaged."

"'Alive'?"

"Not literally. Likely powered by micro–solar panels as opposed to a battery that would already be dead. Light hits it and abracadabra. That's the way everything is headed. And our little friend, wherever he is, is futuristic, a masterpiece of teeny-tiny technology."

"How can you be so sure if you can't find most of it? Just a wing."

"Not just any wing. The angle and flexure joints are ingenious and suggest to me a different flight formation. Not the flight of an angel anymore. But horizontal like a real insect flies. Whatever this thing is and whatever its function, we're talking about something extremely advanced, something I've never seen before. Nothing's been published about it, because I get pretty much every technical journal there is online, plus I've been running searches with no success. By all indications, it's a project that's classified, top secret. I sure hope the rest of it is out there on the ground somewhere, safely covered with snow."

"What was it doing in Norton's Woods in the first place?" I envision the black-gloved hand entering the frame of the hidden video camera, as if the man was swatting at something.

"Right. Did he have it, or did someone else?" She blows on her coffee, holding the mug in both hands.

"And is someone looking for it? Does someone think it's here or think we know where it is?" I ask that again. "Has anyone mentioned to you that his gloves are gone? Did you happen to notice when you were downstairs while Marino was printing the body? It appears the victim put on a pair of black gloves as he arrived at the park, which I thought was curious when I watched the video clips. I assume he died with the gloves on, and so where are they?"

"That's interesting," Lucy says, and I can't tell if she already knew the gloves are missing.

I can't tell what she knows and if she's lying.

"They weren't in the woods when I was walking around yesterday morning," she informs me. "I would have seen a pair of black gloves, saying they were accidentally left by the squad, the removal service, the cops. Of course, they could have been and were picked up by anybody who happened along."

"In the video clips, someone wearing a long black coat walks past right after the man falls to the ground. Is it possible whoever killed him paused just long enough to take his gloves?"

"You mean if they're some type of data gloves or smart gloves, what they're using in combat, gloves with sensors embedded in them for wearable computer systems, wearable robotics," Lucy says, as if it is a normal thing to consider about a pair of missing gloves.

"I'm just wondering why his gloves might be important enough for someone to take them, if that's what's happened," I reply.

"If they have sensors in them and that's how he was control- ling the flybot, assuming the flybot is his, then the gloves would be extremely important," Lucy says.

"And you didn't ask about the gloves when you were down- stairs with Marino? You didn't think to check gloves, clothing, for sensors that might be embedded?"

"If I had the gloves, I would have had a much better chance of finding the flybot when I went back to Norton's Woods," Lucy says. "But I don't have them or know where they are, if that's what you're asking."

"I am asking that because it would be tampering with evidence."

"I didn't. I promise. I don't know for a fact that the gloves are data gloves, but if they are, it would make sense in light of other things. Like what he's saying on the video clip right before he dies," she adds thoughtfully, working it out, or maybe she's already worked it out but is leading me to believe what she's saying is a new thought. "The man keeps saying, 'Hey, boy.'"

"I assumed he was talking to his dog."

"Maybe. Maybe not."

"And he said other things I couldn't figure out," I recall. "'And for you' or 'Do you send one' or something like that. Could a robotic fly understand voice commands?"

"Absolutely possible. That part was muffled. I heard it, too, and thought it was confusing," Lucy says. "But maybe not if he was controlling the flybot. 'For you' could be *four-two*, maybe, as in the number four? 'And' could be *N*, as in north? I'll listen again and do more enhancement."

"More?"

"I've done some. Nothing helpful. Could be he was telling the flybot GPS coordinates, which would be a common command to give a device that responds to voice—if you're telling it where to go, for example."

"If you could figure out GPS coordinates, maybe you could find the location, find where it is."

"Sincerely doubt it. If the flybot was controlled by the gloves, at least partially controlled by sensors in them, then when the victim waved his hand, probably at the moment he was stabbed?"

"Right. Then what?"

"I don't know, but I don't have the flybot, and I don't have the gloves," Lucy says to me while looking at me intently, her eyes directly on mine. "I didn't find them, but I sure wish I had."

"Did Marino mention that someone may have been following Benton and me after we left Hanscom?" I ask.

"We looked for the big SUV with xenon lights and fog lamps. I'm not saying it means anything, but Jack's got a dark-blue Navigator. Pre-owned, bought it back in October. You weren't here, so I guess you haven't seen it."

"Why would Jack follow us? And no. I don't know anything about him buying a Navigator. I thought he had a Jeep Cherokee."

"Traded up, I guess." She drinks her coffee. "I didn't say he would follow you or did. Or that he would be stupid enough to ride your bumper. Except in a blizzard or fog, when visibility's really bad, a rather inexperienced tail might follow too close if the person doesn't know where the target is going. I don't see why Jack would bother. Wouldn't he assume you were on your way here?"

"Do you have an idea why anyone would bother?"

"If someone knows the flybot is missing," she says, "he or she sure as hell's looking for it, and possibly would spare nothing to find it before it gets into the wrong hands. Or the right hands. Depending on who or what we're dealing with. I can say that much based on a wing. If that's why you were followed, it would make me less likely to suspect that whoever killed this guy found the flybot. In other words, it could very well still be missing or lost. I probably don't need to tell you that a top-secret proprietary technical invention like this could be worth a fortune, especially if someone could steal the idea and take credit for it. If such a person is looking for it and has reason to fear it may have come in with the body, maybe this person wanted to see where you were going, what you were up to. He or she might think the flybot is here at the CFC or might think you have it off-site somewhere. Including at your house."

"Why would I have it at my house? I haven't been home."

"Logic has nothing to do with it when someone is in overdrive," Lucy answers. "If I were the person looking, I might assume you instructed your former FBI husband to hide the flybot at your house. I might assume all kinds of things. And if the flybot is still at large, I'm still going to be looking."

I remember what the man exclaimed, can hear his voice in my head. *"What the . . . ? Hey . . . !"* Maybe his startled reaction wasn't due solely to the sudden sharp pain in his lower back and tremendous pressure in his chest. Maybe something flew at his face. Maybe he had on data gloves, and his startled reaction is what caused the flybot to get broken. I imagine a tiny device mid-flight, and then struck by the man's black gloved hand and crushed against his coat collar.

"If someone has the data gloves and looked for the flybot before the snow started, is it really possible the person wouldn't have found it?" I ask my niece.

"Sure, it's possible. Depends on a number of things. How badly damaged it is, for example. There was a lot of activity around the man after he went down. If the flybot was there on the ground, it could have been crushed or damaged further and rendered completely unresponsive. Or it could be under something or in a tree or a bush or anywhere out there."

"I assume a robotic insect could be used as a weapon," I suggest. "Since I don't have a clue what caused this man's internal injuries, I need to think about every possibility imaginable."

"That's the thing," Lucy says. "These days, almost anything you can imagine is possible."

"Did Benton tell you what we saw on CT?"

"I don't see how a micromechanical insect could cause internal damage like that," Lucy answers. "Unless the victim was somehow injected with a micro–explosive device."

My niece and her phobias. Her obsession with explosives. Her acute distrust of government.

"And I sure as hell hope not," she says. "Actually, we'd be talking about nanoexplosives if a flybot was involved."

My niece and her theories about super-thermite, and I remember Jaime Berger's comment the last time I saw her at Thanksgiving when all of us were in New York, having dinner in her penthouse apartment. "Love doesn't conquer all," Berger said. "It can't possibly," she said as she drank too much wine and spent a lot of time in the kitchen, arguing with Lucy about 9/11, about explosives used in demolitions, nanomaterials painted on infrastructures that would cause a horrendous destruction if impacted by large planes filled with fuel.

I have given up reasoning with my phobic, cynical niece, who is too smart for her own good and won't listen. It doesn't matter to her that there simply aren't enough facts to support what has her convinced, only allegations about residues found in the dust right after the towers collapsed. Then, weeks later, more dust was collected and it showed the same residues of iron oxide and aluminum, a highly energetic nanocomposite that is used in making pyrotechnics and explosives. I admit there have been credible scientific journal articles written about it, but not enough of them, and they don't begin to prove that our own government helped mastermind 9/11 as an excuse to start a war in the Middle East.

"I know how you feel about conspiracy theories," Lucy says to me. "That's a big difference between us. I've seen what the so-called good guys can do."

She doesn't know about South Africa. If she did, she would realize there isn't a difference between the two of us. I know all too well what so-called good guys can do. But not 9/11. I won't go that far, and I think of Jaime Berger and imagine how difficult it would be for the powerful and established Manhattan prosecutor to have Lucy as a partner. Love doesn't conquer all. It really is true. Maybe Lucy's paranoia about 9/11 and the country we live in have driven her back into a personal isolation that historically is never broken for long. I really thought Jaime was the one, that it would last. I now feel certain it hasn't. I want to tell Lucy I'm sorry for that and I'm always here for her and will talk about anything she wants, even if it goes against my beliefs. Now is not the time.

"I think we need to consider that we might be dealing with some renegade scientist or maybe more than one of them up to no good," Lucy then tells me. "That's the big point I'm trying to make. And I mean serious no good, extreme no good, Aunt Kay."

It relieves me to hear her call me Aunt Kay. I feel all is right with us when she calls me Aunt Kay, and she rarely does it anymore. I don't remember the last time she did. When I'm her Aunt Kay I can almost ignore what Lucy Farinelli is, which is a genius who is marginally sociopathic, a diagnosis that Benton scoffs at, nicely but firmly. Being marginally sociopathic is like being marginally pregnant or marginally dead, he says. I love my niece more than my own life, but I've come to accept that when she is well behaved, it is an act of will or simply because it suits her. Morals have very little to do with it. It's all about the end justifying the means.

I study her carefully, even though I won't see what's there. Her face never gives away information that could really hurt her.

I say to her, "I need to go ahead and ask you one thing."

"You can ask more than one." She smiles and doesn't look capable of hurting anything or anyone unless you recognize the strength and agility in her calm hands and the rapid changes in her eyes as thoughts flash behind them like lightning.

"You aren't involved in whatever this is." I mean the small white box and the flybot wing inside it. I mean the dead man who is getting an MRI at McLean—someone we may have crossed paths with at a da Vinci exhibition in London months before 9/11, which Lucy incredibly believes was orchestrated from within our own government.

"Nope." She says it simply and doesn't flinch or look the slightest bit uncomfortable.

"Because you're here now." I remind her she works for the CFC, meaning she works for me, and I answer to the governor of Massachusetts, the Department of Defense, the White House. I answer to a lot of people, I tell her. "I can't have—"

"Of course you can't. I'm not going to get you into trouble."

"It isn't just you anymore—"

"No need to have this conversation," she interrupts again, and her eyes blaze. They are so green they don't look real. "Anyway, he doesn't have thermal injury, right? No burns?"

"None that I can see so far. That's correct," I reply.

"Okay. So if someone poked him with a modified shark bang stick? You know, one of those speargun shafts with something like a shotgun cartridge attached to the tip? Only in this case, a tiny, tiny charge containing nanoexplosives?"

I push the power button to start my desktop computer. "It wouldn't look like what I just saw. It would look like a contact gunshot wound minus the patterned abrasion made by the muzzle of a gun. Even if we're talking about using nanoexplosives as opposed to some type of firearm ammunition on the tip of a shaft or something shaftlike, you're right, you'd see thermal injury. There should be burns at the entrance and also to underlying tissue. I assume you're implying something like a flybot could be used to deliver nanoexplosives. Is that what you fear this so-called renegade scientist or more than one of them might be doing?"

"Deliver. Detonate. Nanoexplosives, drugs, poisons. Like I said, let your imagination be the limit what a device like this might be capable of."

"I need to take a look at the security footage that shows the body bag leaking." As I look for files in my computer. "I'm not going to have to go see Ron for that, am I?"

Lucy comes around to my side of the desk and starts typing on my keyboard, entering her system administrator's password that grants complete access to my kingdom.

"Easy as pie." She taps a key to open a file.

"Nobody could get into my files without your knowing."

"Not in cyberspace. But I can't know if someone's been in your physical space, especially since I'm not up here all the time, in fact, not even most of the time, because I work remotely when I can," she says, but I'm not sure I believe she wouldn't know.

In fact, I don't believe it.

"But no way anyone has gotten into your password-protected files," she says, and that I do believe. Lucy wouldn't permit it. "You can monitor the security cameras from anywhere, by the way. Even from your iPhone if you want. All you need is access to the Internet. I found this earlier and saved it as a file. Five-forty-two p.m. That's what time it was yesterday when this was captured by a closed-caption security camera in the receiving area."

She clicks on play and turns up the volume, and I watch two attendants in winter coats pushing a stretcher bearing a black body bag along the lower level's gray tile hallway.

Wheels click as they park the stretcher in front of the cooler, and now I can see Janelle, stocky with short brunette hair, tough-looking with a surprising number of tattoos, as best I recall. Someone Fielding found and hired.

Janelle opens the massive stainless-steel door, and I hear the rush of blowing air.

"Put it . . ." She points, and I notice she is wearing her coat, a dark jacket with *FORENSICS* in large, bright yellow letters on the back. She's in scene clothes, including a CFC baseball cap, as if she's going out in the cold or just came in.

"That tray there?" an attendant asks as he and his partner lift the body bag off the stretcher. The bag bends freely as they carry it, the body inside it as flexible as in life. "Shit, he's dripping. Dammit. He'd better not have AIDS or something. On my pants, my damn shoes."

"The lower one." Janelle directs them to a tray inside the cooler, stepping out of the way and not interested that blood is dripping from the body bag and spotting the gray floor. She doesn't seem to notice.

"Janelle the magnificent," Lucy comments as the video recording ends abruptly.

"Do you have the MLI log?" I want to see what time the medicolegal investigator—in other words, Janelle—came and went yesterday. "Obviously, she was on call during the evening?"

"She worked a double shift on Sunday, worker bee that she is," Lucy says. "Filled in for Randy, who was scheduled for evenings over the weekend but called in sick. Meaning he stayed home to watch the Super Bowl."

"I hope not."

"And Dandy Randy's not here now because of the weather. Supposedly on call at home. Must be nice to have a take-home SUV and get paid for staying home," Lucy says, and I hear the contempt in her flinty tone and see it in the hardness of her face. "I guess you can tell you got your work cut out for you. Assuming you ever quit making excuses for people."

"I don't make them for you."

"That's because there aren't any."

I look at the log Janelle kept yesterday, a template on my video display that has very few fields filled in.

"I don't mean to state what's as plain as the nose on my face, but there's not much you really know about what goes on," Lucy says. "You don't know the finer points of the day-to-day in this place. How could you?" She returns to her side of the desk and picks up her coffee, but she doesn't sit back down. "You haven't been here. You've sort of never been here since we opened for business."

"This is it? This is the entire log for Sunday?"

"Yup. Janelle came in at four. If what she entered into the log is to be believed." Lucy stands there, drinking her coffee, eyeing me. "And she runs with quite a pack, by the way. Forensic fuck buddies. Most of them cops, a few of them data-entry and clerical. Whoever she can be a hero to. You know she's on a dodgeball team? What kind of person plays dodgeball? Someone with finesse."

"If she came in at four, why is she dressed in scene clothes, including her jacket? As if she just came in from the cold?"

"Like I said, if what she entered in the log is to be believed."

"And David was on before that and didn't respond to anything, either?" I ask. "Jack could have sent him to Norton's Woods. David was sitting right here, so why didn't Jack tell him to go to the scene? It's maybe fifteen minutes from here."

"And you don't know that, either." Lucy walks into the bathroom and rinses her mug. "You don't know if David was sitting right here," she says as she walks back out and hovers near my closed office door. "I don't want to be the one to tell you . . ."

"It would seem you are the only one to tell me. No one else is telling me a damn thing," I reply. "What the hell is happening around here? People just show up when they feel like it?"

"Pretty much. The other MEs, the MLIs, in and out, marching to their own drummer. It trickles down from the top."

"It trickles down from Jack."

"At least on your side of things. The labs are another story, because he's not interested in them. Except firearms." She leans against the closed door, slipping her hands into the pockets of her lab coat.

"He's supposed to be in charge in my absence. Jack's the co-director of the entire CFC Port Mortuary." I can't keep the protest out of my tone, the note of outrage.

"Not interested in the labs, and scientists don't pay any attention to him, anyway. Except firearms, like I said. You know Fielding and guns, knives, crossbows, hunting bows. Never met a weapon he didn't love. So he messes with the firearms and toolmark lab and has managed to fuck them up, too. Piss off Morrow until he's on the verge of quitting. I do know he's actively looking for another job, and there's no good reason his lab didn't finish with the Glock the dead guy had on him. The eradicated serial number. Shit. He bolted out of here this morning and didn't bother."

"He bolted out of here?"

"He was driving off when I was returning from Norton's Woods. This was about ten-thirty."

"Did you talk to him?"

"No. Maybe he wasn't feeling well. I don't know, but I don't understand why he didn't make sure someone took care of the Glock. Using acid on a drilled-off serial number? How long does that take to at least try? He must have known it was important."

"He might not have," I answer. "If the Cambridge detective is the only one who talked to him, why would he think the Glock was important? At that time, no one had a clue the man from Norton's Woods was a homicide."

"Well, I guess that's a relevant point. Morrow probably doesn't even know we went to get you, that you're back from Dover. Fielding vanished, too, when he knew damn well there was a major problem that most people with a brain in their head would decide was his fault. He's the one who took the call about the guy in Norton's Woods. He's the one who didn't go to the scene or make sure somebody did. The reason Janelle is dressed for the great outdoors, in my opinion? She didn't get here at four, the time she entered into the log. She got here just in time to let in the attendants and sign in the body and then turned right around and left. I can find out. There will be an entry for when she disabled the alarm to enter the building. Depends on whether you want to make a federal case out of it."

"I'm surprised Marino hasn't made sure I know the extent of the problems." It's all I can think to say. The inside of my head has gone dark.

"Like the boy crying wolf," Lucy says, and it's true.

Marino complains so much about so many people, I scarcely hear him. Now we're back to my failures. I haven't paid attention. I haven't listened. Maybe I wouldn't have listened no matter who told me.

"I've got a few things to take care of. You know how to find me," Lucy says, and she opens my door and leaves it open after she walks out.

I pick up the phone and try Fielding's numbers again. I don't leave any messages this time, and it crosses my mind that his wife isn't answering their home phone, either. She would see my office name and number on caller ID. Maybe that's why she doesn't pick up, because she knows it's me. Or maybe his family has gone somewhere, is out of town. On a Monday night in the middle of a snowstorm, when he knows damn well I've rushed home from Dover to take care of an emergency case?

I walk out and scan my thumb to unlock the door to the right of mine. I stand inside my deputy chief's office and slowly scan it as if it is a crime scene.

11

I picked his office, insisting on one as nice as mine, generously large, with a private shower. He has a river and city view, although his shades are down, which I find unnerving. He must have closed them when it was still light out, and I don't know why he would do that. Not for a good reason, I think. Whatever Jack Fielding has done, it all bodes badly.

I walk around and open each shade, and through expansive glass that is a reflective gray tint, I can make out the blurred lights of downtown Boston and billowing waves of freezing moisture, an icy snow that clicks and bites like teeth. The tops of high-rises, the Prudential and Hancock towers are obscured, and gusting wind moans in low tones around the dome over my head. Below, Memorial Drive is churned up by traffic, even at this hour, and the Charles is formless and black. I wonder how deep the snow is by now and how deep it will get before it moves off to the south. I wonder if Fielding will ever return to this room I designed and furnished for him, and somehow it feels that he won't, even though there is no evidence he's gone for good.

The biggest difference between our work spaces is his is crowded with reminders of the occupant, his various degrees, certificates, and commendations, his collectibles on shelves, autographed baseballs and bats, tae kwon do trophies and plaques, and models of fighter planes and a piece from a real one that crashed. I go over to his desk and survey Civil War relics: a belt buckle, a mess kit, a powder horn, a few minié balls that I remember him collecting during our early days in Virginia. But there are no photographs, and that makes me sad. In some places I can see what's gone in blank spaces of wall where he's not bothered to fill in the tiny holes left from hanging hooks he removed.

It stings that he no longer displays familiar pictures taken when he was my forensic pathology fellow, candid shots of us in the morgue or the two of us out at death scenes with Marino, the lead homicide detective for Richmond PD in the late eighties, the early nineties, when both Fielding and I were just getting started, although in completely different ways. He was the good-looking doctor beginning his career, while I was shifting mine into the private sector, transitioning into civilian life and the role of chief, doing my best not to look back. Maybe Fielding isn't looking back, although I don't know why. His old days were good days compared to mine. He didn't help cover up a crime. He's never had anything on par with that to hide from. Not that I know of, but I have to wonder. What do I know anymore?

Not much, except I sense he's gotten rid of me, maybe gotten rid of all of us. I sense he's gotten rid of more than he ever has before. It is something I'm convinced of without knowing exactly why. Certainly his personal property is still here, his Gore-Tex rain suit on a hanger, and his neoprene hip waders, his dive bag of scuba gear and scene case stowed in a closet, and his collection of police patches and police and military challenge coins. I remember helping him move into this office. I even helped him arrange his furniture, both of us complaining and laughing and then griping some more as we moved the desk, then his conference table, then moved them again and again.

"What is this, Laurel and Hardy?" he said. "You going to push a mule up the stairs next?"

"You don't have stairs."

"I'm thinking of getting a horse," he said as we moved the same chairs we'd just moved earlier. "There's a horse farm about a mile from the house. I could board the horse there, maybe ride it to work, to crime scenes."

"I'll add that to the employee handbook. No horses."

We joked and teased each other, and he looked good that day—vital and optimistic, his muscles straining against the short sleeves of his scrubs. He was just incredibly built and healthy-looking then, his face still boyishly handsome, his dark blond hair messy, and he hadn't shaved for several days. He was sexy and funny, and I remember the whispers and giggles of some of the female staff as they walked past his open door, finding excuses to stare at him. Fielding seemed so happy to be here and with me, and I remember both of us placing photographs and reminiscing about our early days together—photographs that now are gone.

In their place are ones I don't recall. The pictures are promi-
nently arranged on his shelves and walls, formal poses of him
with politicians and military brass, one with General Briggs and
even Captain Avallone, perhaps from the tour Fielding gave her.
He looks wooden and bored. In a photograph of him in tae kwon
do white, mid-flight and kicking an imagined enemy, he looks
angry. He looks red-faced and hateful. As I study recent family
portraits, I decide he doesn't look content in them, either, not
even when he is holding his two little girls or has his arm around
his wife, Laura, a delicate blonde whose prettiness is eroding, as
if a trying existence is mapping its course on her physically, etch-
ing lines and furrows into a topography that once was graceful
and smooth.

She is number three for him, and I can trace his decline as I
scan his captured moments in chronological order. When he married her, he looked energetic, with no sign of a rash, and he didn't
have any unseemly bald patches. I pause to admire how amazing
he was, shirtless and as hard-bodied as stone in running shorts,
washing his Mustang, a '67, cherry red with Le Mans stripes down
the center of the hood. Then as recently as this past fall, the thick-
ening around his middle; the splotchy, flushed skin; the strands
of hair combed back and held in place with gel to hide his alopecia. At a martial arts competition not even a month ago, he
doesn't look as fit or as spiritually balanced in his grandmaster's
uniform and black belt. He doesn't look like someone who finds
joy in beautiful form or technique. He doesn't look like someone
who honors other people or has self-control or respect for any-

thing. He looks dissipated. He looks slightly deranged. He looks perfectly miserable.

Why? I silently ask that earlier photograph of him with his prized car, when he was stunning to behold and seemed carefree and vital, the sort of man it would be easy to fall in love with or to place in charge or to trust with your life. *What changed? What made you so unhappy? What was it this time?* He hates working for me. He hated it the last time, in Watertown, where he didn't stay long, and now the CFC, and he hates that more, it's obvious. This past late summer, when he started looking so bad, is when we finally opened our doors to criminal justice, taking cases. But I wasn't even in Massachusetts then, just one weekend over Labor Day. It can't be my fault. It's always been my fault. I've always blamed myself for Fielding's downfalls, and he's had more of them than I care to count.

I pick him up and he falls again, only harder each time. It gets uglier. It gets bloodier. Again and again. Like a child who can't walk, and I won't accept it until he's injured beyond fixing. The drama that will always end predictably is the way Benton has described it. Fielding shouldn't be a forensic pathologist, and it's because of me that he is. He would have been better off if he'd never met me in the spring of 1988 when he wasn't sure what he wanted in life and I said I know what you should do. Let me show you. Let me teach you. If he'd never come to Richmond, if he'd never run into me, he might have picked a way to spend his days that would have suited him. His career, his life, would have been about him and not about me.

That really is the bottom line, that he does the best he can in an environment totally destructive to him and finally can't take it any longer and decompensates, disintegrates, and remembers why he is what he is and who shaped him, and then I loom as huge in his wretched life as a billboard. His answer to these crises is always the same. He vanishes. One day he simply drops off the radar, and what I find in his wake is awful. Cases he mishandled or neglected. Memos that show his lack of control and dangerous judgment. Hurtful voicemails he didn't bother to delete because he wanted me to hear them. Damaging e-mails and other communications he hoped I'd find. I sit in his chair and start opening drawers. I don't have to rummage long.

The file folder isn't labeled and contains four pages printed at eight-oh-three yesterday morning, February 8, a speech that based on other information in the header and news section is from the Royal United Services Institute's website. A century-old British think tank with satellite offices strategically located around the world, RUSI is dedicated to advanced innovations in national and international security, and I can't imagine Fielding's interest. I can't fathom him caring about a keynote address given by Russell Brown, the shadow secretary of state for defense, on his views about the "defense debate." I skim the conservative member of Parliament's not-so-startling comments that it isn't a given the UK will always act as part of an alliance and the economic impact of the war is catastrophic. He makes repeated allusions to misinformation methodically propagated, which is as close as the respectable MP is going to come to outright accusing the United States of orchestrating the invasion of Iraq and dragging the UK along for the ride.

Unsurprisingly, the speech is political, as is almost everything right now in Britain, which holds its general election in three months. Six hundred and fifty seats are being contested, and a major campaign issue is the more than ten thousand British troops fighting the Taliban in Afghanistan. Fielding isn't military, has never paid much attention to foreign affairs or elections, and I don't know why he would have the slightest interest in what is happening in the UK. I don't recall that he's ever even been to the UK. He's not the sort to be interested in a general election over there or RUSI or any think tank, and knowing him as well as I do, I suspect he intended for me to find this file. He wanted me to see it after he pulled another one of his vanishing stunts. What is it he wants me to know?

Why is he interested in RUSI? And did he come across the speech himself on the Internet, or did someone send it to him? If it was sent to him, by whom? I consider asking Lucy to go into Fielding's e-mail, but I'm not ready to be that heavy-handed, and I don't want to be caught. I can lock the door, but my superuser deputy chief could still walk in, because I don't have confidence that Ron or anyone else will keep Fielding in the security area if he shows up. I have no faith that Ron, who was unfriendly to me and seems to have little regard for me, will detain Fielding or try to get hold of me to ask for clearance. I don't trust that my staff is loyal to me or feels safe with me or follows my orders, and Fielding could reappear at any moment.

That would be like him. To vanish without warning, then show up just as unexpectedly and catch me red-handed, sitting at his desk, going through his electronic files. It's just one more thing he'll use against me, and he's used plenty against me over the years. What has he been doing behind my back? Let's see what else I find, and then I'll know what to do. I look at the time stamp again and imagine Fielding sitting in this very chair at eight-oh-three yesterday morning printing the speech, while Lucy, Marino, Anne, and Ollie, while everybody, was in an uproar because of what was in the cooler downstairs.

How odd that Fielding would be up here in his office while that was going on, and I wonder if he even cared that a man might have been locked inside our refrigerator while still alive. Of course, Fielding would have to care. How could he not? If the worst had turned out to be true, he would be blamed. Ultimately, I would be the one all over the news and likely out of a job, but he would go down with me. Yet he was up here on the seventh floor, in his office and out of the fray, as if he already had his mind made up, and it occurs to me that his disappearance may be related to something else. I lean back in his chair and look around, my attention landing on the pad of call sheets and a ballpoint pen near his phone. I notice faint indentations on the top sheet of paper.

Turning on a lamp, I pick up the pad and hold it at various angles, trying to make out indented writing left like a footprint when someone wrote a note on a top sheet of paper that is no longer there. One thing about Fielding, he doesn't have a light touch, not when he's wielding a scalpel or typing on a keyboard or writing something by hand. For a devotee of martial arts, he is surprisingly rough, is easily frustrated and quick to flare up. He has a childish way of holding a pencil or pen with two fingers on top instead of one, as if he's using chopsticks, and it's not uncommon for him to break lead or nibs, and he's hell on Magic Markers.

I don't need ESDA or a Docustat or vacuum box or some other indented writing-recovery unit to detect what I can see the old-fashioned way in oblique lighting with my own eyes. Fielding's barely legible scribble. What appears to be two separate notes. One is a phone number with a 508 area code and "MVF8/18/UK Min of Def Diary2/8." Then a second one: "U of Sheffield today @ Whitehall. Over and out." I look again, making sure I read the last three words correctly. *Over and out.* The end of a radio transmission, like *Roger Wilco over and out* but also a song performed by a heavy-metal band that Fielding used to play in his car all the time when he first came to Richmond. *"Over and out / every dog has its day."* What he'd sing to me when he'd threaten to quit, when he'd had enough, or when he was teasing, flirting, pretending to be fed up. Did he write *over and out* on a call sheet with me in mind or for some other reason?

I find a legal pad in a drawer and write what I've discovered indented on the pad of call sheets and begin doing the best I can to figure out what Fielding was up to and thinking about, what it is he wants me to know. If I came in here to snoop, I was going to find the printout and the indented writing. He knows me. He would think that way, because he knows damn well how my mind works. The University of Sheffield is one of the top research institutions in the world, and Whitehall is where RUSI is head-quartered, literally in the former Whitehall Palace, the original location of Scotland Yard.

Logging on to Intelliquest, a search engine Lucy created for the CFC, I type in RUSI and the date February 8 and Whitehall. What comes up is the title of a keynote address, *Civilian-Military Collaboration,* the lecture Fielding must be referring to that was delivered at RUSI at ten a.m. UK time, what is now yesterday morning for me. The speaker was Dr. Liam Saltz, the controversial Nobel laureate whose doomsday opinions about military technology make him a natural enemy of DARPA. I wasn't aware he was on the faculty at the University of Sheffield. I thought he was at Berkeley. He used to be at Berkeley, and now he's at Sheffield, I read on the Internet as I think, rather dazed, of the exhibit at the Courtauld in the summer before 9/11, where Lucy and I heard Dr. Saltz lecture. Not long after that, Dr. Saltz, like me, was a vocal critic of MORT.

I ponder the title of the lecture Dr. Saltz delivered not even twenty-four hours ago. *Civilian-Military Collaboration.* That certainly sounds tame for the rabble-rousing Dr. Saltz, who is as jolting as an air-raid siren in his warnings that America's two-hundred-plus-billion-dollar allocation to future combat systems—specifically, unmanned vehicles—has put us on the road to ultimate annihilation. Robots might seem to make sense when you consider sending them into the battlefield, he rails, but what happens when they come home like used Jeeps and other military surplus? Eventually they will find their way into the civilian world, and what we'll have is more policing and surveillance, more insensate machines doing the jobs of humans, only these machines will be armed and equipped with cameras and recording devices.

I've heard Dr. Saltz on the news, painting terrifying scenarios of "copbots" responding to crime scenes and unmanned "robocruisers" pursuing vehicles to write up occupants for traffic violations or hauling people in for outstanding warrants or, God forbid, getting a message from sensors to use force. Robots Tasering us. Robots shooting us to death. Robots that look like huge insects dragging our wounded and dead off a battlefield. Dr. Saltz testifying before the same Senate subcommittee I did but not at the same time. Both of us wreaking havoc for a technology company named Otwahl that I'd completely forgotten about until just hours ago.

I've met him only once, when both of us happened to be on CNN and he pointed at me and quipped, "Autbotsies."

"I beg your pardon," I answered, unclipping my mike as he walked onto the set.

"Robotic autopsies. Someday they'll take your place, my good doctor, maybe sooner than you think. We should have a drink after the show."

He was a bright-eyed man who looked like a lost hippie with his long, graying ponytail and wasted face, and he had the electricity of an exposed live wire. That was two years ago, and I should have taken him up on his invitation and waited around CNN. I should have had a drink with him. I should have gotten better versed in what he believes, because it isn't all crazy. I haven't seen him since then, although I can't escape his presence in the media, and I try to recall if I've ever mentioned him to

Fielding for any reason at all. I don't think so. I can't figure out why I would. Connections. What are they? I search some more.

The University of Sheffield in South Yorkshire has an excellent medical school, that much I already know. *Rerum Cognoscere Causas,* its motto, *To discover the causes of things,* how apropos, how ironic. I need causes. *Research,* and I click on that. Global warming, global soil degradation, rethinking engineering with pioneering computer software, new findings in human embryonic stem cells' DNA changes. I go back to the indented notes on the call sheet.

MVF8/18/UK Min of Def Diary2/8.

MVF is our abbreviation for motor-vehicle fatality, and I instigate another search, this time mining the CFC database. I enter MVF and the date 8/18, August 18 last summer, and a record is returned, the case of a twenty-year-old British man named Damien Patten who was killed in a taxicab accident in Boston. Fielding didn't do the autopsy, one of my other MEs did, and in the narrative I notice that Damien Patten was a lance corporal in the 14th Signal Regiment and was on leave and had come to Boston to get married when he was killed in the taxicab accident. I get a funny feeling. Something registers.

I execute another search using the keywords February 8 and UK Ministry of Defense Diary. I end up on its official news blog, and an entry in the diary lists British soldiers killed in Afghanistan yesterday. I run down the list of casualties, looking for anything that might mean something to me. A lance corporal from 1st Battalion Coldstream Guards. A lance sergeant from 1st Battalion Grenadier Guards. A kingsman from 2nd Battalion Duke of Lancaster's Regiment. Then there is a sapper, or combat engineer, with the Counter-Improvised Explosive Device Task Force, who was killed in the mountainous terrain of northwestern Afghanistan. In the Badghis Province. Where my patient PFC Gabriel was killed on Sunday, February 7.

I execute another search, although one detail I already know without having to look it up is how many NATO troops died in Afghanistan on February 7. At Dover, we always know. It's as routine as preparing for ugly storms, a depressingly morbid report that controls our lives. Nine casualties, and four of them were Americans killed by the same roadside improvised explosive device that turned PFC Gabriel's Humvee into a blast furnace. But again, that was on the seventh, not the eighth. It occurs to me that the British soldier who died on the eighth might have been injured the day before.

I check and I'm right. The IED sapper, Geoffrey Miller, was twenty-three, recently married, and was wounded in a roadside bombing in the Badghis Province early Sunday but died the next day in a military medical center in Germany. Possibly the same roadside bombing that killed the Americans we took care of at Dover yesterday morning—in fact, it's likely. I wonder if Sapper Miller and PFC Gabriel knew each other, and how the British man killed in a taxicab, Damien Patten, might be connected. Was Patten acquainted with Miller and Gabriel in Afghanistan, and what does Fielding have to do with any of this? How are Dr. Saltz or MORT or the dead man from Norton's Woods connected, or are they?

Miller's body will be repatriated this Thursday, returned to his family in Oxford, England. I read on, but I can't find anything else about him, although I certainly am capable of getting more information about a slain British soldier if I need it. I can call the press secretary, Rockman. I can call Briggs, and I should, anyway, I remember. Briggs asked me to—in fact, ordered me—demanding that I keep him informed about the Norton's Woods case, to wake him up if need be the minute I have information. But I won't. No way. Not now. I'm not sure whom I can trust, and as that thought lingers, I realize the trouble I'm in.

What does it say when you can't ask for help from the very people you work with? It says everything, and it's as if the ground is opening up beneath my feet and I'm falling into the unknown, a cold, lightless, empty space where I've been before. Briggs wanted to do an end run, to usurp my authority and transfer the Norton's Woods case to Dover. Fielding has been sneaking around in my absence, meddling in affairs that are none of his business and even using my office, and now he's ducking me, or at least I hope that's all it is. My staff is committing mutiny, and any number of people, strangers to me, seem to know the details of my return home.

It is almost two a.m., and I'm tempted to try the indented telephone number Fielding scribbled on a call sheet and surprise whoever answers, wake the person up and perhaps get a clue as to what is going on. Instead, I do a polite computer search to see who or what the number with the 508 area code might belong to. The report summary shocks me, and for a moment I sit very still and try to calm myself. I try to push back the walls of dismay and confusion crowding in.

■ ■ ■

Julia Gabriel, mother of PFC Gabriel.

On the screen in front of me are her home and business addresses, her marital status, the salary she earns as a pharmacist in Worcester, Massachusetts, and the name of her only child and his age, which was nineteen when he died in Afghanistan on Sunday. I was on the phone with Mrs. Gabriel for the better part of an hour before I autopsied her son, trying to explain as gently as I could the impossibility of collecting his sperm while she raised her voice at me and cried and accused me of personal choices that aren't mine to make and ones I didn't make and would never make.

Saving sperm from the dead and using it to impregnate the living isn't something that causes me a moral dilemma. I really have no personal opinion about what truly is a medical and legal question, not a religious or ethical one, and the choice should be up to those involved, certainly not up to the practitioner. What matters to me is that the procedure, which has become increasingly popular because of the war, is done properly and legally, and my supposed views on posthumous reproduction rights were moot in PFC Gabriel's case, anyway. His body was burned and decomposing, his pelvis so charred that his scrotum was gone and the vas deferens containing semen along with it, and I wasn't about to tell Mrs. Gabriel that. I was as compassionate and gentle as I could be and didn't take it personally as she vented her grief and rage on the last doctor her son would ever see on this earth.

Peter had a girlfriend who was willing to have his children just like his friend was doing, it was a pact they'd made, Mrs. Gabriel went on, and I had no idea whose friend or what she was talking about. Peter's friend told him of another friend who got killed in Boston on his wedding day this past summer, only Mrs. Gabriel never mentioned Damien Patten by name, the British man killed in a taxicab this past August 18. *"All three of them dead now, three young, beautiful boys dead,"* Mrs. Gabriel said to me over the phone, and I had no idea who she was talking about. I think I do now. I think she meant Patten for sure, the friend of the friend whom PFC Gabriel had some sort of pact with. I wonder if the friend of Patten's was this other casualty that Fielding seems to have led me to, Geoffrey Miller, an IED sapper.

All three of them dead now.

Did Fielding discuss the Patten case with Mrs. Gabriel, and who did she talk to first, Fielding or me? She called me at Dover at around quarter of eight. I always fill out a call sheet, and I remember writing down the time as I sat in my small office at Dover's Port Mortuary, looking at the CT scans and their coordinates that would help me locate with GPS precision the frag and other objects that had penetrated the badly burned body of her son. Based on what she said to me as I now try to reconstruct that conversation, she likely talked to Fielding first. That might explain her repeated references to "other cases."

Someone had planted an idea in her head about what we do for other cases. She was under the distinct impression that we routinely extract semen from casualties and in fact encourage it, and I recall being puzzled, because the procedure has to be approved and is fraught with legal complications. I couldn't imagine what had given her such an idea, and I might have asked her about it, had she not been so busy castigating me and calling me names. What kind of monster would prevent a woman from having her dead boyfriend's children or stop the mother of a dead son from being a grandmother? We do it for our other cases, why not her son? she wept. *"I have no one left,"* she cried. *"This is bullshit bureaucracy, go on and admit it,"* she yelled at me. *"Bureaucratic bullshit to cover up yet another hate crime."*

"Anyone home?" Benton is in the doorway.

Mrs. Gabriel called me a military bigot. *"You do unto others as long as they're white,"* she said. *"That's not the Golden Rule but the White Rule,"* she said. *"You took care of that other boy who got killed in Boston, and he wasn't even a U.S. soldier, but not my son, who died for his country. I suppose my son was the wrong color,"* she went on, and I had no idea what she meant or what she was basing such an accusation on. I didn't try to figure it out because it seemed like hysteria, nothing more, and I forgave her for it on the spot. Even though it obviously hurt me badly and I've not been able to put it out of my mind since.

"Hello?" Benton is walking in.

"Another hate crime, only it will be found out and people like you won't get rewarded this time," and she wouldn't explain what she was thinking when she said something so terrible as that. But I didn't ask her to elaborate, and I didn't give her venomous comments much credence at the time, because being yelled at, cursed, threatened, and even attacked by people who are otherwise civilized and sane isn't a new experience. I don't have shatterproof glass installed in the lobbies and viewing rooms of offices where I've worked because I'm afraid of the dead throwing a fit or assaulting me.

"Kay?"

My eyes focus on Benton holding two coffees and trying not to spill them. Why would Julia Gabriel have called here before calling me at Dover? Or did Fielding call her, and in either event, why would he have talked to her? Then I remember Marino telling me about PFC Gabriel being the first casualty from Worcester and the media calling the CFC as if the body was here instead of at Dover, about a number of phone calls here because of the Massachusetts connection. Maybe that's how Fielding found out, but why would he get on the phone with the slain soldier's mother, even if she called here by mistake and needed to be reminded her son was at Dover? Of course she knew that. How could Mrs. Gabriel not know her son was flown into Dover? I can't see any legitimate reason for Fielding to have talked to her or what he possibly could have said that was helpful, and how dare him.

He's not military or even a consultant for the AFME. He's a civilian and has no right to probe into details relating to war casualties or national security or to engage in conversations about such matters, which are plainly defined as classified. Military and medical intelligence are none of his business. RUSI is none of his business. The election in the UK isn't, either. The only thing that should be Fielding's damn business is what he has so resoundingly neglected, which is his enormous responsibility here at the CFC and what should be his damn loyalty to me.

"That's nice of you," I say to Benton in a detached way. "I could use a coffee."

"Where were you just now? Besides in the middle of an imagined fight. You look like you might kill someone."

He comes close to the desk, watching me the way he does when he's trying to read what I'm thinking because he's not about to trust what I say. Or maybe he knows what I have to say is only the beginning of things and that I'm clueless about the rest of it.

"You okay?" He sets the coffees on the desk and moves a chair close.

"No, I'm not okay."

"What's wrong?"

"I think I just discovered what it means when something reaches critical mass."

"What's the matter?" he asks.

"Everything."

lease shut the door." It occurs to me I'm starting to act like Lucy. "I don't know where to begin, so many things are the matter."

Benton closes the door, and I notice the simple platinum band on his left ring finger. Sometimes I'm still caught by surprise that we're married, so much of our lives consumed by each other whether we've been together or apart, and we always agreed we didn't have to do it, to be official and formal, because we're not like other people, and then we did it anyway. The ceremony was a small, simple one, not a celebration as much as a swearing in, because we really meant it when we said until death do us part. After all we'd been through, for us to say it was more than words, more like an oath of office or an ordination or perhaps a summary of what we'd already lived. And I wonder if he ever regrets it. For example, right now does he wish he could go back to how it was? I wouldn't blame him if he thinks about what he's given up and what he misses, and there are so many complications because of me.

He sold his family brownstone, an elegant nineteenth-century mansion on the Boston Common, and he can't have loved some places we've lived or stayed in because of my unusual profession and preoccupations, what is a chaotic and costly existence despite my best intentions. While his forensic psychology practice has remained stable, my career has been in flux these past three years, with the shutting down of a private practice in Charleston, South Carolina, then my office in Watertown closing because of the economy, and I was in New York and then Washington and Dover, and now this, the CFC.

"What the hell is going on in this place?" I ask him as if he knows and I don't understand why he would. But I feel he does, or maybe I'm just wishing it because I'm beginning to experience desperation, that panicky sensation of falling and flailing for something to grab hold of.

"Black and extra-bold." He sits back down and slides the mug of coffee closer. "And not hazelnut. Even though you have quite a stash of it, I hear."

"Jack's still not shown up, and no one has heard from him, I assume."

"He's definitely not here. I think you're as safe in his office as he's been in yours." Benton says it as if he means more than one thing, and I notice how he's dressed.

Earlier he had on his winter coat and in the x-ray room was covered in a disposable gown before heading upstairs to Lucy's lab. I didn't really notice what he was wearing underneath his layers.

Black tactical boots, black tactical pants, a dark red flannel shirt, a rubber waterproof watch with a luminescent dial. As if he's anticipating being out in the weather or someplace that might be hard on his clothes.

"So Lucy told you it appears he's been using my office," I say. "For what purpose I don't know. But maybe you do."

"Nobody's needed to tell me there's a looting mentality at— what is it Marino calls this place? CENTCOM? Or does that just refer to the inner sanctum, or what's supposed to be the inner sanctum, your office. No captain of the ship, and you know what happens. The Jolly Roger flag goes up, the inmates run the asylum, the drunks manage the bar, if you'll excuse me for mixing metaphors."

"Why didn't you say something?"

"I don't work at the CFC. Or for it. Just an invited guest on occasion," he says.

"That's not an answer, and you know it. Why wouldn't you protect me?"

"You mean in the manner you think I should," he says, because it's silly to suggest he wouldn't protect me.

"What has been going on around here? Maybe if you tell me, I can figure out what needs to be done," I then say. "I know Lucy's been catching you up. It would be nice if someone would catch me up. In detail, and with openness and full disclosure."

"I'm sorry you're angry. I'm sorry you've come home to a situation that is upsetting. Your homecoming should have been joyful."

"Joyful. What the hell is joyful?"

"A word, a theoretical concept. Like full disclosure. I can tell you what I've witnessed firsthand, what happened when I met here several times. Case discussions. There have been two that involved me." He stares off. "The first was the BC football player from last fall, not long after the CFC took over the Commonwealth's forensic cases."

Wally Jamison, age twenty, Boston College's star quarterback. Found floating in Boston Harbor on November 1 at dawn. Cause of death exsanguination due to blunt-force trauma and multiple cutting injuries. Tom Booker's case, one of my other MEs.

"Jack didn't do that one," I remind him.

"Well, if you ask him, you might get a different impression," Benton informs me. "Jack reviewed the Wally Jamison case as if it was his. Dr. Booker wasn't present. This was last week."

"Why last week? I don't know anything about it."

"New information, and we wanted to talk to Jack, and he seemed eager to cooperate, to offer a wealth of information."

"'We'?"

Benton lifts his coffee, then changes his mind and sets it back down on Fielding's sloppy desk with all its collectibles that are all about him. "I think Jack's attitude is he may not have done the autopsy, but that's just a technicality. An NFL draft was right up the alley of your ironman freak of a deputy chief."

"'Ironman freak'?"

"But I suppose it was his bad luck to be out of town when Wally Jamison got beaten and hacked to death. Wally's luck was a little worse."

Believed to have been abducted and murdered on Halloween. Crime scene unknown. No suspect. No motive or credible theory.

Just the speculation of a satanic cult initiation. Target a star ath-
lete. Hold him hostage in some clandestine place and kill him
savagely. Chatter on the Internet and on the news. Gossip that's
become gospel.

"I don't give a shit what Jack's feeling is or what's right up his
goddamn alley," says a hard part of me that's old and scarred over,
a part of me that is completely fed up with Jack Fielding.

I realize I'm enraged by him. I'm suddenly aware that at the
core of my unhealthy relationship with him is molten fury.

"And Mark Bishop, also last week. Wednesday was the football player. Thursday was the boy," Benton says.

"A boy whose murder might be related to some initiation.
A gang, a cult," I interject. "A similar speculation about Wally
Jamison."

"*Speculation* being the operative word. Whose speculation?"

"Not mine." I think angrily of Fielding. "I don't speculate
unless it's behind closed doors with someone I trust. I know better than to put something out there, and then the police run with
it, then the media runs with it. Next thing I know, a jury believes
it, too."

"Patterns and parallels."

"You're connecting Mark Bishop and Wally Jamison." It
seems incredible. "I fail to see what they might have in common
besides speculation."

"I was here last week for both case consults." Benton's eyes are
steady on me. "Where was Jack last Halloween? Do you know for
a fact?"

"I know where I was, that's about the only fact I know. While

I've been at Dover, that's all I've known and all I was supposed to know. I didn't hire him so I could goddamn babysit him. I don't know where the hell he was on Halloween. I guess you're going to tell me he wasn't out somewhere taking his kids trick-or-treating."

"He was in Salem. But not with his kids."

"I wouldn't know that and don't know why you do or why it's important."

"It wasn't important until very recently," Benton says.

I stare at his boots again, then at his dark pants with their flannel lining and cargo and rear slash pockets for gun magazines and flashlights, the type of pants he wears when he's working in the field, when he goes to crime scenes or is out on the firing or explosive-ordnance-disposal ranges with cops, with the FBI.

"Where were you before you picked me up at Hanscom?" I ask him. "What were you doing?"

"We have a lot to deal with, Kay. I'm afraid more than I thought."

"Were you dressed in field clothes when you picked me up at the airport?" It occurs to me that he might not have been. He's changed his clothes. Maybe he hasn't done anything yet but is about to.

"I keep a bag in my car. As you know," Benton says. "Since I never know when I might get called."

"To go where? You've been called to go somewhere?"

He looks at me, then out the window at the chalky skyline of Boston in the snowy dark.

"Lucy says you've been on the phone." I continue to prod him for information I can tell I'm not going to get right now.

"I'm afraid nonstop. I'm afraid there's more than I thought," and then he doesn't continue. That's all he's going to say about it. He's headed out somewhere, has someplace to go. It's not a good place. He's been talking to people and not about anything good and he's not going to inform me right now. Full disclosure and joy. When there is such a thing, it is only a taste, a hint of what we don't have the rest of the time.

"You met on Wednesday and then on Thursday. Discussing the Wally Jamison and Mark Bishop cases here at the CFC." I go back to that. "And I assume Jack was in on the Mark Bishop discussion as well. He was involved in both discussions. And you didn't mention this a little while ago when we were talking in the car."

"Not such a little while ago. More than five hours ago. And a lot has happened. There have been developments since we were in the car, as you know. Not the least of which is what we now realize is another murder. Number three."

"You're linking the man from Norton's Woods to Mark Bishop and Wally Jamison."

"Very possibly. In fact, I'd say yes."

"What about the meetings last week? With Jack? He was there," I push.

"Yes. Last Wednesday and Thursday. In your office."

"What do you mean my office? This building? This floor?"

"Your personal office." Benton indicates my office next door.

"In my office. Jack conducted meetings in my office. I see."

"He conducted both meetings in your office. At your conference-room table in there."

"He has his own conference table." I look at the black lacquered oval table with six ergonomic chairs that I got at a government auction.

Benton doesn't respond. He knows as well as I do that Fielding's inappropriate decision to use my personal office has nothing to do with the furniture. I think of what Lucy mentioned about sweeping my office for covert surveillance devices, although she never directly said who might be doing the spying or if anyone was. The most likely candidate for the sort of individual who might bug my office and get away with it is my niece. Maybe motivated by the knowledge that Fielding was helping himself to what isn't rightfully his. I wonder if what's been going on in my private space during my absence has been secretly recorded.

"And you never mentioned this to me at that time," I continue. "You could have told me when it happened. You could have fully disclosed to me that he was using my damn office as if he's the damn chief and director of this goddamn place."

"The first I knew of it was last week when I met with him. I'm not saying I hadn't heard things about the CFC and about him."

"It would have been helpful if I'd known these things you were hearing."

"Rumors. Gossip. I didn't know certain things for a fact."

"Then you should have told me a week ago when you knew it for a fact. On the Wednesday you had your first meeting and discovered it was in my office, in an office Jack didn't have permission to use. What else haven't you told me? What new developments?"

"I'm telling you as much as I can and when I can. I know you understand."

"I don't understand. You should have been telling me things all along. Lucy should have. Marino should have."

"It's not that simple."

"Betrayal is very simple."

"No one is betraying you. Marino and Lucy aren't. I'm certainly not."

"Implying that somebody is. Just not the three of you."

He is quiet.

"You and I talk every day, Benton. You should have told me," I then say.

"Let's see when I might have overwhelmed you with all this, overwhelmed you with a lot of things while you've been at Dover. When you'd call at five a.m. before you'd head over to Port Mortuary to take care of our fallen heroes? Or at midnight when you'd finally log out of your computer or quit studying for your boards?"

He doesn't say it defensively or unkindly, but I get his not-so-subtle point, and it's justified. I'm being unfair. I'm being hypocritical. Whose idea was it that when we have virtually no time for each other we shouldn't dwell on work or domestic minutiae or they will be all that's left? Like cancer, I'm quick to offer my clever medical analogies and brilliant insights when he's the psychologist, he's the one who used to head the FBI's profiling unit at Quantico, he's the one on the faculty of Harvard's Department of Psychiatry. But it's me with all the wisdom, all the profound examples, comparing work and niggling domestic details and emotional injuries to cancers, to scarring, to necrosis, and my prognostications that if we're not careful, one day there's no healthy tissue left and death will follow. I feel embarrassed. I feel shallow.

"No, I didn't approach certain subjects until we were driving here, and now I'm telling you more, telling you what I can," Benton says to me with stoical calm, as if we are in a session of his and any moment he will simply announce we have to stop.

I won't stop until I know what I must. Some things he must tell me. It's not just fairness, it's about survival, and I realize I'm feeling unsure of Benton as if I don't quite know him anymore. He's my husband, and I'm touched by a perception that something has been altered, a new ingredient has been added to the house special.

What is it?

I study what I'm intuiting as if I can taste what has changed.

"I mentioned my concern that Jack's interpretation of Mark Bishop's injuries is problematic," Benton goes on, and he's guarded. He's calculating every word he says as if someone else is listening or he will be reporting our conversation to others. "Well, based on what you've described about the hammer marks on the little boy's head, Jack's interpretation is just damn wrong, couldn't be more wrong, and I suspected it at the time when he was going over the case with us. I suspected he was lying."

"'Us'?"

"I told you I've heard things, but I honestly haven't been around Jack."

"Why do you say 'honestly'? As opposed to *dishonestly*, Benton?"

"I'm always honest with you, Kay."

"Of course you aren't, but now is not the time to go into it."

"Now isn't. I know you understand." And he holds my stare for a long moment. He's telling me to please let it go.

"All right. I'm sorry." I will let it go, but I don't want to.

"I hadn't seen him for months, and what I saw for myself was . . . Well, it was pretty obvious during those discussions last week that something's off with him, severely off," Benton resumes. "He looked bad. His thoughts were racing all over the map. He was hyperfluent, grandiose, hypomanic, aggressive, and red-faced, as if he might explode. I certainly felt he wasn't being truthful, that he was deliberately misleading us."

"What do you mean 'us'?" And it begins to occur to me what I'm picking up.

"Has he ever been in a psychiatric hospital, been in treatment, maybe been diagnosed with a mood disorder? He ever mentioned anything like that to you?" Benton questions me in a way that I find unexpected and unnerving, and I'm reminded of what I sensed in the car when we were driving here. Only now it's more pronounced, more recognizable.

He is acting the way he used to when he was still an agent, when he was empowered by the federal government to enforce the law. I detect an authority and confidence he hasn't manifested in years, a sure-footedness he lacked after his reemergence from protective deep cover. He came back feeling lost, weak, like nothing more than an academician, he often complained. *Emasculated,* he would say. *The FBI eats its young, and they've eaten me,* he would say. *That's my reward for going after an organized-crime cartel. I finally get my life back and don't want what's left of it,* he would say. *It's a husk. I'm a husk. I love you, but please understand I'm not what I was.*

"He ever been delusional or violent?" Benton is asking me, and it isn't just a clinician talking.

I'm feeling interrogated.

"He had to expect you would tell me he's been using my office as if it's his. Or that I'd find out." I think of Lucy again, of spying and covert recordings.

"I know he has a temper," Benton says, "but I'm talking about physical violence possibly accompanied by dissociative fugue, disappearing for hours, days, weeks, with little or no recall. What we're seeing with some of these men and women who return from war, disappearances and amnesia triggered by severe trauma and often confused with malingering. The same thing Johnny Donahue is supposedly suffering from, only I'm not sure how much of it has been suggested to that poor damn kid. I wonder where the idea came from, if someone's suggested it to him."

He says it as if he really doesn't wonder it.

"Jack's certainly famous for coming across as a malingerer, of avoiding his responsibilities going back to the beginning of time," Benton then says.

I created Fielding.

"What haven't you told me about him?" Benton goes on.

I made Fielding what he is. He is my monster.

"A psychiatric history?" Benton says. "Off-limits even to me, even to the FBI. I could find out, but I won't violate that boundary."

Benton and the FBI. One and the same again. Not a street

agent again. I can't imagine that. A criminal investigative analyst, a criminal intelligence analyst, a threat analyst. The Department of Justice has so many analysts, agents who are a combination academic and tactical. If you're going to go to prison or get shot, may as well be at the hand of a cop who's got a Ph.D.

"What might you know about Jack, your protégé, that I don't?" Benton asks me. "Besides that he's a sick fuck. Because he is. Somewhere some part of you knows it, Kay."

I'm Briggs's monster, and Fielding is mine. Going back to the beginning of time.

"I'm well aware of sexual abuse," Benton says blandly, as if he doesn't care what happened to Fielding when he was a child, as if Benton really doesn't give a damn.

Not a psychologist but something else speaking, and I'm sure. Cops, federal agents, prosecutors, those who protect and punish, are hardened to excuses. They judge "subjects" and "persons of interest" by what they do, not by what was done to them. People like Benton don't give a damn about why or if it couldn't be helped, doesn't matter the definitions, distillations, and predictions he so astutely, so skillfully, renders. In his heart Benton has no sympathy for hateful, harmful people, and his years of being a clinician and consultant have been cruel to him, have been unfulfilling and have felt fake, he's confessed to me more than once.

"That much is a matter of public record since the case went to trial." Benton feels the need to tell me something I've never asked Fielding about.

I don't remember when and how I first heard of the special school Fielding attended as a boy near Atlanta. Somehow I know, and all that comes to mind is references he's made to a certain "episode" in his past, that what he experienced with a certain "counselor" makes it excruciatingly difficult for him to handle any tragedy involving children, especially if they were abused. I'm certain I never pushed him to volunteer the details. Back in those days especially, I wouldn't have asked.

"Nineteen seventy-eight," Benton says, "when Jack was fifteen, although he was twelve when it started, went on for several years until they were caught having sex in the back of her station wagon parked at the edge of the soccer field as if she wanted to be caught. She was pregnant. Anther pathetic story about boarding schools, this one, thank God, not Catholic but for troubled teens, one of these private treatment center–slash–academies that has *Ranch* in its name. What the therapist did to get convicted of ten counts of sexual battery on a minor isn't what you haven't told me about Jack."

"I don't know the details," I finally answer him. "Not all of them or even most of them. I don't remember her name, if I ever knew it; didn't know she was pregnant. His child? Did she have it?"

"I've reviewed the case transcripts. Yes. She had it."

"I wouldn't have had a reason to look at the case transcripts." I don't ask why Benton has a reason. He's not going to reveal that to me right now, and maybe he never will. "What a shame there's one more child in the world Jack's raised poorly. Or not at all," I add. "How sad."

"Kathleen Lawler hasn't had such a good life, either," Benton starts to say.

"How sad," I repeat.

"The woman convicted of molesting Jack," he says. "I don't know about the child, a girl, born in prison, given up for adoption. Considering the mutant genetic loading, probably in prison, too, or dead. Kathleen Lawler was in one mess after another, currently in a correctional facility for female offenders in Savannah, Georgia, serving twenty years for DUI manslaughter. Jack communicates with her, is a prison pen pal, although he uses a pen name, and that's not what you haven't told me, because I doubt you know about it. Actually, I can't imagine you do."

"Who else was at the meetings last week?" I'm so cold my fingernails are blue, and I wish I'd brought my jacket in here. I notice a lab coat on the back of Fielding's door.

"It crossed my mind while we were sitting in your office," says Benton, the former FBI agent, the former protected witness and master of secrets, who isn't acting like a former anything anymore.

He's acting like he's investigating a case, not just a consultant on one. I'm convinced that what I suspect is true. He's back with the Feds. Things end where they begin and begin where they end.

"An affective disorder. I've thought hard about it, tried to remember him from the old days. Done a lot of reflecting on the old days." Benton talks matter-of-factly, as if he has no feelings about what he's divulging and accusing me of. "He's never been normal. That's my point. Jack has significant underlying pathology. That's why he was sent off to boarding school. To learn to manage his anger. When he was six years old he stabbed another little kid in the chest with a ballpoint pen. When he was eleven he hit his mother in the head with a rake. Then he was sent to the ranch near Atlanta, where he only got angrier."

"I have no idea what he did when he was growing up," I reply. "It's not a common practice to conduct extensive background checks on doctors one might hire, in fact, was unheard of when I was getting started, when he was getting started. I'm not an FBI agent," I add pointedly. "I don't dig up everything I can about people and go around questioning neighbors they grew up around. I don't question their teachers. I don't track down their pen pals."

I get up from Fielding's desk.

"Although I probably should have. I probably will from now on. But I've never covered up for him," I go on. "Never protected him that way. I admit I've been too forgiving. I admit I've fixed his disasters or tried to. But never covered up something I shouldn't, if that's what you're saying I've done. I would never do anything unethical for him or anyone." *Not anymore,* I add silently. I did it once but never again, and I never did it for Jack Fielding. Not even for myself but for the highest law of the land.

I walk across the office, cold and exhausted and ashamed of myself. I remove Fielding's lab coat from the hook at the top of the closed door.

"I don't know what it is you think I've not told you, Benton. I have no idea what he's involved with or whom. Or his delusions or dissociative states and blackouts. Not in my presence, and he's never shared information like that, if it's true."

I put on the lab coat, and it is huge, and I detect the faint sharp odor of eucalyptus, like Vicks, like Bengay.

"Maybe a mood disorder with a touch of narcissism and intermittent explosive anger," Benton goes on as if I just said nothing. "Or it could be the drugs, maybe his damn performance-enhancement drugs as usual, the sorry bastard. He doesn't represent the CFC well, I'm sorry as hell to make the understatement of the century, and it wasn't lost on Douglas and David, and that got the CFC off on the wrong foot, as long ago as early November, when they got involved in the Wally Jamison kidnapping and murder. You can imagine what's gotten back to Briggs and others. Jack is one inch from ruining everything, and that opens up a place to opportunists. Like I said, it creates a looting mentality."

I pause before a window and look down on the dark, snowy street as if I might find something there that will remind me of who I am. Something to give me strength, something to find comfort in.

"He's done a lot of damage." Benton's voice behind me. "I don't know that it's been intentional. But I suspect some of it has been because of his complicated relationship with you."

Snow is blowing at a sharp angle, hitting the window almost horizontally and making rapid clicks that remind me of fingernails tapping, of something restless and disturbed. When I look at the snow as it hits the glass, it makes me dizzy. It gives me vertigo to look at it and then to look down.

"Is that what this is about, Benton? My complicated relationship with him?"

"I need to know about it. It's better it's me instead of someone else asking you."

"You're saying everything is damaged and ruined because of it. That it's the root of everything wrong." I don't turn around but stare out and down until I can't look at the flying flakes of ice and the road below and the dark river or the volatile winter night any longer. "That's what you believe." I want him to verify what he just said. I want to know if what's been damaged and ruined while I've been gone includes Benton and me.

"I just need to know anything you haven't told me," he answers instead.

"I'm sure you and others need to know." I don't say it nicely as my pulse picks up.

"I understand things from the past don't get resolved easily. I understand complications."

I turn around and meet his stare, and what I see in it isn't just cases and dead people or my mutinous office or my deranged deputy chief. I see Benton's distrust of me and my past. I see him doubting my character and who I am to him.

"I never slept with Jack," I tell him. "If that's what you're trying to find out so someone else is spared the discomfort of asking me. Or is it my discomfort you're so worried about? I never did. It won't come out because it isn't there. If that's what you're trying to ask me, that's your answer. You can pass it along to Briggs, to the FBI, to the attorney general, to whoever you goddamn want."

"I would understand when Jack was your fellow, when both of you were just getting started in Richmond."

"I try not to make it a practice to have sex with people I mentor," I say with a surprising flare of irritability. "I'd like to think I bear no similarity to what's-her-name Lawler, the former therapist locked up in Georgia."

"Jack wasn't twelve when you met him."

"It never happened. I don't do that with people I mentor."

"And when people mentor you?" Benton's eyes are steady on me as I stand by the window.

"That's not why John Briggs and I have a problem," I answer angrily.

13

return to Fielding's desk and sit back down in his chair as I finger something slick and filmy inside one of his lab coat pockets. I pull out a square of transparent plastic that is paper-thin.

"The CFC didn't need to make a bad first impression with the Feds, but I'm confident you'll change it." Benton says it as if he regrets what he's just asked me, as if he's sorry about what he just confronted me with in the line of duty.

I sniff what Fielding must have peeled off a eucalyptus-laced pain-relieving patch, and resentfully think, *Yes, indeed, the Feds. I'm so glad I can change what the goddamn Feds must think of me.*

"I don't want you to feel negative about everything here, everything you've come home to," Benton continues. "It wouldn't be helpful if you are. There is a lot to take care of, but we'll get there. I know we will. I'm sorry our conversation had to move in certain directions. I'm really sorry we had to get into all this."

"Let's talk about Douglas and David." I remind him of names he referred to moments earlier. "Who are they?"

"I have no doubt you'll prevail and make this place work, make it what it was meant to be, which is stellar and unlike anything anywhere. Better than what they have in Australia, in Switzerland, even better than any place where they were doing it first, including Dover, right? I have complete confidence in you, Kay. I don't want you to ever forget that."

The more Benton assures me of his confidence, the less I believe it.

"Law enforcement respects you, the military does," he adds, and I don't believe that, either.

If it were true, he wouldn't have to say it. *So what?* I then think, with hostility that seems to come from nowhere. I don't need people to like or respect me. It isn't a popularity contest. Isn't that what Briggs always says? *It's not a popularity contest, Colonel,* or if he's being more personable, *It's not a popularity contest, Kay,* and he smiles wryly, a steely glint of mischief in his eyes. He doesn't give a shit if anybody likes him, and in fact thrives on people not liking him, and I'm going to start thriving on it, too. The hell with everyone. I know what I need to do, which is something. I will do something, oh, yes, I will. Thinking I'm going to come home to this and just take it, do nothing about it, let whoever it is have his way? No. Hell, no. Not going to happen. Whoever would entertain an idea like that sure as hell doesn't know me.

"Who are Douglas and David?" I again ask, and I sound snappish.

"Douglas Burke and David McMaster," Benton says.

"I don't know them, and who are they to you?" Now I'm the one doing the interrogating.

"FBI's Boston Field Office, Metro Boston Homeland Security. You haven't gotten to know the locals, not key ones, but you will. Including the coast guard. I'm going to help you get to know everyone around here if you'll permit me to. For once I might be useful. I've missed being useful to you. I know you're upset."

"I'm not upset."

"Your face is flushed. You look upset. I don't mean to upset you. I'm sorry I have. But it's something I've needed to know for several reasons."

"And are you satisfied?"

"It's critical to know where you are in all this and who you are in it," he says as I hold the flimsy plastic backing, a square about the size of a cigarette pack.

I lift it up to the light and see Fielding's large fingerprints on the transparent film and smaller ones that must be mine. Fielding is chronically straining muscles, always achy and sore, especially when he's abusing anabolic steroids. When he's back to his old, bad tricks he smells like a damn menthol cough drop.

"What do Homeland Security, the coast guard, have to do with anything we're talking about?" I'm opening desk drawers, looking for Nuprin, Motrin, or Bengay patches, for Tiger Balm, for anything that might confirm what I suspect.

"Wally Jamison's body was floating in the harbor at the coast guard's ISC, their Integrated Support Command. Right there under their nose. Which I believe was the point," Benton replies as he watches me.

"Or the point was the wharf right there that's deserted after dark. One of the few wharves in the area that you can drive a car on. I sure as hell know that area. So do you. We know it, and some of the people who work there probably would recognize us, we've walked around there so many times, right next door to where we stay once in a blue moon when we can get away and be alone and be civil to each other." I sound sarcastic and mean.

"Authorized personnel only. Might I ask what you're looking for? I'm sure it's something that will be in plain view."

"It's my office. This entire place is my office. I'll look at whatever the hell I want. Plain view or not." My pulse is flying, and I feel agitated.

"The wharf isn't open to the public. Not just anybody can drive a car on it," Benton replies as he watches me carefully, worried. "I didn't mean to upset you this much."

"We walk over there all the time and no one asks for our IDs. They're not standing around with submachine guns. It's a tourist area." I'm argumentative and combative, and I don't want to be.

"The coast guard ISC isn't a tourist area. There's a guard gate you have to go through to get out on the pier," Benton says very calmly, very reasonably, and he continues looking at his iPhone. He looks at it and then at me, back and forth, reading both of us.

"I miss it. Let's spend a few days there soon." I try to sound nice because I'm acting awful. "Just the two of us."

"Yes. We will. Soon," he says. "We'll talk and get everything straight."

I imagine it with startling clarity, our favorite suite that reaches out into the water like a fingertip at the Fairmont hotel on Battery Wharf, directly next door to the coast guard ISC. I see the ruffled dark-green water of the harbor and hear it washing against pilings as if I'm there. I hear the creaking of docks, the clanking of rigging lines against masts, and the bass tones of the horns the big ships sound as if all of it is audible inside Fielding's office.

"And we won't answer our phones, and we'll go for walks and get room service and watch the tall ships, the tugboats, the tankers from our window. I would love that. Wouldn't you love it?" But I don't sound nice as I say it. I sound pushy and angry.

"We'll do it this weekend if you want. If we can," he says as he reads something on his iPhone, scrolling down with his thumb.

I move my coffee away and the corner of the desk looks rounded, not squared. Too much caffeine and my heart is beating hard. I feel light-headed and edgy.

"I hate it when you look at your phone all the time," I say before I can stop myself. "You know how much I hate it when we're talking."

"It can't be avoided right now," he says as he looks at it.

"Exit off Ninety-three, get on Commercial Street, and you're right there," I resume arguing. "A convenient way to get rid of a body. Drive it there and dump it in the harbor. Nude, so whatever trace evidence there might have been from the car trunk, for example, was probably washed away." I shut a bottom drawer and sound peculiar to myself as I mutter distractedly, "Pain-relieving patches. None. And I didn't see any in my desk drawers, either. Only chewing gum. I've never been a gum chewer. Well, when I was a little kid. Dubble Bubble at Halloween, with the colorful waxy yellow wrapper that's twisted on the ends."

I see it. I smell it. My mouth waters.

"Here's a secret I've never told anyone. I'd recycle. Chew it and wrap it up again. For days until there was no flavor left."

My mouth is watering, and I swallow several times.

"I stopped chewing gum when I stopped trick-or-treating. See, you've reminded me of trick-or-treating, something I haven't thought of in so many years I can't believe it's just popped into my head. Sometimes I forget I was ever a child. Ever young and stupid and trusting."

My hands are shaking.

"Better not to like something you can't afford, so I didn't make a habit of gum."

I'm trembling.

"Better not to look like you grew up low-class, especially if you did grow up low-class. When have you ever seen me chew gum? I won't. It's low-class."

"Nothing about you is low-class." Benton watches me carefully, guardedly, and I see what is in his eyes. I'm scaring him.

But I can't stop myself. "I've worked damn hard in life not to look low-class. You didn't know me when I was getting started and had no idea what people are really like, people who have complete power over you, people you worship really, and what they're capable of luring you into so that you never feel the same about yourself. And then you bury it like that beating heart under the floorboards in Edgar Allan Poe, but you always know it's there. And you can't tell anyone. Even when it keeps you awake at night. You can't even tell the person you're closest to that there's this cold, dead heart under the floorboards and it's your fault it's under there."

"Christ, Kay."

"It's odd that everything we love seems to be in close proximity to something hateful and dead," enters my mind next. "Well, not everything."

"Are you all right?"

"I'm fine. Just stressed out, and who the hell wouldn't be? Our house is a stone's throw from Norton's Woods, where someone was murdered yesterday, and he may have been at the Courtauld Gallery at the same time Lucy and I were the summer before Nine-Eleven, which she thinks was caused by us, by the way. Liam Saltz was there, too, at the Courtauld, one of the lecturers. I didn't meet him then, but Lucy has him on CD. I can't remember what he talked about."

"I'm curious why you would bring him up."

"A link on a website that Jack was looking at for some reason."

Benton doesn't say anything, and he doesn't take his eyes off me.

"You and I go in The Biscuit when I'm home on weekends, maybe we've been in there at the same time Johnny Donahue and his MIT friend were," I go on and can't keep up with my thoughts. "We love Salem and the oils and candles in the shops there, the same shops that sell iron spikes, devil's bone. Our favorite getaway in Boston is next to where Wally Jamison's body was found the morning after Halloween. Is someone watching us? Does someone know everything we do? What was Jack doing in Salem on Halloween?"

"Wally's body got where it was by boat, not the wharf," Benton replies, and I don't know where he got the information.

"All these things in common. You'd think we live in a small town."

"You don't look good."

"You're sure it was a boat. I feel like I'm having a hot flash." I touch my cheek, press my hand against it. "Lord. That will be next. So much to look forward to."

"More relevant is the fact that someone deliberately dumped his body where the hundred-foot cutters are homeported with guardsmen on board." Benton watches my every move. "And starting around daybreak, support staff and other personnel show up for work and the wharf is a parking lot. All these people getting out of their cars and seeing a mutilated body floating in the water. That's brazen. Killing a little kid in his own backyard while his parents are inside the house is brazen. Killing someone on Super Bowl Sunday in Norton's Woods while a VIP wedding is going on is brazen. Doing all this in our own neighborhoods is brazen. Yes."

"First you know it's a boat. Next you know it was a VIP wedding, not just a wedding but a VIP wedding." I don't ask but state. He wouldn't say it if he didn't know it. "Why was Jack in Salem? Doing what there? You can't even get a hotel room in Salem on Halloween. You can't even drive, there are so many people."

"Are you sure you're all right?"

"Do you think it's personal?" I ask as I obsess about what a small world it is. "I come home and this is my welcome. To have all this ugliness and death and deceit and betrayal practically in my lap."

"To some extent, yes," Benton says.

"Well, thank you for that."

"I said, 'to some extent.' Not everything."

"You said you think it's personal. I want to know exactly how it is personal."

"Try to calm down. Breathe slowly." He reaches for my hand, and I won't let him touch me. "Slowly, slowly, Kay."

I pull away from him, and he returns his hand to his lap, to the iPhone in it that flashes red every other second as messages land. I don't want him to touch me. It's as if I have no skin.

"Is there anything to eat in this place? I can send out for something," Benton says. "Maybe it's low blood sugar. When did you eat last?"

"No. I couldn't right now. I'll be fine. Why do you say 'VIP'?" I hear myself ask.

He looks at his phone again, the tiny red light flashing its alert. "Anne," he says to me as he reads what just landed. "She's on her way, should be here in a few minutes."

"What else? I can download the scan in here, take a look."

"She didn't send it. She tried to call you. Obviously, you're not at your desk. There were undercover agents at the wedding. Protecting a VIP, but obviously he wasn't the one who needed it," Benton says. "Nobody was looking for the one who needed protecting. We didn't know he was going to be there."

I take another deep breath, and I try to diagnose a heart attack, if I might be having one.

"Did the agents see what happened?" Mount Auburn would be the closest hospital. I don't want to go to the hospital.

"Ones stationed by the outside doors weren't looking at him and didn't see it. They saw people rushing around him when he collapsed. There was no reason he was of interest, and the agents maintained their posts. They had to. In case it was some diversionary maneuver. You always maintain your post when you're on a protective detail; with rare exception, you don't divert."

I focus on the discomfort in the center of my chest and my shortness of breath. I'm sweating and light-headed, but there's no pain in my arms. No pain in my back. No pain in my jaw. No radiating pain, and heart attacks don't cause altered thinking. I look at my hands. I hold them in front of me as if I can see what's on them.

"When you saw Jack last week, did he smell like menthol?" I ask, and then I say, "Where is he? What exactly has he done?"

"What about menthol?"

"Extra-strength Nuprin patches, Bengay patches, something like that." I get up from Fielding's desk. "If he's wearing them all the time and reeks of eucalyptus, of menthol, it's usually an indication he's abusing himself physically, tearing the hell out of himself physically in the gym, in his tae kwon do tournaments, has chronic and acute muscle and joint pain. Steroids. When Jack's on steroids, well . . . That's always been the prelude to other things."

"Based on what I saw last week, he's on something."

I'm already taking off Fielding's lab coat. I fold it into a neat square and place it on top of his desk.

"Is there a place you can lie down?" Benton says. "I think you should lie down. The on-call room downstairs. There's a bed. I can't take you home. You can't be there right now. I don't want you going out of this building, not without me."

"I don't need to lie down. Lying down won't help. It will make it worse." I walk into Fielding's bathroom and snatch a trash basket liner from a box under the sink.

Benton is on his feet, watching what I'm doing, keeping an eye on me as I tuck the folded lab coat inside the liner and return to the bathroom. I scrub my hands and face with soap and hot water. I wash any area of skin that might have come into contact with the plastic film I found in Fielding's lab coat pocket.

"Drugs," I announce when I sit back down.

Benton returns to his chair, tensely, as if he might spring up again.

"Something transdermal that certainly isn't Nuprin or Motrin. Don't know what, but I will find out," I let him know.

"The piece of plastic you were touching."

"Unless you poisoned my coffee."

"Maybe a nicotine patch."

"You wouldn't poison me, would you? If you don't want to be married anymore, there are simpler solutions."

"I don't see why he'd be on nicotine unless as a stimulant? I guess so. Something like that."

"It's not something like that. I used to live off nicotine patches and never felt like this, not even when I would light up while I still had a twenty-one-milligram patch on. A true addict. That's me. But not drugs, not whatever this is. What has he done?"

Benton stares at his coffee mug, tracing the AFME crest on

the black glazed ceramic. His silence confirms what I suspect. Whatever Fielding is involved in, it's connected to everything else: to me, to Benton, to Briggs, to a dead football player, to a dead little boy, to the man from Norton's Woods, to dead soldiers from Great Britain and Worcester. Like planes lit up at night, connected to a tower, connected in a pattern, at times seeming at a standstill in the dark air but having been somewhere and going somewhere, individual forces that are part of something bigger, something incomprehensibly huge.

"You need to trust me," Benton says quietly.

"Has Briggs been in contact with you?"

"Some things have been going on for a while. Are you all right? I don't want to go before I know you are."

"This is what I've trained for, made so many sacrifices for." I decide to accept it. Acceptance makes it easier for me to know what to do. "Six months of being away from you, of being away from everyone, of giving up everything so I could come home to something that's been going on for a while. An agenda."

I almost add *just like in the beginning,* when I was barely a forensic pathologist and was too naïve to have a clue about what was happening. When I was quick to salute authority, and worse, to trust it, and much worse, to respect it, and even worse than that, to admire it, and worst of all, to admire John Briggs so much I would do anything he wanted, absolutely anything. Somehow I've managed to land in the same spot. The same thing again. An agenda. Lies and more lies, and innocent people who are disposable. Crimes as coldly carried out as any I've ever seen.

Joanne Rule and Noonie Pieste are graphically in my mind, as real as they've ever been.

I see them on dented gurneys with rust in their welded seams and wheels that stick, and I remember my feet sticking as I walked across an old white stone floor that would not stay clean. It was always bloody in the Cape Town morgue, with bodies parked everywhere, and the week I was there I saw cases as extreme in their grotesqueness as that continent is extreme in its magnificent beauty. People hit by trains and run over on the highway, and domestic and drug deaths in the shantytowns, and a shark attack in False Bay, and a tourist who died from a fall on Table Mountain.

I have the irrational thought that if I go downstairs and walk into my cooler, the bodies of those two slain women will be waiting for me just as they were on that December morning after I'd flown nineteen hours in a small coach seat to get to them. Only they had already been looked at by the time I showed up, and that would have been true if I'd flown Mach II on the Concorde or been a block away from them when they were murdered. It wasn't possible for me to get to them fast enough. Their bodies may as well have been on a movie set, they were so staged. Innocent young women murdered for the sake of a news story, for the sake of power and influence and votes, and I couldn't put a stop to it.

I not only couldn't stop it, I helped make it happen, because I made it possible for it to happen, and I replay what PFC Gabriel's mother said about hate crimes and being rewarded for them. My office at Dover is right next to Briggs's command suite. I remember someone walking past my closed door several times while I was talking to her. Whoever it was paused at least twice. It crossed my mind at the time that someone might be waiting to come in but could hear through the door that I was on the phone and was unwilling to interrupt. The more likely answer is that someone was listening. Briggs has started something, or someone allied with him has, and Benton's right, it's been going on for a while.

"Then these last six months have been nothing more than a political ploy. How sad. How tawdry. How disappointing." My voice is steady, and I sound completely calm, the way I get before I do something.

"Are you okay? Because we should go downstairs if you're okay. Anne is here. We should talk to her, and then I need to go." Benton has gotten up and is near the door, waiting for me with his phone in hand.

"Let me guess. Briggs made sure I got this position so he could keep it open for whomever he really has in mind." I go on and my heart has slowed and my nerves feel steadier, as if they're firing normally again. "Wanted me to keep the seat warm. Or was I the excuse to get this place built, to get MIT, get Harvard, get everybody on board, to justify some thirty million in grants?"

Benton reads something else as messages drop out of the thin air, one after another.

"He could have saved himself a lot of trouble," I say as I get up from the desk.

"You're not going to quit," Benton says, reading what someone has just sent to him. "Don't give them that satisfaction."

"'Them.' Then it's more than one."

He doesn't answer as he types with his thumbs.

"Well, it's always been more than one. Take your pick," I say as we walk out together.

"If you quit, you give them exactly what they want." As he reads and scrolls down on his phone.

"People like that don't know what they want." I shut Fielding's door behind us, making sure it's locked. "They just think they do."

We begin our descent in my bullet-shaped building that on dark nights and gloomy days is the color of lead.

I'm explaining to Benton the indented writing on a pad of call sheets as we glide down in an elevator I researched and selected because it reduces energy consumption by fifty percent. It can't be a coincidence that Fielding was interested in a keynote address Dr. Liam Saltz just gave at Whitehall, I say, while numbers change on a digital display, while we gently sink from floor to floor in the soft glow of LEDs in my environmentally friendly hoisting machine that no one who works here appreciates in the least, from what I've heard. Mostly there are complaints because it is slow.

"He's one extreme, and DARPA's certainly the other, neither of them always right, that's for sure." I describe Dr. Saltz as a computer scientist, an engineer, a philosopher, a theologian, whose sport, whose art, most assuredly isn't war. He hates wars and those who make them.

"I know all about him and his art." Benton doesn't say it in a positive way as we stop gently and the steel door slides open with scarcely a sound. "I certainly remember from that time at CNN when you and I got into a spat because of him."

"I don't remember getting into a spat." We are back in the receiving area, where Ron is sternly alert behind his glass partition, exactly as we left him long hours ago.

In split screens of video displays I see cars parked in the lot behind the building, SUVs that aren't covered with snow and have their headlights on. Agents or undercover police, and I remember windows glowing in MIT buildings rising above the CFC fence, I remember noticing it at the time Benton drove us here, and now I know why. The CFC has been under surveillance, and the FBI, the police, aren't making any effort to disguise their presence now. I feel as if the CFC is on lockdown.

Ever since I walked out of Port Mortuary at Dover, I have been accompanied or locked inside a secured building, and the reason isn't what was presented, at least not the only reason. No one was trying to get me home as quickly as possible because of a body bleeding inside the cooler. That was a priority but certainly not the only one and maybe not even the top one. Certain people used that as an excuse to escort me, certain people, such as my niece, who was armed and playing bodyguard, and I can't believe Benton wasn't involved in that decision, no matter what he did or didn't know at the time.

"Maybe you remember him hitting on you," Benton is saying as we follow the gray corridor.

"You seem to think I'm having sex with everyone."

"Not with everyone," he says.

I smile. I almost laugh.

"You're feeling better," he says, touching my arm tenderly as he walks with me.

Whatever got into me has passed, and I wish it wasn't such a godforsaken hour of the morning. I wish someone was in the trace evidence lab so we could take a look at the plastic film I was exposed to, probably try the scanning electron microscope first, then Fourier transform infrared or whatever detectors it takes to figure out what is on Fielding's pain-relieving patches. I've never taken anabolic steroids and don't know firsthand how that would feel, but I can't imagine it's what I felt upstairs. Not that quickly.

Cocaine, crystal methamphetamine, LSD, whatever could get into my system instantly and transdermally, hopefully nothing like that, either, but what would I know about how that would feel? Not an opioid like fentanyl, which is the most common narcotic delivered by a patch. A strong pain reliever like fentanyl wouldn't have caused me to react the way I did, but again, I'm not sure. I've never been on fentanyl. Everybody reacts differently to medications, and uncontrolled substances can be contaminated with impurities and have variable doses.

"Really. You seem like yourself." Benton touches me again. "How are you feeling? You okay for sure?"

"Worn off, whatever it was. I wouldn't do the case if it wasn't, if I felt even remotely impaired," I tell him. "I guess you're coming to the autopsy room." Since we're headed there.

"A drink. Right." He is back to Liam Saltz. "He bumps into you at CNN and asks you to have a drink with him at midnight. That's not exactly normal."

"I'm not sure how to take that. But I don't feel flattered."

"His reputation with women is on a par with certain politicians who will remain unnamed. What's the buzzword these days? A sexual addiction."

"Well, if you're going to have one."

We walk past the x-ray room, and the door is shut, the red light off because the scanner isn't in use. The lower level is empty and silent, and I wonder where Marino is. Maybe he's with Anne.

"He had any contact with you since then? That was what? About two years ago?" Benton asks. "Or maybe with some of your compatriots at Walter Reed or Dover?"

"Not with me. I wouldn't know about others, except no one involved with the armed forces is a fan of Dr. Saltz's. He's not considered patriotic, which really isn't fair if you analyze what he's actually saying."

"Problem is nobody seems to understand what anybody is saying anymore. People don't listen. Saltz isn't a communist. He's not a terrorist. He hasn't committed treason. He just doesn't know how to curb his enthusiasm and muzzle his big mouth. But he's not of interest to the government. Well, he wasn't."

"Suddenly, he is." I assume that's what Benton will tell me next.

"He wasn't at Whitehall yesterday. Wasn't even in London." Benton waits until now to inform me of this as we pause before the locked double steel doors of the autopsy room. "I don't guess you found that part on the Internet when you were trying to make heads or tails of Jack's indented writing," Benton adds in a tone that is shaded with other meanings. A hint of hostility, not directed at me but at Fielding.

"How do you know where Liam Saltz was or wasn't?" I ask at the same time I think about what Benton mentioned upstairs. He referred to the event at Norton's Woods as a VIP wedding and mentioned a security presence. Undercover agents, Benton told me, although it was during an interval when I wasn't thinking as clearly as I should have been.

"Did his keynote address by satellite on a big video screen. Well attended by the audience at Whitehall," Benton says as if he was there. "He had a complication, a family matter, and had to leave the country."

I think of the man beyond these closed steel doors. A man whose wristwatch when he died may have been set to UK time. A man with an old robot called MORT inside his apartment, the same robot that Liam Saltz and I testified against, persuading people in power to disallow its use.

"Is that why Jack was looking him up, looking up RUSI or whatever he was looking at early yesterday morning?" I ask as I scan open the lock to the autopsy room.

"I'm wondering how that happened, if he got a call and then looked him up or maybe knew he was in Cambridge for some reason," Benton replies. "I'm wondering a lot of things that hopefully will get answered soon. What I do know is Dr. Saltz was here for the wedding. The daughter of his current wife, whose biological father was supposed to give her away, then got the swine flu."

"I text-messaged you," Anne tells me, and she's shrouded in blue as she works on a computer that is contained in a waterproof stainless-steel enclosure, the sealed keyboard mounted at a height suitable for typing while standing. Behind her on the autopsy table of station one, which is now shiny and clean, is the man from Norton's Woods.

"I'm sorry," I say to her abstractedly as I think of Liam Saltz and worry what his connection might be to this dead man, beyond robots, particularly MORT. "My phone's in my office, and I've not been in there," I say to Anne, and then I ask Benton, "Does he have other children?"

"He's at the Charles Hotel," Benton replies. "Someone's on the way to talk to him. But to answer your question, yes, he does. He has a number of children and stepchildren from multiple marriages."

"I wanted to let you know I didn't feel comfortable uploading his scans and e-mailing them," Anne then says to me. "Don't know what we're dealing with and thought it was better to play it extra-safe. If you're going to hang around, you need to cover up." She directs this to Benton. "Got no clue what this one's been exposed to, but he didn't set off any alarms. At least he's not radioactive. Whatever he's got in him isn't, thank God."

"I assume all was quiet at the hospital. No incidents," Benton says to her. "I'm not staying."

"Security escorted us in and out, and we didn't see anyone else—no patients or staff, at any rate."

"You found something in him?" I ask her.

"Trace amounts of metal." Anne's gloved hands move on the computer's keyboard and click the mouse, both freshly overlaid with industrial silicone. Fielding's sloppy presence is noticeably gone from the autopsy room, and I see water in the sink of station one—my station—and a big sponge, the surgical instruments bright and shiny and neatly arranged on the dissecting board. I spot a mop that wasn't here earlier, and a whetstone on a countertop.

"I'm amazed," I say to her as I look around.

"Ollie," she says, clicking the mouse. "I called him, and he drove back and spruced up the place."

"You're kidding."

"It's not that we haven't tried while you were gone. Jack's been using this work space, and we've learned to stay away."

"How can there be metal that didn't show up on CT?" Benton watches her scroll through files she created at the neuroimaging lab, looking for the images she wants from the MRI.

"If it's really small," I explain to him how it's possible. "A threshold size of less than point-five millimeter and I wouldn't expect it to be detected on CT. That's why we wanted to rule out the possibility by using MR, and apparently it's a good thing."

"Although maybe not if he was alive," Anne says, clicking on a file. "You don't want something ferromagnetic in a living person, because it's going to torque. It's going to move. Like metal shavings in the eyes of people involved in professions that expose them to something like that. They may not even know it until they get an MRI. Then they know it; boy, do they ever. Or if they have body piercings they don't tell us about, and we've seen that enough times," she says to Benton. "Or, God forbid, a pacemaker. Metal moves, and it heats up."

"Theories?" I ask her, because I can't imagine an event or a weapon that could create what has just filled the video display.

"Your guess is as good as mine," she answers as we study high-resolution images of the dead man's internal damage, a dark distorted area of signal voids that starts just inside the buttonhole wound and becomes increasingly less pronounced the deeper the penetration inside the organs and soft tissue structures of the chest.

"Because of the magnetic field, even with what must be particles incredibly minute, you're going to get artifact. Right here," I point out to Benton. "These very dark and distorted areas where there's no signal penetration. You get this blooming artifact along the wound track, what's left of the wound track, because the signal's been blown out by metal. He's got some sort of ferromagnetic foreign bodies inside him, all right."

"What could do that?" Benton asks.

"I'm going to have to recover some of it, analyze it." I think of what Lucy said about thermite. It would be ferromagnetic just as bullets are, both metal composites having iron oxide in common.

"Point-five? The size of dust?" Benton's eyes are distracted by other thoughts.

"A little bigger," Anne replies.

"About the size of gunshot residue, grains of unburned powder," I add.

"A projectile like a bullet could be reduced to frag no bigger than grains of gunshot powder," Benton considers, and I can tell he is connecting what I'm saying with something else, and I think of my niece and wonder exactly what she said to him while they were together in her lab earlier. I think of shark bang sticks and nanoexplosives, but there are no thermal injuries, no burns. It wouldn't make sense.

"No projectile I've ever seen," Anne says, and I agree. "Do we know anything more about who he might be?" She means the body on the table. "I wasn't trying to eavesdrop."

"Hopefully soon," Benton replies.

"It sounds like you might have an idea," Anne says to him.

"Our first clue was he showed up at Norton's Woods at the same time Dr. Saltz was inside the building, and that was something to check because of certain interests these two individuals would have in common." He means robots, I suspect.

"I don't think I know who that is," Anne says to him.

"A scientist who won a Nobel Prize and is an expatriate," Benton says, and as I observe him with Anne I'm reminded they are colleagues and friends, that he treats her with an easy familiarity, with trust that he doesn't exhibit around most people. "And if he"—Benton indicates the dead man—"knew Dr. Saltz was coming to Cambridge, the question was how."

"Do we know if he knew that?" I ask.

"Right now we don't for a fact."

"So Dr. Saltz was at the wedding. But this one wasn't dressed for a wedding." Anne indicates the nude dead body on the table. "He had his dog with him. And a gun."

"What I know so far is the bride is a daughter from a different marriage," Benton says as if this detail has been carefully checked. "The daughter's father, who was supposed to give her away, got sick. So she asked her stepfather, Dr. Saltz, at the last minute, and he couldn't physically be in two places at once. He flew into

Boston on Saturday and made his appearance at Whitehall via satellite. A sacrifice on his part. The last thing he felt like doing, I'm sure, was to reenter the U.S. and show up at Cambridge."

"The undercover agents?" I ask. "For him? If so, why? I know he has enemies, but why would the FBI be offering protection to a civilian scientist from the UK?"

"That's the irony," Benton says. "The security at the event wasn't about him, was about those attending the wedding, most of them from the UK because of the groom's family. The groom is Russell Brown's son, David. Both Liam Saltz's stepdaughter Ruth and David attend Harvard Law, which is one reason the wedding was here."

Russell Brown. The shadow secretary of state for defense, whose speech I just read on the RUSI website.

"He shows up at an event like that and is armed," I say as I move closer to the steel table. "A gun with the serial number eradicated?"

"Right. Why?" Benton asks. "To protect himself, or was he a potential assailant? Or to protect himself for a reason that's unrelated to the wedding and the people I've just mentioned?"

"Possibly top-secret technology he was involved in," I offer. "Technology worth quite a lot of money," I add. "Technology people might kill for."

"And maybe did kill for," Anne says as she looks at the dead young man.

"Hopefully, we'll know soon," Benton says.

I look at the dead man rigid on his back, his curled fingers and the position of his arms, his legs, his hands, his head, exactly as they were earlier, no matter how much he has been disturbed during transport and scans. Rigor mortis is complete, but he won't resist me strenuously as I examine him, because he's thin. He doesn't have much muscle fiber for calcium ions to have gotten trapped in after his neurotransmitters quit. I can break him easily. I can bend him to my will.

"I've got to go," Benton says to me. "I know you want to get this taken care of. I'll need your help with something by the time you're ready to get away from here, and you're not to get away on your own. Make sure she calls me," he says to Anne as she labels test tubes and specimen containers. "Call me or call Marino," he adds. "Give us an hour's advance notice."

"Marino will be with you . . . ?" I start to ask.

"We're working on something. He's already there."

I no longer question what Benton is referring to when he says "we," and he looks one more time at me, his eyes meeting mine with the intimacy of a lingering touch, and he leaves the autopsy room. I hear the receding sound of his brisk footsteps along the hard tile corridor, then his voice and another voice as he talks to someone, perhaps Ron. I can't make out a word they are saying, but they sound serious and intense before silence returns abruptly. I imagine Benton has left the receiving area, and on a video display I'm startled by him. Picked up by security cameras, he walks through the bay as he zips up the shearling coat I gave him so long ago I don't remember the year, only that it was in Aspen, where he used to have a place.

I watch him on closed-circuit TV opening the side door that is next to the massive bay door, and then another camera picks him up outside my building as he walks past his green SUV parked in my spot. He gets into a different SUV, dark and big with bright headlights that the snow slashes through, the wipers sweeping side to side, and I can't see who is driving. I watch the SUV in my snow-covered lot, backing up, moving forward, and pausing as the big gate opens, and finally out of sight in the bitter weather at the empty hour of four a.m., with my husband in the passenger's seat, driven by someone, maybe his FBI friend Douglas, both of them headed to a destination that for some reason I've not been told about.

14

nside the anteroom I prepare for battle the way I always do, suiting up in armor made of plastic and paper.

I never feel like a doctor, not even a surgeon, as I get ready to conduct a postmortem examination, and I suspect only people who deal with the dead for a living can understand what I mean by that. During my medical school residencies I was no different from other doctors, tending to the sick and injured on wards and in emergency rooms, and I assisted in surgical procedures in the OR. So I know what it is to incise warm bodies that have a blood pressure and something vital to lose. What I'm about to do couldn't be more different from that, and the first time I inserted a scalpel blade into cold, unfeeling flesh, made my first Y-incision on my first dead patient, I gave up something I've never gotten back.

I abandoned any notion that I might be godlike or heroic or gifted beyond other mortals. I rejected the fantasy that I could heal any creature, including myself. No doctor has the power to cause blood to clot or tissue or bone to regenerate or tumors to shrink. We don't create, only prompt biological functions to work or not work properly on their own, and in that regard, doctors are more limited than a mechanic or an engineer who actually builds some-thing out of nothing. My choice of a medical specialty, which my mother and sister still consider morbid and abnormal, probably has made me more honest than most physicians. I know that when I administer my healing touch to the dead they are unmoved by me or my bedside manner. They stay just as dead as they were before. They don't say thank you or send holiday greetings or name their children after me. Of course I was cognizant of all this when I decided on pathology, but that's like saying you know what com-bat is when you enlist in the marines and get deployed to the mountains of Afghanistan. People don't really know what any-thing is really like until it really happens to them.

I can never smell the acrid, oily, pungent odor of unbuffered formaldehyde without being reminded of how naïve I was to as-sume that the dissection of a cadaver donated to science for teach-ing purposes is anything like the autopsy of an unembalmed person whose cause of death is questioned. My first one took place in the Hopkins hospital morgue, which was a crude place com-pared to what is beyond this room where I am this minute folding my AFME field clothes and placing them on a bench, not bother-ing with the locker room or modesty at this hour. The woman whose name I still recall was only thirty-three and left behind two small children and a husband when she died of postoperative complications from an appendectomy.

To this day I'm sorry she was my science project. I'm sorry she was ever put in a position to be any pathology resident's project, and I remember thinking how absurd it was that such a healthy young human being had succumbed to an infection caused by the removal of a rather useless wormlike pouch from the large intestine. I wanted to make her better. As I worked on her, practiced on her, I wanted her to come to and climb off that scratched-up steel pedestal table in the center of the dingy floor inside that dreary subterranean room that smelled like death. I wanted her alive and well and to feel I'd had something to do with it. I'm not a surgeon. What I do is excavate so I can make my case when I go to war with killers or, less dramatically but more typically, with lawyers.

Anne was thoughtful enough to find a pair of freshly laundered scrubs, size medium and the institutional green I'm accustomed to, and I put them on, then over them a disposable gown, which I tie snugly in back before I pull shoe covers out of a dispenser and cover a pair of rubber medical clogs Anne dug up somewhere. Next are protective sleeves, a hair cover, a mask, and a face shield, and finally I double-glove.

"Maybe you could scribe for me," I say to her as I return to the autopsy room, a big, empty vista of gleaming white and bright steel. Only the three of us are here, if I include my patient on the first table. "In the event I don't get to dictate my findings directly afterward, as it appears I may have to leave."

"Not by yourself," she reminds me.

"Benton took the car key," I remind her.

"Wouldn't stop you, since we have vehicles, so don't try to fool me. When it's time, I'm calling him, and there won't be an argument." Anne can say almost anything and not sound disrespectful or rude.

She takes photographs while I swab the entrance wound on the lower back. Then I swab orifices in the off chance this homicide might involve a sexual assault, although I don't see how, based on what has been described.

"Because we're looking for a unicorn." I seal anal and oral swabs in paper envelopes and label and initial them. "Not your everyday pony, and I'm not going to believe anything, anyway, since I didn't go to the scene."

"Well, nobody did," Anne says. "Which is a shame."

"Even if somebody had, I'd still be looking for a unicorn."

"I don't blame you. I wouldn't trust what anybody says if I were you."

"If you were me." I lock a new blade into a scalpel as she fills a labeled plastic jar with formalin.

"Unless it's me who's talking," she replies without looking at me. "I wouldn't lie or cheat or help myself to things that aren't mine. I would never treat this place as if it belongs to me. Never mind. I shouldn't get into it."

I won't let her get into it. It isn't necessary to put her in a position like that, betraying the people who have betrayed me. I know what it feels like to be put in a position like that. It's one of the worst feelings there is and promotes lying, overtly or by omission, and I know that feeling, too. An untruth that lodges intact in the core of your being like undigested corn found in

Egyptian mummies. There's no getting rid of such a thing, of undoing it, without going in to get it, and I'm not sure I have the courage for that, as I think of the worn wooden steps leading down into the basement of the house in Cambridge. I think of the rough stone walls belowground and the fifteen-hundred-pound safe with its two-inch-thick composite triple-lock door.

"I don't suppose you've heard any rumors about where everybody is," I then say. "When you were with Marino at McLean." I begin the Y incision, cutting from clavicle to clavicle, then long and deep straight down with a slight detour around the navel and terminating at the pubic bone in the lower abdomen. "Did you get any idea of who is in our parking lot and what's going on? Since I seem to be under house arrest for reasons no one has been inclined to make completely clear."

"The FBI." Anne doesn't tell me something I don't know as she walks to the wall where clipboards hang from hooks next to rows of plastic racks for blank forms and diagrams. "At least two agents in the parking lot, and one followed us. Someone did." She collects the paperwork she needs and selects a clipboard after making sure the ballpoint pen attached to it by a cord has ink. "A detective, an agent. I don't know who followed us to the hospital, but someone who clearly had alerted security before we got there." She returns to the table. "When we rolled up at the neuroimaging lab, there were three McLean security guys, most excitement they've had in years. And then this person in an SUV, a dark-blue Ford, an Explorer or an Expedition."

Maybe what Benton just drove away in, and I ask Anne, "Did

he or she get out of the SUV? I assume you didn't talk to whoever it was?" I reflect back soft tissue. The man is so lean he has just the thinnest layer of yellow fat before the tissue turns beefy red.

"It was hard to see, and I wasn't going to walk right up and stare. The agent was still sitting in the SUV when we left and followed us back here."

She picks up rib cutters from the surgical cart and helps me remove the breastplate, exposing the organs and significant hemorrhage, and I smell the beginning of cells breaking down, the faintest hint of what promises to be putrid and foul. The odors emitted by the human body as it decomposes are uniquely unpleasant. It isn't like a bird or an opossum or the largest mammal one can think of. In death we are as different from other creatures as we are in life, and I would recognize the stench of decaying human flesh anywhere.

"How do you want to do this? En bloc? And deal with the metal after we have the organs on the cutting board?" Anne asks.

"I think we need to synchronize what we're doing inch by inch, step by step. Line things up with the scans as best we can, because I'm not sure I'm going to be able to see whatever these ferromagnetic foreign bodies are unless I'm looking right at them with a lens." I wipe my bloody gloved hands on a towel and step closer to the video display, which Anne has divided into quadrants to give me a choice of images from the MRI.

"Distributed a lot like gunshot powder," she suggests. "Although we can't see the actual metal particles because they canceled the signal."

"True. More blooming artifact, more voids at the beginning

than the end. Greatest amount at the entrance." I point my bloody gloved finger at the screen.

"But no residue of anything on the surface," she says. "And that's different from a gunshot wound, a contact wound."

"Everything about this is different from a gunshot wound," I answer.

"You can see that whatever this stuff is, it starts here." She indicates the entrance wound on the lower back. "But not at the surface. Just beneath it, maybe half an inch beneath it, which is really weird. I'm trying to imagine it and can't. If you pressed something against his back and fired, you'd get gunshot residue on the clothes and in the entrance wound, not just an inch inside and then deeper."

"I looked at his clothes earlier."

"No burns or soot, no evidence of GSR," she says.

"Not grossly," I correct her, because not being able to see gunshot residue doesn't mean it isn't there.

"Exactly. Nothing visually."

"What about Morrow? I don't suppose he came downstairs yesterday while Marino had the body in ID, printing him, collecting personal effects. I don't suppose someone thought to ask Morrow to do a presumptive test for nitrites on the clothing, since we didn't know at that time there could be GSR or that there was even an entrance wound that correlates with cuts in the clothing."

"Not that I know of. And he left early."

"I heard. Well, we still can test presumptively, but I'd be really surprised if that's what we're seeing on MR. When Morrow or maybe Phil gets in, let's get them to do a Griess test just to satisfy my curiosity before we move on to something else. I'm betting it will be negative, but it's not destructive, so nothing lost."

It's a simple, quick procedure involving desensitized photographic paper that is treated with a solution of sulfanilic acid, distilled water, and alpha-naphthol in methanol. When the paper is pressed against the area of clothing in question and then exposed to steam, any nitrite residues will turn orange.

"Of course, we're going to do SEM-EDX," I add. "But these days it's a good idea to do more than one thing, since slowly but surely lead is going to disappear from ammunition, and most of these tests are looking for lead, which is toxic to the environment. So we need to start checking for zinc and aluminum alloys, plus various stabilizers and plasticizers, which are added to the gunpowder during manufacturing. Here in the U.S., at any rate. Not so much in combat, where poisoning the environment with heavy metals is considered a fine idea, since the goal is to create dirty bombs, the dirtier the better."

"Not our goal, I hope."

"No, not ours. We don't do that."

"I never know what to believe."

"I do know what to believe, at least about some things. I know what comes back to us when our service people are returned to Dover," I reply. "I know what's in them. I know what isn't. I know what's manufactured by us and what's manufactured by others, the Iraqi insurgency, the Taliban, the Iranians. That's one of the things we do, materials analysis to figure out who is making what, who is supplying it."

"So when I hear these things about weapons or bombs made in Iran . . ."

"That's where it comes from. It's how the U.S. knows. Intelligence from our dead, from what they teach us."

We leave it at that, our talk of the war, because of this other war that has killed a man who is too young to be finished. A man who took an old greyhound for a walk in the civilized world of Cambridge and ended up in my care.

"They've developed some really interesting technology in Texas that I want us to look into." I return to gunshot residue because it is safer to talk about that. "Combining solid phase micro-extraction with gas chromatography coupled with a nitrogen phosphorus detector."

"As Texas should, since it's a state law that everybody carry a gun. Or is it that firearms are tax-deductible, like farming and raising livestock is around here?"

"Well, not quite," I reply. "But we'll want to look into doing something similar at the CFC, since of all places I would expect a growing prevalence of *green* ammunition."

"Of course. Don't pollute the environment while you're doing a drive-by shooting."

"What scientists have come up with at Sam Houston can detect as little as one gunpowder particle, which isn't relevant in this case, since we know this man has metal in him, almost at a microscopic level but plenty of it. Preliminarily, at any rate, Marino should have used a GSR kit on the hands at least. Since this man was armed."

"I do know that he did that much before he printed him," Anne says. "Because of the gun, although no sign it had been fired. But I saw him using a stub on the hands when I walked into ID at one point."

"But not the wound, because you discovered it later. It wasn't swabbed."

"I haven't done anything. I wouldn't have. Not my department."

"Good. I'll take care of it when I get to it, when we turn him over," I decide. "Let's take out the bloc so I can blot the raw surfaces of the injured track. I'm going to use the MRI as my map and blot as much of the metal material as I can, in hopes that even if we can't see it, we're getting some of it. We know it's metal. The question is, what kind of metal and what is it from?"

In wall-mounted steel cabinets with glass doors I find a box of blotting paper while Anne lifts the bloc of organs out of the body and places it on the dissecting board.

"I can't tell you what a problem it is these days, people with metal in them," she comments as she collects organ fragments from the chest cavity, which is opened and empty like a china cup, the ribs gleaming opaquely through glistening red tissue. "Including old bullets of the non-green variety. We get these research subjects in after the hospital's advertised for volunteers, and of course I mean the *normals,* right? All these people who come in and they're just as normal as the day is long, right? And have nothing to report. Uh, right. Like it's real normal to have an old bullet in you."

She returns fragments of the left kidney, the left lung, and the heart to their correct anatomical positions on the bloc of organs as if she's piecing together a puzzle.

"Happens more often than you think," she says. "Well, not more often than someone like you would think, since we see things like that in the morgue all the time. And then you get the old routine that bullets are lead, and lead isn't magnetic, so it's fine to scan the person. Usually, one of the psychiatrists who doesn't know any better and can't seem to remember from one time to the next that, no, wrong again. Lead, iron, nickel, cobalt. All bullets, pellets, are ferromagnetic, I don't care if they're so-called green, they're going to torque because of the magnetic field. That could be a problem if someone's got a fragment in him that's in close proximity to a blood vessel, an organ. God forbid something was left in the brain if some poor person was shot in the head eons ago. Paxil, Neurontin, or the like aren't going to help the poor person's mood disorder if an old bullet relocates to the wrong place."

She rinses a fragment of kidney and places it on the dissecting board.

"We're going to need to measure how much blood is in the peritoneum." I'm looking at the hole in the diaphragm that I saw hours earlier when I followed the wound track during the CT scan. "I'm going to guess at least three hundred MLs, originating through the lacerated diaphragm, and at least fifty MLs in his pericardium, which normally might suggest some time interval before death because of how much he bled. But the severity of these injuries, which are similar to blast injuries? He had no survival time. Only as long as it took for his heart and respiration to quit. If I were willing to use the term *instant death,* this would qualify as one."

"This is unusual." Anne hands me a tiny fragment of kidney

that is hard and brown with tan discoloration and retracted edges. "I mean, what is that? It almost looks fixed or cooked or something."

There is more. As I pull a light closer and look at the bloc of organs, I notice hard, dry fragments of the left lung's lower lobe and of the heart's left ventricle. Using a steel beaker, I scoop pooled blood and hematoma out of the mediastinum, or the middle section of the chest cavity, and find more fragments and tiny, hard, irregular blood clots. Looking closely at the disrupted left kidney, I note perirenal hemorrhage and interstitial emphysema, and more evidence of the same abnormal tissue changes in areas closest to the wound track, areas most susceptible to damage from a blast. But what blast?

"Reminds me of tissue that's been frozen, almost freeze-dried," I say as I label sheets of blotting paper with an abbreviation for the location the sample came from. LLL for left lower lobe and LK for left kidney and LV for left ventricle of the heart.

In the strong light of a surgical lamp and the magnification of a hand lens I can barely make out dark silvery specks of whatever was blasted through this man when he was stabbed in the back. I see fibers and other debris that won't be discernible until they are looked at under a microscope, but I feel hopeful. Something was deposited that likely was unintended by the perpetrator, trace evidence that might give me information about the weapon and the person who used it. I turn the fume hood on the lowest setting so there is nothing more than an exchange of air, and I begin gently blotting.

I touch the sterile paper to the surfaces of fragmented tissue and the edges of wounds, and one by one lay the sheets inside the hood, where the gently circulating air will facilitate evaporation, the drying of blood without disturbing anything adhering to it. I collect samples of the freeze-dried-looking tissue and save them in plasticized cartons and also in small jars of formalin, and I tell Anne we're going to want a lot of photographs and that I'll ask colleagues of mine to look at images of internal damage and of the tannish tough tissue. I'll ask if they've ever seen anything like it before, and as I'm saying all this, I'm wondering who I mean. Not Briggs. I wouldn't dare send anything to him. Certainly not Fielding. No one who works here. No one at all comes to mind except Benton and Lucy, whose opinions won't help or matter. It's up to me whether I like it or not.

"Let's turn him over," I say, and empty of organs, he is light in the torso and head-heavy.

I measure the entrance wound and describe what it looks like and exactly where it is, and I examine the wound track through the bloc of organs, finding every area that was punctured by what I'm now certain was a narrow double- and single-edged blade.

"If you look at the wound, you can clearly see the two sharp ends of it, the corners of the buttonhole made by two sharp edges," I explain to Anne.

"I see." Her eyes are dubious behind her plastic glasses.

"But look here, where the wound track terminates in the heart. Can you see how both ends of the wound are identical, both very sharp?" I move the light closer and hand her a magnifying lens.

"Slightly different from the wound on his back," she says.

"Yes. Because when the blade terminated in the heart muscle, it didn't penetrate as deeply; just the tip went in. As opposed to when these other wounds were made." I show her. "The tip penetrated and was followed by the length of the blade running through, and as you can see, the one end of the wound is just a little blunted and slightly stretched. You especially can see it here, where it penetrated the left kidney and kept going."

"I think I see what you're saying."

"Not what you would expect with a butterfly knife, a boning knife, a dagger, all of which are double-edged, both sides of the blade sharp from tip to handle. This brings to mind something spear-tipped—sharp on both sides at the tip but single-edged after that, like I've seen in some fighting knives or, in particular, something like a bowie knife or bayonet, where the top of the blade has been sharpened on both edges to make penetration easier in stabbings. So what we've got is an entrance that is three-eighths of an inch linear; both ends of the wound are sharp, with one that is slightly more blunted than the other. And the width expands to five-eighths of an inch." I measure, and Anne writes it down on a body diagram.

"So the blade is three-eighths of an inch at the tip, and at its widest it's five-eighths. That's pretty narrow. Almost like a stiletto," she says.

"But a stiletto is double-edged, the entire blade is."

"Homemade? A blade that injects something that explodes?"

"Without causing thermal injury, without causing burns. In fact, what we're seeing is more consistent with frostbite, where the tissue feels hard and is discolored," I remind her as I measure the distance from the wound on the man's back to the top of his head. "Twenty-six inches, and two inches to the left of the mid-spine. Direction is up and anterior, with extensive subcutaneous and tissue emphysema along the track, perforating the transverse process on the left twelfth rib paraspinally. Perforating paraspinal muscle, perirenal fat, left adrenal, left kidney, diaphragm, left lung, and pericardium, terminating in the heart."

"How long a blade for something to perforate all that?"

"At least five inches."

She plugs in the autopsy saw, and we turn the body on its back again. I place a headrest under the neck and incise the scalp from ear to ear, following the hairline so the sutures won't be visible afterward. The top of the skull is white like an egg as I reflect the scalp back and pull the face down like a sock, like something sad, the features collapsing as if he is crying.

I don't realize the sun is up and the arctic front has marched off to the south until I open my office door and am greeted by a clear blue sky beyond tall windows.

I look down seven floors, and there are a few cars moving slowly on the white-frosted furrowed road below, and going the other way, a snowplow truck with its yellow blade held up like a crab claw as it scuttles along, looking for the right spot, then lowering the blade with a clank I can't hear from up here and scraping pavement that's not going to be completely cleared because of ice.

The riverbank is white, and the Charles is the color of old blue bottle glass and wrinkled by the current, and beyond in the distance the skyline of Boston catches the early light, the John Hancock Tower soaring far above any other high-rise, overbearing and sturdy, like a solitary column left standing in the ruins of an ancient temple. I think about coffee, and it is a fleeting urge as I wander into my bathroom and look at the coffeemaker on the counter by the sink and the boxes of K-Cups that include hazelnut.

I'm beyond being helped by stimulants, not sure I'd feel caffeine except in my gut, which is empty and raw. Intermittently, I'm stabbed by nausea, then I'm hungry, then nothing at all, just the gauziness of sleeplessness and the persistent hint of a headache that seems more remembered than real. My eyes burn, and thoughts move thickly but push with force like a heavy surf pounding against the same unyielding questions and tasks to be done. I won't wait for anyone, given a choice. I can't wait. There is no choice. I will overstep boundaries if need be, and why shouldn't I? Boundaries I've set have been stepped on right and left by others. I will do things myself, those things I know how to do. I am alone, more alone than I was because I've changed. Dover has changed me. I will do what is necessary, and it might not be what people want.

It is half past seven, and I've been downstairs all this time because Anne and I took care of other cases after we finished with the Norton's Woods man, whose name we are no closer to discovering, or if it is known, I've not been informed. I know intimate details about him that should be none of my business, but not the most important facts: who he is, what he was and hoped to become, his dreams, and what he loved and hated. I sit down at my desk and check the notes Anne made for me downstairs and add a few of my own, making sure I will remember later he had eaten something with poppy seeds and yellow cheese shortly before he died and the total amount of blood and clot in the left hemithorax was one thousand three hundred milliliters and the heart was disrupted into five irregular fragments that were still attached at the level of the valves.

I will want to emphasize this to the prosecution, it occurs to me, because I'm thinking about court. For me it all ends there, at least on the civilian side of my life. I imagine the prosecutor using inflammatory language I can't use, telling the jury that the man ate cheese and a poppy-seed bagel and took his rescued old dog for a walk, that his heart was blown to pieces, causing him to hemorrhage almost three units of blood or more than a third of all the blood in his body in a matter of minutes. The autopsy didn't reveal the purpose of the man's death, although provisionally, at least the cause of it is simple, and I absently write it down as I continue to ponder and meditate and make plans.

Atypical stab/puncture to the left back.

A pathological diagnosis that seems trite after what I just saw, and one that would give me pause, were I to come across it somewhere. I'd find it cryptic, almost tongue-in-cheek and coy, like a bad joke if one knows the rest of it, the massive blastlike disruption of the organs and that the death is a vicious and calculated homicide. I envision the hem of the long black coat quickly flapping past and what must have happened just seconds before when the person wearing it plunged a blade into the victim's lower back. For an instant he felt the physical response, the shock and pain as he exclaimed, *"Hey . . . !"* and clutched his chest, collapsing on his face on the slate path.

I imagine the person in the black coat quickly bending over to snatch off the man's black gloves and briskly walking away, perhaps tucking the blade up a sleeve or into a folded newspaper or I don't know. But as I imagine it, I believe the person in the long black coat is the killer and was covertly recorded by the dead man's headphones, and it causes me to wonder again who was doing the spying. Did the killer plant micro–recording devices in the victim's headphones so he could be followed? And I imagine a figure in a long black coat walking swiftly through the shaded woods, coming up behind the victim, who couldn't hear anything but the music in his headphones as he's stabbed in the back, and he falls too fast to turn around. I wonder if he died not knowing who did this to him. And afterward? Is it what Lucy proposed? Did the person in the long black coat view the video files and decide it wasn't necessary to delete them from a webcam site somewhere, that in fact it was clever to leave them?

There are reasons for all things, I tell myself what has always been true but never feels that way while I'm in the middle of the problem. There are answers, and I will find them, and while the physics of how the fatal injury was executed may seem difficult to divine, I assure myself there are tracks the killer left behind. I have captured footprints on blotting paper. I will follow them to who did this. *You won't get away with it,* I think, as if I'm talking to the person in the long black coat. *I hope whoever you are, you have nothing to do with me, that you aren't someone I taught to be meticulous and clever.* I have decided that Jack Fielding is on the run or in custody. It even enters my mind that he might be dead. But I'm exhausted. I'm sleep-deprived. My thoughts aren't as disciplined as they should be. He can't be dead. Why would he be dead? I have seen the dead downstairs, and he wasn't among them.

My other patients of the morning were simple enough and asked little of me as I tended to them: a motor-vehicle fatality, and I could smell the booze and his bladder was full, as if he'd been drinking until the moment he left the bar and climbed behind the wheel in a snowstorm that careened him into a tree; a shooting in a run-down motel, and the needle tracks and prison tattoos of yet one more among us who died the way he lived; an asphyxia by a plastic dry-cleaning bag tied around an old widow's neck with an old red satin ribbon, maybe left over from a holiday during better times, her stomach full of dissolved white tablets, and next to the bed an empty bottle of a benzodiazepine prescribed for sleeplessness and anxiety.

I have no messages on my office and cell phones, no e-mails that matter to me at the moment and under the circumstances. When I checked Lucy's lab, she wasn't there, and when I checked with security, I discovered that even Ron has left, replaced by a guard I've never met, gangly and jug-eared like Ichabod Crane, someone named Phil who says Lucy's car isn't in the lot and the instructions are that the security guards aren't to let anyone into the building, not through the lower level or the lobby, without clearing it with me. Not possible, I let Phil know. Employees should be showing up already, or they will be at any minute, and I can't be the gatekeeper. Let anybody in who has a right to be here, I told him before I came upstairs. Except Dr. Fielding, and when I added that, I could tell it wasn't necessary. The guard named Phil clearly was aware that Fielding can't just show up or won't or maybe isn't able to, and besides, the FBI dominates my parking lot. I can see their SUVs clear as the bright, cold day on the video display on my desk.

I swivel my chair around to the polished black-granite countertop behind me, to my arsenal of microscopes and what accompanies them. Pulling on a pair of examination gloves, I slit open one of the white envelopes I sealed with white paper tape right before I came upstairs, and I pull out a sheet of blotting paper that is stained with a generous smear of dried blood that came from the area of the left kidney where I saw a dense collection of metallic foreign bodies in the MRI. Turning on the lamp of my materials microscope, a Leica I have depended on for years, I carefully move the paper to the stage. I tilt the eyetubes to a viewing angle that won't strain my neck and shoulders and realize right away that the settings have been changed for someone much taller than me who is right-handed, someone who drinks coffee with cream and chews spearmint gum, I suspect. The ocular focus and interocular distance have been changed, too.

Switching to left-hand operation and adjusting the height so it is better suited for me, I start with a magnification of 50X, manipulating the focus knob with one hand as I use the other to move the sheet of blotting paper on the stage, lining up the bloody smear until I find what I'm looking for, bright whitish-silver chips and flakes in a constellation of other particles so minute that when I bump the magnification up to 100X, I can't make out their characteristics, only the rough edges and scratches and striations on the largest particles, what looks like unburned metal chips and filings that have been milled by a machine or a tool. Nothing I see reminds me of gunshot residue, doesn't even remotely resemble the flakes, disks, or balls I associate with gunpowder or the ragged fragments or particulate of a projectile or its jacket.

More curious is other debris mixed with blood and its obvious elements, the colorful confetti of detritus that constitutes everyday dust tangled with red cells piled up like coins, and granular leukocytes reminiscent of amoeba that are caught as if frozen in time, swimming and cavorting with a louse and a flea that at a magnified size remind me why seventeenth-century London went into a panic when Robert Hooke published *Micrographia* and revealed the piercing mouthparts and claws of what infested cats and mattresses. I recognize fungi and spores that look like sponges and fruit, spiny pieces of insect legs and insect egg cases that look like the delicate shells of nuts or spherical boxes carved of porous wood. As I move the paper on the stage, I find more hairy appendages of long-dead monsters, such as midges and mites and the wide compound eyes of a decapitated ant, the feathery antenna of what may have been a mosquito, the overlapping scales of animal hair, maybe from a horse or a dog or a rat, and reddish-orange flecks that could be rust.

I reach for the phone and call Benton. When he answers, I hear voices in the background and am subjected to a bad connection.

"A knife sharpened or shaped on something like a lathe, possibly a rusty one in a workshop or basement, possibly an old root cellar where there are mold, bugs, decaying vegetables, probably damp carpet," I say right off as I begin an Internet search on my computer, typing the keywords *knife* and *exploding gases*.

"What was sharpened?" Benton asks, and then he says something to someone else, something like *need the keys* or *need to keep.* "I'm moving, not in a good place," he gets back to me.

"The weapon used to stab him. A lathe, a grinder, possibly old or not taken care of, with traces of rust, based on the metal shavings and very fine particulate I'm seeing. I think the blade was honed, perhaps to make it thinner and to sharpen the tip on both edges, to turn the tip into a spear, so whatever might have been used for sharpening and polishing, a rasp, a file."

"You're talking about power tools that are old and rusty. A lot of rust?"

"Metalworking tools of some type, not necessarily power tools; I'm not in a position to be that detailed. I'm not an expert in metalworking and I don't know how much rust. Just that I found what looks like flakes of it." *Exploding intestines. How to clean your spark plugs. Common gases associated with metalworking and hand-forged knives,* I silently read what is on my computer screen as I then say to Benton, "Not that I pretend to be a trace-evidence examiner, but microscopically it's nothing I've not seen before, just never seen it blown into a body. But then I've never really looked. I've never had a reason to look for something like this, am unaccustomed to using blotting paper internally when someone has been stabbed. I suppose there could be all sorts of invisible fibers, debris, particulate, injected inside people who've been shot, stabbed, impaled, or God knows what."

I type *injection knife* into the search field because as I listen to myself, I'm reminded of remote delivery darts, of weapons powered by CO_2 to fire what's basically a long-range immobilization or tranquilizing missile with a small explosive charge and a hypodermic needle. Why couldn't you do the same thing with a knife, as long as it had a way to be powered and a narrow channel bored through the blade with an outlet hole near the tip?

"I'm walking outside to the car now," Benton says. "Will be there in forty-five minutes to an hour if the traffic's not too bad. The roads aren't bad. One-twenty-eight isn't too bad."

"Well, this wasn't hard." I'm disappointed. Nothing with so much potential for lethal damage should be this easy to find.

"What isn't hard?" Benton says as I look in amazement at an image of a steel combat knife with a gas outlet hole near the tip and a neoprene handle in a foam-lined plastic case.

"A CO_2 cartridge screws into the handle. . . ." I skim out loud. "Thrust the five-inch stainless-steel blade into the target as you use your thumb to push the release button, which it appears is part of the guard hub. . . ."

"Kay? Who's with you right now?"

"Injects a freezing ball of gas the size of a basketball or more than forty cubic inches at eight hundred pounds of pressure per square inch," I go on, looking at images on an elaborate website as I wonder how many people have such a weapon in their homes, their cars, their camping gear, or are walking around with it strapped to their sides. I have to admit it is ingenious, possibly one of the scariest things I've ever seen. "Can drop a large mammal in a single stab . . ."

"Kay, are you by yourself?"

"Freezes wound tissue instantly, thus delaying bleeding and attracting other predators, so if you have to defend yourself against a great white shark, for example, it won't begin bleeding into the water and attracting other sharks until you are well out of the way." I skim and summarize and feel sickened. "It's called a WASP. You can add it to your shopping cart for less than four hundred dollars."

"Let's talk about it when I see you," Benton says over the phone.

"I've never heard of it." I read more about a compressed gas injection knife I can order right now as long as I'm over eighteen years of age. "Advertised for Special Ops, SWAT, pilots who are stranded in open water, scuba divers. Apparently developed to kill large marine predators—as I said, sharks, mammals, maybe whales and those in wet suits. . . ."

"Kay?"

"Or grizzly bears, for example, while you're minding your own business on a friendly hike through the mountains." I make no effort to keep the sarcasm out of my tone, to hide the anger I feel. "And, of course, military, but nothing I've seen in military casualties—"

"I'm on a cell phone," Benton interrupts me. "I'd rather you don't mention this to anyone else. No one in your office, or have you already?"

"I haven't already."

"You're by yourself?" he asks me again.

Why wouldn't I be? But I say, "Yes."

"And maybe you could delete it from your history, empty your cache, in case anybody decides to view your recent searches."

"I can't stop Lucy from doing that."

"I don't care if Lucy does it."

"She's not here. I don't know where she went."

"I know," he says.

"All right, then." He's not going to tell me where she is or where anybody is, it seems. "I'll make evidence rounds, take care of as much as I can and meet you downstairs in back when you get here." I hang up and try to reason through what just happened. I try not to feel hurt by him as I logically sort it out.

Benton didn't sound surprised or especially concerned. He didn't seem alarmed by what I've discovered but by my discovering it and the possibility that I might have told someone else, and that probably means the same thing I've been sensing since I returned home from Dover. Maybe I'm not the one finding things out. Maybe I'm simply the last one to know and nobody wants me to find out anything. What an unexpected predicament to be in, if not an unprecedented one, I think, as I do what Benton asked and empty the cache and clear the history, making it problematic for anyone to see what I've been searching on the Internet. As I do this I wonder who really asked: my husband, or was it the FBI asking? Who was just talking to me and telling me what to do as if I don't know better?

It's almost nine, and most of my staff is already here, those who aren't using the snow as an excuse to stay home or to go somewhere else they'd rather be, such as skiing in Vermont. On the security monitor I've watched cars pull into the lot and seen some people coming through the back door but far more arriving by way of the civilized entrance on the ground floor, through the stone lobby with its formidable carvings and flags, avoiding the dreary domain of the dead on the lower level. The scientists rarely need to meet the patients whose body fluids and belongings and other evidence they test, and then I hear the sounds of my administrator, Bryce, unlocking the door in the hallway that opens onto his adjoining office.

I reseal the blotting paper in a clean envelope and unlock a drawer to gather other items I've been keeping safe as I try not to sink into a dark space, thinking dark thoughts about what I just looked at on a website and what it implies about human beings and their capacity to create imaginative ways to do harm to other creatures. In the name of survival, it crosses my mind, but then rarely is it really about staying alive; instead, it's about making sure something else doesn't, and the power people feel when they can overpower, maim, kill. How terrible, how awful, and I have no doubt about what happened to the man from Norton's Woods, that someone came up behind him and stabbed him with an injection knife, blasting a ball of compressed gas into his vital organs, and if it was CO_2, there is no test that will tell us. Carbon dioxide is ubiquitous, literally as present as the air we exhale, and I envision what I saw on CT, the dark pockets of air that had been blown into the chest and what that must have felt like, and how I will answer the same question I'm always asked.

Did he suffer?

The truthful answer would be no one knows such a thing except the person who is dead, but I would say no, he didn't suffer. I would say he felt it. He felt something catastrophic happening to him. He wasn't conscious long enough to suffer during the agonal last moments of his life, but he would have felt a punch to his lower back accompanied by tremendous pressure in his chest as his organs ruptured, all of it happening at once. That would have been the last thing he felt except possibly a glimmer, a flash, of a panicked thought that he was about to die, and then I stop thinking about it because to obsess and imagine further would become useless and self-indulgent theorizing that is paralyzing and nonproductive. I can't help him if I'm upset.

I'm worthless to anyone if I feel what I feel, just as it was when I took care of my father and became an expert at pushing down emotions that climbed up inside me like some desperate creature trying to get out. "I worry what you have learned, my little Katie," my father said to me when I was twelve and he was a skeleton in the back bedroom, where the air was always too warm and smelled like sickness and light seeped wanly through the slatted shades I kept closed most of the way his last months. "You have learned things you shouldn't ever have to learn but especially at your age, my little Katie," he said to me as I made the bed with him still in it, having learned to wash him religiously so he wasn't overcome by pressure sores, to change his soiled sheets by moving his body, a body that seemed hollowed out and dead except for the heat of his fever.

I would gently rock my father to his side, holding him up on one side, then the other, leaning him against me because he could not get up in the end, couldn't even sit up. He was too weak to help me move him during what his doctor called the blast phase of chronic myeloid leukemia, and at times he enters my mind and I feel the weight of him against me when I'm swathed in protective clothing, peering through protective glasses, at work at my hard steel table.

I fill out lab analysis requests that will need to be signed by each scientist I receipt various items to so I can keep the chain of evidence intact. Then I get up from my desk.

16

nocking once, I open the door that leads into Bryce's
office.

Our shared entrance is directly across from the
door to my private bath, which I've learned to keep open a crack.
When both gray metal doors are shut I have had a tendency to
get mixed up and walk in on Bryce when I'm interested in coffee
or washing up or I find myself about to hand paperwork to a
toilet and a sink. He is at his desk with his chair rolled back and
has taken off his coat, which is draped over the back, but he still
has on his big designer sunglasses that look ridiculously heavy, as
if drawn on with a dark-brown crayon. He struggles with a pair
of L.L.Bean snow boots that don't go with his typically deliberate
ensemble, which today is a navy cashmere blazer, tight black
jeans, a black turtleneck, and a tooled leather belt with a big
silver buckle shaped like a dragon.

"I'll be on the phone and can't be disturbed," I tell him as if I've been here every day for these past six months, as if I've never been gone. "Then I have to leave."

"Is someone going to tell me what's going on around here? And welcome home, boss." He looks up at me, his eyes masked by the big, dark glasses. "I don't suppose the unmarked cars in the parking lot are a surprise party, because I know I'm not throwing one. Not that I wouldn't and wasn't intending to eventually, but whoever they are, they aren't here because of me, and when I asked one of them to be so kind as to give me an explanation and please move his ass so I could park in my spot, he was shall we say *testy*?"

"The case from yesterday morning," I start to say.

"Oh, is that why? Well, no wonder." His face brightens as if what I just said is somehow good news. "I knew it was going to be important, I somehow knew it. But he didn't really die here, please tell me it's not true, that you didn't find anything to suggest anything so outrageous or I guess I'll just start looking for another job right this minute and tell Ethan we're not about to buy that bungalow we've been looking at. I'm sure you've figured out what happened by now, knowing you. You probably figured it out in five minutes."

He pulls off the other boot, moving both of them to the side, and I notice he's spiked his hair and has shaved off the mustache and beard he had when I saw him last. Compactly built, Bryce is slight but strong with a blond choirboy prettiness, to use a cliché, because it happens to be true. He doesn't look like himself with facial hair, which is probably the point, to look like someone else, to be transformed into a formidable and virile character like James Brolin, or to be taken seriously like Wolf Blitzer, heroes of his. My top administrator and trusted right hand has many, a host of famous imagined friends he speaks of easily as if the act of tuning into them on one of his big-screen TVs or saving them with TiVo makes them as real as next-door neighbors.

Seriously good at what he does for me, with degrees in criminal justice and public administration, Bryce Clark at a glance seems misplaced, as if he wandered off the set of *E!,* and I have used this to my advantage over the few years he's worked for me. Outsiders and even people who work here don't always realize that my recovering Mormon compulsive-talking clotheshorse of a chief of staff is not to be trifled with. If nothing else, he's voyeuristic and adores "filling me in," as he puts it. He likes nothing better than to gather information like a magpie and carry it back to his nest. He is dangerous if he detests you. It's unlikely you'll know it. His banter and deliberate affect are a bunker that his more dangerous self hides behind, and in that way he reminds me of my former secretary, Rose. Those who made the mistake of treating her like a silly old woman one day found themselves missing a limb.

"The FBI? Homeland Security? No one I've seen before." Bryce is bent over in his chair as he unzips a nylon gym bag, his stocking feet planted on the floor.

"Probably the FBI—" But he isn't going to let me finish.

"Well, the one who was so rude totally looked the part, all buff in a gray suit and camel-hair coat. I think the FBI fires people if they get fat. Well, good luck hiring in America. Drop-dead good-looking, I'll give him that. Did you see him back there? Do we know his name and what field office he's with? Not anyone I've met from Boston. Maybe he's new."

"Who?" My thoughts run into a wall.

"Lord, you are tired. The agent in that big, bad black Ford Expedition, the spitting image of the football player on *Glee*—oh, you probably don't watch that, either, it's only the best show on TV and I can't imagine you don't love Jane Lynch, unless you don't know who she is, since you probably didn't catch *The L Word,* but maybe *Best in Show* or *Talladega Nights?* My God, what a hoot. The Bureau boy in the black Ford looks exactly like Finn—"

"Bryce . . ."

"Anyway, I saw all the blood, how much the body from Norton's Woods bled inside his pouch, and it was god-awful, and I thought to myself, *This is it. The end of this place.* Meanwhile, Marino's huffing and puffing and about to blow the house down, pitching a fit as only Marino can about someone delivered alive and dying in the fridge. So I told Ethan we might have to tuck away our pennies because I might be unemployed. And the job market right now? Ten percent unemployment or some nightmare like that, and I seriously doubt *Doctor G* is going to hire me because every morgue worker on the planet wants to be on her show, but I would ask you to pick up the phone and recommend me to her, please, if this place goes down the toilet. Why can't we do a reality show? I mean, really. You had your own show on CNN some years ago; why can't we do something here?"

"I need to talk to you about—" But there's no point when he gets like this.

"I'm glad you're here, but sorry you had to come home for

something so god-awful. I stayed awake all night wondering what I was going to tell reporters. When I saw those SUVs behind the building, I thought it was the media, was fully expecting television trucks—"

"Bryce, you need to calm down and maybe take your sunglasses off—"

"But nothing in the news that I know of, and not one reporter has called me or left a message here or anything—"

"I need to go over a few things, and you really need to shut up, please," I interrupt him.

"I know." He takes off his sunglasses as he works his foot into a black high-top sneaker. "I'm just a little overwrought, Dr. Scarpetta. And you know how I get when I'm overwrought."

"Have you heard from Jack?"

"Where's the Mouth of Truth when you need it?" As he ties his sneakers. "Don't ask me to pretend, and I would respectfully request that you inform him I don't answer directly to him anymore. Now that you're home, thank God."

"Why do you say that?"

"Because all he does is order me around as if I work in the drive-through window at Wendy's. He barks and snaps as his hair falls out, and then I wonder if he's going to kick someone, maybe me, or strangle me with his umpteenth-degree black belt or whatever the fuck he has, excuse my French. And it's gotten worse, and we weren't supposed to bother you at Dover. I told everybody to leave you alone. Everybody's told everybody to leave you alone or they'll answer to me. I'm just realizing you've been up all night. You look awful." His blue eyes look me up and down, studying the way I'm dressed, which is in the same khaki cargo pants and black polo shirt with the AFME crest that I put on at Dover.

"I came straight here and don't have anything to change into." I finally get a word in edgewise. "I don't know why you bothered replacing your L.L.Beans with an old pair of Converse left over from basketball camp."

"I know you have a better eye than that, and I know you know I never went to basketball camp, because I always went to music camp every summer. Hugo Boss, half price at Endless-dot-com, plus free shipping," he adds, getting up from his chair. "I'm making coffee, and you want some. And no, I've not heard from Jack, and you don't need to tell me there's a problem and it might have to do with those agents in our parking lot, who obviously have a personality disorder. I don't know why they can't make an effort to be friendly. If I wore a big gun and could arrest people, I'd be Little Miss Sunshine to everyone, smile and be so nice. Why not?" Bryce brushes past me, walking into my office, disappearing into the bathroom. "I can run by your house and pick up a few things if you want. Just tell me. A business suit or something casual?"

"If I get stuck here . . ." I start to say I might take him up on it.

"We really do need to arrange some sort of closet for you, a little haute couture at HQ. Ohhhh, wardrobe?" his voice sings out as he makes coffee. "Now if we had our own show, we'd have wardrobe, hair, makeup, and you'd never find yourself in the same dirty clothes and odiferous of death, not that I'm saying you're . . . Well, anyway. Best of all would be if you went home and straight to bed." As hot water shoots loudly through a K-Cup. "Or I could run out and get you something to eat. I find when I'm tired and sleep-deprived . . ." He emerges from my bathroom with two coffees and says, "Fat. There's a time and a place for everything. Dunkin' Donuts, their croissant with sausage and egg, how 'bout it? You might need two. You actually look a little thin. Life in the military really doesn't suit you, dear boss."

"Are you aware of a woman named Erica Donahue calling here?" I ask him as I return to my desk with a coffee I'm not sure I should drink. Opening a drawer, I search for Advil in hopes there really might be a bottle hiding somewhere.

"She did. Several times." Bryce carefully sips the hot coffee, leaning against the frame of the open doorway that connects us.

When he offers nothing else, I ask, "When did she call?"

"Starting after it was in the news about her son. That was a week ago, I think, when he confessed to killing Mark Bishop."

"You talked to her?"

"Most recently, all I really did was direct her call to Jack again when she was looking for you."

"'Again'?"

"You should get his part from him. I don't know his details," Bryce says, and it's not like him to be careful with me. He's cautious suddenly.

"But he talked to her."

"This was, let me see. . . ." He has a habit of gazing up at the dome as if the answers to all things are there. It's also a favorite delaying tactic of his. "Last Thursday."

"And you talked to her. Before you transferred her call to Jack."

"Mostly I listened."

"What was her demeanor, and what did she say?"

"Very polite, sounded like the upper-class intelligent woman she is, based on what I hear. I mean, there's a ton of stuff about the Donahue family and Johnny Hinckley Junior. He's almost that notorious. . . . *And when he saw what he had done, he holstered his trusty nail gun.* . . . But you probably don't read all this shit on these gore-sites like Morbidia Trivia, Wicked-whatever-pedia, Cryptnotes, or whatever, and I do have to follow them as part of my job, part of my being informed about what's being said out there in sensational sin-loving cyberland."

He's comfortable again. He's uncomfortable only when I probe him about Fielding.

"Mom was an almost famous concert pianist in a former life, played in a symphony orchestra. I think in San Francisco," Bryce goes on. "I happened to notice some Twittering about her being taught by Yundi Li, but I seriously doubt Li gives lessons, and he's only twenty-eight, so I don't believe it for a second. Of course she's in an uproar, can you imagine? They say her son is a savant, has these bizarre abilities, like knowing tire treads. The detective from Salem, Saint Hilaire, who is anything but, and you don't know him yet, was talking about it. Apparently, Johnny Donahue can look at a tread pattern in a dirt parking lot and go, 'That's a Bridgestone Battle Wing front motorcycle tire.' I just came up with that because Ethan has those on his BMW, which I wish he didn't love so much, because to me they're all donorcycles. Supposedly, Johnny can do math problems in his head, and I'm not talking if a banana costs eighty-nine cents how much is a bunch of six? More Einsteinian, like what is nine times a hundred and three to the square root of seven or something? But then you probably know all this. I'm sure you've been keeping up with the case."

"What exactly did she want to discuss with me? Did she tell you?" I know Bryce. He wouldn't hand off someone like Erica Donahue without letting her talk until she ran out of words or patience. He's too much of a snoop, his mind a chatterbox gossip mill.

"Well, obviously he didn't do it, and if someone would really look into the facts without having their mind made up, they'd see all the inconsistencies. The conflicts," Bryce replies, blowing on his coffee, not looking at me.

"What conflicts, exactly?"

"She says she talked to him the day of the murder at around nine in the morning, before he headed off to that café in Cambridge that's now become so famous right around the corner from you?" Bryce continues. "The Biscuit? Lines out the door because of all the publicity. Nothing like a murder. Anyway, he wasn't feeling well that day, according to Mom. Has terrible allergies or something and was complaining his pills or shots or whatever weren't working anymore, and he was dosing up big-time and felt *punk* is the word she used. So I guess if someone has itchy eyes and a runny nose, he's not going to kill anyone. I didn't want to tell her that a jury wouldn't put much stock in a sneezy defense—"

"I need to make a call and then make my rounds," I cut him off before he digresses the rest of the day. "Can you check with Trace Evidence and see if Evelyn is in, and if so, please tell her I have a few things that are rather urgent. What I've got needs to start with her and then fingerprints, then DNA, then toxicology, then one item in particular will come back up here to Lucy's lab. There was no one over there a while ago. What about Shane, are we expecting him, because I'm going to need an opinion about a document?"

"It's not like we're a rugby team stranded in a blizzard in the Andes and are going to resort to cannibalism, for God's sake."

"It was quite a storm all night."

"You've been down south too long. There's what? Eight inches? A bit icy but nothing for around here," Bryce says.

"Actually, if you could ask Evelyn to come upstairs immediately and let her into Jack's office." I decide I'm not going to wait as I remember the lab coat folded up inside the trash-can liner.

I explain to Bryce what's in the pocket and that I want it checked right away on SEM and I also want a nondestructive chemical analysis.

"Be very, very careful not to open the bag and touch anything," I say to Bryce. "And tell Evelyn there are fingerprints on the plastic film. Meaning there will also be DNA."

With my administrator silently out of range on the other side of our shared shut door, I decide to hold off calling Erica Donahue until I have a chance to think about what I'm going to do. I need to think about everything.

I want to reread her letter and make sure of my intentions, and as I ponder and remember what's happened since I left Dover, as

I look out at the bright blue sky of a new day, I know I'm still hungover from the last mother I dealt with. I feel poisoned by the memory of Julia Gabriel on the phone as someone loitered outside my closed door at Port Mortuary. The names she called me and what she accused me of were bitter and vile, but I didn't really let it get to me in a way that gave power to her words until I found what I did in Fielding's office. Since then a shadow that is chilled and dark like a sunless part of the moon is at the back of my thoughts and moods. I don't know what is being said or decided about me or what has been resurrected like some cold-blooded thing that never died and now is stirring.

What records have been found, and what has been gone through that I have secretly feared all these years and at the same time forgotten? Although the truth was always there, like something unseemly out of sight in a closet, something that I never look for but, if reminded, I know it's not gone, because it was never thrown out or returned to its rightful owner, which should never have been me. But the ugly matter was handed over as if it was mine. And it was left hanging. As long as what was done in South Africa stayed hidden in my closet instead of where it belonged, I'd be fine, was the message I got when I returned to Walter Reed after working those two deaths and was thanked for my service to the AFIP, to the air force, and was free to leave early. Debt paid in full. They had just the position for me in Virginia, where I would prosper as long as I remembered loyalty and took my dirty laundry with me.

Has it happened again? Has Briggs done the same thing to me again and soon will send me packing? Where this time? Early retirement crosses my mind. It's all coming out with more ugliness piled on, and that's not survivable, I decide, because I don't know what else to think. Briggs has told someone, and someone told Julia Gabriel, who has accused me of hatred, prejudice, callousness, dishonesty, and I must remember that this noxious miasma permeates any decisions I might make right now, that and fatigue. *Be exceedingly careful. Use your head. Don't give yourself up to emotions, and easy as pie* drifts through my mind. What Lucy said about security recordings, and I pick up my phone and buzz Bryce.

"Yes, boss," he says brightly, as if we haven't chatted in days.

"Our security recordings from the closed-circuit cameras everywhere," I say. "When was Captain Avallone here from Dover? I understand Jack gave her a tour."

"Oh, Lord, that was a while ago. I believe November. . . ."

"I recall she went home to Maine the week of Thanksgiving," I tell him. "I know she was gone from Dover that week because I had to stay. We were shorthanded."

"That sounds about right. I think she was here that Friday."

"Were you with them on the grand tour?"

"I was not. I wasn't invited. And Jack spent a lot of time with her in your office, just so you know. In there with the door shut. They ate lunch in there at your table."

"This is what I need you to do," I tell him. "Get hold of Lucy, text-message her or whatever you need to do, and let her know I want a review of every security recording that has Jack and Sophia on it, including anything in my office."

"In your office?"

"How long has he been using it?"

"Well . . ."

"Bryce? How long?"

"Pretty much the entire time. He helps himself when he wants to impress people. I mean, he doesn't use it for his casework very often, mostly when he's being ceremonial. . . ."

"Tell Lucy I want recordings of my office. She'll know exactly what I mean. I want to see what Jack and the captain were talking about."

"How delicious. I'll get right on it."

"I'm about to make an important call, so please don't disturb me," I then say. As I hang up, I realize Benton will be here soon.

But I resist the temptation to rush. Wise to slow down, to allow thoughts and perceptions to sort themselves out, to strive for clarity. *You're tired. Exercise caution, and play it smart when you're this tired.* There's one way to do this right, and every other way is wrong. You won't know the right way until it happens, and you won't recognize it if you're wound up and muddled. I reach for my coffee but change my mind about that, too. It won't help at this point, will only make me jittery and upset my stomach more. Pulling another pair of examination gloves out of a box on the granite counter behind my desk, I remove the document from the plastic bag I sealed it in.

I slide the two folded sheets of heavy paper out of the envelope I slit open in Benton's SUV as we drove through a blizzard what now seems like a lifetime ago but has only been twelve hours. In the light of morning and after so much has happened, it seems more unusual than it did that this classical pianist whom Bryce described as intelligent and reasonable would have used duct tape on her fine engraved stationery. Why not regular tape that is transparent instead of this ugly wide strip of lead-gray across the back? Why not do what I do when I enclose a private memo in an envelope and simply sign your name or initials over the seal of the flap? What was Erica Donahue afraid would happen? That her driver might want to read what she wrote to someone named Scarpetta whom he apparently had never heard of?

I smooth open the pages with my cotton-gloved hand and try to intuit what the mother of a college boy who has confessed to murder transferred to the keys of her typewriter, as if what she felt and believed as she composed her plea to me is a chemical I can absorb that will get me into her mind. It occurs to me I've come up with such an analogy because of the plastic film I found in the pocket of Fielding's lab coat. Hours beyond that unnerving druggy experience, I can see just how bad it really was and that I could not have been myself with Benton, and how uncomfortable it must have been for him. Maybe that's why he's being so secretive and is lecturing me about divulging information to whoever happens to be nearby, as if I, of all people, don't know better. Maybe he doesn't trust my judgment or self-control and fears that the horrors of war changed me. Maybe he's not so sure that the woman who came home to him from Dover is the one he knows.

I'm not who you used to know floats through my head. *I'm not sure you ever knew me* is a whisper in my thoughts, and as I read the neat rows of single-spaced type, I find it remarkable that in two pages there isn't one mistake. I see no evidence of white-out or correction tape, no misspellings or bad grammar. When I think back to the last typewriter I used, a dusky pink IBM Selectric I had in

Richmond the first few years I was there, I remember my chronic aggravation with ribbons that broke or having to swap out the golf ball–like element when I wanted to change fonts, and dealing with a dirty platen that left smudges on paper, not to mention my own hurried fingers hitting the wrong keys, and while my spelling and grammar are good, I'm certainly not infallible.

As my secretary Rose used to say when she'd walk in with my latest effort typed on that damn machine, *"And on what page is this in Strunk and White, or maybe it's in the MLA style guide and I just can't find it? I'll redo it, but every time you type something yourself?"* And she'd flap her hand in that characteristic gesture of hers that said to me *Why bother?,* and then I stop those thoughts because it makes me sad when I think about her. I've missed Rose every day since she died, and if she were here right now, somehow things would be different. Things would feel different, if nothing else. For me she was my clarity. For her I was her life. No one like Rose should be gone from this earth, and I still can't believe it, and now is not a good time to think about the blond young man in black high-top sneakers sitting next door instead of her. I need to focus. Focus on Erica Donahue. What will I do with this woman? I am going to do something, but I must be shrewd.

She must have typed her letter to me more than once, as many times as it took to make it impeccable, and I'm reminded that when her driver rolled up in the Bentley he didn't seem to know that the intended recipient of the envelope sealed with duct tape is a woman, and indeed seemed to think a silver-haired man was me. I remind myself that the mother of Johnny Donahue also doesn't seem aware that the forensic psychologist evaluating him, this same silver-haired man, is my husband, and also contrary to what's in her letter, there is no unit for the "criminally insane" at McLean, nor has anyone deemed that Johnny is criminally insane, which is a legal term and not a diagnosis. According to Benton, she also has other facts wrong.

She has confused details that may very well hurt her son, possibly damaging an alibi that potentially is his strongest. Claiming he left The Biscuit in Cambridge at one p.m. instead of at two, as Johnny maintains, she has made it far more believable that he could have found transportation and gotten to Salem in time to kill Mark Bishop around four that afternoon. Then there is her reference to her son reading horror novels and enjoying horror films and violent entertainment, and finally what she said about Jack Fielding and a nail gun and a satanic cult, none of that correct or proven.

Where did she get those dangerous details—where, really? I suppose Fielding could have put such ideas in her head when he talked to her on the phone, if it's true he's the one now spreading these rumors, that he's lying, which is what Benton seems to think. Regardless of what Fielding did or didn't do or his truths or untruths or his reasons for anything that is happening, my questions come back to the mother of Johnny Donahue. I make myself bring all of it back to her, because what I fail to see is motivation that is logical. Her delivering this letter to me really doesn't sit well at all. It feels off. It feels wrong.

For one so meticulous about typos and sentence construction, not to mention the attention she must pay to her music, it strikes me that she doesn't seem to care nearly as much as she should about the facts of her son's confession to one of the most heinous acts of violence in recent memory. Every detail counts in a case like this, and how could an intelligent, sophisticated woman with expensive lawyers not know that? Why would she take the chance of divulging anything to someone like me, a complete stranger, especially in writing, when her son faces being locked up for the rest of his life in a forensic psychiatric facility like Bridgewater or, worse, in a prison, where a convicted child-killer with Asperger's, a so-called savant who can work the most difficult math problems in his head but is impaired when it comes to everyday social cues, isn't likely to survive very long?

I refresh myself on all these facts and relevant points at the same time I realize I'm feeling and behaving as if they matter to me. And they shouldn't. I'm supposed to be objective. *You don't take sides, and it's not your job to care,* I tell myself. *You don't care about Johnny Donahue or his mother one way or the other, and you're not a detective or the FBI,* I think sternly. *You're not Johnny's defense attorney or his therapist, and there's nothing for you to get involved in,* I then say to myself severely, because I don't feel convinced. I'm struggling with impulses that have become impossibly strong, and I'm not sure how to turn them off or if I can or should. I do know I don't want to.

Some of what I've grown accustomed to not only at Dover but on non-combat-related matters that are the jurisdiction of the AFME or what basically is the federal medical examiner is far too compatible with my true nature, and I don't want to go back to the staid old way of doing things. I'm military and I'm not. I'm civilian and I'm not. I've been in and out of Washington and lived on an air force base and routinely been sent on recovery missions of air crashes and accidents during training exercises and deaths on military installations or fatalities involving special forces, the Secret Service, a federal judge, even an astronaut in recent months, handling a multitude of sensitive situations I can't talk about. What I'm feeling is the *not* part of the equation. I'm not any one thing, and I'm not feeling at all inclined to surrender to limitations, to sit on my hands because something isn't my department.

As an officer involved in medical intelligence, I'm expected to investigate certain aspects of life and death that go far beyond the usual clinical determinations. Materials I remove from bodies, the types of injuries and wound ballistics, the strengths and failures of armor, and infections, diseases, lesions, whether from parasites or sand fleas, and extreme heat, dehydration, and boredom, depression, and drugs are all matters of national defense and security. The data I gather aren't just for the sake of families and usually aren't destined for criminal court but can have a bearing on the strategies of war and what keeps us safe domestically. I'm expected to ask questions. I'm expected to follow leads. I'm expected to pass along information to the surgeon general, the Department of Defense, to be intensely industrious and proactive.

You're home now. You don't want to come across as a colonel or a commander, certainly not as a prima donna. You don't want to get a case null *prossed or thrown out of court. You don't want to cause trouble. Isn't there enough already? Why would you encourage more? Briggs doesn't want you here. Be careful you don't justify his position. Your own staff doesn't seem to want you here or know you're here. Don't make it easy for you not to be. Your only legitimate purpose in contacting Erica Donahue is to ask her kindly not to contact you or your office again, for her own good, for her own protection.*

I decide to use those exact words, and I almost believe my motivation as I call the home phone number typed at the end of her letter.

17

The person who answers doesn't seem to understand what I'm saying, and I have to repeat myself twice, explaining that I'm Dr. Kay Scarpetta and I'm responding to a letter I just received from Erica Donahue, and is she available, please?

"I beg your pardon," the well-modulated voice says. "Who is this?" A woman's voice, I'm fairly sure, although it is low, almost in the tenor range, and could belong to a young man. In the background a piano plays, unaccompanied, a solo.

"Is this Mrs. Donahue?" I'm already getting an uncomfortable feeling.

"Who is this, and why are you calling?" The voice hardens and enunciates crisply.

I repeat what I said as I recognize a Chopin étude, and I remember a concert at Carnegie Hall. Mikhail Pletnev, who was stunning in his technical mastering of a composition that is very hard to play. The music of someone detailed and meticulous who likes everything just so. Someone who isn't careless and doesn't make mistakes. Someone who wouldn't mar a fine engraved envelope by slapping on duct tape. Someone who isn't impulsive but very studied.

"Well, I don't know who this really is," says the voice, what I now believe is Mrs. Donahue's voice, stony and edged with distrust and pain. "And I don't know how you got this number, since it's unlisted and unpublished. If this is some sort of crank call, it's absolutely outrageous, and whoever you are, you should be ashamed of yourself—"

"I assure you this is not a crank call," I interrupt before she can hang up on me as I think about her listening to Chopin, Beethoven, Schumann, worrying her life away, agonizing over a son who probably has caused her anguish since she gave birth to him. "I'm the director of the Cambridge Forensic Center, the chief medical examiner of Massachusetts," I explain authoritatively but calmly, the same voice I use with families who are on the verge of losing control, as if she is Julia Gabriel and about to shriek at me. "I've been out of town, and when I arrived at the airport last night, your driver was there with your letter, which I've carefully read."

"That's absolutely impossible. I don't have a driver, and I didn't write you a letter. I've written no one at your office and have no idea what on earth you're talking about. Who is this? Who really, and what do you want?"

"I have the letter in front of me, Mrs. Donahue."

I look at it on top of my desk and smooth it open again, being careful and deliberate as it nags at me to ask her about Fielding and why she called him and what he said to her. It nags at me that I don't want her to hate me or think I'm unfeeling or anything other than honest. It's possible Fielding disparaged me to her the same way I suspect he did with Julia Gabriel. I'm close to asking, but I stop myself. What has been said, and what has Erica Donahue been led to believe? But not now. *Self-control,* I tell myself.

Mrs. Donahue asks indignantly, "What does it say that's supposedly from me?"

"A creamy rag paper with a watermark." I hold the top sheet of paper up to my desk lamp, adjusting the shade so the bulb shines directly through the paper, showing the watermark clearly, like the inner workings of a soft-shell crab showing through pearly skin. "An open book with three crowns," I say, and I'm shocked.

I don't let her hear it in my voice. I make sure she can't begin to sense what is racing through my mind as I describe to her what I'm seeing, like a hologram, in the sheet of paper I hold up to the light: an open book between two crowns, with a third crown below, and above that three cinquefoil flowers. And it is the flowers Marino neglected to mention that so glaringly aren't Oxford's coat of arms, that so glaringly aren't the coat of arms for the online City University of San Francisco. What I'm looking at isn't what Benton found on the Internet early this morning while all of us were in the x-ray room, but it's what I saw on the gold signet ring I took out of the evidence locker before I came upstairs after looking at the dead man's clothes.

I open the small manila envelope and shake the ring out into the palm of my gloved hand. The gold catches the lamplight and is bright against white cotton as I turn it different ways to look at it, noting it is badly scratched and the bottom of the band is worn thin. The ring looks old, like an antique, to me.

"Well, that sounds like my crest and my paper. I admit it does," Mrs. Donahue is saying over the phone, and then I read to her the Beacon Hill address engraved on the envelope and letterhead, and she confirms it also is hers. "My personal stationery? How is that possible?" She sounds angry, the way people get when they're scared.

"What can you tell me about your crest? Would you mind explaining it to me?" I ask.

I look at the identical crest engraved in the yellow-gold signet ring that I now hold under a hand lens. The three crowns and the open book are large in the magnifying glass, and the engraving is almost gone in spots, the five-petal flowers, the cinquefoils especially, just a ghost of what was once deeply etched because of the age of the ring, which has been subjected to wear and tear by someone, or perhaps by a number of people, including the man from Norton's Woods, who was wearing it on the little finger of his left hand when he was murdered. There can be no mistake he had it on, that the ring came in with his body. There was no mix-up by police, a hospital, a funeral home. The ring was there when Marino removed the man's personal effects yesterday morning and locked them up and kept the key until he turned it over to me.

"My family name is Fraser," Mrs. Donahue explains. "It's my family coat of arms, that particular emblazon for Jackson Fraser, a great-grandfather who apparently changed the design to incorporate elements such as Azure in base, a border Or, and a third crown Gules, which you can't see unless you're looking at a replica of the coat of arms that displays the tinctures, such as what is framed in my music room. Are you saying someone wrote a letter on my stationery and had a driver hand-deliver it to you? I don't understand or see how it's possible, and I don't know what it means or why someone would do something like that. What kind of car was it? We certainly don't have a driver. I have an old Mercedes, and my husband drives a Saab and isn't in the country right now, anyway, and we've never had a driver. We only use drivers when we travel."

"I'm wondering if your family coat of arms is on anything else. Embroidered, engraved, besides being framed on the wall in your music room, anywhere else it might appear. If it's known or published, if someone could have gotten hold of it." No matter how I phrase it, it sounds like a peculiar thing to quiz her about.

"Get hold of it to do what ultimately? What goal?"

"Your stationery, for example. Let's think about that and what the ultimate goal might be."

"Is what you have engraved or printed?" she then asks. "Can you tell the difference between engraved and printed by looking at what you have?"

You don't know who he is, I'm thinking. *You don't know that the man who died wearing that ring isn't a member of her family, a relative,* and I remember Benton saying Johnny Donahue has an older brother who works at Langley. What if he happened to be in Cambridge yesterday, staying at an apartment near Harvard, maybe a friend's apartment that has an obsolete packbot in it, a friend with a greyhound, a friend who perhaps works in a robotics lab? What if the older brother or some other man significant to Mrs. Donahue had just been overseas, in the UK, and had flown back here unexpected and is dead and she doesn't know, the Donahue family doesn't know? What does Johnny's brother look like?

Don't ask her.

"The stationery is engraved," I answer Mrs. Donahue's question.

What if her family is somehow connected with Liam Saltz or with someone who might have attended his daughter's wedding on Sunday? Might the Donahues have a connection to a member of Parliament named Brown?

Stay away from it.

"Well, you can't pull engraved stationery out of a hat, have it made in a minute," Mrs. Donahue is saying.

Now I'm looking at the envelope, at the duct tape on the back that I didn't cut through, that I thought to preserve.

"Especially if you don't have the copperplates," she adds.

We use sticky-sided tape all the time in forensics, to collect trace evidence from carpet, from upholstery, to lift fibers, paint chips, glass fragments, gunshot residue, minerals, even DNA and fingerprints, from all types of surfaces, including human bodies. Anybody could know that. Just watch television. Just Google "crime scene investigative techniques and equipment."

"If someone got hold of my copperplates? But who? Who could have them?" she protests. "Without those, it would take weeks. And if you do press proofs, which of course I do, add several more weeks. This makes no sense."

She wouldn't put duct tape on the back of her elegant envelope that took many weeks to engrave. Not this precise, proud woman who listens to Chopin études. If someone else did, then I might have an idea why. Especially if it was someone who knows me or knows the way I think.

"And yes, the crest is on a number of things. It's been in my family for centuries," she adds, because she wants to talk. There is much pent up inside her, and she wants to let it out.

Allow it.

"Scottish, but you probably guessed that based on the name," she then says. "Framed on the wall in the music room, as I mentioned, and engraved on some of my family silverware, and we did have some silver stolen years ago by a housekeeper who was fired but never charged with anything because we really couldn't prove it to the satisfaction of the Boston police. I suppose my family silver could have ended up in a pawnshop around here. But I don't see what that could have to do with my stationery. It sounds as if you're implying someone might have made engraved stationery identical to mine with the goal of impersonating me. Or someone stole it. Are you suggesting identity theft?"

What to say? How far do I go?

"What about anything else that might have been stolen, anything else with your family crest on it?" I don't want to directly ask her about the ring.

"Why do you ask? Is there something else?"

"I have a letter that is supposedly from you," I reiterate instead of answering her questions. "It's typed on a typewriter."

"I still use a typewriter," she verifies, and sounds bewildered. "But usually I write letters by hand."

"Might I ask with what?"

"Why, a pen, of course. A fountain pen."

"And the type style on your typewriter, which is what kind? But you might not know the typeface. Not everybody would."

"It's just an Olivetti portable I've had forever. The typeface is cursive, like handwriting."

"A manual one that must be fairly old." As I look at the letter, at the distressed cursive typeface made with metal typebars striking an inked ribbon.

"It was my mother's."

"Mrs. Donahue, do you know where your typewriter is?"

"I'm going to walk over there, to the cabinet in the library where it's kept while I'm not using it."

I hear her moving into another area of the house, and it sounds as if she sets what must be a portable phone down on a hard surface. Then a series of doors shut, perhaps cabinet doors, and a moment later she is back on with me and almost breathless as she says, "Well, it's gone. It's not here."

"Do you remember when you saw it last?"

"I don't know. Weeks ago. Probably around Christmas. I don't know."

"And it wouldn't be someplace else. Perhaps you moved it or someone borrowed it?"

"No. This is terrible. Someone took it and probably took my

stationery, too. The same one who wrote to you as if it was me. And I didn't. I most assuredly didn't."

The first person to come to mind is her own son Johnny. But he is at McLean. He couldn't possibly have borrowed her typewriter, her pen, her stationery, and then hired a man and a Bentley to deliver a letter to me. Assuming he could have known when I was flying in last night on Lucy's helicopter, and I'm not going to ask his mother about that, either. The more I ask her, the more information I give.

"What's in the letter?" she persists. "What did someone write as if it's from me? Who could have taken my typewriter? Should we call the police? What am I saying? You are the police."

"I'm a medical examiner," I correct her matter-of-factly as Chopin's tempo quickens, a different étude. "I'm not the police."

"But you are, really. Doctors like you investigate like the police and act like the police and have powers they can abuse like the police. I talked to your assistant, Dr. Fielding, about what's being blamed on my son, as I know you're very well aware. You must know I've called your office about it and why. You must know why and how wrong it is. You sound like a fair-minded woman. I know you haven't been here, but I must say I don't understand what's been condoned, even from a distance."

I swivel around in my chair, facing the curved wall behind me that is nothing but glass, my office shaped exactly like the building if you laid it on its side, cylindrical and rounded at one end. The morning sky is bright blue, what Lucy calls severe clear, and I notice something moving in the security display, a black SUV parking in back.

"I was told you called to speak to him," I reply, because I can't say what is about to boil out of me. What isn't fair? What have I condoned? How did she know I haven't been here? "I can understand your concern, but—"

"I'm not ignorant," Mrs. Donahue cuts me off. "I'm not ignorant about these things, even if I've never been involved in anything so awful ever before, but there was no reason for him to be so rude to me. I was within my rights to ask what I did. I fail to understand how you can condone it, and maybe you really haven't. Maybe you aren't aware of the entire sordid mess, but how could you not be? You're in charge, and now that I have you on the phone, perhaps you can explain how it's fair or appropriate or even legal for someone in his position to be involved in this and have so much power."

The word *careful* flashes in my mind, as if there is a warning light in my head flashing neon-red.

"I'm sorry if you feel he was rude or unhelpful." I abide by my own warning and am careful. "You understand we can't discuss cases with . . ."

"Dr. Scarpetta." Sharp piano notes sound as if responding to her or the other way around. "I would never and I most assuredly did not," she says emotionally. "Will you excuse me while I turn this down? You probably don't know Valentina Lisitsa. If only I could just listen and not have all these other dreadful things banging in my head, like pots and pans banging in my head! My stationery, my typewriter. My son! Oh, God, oh, God." As the music stops. "I didn't ask Dr. Fielding prying questions about someone who was murdered, much less a child. If that's what he's told you I called about, it's absolutely untrue. Well, I'll just say it. A lie. A damn lie. I'm not surprised."

"You called wanting to speak to me," I say, because that's all I really know other than her claims to Bryce about Johnny and his innocence and allergies. She obviously has no idea I've not talked to Fielding, that no one has, it seems. And the more I downplay what she's saying or outright ignore it, the louder she'll get and the more she'll volunteer.

"Late last week," she says with energy. "Because you're in charge and I've gotten nowhere with Dr. Fielding, and of course you understand my concern, and this really is unacceptable if not criminal. So I wanted to complain, and I'm sorry about your coming home to that. When I realized who you are, that it wasn't some crank call, my first thought was it's about my filing a complaint with your office, not anything as official as I'm making it sound, at least not yet, although our lawyer certainly knows and the CFC's legal counsel certainly knows. And now maybe I won't need to file anything. It depends on what you and I agree upon."

Agree upon about what? I think but I don't ask. She knew I was coming home, and that doesn't fit with what she supposedly wrote to me, either. But it fits with a driver meeting me at Hanscom Field.

"What is in the letter? Can you read it to me? Why can't you?" she says again.

"Is it possible someone else in your family might have written to me on your stationery and borrowed your typewriter?" I suggest.

"And signed my name?"

I don't answer.

"I'm assuming I supposedly signed whatever you got or you'd have no reason to think it's from me other than an engraved address, which could be my husband, who unavoidably is in Japan on business, has been since Friday, although it is the most inopportune time to be away. He wouldn't write such a thing, anyway. Of course he wouldn't."

"The letter purports to be from you," I reply, and I don't tell her it is signed "Erica" above her name typed in cursive and that the envelope is addressed in an ornate script in the black ink of a fountain pen.

"This is very upsetting. I don't know why you won't read it to me. I have a right to know what someone said as if they're me. I suppose our attorney will have to deal with you after all, the attorney representing Johnny, and I assume it's about him, this letter that's a lie, a fraud. Probably the dirty trick of the same ones who are behind all this. He was perfectly fine until he went there, and then he became Mr. Hyde, which is a harsh thing to say about your own child. But that's the only way I can think to say it so you understand how dramatically he was altered. Drugs. It must be, although the tests are negative, according to our lawyer, and Johnny would never take them. He knows better. He knows what thin ice he already skates on because of his unusualness. I don't know what else it could be except drugs, that somebody introduced him to something that changed him, that had a terrible effect, to deliberately destroy his life, to set him up. . . ."

She continues to talk without pause, getting increasingly upset, as a knock sounds on my outer door and someone tries the knob, then at the same time Bryce opens our adjoining door and I shake my head no at him. *Not now.* Then he whispers that Benton is at my door, and can he let him in? And I nod, and he shuts one door and another opens.

I put Mrs. Donahue's call on speakerphone.

Benton closes the door behind him as I hold up the letter to indicate whom it is I'm talking to. He moves a chair close to me while Mrs. Donahue continues to speak, and I jot a note on a call sheet.

Says didn't write it—not her driver or Bentley.

". . . at that place," Mrs. Donahue's voice sounds inside my office as if she is in it.

Benton sits and has no reaction, and his face is pale, drained, and exhausted. He doesn't look well and smells of wood smoke.

"I've never been there because they don't allow visitors unless they have some special event for staff. . . ." her voice continues.

Benton picks up a pen and writes on the same call sheet *Otwahl?* But it seems perfunctory when he does it. He doesn't seem particularly curious.

"And then you have to go through security on a par with the White House, or maybe more extreme than that," Mrs. Donahue says, "not that I know it for a fact, but according to my son, who was frightened and a wreck the last few months he was there. Certainly since summer."

"What place are you talking about?" I ask her as I write another note to Benton.

Typewriter missing from her house.

He looks at the note and nods as if he already knew that Erica Donahue's old Olivetti manual typewriter is gone, possibly stolen, assuming what she's just told me is true. Or maybe he somehow knows she's told me this, and then it intrudes upon my thoughts that my office probably is bugged. Lucy's saying she has swept my office for covert surveillance devices likely means she planted them, and my attention wanders around the room, as if I might find tiny cameras or microphones hidden in books or pens or paperweights or the phone I'm talking on. It's ridiculous. If Lucy has bugged my office, I'm not going to know. More to the point, Fielding wouldn't know. I hope I catch him saying things to Captain Avallone, not realizing the two of them were being recorded secretly. I hope I catch both of them in the act of conspiring to ruin me, to run me out of the CFC.

". . . where he had his internship. That technology company that makes robots and things nobody is supposed to know about . . ." Mrs. Donahue is saying.

I watch Benton fold his hands in his lap, lacing his fingers as if he is placid when he's anything but low-key and relaxed. I know the language of how he sits or moves his eyes and can read his restiveness in what seems the utter stillness of his body and mood. He is stressed-out and worn-out, but there is something else. Something has happened.

". . . Johnny had to sign contracts and all these legal agreements promising he wouldn't talk about Otwahl, not even what its name means. Can you imagine that? Not even something like that, what *Otwahl* means. But no wonder! What these damn people are up to. Huge secret contracts with the government, and greed. Enormous greed. So are you surprised things might be missing or people are being impersonated, their identities stolen?"

I have no idea what *Otwahl* means. I assumed it was the name of a person, the one who founded the company. Somebody Otwahl. I look at Benton. He is staring vacantly across the room, listening to Mrs. Donahue.

". . . Not about anything, certainly not what goes on, and anything he did there belongs to them and stays there." She is talking fast, and her voice no longer sounds as though it is coming from her diaphragm but from high up in her throat. "I'm terrified. Who are these people, and what have they done to my son?"

"What makes you think they've done something to Johnny?" I ask her as Benton quietly, calmly writes a note on the call sheet, his mouth set in a firm, thin line, the way he looks when he gets like this.

"Because it can't be coincidental," she replies, and her voice reminds me of the cursive typeface of her old Olivetti. Something elegant that is deteriorating, fading, less distinct and slightly bleary. "He was fine and then he wasn't, and now he's locked up at a psychiatric hospital and confessing to a crime he didn't commit. And now this," she says hoarsely, clearing her throat. "A letter on my stationery or what looks like my stationery, and of course it's not from me and I have no idea who delivered it to you. And my typewriter is gone. . . ."

Benton slides the call sheet to me, and I read what he wrote in his legible hand.

We know about it.

I look at him and frown. I don't understand.

". . . Why would they want him accused of something he didn't do, and how have they managed to brainwash him into thinking he murdered that child?" Mrs. Donahue then says yet again, "Drugs. I can only assume drugs. Maybe one of them killed that little boy and they need someone as a scapegoat. And there was my poor Johnny, who is gullible, who doesn't read situations the way others do. What better person to pick on than a teenager with Asperger's. . . ."

I am staring at Benton's note. *We know about it.* As though if I read it more than once I'll comprehend what it is he knows about or what it is that he and his invisible others, these entities he refers to as "we," know about. But as I sit here, concentrating on Mrs. Donahue and trying to decipher what she is truly conveying while I cautiously extract information from her, I have the feeling Benton isn't really listening. He seems barely interested, isn't his typically keen self. What I detect is he wants me to end the call and leave with him, as if something is over with and it's just a matter of finishing what has already ended, just a matter of tying up loose ends, of cleaning up. It is the way he used to act when a case had wrung him out for months or years and finally was solved or dropped or the jury reached a verdict, and suddenly everything stopped and he was left harried but spent and depressed.

"You started noticing the difference in your son when?" I'm not going to quit now, no matter what Benton knows or how spent he is.

"July, August. Then by September for sure. He started his internship with Otwahl last May."

"Mark Bishop was killed January thirtieth." It is as close as I dare come to pointing out the obvious, that what she continues to claim about her son being framed doesn't make sense, the timing doesn't.

If his personality began changing last summer when he was working at Otwahl and yet Mark Bishop wasn't murdered until January 30, what she's suggesting would mean someone programmed Johnny to take the blame for a murder that hadn't happened yet and wouldn't happen for many months. The Mark Bishop case doesn't fit with something meticulously planned but as a senseless and sadistic violent attack on a little boy who was at home, playing in his yard, on a weekend late afternoon as it was getting dark and no one was looking. It strikes me as a crime of opportunity, a thrill kill, the evil game of a predator, possibly one with pedophilic proclivities. It wasn't an assassination. It wasn't the black-ops takeout of a terrorist. I don't believe his death was premeditated and executed with a very certain goal in mind, such as national security or political power or money.

". . . People who don't understand Asperger's assume those who have it are violent, are almost nonhuman, don't feel the same things the rest of us do or don't feel anything. People assume all sorts of things because of what I call *unusualness,* not sickness or derangement but unusual. That's the disadvantage I mean." Mrs. Donahue is talking rapidly and with no ordered sequence to her thoughts. "You point out behavior changes that are alarming and other people think it's just him. Just Johnny because of his unusualness, which is a sad disadvantage, as if he needed yet one more disadvantage. Well, that's not what this is, not about his unusualness. Something horrific got started when he did at that place, at Otwahl last May. . . ."

It also enters my mind what Benton mentioned hours earlier, that Mark Bishop's death might be connected to others: the football player from BC, who was found in the Boston Harbor last November, and possibly the man who was murdered in Norton's Woods. If Benton is right, then Johnny Donahue would have to be framed for all three of these homicides, and how could he be? He was an inpatient at McLean when the killing occurred in Norton's Woods, for example. I know he couldn't have committed that homicide, and I fail to see how he could be set up to take the blame for it unless he wasn't on the hospital ward, unless he was on the loose and armed with an injection knife.

Benton writes another note. *We need to go.* And he underlines it.

"Mrs. Donahue, is your son on any medications?" I ask.

"Not really."

"Prescription or perhaps over-the-counter medications?" I inquire without being pushy, and it requires effort on my part, because my patience is frayed. "Maybe you can tell me anything at all he might have been taking before he was hospitalized or any other medical problems he might have."

I almost say "might have had," as if he is dead.

"Well, a nasal spray. Especially of late."

Benton raises his hands palms up as if to say *This isn't news.* He knows about Johnny's medication. His patience is frayed, too, and signs of it are breaking through his imperviousness. He wants me to get off the phone and to go with him right now.

"Why of late? Was he having respiratory problems? Allergies? Asthma?" I ask as I pull a pair of gloves out of the dispenser and hand them to Benton. Then I give him the manila envelope containing the ring.

"Animal dander, pollens, dust, gluten, you name it, he's allergic, has been treated by allergists most of his life. He was doing fine until late summer, and then nothing seemed to work very well anymore. It was a very bad season for pollens, and stress makes things worse, and he was increasingly stressed," she says. "He did start using a spray again that has a type of cortisone in it. The name just fled from me. . . ."

"Corticosteroid?"

"Yes. That's it. And I've wondered about it in terms of it affecting his moods, his behavior. Things such as insomnia, ups and downs, and irritability, which, as you know, became extreme, culminating in him having blackouts and delusions, and ultimately our hospitalizing him."

"He started using it again? So he's used the corticosteroid spray before?"

"Certainly, over the years. But not since he started a new treatment, which meant he didn't need shots anymore. For about a year it was like a magical cure; then he got bad again and resumed the nasal spray."

"Tell me about the new treatment."

"I'm sure you're familiar with drops under the tongue."

I'm aware that sublingual immunotherapy has yet to be approved by the FDA, and I ask, "Is your son part of a clinical trial?" I scribble another note to Benton.

Spray and drops to the labs stat. And I underlined *stat,* which means *statim,* or immediately.

"That's right, through his allergist."

I look at Benton to see if he knows about this, and he glances at my note as he puts on the gloves, and next he glances at his watch. He's going to look at the ring only because I asked him to. It's as if he's already seen it or already knows it isn't important or has his mind made up. Something has ended. Something has happened.

". . . What's called an off-label use that his doctor supervises, but no more trips to his office for shots every week," Mrs. Donahue says, and she seems momentarily soothed as she talks about her son's allergies instead of everything else, her pain in remission, but it won't last.

If someone has tampered with Johnny's medications, it might explain why his allergies got bad again. What he was placing under his tongue or spraying up his nose might have been sufficiently altered chemically to render the medications ineffective, not to mention extremely harmful. I look at Benton as he examines the signet ring. He has no expression on his face. I hold up a sheet of stationery so he can see the watermark. He has no visible reaction, and I notice a cobweb in his hair. I reach over and remove it, and he returns the ring to the envelope. He meets my eyes and widens them the way he does at parties and dinners when he's telegraphing *Let's go now.*

". . . Johnny takes several drops under his tongue daily, and for a while had excellent results. Then it stopped working as well, and he's been miserable at times. This past August he resumed the spray but only seemed to get worse, and along with it were these very disturbing changes in his personality. They were noted by others, and he did get in trouble for acting out, was kicked out of that class, as you know, but he wouldn't have harmed that child. I don't think Johnny was even aware of him, much less would do something. . . ."

Benton takes off the gloves and drops them in the trash. I point at the envelope, and he shakes his head. *Don't ask Mrs. Donahue about the ring.* He doesn't want me to mention it, or maybe it isn't necessary for me to bring it up to her because of what Benton knows that I don't, and then I notice his black tactical boots. They are covered with gray dust that wasn't there earlier when we were talking in Fielding's office. The legs of his black tactical pants also are quite dusty, and the sleeves of his shearling coat are dirty, as if he brushed up against something.

". . . It was the main thing I wanted to ask, more of a personal matter directed at him as a man who teaches martial arts and is supposed to abide by a code of honor," Mrs. Donahue says, grabbing my attention back, and I wonder if I've misunderstood her. I can't possibly have heard what I just did. "It was that more than the other, not at all what you assumed or what he told you. Lying, I'm sure, because as I've said, if he claims I called him to ask for details about what was done to that poor child, then he was lying. I promise I didn't ask about Mark Bishop, who wasn't known to us personally, by the way. We only saw him there sometimes. I didn't ask for information about him. . . ."

"Mrs. Donahue, I'm sorry. You're cutting in and out." It's not really true, but I need her to repeat what she said and to clarify.

"These portable phones. Is this better? I'm sorry. I'm pacing as I talk, pacing all over the house."

"Thank you. Could you please repeat the last few things you said? What about martial arts?"

I listen with another jolt of disbelief as she reminds me of what she assumes I know, that her son Johnny is acquainted with Jack Fielding through tae kwon do. When she called this office several times to talk to Fielding and eventually to complain to me, it is because of this relationship. Fielding was Johnny's instructor at the Cambridge Tae Kwon Do Club. Fielding was Mark Bishop's instructor, taught a class of Tiny Tigers, but Johnny didn't know Mark, and certainly they weren't in the same class, weren't taught together, Mrs. Donahue is adamant about that, and I ask her when Johnny started taking lessons. I tell her I'm not sure about the details and must have an accurate account if I'm to deal appropriately and fairly with her complaint about my deputy chief.

"He's been taking lessons since last May," Mrs. Donahue says while my thoughts scatter and bounce like caroms. "You can understand why my son, who's never really had friends, would be easily influenced by someone he adores and respects. . . ."

"Adores and respects? Do you mean Dr. Fielding?"

"No, not hardly," she says acidly, as if she truly hates the man. "His friend was involved in it first, has been for quite some time. Apparently, a number of women are quite serious about tae kwon do, and when she began working with Johnny and they became friends, she encouraged him, and I wish he hadn't listened. That and, of course, Otwahl, that place and whatever goes on there, and look what's happened. But you can certainly imagine why Johnny would want to be powerful and able to protect himself, to feel less picked on and alone when the irony, of course, is that those days for him really were gone. He wasn't bullied at Harvard. . . ."

She goes on, rambling and less crisp and commanding now, and her despair is palpable. I can feel it in the air inside my office as I get up from my desk.

". . . How dare him. That certainly constitutes a violation of his medical oath if anything does. How dare him continue to be in charge of the Mark Bishop case in light of what we all know the truth is," she says.

"Can you be specific about what truth you're referring to?" I look out my windows at the blindingly bright morning. The sun and the glare are so intense, my eyes water.

"His bias." Her voice sounds behind me, on speakerphone. "He's never been fond of Johnny or particularly nice to him, would make tactless comments to him in front of the others. Things such as 'You need to look at me when I'm talking to you instead of at the goddamn light switch.' Well, as I'm sure you're aware, because of Johnny's unusualness, his attention gets caught up on things that don't make sense to others. He has poor eye contact and can be offensive because people don't understand it's just the way his brain works. Do you know much about Asperger's, or has your husband . . ."

"I don't know much." I don't intend to get into what Benton has or hasn't told me.

"Well, Johnny gets fixated on a detail of no significance to anyone else and will stare at it while you're talking to him. I'll be telling him something important and he's looking at a brooch or a bracelet I'm wearing, or he makes a comment or laughs when he shouldn't. And Dr. Fielding berated him about laughing inappropriately. He belittled him in front of everyone, and that's when Johnny tried to kick him. Here this man has however many degrees of a black belt someone can have, and my son, who weighs all of a hundred and forty pounds, tried to kick him, and that was when he was forced to leave the class for good. Dr. Fielding forbade him from ever coming back and threatened to blackball him if he tried to take lessons anywhere else."

"When was this?" I hear myself as if I'm someone else speaking.

"The second week of December. I have the exact date. I have everything written down."

Six weeks before Mark Bishop was murdered, I think, dazed, as if I'm the one who has been kicked. "And you suggested to Dr. Fielding—" I start to say to the phone on my desk as if I'm looking at Mrs. Donahue and she can see me.

"I certainly did!" she says excitedly, defiantly. "When Johnny started babbling his nonsense about having killed that boy during a blackout and that their tae kwon do instructor did the autopsy! Can you imagine my reaction?"

Their tae kwon do instructor. Who else is she referring to? Johnny's MIT friend, or are there others? Who else might Fielding have been teaching, and what could have caused Johnny Donahue to confess to a murder Benton believes he didn't commit? Why would Johnny think he did something so horrific during a so-called blackout? Who influenced him to the extent he would admit to it and offer details such as the weapon being a nail gun when I know for a fact that isn't true? But I'm not going to ask Mrs. Donahue anything else. I've gone too far; everything has gone too far. I've asked her more than I should, and Benton already knows the answers to anything I might think of. I can tell by the way he's sitting in his chair, staring down at the floor, his face as hard and dark as my building's metal skin.

18

hang up the phone and stand before my curved wall of glass, looking out at a patchwork of slate tiles and snow punctuated by church steeples stretching out before me in the kingdom of CFC.

I wait for my heart to slow and my emotions to settle, swallowing hard to push the pain and anger back down my throat, distracting myself with the view of MIT, and beyond it, Harvard and beyond. As I stand inside my empire of many windows and look out at what I'm supposed to manage if the worst happens to people, I understand. I understand why Benton is acting the way he is. I understand what has ended. Jack Fielding has.

I vaguely remember him mentioning not long after he moved here from Chicago that he had volunteered at some tae kwon do club and couldn't always be available to do cases on weekends or after hours because of his dedication to teaching what he referred to as his art, his passion. On occasion he would be gone to tournaments, he told me, and he assumed he would be granted "flexibility." As acting chief during my long absences, he expected flexibility, he reiterated, almost lecturing me. The same flexibility I would have if I were here, he stated, as if it was a known fact that I have flexibility when I'm home.

I remember being put off by his demands, since he's the one who called me asking for a job at the CFC, and the position I foolishly agreed to give him far surpasses any he's ever had. In Chicago he wasn't afforded much status, was one of six medical examiners and not in line for a promotion of any kind, his chief confided in me when we spoke of my hiring Fielding away from there. It would be a tremendous professional opportunity and good for him personally to be around family, the chief said, and I was deeply moved that Fielding thought of me as family. I was pleased that he had missed me and wanted to come back to Massachusetts, to work for me like in the old days.

And the irony that should have infuriated me, and one I certainly should have pointed out to Fielding instead of indulging him as usual, was this notion of flexibility, as if I come and go as I please, as if I take vacations and run off to tournaments and disappear several weekends each month because of some art or passion I have beyond what I do in my profession, beyond what I do every damn day. My passion is what I live every damn day, and the deaths I take care of every damn day and the people the deaths leave behind and how they pick up and go on, and how I help them somehow do that. I hear myself and realize I've been saying these things out loud, and I feel Benton's hands on my shoulders as he stands behind me while I wipe tears from my eyes. He rests his chin on top of my head and wraps his arms around me.

"What have I done?" I say to him.

"You've put up with a lot from him, with way too much, but it's not you who's done anything. Whatever he was on, was taking and probably dealing . . . Well. You had a brush with it earlier, so you can imagine." He means whatever drugs Fielding might have used to saturate his pain-relieving patches, and whatever drugs he might have been selling.

"Have you found him?" I ask.

"Yes."

"He's in custody? He's been arrested? Or you're just questioning him?"

"We have him, Kay."

"I suppose it's best." I don't know what else to ask except how Fielding is doing, which Benton doesn't answer.

I wonder if Fielding had to be placed in a four-point restraint or maybe in a padded room, and I can't imagine him in captivity. I can't imagine him in prison. He won't last. He will bat himself to death against bars like a panicked moth if someone doesn't kill him first. It also crosses my mind that he is dead. Then it feels he is. The feeling settles numbly, heavily, as if I've been given a nerve block.

"We need to head out. I'll explain as best I can, as best we know. It's complicated; it's a lot," I hear Benton say.

He moves away, no longer touching me, and it is as if there is nothing holding me here and I will float out the window, and at the same time, there is the heaviness. I feel I've turned into metal or stone, into something no longer alive or human.

"I couldn't let you know earlier as it became clear, not that all of it is clear yet," Benton says. "I'm sorry when I have to keep things from you, Kay."

"Why would he, why would anyone . . . ?" I start to ask questions that can never be answered satisfactorily, the same questions I've always asked. Why are people cruel? Why do they kill? Why do they take pleasure in ruining others?

"Because he could." Benton says what he always does.

"But why would he?" Fielding isn't like that. He's never been diabolical. Immature and selfish and dysfunctional, yes. But not evil. He wouldn't kill a six-year-old boy for fun and then enjoy pinning the crime on a teenager with Asperger's. Fielding's not equipped to orchestrate a cold-blooded game like that.

"Money. Control. His addictions. Righting wrongs that go back to the beginning of his time. And decompensating. Ultimately destroying himself because that's who he was really destroying when he destroyed others." Benton has it all figured out. Everybody has it figured out except me.

"I don't know," I mutter, and I tell myself to be strong. I have to take care of this. I can't help Fielding, I can't help anyone, if I'm not strong.

"He didn't hide things well," Benton then says as I move away from the window. "Once we figured out where to look, it's become increasingly obvious."

Someone setting people up, setting up everything. That's why it's not hidden well. That's why it's obvious. It's supposed to be obvious, to make us think certain things are true when maybe they aren't. I won't accept that the person behind all this is Fielding until I see it for myself. *Be strong. You must take care of it. Don't cry over him or anyone. You can't.*

"What do I need to bring?" I collect my coat off a chair, the tactical jacket from Dover that isn't nearly warm enough.

"We have everything there," he says. "Just your credentials in case someone asks."

Of course they have everything there. Everything and everyone is there except me. I collect my shoulder bag from the back of my door.

"When did you figure it out?" I ask. "Figure it out enough to get warrants to find him? Or however it's happened?"

"When you discovered the man from Norton's Woods was a homicide, that changed things, to say the least. Now Fielding was connected to another murder."

"I don't see how," I reply as we walk out together, and I don't tell Bryce I'm leaving. At the moment I don't want to face anyone. I'm in no mood to chat or to be cordial or even civilized.

"Because the Glock had disappeared from the firearms lab. I know you haven't been told about that, and very few people are aware of it," Benton says.

I remember Lucy's comments about seeing Morrow in the back parking lot at around ten-thirty yesterday morning, about a half hour after the pistol was receipted to him in his lab, and he couldn't be bothered with it, according to Lucy. If she knew about the missing Glock, she withheld that crucial information, and I ask Benton if she deliberately lied by omission to me, the chief, her boss.

"Because she works here," I say as we wait for the elevator to climb to our floor. It is stuck on the lower level, as if someone is holding open the door down there, what staff members sometimes do when they are loading a lot of things on or off. "She works for me and can't just keep information from me. She can't lie to me."

"She wasn't aware of it then. Marino and I knew, and we didn't tell her."

"And you knew about Jack and Johnny and Mark. About tae kwon do." I'm sure Benton did. Probably Marino, too.

"We've been watching Jack, been looking into it. Yes. Since Mark was murdered last week and I found out Jack taught him and Johnny."

I think of the photographs missing from Fielding's office, the tiny holes in the wall from the hanging hooks being removed.

"It began to make sense that Jack took control of certain cases. The Mark Bishop case, for example, even though he hates to do kids," Benton goes on, looking around, making sure no one is nearby to overhear us. "What a perfect opportunity to cover up your own crimes."

Or some other person's crimes, I think. Fielding would be the sort to cover for someone else. He desperately needs to be powerful, to be the hero, and then I remind myself to stop defending him. *Don't unless you have proof.* Whatever turns out to be true, I'll accept it, and it occurs to me that the photographs missing from Fielding's office might have been group poses. That seems familiar. I can almost envision them. Perhaps of tae kwon do classes. Pictures with Johnny and Mark in them.

I wonder but don't ask if Benton removed those photographs or if Marino did, as Benton continues to explain that Fielding went to great lengths to manipulate everyone into believing that Johnny Donahue killed Mark Bishop. Fielding used a compromised, vulnerable teenager as a scapegoat, and then Fielding had to escalate his manipulations further after he took out the man from Norton's Woods. That's the phrase Benton uses. *Took out.* Fielding took him out and then heard about the Glock found on the body and realized he'd made a serious tactical error. Everything was falling apart. He was losing it, decompensating like Ted Bundy did right before he was caught, Benton says.

"Jack's fatal mistake was to stop by the firearms lab yesterday morning and ask Morrow about the Glock," Benton continues. "A little later it was gone and so was Jack, and that was impulsive and reckless and just damn stupid on his part. It would have been better to let the gun be traced to him and claim it was lost or stolen. Anything would have been better than what he did. It shows how out of control he was to take the damn gun from the lab."

"You're saying the Glock the man from Norton's Woods had is Jack's."

"Yes."

"It's definitely Jack's," I repeat, and the elevator is moving now, making a lot of stops on its way up, and I realize it is lunchtime. Employees heading to the break room or heading out of the building.

"Yes. The dead man has a gun that could be traced to Fielding once acid was used on the drilled-off serial number," Benton says, and it's clear to me that he knows who the dead man is.

"That was done. Not here." I don't want to think of yet something else done inside my building that I didn't know.

"Hours ago. At the scene. We took care of the identification right there."

"The FBI did."

"It was important to know immediately who the gun was traced to. To confirm our suspicions. Then it came here to the CFC and is safely locked up in the firearms lab. For further examination," Benton says.

"If Jack is the one who murdered him, he should have realized the problem with the Glock when he first was called about the case on Sunday afternoon," I reply. "Yet he waited until Monday morning to be concerned about a gun he knew could be traced to him?"

"To avoid suspicion. If he'd started asking the Cambridge police a lot of questions about the Glock prior to the body being transported to the CFC, or demanded that the gun be brought in immediately when the labs were closed, it would have come across as peculiar. Antennas would have gone up. Fielding slept on it and by Monday morning was probably beside himself and planning what he was going to do once the gun was brought in. He would take it and flee. Remember, he hasn't been exactly rational. It's important to keep in mind he's been cognitively impaired by his substance abuse."

I think about the chronology. I reconstruct Fielding's steps yesterday morning, based on information from his desk drawer and the indented writing on his call-sheet pad. Shortly after seven a.m. it seems he talked to Julia Gabriel before she called me at Dover, and about a half hour later he entered the cooler, and minutes after that he told Anne and Ollie the body from Norton's Woods was inexplicably bloody. It seems more logical to consider it was at this point that Fielding recognized the dead man and realized the Glock he'd heard about from the police would be traced to him. If he didn't recognize the dead man until Monday morning, then Fielding didn't kill him, I say to Benton, who replies that Fielding had a motive I couldn't possibly know about.

The dead man's stepfather is Liam Saltz, Benton informs me. It was confirmed a little while ago when an FBI agent went to the Charles Hotel and talked to Dr. Saltz and showed him an ID photograph Marino took of the man from Norton's Woods. He was Eli Goldman, age twenty-two, a graduate student at MIT and an employee at Otwahl Technologies, working on special micro-mechanical projects. The video clips from Eli's headphones were traced to a webcam site on Otwahl's server, Benton tells me, but he won't elaborate on who did the tracing, if Lucy might have.

"He rigged up the headphones himself?" I ask as the elevator finally gets to us and the doors slide open.

"It appears likely. He loved to tinker."

"And MORT? How did he get that? And what for? More tinkering?" I know I sound cynical.

I know when people have their damn minds made up, and I'm not ready for my mind to be made up. Not one damn thing should be decided this fast.

"A facsimile, a model he made as a boy," Benton explains.

"Based on photographs his stepfather had taken of the real thing when he was lobbying against it some eight or nine years ago when you and Dr. Saltz testified before the Senate subcommittee. Apparently, Eli was making models of robots and inventing things since he was practically in diapers."

We slowly sink from floor to floor while I ask why Otwahl would hire the stepson of a detractor like Liam Saltz, and I want to know what Otwahl means, because Mrs. Donahue said the name meant something. "O. T. Wahl," Benton replies. "A play on words, because the last name of the company's founder is Wahl. *On the Wall,* as in a fly on the wall, and Eli's last name isn't Saltz," Benton adds, as if I didn't hear him when he told me it's Goldman. Eli Goldman. But Otwahl would have done a background check on him, I point out. Certainly they would have known who his stepfather is, even if their last names aren't the same.

"MORT was a long time ago," Benton says as the elevator doors open on the lower floor. "And I don't know that Otwahl had a clue Eli and his stepdad were philosophically simpatico."

"How long had Eli worked there?"

"Three years."

"Maybe three years ago Otwahl wasn't doing anything that Eli or his stepfather would have been concerned about," I suggest as we walk along gray tile while Phil the security guard watches us from behind his glass partition. I don't wave at him. I'm not friendly.

"Well, Eli was worried and had been for months," Benton says. "He was about to give his stepfather a demonstration of technology that he wasn't going to approve of at all, a fly that could be a fly on the wall and spy and detect explosives and deliver them or drugs or poisons or who knows what."

Nanoexplosives or dangerous drugs delivered by something as small as a fly, I think, as we walk past staff I've not seen in months. I don't stop to chat. I don't wave or say hello or even have eye contact.

"He's about to give his stepfather important information like that and conveniently dies," I reply.

"Exactly. The motive I mentioned," Benton says. "Drugs," he says again, and then he tells me more, gives me details the FBI learned from Liam Saltz just a few hours earlier.

I feel sad and upset again as I envision what Benton is saying about a young man so enamored of his famous stepfather that whenever they were to see each other, Eli always set his watch to it, mirroring Dr. Saltz's time zone in anticipation of their reunion, a quirk that has its roots in Eli's poignant past of broken homes and parental figures missing in action and adored from afar. I remember what I watched on the video clips, Eli and Sock walking to Norton's Woods, and then I imagine Dr. Saltz emerging from the building in the near dark after a wedding Eli wasn't invited to. I imagine the Nobel laureate looking around and wondering where his stepson was, having no idea of the terrible truth. Dead. Zipped up inside a pouch and unidentified. A young man, barely more than a boy. Someone Lucy and I may have crossed paths with at an exhibit in London the summer of 2001.

"Who killed him, and what for?" I say as we pass through the empty bay, the CFC van-body truck gone. "I don't see how what you've just said explains Eli being murdered by Jack."

"It all points in the same direction. I'm sorry. But it does."

"I just don't see why and for what." I open the door leading outside, and it is too beautiful and sunny to be so cold.

"I know this is hard," Benton says.

"A pair of data gloves?" I say as we begin to pick our way over snow that is glazed and slick. "A micromechanical fly? Who would stab him with an injection knife, and why?"

"Drugs." Benton goes back to that again. "Somehow Eli had the misfortune of getting involved with Jack or the other way around. Strength-enhancing, very dangerous drugs. Probably was using and selling, and Eli was the supplier, or someone at Otwahl was. We don't know. But Eli being killed while he was out there with a flybot and about to meet his stepfather wasn't a coincidence. It's the motive, I mean."

"Why would Jack be interested in a flybot or a meeting?" I ask as we move very slowly, one step at a time, my feet about to go out from under me. "A damn ice-skating rink," I complain, because the parking lot wasn't plowed and it needs to be sanded. Nobody has been running this place the way it ought to be run.

"I'm sorry, we're way over here." We head slowly toward the back fence. "But that's all there was. The drug connection," Benton then says. "Not street drugs. This is about Otwahl. About a huge amount of money. About the war, about potential violence on an international and massive scale."

"Then if what you're saying is right, it would seem to imply Jack was spying on Eli. Rigged up the headphones with hidden recording devices and followed him to Norton's Woods. That would make sense if the murder was to stop Eli from showing his stepfather the flybot or turning it over to him. How else would

Jack know what Eli was about to do? He must have been spying on him, or someone was."

"I doubt Jack had anything to do with the headphones."

"My point exactly. Jack wouldn't be interested in technology like that or capable of it, and he wouldn't be interested in a place like Otwahl. You're not talking about the Jack I know. He's much too limbically driven, too impatient, too simple, to do what you've just described." I almost say *too primitive,* because that has always been part of his charm. His physicality, his hedonism, his linear way of coping with things. "And the headphones don't make sense," I insist. "The headphones make me think someone else might be involved."

"I understand how you feel. I can understand why you'd want to think that."

"And did Dr. Saltz know his adoring stepson was into drugs and had an illegal gun?" I ask. "Did he happen to mention the headphones or other people Eli might have been involved with?"

"He knew nothing about the headphones and not much about Eli's personal life. Only that Eli was worried about his safety. As I said, he'd been worried for months. I know this is painful, Kay."

"Worried about what, specifically?" I ask as we walk very slowly, and someone is going to get hurt out here. Someone is going to slip and break bones and sue the CFC. That will be next.

"Eli was involved in dangerous projects and surrounded by bad people. That's how Dr. Saltz described it," Benton says. "It's a lot to explain and not what you might imagine."

"He knew his stepson had a gun, an illegal one," I repeat my question.

"He didn't know that. I assume Eli wouldn't have mentioned it."

"Everyone seems to be doing a lot of assuming." I stop and look at Benton, our breath smoking out in the brightness and the cold, and we are at the back of the parking lot now, near the fence, in what I call the hinterlands.

"Eli would know how Dr. Saltz feels about guns," Benton says. "Jack probably sold the Glock to him or gave it to him."

"Or someone did," I reiterate. "Just as someone must have given him the signet ring with the Donahue crest on it. I don't suppose Eli was also involved in tae kwon do." I look around at SUVs that don't belong to the CFC, but I don't look at the agents inside them. I don't look at anyone as I shield my eyes from the sun.

"No," Benton answers. "The football player wasn't, either, Wally Jamison, but he used the gym where they're held, used Jack's same gym. Maybe Eli had been to that gym, too."

"Eli doesn't look like someone who uses a gym. Hardly a muscle in his body," I comment as Benton points a key fob at a black Ford Explorer that isn't his and the doors unlock with a chirp. "And if Jack killed him, why?" I again ask, because it makes no sense to me, but maybe it's my fatigue. No sleep and too much trauma, and I'm too tired to comprehend the simplest thing.

"Or maybe the connection has to do with Otwahl and Johnny Donahue and other illegal activities Jack was involved in that you're about to find out. What he was doing at the CFC, how he was earning his money while you were gone." Benton's voice is hard as he says all that while opening my door for me. "Don't know everything but enough, and you were right to ask what Mark

Bishop was doing in his backyard when he was killed. What kind of playing he was doing. I almost couldn't believe it when you asked me that, and I couldn't tell you when you asked. Mark was in one of Jack's classes, as Mrs. Donahue implied, for three- to six-year-olds, had just started in December and was practicing tae kwon do in his yard when someone, and I think we know who, appeared, and again, you're probably right about how it happened."

As he goes around to the driver's side to get in, and I dig in my bag for my sunglasses, impatient and frustrated as a lipstick, pens, and a tube of hand cream spill on the plastic floor mat. I must have left my sunglasses somewhere. Maybe in my office at Dover, where I can scarcely remember being anymore. It seems like forever ago, and right now I am sickened beyond what I could possibly describe to anyone, and it doesn't please me to hear I was right about anything. I don't give a damn who is right, just that someone is, and I don't think anybody is. I just don't believe it.

"A person Mark had no reason to distrust, such as his instructor, who lured him into a fantasy, a game, and murdered him," Benton goes on as he starts the SUV. "And then trumped up a way to blame it on Johnny."

"I didn't say that part." I stuff items back into my bag as I grab my shoulder harness and fasten up, then I decide to take my jacket off, and I undo the seat belt.

"What part?" Benton enters an address in the GPS.

"I never said Jack trumped up a way to make Johnny believe he drove nails into Mark Bishop's head," I reply, and the SUV is warm from when Benton drove it here, and the sun is hot as it blazes through glass.

I take off my jacket and toss it in back, where there is a large, thick box with a FedEx label. I can't tell whom it is for and I'm not interested, probably some agent Benton knows, probably whoever Douglas is, and I suppose I'll find out soon enough. I fasten my shoulder harness again, working so hard I'm practically out of breath, and my heart is pounding.

"I didn't mean that part was from you. There are a lot of questions. We need you to help us answer everything we possibly can," Benton says.

We begin backing up, pulling out of my parking lot, waiting for the gate to open, and I feel handled. I feel humored. I'm not sure I remember ever feeling so nonessential in an investigation, as if I'm an obstruction and a nuisance people have to be politically correct with because of my position, but not taken seriously and unwanted.

"I thought I'd seen it all. I'm warning you, it's bad, Kay." Benton's voice has no energy as he says that. It sounds hollow, like something gutted.

19

he gray frame house with the old stone foundation and a cold cellar in back were built by a sea captain in centuries past. The property is scrubbed and eroded by harsh weather, directly exposed to what blows in from the sea, and sits alone at the end of a narrow, icy street coarsely sanded by city emergency crews. Where branches have snapped, ice is shattered on the frozen earth and sparkles like broken glass in a high sun that offers no warmth, only a blinding glare.

Sand makes a gritty sound against the underside of the SUV while Benton drives very slowly, looking for a place to park, and I look out at the brightness of the sandy road and the heaving deep blue of the sea and the paler blue of the cloudless sky. I no longer feel the need for sleep or that I could if I tried. Having last gotten up at quarter of five yesterday morning in Delaware, I have been awake some thirty hours since, which isn't unheard of for me, isn't really remarkable if I pause to calculate how often it happens in a profession where people don't have the common courtesy to kill or to die during business hours. But this is a different type of sleeplessness, foreign and unfamiliar, with the added excitement bordering on hysteria from being told, or having it implied at least, that I've lived much of my life with something deadly and I'm the reason it turned deadly.

No one is stating such a thing in exactly those words, but I know it to be true. Benton is diplomatic, but I know. He's not said it's my fault people are brutally dead and countless others have been disrespected and defiled, not to mention those harmed by drugs, people whose names we may never know, guinea pigs or "lab rats," as Benton put it, for a malevolent science project involving a potent form of anabolic steroid or testosterone laced with a hallucinogenic to build strength and muscle mass and enhance aggression and fearlessness. To create killing machines, to turn human beings into monstrosities with no frontal cortex, no concept of consequences, human robots that savagely kill and feel no remorse, feel virtually nothing at all, including pain. Benton has been describing what Liam Saltz told the FBI this morning, the poor man bereft and terrified.

Dr. Saltz suspects Eli got involved with a treacherous and unauthorized technology at Otwahl, found himself in the midst of DARPA research gone bad, gone frighteningly wrong, and was about to warn his humanitarian Nobel laureate stepfather and to offer proof and to beg him to put a stop to it. Fielding put a stop to Eli because Fielding was using these dangerous drugs, perhaps helping to distribute them, but mostly my deputy chief with his lifelong lust for strength and physical beauty and his chronic aches and pains was addicted. That's the theory behind Fielding's vile crimes, and I don't believe it is that simple or even true. But I do believe other comments Benton has continued to make. I was too good to Fielding. I've always been too good to him. I've never seen him for what he is or accepted his potential to do real harm, and therefore I enabled him.

Snow turned to freezing rain where the ocean warms the air, and the power is still out from downed lines in this area of Salem Neck called Winter Island, where Jack Fielding owns a historic investment property I had no idea about. To get to it you have to pass the Plummer Home for Boys, a lovely mossy green mansion set on a gracious spread of lawn overlooking the sea, with a distant view of the wealthy resort community of Marblehead. I can't help but think about the way things begin and end, the way people have a tendency to run in place, to tread water, to really not get beyond where and how it all started for them.

Fielding stopped his life where it took off for him so precipitously, in a picturesque setting for troubled youths who can no longer live with their families. I wonder if it was deliberate to pick a spot no more than a stone's throw from a boys' home, if that factored into his subconscious when he decided on a property I'm told he intended to retire to or perhaps sell for a profit in the future when the real-estate market turns around and after he'd finished much-needed improvements. He'd been doing the work on the house and its outbuilding himself and doing it poorly, and

I'm about to see the manifestation of his disorganized, chaotic mind, the handiwork of someone profoundly out of control, Benton has let me know. I'm about to see the way my enabled protégé lived and ended.

"Are you still with us? I know you're tired," Benton says as he touches my arm.

"I'm fine." I realize he's been talking and I tuned him out.

"You don't look fine. You're still crying."

"I'm not crying. It's the sun. I can't believe I left my sunglasses somewhere."

"I've said you can have mine." His dark glasses turn toward me as he creeps along the sandy, gritty-sounding road in the glaring sun.

"No, thank you."

"Why don't you tell me what's going on with you, because we're not going to have a chance to talk for a while," he says. "You're angry with me."

"You're just doing your job, whatever it is."

"You're angry with me because you're angry at Jack, and you're afraid to be angry at him."

"I'm not afraid of what I feel about him. I'm more afraid of everyone else," I reply.

"Meaning what, exactly?"

"It's something I sense, and you don't agree with me, so we should leave it at that," I say to him as I look out the window at the cold, blue ocean and the distant horizon, where I can make out houses on the shore.

"Maybe you could be a little more specific. What do you sense? Is this a new thought?"

"It isn't. And it's nothing anybody wants to hear," I answer him as I stare out at the bright afternoon while we continue to troll for a place to park.

I'm not really helping him look for a spot. Mostly I'm sitting and staring out the window while my mind goes where it wants to, like a small animal darting about, looking for a safe place. Benton probably thinks I'm pretty useless. He's aided and abetted my uselessness by waiting this long to come get me for something that's been going on for hours. I'm showing up in medias res, as if this is a musical or an opera and it's no big deal for me to wander in during the middle or toward the end, depending on which act we're in.

"Christ, this is ridiculous. You would think someone would have left us something. I should have had Marino put cones out, save us something." Benton vents his anger at parked cars and the narrow street, then says to me, "I want to hear whatever it is. New thought or not. Now, while we have a minute alone."

There is no point in saying the rest of it, of telling him again what I sense, which is a calculating, cruel logic behind what was done to Wally Jamison, Mark Bishop, and Eli Goldman, behind what happened to Fielding, behind everything, a precisely formulated agenda, even if it didn't turn out as planned. Not that I know the plan in its entirety, maybe not even most of it, but what I sense is palpable and undeniable, and I won't be talked out of it. *Trust your instincts. Don't trust anything else. This is about power.*

The power to control people, to make them feel good or frightened or to suffer unbearably. Power over life and death. I'm not going to repeat what I'm sure sounds irrational. I'm not going to tell Benton yet again that I sense an insatiable desire for power, that I feel the presence of a murderous entity watching us from a dark place, lying in wait. Some things are over, but not everything is, and I don't say any of this to him.

"I'm just going to have to tuck it in here, and the hell with it." He isn't really talking to me but to himself, easing as close to a rock wall as he can so we don't stick halfway out into the slick, sandy street. "We'll hope some yahoo doesn't hit me. If so, he'll be in for an unpleasant surprise."

I suppose he means it wouldn't be fun to realize the door you just dinged or the bumper you just scraped or the side you just swiped is the property of the FBI. The SUV is a typical government vehicle, black with tinted glass and cloth seats, and emergency strobes hidden behind the grill, and on the floor in back are two coffee cups neatly held in place inside their cardboard to-go box along with a balled-up food bag. The war wagon of a busy agent who is tidy but not always in a convenient spot to toss out trash. I didn't know that Douglas was a woman until Benton referred to the special agent who's assigned this car as "she" a little while ago while he was telling me about *her* running the license plate of the Bentley that met us at Hanscom last night, a 2003 four-door black Flying Spur personally owned by the CEO of a Boston-based niche service company that supplies "discreet concierge-minded chauffeurs" who will drive any vehicle requested, explaining why the Bentley didn't have a livery license plate.

The reservation was made online by someone using an e-mail address that belongs to Johnny Donahue, an inpatient at McLean with no Internet access when the e-mail was sent yesterday from an IP address that is an Internet café near Salem State College, which is very close to here. The credit card used belongs to Erica Donahue, and as far as anybody knows, she doesn't do anything online and won't touch a computer. Needless to say, the FBI and the police don't believe she or her son booked the Bentley or the driver.

The FBI and the police believe Fielding did, that he likely got access to Mrs. Donahue's credit card information from payments she made to the tae kwon do club for lessons her son took until he was told not to come back after he tried to kick his instructor, my deputy chief, a grandmaster with a seventh-degree black belt. It isn't clear how Fielding might have gained access to Johnny's e-mail account unless he somehow manipulated the vulnerable and gullible teenager into giving him the password at some point or learned it by some other means.

The chauffeur, who isn't suspected of anything except not bothering to research Dr. Scarpetta before he delivered something to her, received the assignment from dispatch, and according to dispatch, no one who works at the elite transportation company ever met the alleged Mrs. Donahue or talked to her over the phone. In the notes section of the online reservation, an "exotic luxury car" was requested for an "errand," with the explanation that further instructions and a letter to be delivered would be dropped off at the private driving company's headquarters. At approximately six p.m., a manila envelope was slipped through the mail slot in the front door, and some three hours later, the chauffeur showed up at Hanscom Field with it and decided that Benton was me.

We get out into the cold, clean air, and ice is everywhere, lit up by the sun as if we are inside an illuminated crystal chandelier. Shielding my eyes with my hand, I watch the dark-blue sea as it rolls and contracts like muscle, pushing itself inland to smash and boil against a rock-strewn shore where no one lives. Right here a sea captain once looked out at a view that I doubt has changed much in hundreds of years, acres of rugged coastline and beach with copses of hardwood trees, untouched and uninhabitable because it is part of a marine recreational park, which happens to have a boat launch.

A little farther down, past the campground, where the Neck wraps around toward the Salem Harbor, is a yacht yard where Fielding's twenty-foot Mako was shrink-wrapped and on a jack stand when police found it this morning. I'm vaguely aware he has a dive boat because I've heard him mention it, but I didn't know where he keeps it. I never would have imagined twenty-four hours ago that it might become the focus of a homicide investigation, or that his dark-blue Navigator SUV with its missing front license plate would, or that his Glock pistol with its drilled-off serial number would, or that everything Fielding owns and has done throughout his entire existence would.

Overhead, an orange Dauphin helicopter, an HH-65A, also known as a Dolphin, beats low across the cold blue sky, its enclosed Fenestron ten-bladed tail rotor making a distinctive modulated sound that is described as low noise but to me has a quiet high pitch, is ominously whiny, reminding me a bit of a C-17. Homeland Security is conducting air surveillance, and I've been told that, too. I don't know why federal law enforcement has taken to the air or the land or the sea unless there is a concern about the overall security of the Salem Harbor, a significant port with a huge power plant. I have heard the word *terrorism* mentioned, just in passing by Benton and also by Marino when I had him on the phone a few minutes ago, but these days I hear that word a lot. In fact, I hear it all the time. Bioterrorism. Chemical terrorism. Domestic terrorism. Industrial terrorism. Nanoterrorism. Technoterrorism. Everything is terrorism if I stop to think about it. Just as every violent crime is hateful and a hate crime, really.

I continue going back to Otwahl, everything leading me back to Otwahl, my thoughts carried on the wing of a flybot or, as Lucy puts it, not a flybot but the holy grail of flybots. Then I think about my old nemesis MORT, a life-size model of it perched like a giant mechanical insect inside a Cambridge apartment rented by Eli Goldman, and next I worry about the controversial scientist Dr. Liam Saltz, who must be heartbroken beyond remedy. Maybe he simply got caught in one of those ghastly coincidences that happens in life, his tragic misfortune to be the stepfather of a brilliant young man who slipped into bad science, bad drugs, and illegal firearms.

A kid too smart for his own good, as Benton puts it, murdered while wearing an antique signet ring missing from Erica Donahue's house, just as her stationery is missing, and her typewriter and a fountain pen, items that Fielding must have gotten hold of somehow. He must have gotten his hands on all sorts of things from the rich Harvard student he bullied, Johnny Donahue, and it doesn't matter if it all feels wrong to me. I can't prove that Fielding didn't exchange the gold ring for drugs. I can't prove he didn't exchange the Glock for drugs. I can't say that's not why Eli had the ring and the gun, that there's some other reason far more nefarious and dangerous than what Benton and others are proposing.

I can say and have said that Eli Goldman was an obstruction to the mercenary progress of a company like Otwahl, and Otwahl is the common denominator in everything, more so than tae kwon do or Fielding. As far as I'm concerned, if Fielding is as directly and solely responsible as everyone is claiming, then we should be taking a very hard and different look at Otwahl and wonder what he had to do with the place beyond being a user or a research subject or even someone who helped distribute experimental drugs until they brought about his complete annihilation.

"Otwahl and Jack Fielding," I said to Benton a little while ago. If Fielding is guilty of murder and case-tampering and obstruction of justice and all sorts of lies and conspiracies, then he's intimately connected with Otwahl, right down to its parking lot, where his Navigator likely got tucked out of sight last night during a blizzard. "You have to make that connection in a meaningful way," I repeatedly told Benton on our drive to this desolate spot that is achingly beautiful and yet ruined, as if Fielding's property is an ugly stain on the canvas of an exquisite seascape.

"Otwahl Technologies and an eighteenth-century sea captain's house on Salem Neck," I said to my husband, and I asked his opinion, his honest and objective opinion. After all, he should have a very well-informed and completely objective opinion because of his alliance with the well-informed and completely objective *we*'s, as I stated it, these anonymous comrades of his, the shadowy rank and file of an FBI he doesn't belong to anymore, he claims, and of course I don't believe him. He is FBI, all right, as secretive and driven as I remember him from times long past, and maybe I could put up with that if I didn't feel so utterly alone.

He's not even listening to me anymore, pretty much checked out when I made the comment a few minutes ago that Fielding must have some link to Otwahl beyond his teaching martial arts to a few brainy students who had internships with the technology behemoth. The connection must be more than just drugs, I said. Drug-impregnated pain-relieving patches can't be the entire explanation for what I'm about to find inside a tiny stone outbuilding that Fielding was turning into a guest quarters before he supposedly found another use for it that has earned it several new names.

The Kill Cottage, I think darkly, bitterly. *The Semen's House,* I think cynically.

Destined to be Salem's latest attraction during Halloween, which lasts all of October, with a million people making a pilgrimage here from all over the land. Another example of a place made famous by atrocities that don't seem real anymore, tall tales, almost cartoonish, like the witch on her broom depicted on the Salem logo that is on police patches and even painted on the police cruiser doors. Be careful what you hate and murder, because one day it will own you. The Witch City, as people have dubbed the place where those men and women were herded up to what is now called Gallows Hill Park, a spot similar to where Fielding bought a sea captain's house. Places that don't change much. Places that are now parks. Only Gallows Hill is ugly, and it should be. An open field ravaged by the wind, and barren. Mostly rocks, weeds, and patchy, coarse grass. Nothing grows there.

Thoughts like these are solar flares, and peak and spike with a timing I can't seem to control, as Benton touches my elbow, then grips it firmly, while we cross the sandy dead-end street that has turned into a parking lot of law-enforcement vehicles, marked and unmarked, some with the Salem logo, silhouettes of witches straddling their brooms. Pulled up close to the sea captain's house, almost right up against the back of it, is the CFC's white van-body truck that Marino drove here hours earlier while I was in the autopsy room and then upstairs, having no idea what was happening some thirty miles northeast. The back of the truck is open, and Marino is inside, wearing green rubber boots and a bright yellow hard hat and a bright yellow level-A suit, what we use for demanding jobs that require protection from biological and chemical hazards.

Cables snake over the diamond-steel floor and out the open metal doors, over the unpaved icy drive, and disappear through the front of the stone cottage, what must have been a charming, cozy outbuilding before Fielding turned it into a construction site of exposed foundation blocks, the ground frozen with ice that is gray. The area behind the sea captain's house is an eyesore of spilled cement and toppled piles of lumber and bricks, and rusting tools, shingles, weather stripping, and nails everywhere. A wheelbarrow is covered loosely with a black tarp that flaps, the entire perimeter strung with yellow crime scene tape that shakes and jumps in the wind.

"We got enough juice in this thing for lights and that's it, got about a hundred and twenty minutes of run time left," Marino says to me as he digs inside a built-in storage bin.

What he's referring to is the auxiliary power unit, the APU, which can keep the truck's electrical system running while the engine is off and supplies a limited amount of emergency power externally.

"Assuming the power doesn't come back on, and maybe we'll get lucky. I've heard it could anytime, the main problem being those poles knocked over by snapped-off trees you probably drove past on Derby Street on your way here. But even if we get the electricity back, it won't help much in there." He means in the stone outbuilding. "No heat in there. It's cold as shit, and after a while it gets to you, I'm just telling you," he says from inside the truck while Benton and I stand outside in the wind and I flip up the collar of my jacket. "Cold as our damn fridge at the morgue, if you can imagine working in there for hours."

As if I've never worked a scene in frigid weather and am unfamiliar with a morgue cooler.

"Course, there are some advantages to that if the power goes out, which it's going to do in these parts when you get storms, and he didn't have a backup generator," Marino continues.

He means that Fielding didn't.

"And that's a lot of money to lose if the freezer quits. Which is why plugging in a space heater and turning it on high was for the obvious reason of ruining the DNA so we'd never know who he'd taken the shit from. Do you think that's possible?" he asks me.

"I'm not sure which part of it—" I start to say.

"That we won't ID them. Possible we won't?" Marino continues talking nonstop, as if he's been drinking coffee since I saw him last. His eyes are bloodshot and glassy.

"No," I reply. "I don't think it's possible. I think we'll find out."

"So you don't think it's as worthless as tapioca."

"Christ," Benton says. "I could have done without that. Christ, I wish you'd stop with the fucking food analogies."

"Low copy number." I remind Marino we can get a DNA profile from as little as three human cells. Unless virtually every cell is degraded, we'll be okay, I assure him.

"Well, it's only fair we really try." Marino talks to me as if Benton's not here, directing his every comment to me as if he's in charge and doesn't want to be reminded of my FBI or former FBI husband. "I mean, what if it was your son?"

"I agree we have to ID them and let their next of kin know," I reply.

"And get sued, now that I think of it," Marino reconsiders. "Well, maybe we shouldn't tell anyone. Seems to me we just need to know who it came from. Why tell the families and open a can of worms?"

"Full disclosure," Benton says ironically, as if he really knows what that is. He is looking at his iPhone, reading something on it, and he adds, "Because a lot of them probably already know. We're assuming Fielding arranged with them up front to pay for the service he was offering. It's not possible to hide anything."

"We're not going to," I answer. "We don't hide things, period."

"Well, I'll tell you. I'm thinking we really should install cameras inside our cooler, not just outside in the hall and the bay and certain rooms but actually in there," Marino says to me, as if it has always been his belief that we should have cameras inside the coolers, probably inside the freezer, too. In fact, he's never mentioned the idea before now. "I wonder if cameras would work in a cooler. . . ." he is saying.

"They work outdoors. It gets colder in the winter around here than it is in the cooler," Benton comments dully, barely listening to Marino, who is full of himself, enjoying his role in the drama that has unfolded, and he's never liked Fielding. I can't think of a bigger *I told you so.*

"Well, we got to do it," Marino says to me. "Cameras and no more of this shit, of people doing shit they think they can get away with."

I look behind us at boots and shoes lined up outside the opening that leads into the cottage. The Kill Cottage, the Semen's Cottage. Some cops are calling it the Little Shop of Horrors.

"Cameras," I hear Marino as I stare at the stone cottage. "If we had them in the cooler, we'd have it all on tape. Well, hell, maybe it's a good thing. Shit, imagine if something like that got leaked and ended up on YouTube. Fielding doing that to all these dead bodies. Jesus. I bet you have cameras like that at Dover, though."

He hands us folded bright yellow suits like his.

"Dover must have cameras in the coolers, right?" he goes on. "I'm sure DoD would spring for it, and nothing like the present to ask, right? In light of the circumstances, I don't think anything's off the table when it comes to beefing up security at our place. . . ."

I realize Marino is still talking to me, but I don't answer because I'm worrying about what's in the cab of the truck. I'm suddenly overwhelmed by pity as I stand outside in the cold and wind and glare, my level-A suit folded up and tucked under my arm while Benton is putting his on.

And Marino goes on quite cheerfully, as if this is quite the carnival. ". . . Like I said, a good thing it's cold. I can't imagine working this on one of those ninety-degree days like we used to get in Richmond, where you can wring water out of the air and nothing's stirring. I mean, what a fucking pig. Don't even look at the toilet in there; probably the last time it was flushed was when they were still burning witches around here. . . ."

"They were hanged," I hear myself say.

Marino looks at me with a blank expression on his big face, and his nose and ears are red, the hard hat perched on top of his bald head like the bonnet of a yellow fireplug.

"How's he doing?" I indicate the cab of the truck and what's inside it.

"Anne's a regular Dr. Dolittle. Did you know she wanted to be a vet before she decided to be Madame Curie?" He still says *curry,* like curry powder, no matter how many times I've told him it's *Cure-ee,* like the element curium that's named after Madame *Cure-ee.*

"I tell you what, though," he then says to me. "It's a good thing the heat hadn't been off in the house more than five, six hours before anybody got here. Dogs like that don't have much more hair than I do. He'd dug himself under the covers in Fielding's rat's nest of a bed and was still shivering like he was having a seizure. Of course, he was scared shitless. All these cops, the FBI storming in with all their tactical gear, the whole nine yards. Not to mention I've heard that greyhounds don't like to be left alone, have, what do you call it, separation anxiety."

He opens another storage bin and hands me a pair of boots, knowing my size without asking.

"How do you know it's Jack's bed?" I ask.

"It's his shit everywhere. Who else's would it be?"

"We need to be sure of everything." I'm going to keep saying it. "He was out here in the middle of nowhere. No neighbors, no eyes or ears, the park deserted this time of year. How do you know for a fact he was alone out here? How can you be absolutely certain he didn't have help?"

"Who? Who the hell would help him do something like this?" Marino looks at me, and I can see it on his big face, what he thinks. I can't be rational about Fielding. That's exactly what Marino thinks, probably what everybody thinks.

"We need to keep an open mind," I reply, then I indicate the cab of the truck again and ask again about the dog.

"He's fine," Marino says. "Anne got him something to eat,

chicken and rice from that Greek diner in Belmont, made him a nice comfy bed, and the heat's blasting, feels like an oven, probably sucking up more to keep his skinny ass warm than we're using in the cellar. You want to meet him?"

He hands us heavy black rubber gloves and disposable nitrile ones, and Benton blows on his hands to warm them as he continues text-messaging and reading whatever is landing on his phone. He doesn't seem interested in anything Marino and I are saying.

"Let me take care of things first," I tell Marino, because I don't have it in me at the moment to see an abandoned dog that was left alone in a pitch-dark house with no heat after his master was murdered by the person who stole him. Or so the theory goes.

"Here's the routine," Marino then says, grabbing two bright yellow hard hats and handing them to us. "Over there, where you'll see plastic tubs for decon." He points at an area of dirt near a sheet of plywood that serves as the cottage's front door. "You don't want to track anything beyond the perimeter. Suits and boots go on and off right over there."

Lined up next to three plastic tubs filled with water is a bottle of Dawn dishwashing detergent and rows of footwear, the boots and shoes of the people inside, including what I recognize as a pair of tan combat boots, men's size. Based on what I'm seeing, there are at least eight investigators working the scene, including someone who might be army, someone who might be Briggs. Marino bends over to check the status display on the diamond-steel-encased APU in the back of the truck, then thuds down the diamond-steel steps out into the glare and sparkle of ice that coats bare trees as if they have been dipped in glass. Hanging everywhere are long, sharp icicles that remind me of nails and spears.

"So what you can do is put your gear on now," Marino says for my benefit as Benton wanders off, busy with his phone, communicating with someone and not listening to us.

Marino and I begin walking to the cottage, careful not to slip on ice that is frozen unevenly over rutted dirt and mud and debris that Fielding never cleaned up.

"Leave your shoes here," Marino tells me, "and if you need to use the facilities or go out for fresh air, just make sure you swish your boots off before you go back in. There's a lot of shit in there you don't want to be tracking everywhere. We don't even know exactly what shit, could be shit we don't know about, my point is. But what we do know isn't something you want to be tracking all over, and I know they say the AIDS virus can't live very long postmortem or whatever, but don't ask me to find out."

"What's been done?" I unfold my suit, and the wind almost blows it out of my hands.

"Things you're not going to want to do and shouldn't be your problem." Marino works his huge hands into a pair of purple gloves.

"I'll do anything that needs to be done," I remind him.

"You're going to need your heavy rubber gloves if you start touching a lot of stuff in there." Marino puts those on next.

I feel like snapping at him that I'm not here to sightsee. Of course I'll be touching things. But I don't intend to stoop to saying I've shown up to work a crime scene as if I'm one of the troops reporting to Marino and will be saluting him next. It's not that I don't understand what Marino is doing, what Benton is doing, what everyone is doing. Nobody wants me guilty of the very thing Mrs. Donahue accused Fielding of, ironically. Not that I want to have a conflict, either, and I understand I shouldn't be the one examining someone who worked for me and who, as rumor has it, I had sex with at some point in my life.

What I don't understand is why I'm not bothered more than I am. The only sadness I'm aware of right now is what I feel about a dog named Sock who is sleeping on towels in the cab of the CFC truck. If I see the dog I'm afraid I'll break down, and every other thought is an anxious one about him. Where will he go? Not to an animal shelter. I won't allow that. It would make sense if Liam Saltz took him, but he lives in England, and how would he get the dog back to the UK unless it is in the cargo area of a jet, and I won't permit that, either. The pitiful creature has been through enough in this life.

"Just be careful." Marino continues his briefing as if I don't know a damn thing about what is going on around here. "And just so you know, we got the van making runs back and forth like clockwork."

Yes, I know. I'm the one who set it up. I watch Benton wander back toward the truck, talking to someone on his phone, and I feel forgotten. I feel extraneous. I feel I'm not helpful or of interest to anything or anyone.

"Pretty much nonstop, already thirty or forty DNA samples in the works, a lot of it not completely thawed, so maybe you're right and we'll be lucky. The van makes an evidence run and then turns around and comes right back, is on its way back here now even as we speak," Marino says.

I bend over and untie one of my boots.

"Anne drives like a damn demon. I didn't know that. I always figured she'd drive like an old lady, but she's been sliding in and out of here like the damn thing's on skis. It's something," Marino says, as if he likes her. "Anyway, everybody's working like Santa's helpers. The general says he can bring in backup scientists from Dover. You sure?"

At the moment I don't know what I want, except a chance to evaluate the situation for myself, and I've made that clear.

"It's not your decision," I answer Marino, untying my other boot. "I'll handle it."

"Seems like it would be helpful to have AFDIL." Marino says it in a way that makes me suspicious, and I eye the tan combat boots by the decon tubs.

It's awkward enough that Briggs is here, and it enters my mind that he might not be the only one who's shown up from Dover.

"Who else?" I ask Marino as I lean against cinder blocks for balance. "Rockman or Pruitt?"

"Well, Colonel Pruitt."

Another army man, Pruitt is the director of the Armed Forces DNA Identification Laboratory, AFDIL.

"He and the general flew in together," Marino adds.

I didn't ask either of them to come, but they didn't need me to ask, and besides, Marino asked, at least he admitted to inviting

Briggs. Marino told me about it during the drive here, over the phone. He said by the way he hoped I didn't mind that he took the liberty, especially since Briggs supposedly had been calling and I supposedly hadn't been answering, so Briggs hunted down Marino. Briggs wanted to know about Eli, the man from Norton's Woods, and Marino told him what was known about the case and then told him "everything else," Marino informed me, and he hoped I didn't mind.

I replied that I did mind, but what's done is done. I seem to be saying that a lot, and I said as much to Marino while I was on the phone with him during the car ride here. I said certain things were done because Marino had done them, and I can't run an office like that, although what was implicit but not stated was that Briggs is here for that very reason. He's here because I can't run an office. Not like that. Not at all. If I could run the CFC as the government and MIT and Harvard and everyone expected, nobody would be working this crime scene, because it wouldn't exist.

My yellow suit is stiff and digs into my chin as I pull my green rubber boots on, and Marino moves the makeshift plyboard door out of the way. Behind it is a wide sheet of heavy translucent plastic nailed to the top of the door frame, hanging like a curtain.

"Just so we're clear, I'm maintaining the chain of custody," I tell him the same thing I said earlier. "We're doing this the way we always do it."

"If you say so."

"I do say so."

I have a right to say so. Briggs isn't above the law. He has to honor jurisdiction, and for better or for worse, this case is the jurisdiction of Massachusetts and the principalities where the crimes have occurred.

"I just think any help we can get . . ." Marino says.

"I know what you think."

"Look, it's not like there's going to be a trial," he then says. "Fielding saved the Commonwealth a lot of fucking money."

20

The air is heavy with the smell of wood smoke, and I notice that the fireplace in the far wall is crammed with partially burned pieces of lumber topped by billowy clouds of whitish-gray ash, delicate, as if spun by a spider, but in layers. Something clean-burning, like cotton cloth, I think, or an expensive grade of paper that doesn't have a high wood-pulp content.

Whoever built the fire did so with the flue closed, and the assumption is that Fielding did, but no one seems quite sure why, unless he was out of his mind or hoping that eventually his Little Shop of Horrors would burn to the ground. But if that was his intention, he certainly didn't go about it in the right way, and I make a mental note of a gas can in a corner and cans of paint thinner and rags and piles of lumber. Everywhere I look I see an opportunity for starting a conflagration easily, so the fireplace makes no sense unless he was too deranged in the end to think clearly or wasn't trying to burn down the building but to get rid of something, perhaps to destroy evidence. Or someone was.

I look around in the uneven, harsh illumination of temporary low-voltage extension lights hanging from hooks and mounted on poles, their bulbs enclosed in cages. Strewn over an old scarred, paint-spattered workbench are hand tools, clamps, drill bits, paintbrushes, plastic buckets of L-shaped flooring nails and screws, and power tools, such as a drill with screwdriver attachments, a circular saw, a finishing sander, and a lathe on a metal stand. Metal shavings, some of them shiny, and sawdust are on the bench and the concrete floor, everything filthy and rusting, with nothing protecting Fielding's investment in home improvement from the sea air and the weather but heavy plastic and more plyboard stapled and nailed over windows. Across the room is another doorway that is wide open, and I can hear voices and other sounds drifting up from stairs leading down into the cellar.

"What have you collected in here?" I ask Marino as I look around and imagine what I saw under the microscope. If I could magnify samples from Fielding's work space, I suspect I would see a rubbish dump of rust, fibers, molds, dirt, and insect parts.

"Well, it's obvious when you look at the metal shavings some of them are recent because they haven't started rusting and are really shiny," Marino replies. "So we got samples, and they've gone to the labs to find out if under the scope they look anything like what you found in Eli Saltz's body."

"His last name isn't Saltz," I remind him for the umpteenth time.

"You know, to compare tool marks," Marino says. "Not that there's much of a reason to doubt what Fielding did. We found the box."

The box the WASP came in.

"A couple spent CO-two cartridges, a couple extra handles, even the instruction book," Marino goes on. "The whole nine yards. According to the company, Jack ordered it two years ago. Maybe because of his scuba diving." He shrugs his big shoulders in his big yellow suit. "Don't know, except he didn't order it two years ago to kill Eli. That's for damn sure. And two years ago Jack was in Chicago, and I guess you might ask what he needed a WASP for." Marino walks around in his big green boots and keeps looking at the opening to the stairs leading down, as if he's curious about what's being said and done down there. "The only thing that will kill you in the Great Lakes that I know of is all the mercury in the fish."

"It's with us. We have the box and the CO-two cartridges. We have all of it." I want to know which labs. I want to make sure Briggs isn't sending my evidence to the AFME labs in Dover.

"Yeah, all that stuff. Except the knife that was in the box, the WASP itself. It still hasn't shown up. My guess is he ditched it after stabbing the guy, maybe threw if off a bridge or something. No wonder he didn't want anyone going to the Norton's Woods scene, right?" Marino's bloodshot eyes look at me, then distractedly look around, the way people act when nothing they are looking at is new. He'd been here many hours before I showed up.

"What about in here?" I squat in front of the fireplace, which is open and built of old firebrick that is probably original to the building. "What's been done here?" My hard hat keeps slipping over my eyes, and I take it off and set it on the floor.

"What about it?" Marino watches me from where he's standing.

I move my gloved finger toward the whitish ashes, and they are weightless, lifting and stirring as the air moves, as if my thoughts are moving them. I contemplate the best way to preserve what I'm seeing, the ashes much too fragile to move in toto, and I'm pretty sure I recognize what has happened in the fireplace, or at least some of what occurred. I've seen this before but not recently, maybe not in at least ten years. When documents are burned these days, usually they were printed, not typed, and were generated on inexpensive copying paper with a high wood-pulp content that combusts incompletely, creating a lot of black sooty ash. Paper with a high cotton-rag content has a completely different appearance when it is burned, and what comes to mind immediately is Erica Donahue's letter that she claims she never wrote.

"What I recommend," I say to Marino, "is we cover the fireplace so the ashes aren't disturbed. We need to photograph them in situ before disturbing them in any way. So let's do that before we collect them in paint cans for the documents lab."

His big booted feet move closer, and he says, "What for?"

What he's really asking is why I am acting like a crime scene investigator. My answer, should I give one, which I won't, is because somebody has to.

"Let's finish this the way it should be done, the way we know how and have always done things." I meet his glassy stare, and what I'm really saying is nothing is over. I don't care what everyone assumes. It's not over until it is.

"Let's see what you've got." He squats next to me, our yellow suits making a plastic sound as we move around, and their faint odor reminds me of a new shower curtain.

"Typed characters on the ash." I point, and the ashes stir again.

"Now you're a psychic and ought to get a job in one of the magic shops around here if you can read something that's been burned."

"You can read some of it because the expensive paper burns clean, turns white, and the inked characters made by a typewriter can be seen. We've looked at things like this before, Marino. Just not in a long time. Do you see what I'm looking at?" I point, and the air moves and the ashes stir some more. "You can actually see the inked engraving of her letterhead, or part of it. Boston and part of the zip code. The same zip code on the letter I got from Mrs. Donahue, although she says she didn't write it and her typewriter is missing."

"Well, there's one in the house. A green one, an old portable on the dining-room table." He gets up and bends his legs as if his knees ache.

"There's a green typewriter next door?"

"I figured Benton told you."

"I guess he couldn't tell me everything in an hour."

"Don't get pissed. He probably couldn't. You won't believe all the shit next door. Appears when Fielding moved here he never really moved his shit in. Boxes everywhere. A fucking landfill over there."

"I doubt he had a portable typewriter. I doubt that's his."

"Unless he was in cahoots with the Donahue kid. That's the theory of where a lot of shit has come from."

"Not according to his mother. Johnny disliked Jack. So how does it make sense that Jack would have Mrs. Donahue's typewriter?"

"If it's hers. We don't know it is. And then there's the drugs," Marino says. "Obviously, Johnny's been on them since about the time he started taking tae kwon do lessons from Fielding. One plus one equals two, right?"

"We're going to find out what adds up and what doesn't. What about stationery or paper?"

"Didn't see any."

"Except what seems to be in here." I remind him it appears some of Erica Donahue's stationery might have been burned, or maybe all of it was, whatever was left over from the letter someone wrote to me, pretending to be her.

"Listen . . ." Marino doesn't finish what he's about to say.

He doesn't need to. I know what he's going to say. He's going to remind me I can't be reasonable about Fielding, and Marino thinks he should know, all right. Because of our own history. Marino was around in the early days, too. He remembers when Fielding was my forensic pathology fellow in Richmond, my pro-tégé, and in the minds of a lot of people, it seems, a lot more than that.

"This was here just like this?" I then ask, indicating a roll of lead-gray duct tape on the workbench.

"Okay. Sure," he says as he squats by an open crime scene case on the floor and gets out an evidence bag, because the roll of tape can be fracture-matched to the last strip torn off it. "So tell me how the hell he might have gotten hold of it, and what for?"

He means Fielding. How did Jack Fielding get hold of Erica Donahue's typewriter, and what was his purpose in writing a letter allegedly from her and having it hand-delivered to me by a driver-for-hire who usually works events like bar mitzvahs and weddings? Did Johnny Donahue give Fielding the typewriter and stationery? If so, why? Maybe Fielding simply manipulated Johnny. Lured him into a trap.

"Maybe a last-ditch effort to frame the kid," Marino then says, answering his own question and voicing what I'm pondering and about to dismiss as a possibility. "A good question for Benton."

But Benton is off somewhere, talking on his phone or maybe conferring with his FBI compatriots, maybe with the female agent named Douglas. It bothers me when I think about her, and I hope I'm just paranoid and raw and have no reason to be concerned about the nature of his relationship with Special Agent Douglas. I hope the extra coffee cup in the back of her SUV wasn't Benton's, that he hasn't been riding around with her, spending a lot of time with her while I was at Dover and then before that, in and out of Washington. Not just an enabler and a bad mentor, now I'm a bad wife, it occurs to me. Everything feels wrecked. It feels over with. It feels as if I'm working my own death scene, as if the life I knew somehow didn't survive while I was away, and I'm investigating, trying to reconstruct what did me in.

"This is what we need to do right now," I tell Marino. "I assume no one has touched the typewriter, and is it an Olivetti, or do you know?"

"We've been pretty tied up over here." What he's saying is that the police have more important matters to tend to than an old manual typewriter. "We found the dog in there, like I told you. And a bedroom it appears Fielding was using, and you can tell he was in and out living here, but this is where it happened." He indicates the outbuilding we're in. "The typewriter's in a case on the dining-room table. I opened it to see what was inside, but that's it."

"Swab the keys for DNA before you pack it up and transport it to the labs, and I want those swabs going out on the next evidence run the van makes. I want those swabs analyzed first, because they might tell us who wrote that letter to me," I tell him.

"I think we know who."

"Then the typewriter goes to Documents so we can compare the typeface to what's on the letter I got, a cursive typeface, and we'll analyze the duct tape that's on the envelope and see if it came from the roll we just found and what trace is on it or DNA or fingerprints or who knows what. Don't be surprised if it points to the Donahues. If trace is from their house or fingerprints or DNA is from that source."

"Why?"

"Framing their son."

"I didn't know Jack was that damn smart," Marino says.

"I didn't say he framed anyone. I've not tried and convicted him or anyone," I reply flatly. "We have his DNA profile and fingerprints for exclusionary purposes, just as we have all of ours. So he should be easy to include or exclude, and any other profiles, and if there are? If we find DNA from more than one source, which we certainly should expect? We run the profiles through CODIS immediately."

"Sure. If that's what you want."

"We run them right away, Marino. Because we know where Jack is. But if anyone else is involved, including the Donahues? We can't waste time."

"Sure, Doc. Whatever you want," Marino says, and I can read his thoughts.

This is Jack Fielding's house, it's his Kill Cottage, his Little Shop of Horrors. Why go to all this trouble? But Marino's not going to say it to me. He's assuming I'm in denial. I'm holding out the remote and irrational hope that Fielding didn't kill anyone, that someone else magically was using his property and his belongings and is responsible for all of this, someone other than Fielding, who is the victim and not the monster everyone now believes he is.

"We don't know if his family's been here," I remind Marino patiently and quietly, but in a sobering tone. "His wife, his two little girls. We don't know who's been in the house and touched things."

"Not unless they've been coming here from Chicago to stay in this dump."

"When exactly did they move out of Concord?" That's where his family was living with him, in a house Fielding had rented that I helped him find.

"Last fall. And it fits with everything," Marino makes yet one more assumption. "The football player and what happened after

Fielding's family moved back to Chicago and he came here, fixing up this place while he was living in it like a hobo. He could have sent you a goddamn e-mail and let you know it wasn't working out for him personally around here. That his wife and kids bolted not long after the CFC started taking cases."

"He didn't tell me. I'm sorry he didn't."

"Yeah, well, don't say I should have." Marino seals the roll of duct tape in a plastic evidence bag. "It wasn't my business. I wasn't going to start out my new career here by ratting on the staff and telling you that Fielding was the usual fuck-up right out of the box and you sure as hell should have expected it when you thought it was such a brilliant idea to take him back."

"I should have expected this?" I hold Marino's bloodshot, resentful stare.

"Put on your hard hat before you go down. There's a lot of shit hanging from the ceilings, like all these damn lights strung up like it's Christmas. I got to go back out to the truck, and I know you need a minute."

I adjust the ratchet of my hard hat, making it tighter, and the reason Marino isn't going into the cellar with me isn't because I need a minute. It isn't because he's sensitive enough to offer me a chance to deal with what's down there without him by my side, breathing down my neck. That might be what he's talked himself into, but as I listen to him swishing his boots in the tubs just outside the door, stepping in and out of the water, I can only imagine how distasteful a scene like this must be to him. It has little to do with the unpleasantness of body fluids thawing and breaking down or even his squeamishness about hepatitis or HIV or some other virus and everything to do with how the body fluids got here. Marino's ablution in the plastic tubs filled with water and dishwashing fluid are his attempt to cleanse himself of the guilt I know he feels.

He never saw Fielding doing any of it, and that's the problem Marino faces. The way he would think about it is he should have noticed, and as I've explained to Benton while we were driving here and then explained to Marino over the phone, the extraction of sperm isn't much different from a vasectomy, except when such a procedure is performed on a dead body, it's even quicker and simpler, for obvious reasons. No local anesthesia is needed, and the doctor doesn't have to be concerned with how the patient is feeling or if he might have second thoughts or any other emotional response.

All Fielding had to do was make a small puncture on one side of the scrotum and inject a needle into the vas deferens to extract sperm. He could have done this in minutes. He probably didn't do it during the autopsy but before it by going into the cooler when nobody was around, making certain he got to the body as quickly after death as possible, which in retrospect might explain why he noticed the man from Norton's Woods was bleeding before anybody else did. Fielding went into the cooler first thing when he got to the building early Monday morning to acquire his latest involuntary sperm donation, and that's when he noticed blood in the tray under the body bag. So he walked rapidly down the corridor and notified Anne and Ollie.

If anybody would have noticed something like this going on during the six months I was at Dover it was Anne, I told Marino.

She never saw what Fielding was doing or had a clue, and we know he extracted sperm from at least a hundred patients based on what has been found in a freezer in the cellar and what's broken all over the floor, potentially a hundred thousand dollars, maybe much more, depending on what he charged and if he did it on a sliding scale, taking into account what the family or other interested party could afford. Liquid gold, as cops are calling what Fielding was selling on a black market of his own creation, and I can't stop thinking about his choice of Eli as an involuntary donor, assuming this was Fielding's intention, and we'll never really know.

But at the time Fielding went into the cooler yesterday morning, there was only one young male body fresh enough to be a suitable candidate for a sperm extraction, and that was Eli Goldman. The other male case was elderly, and it's highly unlikely he had loved ones who might be interested in buying his semen, and a third case was a female. If Fielding murdered Eli with the injection knife, would he then be so brazen and reckless as to take the young man's sperm, and who was he planning to sell it to without incriminating himself? If he'd tried something like that, he may as well have confessed to the homicide.

It continues to tug at my thoughts that Fielding didn't know who the unidentified dead young male was when he was notified about the case on Sunday afternoon. Fielding didn't bother going to the scene, wasn't interested, and had no reason at that time to be interested. I continue to suspect he didn't have a clue until he walked into the cooler, and then he recognized Eli Goldman because they had a connection somehow. Maybe it was drugs, and that's why Eli had one of Fielding's guns. Maybe Fielding had given or sold the Glock to Eli. For sure someone did. Drugs, the gun, maybe something else. If only I could have been in Fielding's mind when he walked into the cooler at shortly after seven yesterday morning. Then I would know. I would know everything.

I move a hanging light out of my way so it doesn't knock my hard hat as I go down stone steps in my bulky yellow suit and big rubber boots.

A cold sweat is rolling down my sides, and I am worrying about Briggs and what it will be like when I'm confronted with him, and I'm worrying about a greyhound named Sock. I am worrying about everything I can possibly worry about because I can't bear what I'm about to see, but it is better this way, and as much as I complain about Marino, he really did do the right thing. I wouldn't have wanted Fielding's body transported to the CFC. I wouldn't want to see it for the first time in a pouch on a steel gurney or tray. Marino knows me well enough to decide that given the choice, I would demand to see Fielding the way he died, to satisfy myself that it was exactly as it appears, and that what Briggs determined when he examined the body hours earlier is the same thing I observe and that Briggs and I share the same opinion about Fielding's cause and manner of death.

The cellar is whitewashed stone with a vaulted stone ceiling and no windows, and it is too small a space for so many people, all of them dressed the way I am, in bright yellow with thick black gloves and green rubber boots and bright yellow hard hats. Some people have on face shields, others surgical masks, and I recognize my own scientists, three from the DNA lab, who are swabbing an area of the stone floor that is littered with shattered glass test tubes and their black plastic stoppers. Nearby is the space heater Marino mentioned, and an upright stainless-steel laboratory cryogenic freezer, the same make and model that we use in labs where we have to store biological samples at ultra-low temperatures.

The freezer door is open wide, the adjustable shelves inside empty because someone, presumably Fielding, removed all the specimens and smashed them to the stone floor, then turned on the space heater. I notice partial labels adhering to glass fragments on a floor that is otherwise clean, the cellar appearing whitewashed with something nonglossy, like primer, like a wine-maker's cave that has been turned into a laboratory with a steel sink and steel countertop, racks for test tubes, and large steel tanks of liquid nitrogen, and central to the main room I'm in, a long metal table that Fielding probably was using for shipping and several chairs, one of them pulled out a little, as if someone might have been sitting in it. I look at the chair first, and I look for blood, but I don't see any.

The table is covered with white butcher paper, and arranged on it are pairs of elbow-length bright-blue cryogloves, ampoules, rollerbases, smudge-proof pens, and long corks and measuring sticks for storage canisters, and stacked underneath are white cardboard boxes called CryoCubes, which are inexpensive vapor shippers we typically use for sending biological materials that are placed inside an aluminum canister, where they can remain frozen at minus 150 degrees centigrade for up to five days. These special packing containers can also be used to ship frozen semen, and in fact are often referred to as "semen tanks" and are favored by animal breeders.

I can only assume that Fielding's equipment and materials for his illegal and outrageous cottage industry were purloined from the CFC, that in the dark of night or after hours, he somehow managed to sneak what he wanted out of the labs without security batting an eye. Or it is possible he simply ordered what he needed and charged it to us but had it shipped directly here, to the sea captain's house. Even as I'm piecing together what he might have done, he is so close to me I could touch him, under a disposable blue sheet on his clean white primer–painted floor that is stained with blood at one edge of the plasticized paper, a spot of blood that is part of a large pool under his head, based on what I know. From where I'm standing, I can see the blood has begun to separate and coagulate, is in the early stages of decomposition, a process that would have been dramatically slowed because of the ambient temperature in the cellar. It is cold enough to see your breath, as cold as a morgue refrigerator.

The flashgun of a camera goes off, and then goes off again as a broad-shouldered figure in blaze yellow photographs the one area of whitewashed wall down here that is blackened and foul, where a total station on a bright yellow tripod has been set up, and I'm guessing the electro-optical distance-measuring system has already mapped the scene, recording the coordinate data of every feature, including what Colonel Pruitt is photographing. He catches me looking at him and lowers the camera to his side as I walk over to a wall where I smell death, the faintest musty, pungent stench of blood that has broken down and dried over months in a sunless, cold environment. I smell mildew. I smell dust, and I notice piles of torn dirty carpet and plywood nearby against a different wall, and I can tell by dust and dirt on the white floor that the carpet and wood was recently dragged to where it is.

Bolted into stone at the height of my head are a series of steel screw-pin anchor shackles that I associate with sling assemblies used in hoisting. Based on coils of rope, grease guns, clamps, a cargo trolley, and grab hooks and swivel rings in the ceiling, I surmise that Fielding devised a creative rig for changing out the heavy tanks of liquid nitrogen, and at some point the system was perverted into one I suspect he never intended when he began extracting semen and selling it.

"From what I'm able to figure out so far, the main thing used was the splitting maul, which would account for both the blunt-force and cutting injuries," Pruitt begins without so much as a hello, as if our meeting here is normal, nothing more than a continuum of our time together at Dover. "Basically, a long-handled sledgehammer on one side, the other side sharp like an ax. It was under carpet and wood, along with a Boston College letter jacket, a pair of sneakers, other items of clothing that we think were Wally Jamison's. This entire area was under that stuff over there." He indicates the carpet and wood that was moved, what I surmise was used to cover the crime scene. "All of it, including the splitting maul, of course, has been packaged and sent to your place already. Did you see the weapon yet?" Pruitt says, shaking his head.

"No."

"Can't imagine someone coming after me with something like that. Jesus. Shades of Lizzie Borden. And pieces of bloody rope from being strung up." He points to the shackles and rings bolted into stone that is crusty and black with old blood, and I almost imagine I can smell fear down here, the unimaginable terror of the football player tortured and murdered on Halloween.

"Why didn't he clean this up?" I ask the first question that comes to mind as I look at a scene that doesn't appear to have been touched after Wally Jamison was brutally and sadistically murdered down here.

"I guess he took the path of least resistance and just covered everything up with plyboard and old carpet," Pruitt replies. "That's why there's a lot of dirt and fibers everywhere. Appears after the homicide, he didn't bother washing things down at all. Just heaped old carpet on top and leaned all these boards against the wall." He points again to the pile of old torn carpet of different colors, and near it, the large sheets of plyboard stacked on the white floor near a closed access door that leads outside the cellar.

"I don't know why he wouldn't have washed it down," I repeat. "That was three months ago. He just left a crime scene, practically left it like a time capsule? Just threw carpet and plyboard over it?"

"One theory is he got off on it. Like people who photograph

or film what they do so they can continue getting off on it after the fact. Every time he came down here, he knew what was behind the boards and carpet, what was hidden under them, and got off on it."

Or someone got off on it, I think. Jack Fielding has never gotten off on gore. For a forensic pathologist, he was actually rather squeamish. Benton will say it was the influence of drugs. Everyone is probably saying that, and maybe it's true. Fielding was altered, that much I don't doubt.

"Some of us can help you with this, you know," Pruitt then says, looking at me through a plastic face shield that clouds up intermittently as he breathes the cold cellar air. His hazel eyes are alert and friendly as they look at me, but he is troubled. How could anybody not be, and I wonder if he senses what I do. I wonder if he has a feeling in his gut that something is wrong with all this. I wonder if he's asking the question I am right now as I look at the blackened whitewashed wall with the rusting shackles bolted into the stone.

Why would Jack Fielding do something like this?

Extracting semen to sell to bereft families is almost understandable. One can easily blame greed or even a lust for the gratification, the power he must have felt when he was able to give back life where it had been taken. But as I envision the photographs, video recordings, and CT scans I've seen of Wally Jamison's mutilated body, I'm reminded of what went through my thoughts at the time. His murder seemed sexually and emotionally driven, as if the person who swung the weapon at him had feelings for him, certainly had a rage that didn't quit until Wally was lacerated, sliced, cut, and contused beyond recognition and bled to death. Afterward, his nude body was transported, probably by boat, probably by Fielding's boat, and dumped in the harbor at the coast guard station, an act that Benton describes as brazen, as a taunt to law enforcement. And that doesn't sound like Fielding, either. For such a fierce, muscle-bound grandmaster, he was rather much a coward.

"Thank you. Let's see what's needed," I say to Pruitt.

"Well, you know the DNA that's needed. Hundreds of samples already, not just the semen that needs to be reconnected with its donor but everything else being swabbed."

"I know. It's a huge job and will go on for quite a while because we don't know what's happened in here. Just part of it. What was in the freezer and then whatever else was done in addition to what I'm supposing must have been the homicide of the BC student, Wally Jamison." As I say his name I envision him, square-jawed with curly black hair and bright blue eyes, and powerfully built. Then what he looked like later. "What time did you get here?"

"John and I flew in early, got here about seven hours ago."

I don't ask him where Briggs is now.

"He did the external exam and will go over those details with you when you're ready," Pruitt adds.

"And nobody had touched him prior to that?" Fielding's body was discovered shortly after three a.m. Or that's what I've been told.

"When John and I got here, the body was covered just like he is now. The Glock isn't here. After the FBI restored the eradicated serial number, the gun was bagged and is now at your labs," Pruitt tells me what Benton did.

"I didn't know about it until a little while ago. When I was being driven here."

"Look. If I'd been here at three a.m. and it was up to me?" He starts to say he would have told me everything that was going on. "But the FBI wanted to keep things contained, since no one's been sure if he was a lone wolf." He means if Fielding was. "Because of all the other factors, like Dr. Saltz and the MP and so on. The fear of terrorism."

"Yes. Only not the brand of terrorism the Bureau usually has to worry about. This is a different brand of terrorism," I comment. "It feels personal. Doesn't it feel personal? What are you thinking about all this?"

"Nobody had touched the body when the police, the FBI found it." Pruitt doesn't want to tell me what he thinks about it. "I do know he was the same temperature as the room by then, had been down here for a while, but you should talk to John about it."

"You're saying his body was the same temperature as the ambient air at three a.m."

"It's forty degrees, or around that. Maybe a few degrees warmer because of all the people down here. But you need to get the details from John."

Pruitt stares off at the human-shaped mound draped with a blue sheet on the other side of the cellar, near the freezer, near thawing fluids on the stone floor, where investigators have knee

pads on and are collecting one shard of glass at a time and swabbing, and packaging each item separately in paper envelopes that
they label with permanent markers. I won't do the calculations
until I check the body, but already what I'm hearing adds to what
I suspect. Something is wrong.

21

he stain on the whitewashed wall is an ugly darkness some six feet above the stone floor, probably where Wally Jamison's head and neck were when he was shackled and beaten and cut to death.

Spraying out from the largest stain are a constellation of pinpoint spatters, tiny black marks that at close inspection are elongated, are angled, the cast-off blood from the weapon as it was repeatedly swung, as it was repeatedly bloodied from impacting with human flesh, and I envision the wood-splitting maul Pruitt mentioned, and I agree with him. What a terrible way to die. Then I think of the injection knife. Another horrendous way to die. Sadism.

"He should have had a system of keeping track of the samples," I say to Pruitt as I watch the investigators in bright yellow, on their hands and knees, some of them people I don't know. Maybe Saint Hilaire from Salem. Maybe Lester "Lawless" Law from Cambridge. I'm not sure who is here, really, just that the FBI is working in conjunction with a special task force comprising investigators from various departments who are members of the North Eastern Massachusetts Law Enforcement Council, NEMLEC. "If he really was selling extracted semen," I continue my train of thought, "I would assume he had a way of logging the specimens." I direct his attention to bits of gummy labels still adhering to broken glass on the floor. "Finding information like that will help us with identification, maybe preliminarily supply it, and then we can verify through DNA. If all of the specimens came from CFC cases, we should have DNA on blood-spot cards in each case file."

"I know Marino is looking into that, has somebody pulling every case of young males who would have been viable candidates. Especially if Fielding did the autopsies."

"With all due respect, that was my direction, not Marino's." I hear the defensiveness I can't keep out of my tone, but I've had enough of my new self-appointed acting chief Pete Marino. I've had enough references that imply he runs my office.

"We've not found a log yet," Pruitt adds. "But Farinelli's over there with his laptop, which was as dead as he was when we got here. Maybe the log will be on that."

It always seems strange when investigators refer to my niece by her last name. Lucy must be next door in the house, where there are no lights or heat, unless the power has come back on. I realize that down here I might not know, since we are using auxiliary lights brought in and set up. I walk over to an open Pelican case near the bottom of the stairs and find a flashlight, then return to the wall to shine the light over bloodstains to see what else they have to tell me before I look at the person who supposedly caused them, my deputy chief, working alone in his Kill Cottage. *My deputy chief, the lone wolf who had no help in all this,* I think skeptically and with growing anger at the police, the FBI, at everyone who started working the scene without me.

Below the darkest area on the whitewashed wall is a corresponding dark area on the whitewashed floor, a myriad of drips that combine into a solid stain, what I can tell was a pool of blood that is almost black and flaking, much of it having soaked into the porous whitewashed stone. Some of the drops at the edge of the large stained area are perfectly round, with only a small amount of distortion or scalloping around the edges from the roughness of the stone, passive spatters from the victim bleeding. Other stains are smeared from someone, possibly the assailant, stepping on them or dragging something over them while they were still wet. Maybe dragging carpet and plyboards over them, I think. The only bloodstains that show a direction of travel are those on the wall and the ceiling, black and elongated or with a teardrop shape, and I believe most of these were projected by the repeated swings and impacts of the weapon.

The victim was upright when he bled, shackled to the wall, it would seem, and what I can't tell is the timing of at least one blow that I know was fatal. Did it happen early on or later? *The earlier, the better,* I can't help but think as I imagine what was done, as I reconstruct the pain and suffering and most of all his terror.

I hope he hadn't been subjected to the abuse for long when an artery was breached, most likely the carotid on the left side of his neck. The distinctive wave pattern on the wall is from arterial blood spurting out under high pressure in rhythm to the beats of his heart, and I remember photographs I saw, the deep gashes to his neck.

Wally Jamison would have lived only minutes after receiving such an injury, and I wonder how long the cutting and beating went on after it was too late to hurt him anymore. I wonder about the rage and what the connection might have been between Wally Jamison and Jack Fielding. It had to be more than that they simply went to the same gym. Wally wasn't involved in martial arts, and as far as anyone knows, he wasn't acquainted with Johnny Donahue or Eli Goldman or Mark Bishop. He didn't work or intern at Otwahl, either, and apparently had nothing to do with robotics or other technologies. What I know about Wally Jamison is that he was from Florida, a senior at BC, where he was majoring in history and somewhat of a celebrity because of football, and a partier, a ladies' man. I can't come up with a single reason why Fielding might have known him, unless it was some chance encounter they had, perhaps because of the gym and then perhaps drugs, the hormonal cocktail Benton mentioned.

Wally Jamison's toxicology was negative for illegal or therapeutic drugs or alcohol, but we don't routinely test for steroids unless we have reason to suspect a death may be related to them. Wally's cause of death wasn't a question. There certainly was no reason to think steroids killed him, at least not directly, and now it may be too late to go back. We're not going to get another sample of his urine, although we can try testing his hair, where the molecules of drugs, including steroids, might have accumulated inside the hair shaft. A test like that would be a long shot for detecting steroids, and it isn't going to tell us if Wally got them from Fielding or knew Fielding or was murdered by him. But I'm willing to try anything, because as I look around this cellar and see the shape of Fielding's body under a sheet on the floor, I want to know why. I have to know and won't accept that he was crazy, that he'd lost his mind. That's just not good enough.

Returning to the Pelican case near the stairs, I find a pair of knee pads and put them on before kneeling by the rounded blue sheet, and when I pull it back from Jack Fielding's face, I'm not prepared for how present he looks. That's the word that comes to mind, *present,* as if he's still here, as if he's asleep but not well. There is nothing vital or vibrant about him, and my brain races through the details I'm seeing, the stiff strands of hair from the gel he used to hide his baldness, the red splotches on his face, which is puffy and pale, and I pull the sheet off, and it rustles as I move it out of my way. I sit back on the heels of my rubber boots and look him over, taking in his gelled sandy-brown hair that was thinning on top and gone in spots, and the dried blood around his ear and pooled under his head.

I imagine Fielding pointing the barrel of the Glock inside his left ear and pulling the trigger. I try to get into his mind, try to conjure up his last thoughts. Why would he do that? Why his ear? The side of the head is common in gunshot suicides, but not the ear, and why his left side and not his right? Fielding was right-handed. I used to tease him about having what I called "extreme handedness" because he couldn't do anything useful with his left hand, nothing that required any degree of dexterity or skill. He certainly didn't shoot himself in his left ear while holding the pistol in his right hand, not unless he'd become a contortionist in my absence, and maybe that will be one more speculation everyone will come up with. But I need to check the angle. I point my right finger into my left ear canal as best I can, pretending my index finger is the barrel of the Glock.

"Things really aren't that bad," a deep voice says. "It hasn't come to that, has it?" General John Briggs says.

I look up at him standing over me, his legs spread, his hands behind his back, big and bulky in bright yellow, but he's not wearing a face shield or gloves or a hard hat, his face ruggedly compelling, hawklike, it's been described as, and shadowed with stubble. He's a dark man, and no matter how often he shaves, he always looks as if he needs to, his eyes the same dark gray as the titanium veneer on my building, his black hair thick with very little gray for his age, which is exactly sixty.

"Colonel," he then says, and he squats next to me and picks up the flashlight I was using earlier and had left upright on the stone floor. "I imagine you're wondering the same thing I am." He turns on the light.

"I seriously doubt it," I reply as he shines the light inside Fielding's left ear.

"I'm wondering where he was," Briggs says. "Looking for high-velocity spatter, something to indicate if he was right here? Because why? Was he standing by his cryogenic freezer and just stuck a gun in his ear?"

I take the light from him so I can direct it where I want as I look inside Fielding's ear, and mostly what I see is dark dried blood that is crusty, but as I lean closer I can make out the small black entrance wound, a contact wound, and that is elongated. It is angled. A large amount of blood is under his head, a dried pool of it that is thick and looks sticky because the cellar is moist, and I smell blood that is beginning to break down, the sweetish foul odor that is faint, and I detect alcohol. It wouldn't surprise me if Fielding was drinking in the end. Whether he shot himself or someone else did, he probably was compromised, and I remember the big SUV with the xenon lights that tailed Benton and me some sixteen hours ago while we were driving through a blizzard to the CFC. The current assumption is that Fielding was in that SUV, that it was his Navigator and he'd removed the front plate so we couldn't tell who was behind us.

Nobody has satisfactorily offered why he might have decided to tail Benton and me or how he managed to disappear instantly, seemingly into thin air, after Benton stopped in the middle of the snowy road in hopes whoever was on our bumper would pass us. I seem to be the only one consumed by the fact that Otwahl Technologies is very close to the area where the big SUV with xenon lights and fog lamps vanished, and if someone had a gate opener or code to that place or was familiar to the private police, that person could have tucked the Navigator in there, rather much like vanishing in the Bat Cave, is how I described it to Benton, who didn't seem impressed. *"Why would Jack Fielding have that kind of access to Otwahl?"* I asked Benton as we were driving here. *"Even if he was involved with some of the people who work there, would he have access to its parking lot? Could he have pulled in so quickly and been confident the private police who patrol the grounds would have been fine with it?"*

"With all the white-painted surfaces in here," Briggs is saying to me, "you'd think we could find something that might indicate where the shooting occurred."

I look at Fielding's hands. They are as cold as the stone in the cellar, and he is completely rigorous. As muscle-bound as he is, it is like moving the arms of a marble statue as I shine the flashlight on his thick, strong hands, examining them, noting his clean, trimmed nails and surprised by them. I expected them to be dirty, as crazy and out of control as everyone believes he was. I notice his calluses, which he's always had from using free weights in the gym or working on his cars or doing home repairs. It appears he died holding the pistol in his left hand, or it is supposed to look like he did, his fingers curled tightly and the impression in his palm made by the Glock's nonslip stippled grip. But I don't notice a fine mist of blood that might have blown back on his skin when he pulled the trigger. Back spatter is an artifact that can't be staged or faked.

"We'll do GSR on his hands," I comment, and I notice that Fielding isn't wearing his wedding band. The last time I saw him, he had it on, but that was in August, and he was still living with his family, from what I understand.

"The muzzle of the gun had blood," Briggs tells me. "Internal muzzle staining from blood being sucked in."

The phenomenon is caused by explosive gases when the barrel of a gun is pressed against the skin and fired.

"The ejected cartridge case?" I inquire.

"Over there." He indicates an area of the whitewashed floor about five feet from Fielding's right knee.

"And the gun? In what position?" I slide my hands under Fielding's head and feel the hard lump of jagged metal under the scalp above his right ear, where the bullet exited his skull and is trapped under his skin.

"Still gripped in his left hand. I'm sure you noticed the way his fingers are curled and the impression of the grip in his palm. We had to pry the gun out of his hand."

"I see. So he shot himself with his left hand even though he's right-handed. Not impossible but unusual, and he either was already lying right here on the floor when he did it or fell with the gun still gripped in his hand. A cadaveric spasm and he clenched it hard. And fell neatly on his back just like this. Well, that's quite a thing to imagine. You know me and cadaveric spasms, John."

"They do happen."

"Like winning the lottery," I answer. "That happens, too. Just never to me."

I feel fractured bone shift beneath my fingers as I gently palpate Fielding's head and envision a wound path that is upward and slightly back-to-front, the bullet lodging approximately three inches from the lower angle of his right jaw.

"He shot himself like this?" I turn my left hand into a gun again, and point my purple nitrile–gloved index finger at an awkward angle, as if I'm going to shoot myself in the left ear. "Even if he held the pistol in his left hand when he wasn't left-handed, it's slightly awkward and unusual, the way my elbow has to be down and behind me, don't you think? And I might expect a fine mist of back spatter on his hand. Of course, these things aren't set in stone," I say inside Fielding's white-painted stone cellar.

"Odd thing about shooting yourself in the ear," I comment, "is people generally are squeamish because of the anticipated noise, not rational, because you're about to die anyway, but it's human nature. Like shooting yourself in the eye. Almost nobody does."

"You and I need to talk, Kay," Briggs says.

"And most of all, the timing of when the cryogenic freezer was gone into," I then say. "And the space heater turned on and what was burned upstairs, possibly Erica Donahue's stationery. If Jack did all that before he killed himself, then why is there no semen or broken glass on the floor under him?" I am manipulating Fielding's big body, and he is deadweight, completely stiff and unwilling as I move him a little, looking under him at a floor that is white and clean. "If he came down here and broke all these test tubes and then shot himself in the ear, there should be glass and semen under his body. It's all around him but none under him. There's a shard of glass in his hair." I pick it out and look at it. "Someone broke all this after he was dead, after he was already lying here on the floor."

"He could have gotten glass in his hair when he broke test tubes, violently smashed everything," Briggs says, and he sounds patient and kind, for him. He almost seems to feel sorry for me. My insecurities again.

"Do you have your mind made up, John? You and everyone else?" I look up into his compelling face.

"You know damn better than that," he says. "We have a lot to talk about, and I'd rather not do it here in front of the others. When you're ready, I'll be next door."

The power came back on in Salem Neck at about half past two, about the time I was finishing with Jack Fielding, kneeling next to him on that cold stone floor until my feet started tingling and my knees were aching and burning, despite the pads I had on.

The flush-mounted lights in his old outdated kitchen are illuminated, the house quite chilly but with the promise of warmth in the forced air I feel coming out of floor vents as I walk around in my tactical boots and field clothes and jacket, having taken off my protective gear except for disposable gloves. The white porcelain sink is filled with dishes, and the water is scummy with soap, a coagulated slick of yellowish grease floating on it, and the sheer yellow curtain covering the window over the sink is stained and dingy.

Wherever I look I find remnants of food and garbage and hard drinking and am reminded of the squalor of countless scenes I've worked, of their rot and spoilage, their musty, mildewy smells, of how often it is that the life preceding the death was the real crime. Fielding's last months on earth were far more tortured than he deserved, and I can't accept that he wanted anything he made for himself. This is not what he scripted for his ultimate destiny, it's not what he was born to, and I continue thinking of that favorite phrase of his when he would remind me he wasn't *born to* this or *born to* that, especially if I asked him to do something he found distasteful or boring.

I pause by a wooden table with two wooden chairs beneath a window that faces the icy street and the choppy dark-blue water beyond it, and the table is deep in old newspapers and magazines that I spread around with my gloved hand. The *Wall Street Journal*, the *Boston Globe*, the *Salem News*, as recent as Saturday, I note, and I recall seeing several papers covered with ice on the sidewalk in front, as if they were tossed there and no one brought them inside the house before the big storm. There are about half a dozen *Men's Health* magazines, and I notice the mailing labels are for Fielding's Concord address. The January and February issues were forwarded here, as was a lot of other mail in the pile I sift through. I recall that Fielding's rental of the house in Concord began almost a year ago, and based on the clutter and furniture I recognize as his and what I've been told about his domestic problems, it would make sense that he didn't renew the lease. He relocated to a drafty antique house that is completely lacking in charm because of the run-down condition it's in, and while I can imagine what he envisioned when he fell in love with the place, something changed for him.

What happened to you? I look around at the squalor he's left in his wake. *Who were you in the end?* I envision his dead hands and remember their coldness and their rigor and how heavy they felt as I held them. They were clean, his nails well kempt, and that very small detail doesn't seem to fit with everything else I'm seeing. *Did you make this appalling mess? Or did someone else? Has some other person who is slovenly and crazed been inside your house?* But I also know that consistency really is the hobgoblin of little minds, that what Ralph Waldo Emerson wrote is true. People aren't easily explained or defined, and what they do isn't always consistent. Fielding may very well have been falling apart along with everything around him but was still vain enough to have good hygiene. It could be true.

But I'm not going to know. His CT scan, his autopsy won't tell me. There's so much I won't know, including why he never told me about his place in Salem. Benton says that Fielding purchased the house right after he moved to Massachusetts, which was a year ago this past January, but he never mentioned it to me. I'm not sure he was hiding anything criminal he was up to or intended to be up to, but rather I have a feeling he wanted something that was just his, something that didn't concern me and that I had no opinion about and wasn't going to improve or change or help him with. He didn't want my mentoring him as he set about to turn an eighteenth-century sea captain's safe harbor into his own or into an investment or whatever he originally dreamed of having all to himself.

If that's the truth, then how sad, I think as I look out at water sparkling like sapphires, rolling and crashing against the gray, rocky shore across the icy, sandy street. I walk through a wide opening that once had pocket doors, into a dining room of exposed dark oak beams in a white plaster ceiling that is water-stained, noting that the tarnished brass hanging onion lantern belongs in an entryway, not over the walnut table, which is dusty and surrounded by chairs that don't match and need new upholstery. I don't blame Fielding for not wanting me here. I'm too critical, too sure of my goddamn good taste and informed opinions, and it's no wonder I drove him to distraction. Not just an enabler but also a bad mother when I had no right to even be a good one. It wasn't my place to be anything to him except a responsible boss, and if he were here I would tell him I'm sorry. I would ask him to forgive me for knowing him and caring, because what help was it? What damn good did I do?

I focus on a disturbed area of dust at one end of the table, where someone was eating or working, perhaps where the Olivetti typewriter was, and the chair in front of it is in better shape than the others. Its faded, threadbare red-velvet cushion is intact and probably safe to sit on, and I think about Fielding in here typing. I try to place him at this table with its old casement windows, the view in here a dreary one of the gravel drive, and it's impossible for me to envision him hunched over in a small chair beneath a hanging lantern, typing a two-page letter over and over on engraved watermarked paper until he had a final version that was flawless.

Fielding and his big, impatient fingers, and he was never much of a typist, was self-taught, what he called "hunt and pick" instead of hunt and peck, and the point of that document supposedly from Erica Donahue is illogical if it came from him. Considering the condition Fielding was in, based on what Benton saw when he met with him last week in my office, it doesn't seem plausible to me that my deputy chief would have gone to such lengths to set up and frame a Harvard student for Mark Bishop's homicide. Why would Fielding have killed that six-year-old boy? I don't buy what Benton says, that Fielding was killing himself as a child when he drove nails into Mark Bishop's head. Fielding was putting an end to his own childhood of abuse, Benton told me, and I'm not persuaded.

But I have to remind myself that there are many things in life that make sense to the people who are doing them while the rest of us never figure it out. Even when we're told why, the explanation often doesn't fit with any template that has rhyme or reason. I pause before a casement window, not quite ready to leave this room and enter the next one, where I can hear Briggs walking around in his desert boots. He is talking to someone on his phone, and I pull out mine to check my text messages and see that there is one from Bryce.

Can U call Evelyn!?

I try her in the trace evidence lab and another microscopist answers, a young scientist named Matthew.

"You anywhere near a computer?" Matthew's voice, confident and tense with excitement. "Evelyn's just down the hall in the ladies' room, but we want to send you something totally weird, and I keep thinking it's a mistake or like the weirdest contamination ever. You know a hair is about eighty thousand nanometers, right? So imagine something four nanometers, in other words, a hair would be twenty thousand times the diameter of what we found. And it's not organic, even though the elemental fingerprint is mostly pure carbon, but we've also detected trace residues of what appears to be phencyclidine. . . ."

"You found PCP?" I interrupt his breathless talk.

"PCP, angel dust, a really trace amount, just a minuscule amount. Using FTIR. At a magnification of one hundred, just plain ol' light microscopy, and you can see the granules and a lot of other microscopic debris, especially cotton fibers, on the backing of the pain-relieving patch, okay? Probably some of these granular structures are PCP, maybe Nuprin, Motrin, too, whatever the patch originally was, possibly other chemicals there."

"Matthew, slow down."

"Well, at one hundred and fifty thousand X with SEM you'll see what I'm talking about as big as a bread box, Dr. Scarpetta, what we want to send you."

"Go ahead, and if nothing else, I'll go out to the truck and log in. Send PDFs, though, and I'll try on my iPhone. What are you talking about, exactly?"

"Sort of like buckyballs, like a dumbbell made out of buckyballs but with legs. It's definitely man-made, about the size of a strand of DNA, like I said, four nanometers and pure carbon, except for whatever it was meant to deliver. And also traces of polyethylene glycol that we're conjecturing was the outer coating for what was meant to be delivered."

"Explain the *meant-to-deliver* part. Something built on nanoscale to deliver a trace amount of PCP or what?"

"This isn't my area, obviously, and we don't have an AFM, an atomic force microscope, here, hint, hint. Because I'd say we've just entered a new day where we have to start looking for things like this, things you might need to magnify millions of times. And in my opinion, something like an AFM would have to have been used to assemble this, do the nanoassembly, to manipulate the nanotubes, the nanoparticles, while you're trying to get them to stick together, using a nanoprobe or whatever. Well, we could probably handle a lot of this with SEM, but an AFM would be a good idea if this is what's headed down the pike and about to slam into us head-on, Dr. Scarpetta."

"You don't know what you've found, but it's a nanobot of some type, possibly, in your opinion, for the delivery of a drug or drugs? You found one on the film backing that was in the lab coat pocket?" I don't say whose lab coat.

"Just one admixed with the particulate and fibers and other debris because we didn't analyze the entire piece of film, just the specimen we mounted on a stub. The rest of the plastic film's at fingerprints right now, and then it's going to DNA, then to GC-Mass-Spec," Matthew says. "And it's broken or degraded."

"What is?"

"The nanobot. Or it looks broken, or maybe it's deteriorating, like it was supposed to have eight legs but I'm seeing four on one side and two on the other. I'm e-mailing this to you now, a couple photographs we took so you can see it for yourself."

I'm able to pull up the images on my iPhone, and it is an in-explicable feeling to note the eerie symmetry, to have it enter my mind that the nanobot looks like a molecular version of a micro-mechanical fly. I can't know if Lucy's holy grail of flybots looks like this nanobot magnified thousands of times, but the artificial structure in the photographs is insectlike with its grayish, bucky-ball elongated body. The delicate nanowire arms or legs that are still intact are bent at right angles with gripperlike appendages on the tips, possibly for grabbing onto the walls of cells or burrowing into blood vessels or organs, to find the target, in other words, and adhere to it while delivering medicine or perhaps illegal drugs destined for certain brain receptors.

No wonder Johnny Donahue's drug screen was negative, it occurs to me. If nanobots were added to his sublingual allergy extracts or, better yet, to his corticosteroid nasal spray, the drugs might have been below the level of detection. More astonishingly, the drugs may not have penetrated the blood-brain barrier at all, but would have been programmed to bind to receptors in the frontal cortex. If the drugs never entered the bloodstream, they wouldn't have been excreted in urine. They wouldn't have ended up in hair, and that's the point of nanotechnology's use in medicine, to treat diseases and disorders with drugs that aren't systemic and therefore are less harmful. As is true with everything else, whatever can be used for good most assuredly will be used for evil.

Fielding's living room is bare floors and walls, and stacked almost to the ceiling are dusty brown boxes, all the same size, with the moving company Gentle Giant's logo on the sides, scores of cartons in cubed piles as if they've never been touched since they were carried in here.

In the midst of this cardboard bunker Briggs sits, reminding me of a Matthew Brady photograph of a Civil War general, in his muted sandy-green fatigues and boots, a Mac notebook in his lap, his broad-shouldered back straight against the straight-back chair. I decide it would be like him to sit and make me stand, to choreograph our conversation so I feel small and subservient to him, but he gets up, and I tell him no, thank you, I'll stand. So both of us do, moving to a window, where he places his laptop on a sill.

"I find it interesting he has a wireless network in here," Briggs says right off, looking out at the view of the ocean and the rocks across the icy street that is covered with tan sand. "With all you've seen in here, would you expect him to have wireless?"

"Maybe he wasn't the only person in here."

"Maybe."

"At least you'll entertain the possibility. That's more than anybody else seems to be doing." I place my iPhone on the windowsill so he can see what is in the small display, and he looks at it, and then he looks away.

"Imagine two types of nanobots," he says, as if he's talking to someone on the other side of the wavy old window, as if his attention is out there on the sunlight and sparkling water and not on the woman standing next to him, a woman who always feels young and insecure with him, no matter her age or who she grew up to become.

"A nanobot that is biodegradable," he says, "that vanishes at some point after delivering a minute dose of a psychoactive drug, and then a second type of nanobot that self-replicates."

I always feel like someone else with Briggs, someone other than myself, and as I stand next to him, our sleeves touching and feeling his heat, I think of the wonderful and the terrible ways he has shaped me.

"The self-replicating one is what worries us most. Imagine if you got something like that inside you," he says, and what's inside me is the irresistible force that is General John Briggs, and I understand what Fielding felt and how much he must have revered and resented me.

I understand how awful and wonderful it is to be overwhelmed by someone. Like a drug, it occurs to me. An addiction you desperately want to get over and desperately want to keep. Briggs will always have the same effect on me, I think. I won't get over it in this life.

"And the self-replicating nanobot enables the sustained release of something like testosterone," Briggs says, and I feel his energy, the intensity of him, and I'm aware of how close we are standing to each other, drawn to each other, just as we've always been and should never have been. "A drug like PCP couldn't replicate, of course, so that would be a dead-end hit, would be repeated only as the subject repeats his or her nasal spray or injections or applies a new transdermal patch impregnated with biodegradable nanobots. But something your body naturally produces could be programmed to replicate, so the nanobot is replicating, flowing freely through the body, through your arteries, latching onto target areas, like the frontal cortex of your brain, without the need of a battery. Self-propelled and replicating."

Briggs looks at me, and his eyes are hard but there is something in them that he's always held for me, an attachment that is as constant as it is conflicted. I'm vividly reminded of who we were at Walter Reed, when our futures held mystery and limitless possibility, when he was older and profoundly formidable to me and I was a prodigy. He called me Major Prodigy, and then I returned from South Africa and went to Richmond and he didn't call me at all, not for years. What we had with each other was complex and unfathomable, and I'm reminded all over again when I'm with him.

"We wouldn't need wars anymore," he says. "Not the sort of wars you and I know, Kay. We're on the threshold of a new world where our old wars will seem easy and humane."

"Jack Fielding wasn't that kind of scientist," I reply. "He didn't manufacture those patches and probably would have been extremely resistant and unnerved had someone attempted to entice him into using drugs delivered by nanobots. I would be stunned if he even knew what a nanobot is or would have a clue this was what he was letting loose in his system. He probably thought he was taking some new form of steroid, a designer steroid, something that would help him in his bodybuilding, help alleviate his chronic pain from decades of overuse, help him fight aging. He hated getting older. Getting old wasn't an option to him."

"Well, he won't have to worry about it."

No, he won't, that's for sure. What I say is, "I don't accept that he killed himself because he didn't want to get old. I haven't accepted he killed himself, and have extreme doubts about it."

"I understand you got an exposure to one of his patches," Briggs then says, "and I'm sorry about that, but if you hadn't, you wouldn't know the rest of it. Kay Scarpetta high. Now, that's quite a thought. I'm sorry I wasn't there to see that."

Benton must have told him.

"This is what we're up against, Kay," Briggs says. "Our brave new world, what I call neuroterrorism, what the Pentagon is calling it, the big fear. Make us crazy and you win. Make us crazy enough and we'll kill ourselves, saving the bad guys the trouble. In Afghanistan, give our troops opium, give them benzodiazepines, give them hallucinogenics, something to take the edge off their boredom, and then see what happens when they climb into their choppers and fighter jets and tanks and Humvees. See what happens when they come home addicts, come home deranged."

"Otwahl," I comment. "We're developing weapons like this?"

"*We* aren't. That's not what DARPA's paying all these millions for, dammit. But someone at Otwahl is, and we don't think it's just one. A cell of superbrains engaging in experiments not authorized or approved, and in fact as dangerous as it gets."

"I assume you know who."

"Damn kids," he says, gazing out at the bright afternoon. "Seventeen, eighteen, with IQs off the charts and full of passion but nothing home up here." He taps his forehead. "I don't need to tell you about boys especially, their frontal lobes not done, like a halfbaked cookie until they're in their early to mid-twenties, and yet there they are, fucking around in nanotech labs or with superconductors and robotics and synthetic biology, you name it. Difficult enough we give them guns and throw them into stealth bombers, but we have rules," he says in a hard tone. "We have structures, regimens, leadership, the strictest of supervision, but what the hell do you think goes on at a place like Otwahl where the objective isn't national security and discipline but money and ambition? Those damn whiz kids like Johnny Donahue and his gang over there don't know shit about Afghanistan or Pakistan or Iraq, for Christ's sake. They've never set foot on a military base."

"I don't see Jack's connection to it beyond his teaching martial arts to a few of them." The sky is a spotless deep turquoise, and below it, the blue ocean heaves.

"He got tangled up with them, and my guess is unwittingly became a science project. You know all too well what goes on with research projects and clinical trials, only the type we're familiar with are supervised and strictly monitored by human-study review boards. So where do you get volunteers if you're an eighteen-year-old Harvard or MIT technical engineer at Otwahl? We can only guess that Jack made his contacts likely through the gym, through tae kwon do. All of us are painfully aware of his lifelong problems with substance abuse, mainly steroids, so now someone is going to deliver the elixir of life, the fountain of youth, through pain-relieving patches. But he sure as hell didn't get what he bargained for. Neither did Wally Jamison, Mark Bishop, or Eli Goldman."

"Wally Jamison didn't work at Otwahl."

"For a while he dated someone who does. Dawn Kincaid, another one of the neuroterrorists over there."

"Johnny Donahue's best friend," I say. "And where is she right now?" I ask. "It seems everyone you've mentioned is dead. Except her." I feel an alarm going off inside me.

"Missing in action," Briggs says. "Didn't show up at Otwahl yesterday or today, supposedly is on vacation."

"I'm sure."

"Exactly. We'll find her and get the rest of the story, because no question she's going to be the one to tell it, since her expertise is nanoengineering, nanoscale chemical synthesis. Based on what we've learned, she's likely the one developing these nasty little nanobots that found their way to Jack Fielding and turned him into a Mr. Hyde, to put it mildly."

"Mr. Hyde," I repeat. "The same thing Erica Donahue says happened to her son," I point out. "Only I doubt Johnny killed anyone."

"He didn't kill that boy."

"You're convinced Jack did."

"Out of control, sloppy," Briggs says.

"And then he killed Eli." My comment hangs in the air, and I wonder if it sounds as hollow to Briggs as it does to me. I wonder if he can hear how strongly I don't believe it.

"You realize this is because of the damn swine flu." He continues staring out at the day blazing beyond dusty old glass. "If the stepdaughter's biological father hadn't gotten sick, Liam Saltz wouldn't have had the pleasure of giving her away at her wedding, and he wouldn't have come to the U.S., to Cambridge, to Norton's Woods, at the last minute. And Jack wouldn't have had to stab Eli in the back with a damn injection knife."

"To stop him from telling Dr. Saltz what you're telling me."

"We can't ask Jack, unfortunately."

"Maybe I could understand it if Eli was going to tell Dr. Saltz or someone that Jack was selling semen he was stealing from dead bodies. Maybe that would be a motive."

"We don't know what Eli knew. But he likely was aware of Jack and his drugs, obviously was well enough acquainted with him to have one of his guns. That must have been a bad feeling when Jack found out from the Cambridge police that the dead man had a Glock on him with an eradicated serial number."

"Sounds like Marino's filled you in. Told you all this as if it's an irrefutable case history. And it's not. It's a theory. We don't have tangible evidence that Jack killed anyone."

"He knew he was in trouble. That much I think is safe to say," Briggs replies.

"As much as anything is safe to say. I agree he wouldn't have removed the Glock from the lab had he not feared he had a problem. My question is whether he was covering for himself or for someone else."

"He knew damn well we'd restore the serial number, that we'd trace the pistol to him."

"'We,'" I reply. "I've been hearing that word a lot of late."

"I know how you feel about it." Briggs plants his hands on the windowsill and leans forward, as if his lower back aches. "You think I'm trying to take something away from you. You believe it." He smiles grimly. "Captain Avallone came here last fall."

"Someone that junior? So it wouldn't raise suspicions?"

"Exactly, to appear casual, an informal drop-in while she was on her way somewhere else. When the fact is we were hearing things we didn't like about how your second in command was running the CFC. And I don't need to tell you we have a vested interest. The AFME does, DoD does, a lot of people do. It isn't yours to ruin."

"It isn't mine at all," I answer. "Obviously, I did a terrible job before I even started—"

"You haven't done a terrible job," he cuts me off. "I'm just as much to blame. You picked Jack or, better put, gave in to his wish to come back, and I didn't get in your way, and I sure as hell should have. I didn't want to step on you, and I should have stepped all over you about that decision you made. I figured in four months you'd be home, and I honestly didn't imagine the havoc that man could cause in such a short period of time, but he was mixed up with the Otwahl Technologies Rat Pack, doing drugs and losing it."

"Is that why you delayed my leaving Dover? So you could find time to replace the leadership at the CFC? Find time to replace me?" I say it as bravely as I can.

"The opposite. To keep you out of it. I didn't want you tarred by it. I delayed you as many times as I could without an out-and-out abduction, and then the father of the bride in London gets the damn swine flu, and a dead body starts bleeding. And your niece shows up in her chopper at Dover, and I tried to get you to stay by offering to transport the body to Dover, but you wouldn't, and that was the end of it. And here we are again."

"Yes, again."

"We've been in our messes before. And we probably will again."

"You didn't send Lucy to pick me up."

"I did not. And I don't think she's likely to take orders from me. Thank God she never thought about enlisting. Would end up in Leavenworth."

"You didn't ask her to bug my office."

"A suggestion made in passing so we could know exactly what Jack was doing."

"Your making a suggestion in passing is like a cannibal off-handedly inviting someone to dinner," I reply.

"Quite an analogy."

"People pay attention to your suggestions, and you know it."

"Lucy pays attention if it suits her."

"What about Captain Avallone? Did she conspire with Jack, conspire against me?"

"Never. I told you why she showed up last November for her tour. She's quite loyal to you."

"So loyal that she told Jack about Cape Town." I surprise myself by saying it out loud.

"That never happened. Sophia knows nothing about Cape Town."

"Then how did Julia Gabriel know?"

"When she was yelling at you? I see," he says, as if I've just answered a question I didn't know he'd asked. "I stopped outside your door to have a word with you and could hear you talking on the phone, could hear you were somewhat intensely involved. She talked to me, too. Talked to a number of people after getting word on the grapevine that we routinely extract semen at Dover, that every medical examiner's office does this routinely, which is utter bullshit. We would never do such a thing unless it was absolutely proper and approved. She got this impression because Jack was covertly doing that at the CFC and had done so in the case of the man who got killed in a Boston taxicab on his wedding day. Someone connected to Mrs. Gabriel's son. And I think you can understand how she got the idea that her son Peter should get the same special treatment."

"She knows nothing about me personally. She didn't mean it personally. You're sure."

"Why would you believe these negative things about you personally?" he says.

"I think you know why, John."

"No damn way she was referring to anything specific. She's an angry, militant woman and was just venting when she called you the same names she called me, called several other people at Dover. Bigots. Racists. Nazis. Fascists. A lot of staff got christened a lot of ugly names that morning."

Briggs steps back away from the window and collects his laptop off the sill, his way of saying he has to go. He can't have a conversation that lasts more than twenty minutes, and in fact the one we just had is lengthy for him and has tried his patience and gotten too close to too many things.

"One favor you could do for me that would be greatly appreciated," he says. "Please stop telling people I thought MORT was the best thing since sliced bread."

Benton, I think. I guess the two of them have gotten quite cozy.

"Not so, but I understand your remembering it that way, and I'm sorry we butted heads about it," Briggs goes on. "However, given a choice of a robot dragging a dead body off the battlefield and a living person risking his life and limb to do it? That's what I call a Sophie's choice. No good choice, only two bad ones. You weren't right, and I wasn't, either."

"Then we'll leave it at that," I answer. "Both of us made bad decisions."

"It's not like we hadn't made them before," he mutters.

He walks with me out of the sea captain's house, passing through rooms I've already been in. Every space seems empty and depressing, as if there never was anybody home. It doesn't feel that Fielding ever lived here, just parked himself as he worked demonically on his renovations and labored secretly in his cellar, and I just don't know what drove him. Maybe it was money. He'd always wanted money and was never going to get it in our trade, and that bothered him about me, too. I do better than most. I plan well, and Benton has his inheritance, and then there is Lucy, who is obscenely rich from computer technologies she's been selling since she was no older than the neuroterrorists Briggs just talked about. Thank God Lucy's inventions are legal, as best I know.

She's inside the CFC truck with Marino and Benton, and the yellow suits and hard hats are off, and everyone looks tired. Anne has driven off in the van again, making another delivery to the labs while more evidence waits for her here, white boxes filled with white paper evidence bags.

"There's a package for you in your car," Briggs says to me in front of the others. "The latest, greatest level four-A armor, specifically designed for females in theater, which would be fine if you ladies would bother with the plates."

"If the vest isn't comfortable," I start to say.

"I think it is, but I'm built a little different from you. Problem's going to be if it won't completely close on the sides. We've seen that too many times, and the projectile finds that one damn opening."

"I'll try it out for you," Lucy offers.

"Good," Marino says to her. "You put it on, and I'll start shooting, see if it works."

"Or trauma from blunt force, which is what most people seem to forget about," I tell Briggs. "The round doesn't penetrate the body armor, but if the blunt force from the impact goes as deep as forty-four millimeters, it's not survivable."

"I haven't been to the range in a while," Lucy chats with Marino. "Maybe we can borrow Watertown's. You been to their new one?"

"I bowl with their range master."

"Oh, yeah, your team of cretins. What's it called? Gutter Balls."

"Spare None. You should bowl with us sometime," Marino says to Briggs.

"Would it be acceptable to you, Colonel, if AFDIL sends in backup scientists to help out at the CFC, for God's sake?" Briggs is saying to me. "Since it seems we have an avalanche of evidence that just keeps coming."

"Any help would be greatly appreciated," I reply. "I'll work on the vest right away."

"Get some sleep first." Briggs says it like an order. "You look like hell."

assachusetts Veterinary Referral Hospital has twenty-four-hour emergency care, and although Sock doesn't seem to be in any distress as he snores curled up like a teacup dog, a Chihuahua or poodle that can fit in a purse, I need to find out what I can about him. It is almost dark, and Sock is in my lap, both of us in the backseat of the borrowed SUV, driving north on I-95.

Having identified the man who was murdered while walking Sock, I intend to bestow the same kindness toward the rescued race dog, because no one seems to know where he came from. Liam Saltz doesn't know and wasn't aware his stepson Eli had a greyhound, or any pet. The superintendent of the apartment building near Harvard Square told Marino that pets aren't allowed. By all accounts, when Eli rented his unit there last spring, he didn't have a dog.

"This doesn't really need to be done tonight," Benton says as we drive and I pet the greyhound's silky head and feel great pity for him. I'm careful about his ragged ears because he doesn't like them touched, and he has old scars on his pointed snout. He is quiet, like something mute. *If only you could talk,* I think.

"Dr. Kessel doesn't mind. We should just do it while we're out," I reply.

"I wasn't thinking about whether some vet minded or not."

"I know you weren't." As I stroke Sock and feel that I might want to keep him. "I'm trying to remember the name of the woman who is Jet Ranger's nanny."

"Let's not go there."

"Lucy's never home, either, and it works out just fine. I think it's Annette, or maybe Lanette. I'll ask Lucy if Annette or Lanette could stop by during the day, maybe first thing each morning. Pick up Sock and take him to Lucy's place so he and Jet Ranger can keep each other company. Then Annette or whatever her name is could bring Sock back to Cambridge at night. What would be so hard about that?"

"We'll find Sock a home when the time is right." Benton takes the Woburn exit, the sign illuminating an iridescent green as our headlights flash over it and he slows down on the ramp.

"You're going to have a lovely home," I tell Sock. "Secret Agent Wesley just said so. You heard him."

"The reason you can't have a dog is the same reason it's always been a bad idea," Benton's voice says from the dark front seat. "Your IQ drops about fifty points."

"It would be a negative number, then. Minus ten or something."

"Please don't start baby talk or gibberish or whatever it is you speak to animals."

"I'm trying to figure out where to stop for food for him."

"Why don't I drop you off and I'll run to a convenience store or market and pick up something," Benton then says.

"Nothing canned. I need to do some research first about brands, probably a small-batch food for seniors because he's not a spring chicken. Speaking of, let's do chicken breasts, white rice, whitefish like cod, maybe a healthy grain like quinoa. So I'm afraid you'll need a real grocery store. I think there's a Whole Foods somewhere around here."

Inside Mass Vet Referral, I'm shown along a long, bright corridor lined with examination rooms, and the technician who accompanies us is very kind to Sock, who is rather sluggish, I notice. He is light on his small feet, slowly ambling along the corridor as if he's never run a race in his life and couldn't possibly.

"I think he's scared," I say to the tech.

"They're lazy."

"Who would think that of a dog that can run forty miles an hour?" I comment.

"When they have to, but they don't want to. They'd rather sleep on the couch."

"Well, I don't want to tug him. And his tail's between his legs."

"Poor baby." The tech stops every other second to pet him.

I suspect Dr. Kessel alerted the staff of the greyhound's sad circumstances, and we've been shown nothing but consideration and compassion and quite a lot of attention, as if Sock is famous, and I sincerely hope he won't be. It wouldn't be helpful if news of him became public, becoming chatter on the Internet and voyeurism or the usual tasteless jokes that seem to crop up around me. Do I take Sock to the morgue? Is Sock being trained as a cadaver dog? What does Sock do when I come home smelling like dead bodies?

He doesn't have a fever, and his gums and teeth are healthy, his pulse and respiration are normal, and no sign of a heart murmur or dehydration, but I won't allow Dr. Kessel to draw blood or urine. We'll reserve a thorough checkup for another time, I suggest, because the dog doesn't need more trauma. "Let him get to know me before he associates me with pain and suffering," I suggest to Dr. Kessel, a thin man in scrubs who looks much too young to have finished veterinary school. Using a small scanner he calls a wand, he looks for a microchip that might have been implanted under the skin of Sock's bony back as the dog sits on the examination table and I pet him.

"Well, he's got one, a nice little RFID chip right where it ought to be over his shoulders," Dr. Kessel says as he looks at what appears in the wand's display. "So what we have is an ID number, and let me give the National Pet Registry a quick call and we'll find out who this guy belongs to."

Dr. Kessel makes the call and takes notes. Momentarily, he hands me a piece of paper with a phone number and the name Lost Sock.

"That's quite a name for a race dog, huh, boy?" the vet says to him. "Maybe he lived up to it and that's why he got put out to pasture. A seven-seven-zero area code. Any idea?"

"I don't know."

He goes to a computer on a countertop and types the area code into a search field and says, "Douglasville, Georgia. Probably a vet's office there. You want to call from here and see if it's open? You're a long way from home," he says to Lost Sock, and I already know I won't call him that.

"You won't be lost ever again," I tell him as we return to the car, because I don't want to make the phone call in front of an audience.

The woman who answers simply says hello, as if I've reached a home number, and I tell her I'm calling about a dog that has this phone number on a microchip.

"Then he's one of our rescues," she says, and she has a Southern drawl. "Probably from Birmingham. We get a lot of them retired from the racetrack there. What's his name?"

I tell her.

"Black and white, five years old."

"Yes. That's correct," I reply.

"Is he all right? Not hurt or anything? He hasn't been mistreated."

"Curled up in my lap. He's fine."

"A sweetheart, but they all are. The nice thing about him is he's cat- and small dog–tolerant and does fine with children as long as they don't yank or tug on his ears. If you hold on a minute, I'll pull him up on my computer and see what I can find out about where he's supposed to be and with whom. I remember a student took him but can't think of her name. Up north. He was wandering loose or what? And where are you calling from? I know he's been trained and socialized, went through the program with flying colors, so you have a really nice dog, and I'm sure his owner must be just beside herself looking for him."

"'Trained and socialized'?" I ask as I think about Sock being owned by a female student. "What program? Is your rescue group involved in a special program of some sort that takes greyhounds to retirement communities or hospitals, something like that?"

"Prisons," she says. "He was released from the racetrack last July and went through our nine-week program where inmates do the actual training. In his case, he went to the Georgia Prison for Women in Savannah."

I remember Benton telling me about the woman incarcerated in a prison located in Savannah, the therapist convicted of molesting Jack Fielding when he was a troubled boy and sent to live on a ranch near Atlanta.

"We got involved with them because they were already training bomb-sniffing dogs, and we thought why not see if they want to do something a little more warm and fuzzy," the woman says, and I put her on speakerphone and turn up the volume, "like taking one of these sweet babies. The inmate learns patience and responsibility, and what it feels like to be loved unconditionally, and the greyhound learns commands. Anyway, Lost Sock was trained by a female inmate at the Georgia Prison for Women who said she wanted him when she finally gets out, but I'm afraid that won't be for a while. He was then adopted by someone she recommended, the young woman in Massachusetts. Do you have something to write with?"

She gives me the name Dawn Kincaid and several phone numbers. The address is the one where we just were in Salem, Jack

Fielding's house. I seriously doubt Dawn Kincaid lived there all of the time, but she may have been there often. I doubt she was living with Eli Goldman all of the time, either, but it could be that he babysat her dog. Obviously, he knew her, both of them at Otwahl, and I remember that Briggs said Dawn Kincaid's area of expertise was chemical synthesis and nanoengineering. Anyone who is an expert in nanoengineering likely would consider it child's play to rig a pair of headphones with hidden micro audio and video recorders. She likely would have had easy access to Eli's headphones and portable satellite radio. She worked with him. Her dog was in his apartment, meaning she may have been a frequent visitor there. She may have stayed there. She might have a key.

Bryce is still at the CFC when I reach him, and I tell him I made a photocopy of Erica Donahue's letter before it was submitted to the labs, and to please find the file and read the phone numbers. I jot them down and ask what's going on with the DNA lab.

"Working around the clock," Bryce says. "I hope you're not coming back here tonight. Get some rest."

"Did Colonel Pruitt return to Dover, or is he at the labs?"

"I saw him a little while ago. He's here with General Briggs, and some of their people are coming from Dover. Well, they're your people, too, I guess. . . ."

"Get hold of Colonel Pruitt and ask him if per my directive the profiles from the typewriter are going into CODIS immediately, before everything else. Maybe they already have? He'll know what I mean. But what's really important is I want a familial search done, checking any profiles against Jack Fielding's exclusionary DNA, and a familial search done in CODIS that includes a comparison with the profile of an inmate at the Georgia Prison for Women in Savannah. Her name is Kathleen Lawler." I spell the name for him. "A repeat offender . . ."

"Where?"

"The women's prison near Savannah, Georgia. Her DNA should be in the CODIS database. . . ."

"What's that got to . . . ?"

"She and Jack had a child together, a girl. I want a familial search to see if we get a match with anything recovered. . . ."

"He what? He what with who?"

"And the latent prints on the plastic film . . ." I start to say.

"Okay. Now you're scrambling my brains. . . ."

"Bryce. Get unscrambled and be quiet, and you'd better be writing this down."

"I am, boss."

"I want the prints from the film compared to Fielding and to me, and I want DNA done ASAP on that, too. See who else might have touched the film. Maybe whoever made or altered the patch the film came from. And my guess is Otwahl might print its employees, have their prints on file over there. A place that security-minded. It's really important we know exactly who supplied those tampered-with patches. Colonel Pruitt and General Briggs will understand all this."

Next I get Erica Donahue on the phone as Benton drives through Cambridge, taking the same roads Eli did the last time he walked here with Sock on Sunday, on his way to meet his stepfather, to blow the whistle on Otwahl Technologies to a man who could do something about it.

"A welcome guest meaning how often?" I ask Mrs. Donahue after she tells me over speakerphone that Dawn Kincaid has been to the Donahues' home on Beacon Hill many times and is always a welcome guest. The Donahues adore her.

"For dinner or just dropping by, especially on the weekends. You know she came up the hard way, had to work for everything and has had so much misfortune, her mother killed in a car crash, and then her father dying tragically, I forget from what. Such a lovely girl, and she's always been so sweet to Johnny. They met when he started at Otwahl last spring, although she's older, in a Ph.D. program at MIT, transferred from Berkeley, I believe, and just incredibly bright and so attractive. How do you know her?"

"I'm afraid I don't. We've not met."

"Johnny's only friend, really. Certainly the closest one he's ever had. But not romantic, although I've hoped for it, but I don't think that will ever be. I believe she's seeing someone else at Otwahl, a scientist she's working with there."

"Do you know his name?"

"I'm sorry, I don't recall it if I ever knew. I think he's originally from Berkeley as well, and then ended up here because of MIT and Otwahl. A South African. I've heard Johnny rather rudely refer to the Afrikaans nerd Dawn dates, and some other names I won't repeat. And before that it was a dumb jock, according to my son, who's a bit jealous. . . ."

"A dumb jock?" I ask.

"A terribly rude thing to say about someone who died so tragically. But Johnny lacks tact. That's part of his unusualness."

"Do you know the name of the man who died?"

"I don't remember. That football player they found in the harbor."

"Did Johnny talk about that case with you?"

"You're not going to imply that my son had something to do with—"

I calmly reassure her I'm not implying anything of the sort, and I end the call as the SUV crunches through the frozen snow blanketing our Cambridge driveway. At the end of it, under the bare branches of a huge oak tree, is the carriage house, our remodeled garage, its double wooden doors illuminated in our headlights.

"You heard that for yourself," I say to Benton.

"It doesn't mean Jack didn't do it. It doesn't mean he didn't kill Wally Jamison or Mark Bishop or Eli Goldman," he says. "We need to be careful."

"Of course we need to be careful. We're always careful. None of this you already knew?"

"I can't tell you what a patient told me. But let's put it this way, what Mrs. Donahue just said is interesting, and I didn't say I'm convinced about Fielding. I'm saying we just need to be careful because we don't know certain things for a fact right now. But we will. I can promise you that. Everyone's looking for Dawn Kincaid. I'll pass this latest information along," Benton says, and what he's really saying is there's nothing we can do about it or nothing we should do about it, and he's right. We can't go out

like a two-party posse and track down Dawn Kincaid, who probably is a thousand miles from here by now.

Benton stops the SUV and points a remote at the garage. A
wooden door rolls up, and a light goes on inside, illuminating his
black Porsche convertible and three other empty spaces.

He tucks the SUV next to his sports car, and I slip the lead over
Sock's long, slender neck and help him out of my lap, then out of
the backseat and into the garage, which is very cold because of the
missing window in back. I walk Sock across the rubberized flooring and look through the gaping black square and at our snowy
backyard beyond it. It is very dark, but I can make out disturbed
snow, a lot of footprints, the neighborhood children again using
our property as a shortcut, and that's going to stop. We have a
dog, and I will get the backyard walled or fenced in. I will be the
mean, crabby neighbor who doesn't allow trespassing.

"What a joke," I comment to Benton as we walk out of the
detached garage and onto the slick, snowy driveway, the night
sharply cold and white and very still. "You decide to get an alarm
system for the garage. So we have one that doesn't work and anybody could climb right in. When are we getting a new window?"

We head to the back door, walking carefully over crusty
snow, which Sock clearly doesn't like, snatching his paws up as if
he's walking over hot coals and shivering. Dark trees rock in the
wind, the night sky scattered with stars, the moon small and
bone-white high above the roofs and treetops of Cambridge.

"It sucks," he says, shifting the bag of groceries to his other arm as he finds the door key. "I'll make sure to get them out here tomorrow. It's just I haven't been around and someone has to be home."

"How big a deal to get fencing in back for Sock? So we can let him out and not be afraid he'll run off."

"You told me he doesn't like to run." Benton unlocks the door of the glassed-in porch.

Beyond it are the dark shapes of trees in Norton's Woods. The timber building with its three-tiered metal roof hulks darkly against the night, no lights on inside. I feel sad as I look at the American Academy of Arts and Sciences headquarters and think of Liam Saltz and his slain stepson. I wonder if the maimed flybot is still out there somewhere, buried and frozen, no longer alive, as Lucy put it, because the sun can't find it. I have a funny feeling someone has it. Maybe the FBI, I decide. Maybe people from DARPA, from the Pentagon. Maybe Dawn Kincaid.

"I think we need boots for him," I say. "They make little booties for dogs, and he needs something like that so he doesn't cut his paws on the ice and frozen snow."

"Well, he won't go very far in this cold." Benton opens the door and the alarm begins to beep. "Trust me. You'll have a hard time making him go out in this weather. I hope he's housebroken."

"He needs a couple of coats. I'm surprised Eli or Dawn or whoever didn't have coats for him. Greyhounds need them up here. This really isn't the right part of the world for greyhounds, but it is what it is, Sock. You're going to be warm and well fed and fine."

Benton enters the code on the keypad and resets the alarm

the instant he's shut the door behind us, and Sock leans against my legs.

"You build a fire, and I'm making drinks," I tell Benton. "Then I'll cook chicken and rice or maybe switch to cod and quinoa but not right now. He's been eating chicken and rice all day, and I don't want him sick. What would you like? Or maybe I should ask what's in the house."

"Some of your pizza's still in the freezer."

I turn on lights, and the stained-glass windows in the stairwell are dark but will be gorgeous from the outside, backlit by lights inside the house. I imagine the French wildlife scenes brilliantly lit up when I take Sock out at night and how cheerful that will be. I imagine playing with him in the backyard in the spring and summer, when it's warm, and seeing the vibrant windows lit up at night and of how peaceful and civilized that will be. Living on the edge of Harvard and coming home from the office to my old dog, and I'll plant a rose garden in back, and I think how good that sounds.

"Nothing to eat for me right now," Benton says, taking off his coat. "First things first. A very strong drink, please."

He goes into the living room, and Sock's nails click against hardwood, then are silent on rugs as we pass from room to room and into the kitchen, where I feel him leaning against my legs as I open dark cherry cabinets above stainless-steel appliances. Wherever I move, he moves and presses against me, pushing against the back of my legs as I get out tumblers, then ice from the freezer, and then a bottle of our very best Scotch, a Glenmo-rangie single-malt aged twenty-five years that was a Christmas gift from Jaime Berger. My heart aches as I pour drinks and think of Lucy and Jaime breaking up and of people who are dead, and of what Fielding did to his life, and now he's dead. He'd been killing himself all along, and then someone finished it for him, stuck a Glock in his left ear and pulled the trigger, most likely when he was standing near the cryogenic freezer, where he stored ill-gotten semen before shipping it to wives, mothers, and lovers of men who died young.

Who would Fielding trust so much as to allow the person into his cellar, to share his illegal venture capitalism with, to let borrow his sea captain's house and probably everything he owned? I remember what his former boss told me, the chief in Chicago. He commented he was glad Jack was moving to Massachusetts to be near family, only he wasn't referring to Lucy, Marino, and me, not to any of us, not even to his current wife and their two kids. I have a feeling the chief meant someone I never knew existed before now, and if I weren't so selfish and egotistical, maybe the thought would have occurred to me sooner.

How typical of me to assume such importance in Fielding's life, and he wasn't thinking of me at all when he told his former chief what he did about family. Fielding probably meant the daughter from his first love, probably the first woman he ever had sex with, the therapist at the ranch near Atlanta who bore his daughter, and then gave her up just as Fielding was given up. A girl with genetic loading, as Benton put it, that would land her in prison if she didn't end up dead. And she moved here last year from Berkeley, and then Fielding moved back here from Chicago.

"Nineteen seventy-eight," I say as I walk into the dark, cozy living room of built-in bookcases and exposed old beams. The lights are out, and a fire crackles and glows on the brick hearth, and sparks swarm as Benton moves a log with the poker. "She would be about Lucy's age, about thirty-one." I hand him a tumbler of Scotch, a generous pour with only a few cubes of ice. The whisky looks coppery in the firelight. "Do you think it's her? That Dawn Kincaid is his biological daughter? Because I do. I hope you didn't already know about her."

"I promise I didn't. If it's true."

"You really weren't focused on Dawn Kincaid or a child Fielding had with the woman in prison."

"I really wasn't. You need to remember how recent this all has been, Kay." We settle next to each other on the sofa, and then Sock settles in my lap. "Fielding wasn't on anybody's radar until last week, at least not for anything criminal, nothing violent. But I should have gone to the trouble to find out about the baby adopted," Benton says, and he sounds slightly angry with himself. "I know I would have eventually, and I hadn't yet because it didn't seem important."

"In the grand scheme of things and at the time, it wasn't. I'm not trying to put you on the defensive."

"I knew from the records I reviewed that the baby, a girl, was given up for adoption while the mother was in prison the first time. An adoption agency in Atlanta," he says. "Maybe like some adopted children, she set about to find out who her biological parents were."

"As smart as she is, that probably wasn't hard."

"Christ." Benton takes a swallow of Scotch. "It's always the one thing you think doesn't matter, the one thing you think can wait."

"I know. That's almost always how it works out. The detail you don't want to bother with."

We sit on the sofa, looking at the fire, and Sock is curled up on top of me. He is attached to me. He won't let me out of his sight. He has to be touching me, as if he's certain I'll disappear and he'll be abandoned in a run-down house again where horrible things happen.

"I think there is a very good probability that's what the DNA is going to tell us about Dawn Kincaid," Benton continues in a flat tone. "I wish we could have known it before, but there wasn't a reason to look."

"You don't have to keep saying that. Why would you have looked? What would a baby he fathered when he was a teenager have to do with what's gone on?"

"Obviously, it might have."

"Twenty-twenty hindsight."

"I knew he was writing Kathleen Lawler, e-mailing her, but there's nothing criminal about that, nothing even suspicious, and no mention of anyone by the name of Dawn, just an *interest* they had in common. I recall that phrase, the interest they shared. I thought he fucking meant crime, maybe their old crime and how it changed who they were forever, that was the *interest* they had in common," he says ruefully, trying to figure it out as he talks. "Now I have to wonder if the interest they shared might be their child, might even be Dawn Kincaid. Just unfortunate that Jack never got past that part of his life, that he was still connected to

Kathleen Lawler, and probably she to him. And then a daughter who got his intelligence, his good parts and his bad parts. And the mother's good and really bad parts. And who the hell knows all the places that daughter's been bounced around to but never lived with her father, who I suspect she never knew while she was growing up. Of course, this is complete speculation on our part."

"Not really. It's like an autopsy. Most of the time it tells me what I already know."

"I'm afraid we might know. I'm afraid we really might, and it's a horror story, really. Talk about bad seed and the sins of the father."

"Some would say it was the sins of the mother in this case."

"I should make some phone calls," Benton says as he drinks and sits in front of the fire, staring into it.

He is angry with himself. He can't tolerate missing that one thing, as he calls it. In his mind, he should have made it a burning priority to track down a baby born to a woman in prison more than thirty years ago, and that really is unreasonable. Why would he think it mattered?

"Jack never mentioned Dawn Kincaid to me or a daughter who was given up for adoption, absolutely nothing like that. I had no idea." The whisky has heated me up, and I pet Sock, feeling the bumps of his ribs, like a washboard, and feeling the sadness that has settled inside me and won't go away. "I seriously doubt she ever lived with him until maybe very recently, don't see how. Not in Richmond, absolutely not. And it's unlikely his wives would have allowed a daughter from that early criminal liaison to be part of their lives, assuming they knew. He probably didn't tell them, except to allude to his difficulty with cases involving dead children. If he even said that much to the women in his life."

"He said it to you."

"I wasn't just a woman in his life. I was his boss."

"That's not all."

"Please not again, Benton. Really. It's getting to be ridiculous. I know you're in a mood and both of us are tired."

"It's the thought of you not being honest with me. I don't care what you did back then. I don't have a right to care about what you did before we were together."

"Well, you do care, and you have a right to care about anything you want. But how many times do I have to tell you?"

"I remember the first time we socialized."

"How dated that sounds, no pun intended. Like two people on a Sunday night in the fifties." I reach for his hand.

"Nineteen eighty-eight, that Italian place in the Fan. Remember Joe's?"

"Every time I was out with the cops, that's where we'd end up. Nothing like a big plate of baked spaghetti after a homicide scene."

"You hadn't been the chief long." Benton talks to the fire, and he strokes my hand gently, both of our hands resting on top of Sock. "I asked you about Jack because you were so industrious about him, so vigilant, so focused, and I thought it was unusual. The more I probed, the more evasive you got. I've never forgotten it."

"It wasn't because of him," I answer. "It was because of the way I felt about me."

"Because of Briggs. Not an easy man to be under. And I don't mean that the way it just came out. Not that you would necessarily be the one under him or anyone. Probably on top."

"Please don't be snide."

"I'm teasing you, and both of us are too tired and frayed around the edges for teasing. I apologize."

"What happened is my fault, anyway. I won't blame him or anyone," I continue. "But he was God back then. To someone like me. I was really very sheltered. I think all I'd ever done was go to school, study, consumed by residencies, Lord, how many years of them, like a long dream of working hard and rarely sleeping, and of course doing what I was told by people in authority. In the early days hardly questioning it. Because I felt I didn't deserve to be a doctor. I should have run my father's small grocery store, been a wife and mother, lived simply, like everyone else in my family."

"John Briggs was the most powerful person you'd ever come across. I can see why," Benton says, and I sense he might know Briggs better than I've imagined. I wonder how much they've talked these past six months, not only about Fielding but about everything.

"Please don't be threatened by him," I'm saying as I wonder what Benton knows about Briggs and, most of all, what Benton knows about me. "My past with him doesn't matter anymore. And it was about my perception, anyway. I needed him to be powerful. I needed that back then."

"Because your father was anything but powerful. All those years he was ill, with you taking care of him, taking care of everyone. You wanted someone who would take care of you for once."

"And when you get what you want, guess what happens. John took terrible care of me. Or it would be more accurate if I said that I took terrible care of myself. I knew—better yet, was persuaded—to go against my conscience and to be led into something that wasn't right."

"Politics," Benton says as if he knows.

"What would you know about what happened back then?" I look at him, and shadows move on his keenly handsome face in the firelight.

"I think it's something like two years' service for every year of medical or law school paid for by the military. So unless my math is really bad, you owed the U.S. government eight years of service with the air force, more specifically, the AFIP, AFME."

"Six. I finished Hopkins in three years."

"Okay, that's right. But you served what, a year? And every time I've asked about it, you give me the same song and dance about the AFIP wanting to set up a fellowship program in Virginia and they decided to plant you there as chief."

"We did start an AFIP fellowship program. In those days there weren't that many offices if you were AFIP and wanted to specialize in forensics. So we added Richmond. And now, of course, us. The CFC. We'll be gearing up for that soon. Any minute I've got to get that going."

"Politics," Benton says again as he takes a drink of Scotch. "You've always felt guilty about something, and for the longest time I thought it was Jack. Because you'd had an affair with him, repeating his original injury. A powerful woman in charge of him has sex with him, victimizing him again, returning him to the scene of the original crime. For you? That would have been unpardonable."

"Except I didn't."

"You promise."

"I promise."

"Well, you did something." He's not going to stop until we have it before us.

"Yes, I did, but it was before Jack," I answer.

"You did what you were ordered to do, Kay. And you've got to let it go," he says, because he knows. It's obvious he does.

"I never told their families," I reply, and Benton doesn't say anything. "The two women murdered in Cape Town. I couldn't call their families and tell them what really happened. They think it was racism, gang members during Apartheid. A high crime rate of blacks killing whites suited certain political leaders back then. They wanted it to be true. The more, the better."

"Those leaders are gone now, Kay."

"You should make your phone calls, Benton. Call Douglas or whoever and tell them about Dawn Kincaid and who she probably is and the tests I've ordered."

"The Reagan administration is long gone, Kay." Benton's going to make me talk about it, and I'm convinced it's been talked about before. Briggs probably said something to him because Briggs knows damn well how haunted I am.

"What I did isn't long gone," I reply.

"You didn't do a damn thing that was wrong. You had nothing to do with their deaths. I don't have to know all the details to say that much," Benton says as he laces his fingers in mine, our joined hands gently rising and sinking in rhythm to Sock's breathing.

"I feel as if I had everything to do with it," I answer.

"You didn't," he says. "Other people did, and you were forced to be silent. Do you know how often it is I can't tell what I know? My whole life has been like that. The alternative is to make things worse. That's the test. Does telling make it worse and cause others to be persecuted and killed. *Primum non nocere.* First, do no harm. That's what I weigh everything against, and I sure as hell know you do the same."

I don't want a lecture right now.

"Do you think she did it?" I ask as Sock breathes slowly, contentedly, as if he's lived here always and is home. "Killed all of them?"

"Now I'm wondering." He looks at his drink, and it turns the color of honey in the firelight.

"To put Jack out of his misery?"

"She probably hated him," Benton says. "That's why she would have been drawn to him, wanted to get to know him as an adult, if that's what she did."

"Well, I don't think he shackled Wally Jamison in his cellar and hacked him to death. If Wally came to the house in Salem willingly, probably it was upon Dawn's invitation, to see her. Maybe play out some fantasy, a game, a macabre sex game on Halloween. Maybe she did a similar thing to Mark Bishop, and when she has them under control, under her spell, exactly where she wants them, she strikes. A rush, a thrill, for someone diabolical like that."

"Liam Saltz's second wife, Eli's mother, is South African," Benton says. "As is her husband from that earlier marriage, Eli's biological father, and Eli was wearing a ring that likely was taken from the Donahue house, likely taken by Dawn along with the typewriter, the stationery. Maybe used the duct tape to collect fibers, trace evidence, DNA from the Donahue house, while she was at it. Make it look like the letter really did come from the mother, making sure that Johnny's alibi was weakened further by it."

"Now you're thinking irrationally like me," I reply wryly. "That's what I believe happened, or close to it."

"The game," Benton muses in that tone he has when he hates what someone has done. "Games and more games, elaborate, intricate dramas. I can't wait to meet the fucking bitch. I really can't wait."

"Maybe you've had enough Scotch."

"Not half enough. Who better to manipulate Johnny Donahue than someone like that, some attractive brain trust of a woman who's older? To plant the idea in that poor kid's head that he murdered a six-year-old while he was delusional and having memory lapses because of drugs she was spiking his meds with? Spiking Fielding's meds with. Who knows who else? A poisonous person who destroys the people she's supposed to love, pays them back for every crime committed against her, and you pile on her genetic predisposition and maybe the same cocktail Fielding was on?"

"That would be the perfect storm, as they say."

"Let's see what kind of killing machine I can be and get away with it," he says in that tone of his, and if I could look into his eyes, I know what would be in them. Complete contempt. "And after it's ended, no one is left standing but her. Fucking bulletproof."

"You could be right." And I remember the box I left in the car. "Why don't you make your phone calls."

"Borderline, sadistic, manipulative, narcissistic."

"I guess some people are everything." I set down my glass on the coffee table and ease Sock off my lap and onto the rug.

"Some people just about are."

"I forgot the box Briggs left for me," I say as I get up from the sofa. "And I'll take Sock out back. You ready to go potty?" I ask the dog. "Then I'll warm up pizza. I don't suppose we have anything for salad. What the hell have you eaten the entire time I've been gone? Let me guess. You run over to Chang An for Chinese food and live on that for the next three days."

"That would be really good right now."

"You've probably been doing it every week."

"I'd rather have your pizza anytime."

"Don't try to be nice," I reply.

I walk into the kitchen for Sock's lead and slip it around his neck and find a flashlight in a drawer, an old Maglite that Marino gave me aeons ago, long and black aluminum, powered by fat D batteries, reminding me of the old days, when police used to carry flashlights the size of nightsticks instead of everything being so small, like the SureFire lights Lucy likes and what Benton keeps in his glove box. I disarm the alarm system and worry about Sock, about how cold it is, realizing as we go down the back steps in the dark that I didn't bother with a coat for me, and I notice that the motion-sensor light attached to the garage is out. I try to remember if it was out an hour or so ago when we got home, but I'm not sure. There is so much to fix, so much to change, so much to do. Where will I start when tomorrow comes?

Benton didn't lock the door to the detached garage, because what would be the point with an open window the size of a big-screen TV? Inside the remodeled carriage house it is dark and bitterly cold, and air blows in through the open black square that I can barely make out, and I turn on the Maglite and it doesn't work. The batteries must be dead, and how stupid of me not to check before I left the house. I point the key at the SUV, and the lock chirps but the interior light doesn't go on because it's a damn Bureau car, and Special Agent Burke isn't about to have an interior light that comes on. I feel around on the backseat for the box, which is quite large, and I realize it won't be easy to carry it and deal with Sock. In fact, I can't.

"I'm sorry, Sock," I say to the dog as I feel him shivering against my legs. "I know it's cold in here. Just give me a minute. I'm so sorry. But as you're discovering, I'm a very stupid person."

I use the car key to slit the tape on top of the box and pull out a vest that is familiar even if I've not examined this particular brand, but I recognize the feel of tough nylon and the stiffness of ceramic-Kevlar plates that Briggs or someone has already inserted into the internal pockets. I tear open the Velcro straps on the sides to open up the vest so I can sling it over my shoulder. I feel the weight of the vest draped over me as I shove the car door shut, and Sock jumps away from me like a rabbit. He yanks the lead out of my hand.

"It's just the car door, Sock. It's all right, come here, Sock. . . ."
I start to call out at the same time something else moves inside
the garage near the open window, and I turn around to see what
it is, but it is too dark to see anything.

"Sock? Is that you over there?"

The dark, frigid air moves around me, and the blow to my
back feels like a hammer hitting me between my shoulder blades,
as if a loud hissing dragon is attacking me, and I lose my balance.

A piercing scream and hissing, and a warm, wet mist spatters
my face as I fall hard against the SUV and swing with all my
might at whatever it is. The Maglite cracks like a bat against
something hard that gives beneath the weight of the blow and
then moves, and I swing again and hit something again, something that feels different. I smell the iron smell of blood and taste
it on my lips and in my mouth as I swing again and again at air,
and then the lights are on and the glare is blinding and I'm covered with a fine film of blood as if I've been spray-painted with
it. Benton is inside the garage, pointing a pistol at the woman in
a huge black coat facedown on the rubberized floor. I notice blood
pooling under her bloody right hand, and near it, a severed fingertip with a glittery white French nail, and near that, a knife
with a thin steel blade and a thick black handle with a release
button on the shiny metal guard.

"Kay? Kay? Are you all right? Kay! Are you all right?"

I realize Benton is shouting at me as I crouch by the woman
and touch the side of her neck and find her pulse. I make sure she
is breathing and turn her over to check her pupils. Neither of
them is fixed. Her face is bloody from the Maglite smashing into

it, and I am startled by the resemblance, the dark blond hair cut very short, the strong features, and the full lower lip that look like Jack Fielding's. Even the small ears close to the sides of her head look like his, and I feel the strength in her upper body, her shoulders, although she isn't a large person, maybe five-foot-six or -seven and slender but with large bones like her dead father. All this is flooding my senses as I tell Benton to rush into the house and call 911, and to bring a container of ice.

23

A warm front moved in during the night and brought more snow, this time a gentle snow that falls silently, muting all sound, covering everything that is ugly, softly rounding whatever is sharp and hard.

I sit up in bed inside the master bedroom on the second floor of the house in Cambridge, and snow is coming down, piling in the bare branches of an oak tree on the other side of the big window nearest me. A moment ago a fat gray squirrel was there, perfectly balanced on the smallest twig, and we were eye to eye, his cheeks moving as he stared through the window at me while I sifted through the paperwork and photographs in my lap. I smell old paper and dust and the medicine smell of the wipes I used on Sock, who I suspect hadn't had his ears cleaned in recent memory, maybe not ever, not the way I cleaned them. He didn't like it at first, but I talked him into it with a soft voice and a sweet-potato treat that Lucy brought by when she gave me a container of the same wipes she uses on her bulldog. The miconazole-chlorhexidine is good for pachydermatis, I made the mistake of mentioning to my niece very early this morning when she stopped by to check on me.

Jet Ranger wouldn't appreciate being called a pachyderm, Lucy retorted. He's not an elephant or a hippopotamus, and there's only so much one can do about his weight. She has him on a new diet for seniors, but he can't exercise because of his bad hips, and the snow gives him a rash on his paws for some reason, and his legs are too short for snow this deep, so he can't go on even the briefest walk this time of year, she went on and on, and I'd truly offended her. But that's the way Lucy can get when she's worried and scared, and most of all she's upset she wasn't here last night. She's angry she wasn't here to deal with Dawn Kincaid, but I'm not sorry in the least. I can't say I'm proud of myself for giving someone a linear skull fracture and a concussion, but if Lucy had been in the garage instead of me, there would be one more person dead. My niece would have killed Dawn Kincaid for sure, probably shot her, and there are enough people dead.

It's also possible that Lucy wouldn't have survived the encounter, I don't care what she says. It depends on two details that made the difference in my still being here and Dawn Kincaid being locked up on the forensic ward of an area hospital. I don't think she was expecting me to walk into the garage. I think she was lurking on the other side of the gaping window, waiting for me to take Sock into the dark backyard. But I surprised her by entering the garage first to get what I'd left in the car, and by the time she slipped through the big space where the window was supposed to be, I'd already opened the box and slung the level IV-A tactical vest over my shoulder. When she stabbed at my back with the injection knife, it hit a nylon-covered ceramic-Kevlar plate, and the terrific jolt caused by that absolute stopping action caused her fingers to slide along the blade. She cut three fingers to the bone and severed the tip of her pinkie at the same time she was releasing the CO_2, and a mist of her blood sprayed all over me.

My point to Lucy was that unless she'd caused Dawn to lose the surprise element for the attack and unless Lucy also just happened to have on body armor or at least have it draped over her torso, she might not have been as fortunate as I was. So my niece should stop saying it's a damn shame she wasn't here last night, claiming that she sure as hell would have taken care of things, as if I didn't, because I did, even though it was luck. I think I took care of things just fine and only hope I can take care of a far more important matter that hasn't killed me yet but at times has certainly felt like it might.

"She'd told me there had been catcalls and ugly comments," Mrs. Pieste is telling me over the phone as I go over her daughter's case with her. "Calling her a Boer. Telling the Boers to go home, and as you know, that's Afrikaans for farmer but it's really meant to disparage all white South Africans. And I kept telling the man from the Pentagon that I didn't care about the reason, whether it was Noonie and Joanne being white or American or assumed to be South African. And, of course, they weren't South African. I didn't care why. I just didn't want to believe the suffering he described."

"Do you remember who that man from the Pentagon was?" I ask.

"A lawyer."

"It wasn't a colonel in the army," I hope out loud.

"It was some young lawyer at the Pentagon who worked for the secretary of defense. I don't remember his name."

Then it wasn't Briggs.

"A fast-talking one," Mrs. Pieste adds disdainfully. "I remember I didn't like him. But I wouldn't have liked anybody who told me the things he did."

"The only comfort I can offer out of all of this," I repeat, "is Noonie and Joanne didn't suffer the way you've been led to believe. I can't say with absolute certainty that they weren't aware of being smothered, but it is extremely likely they weren't aware because they were drugged."

"But that would have been tested for," Mrs. Pieste's voice says, and she has a Massachusetts accent, can't pronounce R's, and I didn't realize she's originally from Andover. After Noonie's murder, the Piestes moved to New Hampshire, I just found out.

"Mrs. Pieste, I think you understand nothing was tested as it was supposed to be," I reply.

"Why didn't you?"

"The medical examiner in Cape Town—"

"But you signed the death certificate, Dr. Scarpetta. And the autopsy report. I have copies that lawyer from the Pentagon sent me."

"I didn't sign them." I refused to sign documents that I knew were a lie, but knowing they were a lie made me guilty of it anyway. "I don't have copies, as hard as that probably is for you to believe," I then say. "They weren't supplied to me. What I have are my own notes, my own records, which I mailed back to the U.S. before I left South Africa because I worried my luggage would be gone through, and it was."

"But you signed what I have."

"I promise I didn't," I reply calmly but firmly. "My guess is certain people made certain my signature was forged on those falsified documents in the event I decided to do what I'm doing now."

"If you decided to tell the truth."

It's so hard to hear it stated so bluntly. The truth. Implying what I've told or not told over the years makes me a liar.

"I'm sorry," I tell her again. "You had a right to know the truth back then, at the time of your daughter's death. And the death of her friend."

"I can see why you didn't say anything back then, though," Mrs. Pieste says, and she sounds only slightly upset. Mostly she sounds interested and relieved to be talking about something that has dominated her life for most of it. "When people do things like this, no telling where they'll stop. Well, there's no limit. Other people would have gotten hurt. Including you."

"I wouldn't have wanted anybody else to get hurt," I reply, and I feel worse if what she's saying is that I was silent out of fear for my own safety. I was afraid of a lot of things and a host of people I couldn't see. I was afraid of other people dying, of people being wrongly accused.

"I hope you understand that when I read the death certificate and autopsy report, not that I understand most of the medical terms, well, one would think the findings are yours," Mrs. Pieste says.

"They absolutely weren't, and they are false. There was no tissue response to the injuries. All of it was postmortem. In fact, hours after the deaths, Mrs. Pieste. What was done to Noonie and Joanne occurred many hours after they had died."

"If there wasn't a test for drugs, then how can you be sure they were given something?" her voice goes on, and I hear the sound of another phone being picked up.

"This is Edward Pieste," a man's voice says. "I'm on, too. I'm Noonie's father."

"I'm so sorry for your loss." It sounds weak, perfectly insipid. "I wish I had exactly the right words to say to both of you. I'm sorry you were lied to and that I permitted it, and although I won't make excuses . . ."

"We understand why you couldn't say what happened," the father replies. "The feelings back then, and our government secretly in collusion with those who wanted to keep Apartheid alive. That's why Noonie was making that documentary. They wouldn't let the film crew into South Africa. Each of them had to go in as if they were tourists. A big dirty secret, what our government was doing to support the atrocities over there."

"It wasn't that big of a secret, Eddie." Mrs. Pieste's voice.

"Well, the White House put on the good face."

"I'm sure they told you about the documentary Noonie was making? She had such a future," Mrs. Pieste says to me as I look at a picture of her daughter that I wouldn't want the Piestes to ever see.

"About the children of Apartheid," I reply. "I did see it when it aired here."

"The evils of white supremacy," she says. "Of any supremacy, period."

"I missed the first part of what the two of you have been talking about," Mr. Pieste says. "Was out shoveling the driveway."

"He doesn't listen," his wife says. "A man his age shoveling snow, but he's the hard head." She says it with sad affection. "Dr. Scarpetta was telling me Noonie and Joanne were drugged."

"Really. Well, that's something." He says it with no energy in his tone.

"I got to the apartment several days after their deaths and did a retrospective. It was staged, of course; their crime scene was staged," I explain. "But there were beer cans, plastic cups, and a wine bottle in the kitchen trash, a bottle of white wine from Stellenbosch, and I managed to get the cans, the bottle, and cups along with other items, and have them sent back to the States, where I had them tested. We found high levels of GHB in the wine bottle and two of the cups. Gamma hydroxybutyric acid, commonly known as a date-rape drug."

"They did say there was rape," Mr. Pieste says with the same empty affect.

"I don't know for a fact that they were raped. There was no physical sign of it, no injuries except staged ones inflicted postmortem, and swabs I had tested privately here in the U.S. were negative for sperm," I reply, looking through photographs of the nude bodies bound to chairs I know the women weren't sitting in when they were murdered. I look at close-ups showing a livor mortis pattern that told me the women were lying in bed on rumpled sheets for at least twelve hours after death.

I go through photographs I took with my own camera of hacking and cutting injuries that barely bled, and ligatures that scarcely left a mark on the skin because the brutes behind all this were too ignorant to know what the hell they were doing, someone hired or assigned by government or military operatives to spike a bottle of local wine and have drinks with the women, possibly a friend or they thought the person was friendly or safe, when, of course, he was anything but, and I tell them that serology tests I had done after I got home indicated the presence of a male. Later, when I had DNA testing done, I got the profile of a European or white male who remains unknown. I can't say for a fact it is the profile of the killer, but it was someone drinking beer inside the apartment, I add.

As much as one can reconstruct anything, I tell the Piestes what I think happened, that after Noonie and Joanne were drugged and groggy or unconscious, their assailant helped them to bed and smothered them with a pillow, and I based this on pinpoint hemorrhages and other injuries, I explain. Then for some reason this person must have left. Maybe he wanted to come back later with others involved in the conspiracy, or it could be that he waited inside the apartment for his compatriots to arrive, I don't know. But by the time the women were bound and cut and mutilated so savagely, they had been dead for a while, and it couldn't have been more obvious to me when I finally saw them.

"Up here we got about four inches already," Mr. Pieste says

after a while, after he's heard enough. "That on top of ice. Did you get the ice down there in Cambridge?"

"I guess we should complain about this to someone," Mrs. Pieste says. "Does it matter how long it's been?"

"It never matters how long it's been when you're talking about the truth," I reply. "And there's no statute of limitation on homicide."

"I just hope they didn't lock up someone who shouldn't have been," Mrs. Pieste then says.

"The cases have remained unsolved. Attributed to black gang members but no arrests," I tell them.

"But it was probably someone white," she says.

"Someone white was drinking beer inside the apartment, that much I can say with reasonable certainty."

"Do you know who did it?" she asks.

"Because we would want them punished," her husband says.

"I only know the type of people who likely did it. Cowardly people all about power and politics. And you should do what you feel, what's in your heart."

"Eddie, what do you think?"

"I'll write a letter to Senator Chappel."

"You know how much good that will do."

"Then to Obama, Hillary Clinton, Joe Biden. I'll write everyone," he says.

"What will anybody do about it now?" Mrs. Pieste says to her husband. "I don't know that I can live through it again, Eddie."

"Well, I need to go clear the walk again," he says. "Got to stay on top of the snow, and it's really coming down. Thank you for your time and trouble, ma'am," he says to me. "And for going ahead and telling us. I know that wasn't an easy decision, and I'm sure my daughter would appreciate it if she was here to tell you herself."

After I hang up, I sit on the bed for a while, the paperwork and photographs back in the gray accordion file they've been in for more than two decades. I'll return the file to the safe in the basement, I decide. But not now. I don't feel like going down into the basement and into that safe right now, and I think someone has just pulled into our driveway. I hear snow crunching, and I'm not in a good state of mind to see whoever it is. I'll stay up here for a little while longer. Maybe make a grocery list or contemplate errands or just pet Sock for a minute or two.

"I can't take you for a walk," I tell him.

He is curled up next to me, his head on my thigh, unperturbed by the sad conversation he just overheard and having no idea what it says about the world he lives in. But then he knows cruelty, maybe knows it better than the rest of us.

"No walks without a coat," I go on, petting him, and he yawns and licks my hand, and I hear the beeping of the alarm being disarmed, then the front door shuts. "I think we're going to try boots," I tell Sock as Marino's and Benton's voices drift up from the entryway. "You probably aren't going to like these little shoes they make for dogs and are likely to get quite annoyed with me, but I promise it's a good thing. Well, we have company." I recognize Marino's heavy footsteps on the stairs. "You remember him from yesterday, in the big truck. The big man in yellow who gets on my nerves most of the time. But for future reference, you have no reason to be afraid of him. He's not a bad person, and as you may be aware, people who have known each other for a very long time tend to be ruder to each other than they are to people they don't like half as much."

"Anybody home?" Marino's big voice precedes him into the bedroom as the doorknob turns, and then he knocks as he opens the door. "Benton said you was decent. Who were you talking to? You on the phone?"

"He's clairvoyant, then," I reply from the bed, where I'm under the covers, nothing but pajamas on. "And I'm not on the phone and wasn't talking to anyone."

"How's Sock? How ya doing, boy?" he then says before I can answer. "How come he smells funny? What did you put on him, flea medicine? This time of year? You look okay. How are you feeling?"

"I cleaned his ears."

"So, how are you doing, Doc?"

Marino looms over me, and his presence seems larger than usual because he's in a heavy parka and a baseball cap and hiking boots while I'm in nothing but flannel, modestly tucked under a blanket and a duvet. He has a small black case in his hands that I recognize as Lucy's iPad, unless he's managed to get one of his own, which I doubt.

"I didn't get hurt. There's nothing wrong with me. I've just been staying in this morning, taking care of a few things," I say to him. "I'm assuming Dawn Kincaid is fine. Last I heard, she was stable."

"Stable? You're joking, right?"

"I'm talking about her physical condition. The reattachment of her finger and the damage to the rest of them, the other three that were cut so severely. It's probably a good thing for her it was so cold in the garage. And, of course, we thought to pack her hand and her severed finger in ice. I'm hoping that helped. Do you know? I haven't heard a word. What's her status? I've not heard any reports since she was admitted last night."

"You're kidding, right?" Marino's eyes look at me, and they're just as bloodshot as they were yesterday in Salem.

"I'm not kidding. Nobody's told me a word. Benton said earlier he would check, but I don't think he has."

"He's been on the phone with us all morning."

"Maybe you'd be so kind as to call the hospital and check."

"Like I give a flying fuck if she loses a finger or all of her damn fingers," Marino says. "Why would you give a fuck? You afraid she'll sue you? That must be it, and wouldn't that figure? She probably will. Will sue you for maybe losing the use of her hand so she can't build nanobots or whatever anymore, a psycho like that. I guess psychopaths are stable in the mental illness sense of the word. Can you be crazy and a psychopath? And still be put together well enough to work at a place like Otwahl? Her case is going to be one big damn problem. If she gets out, well, can you imagine?"

"Why would she get out?"

"I'm just telling you the case is going to be a problem. You won't be safe if she's on the loose again. None of us will be."

He helps himself to the foot of the bed, and the bed sinks and it feels like I'm suddenly sitting uphill as he makes himself comfortable, petting Sock and informing me that the police and the FBI found the "rat hole" Dawn Kincaid had rented, a one-bedroom apartment in Revere, just outside of Boston, where she stayed when she wasn't with Eli Goldman or with her biological father, Jack Fielding, or whoever else she had entangled in her web at any point in time. Marino slips the iPad out of its case and turns it on as he lets me know that he and Lucy and quite a number of other investigators have been searching the rat-hole apartment for hours, going through Dawn's computer and everything she has, including everything she's stolen.

"What about her mother?" I ask. "Has anybody talked to her?"

"Dawn's been in contact with her for a number of years, visiting her in prison down there in Georgia now and then. Reconnected with her and with Fielding on and off over the years. Latches on when she wants something, a first-class manipulator and user."

"But does the mother know what's happened up here?"

"Why do you care what a fucking child molester thinks?"

"Her relationship with Jack wasn't that simple. It's not as easily explained as you so eloquently just put it. I'd hate for her to hear about him on the news."

"Who gives a shit."

"I never want anybody to find out that way," I reply. "I don't care who it is. Her relationship with him wasn't simple," I repeat. "Relationships like that never are."

"Plain and simple to me. Black and white."

"If she hears it on the news," I reply, and I realize I'm perseverating. "I always hate for that to happen. Such an inhumane way for people to find out terrible things like this. That's my concern."

"A klepto," Marino then says, because his only interest is the case and what the investigators have been discovering at Dawn Kincaid's apartment.

Apparently, she is a bona fide klepto, to quote Marino. Someone who seemed to have taken souvenirs from all sorts of people, he goes on, including items stolen from people we have no idea about. But some of what investigators have found so far has been identified as jewelry and rare coins from the Donahue house, and also several rare autographed musical manuscripts that Mrs. Donahue had no idea were missing from the family library.

Recovered from a locked chest in a closet in Dawn's apartment were guns believed to have been removed from Fielding's collection, and his wedding band. Also in this same trunk, a martial-arts carry bag, I'm told, and inside it, a black satin sash, a white uniform, sparring gear, a lunch bag filled with rusty L-shaped flooring nails, and a hammer, and a pair of boy's Adidas tae kwon do shoes believed to be the ones Mark Bishop was wearing while practicing kicks in his backyard the late afternoon he was killed. Although no one is quite certain how Dawn lured the boy into lying facedown and allowing her to play some gruesome game with him that included "pretending" to hammer nails into his head, or more specifically, the first nail.

"The one that went in right here," Marino continues speculating, pointing to the space between the back of his neck and the base of his skull. "That would have killed him instantly, right?"

"If we must use that phrase," I reply.

"I mean, she probably helped him in some of Fielding's Tiny Tiger classes, maybe?" he continues to spin the story. "So the kid's familiar with her, looks up to her, and she's hot, I mean really good-looking. If it was me, I'd tell the kid I'm going to show him a new move or something and to lie down in the yard. And of course the kid's going to do what an expert says, what someone teaching him says, and he lies down and it's almost dark out and then boom! It's over."

"Someone like that can never get out," I reply. "She'll do more and do it worse next time, if that's even possible."

"Denying everything. She's not talking, except to say Fielding did it all and she's innocent."

"He didn't."

"I'm with you."

"She's going to have a hard time explaining what's in her apartment," I point out, as I continue going through photographs. Marino must have taken hundreds.

"She's good-looking and charming and smart as hell. And Fielding's dead."

"Incriminating." I've said this several times as I look through the photographs on the iPad. "Should be very helpful to the pros-ecution. I'm not sure why you think the case will be a problem."

"It's going to be. The defense will pin it all on Fielding. The psycho bitch will get a dream team of big-shot lawyers, and they'll make the jury believe Fielding did all of it." Marino leans closer to me, and the slope of the bed changes again, and Sock is snoring quietly, not interested in his former owner or her rat hole, which has a dog bed in it, Marino shows me.

He leans close to me, clicking through several photographs of the dog's plaid bed and several toys, and I indicate I'd rather look at the photographs myself. He and Sock are on top of me, and I'm feeling smothered.

"I just thought I'd show you, since I'm the one who took them," Marino says.

"Thank you. I'll manage. You did a very good job with the photographs."

"Point is, it's obvious the dog stayed here." Marino means Sock stayed in Dawn Kincaid's rat hole. "And also with Eli and with Fielding," he adds. "To give her credit, I guess she liked her dog."

"She left him in Jack's house with no heat and all alone." I click through photographs that are overwhelmingly incriminating.

"She doesn't give a shit unless it suits her. When it doesn't, she gets rid of it one way or another. So she cared about him when it suited her."

"That's the more likely story," I agree.

I look at photographs of an unmade double bed, then other pictures of a tiny bedroom shockingly filled with junk, as if Dawn Kincaid is a hoarder.

"Plus, she had another reason to leave him," Marino goes on. "If she leaves the dog at Fielding's house, then maybe we think he's the one who killed everyone, then killed himself. The dog is there. His red leash is there. The boat that was probably used to dump Wally Jamison's body is there, and Wally's clothes and the murder weapon are in Fielding's basement. The Navigator with the missing front plate is there. You're supposed to think Fielding was following you and Benton when you left Hanscom. Fielding's deranged. He's watching you. He's following you, trying to intimidate you, or spying, or maybe he was going to kill you, too."

"He was dead by the time we were followed. Although I can't be exact about time of death, I'm calculating he'd been dead since Monday afternoon, probably was murdered not long after he got home to Salem after leaving the CFC with the Glock he'd removed from the lab. It was Dawn in the Navigator tailing us Monday night. She's the one deranged. She rode our bumper to make sure we knew we were being followed, then disappeared, probably ducked out of sight in Otwahl's parking lot. So eventually we'd think it was Jack, who in fact already had been murdered by her with a pistol she probably gave to her boyfriend, Eli, before she murdered him, too. But you're right. It's likely she tried to set things up so all of it got blamed on Jack, who isn't around to defend himself. She set up Jack and made it look like he was setting up Johnny Donahue. It's terrifying."

"You got to make the jury buy it."

"That's always the challenge, no matter the case."

"It's bad the dog was at Fielding's house," Marino repeats. "It connects him to Eli's murder. Hell, it's on video clips that Eli was walking the dog when he was whacked."

"The microchip," I remind him. "It traces back to Dawn, not to Jack."

"Doesn't mean anything. He kills Eli and then takes the dog, and the dog would know Fielding, right?" Marino says, as if Sock isn't inches away from him, sleeping with his head on my leg. "The dog would be familiar with Fielding because Dawn was staying over there in Salem, had the dog at Fielding's house some of the time or whatever. So Fielding kills Eli, then takes the dog as he walks off, or this is what Dawn wants us to think."

"It's not what happened. Jack didn't kill anyone," as I conclude that Dawn's apartment has the same brand of squalor that I observed at Fielding's house in Salem.

Clutter and boxes everywhere. Clothes piled in mounds and strewn in odd places. Dishes piled in the sink. Trash overflowing. Mounds of newspapers, computer printouts, magazines, and on a dining-room table, a large number of items tagged and placed there by police, including a GPS-enabled sports watch that is the same model as one I gave Fielding for his birthday several years ago, and a Civil War military dissection set in a rosewood case that is identical to one I gave him when he worked for me in Richmond.

There is a close-up of a pair of black gloves, one of them with a small black box on the wrist, what Marino describes as lightweight flexible wireless data gloves with built-in accelerometers, thirty-six sensors, and an ultra-low-profile integrated transmitter-receiver, only I have to infer all this, sift it out of his mispronunciations and mangled descriptions. The gloves, which were closely examined by both Briggs and Lucy at the scene, are clearly intended for gesture-based robotic control—specifically, to control the flybot that Eli had with him when he was murdered by the woman who had given him the stolen signet ring he was wearing when his body came to the CFC.

"Then the flybot was in her apartment," I presume. "And did Benton offer you any coffee?"

"I'm coffeed out. Some of us haven't been to bed yet."

"I'm in bed working. Doesn't mean I've slept."

"Must be nice. I'd like to stay home and work in bed." He takes the iPad from me and searches through files.

"Maybe we could adjust your job description. You can stay home and work in bed a certain number of days each year, depending on your age and decrepitude, which we'll have to evaluate. I suppose I'll be the one to evaluate it."

"Oh, yeah? Who's gonna evaluate yours?" He finds a photograph he wants me to see.

"Mine doesn't need evaluating. It's obvious to one and all."

He shows me a close-up of the flybot, only at a glance it's hard to know what it is, just a shiny, wiry object on a square of white paper on Dawn Kincaid's dining-room table. The micromechanical device could be an earring, it occurs to me. A silver earring that was stepped on, which is exactly what is suspected, Marino tells me. Lucy thinks the flybot was stepped on while the EMTs were working on Eli, then later Dawn found it when she returned to Norton's Woods, possibly wearing the same long black wool coat that she had on in my garage, a coat that I believe was Fielding's. A witness claims to have observed a young man or woman, the person wasn't sure which, in a big black coat walking around Norton's Woods with a flashlight, several hours after Eli Goldman died there. The individual in the big coat was out there alone, and the person who saw him or her thought it was strange because he or she did not have a dog and seemed to be looking for something while making odd hand gestures.

"It must have been huge on her and practically dragged on the ground," Marino says, getting up from the bed. "I'm not saying she was trying to look like a man, but with her short hair and the big coat, and a hat and glasses on or whatever? As long as you don't see her rack. She's got quite a rack. Has that in common with her dad, right?"

"I've never known Jack to have large breasts."

"I mean both of them built."

"So she returned when she assumed it was safe to do so, and even though the flybot was badly damaged, it responded to radio frequency signals sent by the data gloves?" I turn off the iPad and hand it to him.

"I think she just saw it on the ground, think it was shiny in the flashlight and she found it that way. Lucy says the bug is DOA. Squashed."

"Do we know exactly what it does or was supposed to do?"

Marino shrugs, towering over me again, still in his parka, which he hasn't bothered to unbutton, as if he didn't intend to stay long. "This isn't my area of expertise, you know. I didn't understand half of what they were talking about, Lucy and the general. I just know the potential for whatever this thing is supposed to do is something to be concerned about, and DoD intends to do some sort of inspection of Otwahl to see what the hell is really going on over there. But I'm not sure we don't already know exactly what the hell is going on over there."

"Meaning what?"

He returns the iPad to its case and says, "Meaning I worry there's R-and-D going on that the government damn well knows about but just doesn't want anyone else to know, and then you get kids out of control and the shit hits the fan. I think you get my drift. When are you coming back to work?"

"Probably not today," I tell him.

"Well, we got a shitload of things to do and undo," he says.

"Thanks for the warning."

"Buzz me if you need something. I'll call the hospital and let you know how the psycho's doing."

"Thanks for stopping by."

I wait until the sound of his heavy footsteps stops at the front door, and then the door shuts again, and then a pause, and Benton resets the alarm. I hear his footsteps, which are much lighter than Marino's, as he walks past the stairs, toward the back of the house where he has his office.

"Come on, let's get up," I say to Sock, and he opens his eyes and looks at me and yawns. "Do you know what bye-bye means? I guess not. They didn't teach you that at the prison. You just want to sleep, don't you? Well, I've got things to do, so come on. You're really quite lazy, you know. Are you sure you ever won a race or even ran in one? I don't think I believe it."

I move his head and put my feet on the floor, deciding there must be a pet shop around here that has everything a skinny, lazy old greyhound might need for this kind of weather.

"Let's go for a ride." I talk to Sock as I find my slippers and a robe. "Let's see what Secret Agent Wesley is doing. He's probably in his office on the phone again, what do you bet? I know, he's always on the phone, and I agree, it's quite annoying.

"Maybe he'll take us shopping, and then I'm going to make a very nice pasta, homemade pappardelle with a hearty Bolognese sauce, ground veal, red wine, and lots of mushrooms and garlic.

"I need to explain up front that you only get canine cuisine; that's the rule of the house. I'm thinking quinoa and cod for you today." I continue talking as we go down the stairs. "That will be a nice change after all that chicken and rice from the Greek diner."